D1187772

DATE DUE FOR RETURN

THE
SELF PSYCHOLOGY
OF
ADDICTION
AND ITS
TREATMENT

THE
SELF PSYCHOLOGY
OF
ADDICTION
AND ITS
TREATMENT

NARCISSUS IN WONDERLAND

RICHARD B. ULMAN AND HARRY PAUL

Routledge
Taylor & Francis Group
New York   London

Routledge is an imprint of the
Taylor & Francis Group, an informa business

Routledge
Taylor & Francis Group
270 Madison Avenue
New York, NY 10016

Routledge
Taylor & Francis Group
2 Park Square
Milton Park, Abingdon
Oxon OX14 4RN

© 2006 by Richard B. Ulman and Harry Paul
Routledge is an imprint of Taylor & Francis Group, an Informa business

Printed in the United States of America on acid-free paper
10 9 8 7 6 5 4 3 2 1

International Standard Book Number-10: 1-58391-307-6 (Hardcover)
International Standard Book Number-13: 978-1-58391-307-9 (Hardcover)
Library of Congress Card Number 2005001367

Library of Congress Cataloging-in-Publication Data

Ulman, Richard B.
     The self psychology of addiction and its treatment : Narcissus in wonderland /
Richard B. Ulman and Harry Paul.
          p. cm.
     Includes bibliographical references and index.
     ISBN 1-58391-307-6 (hardback)
     1. Substance abuse. 2. Self psychology. I. Paul, Harry. II. Title.

RC564.U46 2005
616.86--dc22   2005001367

Visit the Taylor & Francis Web site at
http://www.taylorandfrancis.com

and the Routledge Web site at
www.routledgementalhealth.com

We dedicate our book to our fellow addicts who already are in recovery, who are seeking recovery, who are without recovery, or who are beyond recovery.

Contents

Part IV: *Findings and Conclusions*

Acknowledgments

The first and main author (RBU) wants to acknowledge my wife, Triss R. Ulman, who has made extraordinary sacrifices without which it would have been impossible for me to complete the writing of this book. On a very personal level, I want Triss to know how much she has meant to me as, ensconced alone in my study, I spent hours, days, weeks, months, and years working on this book. She has been my special angel in her unbelievable capacity to make self-sacrifices in sharing me with my muses, and, in the process, giving up precious time together as a married couple. Without her angelic devotion and dedication to me as a writer I never would have found the courage and fortitude that were so necessary in persevering, often in very adverse circumstances, in transforming this book from a fantasy into a reality.

I also want to acknowledge all my English bulldogs—past and present—whose presence has functioned for me as "transitional selfobjects."

For the second and contributing author (HP), this book represents the culmination of a significant personal and professional journey. Intellectually and emotionally, it has been profoundly challenging for me to engage in this project, and it would never have become a reality if not for the love, dedication, and guidance of a number of people, whom I wish to thank. Foremost, I offer to my wife, Amy, all of my love and affection. For over 30 years, she has been a wonderful partner and my best friend. Her unwavering support enabled me to cope with the emotional and intellectual challenges of engaging in this project. The solitary experience of writing has always been mediated by her loving presence. As I sat writing for long periods of time, I never felt alone.

I am forever grateful to Amy and my two sons, Scott and Jordan, all of whom gave up family outings and trips so that I could face the challenge of writing this book. My children have always been an inspiration to me and it has been a joy being their father. Every once in a while over the last 15 years one of them, either Scott or Jordan, turned to me and asked: "How's the book coming?" Obviously, they felt some sense of disbelief that we would ever finish the book. Thank you both for your patience, understanding, and encouragement.

Also I would like to acknowledge the loving and enduring friendship with the first and main author (RBU). He was there metaphorically, so to speak, to catch me when I faltered and lost my balance in my writing endeavor. In breaking my fall, he carried me through some of the perilous twists and turns of contributing to this manuscript. Our selfobject relationship has pushed me to become a better human being and a better thinker.

Both of us want to acknowledge the sense of empathic understanding and responsiveness that we have experienced from our fellow members—faculty and candidates alike—at the Training and Research Institute for Self Psychology (TRISP). TRISP has served as a "group" or "collective selfobject" for us during the incredibly long period in which we have been at work on our book. As such, it nourished us narcissistically and, in the process, sustained our respective senses of self in what we experienced, at times, as an otherwise unempathic and sometimes even antipathetic environment.

Both authors want to acknowledge Anne Tierney, our tireless typist, who has made a truly heroic effort in typing and retyping the endless drafts of the different versions of this book. The writing of this book would never have come to fruition without her inestimable contributions. We also want to express our gratitude to Jack Sherin of Jack Sherin Design for his creative and imaginative cover to our book, which graphically depicts what we had in mind in subtitling our book—*Narcissus in Wonderland*.

In addition we want to acknowledge several key individuals who have been extremely instrumental in the writing of this book. We want to thank from the bottom of our hearts David W. Krueger, M.D., who championed this book with Routledge from its first stage as a book proposal to its final stage as a completed book manuscript. We also want to pay special tribute to George P. Zimmar, Ph.D., Publishing

Director at Routledge, who has demonstrated rare forbearance and exceptional understanding as we went well beyond the original deadline and length in finishing our book. We can only hope that his faith and trust in us and our book will be rewarded richly by the reception and response of those professionals in the mental health field who have an interest as well as a need to better understand and treat addicted patients. And finally, we want to express our gratitude to Bernadette Capelle, Katherine Mortimer, Shannon Vargo, Dana Bliss, and Mimi Williams, all of whom helped to shepherd our book through the sometimes perilous publishing process.

Finally, we want to express our deepest gratitude to Kenneth David Burrows, Esq. of Bender Burrows & Rosenthal, LLP, a friend of long-standing, who helped us in negotiating our book contract. Of equal, if not greater importance, he provided us with invaluble guidance in navigating our way safely in our highly litigious society. For authors such as ourselves who were writing a manuscript that involves extremely personal and sensitive material, this was of invaluable assistance.

Introduction

We base our book on three previously published chapters that appear in various volumes in the series *Progress in Self Psychology*. We refer to these three contributions as the "addiction paper trilogy" (Ulman & Paul 1989, 1990, 1992). These papers constitute what was then our latest thinking regarding a self-psychological understanding of and approach to working psychoanalytically with addicted patients, all of whom suffer from a variety of addictive disorders.

These different yet interrelated forms of addiction include alcoholism, drug or substance abuse, eating disorders, and, more specifically bulimia and compulsive overeating, as well as compulsive gambling and sexual behavior. We feel that these five kinds of addiction represent the major forms of this disorder. We discuss, as part of our trilogy, six representative (that is, typical, graphic, and illustrative) psychotherapy case histories covering the five major types of addiction.

Our current work builds on and strengthens the psychoanalytic foundations of our self-psychological understanding and approach to working psychotherapeutically with a wide variety of addicted patient. We divide our book into four major parts. In the first part of our book (Part I), which includes Chapters 1 to 3, we introduce the reader to our current self-psychological ideas on understanding and treating addiction. In Chapter 1, we place our thinking in a relevant historical context by using contemporary portrayals of addiction in both the popular media as well as more professional literature.

We also locate our ideas for the reader in a pertinent metaphorical context by linking the ancient Greek myth of Narcissus with Lewis J. Carroll's fable for children, *Alice's Adventures in Wonderland* (1865). We link the myth of Narcissus, who is captivated by his own self-image as it appears to him in the reflecting pool, and, who, as a result, withers away and starves to death, with Alice who swallows a magic pill and drops down the rabbit hole into a strange and wondrous world. We combine the myth of Narcissus with the story of Alice in Wonderland as the basis for the subtitle of our book *Narcissus in Wonderland.* The typical addicted patient is, we argue, both narcissistically disordered and lost in a version of wonderland. As such, an addicted patient is, we believe, a modern day Narcissus, who is lost in a phantasmagorical wonderland in which he or she undergoes a pathological metamorphosis or transmogrification.

We illuminate some of the main ideas of our work by referring to past depictions and descriptions of addiction as they appear in literature, poetry, and scientific papers. For example, we cite Robert Louis Stevenson's work of fiction, *The Strange Case of Dr. Jekyll and Mr. Hyde* (1886), which we read as a cautionary tale warning against the dangers of dabbling and experimenting with magic potions that literally induce a metamorphosis and transmogrification.

We also mention Samuel Taylor Coleridge's poem "Kubla Khan" written under the influence of cocaine (see Weissman, 1989). And finally, we make note of Freud's addiction to cocaine, which occurred as a result of his personal attempt to discover a medical anesthesia for relieving intractable physical pain (see Byck in Freud, 1974, on Freud's so-called "Cocaine Papers").

Coleridge and Freud are both characteristic of the artists and scientists from the 19th and 20th centuries who had personal encounters with addiction. Consequently, they acquired first-hand knowledge of the disastrous effects of addiction. The same is true for the two authors of this current work, both of whom are recovering addicts with many, many years of recovery. We, like Coleridge and Freud, have had our own and respective trips down the metaphorical rabbit hole into an addictive wonderland. Yet, our falls into and recoveries from our respective addictions have helped us to empathically understand and work self-psychologically with our population of addicted patients.

In Chapter 2, we introduce the reader to our self-psychological model of a psychoanalytic understanding of and approach to working psychotherapeutically with addicted patients. Our model consists of four components: a phenomenology of addiction or *what* is addiction; an etiology and pathogenesis of addiction or *when* are the origins and *where* are the developmental pathways leading to addiction; a typology of addiction or *who* are the various types of addict; and a therapeutics of addiction or *how* does a psychotherapist work psychotherapeutically with an addicted patient.

In Chapter 3, we position our self-psychological model of addiction within the vast literature on addiction, which includes psychoanalytic, psychiatric, and psychological materials. More specifically, we present the reader with a general overview of this enormous body of work on addiction.

We also explore and connect our model with Kohut's thinking on addiction, which is scattered throughout his self-psychological writings. In this chapter, we attempt, therefore, to find the proper place for our model within the general literature on addiction, and especially, in relation to Kohut's thinking.

In the second part of the book (Part II), we return to our six original and representative psychotherapy case histories as they first appeared in the respective volumes of the series *Progress in Self Psychology*. However, we have had the advantage of considerable additional time (that is, 15 years) to work with these six addicted patients. This allows us to present the reader with an expanded and more psychoanalytically in-depth version of these psychotherapy case histories. Each chapter in the second part (that is, Chapters 4 to 6) contains two expanded and detailed versions of our original cases.

In Part II we follow the original chronological order in which we first presented our cases. In so doing, we provide the reader with an opportunity to join us in a psychoanalytic journey beginning with the first presentation of our ideas in the addiction paper trilogy and culminating in the most recent developments in our thinking. The order in which we discuss our original, and by now significantly revised, psychotherapy case histories is as follows: in Chapter 4 we present the cases of Teddy (an alcoholic and rageaholic) and Mary (a bulimic and compulsive overeater); in Chapter 5 we discuss the cases of Joe (an alcoholic Vietnam veteran suffering from posttraumatic stress disorder, or PTSD) and JoAnn (another patient with an eating disorder, who is also addicted to exercise); and in Chapter 6 we describe the cases of Travis (a drug and sex addict who, in the past and until he is in the midst of his psychotherapy, is addicted to violence) and Errol (a compulsive gambler and sex addict).

In all six of these cases, we employ an "empathic-introspective stance" (Kohut, 1977b, p. xiii) as a means of gaining access to the unconscious fantasy lives of our addicted patients. We discover that unconsciously they are organized in terms of a specific type of archaic narcissistic fantasy. This is a megalomaniacal fantasy of possessing magically endowed things and activities (or, ATMs, that is, addictive trigger mechanisms). The abuse of these ATMs engenders within the unconscious mind of an addict a fantasy of being a megalomaniacal self and as gifted with magical control over the forces of nature, and especially those that govern human nature.

The megalomaniacal fantasies of magical control, which our six addicted patients entertain and indulge in, are the crux of what we term the Narcissus complex, which we distinguish from Freud's Oedipus complex. The latter is organized unconsciously in the lives of patients on the basis of psychosexual and aggressive fantasies as well as the defenses against these illusions. We are not asserting that our addicted patients do not suffer from an Oedipus complex.

Instead, and in line with the thinking of Kohut and his self-psychological followers, we argue only that the unconscious crux of the psychic maladies of our addicted patients is best understood and treated psychotherapeutically in terms of the Narcissus complex. It is our opinion that our addicted patients may be accurately and justifiably referred to in common parlance as "fantasy junkies" and "control freaks" *par excellence.*

There is within the field of addiction studies a popular and in vogue notion of the so-called "self-medication hypothesis" (see Khantzian 1975, 1978, 1983, 1985). In contrast to this hypothesis, we believe that addicts intentionally, albeit unconsciously, induce within themselves hypnotic, trance-like, and fugue-like conditions of a dissociative nature. In other words, we contend that addicts, rather than merely self-medicating by various addictive means, are better understood as practicing a form of self-hypnosis.

We originally referred to this hypnoid defense as dissociative anesthesia, whereas we now describe it as addictive metamorphosis or phantasmagorical transmogrification. Both of these latter terms denote an addictive state of mind. In such an altered state of consciousness an addict imagines himself or herself as the supreme ruler or master of the psychic universe made up of unconscious thoughts and emotions.

From our self-psychological perspective, there is a tragic irony to an addict's fantasy of a megalomaniacal self and as endowed with magical control. An addict imagines that he or she controls agents, or ATMs, that induce the hypnotic illusion of being in complete control of his or her psychic reality. This tragic irony, we maintain, consists of the following fact. An addict, rather than achieving total control over the psychic forces governing his or her emotional life and affairs, ultimately and tragically feels like he or she has lost control and is out of control over these powerful psychic forces. Therefore, an addicted patient, who suffers from the Narcissus complex in the form of a fantasy, being megalomaniacal self and as empowered with magical control, actually experiences his or her life as increasingly unmanageable and intolerable.

In the third part of the book (Part III), we provide the reader with a selective and critical review of literature, including psychoanalytic, psychiatric, and psychological, which is relevant for each of the four components of our self-psychological model of addiction (that is, phenomenology, etiology and pathogenesis, typology, and therapeutics). This review enriches the reader's appreciation of the central ideas making up the four components of our model.

In Chapter 7, we uncover the roots of our phenomenology of addiction in the work of a variety of authors. We explain our phenomenology in terms of addictive metamorphosis and phantasmagorical transmogrification. Such addictive states of mind are based in the unconscious mind of an addict on a powerful fantasy of being a megalomaniacal self and empowered with magical control. This unconscious fantasy radically, albeit temporarily and at great psychological cost, alters mind, mood, consciousness, and sensation, and hence an addict's subjective experience of self in relation to the selfobject milieu.

In Chapter 8, we examine a body of literature that serves as a background for our etiology and pathogenesis of addiction. We base the latter on our thinking about a particular form of arrest in psychological development. On the basis of such an arrest, what we describe as healthy "transitional selfobject" things and activities undergo an unhealthy change in their use by a future addict. Over time, transitional selfobjects (things and activities) undergo for an "addiction-prone personality" (Kohut, 1978e [1976], p. 850) a pathological mutation into ATMs.

The psychological arrest in selfobject development occurs in the context of what we label as the narcissistic exchange process. The pathogenic derailment of this unconscious process entails a child exchanging the selfobject functioning of human caregivers for the selfobject-like functioning of nonhuman things and activities. A child, who, as a result of a lack of empathy (that is, an empathic failure) or downright antipathy on the part of the selfobject milieu, is prone to addiction of some type at some point later in life.

An addiction-prone child fails to proceed through the narcissistic exchange process in a natural and healthy fashion. Thus, such a child does not reinvest the narcissistic capital, which is originally derived from early human caregivers, back into nonhuman things or activities (that is, transitional selfobjects) as well as later human caregivers.

Instead, this child remains arrested developmentally at a phase or style of over-investment of narcissistic capital in nonhuman, or at best semi-human, things and activities. This narcissistic over-investment on the part of a child leads to the virtual exclusion of reinvestment of this narcissistic currency back into the selfobject milieu of other human beings as well as healthy nonhuman entities. (See Kohut, 1977b, p. 56 on the crucial distinction between human and nonhuman selfobject, which inexplicably is neither referred to nor discussed by self psychologists.)

We present the psychotherapy case history of Megworth, a young child seen in family psychotherapy, as an example of what can, and, unfortunately, often does go awry in an "addict family" (Chein et al., 1964). The case of Megworth, or Meggy, provides graphic and illustrative evidence (that is, he is representative) of the early emergence in a child of an archaic and a fantasy of being a megalomaniacal self and as possessing magical control. Such an archaic narcissistic fantasy, although phase-appropriate during childhood and even into early adolescence, fails to undergo healthy development into a narcissistically mature and normal sense of mastery. The case of Meggy allows us to take the reader into the unconscious fantasy life of a child to see the etiological origins and pathogenic pathways that may lead, later in life, into addiction.

In Chapter 9, we pursue a discussion of the literature that sets the context for both our typology and therapeutics of addiction. Both our typology and therapeutics revolve around the introduction of our eighth representative psychotherapy case history—that of Byron, an adult male addicted patient who epitomizes Narcissus in wonderland. Byron, during the course of this still ongoing psychoanalytic psychotherapy, is addicted to all five major forms of addiction—either singly or in various combinations.

In this sense, Byron is, therefore, truly representative of the types of addicted patient practitioners often encounter in the context of their private practices. Moreover, he is representative of the increasing number of patients who suffer from some form of bipolar spectrum disorder as well as addiction. In the course of our discussion of Byron as representative of different types of addicted patient, we go beyond our earlier bipolar typology of addiction (see Chapter 2) to a "bioself-psychological typology" of addiction. The latter combines and synthesizes Kohut's notion of the bipolar self, as originally spelled out in *The Restoration of the Self*

(1977b), with the thinking within the ranks of biological psychiatrists and neuroscientists about the topic of the bipolar spectrum disorder.

The case of Byron also serves as a focal point for our description of the literature that most clearly informs our self-psychological approach to using psychoanalytic psychotherapy in working with addicted patients. To be more specific, we organize our therapeutics of addiction on the basis of the notion of the "transference-countertransference neurosis" as initially conceptualized by Ulman & Stolorow (1985) and subsequently developed by Ulman and co-workers (see Miliora & Ulman, 1996a,b; Ulman & Brothers, 1987, 1988; Ulman & Miliora, 2000; Ulman & Paul, 1989, 1990, 1992).

In our discourse on the psychotherapy of Byron, we expand upon the original notion of the transference-countertransference neurosis. We expand it to include archaic narcissistic fantasies, and, in particular, a fantasy of being a megalomaniacal self and as empowered with magical control, which are shared respectively by patient and psychotherapist. We refer to these types of shared fantasy as intersubjective fantasies, and thus introduce and integrate an intersubjective perspective to our self-psychological therapeutics.

Another important aspect of our therapeutics concerns a psycho-analytic discovery by Sterba (1934) of what he refers to as "therapeutic dissociation." In the case of Byron, our psychoanalytic psychotherapy reveals the appearance and presence of therapeutic dissociation in patient and psychotherapist alike. In line with Sterba's original concept of therapeutic dissociation, the psychoanalytic psychotherapy of Byron reveals what we coin as the "psychopharmacotherapeutic effect" (Mas, 2000) of the transitional selfobject transference fantasy. The psychop-harmacotherapeutic effect of the transference may entail one of the following medicinal actions: antianxiety, antidepressant, anti-mania, shame-relieving, and/or anti-panic.

For an addicted patient, the psychopharmacotherapeutic effects of the selfobject transference fantasy take over and replace the selfobject-like effects of ersatz selfobjects or ATMs. In the context of therapeutic dissociation, this takeover is based on the psychophar-macotherapeutic effect of the transference. It enables an addicted patient to replace the ersatz selfobjects in the form of ATMs with genuine transitional selfobject things and activities in the form of the psychotherapist and the psychotherapy.

In the last part of the book (Part IV) namely, Chapter 10, we conclude our study by establishing a linkage between addiction and trauma as mediated by fantasy, dissociation, and control. We establish this interrelationship between addiction and trauma to add to and strengthen the growing awareness and documentation within the mental health field, and, more specifically, within the subfields of addiction and trauma studies—an important connection. There are crucial diagnostic, clinical, and psychotherapeutic links between addiction and trauma. We believe that all eight of our psychotherapy case histories provide further proof of the existence of what Evans and Sullivan (1995) describe as the "addicted survivors of trauma."

Part I

An Introduction to a Self-Psychological Model and Theory of Addiction

Chapter 1

Narcissus in Wonderland

THE NARCISSUS COMPLEX

The subtitle of this book, *Narcissus in Wonderland*, is more than a catchy phrase. We have borrowed the character of Narcissus from ancient Greek mythology, and in so doing, we have located this mythical figure in the wonderland of Lewis J. Carroll's famous book for children, *Alice's Adventures in Wonderland* (1865). In transporting Narcissus to wonderland, we are constructing a self-psychological allegory about the addicted patient as narcissistically disordered. Such a person is a lost soul who wanders aimlessly in an addictive "wonderland."

According to Greek mythology (see, for example, Grimal, 1990; see also, Doty, 1993), Narcissus starved to death because he became so enamored and transfixed by his own image as it was reflected in a pool of water. The myth of Narcissus warns us that individuals can destroy themselves in the process of becoming fatally infatuated by the sight of their own reflected images. In moving from the mythological to the psychological, we can undertake a self-psychological reinterpretation of the underlying message of the story of Narcissus.

Our self-psychological reinterpretation would read as follows: early developmental forms of narcissism, and, especially those expressed as archaic narcissistic fantasies (see Ulman & Brothers, 1987, 1988 for a full explanation on the nature and function of these unconscious presences), possess the inherent power to induce a hypnoid state or hypnotic-like trance in an individual (see Abse, 1966; see also Dickes & Papernik, 1977, and Laplanche & Pontalis, 1988). In such a trance-like state, a person may become so mesmerized and self-absorbed as to

3

become oblivious and indifferent to normal concerns about health and well-being.

Moreover, our self-psychological perspective emphasizes the importance of the fact that psychologically Narcissus loses himself in an image as reflected back to him by a pool of water. In the context of the Greek myth of Narcissus, the pool of water, although an inanimate and non-living thing, takes on animate and almost semi-human qualities. It does so because it reflects back to Narcissus an image of his own human face. In this sense, therefore, Narcissus relates to and uses the pool of water almost as if it were another animate and living being.

According to Strozier (in Kohut, 1985), Kohut had a keen interest in *Alice's Adventures in Wonderland* "from which he could always lovingly quote long passages" (p. 5). Thus, for the purpose of our study, we deem it fitting to bring together Narcissus from Greek myth and Alice from Wonderland. Together they create our self-psychological allegory about narcissism and addiction.

Moreover, there is a significant, yet somewhat obscure, etymological connection between narcissism and addiction. The words narcissism and narcotic, although seemingly unrelated, actually have the same Greek root, namely *narke*. The latter can be translated as numbness or numbing. It would appear, therefore, that both words refer to a kind of deadening of sensation or dulling of awareness. Indeed, narcissism and narcosis (a general term referring to any drug- or chemically induced stupor or state of unconsciousness) have similar implications. They both imply that consciousness or subjective awareness have been altered in the direction of self-absorption in the former and obliviousness in the latter.

Narcissism and narcosis (as synonymous with addiction) may be compared like this: in the case of narcissism an archaic form of self-love functions like a narcotic drug that induces a state of enraptured self-absorption; whereas, in the case of narcosis, a drug or other substance produces a narcissistic state of bliss characterized by an ecstatic trance and euphoric obliviousness. (See Rosenman, 1981, p. 545, for support of our connection between Narcissus and addiction.)

The Narcissus in wonderland of this book is an addict who is in love with an image of the self as dissociatively altered in the reflecting pool of narcissistic fantasy and mood. And, the wonderland that Narcissus inhabits is a domain in which magic and illusion reign supreme. A variety of psychoactive things and activities serve for an addict as magic wands creating spells that arise in the context of the dissociative alteration of conscious awareness. Narcissus, like Alice, undergoes many strange and bizarre adventures in an altered state of mind in which the surreal and fantastic become the norm.

We use our self-psychological allegory, in which we place the mythical character of Narcissus in Carroll's magical Wonderland, to focus on a previously hidden and unconscious complex—the *Narcissus complex*. (See Hamilton, 1982, for a discussion of the importance of the myths of Narcissus and Oedipus for psychoanalytic theory; see also Rosenman, 1981, as well as Bruhm, 2001; Dufresne, 1996; Jacoby, 1985; Schwartz-Salant, 1982, for both Freudian and Jungian discussions on the importance of the myth of Narcissus to an understanding of narcissistic psychopathology.) This psychic constellation is analogous to and modeled after Freud's famous Oedipus complex, which he discovered as the unconscious basis for both neurosis and psychosis. From his classical perspective, Freud (1953 [1916–1917]) argues that psychosexual and aggressive fantasies are the unconscious bedrock of the Oedipus complex and its accompanying neurotic and psychotic psychopathology.

In a clear anticipation of our concept of the Narcissus complex, Tartakoff (1966) contends that "infantile narcissistic fantasies" (p. 232) are at the unconscious core of what she calls the "Nobel Prize Complex" (p. 236). Tartakoff coins this evocative term in the course of describing the unconscious fantasy lives of a group of psychoanalytic patients. These patients are "exemplified by individuals who ... entertain ambitious goals: e.g., the wish to be President, to attain great wealth, to become a social leader or to win an 'Oscar'" (p. 236). According to Tartakoff, two of the "infantile narcissistic fantasies" that unconsciously organize the "Nobel Prize Complex" are: "(1) the active, omnipotent fantasy of being the 'powerful one,' with grandiose features; and (2) the passive fantasy of being the 'special one,' chosen by virtue of exceptional gifts" (p. 237).

In linking the "infantile narcissistic fantasies" with the "Nobel Prize Complex," first, she warns: "Nonetheless, whenever autonomous functioning remains irrevocably associated with *grandiose narcissistic fantasies* fostered in childhood, true autonomy may not be achieved no matter how great the individual's potentialities" (p. 246, emphasis added). Then, she adds: "In this instance, *one is reminded of an addiction* which is characterized by an insatiable desire to recover an infantile state of gratification which can never be fulfilled in reality" (pp. 246–47, emphasis added).

We maintain, building on Tartakoff's work, that an unconscious system of archaic narcissistic fantasies make up the Narcissus complex.

The latter is expressed symptomatically or characterologically in the form of an addiction. More specifically, we believe that a fantasy of being a megalomaniacal self and empowered with magical control is at the center of the underlying system of illusions constituting the Narcissus complex. (For some recent studies of megalomania, see Lifton, 1999, and Steiner, 1999.)

In the case of addiction, such a narcissistic fantasy centers on a narcissistic illusion of a megalomaniacal being that possesses magical control over psychoactive agents (things and activities). These latter entities allow for the artificial alteration of the subjective reality of the sense of both one's self and one's personal world. Under the influence of these intoxicating fantasies, an addict imagines being like a sorcerer or wizard who controls a magic wand capable of manipulating the forces of nature, and particularly those forces of human nature. Eventually, a person becomes a captive of these addictive fantasies and then becomes an addict lost in a wonderland. A recent film by Darren Aronofsky entitled *Requiem for a Dream*—a movie based on a 1978 novel by Hubert Selby with the same title— presents a contemporary cinematic portrayal of addiction that is amazingly consistent with our own view. The main characters in this film are addicted to a variety of things and activities; however, all as different means to a similar *end*, namely, entering into an addictive fantasy state, or self-state. The characters from this movie are, therefore, remarkably similar to our addicted patients in being "fantasy junkies."

The primary nature of their addiction, like that of our addicted patients, is therefore, to a fantasy [the end] rather than to any particular thing or activity [the means]. In both instances, fantasy assumes primacy in being the unconscious determinant of addiction, whereas the things and activities assume only a secondary status.

We are not alone in recognizing the importance of the myth of Narcissus (in contrast to Freud's focus on the myth of Oedipus) to a psychoanalytic understanding of modern life and thought. First, there is Lasch's famous book, *The Culture of Narcissism: American Life in an Age of Diminishing Expectations* (1979). In another instance, Alford (1988) analyzes the Greek myth of Narcissus as a basis for applying the psychoanalytic concept of narcissism to the study of modern schools of political theory. Or, to take another good example, Berman (1990) employs the Narcissus myth as the means by which he conducted his applied psychoanalytic study of narcissism as a hidden yet central dimension in the text of many modern novels.

And, Shay (1994) in his work, *Achilles in Vietnam: Combat Trauma and the Undoing of Character*, takes the Greek mythical figure of Achilles as a point of departure for an examination of posttraumatic stress disorder (PTSD) in Vietnam combat veterans. In essence, he argues that the Vietnam combat veteran is analogous to Achilles in being a modern-day version of the mythical warrior. And, like Achilles, the veteran of the Vietnam War is cursed with a fatal flaw—namely, an Achilles heel—that exposes him to emotional breakdown in the heat of battle. More specifically, Shay draws a parallel between Achilles and the Vietnam combat veteran in a fashion analogous to the way in which we compare Narcissus to an addict.

We follow the lead of Lasch, Alford, Berman, and Shay in utilizing Greek mythology to gain a psychoanalytic understanding of the unconscious dimension of modern phenomenon taking place in the contemporary world. In this sense, we are also following in Freud's footsteps in returning to antiquity to understand modernity. (Nussbaum, 1994, turns this intellectual perspective on its head, so to speak. She takes modern thought on the nature of psychotherapy and the psychotherapeutic process as a lens through which to illuminate ancient Greek insights on psychic maladies and their remedy.)

ALICE IN WONDERLAND

Our notion of Alice as an addict lost in a wonderland in which both conscious awareness and subjective experience are radically changed by mind altering agents is not original to our work. The idea is inspired by the lyrics of a song, "Go Ask Alice," by Jefferson Airplane, a popular rock group of the 1960s. The group sings about Alice's adventures in Wonderland and the strange effects of mind and mood altering substances on her subjective sense of herself and her immediate surroundings.

For example, they sing about one drug making Alice bigger and another making her smaller. Clearly, there is an important implication based on the drug-induced distortions in Alice's physical size. It stands as a metaphor related to the psychoactively induced metamorphosis which Alice undergoes as a result of using these potent agents.

Jefferson Airplane is not alone in reinterpreting Carroll's *Alice's Adventures in Wonderland* as an allegory for the dangers of addiction. Martha Morrison (1989) entitles her moving, autobiographical account of her hard won victory over drug addiction—*White Rabbit: A Doctor's*

Story of Her Addiction and Recovery. She uses the "White Rabbit" and the "Mad Hatter" of Carroll's *Alice* for purposes similar to that of Jefferson Airplane.

In fact, Morrison begins her book with a long quote from the lyrics of "Go Ask Alice" written by Grace Slick; thereby making a clear connection between her book and the song. These lyrics describe the strange world Alice explores during her substance-induced trip. The lyrics include references to several addictive substances, such as pills, hashish, and mushrooms, all of which were drugs fads in the 1960s.

Both Slick and Morrison reinterpret Carroll's story of *Alice* on the basis of allegory. Both view it as a literary device alluding to the mind-altering and reality-bending effects of drugs. And, both song writer and autobiographer interpret the *Alice* story as containing an implicit warning to those considering or already using addictive drugs: an individual who uses these psychoactive agents can become an unwitting captive of an altered state of consciousness from which it is not so easy to escape.

We agree with Slick and Morrison regarding the underlying meaning of *Alice's Adventures in Wonderland.* We also read it as a story warning about the dangers to a person who enters an addictive state of mind, with little or no regard for the deleterious effects to one's mental health and well-being. From this vantage point, the story of *Alice* may be reinterpreted as follows: an individual who repeatedly alters conscious-ness over a long period of time through the addictive abuse of psycho-active agents may experience an initial sense of pleasure and euphoria; however, eventually, such a form of addictive repetition leads to the serious warping and distortion of a person's sense of the subjective reality of self and the world.

From the perspective of the 1960s, we understand Slick and Morrison as reinterpreting Carroll's story as a cautionary tale: it warns us that if we foolishly alter our state of mind, as Alice does through the careless use of magical potions, we risk becoming unwitting captives of these potent agents. As a result, we may lose ourselves in a surreal world which has been *transmogrified* from a blissful wonderland into a mortifying hell.

Unlike several other well-known literary artists and poets of the 18th and 19th centuries, it appears that Carroll was neither a user nor abuser of addictive drugs, such as cocaine and opium, both of which were commonly abused during that era. Yet, he is reputed to have had a perverse fascination with young girls—one bordering on what some might describe as a pedophilic perversion.

In a fashion similar to an addict, Carroll appears to have been obsessed, not, however, with drugs but with young girls; in addition, in some instances he was quite compulsive in his behavior toward them. For example, he was especially fond of taking pictures of nude little girls (J. Jackson, personal communication, 1993; see also Cohen, 1995, for a recent biography of Carroll). In this sense, Carroll is like an addict—both mentally obsessed with a particular thing and very compulsive in his behavior as regards it.

In the context of our current discussion, Carroll's story about *Alice's Adventures in Wonderland* may be viewed as symbolic of his unusual fascination with little girls. (See Greenacres, 1955b; Grotjahn, 1947; Schilder, 1938; Skinner, 1947 for psychoanalytic studies of Carroll and *Alice's Adventure in Wonderland*. See also, Wullschläger, 1995, for a study of Carroll's life and personal fantasies). As such, the story is reflective of both the obsessive and compulsive nature of Carroll's preoccupation with young girls.

It appears that both perversion and addiction share obsessive-compulsive characteristics. Perhaps this helps to account for the respective positions of Jefferson Airplane and Martha Morrison regarding the allegorical nature of Carroll's story. Indeed, they believe it is an allegory that Carroll intended as a warning. He warns about the inherent dangers attendant to the use (abuse) of psychoactive agents that radically alter one's sense of the subjective reality of oneself and one's personal world.

However, Carroll is by no means the only 18th/19th century author who can be interpreted as writing allegorically about drug-induced states of *phantasmagorical transmogrification*. For example, Robert Louis Stevenson's *The Strange Case of Dr. Jekyll and Mr. Hyde*, originally published in 1886, may be read similarly as an allegorical story about Stevenson's probable experiences with cocaine (see, for example, Schultz, 1971). Or, to cite another instance, Samuel Taylor Coleridge's "Kubla Khan," written in the late 1790s, may be interpreted as an allegorical description of his experiences with opium (see, for example, Marcovitz, 1964; Weissman, 1989).

Moreover, both Stevenson's *Dr. Jekyll and Mr. Hyde* and Coleridge's "Kubla Khan" were probably written in the midst of each author's abuse or dependence on, respectively, cocaine and opium. In addition, both works appear to have been imaginative creations emanating from the dreams of these two authors.

Writing about Stevenson, Schultz (1971) notes: *"Jekyll and Hyde* was the product of a *fantastic dream"* (p. 91, emphasis added). Marcovitz (1964) observes about "Kubla Khan" that Coleridge was "an opium addict and ... he had said that the poem was dreamed during an opium sleep" (p. 411). Marcovitz adds: "On re-reading the poem, it suddenly appeared to me as a dream epitomizing the psychology of addiction" (p. 411).

We take seriously the suggestions of both Schultz and Marcovitz concerning the dream-like, and hence, unconscious origins of *Dr. Jekyll and Mr. Hyde* and "Kubla Khan." It is possible, therefore, that by employing the standard technique of psychoanalysis we can analyze these works as if they were dreams. Thus, we can arrive at a psycho-analytic interpretation of these works as the unconscious expression of the addictive fantasies of the respective authors. For example, Marcovitz states:

> I believe that the poem provides us with the most elegant example in all literature of *the fantasy which the addictive drug fulfills*, together with the evidence for the belief in the power of the dream, that is, of the addictive drug, to bring a fulfillment greater than any reality. (p. 424, emphasis added)

Earlier, Marcovitz argues that this fantasy is in "essence ... the psychology of the addict." He (Marcovitz, 1974) continues:

> In his repetitions of the addictive behavior the addict each time tries not only to re-create the feeling of well-being, but *also to recapture the lost dream* with which he will attain the fulfillment of all his desires and the relief of his distress." (p. 424)

The heroine and heroes in the works of Carroll, Stevenson, and Coleridge are transported as if by magic to a surreal world. Or, in the case of Dr. Jekyll, he is *metamorphized* into a strange creature. Further-more, the main character in all three of these literary works undergoes a drug-induced experience.

This episode entails a dissociative alteration of the subjective reality of the sense of self as evidenced by mysterious feelings and behavior. (See also Garcia, 1990, on the role of dissociation in Stevenson's *Dr. Jekyll and Mr. Hyde.*) The dissociated heroine and heroes of these various tales are under the spell of fantasy, and, consequently, are *anesthetized* against the misery and drudgery of their otherwise humdrum lives. In this sense, therefore, they are like Alice in that they are characters who are like Narcissus. Like Narcissus, they find themselves lost in a wonderland of both *addictive dissociation* and *anesthetization.*

As is evident from the cases of Coleridge and Stevenson, from the late 18th century to the 19th century many writers and artists experimented and, in some cases, became addicted to psychoactive drugs such as opium and cocaine. (See Milligan, 1995, for a discussion of the role of opium in 19th century English culture.) In the late 19th century, the founder of psychoanalysis, Sigmund Freud, himself experimented with and apparently became temporarily addicted to cocaine. However, Freud is unlike his cohorts in the literary world. These writers resorted to fictive accounts as a discreet means of chronicling their personal experiences with highly addictive drugs. In dramatic contrast, Freud records the results of his scientific experiments with cocaine openly in a series of articles subsequently referred to as the "Cocaine Papers."

Moreover, Freud, always the scientist *par excellence*, is unlike his counterparts in the literary world in still another sense. They are content to make up allegorical stories about the effect of mind and mood altering agents on psyche and soul. (See Boon, 2002, and Plant, 1999, for a description of post-Romantic writers such as Coleridge and Freud as well as others who provide fictional and factual accounts of their personal experiences with powerful, and highly addictive, drugs such as, respectively, opium and cocaine.) Instead, Freud originally experimented with cocaine in the hopes of finding a drug that might function as a much needed antidepressant. (See Bernfeld, 1953, and Byck in Freud, 1974, for an analysis of Freud's use of cocaine as an antidepressant drug, as well as his place in the annals of medical history as, paradoxically, a forerunner of modern psychopharmacology.)

It is an ironic twist of historical fact that Freud, the consummate psychoanalyst, discovered in cocaine a possible and early psychopharmacological remedy for unconscious suffering. Freud stumbled upon, in his experiments with cocaine, the connection between brain and mind. However, the case of Freud's probable dependence on cocaine illustrates the dangers of relying too heavily on these addictive agents. Psychoactively induced forms of dissociation and anesthetization, and the appeal and cravings for such a phantasmagorical transmorgrification, are major determinants of addiction. At least for a short period of time, Freud himself apparently became a prime example of a Narcissus in wonderland.

NARCISSUS IN WONDERLAND

We are implying, by the subtitle of our book, that Narcissus has been transported figuratively from Greek myth and placed instead in a storybook wonderland. We are employing our book, therefore, to focus attention on an underlying yet crucial connection. We contend that there is a vital link between fantasy and addiction. The Narcissus in wonderland of our book stands, metaphorically, for all addicts. In a psychological sense, addicts, just like Alice, drop down the rabbit hole into what seems to be at first glance a fantastic world of magic and illusion. Temporarily at least, an addict can in such a world dissociate from and anesthetize against all the ills and pains of daily living.

In the last resort, however, an addict may suffer the same fate as Narcissus. An addict, like Narcissus, withers away and dies a psychic death, as a result of becoming so self-absorbed by the mesmerizing reflection in the mind's eye of one's own glorious self-image. Unlike Narcissus, however, an addict is transfixed by a narcissistically inflated and over-exaggerated image of the self.

This unrealistic self-image appears in a reflecting pool of the mind, and, more specifically, a mental pond composed of narcissistic fantasies and moods. Such transfixation is often the tragic outcome of the Narcissus complex in which an addict is trapped in a surreal wonderland constituted by narcissistic fantasy and mood. From our perspective, an addict enters into a hypnoid or dissociated state involving an archaic narcissistic fantasy of being a self as a megalomaniacal being. In such a state of self(auto)-hypnosis, an addict replays psychoactive fantasy tapes (that is, imaginary scenarios) in a mesmerizing fashion on a projection screen of the mind. (See Edelson, 1988, on the "cinematic model" of the unconscious mind as a view that is especially compatible with our conceptualization of the unconscious.)

Another essential similarity may be drawn between the myth of Narcissus and dissociative anesthesia, or what we now refer to as either addictive metamorphosis or phantasmagorical transmogrification. This similarity is critical to understanding the fantastic nature of the Narcissus complex. According to Greek myth, Narcissus loses himself in his own self-image as reflected in a pool of water. Narcissus does not interact with others in a normal and healthy fashion. Instead, Narcissus substitutes for such real and human interaction an illusory connection to an inanimate body of water, namely a reflecting pool.

The latter functions for Narcissus as a semi-human thing in the presence of which he falls madly (that is, infatuatedly and insanely) in love with himself.

Similarly, and as part of the Narcissus complex, an addict substitutes inanimate things and activities (regardless of how humanoid or android an addict imagines them as being) for interaction with other, living beings. And, in the end, an addict becomes a victim of the same fate as that which befalls Narcissus. Like Narcissus, an addict lives out an emotionally impoverished life consisting of bare subsistence on narcissistic illusions. An addict, in a fashion analogous to Narcissus, psychologically withers away in such a vacuous existence and in the absence of the psychic nourishment provided by interaction with real-life, human beings.

The Self Psychology of Addiction and Its Treatment: Narcissus in Wonderland reports on the outcome of our self-psychological study of the unconscious fantasy lives of a representative sample of addicted patients. The findings of our investigation are based on psychoanalytic data gathered during many years of treating these patients in self-psychological psychotherapy. We maintain that, from a methodological perspective, addiction constitutes an excellent opportunity for the psychoanalytic researcher to shed light on the otherwise dark and murky world of unconscious fantasy. Focusing on fantasy allows us to arrive at a self-psychological understanding of the unconscious dimensions of addiction as well as a self-psychological (and intersubjective) approach to its treatment.

In essence, we discovered that an archaic form of narcissism, namely, megalomania, is at the unconscious bottom of addiction. The notion of megalomania has fallen into ill-repute within psychoanalysis, and more specifically among self-psychologists (see, for example, Shane & Shane, 1990, p. 82). Yet, despite its notoriety, the idea of megalomania, and more specifically, a fantasy of being a megalomaniacal self and as gifted with a form of magical control, constitutes our main contribution to the psychoanalysis of addiction.

We have borrowed our notion of megalomania from Freud's (1958 [1911]) famous study of the case of Schreber. (Lothane, 1992, has studied Freud's analysis of this case using a massive examination of all the relevant historical records and documents of that period. Relying on this critical reassessment, Lothane finds Freud's analysis to be seriously flawed and inaccurate. Yet, the exhaustive nature of Lothane's work notwithstanding, he cites and discusses megalomania in only one context, and that single instance concerns a passing reference by Freud to the notion of megalomania in a letter he had written to Abraham. It follows, therefore, that Lothane does not go into any detail at any point regarding the importance of megalomania to Freud's analysis of the case of Schreber.)

There are clearly important differences between our self-psychological reinterpretation of megalomania and Freud's classical understanding of the term. (See Rosenfeld, 2000, for a fictional account of what a particular author conjures up as Freud's own tendency toward megalomania, as Freud himself had construed it.) Freud understands megalomania in the context of his study of psychosis.

In contrast, we understand megalomania on the basis of our examination of addiction. Moreover, from our self-psychological perspective we conceive of megalomania and, again more specifically, a fantasy of being a megalomaniacal self that wields magical control, as a phase-appropriate aspect of narcissism in its normal development from archaic to mature forms. In contradistinction, Freud from his classical psychoanalytic perspective views megalomania as pathological by definition and as a key feature of paranoid psychosis.

However, despite these significant differences, there are still some crucial similarities between our position and that of Freud. For example, we, like Freud, view those individuals who harbor megalomaniacal ideas as prone to either narcissistic illusions or delusions of being godlike. (See, for example, Scull, 2005, for a description and analysis of this little discussed phenomenon in the field of medicine. Such persons imagine that they possess a magical ability to control the very nature of reality.

Nonetheless, there is a subtle yet profound difference between an addict and a psychotic. An addict entertains megalomaniacal illusions, whereas a psychotic concocts megalomaniacal delusions. Another way of looking at this difference is as follows. On the one hand, the megalomaniacal illusions of an addict extend only to magical control over very specific things and activities. As part of the mental act of magical thinking, an addict imagines these entities as being endowed with the illusory power to transform human nature as expressed in fantasy and mood. On the other hand, the megalomaniacal delusions of a psychotic extend to magical control over the entire range of physical forces of nature.

We focus on megalomania in an attempt to resurrect it, so to speak, from a psychoanalytic graveyard, where, in our opinion, it has been buried prematurely. In the process, we are also trying to "depathologize" it (that is, to conceive of it as a normal feature in the developmental unfolding of healthy narcissism). We are following in the footsteps of Heinz Kohut, who endeavored to depathologize the similar and related concepts of grandiosity and omnipotence. (See Eigen, 2004 [1986], on the problem inherent in Kohut's absorption [and elimination] of Freud's idea of megalomania into the former's formulation of grandiosity and omnipotence.)

Thus, from our self-psychological perspective we conceive of megalomania as one of the phase-appropriate forms of archaic narcissism. Like other archaic forms of narcissism, it may become developmentally arrested in the context of a selfobject milieu that is lacking in empathy (or is antipathetic). In certain instances, such a developmental arrest may lead, later in life, to addiction. In the case of an addict, megalomania manifests itself primarily in an archaic narcissistic fantasy of being a megalomaniacal self endowed with a form of magical control over psychoactive agents (things and activities). An addict imagines that the possession of these entities will usher in a metamorphosis or transmogrification into a radically new and different state of being; that is, a fantasy of being a megalomaniacal self.

In essence, a two-way street may be said to run between the fields of addiction studies and self psychology. In one direction, the study of addiction may benefit enormously from the inclusion of a self-psychological perspective on the nature and role of archaic narcissistic fantasy and accompanying moods of narcissistic bliss and mortification. In the other direction, self psychology can gain considerably from the study of addiction as a prime example of a narcissistic (behavior) disorder. (See Kohut, 1977b, for a discussion of the crucial, yet until recently, rarely cited distinction between narcissistic personality and behavior disorders.)

As a paradigmatic example of Narcissus in wonderland, an addict undergoes a dissociative alteration of consciousness similar, although not identical, to that experienced by Alice. As already noted, we (Ulman and Paul, 1992) have previously referred to this change of consciousness as "dissociative anesthesia," or what we now refer to as addictive metamorphosis or phantasmagorical transmogrification. This anesthetized state of dissociation is based on a self-induced alteration of the sense of the subjective reality of oneself in relation to one's personal world (see Drover et al., 2002; John & Prichep, 2005; John et al., 2001; Mashour, 2006; and Rondshagen et al., 2004 for studies and discussions of the effect of and inter-relationships among anesthesia, consciousness and the unconscious).

We distinguish such an artificially induced state from similar states that occur naturally and spontaneously. An addictive state of mind is based, in our opinion, on autohypnosis. It arises from the sudden appearance in normal, waking consciousness of otherwise unconscious fantasies and accompanying moods (see Paul and Carson, 1997; see also Bollas, 1978; Freedman, 1985).

Anticipating our position, Siegel (1989) in his study *Intoxication* suggests that both dissociation and anesthetization are definitive of the addictive experience. In referring to various forms of drug use, Siegel stresses that "this *dissociation*, not unlike the trance from dizziness or *anesthesia* from nitrous oxide ... is so attractive to many users" (p. 219, emphasis added). Siegel continues: "They have dreamlike experiences in which they feel as though they were in a different place, in a different time" (p. 219).

Siegel focuses, in his depiction of intoxication, on the state of being simultaneously dissociated and anesthetized. His description of a person's subjective experience of being intoxicated is a state of mind that is characteristic of addiction. It sounds remarkably similar to the description provided by Carroll concerning Alice's alteration of consciousness in Wonderland.

An addict is in a state of mind dissociatively altered. In such a hypnogogical state of consciousness, an addict imaginatively relives childhood fantasies of "control over a narcissistically experienced world" (Kohut, 1978d [1972], p. 657) and affectively re-experiences early moods (affect and sensation) of narcissistic bliss. Such ideational reliving and affective re-experiencing occur simultaneously and on three distinct yet interrelated levels including those of cognition, emotion, and senses.

On a cognitive level, fantasies of being a megalomaniacal and as exercising magical control are activated and heightened, and temporarily pervade consciousness in such a way as to produce a hypnoid or dissociated self-state. We have extrapolated from Kohut's (1977b) notion of "self-state dreams" (pp. 109–110) in our formulation of what we now refer to as a "self-state fantasy." The latter idea constitutes more refined and theoretically advanced formulations of the unconscious domain of experience, which we previously indicated by the concept of archaic narcissistic fantasy.

Our description of the alteration of cognition is not intended to imply that an addict is conscious or self-aware of the presence of archaic narcissistic fantasies, or self-state fantasies. Because these fantasies emerge in a dreamlike state, an addict remains consciously unaware of either their presence or their meaning. In essence, an addict engages in an unconscious process involving what some analysts (see, for example, Brenner, 1994, pp. 822, 823, 834; Dickes and Papernik, 1988, pp. 640, 652; Ferguson, 1990, pp. 430, 433), who have returned to ideas in Breuer and Freud's *Studies on Hysteria* (1953 [1893–1895]), have termed the "hypnoid defense."

This unconscious mechanism of defense involves the dissociative alteration of subjective awareness. Such a radical change in conscious awareness is based on the temporary take over of subjectivity by powerful fantasies. In conditions such as dissociative identity disorder (DID), or what previously had been referred to as multiple personality disorder (MPD), this unconscious defense mechanism occurs in a spontaneous fashion. In the case of addiction it occurs artificially as a result of the use of some mind and mood altering agent. As a result, and over time, an addict may attain, however dimly, a vague awareness of a facsimile of these fantasies.

In contrast, an addicted patient may gain some greater familiarity with and appreciation of the true nature of these addictive fantasies and moods as they are therapeutically revived in the form of a transitional selfobject transference. Clinically speaking, the revival in the transference of these fantasies and moods is the primary source and means by which we psychoanalytically reconstruct the unconscious meaning of the Narcissus complex. Outside of the analytic setting, an addict can evoke a fantasy of being a megalomaniacal self without, however, knowing or understanding much about them. Thus, under (ab)normal circumstances, an addict is subjectively aware of (or consciously experiences) only a faint hint of the presence of a fantasy of being a megalomaniacal self.

On an affective level, intense moods of narcissistic bliss and rapture including euphoria, ecstasy, and elation (see Lewin, 1950, for an original and pioneering psychoanalytic study of these narcissistic affects), which accompany addictive fantasies, temporarily become the dominant emotions. The exquisite pleasure and emotional numbing derived from these instances of affective re-experiencing are crucial in producing the anesthetization that characterizes addictive metamorphosis. The narcissistic pleasure attendant to phantasmagorical transmogrification, despite being crass and hedonistic, serves for an addict to reinforce the desire to repeat the numbing (that is, narcotic) experience of the addictive state of mind.

And finally, as part of addictive metamorphosis appealing sensations flood the brain and body on a sensorial level. The pleasurable nature of these physical sensations is a third kind of psychic reinforcer that habituates an addict to constantly repeat and prolong the addictive state of mind.

We must distinguish our view of the addictive dissociation, which entails a trance-like reliving of fantasy and fugue-like re-experiencing of mood, from the dissociation typical of the reliving and re-experiencing symptoms characteristic of other psychiatric disorders such as posttraumatic stress disorder (PTSD). First, in the case of addictive dissociation, a person has an illusionary experience based on a past imagined as intensely pleasant. In the case of stress-induced dissociation, a person imagines being back in a past experienced as extremely traumatic.

And second, an addict unconsciously induces a hypnoid state consisting of an imaginative reliving and affective re-experiencing, which together produce a desired alteration of consciousness. (See Abse, 1966; Brody, 1964; Dickes & Papernik, 1977; LaPlanche & Pontalis, 1988; Leowald, 1980 [1955]; Stamm, 1962; and Stein, 2003 for discussions of the hypnoid and trance states.) Obviously, and in striking contrast, a trauma survivor unintentionally undergoes ideational reliving and affective re-experiencing. The PTSD symptoms, which are characteristic of this reliving and re-experiencing, are clearly unwanted and undesired. Thus, addictive dissociation and anesthetization may be contrasted to traumatic dissociation and numbing as follows: as part of the addictive process, an addict undergoes an illusory experience of intense yet self-destructive pleasure; whereas as part of the traumatic process, a trauma survivor undergoes an illusory experience of intense and debilitating pain.

Special Features of the Study

The special features of our study consist of its distinct clinical depth and breadth. First, our study is one of only a few of the self-psychological theories of addiction that are fantasy-based. As such, it is capable of penetrating psychoanalytically to the phantasmagorical depths of the unconscious mind. Second, our study is derived from psychoanalytic psychotherapy with a broad range of patients suffering from all five of the major forms of addiction (that is, alcoholism, drug abuse, eating disorders, as well as compulsive gambling and sex). In gathering and analyzing our clinical data, we formulated a self-psychological model of addiction that is both systematic and comprehensive.

The lengthy and in-depth nature of the psychoanalytic research on which our study is based distinguishes it from other works in the field. These works typically offer a psychoanalytic theory of addiction, without, however, presenting the details and discussing the exact nature of the psychoanalytic approach to treating addiction. The absence of such clinical data as part of case studies (as distinct from case histories) imposes serious limits on the clinical applicability of such studies, regardless of their respective theoretical merits and clinical insights.

Third and finally, our study is distinct because it has been conducted by two psychoanalysts who were themselves addicts, yet who are in full and long-term recovery. As recovering addicts, we have developed an intimate affinity for and empathy with our addicted patients. We have our own experience with and personal knowledge of the intoxicating fantasies and inebriating moods that are such an integral yet often hidden feature of the addictive state of mind. The fact of having been once addicted ourselves, combined with our psychotherapeutic experience (gained during the course of many years of treating addicts), allows us to ground our "experience-distant" theorizing in a clinical reality which is "experience-near." (See Kohut, 1977b, for a discussion of the distinction between "experience-distant" and "experience-near" theorizing.)

Organizational Format

Narcissus in Wonderland is organized so that the reader can follow the natural evolution of our thinking on addiction. This line of thinking makes up the theoretical and clinical backbone of the book. The origins of our current thinking on addiction can be traced back to three separately published papers on the topic (Ulman & Paul, 1989, 1990, 1992), or what we now call the "addiction paper trilogy."

The book is divided into four major parts—(1) an introductory section; (2) a section consisting of a detailed presentation of six representative treatment case histories; and (3) a section connecting the four components of our self-psychological model of addiction (that is, the phenomenology, etiology and pathogenesis, typology, and therapeutics) to relevant and pertinent literature; and (4) a summary of the major findings of our work. The first part of the book consists of three chapters: the current, introductory chapter (Chapter 1), a chapter describing our self-psychological model of addiction (Chapter 2), and a chapter discussing the theoretical and, more specifically, Kohutian origins of our model (Chapter 3).

The second part of the book also is composed of three interrelated chapters which, taken together, retrace the chronology of our previous treatment case histories. Each one of these three chapters (Chapters 4, 5, and 6) present expanded and more psychoanalytically in-depth versions of our earlier treatment case histories—that is, the six therapy cases from our earlier addiction paper trilogy. These chapters, each one of which consists of two cases, follow our work with addicted patients as it unfolded chronologically over the course of many years.

Hence, the first of these three chapters (Chapter 4) presents a revised version of our earliest work with two addicted patients—one of which (Teddy) is alcoholic, whereas the other (Mary) is eating disordered. The second of these chapters (Chapter 5) records a new version of our later work with two other addicted patients—Joe who suffers from alcoholism, and JoAnn who is afflicted with an eating disorder. The final chapter (Chapter 6) of this second part involves an updated discussion of our relatively more recent psychotherapy with the last two of our six representative treatment case histories. These two addicted patients—named Travis and Errol—are disturbed by a serious problem with drug abuse and sex addiction in the case of the former and compulsive gambling and sex addiction in the case of the latter.

In presenting the cases in this particular order we follow the natural course of our psychoanalytic therapy with these addicted patients. Moreover, in so doing we enable the reader to join us as we retrace the steps we took in deepening our self-psychological understanding of the unconscious (phantasmagorical) dynamics of addiction and in enhancing our intersubjective approach to the psychotherapeutic treatment of the addicted patient.

There are several advantages to the reader in following the organic evolution of our theoretical and clinical thinking. First, the reader joins us as we learn from our inevitable missteps and mistakes and, in the process, advance in our endeavor to better understand and more effectively treat our addicted patients. Second, we place the case histories in the middle part of the book in order to provide the reader with an empirical and, more specifically, clinical point of reference. The reader can grasp from this reference point the psychotherapeutic implications of the previous more abstract and theoretical discussion of our self-psychological model of addiction.

The six psychotherapy cases also serve as a natural bridge to the third part of the book. In this section of our work, we present the reader with an historical context within which to locate our model. In the first two chapters (Chapters 7 and 8) in this section, we review and integrate literature relevant to the components of our model dealing, respectively, with the phenomenology as well as the etiology and pathogenesis of addiction. In this latter chapter (Chapter 8), we describe the case of a child, Megworth or Meggy, to provide a graphic illustration of the etiology and pathogenesis of addiction.

In the last chapter of this section (Chapter 9) we present both a bioself-psychological typology of addiction and psychotherapeutic approach to its treatment. As part of Chapter 9, we discuss the case of Byron as a representative example of our bioself-psychological typology and psychotherapeutic approach.

In reviewing and discussing all this literature, we hope to give the reader a clear picture of how our self-psychological model of addiction emerged from our extensive and in-depth reading of the works of other authors, all of whom dealt with subject matters related to our own clinical work and theorizing. In other words, we want to make it abundantly clear to the reader that our self-psychological model of addiction did not emerge in an historical vacuum. On the contrary, it developed gradually and slowly, as we incorporated the important ideas and thinking of many other theorists and clinicians who preceded us in studying addiction primarily from a psychoanalytic perspective and secondarily from a nonpsychoanalytic vantage point. All of these points of view contributed enormously to the theoretical construction of our self-psychological model of addiction, and we are, therefore, deeply indebted to all of them.

In the fourth and concluding chapter of the book (Chapter 10) we examine the theoretical as well as clinical interconnection that links addiction and trauma. We employ the concepts of fantasy, control, and dissociation as mediating variables through which it is possible to establish a bioself-psychological relationship between addiction and trauma. In the course of our concluding discussion, we come full circle to an earlier work on trauma (see Ulman & Brothers, 1988). *The Shattered Self* (Ulman & Brothers, 1988) and *Narcissus in Wonderland* constitute the two pillars upon which we construct a theoretical bridge linking trauma to addiction and vice versa.

Chapter 2

A Self-Psychological Model of Addiction

INTRODUCTION

Our self-psychological model of addiction is multifaceted and fantasy-based. (See, for example, Brody, 2003; Eisch and Mandyam, 2004; Hyman, 2005; Massing, 2000; O'Neil, 2003; Satel, 1999, 2000; Satel and Goodwin, 1998; and Volkow, 2004 for a discussion of the hotly contested debate about the best and more accurate way of viewing addiction as either a complex mental [that is, psychic] disorder or a biological disease of the brain.) It consists of four separate yet interrelated components which, when utilized together, allow us to focus specifically on the phenomenology, etiology and pathogenesis, typology, and treatment of addiction. We employ each of these components to examine an essential and critical aspect of addiction. Each component of our model is designed to answer one of four research questions: (1) *what* (phenomenology) is the nature of addiction; (2) *when* and *where* (etiology and pathogenesis) does addiction begin; (3) *who* (typology) is an addict; and (4) *how* (therapeutics) is an addicted patient treated most effectively.

Our proposed model rests on one key concept—namely that of fantasy. We explore fantasy as it achieves expression in an addict's conscious and unconscious mental life. (See Paul and Carson, 1997, on the critical relationship between fantasy and the influence of addictive substances.) We borrow our basic conception of fantasy from classical psychoanalysis; our model incorporates a distinctly self-psychological perspective on narcissism, one which centers primarily on the concept of "archaic narcissistic fantasy" (Ulman & Brothers, 1988), or self-state fantasy.

These ephemeral yet powerful psychic presences are typically expressed (consciously and unconsciously) as phantasmagorical visions of the self in relation to others. These other persons are subjectively experienced, however, as extensions of or as additions to the self, that is, as selfobjects. Later in this chapter, we will have more to say about the nature and function of selfobjects, both human and nonhuman.

From our self-psychological perspective, we refer to these fantasies as *archaic* because they originate in childhood experiences of the person in relation to and in connection with caretakers who function as selfobjects. In addition, we view these fantasies as archaic because there has been a developmental failure in their transformation and, hence, in modulating and tempering them. In other words, these imaginary visions—or mental images of the self in relation to a selfobject milieu—are archaic because they retain a highly phantasmagorical (magical and illusory) quality. In adulthood, these fantasies lend an archaic and narcissistic quality to the unconscious organization of subjective experience whereby an individual is prone to being unusually self-indulgent, self-absorbed, egocentric, and idiosyncratic.

According to our self-psychological point of view, these fantasies are *narcissistic* because they are extremely self-referential and solipsistic; they evidence little regard for practical reality or the feelings of others. These self-centered fantasies may be seen as consisting of the following imaginary scenarios: (1) the mirroring scenario entails a vision of oneself as grandly exhibiting himself or herself before an awestruck audience of worshipful admirers; (2) the idealizing scenario involves a vision of oneself as merged with an omnipotent figure or omniscient presence; and (3) in the twinship scenario one envisions oneself as joined by or allied with an alter ego or identical twin. (We should note that we have added a fourth scenario to this original series of selfobject fantasies, namely the megalomaniacal scenario in which one envisions oneself as in control of magically endowed [nonhuman] things and activities which are imagined as being capable of altering the laws of human nature.) We refer to this illusionary vision of oneself as a fantasy of being a megalomaniacal self and as wielding magical control.

At the outset, we must clarify some important aspects of these illusory and phantasmagorical visions. We maintain that there are six critical features that distinguish these prototypical fantasy scenes. First, we view them as central to unconscious organization and determination of both how a person thinks and feels about oneself as well as how a person acts and behaves. Thus, we construe these fantasies not as mere psychic epiphenomena, but rather as crucial to the overall functionality (or dysfunctionality) of the personality. (For psychoanalytic studies of the critical role of fantasy in personality, society, life, and art, see, for example, Adams, 2001, 2004; Adelman, 1992; Bader, 2002; Bloch, 1978; Breineis, 1990; Donald, 1989; Ellman & Reppen, 1997; Franklin, 2000; Freeman & Kupfermann, 1988, Gediman, 1995, Jacobs, 2000, Johnston, 1997; Kipnis, 1996; Levin, 1993; Person, 1995; Pleiz, 1997; Segal, 1985; Steiner, 2003; Theweleit, 1987; Warner, 2002; Weininger, 1989; Weissmann, 2004; and Wullschläger, 1995.)

Second, these fantastic visions may find expression at either unconscious or conscious levels of awareness, in pathological or nonpathological forms, and in a variety of modalities and mediums. We are suggesting, therefore, that there is a *continuum of expression* ranging from the unconscious to the conscious and covering a number of different *modes of expression* including the creative and artistic, the symptomatic and characterological, the mental and behavioral.

For example, as regards the mental mode, fantasy may be expressed on an unconscious level in the form of dreams, addictive states, or fugue and trance states. On a more conscious level, it may find expression in the form of daydreams, reverie, or other kinds of waking imaginings. Or, to take still another instance, fantasy may be expressed behaviorally either at an unconscious level of enactment in the form of reliving experiences or at a conscious level of enactment in the form of play and games.

We employ a number of similar terms such as illusory, magical, phantasmagorical, and imaginary in our discussion of the different ways, mediums, and modalities as well as the various levels of awareness or enactment in which fantasy can be expressed. (See Arlow 1969a,b; 1991 [1977] for the classic and pioneering psychoanatic work on the various ways in which unconscious fantasy finds expression in conscious awareness and behaviour.) For the purpose of our work, we consider all of these terms to be equivalent.

Such dereistic visions are based on what classical psychoanalysis has traditionally construed as "primary process" thinking. According to classical psychoanalysis, such thought is determined by cognitive principles quite different in nature from those governing thought based on more realistic and practical principles, or "secondary process." Primary process thinking in the form of fantasizing is a dereistic mental activity in that it "follows a totally subjective and idiosyncratic system of logic and fails to take the facts of reality or experience into consideration" (Kaplan & Sadock, 1991, p. 51). In other words, primary process thought, or fantastic (magical) thinking, is based on a private form of illogic that is not subject to rules of logical thought derived from common sense, trial-and-error, induction and deduction, cause-and-effect, and so forth.

Or, to make the same point in Piagetian terms, fantasizing is "egocentric" thought in that it is completely self-centered and without significant reference to a consensually-validated notion of reality. Such magical thinking is both a form of mental activity and an ideational-affective content of the mind. The mental imagery flowing from such thought processes is derived from an early childhood world of make-believe, pretend, and illusion.

Third, these fantastic visions always involve a specific set of not only mental images, but also accompanying affects (feelings or emotions) as well as sensations. In our study, these affects are referred to, respectively, as moods of *narcissistic bliss* (see also Ostow, 1967, pp. 36–37 on "narcissistic tranquility") or "narcissistic mortification" (Eidelberg, 1959; Kohut, 1971; Lax, 1997). The narcissistic state of bliss may consist of a variety of feelings and sensations including euphoria, ecstasy, elation, exhilaration, exuberance, as well as a tingly sensation or light-headedness. Correspondingly, the narcissistic state of mortification may consist of various feelings and sensations of embarrassment, humiliation, and shame; queasiness, racing or pounding heart, and sweaty palms; self-loathing, self-hate, and self-contempt; imploding into the dark abyss of a psychic black hole; falling apart or going to pieces; losing control or being out of control; flying off the handle and exploding.

Fourth, archaic narcissistic fantasies and the accompanying affective states are essentially Janus-faced or two-sided (see Miliora & Ulman, 1996a). Thus, they may be expressed in either a positive and hopeful version with accompanying pleasant feelings and sensations or in a negative or dreaded version with accompanying unpleasant emotions and sensations. The dichotomous and dualistic nature of these emotion-laden fantasies entails an action which is inherently dialectical. Such a dialectic of positive and negative versions either flip-flops erratically, as, for example, in the case of addiction, or switches in a more orderly fashion as, for instance, in healthy psychological functioning.

Fifth, the manner and conditions under which these pleasant and unpleasant fantasy visions succeed one another and flip-flop or switch positions in a person's unconscious mind are crucial to determining the relative degree of mental illness or well-being. Likewise, the extent to which these imaginary scenarios have undergone developmental trans-formation from archaic to mature forms is also critical to determining the overall nature of mental health. Even an individual who is moderately healthy is never completely free of the seductive and captivating powers of the archaic form of these fantasies. However, the more a person has been able to realize and actualize some more realistic version of these fantasies, the more that individual may be said to have achieved a normal and expectable level of emotional health as well as psychological maturity.

Sixth, and finally, it is important to stress that our description of these fantasies is not based on mere idyll and abstract speculation. On the contrary, our depiction derives from the clinical examination of these fantasies as we have psychoanalytically reconstructed them in the context of over 25 years of psychoanalytic psychotherapy with a wide variety of addicted patients. Such psychoanalytic therapy, with its focus on transference, resistance, genetic reconstruction, dreams, free association, and behavioral enactment, is well-suited for illuminating the often oth-erwise obscure presence and hidden mental action of these "central organizing fantasies" (Nurnberg & Shapiro, 1983), "core fantasies" (Ches-sick, 1994, pp. 288–94; see also, Chasseguet-Smirgel & Goyena, 1993, on "core fantasy"), or "global fantasies" (Shane & Shane, 1990).

In addition, the unique aspects of psychoanalytic therapy are, to varying degrees, all essentially dissociative in nature. The main effects of psychoanalytic therapy entail a clinical alteration of normal, waking consciousness as fantasy pervades and influences it. Each of these various affects involves a fantasy-based alteration of consciousness.

These clinically-determined phenomena are, therefore, dissociative in a fashion somewhat similar to the dissociation that defines the addictive experience. Like addictive dissociation, the various forms of psychoanalytic dissociation may be viewed as an unconscious means of reliving fantasy as well as re-experiencing accompanying affect and sensation. Thus, the illusory (that is, fantasy-based) nature of the psy-choanalytic experience is an ideal psychotherapeutic medium for gaining empathic access to a crucial domain of unconscious mental life. Hence, a psychotherapist can gain a glimpse or a clinical facsimile of the fantasies and moods that psychically determine the dissociating and anesthetizing effects of the addictive state of mind.

Based on these six distinct features, our study defines the "addictive process" (Goodman, 1993) as characterized by: (1) the (ab)use or misuse of magically-endowed things or activities (addictive trigger mechanisms, or ATMs) which leads to (2) pathological self-absorption in "psychoactive fantasy tapes" (archaic narcissistic fantasies, or self-state fantasies) which, in turn, creates (3) dissociation and anesthetization as part of an artificially induced hypnoid defense, that is, a fugue or trance.

ATMs serve as magically endowed agents by which an addict can indulge in narcissistic fantasies and moods. Under normal circumstances, these fantasies and moods are usually too ephemeral and vague to achieve spontaneous and conscious expression in any way other than by artificial (or sometimes creative and artistic) means. ATMs set off these psychoactive fantasy tapes by a variety of artificial means including biochemical, physiological, and behavioral.

From a descriptive (rather than judgmental) point of view, our study views an addict as the quintessential narcissist. An addict, who is self-involved and self-absorbed, has little awareness of the presence of other persons or things as independent entities. For an addict, they do not exist in an environment experienced as separate and distinct.

Having an unconscious fantasy of oneself as being megalomaniacal, an addict is self-deceived, and thus imagines that it is really possible to magically control and manipulate a "narcissistically perceived reality, a narcissistic ... view of the world." (Kohut, 1978d [1972] p. 644–45), "a narcissistically experienced archaic environment" (Kohut, 1978d [1972], p. 656), or a "narcissistic universe" (Kohut, 1978e [1976], p. 834). To quote from Kohut (1978e [1976]), narcissistically disturbed individuals, including an addict, "understand the environment in which they live only as an extension of their own *narcissistic universe*" (p. 834, emphasis added). He elaborates: "They understand others only insofar—but here with the keenest empathy!—as they can serve as *tools* toward their own narcissistic ends or insofar as they interfere with their own purposes" (p. 834, emphasis added).

Thus, for an addict, other people, things, and activities exist only as "tools" to be exploited for the purpose of "*re-establishing control* over a narcissistically experienced world" (Kohut, 1978d [1972], p. 657, emphasis added). In this regard, and depending on the circumstance, for an addict everyone and everything may serve as narcissistic artifacts, which are manipulated by an addict as if they are parts of the self. As such, an addict manipulates them with an unconscious intention of altering subjectivity.

Before briefly describing the four interrelated components of our proposed model, it is first necessary to place our model within a relevant conceptual context. As noted, our study views addiction as a (sub)type of narcissistic behavior disorder. Adopting such a perspective automatically places our model of addiction conceptually within the theoretical camp of those clinicians who conceive of addiction as a symptom of a psychological disorder. These theorists may be contrasted with those who conceptualize addiction primarily as a physical or biochemical *disease.* (See Berger, 1991; J. Brody, 2003; and Satel & Goodwin, 1998 for a thorough discussion of this distinction and convincing arguments in favor of the superiority of the former position over the latter.)

Moreover, our view of addiction as a psychological symptom or disorder (rather than as a physical or organic disease) situates our model squarely within the theoretical camp of those clinicians who subscribe to a psychoanalytic perspective. From such a vantage point, it follows that addiction, as a symptom of or as a type of narcissistic behavior disorder, has an unconscious meaning and function. Moreover, because it has such import, it may be interpreted and analyzed using the same psychoanalytic techniques traditionally employed in understanding a neurotic symptom such as, for example, hysterical blindness.

Although we adopt a psychoanalytic perspective on addiction, our proposed model does not discount the significance of biochemistry, physiology, and behavior, all of which are so integral to the position of those theorists who view addiction as a disease. On the contrary, our model gives all of these factors an important role in the "addictive process." From our self-psychological point of view, ATMs are viewed as magical agents that enable an addict to indulge via artificial means in archaic narcissistic fantasies and moods of narcissistic bliss. As ersatz selfobjects, ATMs serve as a means by which an addict takes advantage of biochemical, physiological, and behavioral pathways, all of which lead to neuroanatomically sensitive areas of the brain.

We are suggesting, therefore, that at the center of the addictive process there is a chain reaction of psychosomatic proportions. This chain reaction involves both the brain (that is, a somatic entity) and the unconscious mind (that is, a psychological phenomenon). It starts when ATMs act, either directly or indirectly, on specific areas of the brain, thus causing a powerful surge of cerebral activity. This neuroanatomical burst serves, in turn, as the basis for a further psychological (unconscious) reaction involving the mobilization of latent fantasies and moods.

Moreover, in stressing these biochemical, physiological, and behavioral factors, our proposed model contributes to the emerging and important synthesis of biological psychiatry, psychoanalysis, and the neurosciences. (For examples of this important trend, see Brockman, 1998; Cozolino, 2002; Fauconnier & Turner, 2002; Gedo, 1991; Harris, 1998; Joseph, 1992; Kandel, 2005; Kaplan-Solms & Solms, 2002; Kircher & David, 2003; Levin, 1991; L. Miller, 1991; Shevrin et al., 1996; and Vaughan, 1997.) From a self-psychological perspective, our work furthers this synthesis by formulating a *"bioself-psychological"* theory (see Miliora & Ulman, 1996b for a description of this theoretical perspective). Such a theory envisions the self of an individual as the by-product of an intricate and complicated interaction between both the brain and the mind. (See for alternative views Eccles, 1994, for a discussion of *How the Self Controls Its Brain*; see also Restak, 1991, on *The Brain Has a Mind of Its Own*; as well as Feinberg, 2001, on *Altered Egos: How the Brain Creates the Self*.) Together this organ and entity evolve and interact to create character and personality. More specifically, both brain and mind create fantasy, affect, and sensation, all of which imbue subjective experience with its highly personal meaning.

PHENOMENOLOGY

The phenomenological component of our model focuses on the nature of addiction, or *what* is addiction as a psychological phenomenon? In raising this theoretical query, we divide addiction as a psychological phenomenon into several interrelated dimensions: cognitive, affective, sensorial, and environmental. Through the multiple lens of this focus, we view the nature of addiction in terms of what we referred to previously as *dissociative anesthesia*. (In the field of anesthesiology, there is a basic distinction between general anesthesia, which puts the patient to sleep, and local anesthesia, which leaves the patient awake yet dissociated. See, for example, Corssen & Domino, 1966, for a discussion of "dissociative anesthesia" in the context of anesthesiology.)

As a psychopathological process inherent in all addictions, addictive anesthesia involves: (1) the *dissociative* alteration of cognition or thought based on the unconscious reliving of fantasies of early childhood; and, (2) the *anesthetization* of painful affect and sensation generated by the pleasurable re-experiencing of the mood of narcissistic bliss. This kind of dissociative reliving of fantasy entails what Abse (1966) referred to as a "hypnoid state." Adumbrating our thinking, Abse observed:

> We thus see anyway that in fugue the dissociation is dynamically related to a *wish phantasy*, with adherent feelings of well-being assuming dominance of consciousness and replacing consciousness of frustration and feelings of ill-being (p. 138, emphasis added).

We have applied Abse's concept of the hypnoid state to our view of addiction as essentially fantasy-based. Consequently, we envision an addict employing psychoactive agents to enter into a hypnoid state characterized by fugue or trance. We employ the concept of self-hypnosis, or the hypnoid defense, to indicate that an addict relies or depends on a special class of things and activities (ATMs). These entities serve as the artificial means by which an addict induces an altered state of consciousness similar to the fugue or trance state attendant to hypnosis. In fact, in the field of hypnosis there is a phenomenon referred to as "hypnotic anesthesia" (Gregory, 1987), which is similar to our notion of dissociative anesthesia. (See also Orlandini, 2004, who refers to the "analgesia principle" in the context of discussing Freud's original concept of the repetition compulsion. And, more specifically, Orlandini conjectures that, according to Freud, this principle helps to explain the means by which a person attempts unconsciously to achieve a psychic state of analgesia. This unconscious self-state dulls and numbs emotional pain.)

There is a striking similarity between our original notion of dissociative anesthesia and Orlandini's conception of the analgesia principle. More importantly, Orlandini's thinking has relevance for our theory of addiction. His notion of the analgesia principle is consistent with our thinking regarding an addict's desperate desire to escape to a private world of unconscious fantasy. In such a magical realm, pleasure serves as an analgesic agent by which it is possible for an addict to dissociate from overwhelming psychic pain.

In a sense, then, an addict unwittingly serves as his or her own hypnotist. Thus, in this role, an addict uses ATMs as aids to induce a hypnotic or hypnoid state. In this regard, we are suggesting, therefore, that it is best to conceptualize addiction as a kind of *self-hypnosis* rather than as a type of "self-medication" (Khantzian, 1985; see also Khantzian, 1999).

In our opinion, Khantzian's by now very popular and widely accepted notion of "self-medication" does not go far enough as an explanation of addiction. If addiction were merely a form of self-medication, then the analgesic effect (that is, the numbing or dulling of pain without the loss or alteration of consciousness) would be sufficient. However, an addict wants more than just the absence of pain; an addict needs to dissociate as a means of anesthetizing. Or, more precisely, an addict desires to radically alter the normal and reality-based sense of the self and the world, all as part of undergoing an addictive metamorphosis or phantasmagorical transmogrification.

Dissociative anesthetization occurs because of the psychoactive effects of specific agents. These effects include, for example, antianxiety tranquilization and sedation, antidepressant stimulation, de-aggressivization or pacification, and shame-relieving humanization. In the context of megalomania (that is, a narcissistic illusion of being a megalomaniacal self as wielding magical control), the effect entails an anti-panic sense of being in control, which counteracts the panic attendant to a sense of having lost control and/or being out of control. However, and paradoxically, rather than "re-establishing control," an addict experiences an increasing sense of loss of control, leading to still further and ill-fated efforts at reinstituting the illusion of control.

The selection, use, and eventual abuse by an addict of a particular agent (or various combinations of ATMs) are, to a large extent, dependent on the psychoactive effect of specific ATM(s). We have referred to this as the *psychoactive specificity* of an ATM(s). An addict selects and abuses a particular ATM because of the objective effect of a particular psychoactive agent.

However, the concomitant subjective and illusory experience of an addict should not be confused with the psychoactive effectiveness of a given agent. Addictive things and activities are, ultimately, unreliable means by which an addict makes a futile attempt to assert a sense of pseudo-independence and domination. According to our notion of the dialectical bipolarity of fantasy and mood, an addict flip-flops between a fantasy of being a lost soul out to sea with feelings of narcissistic mortification, and a fantasy of being the master of his or her own ship with feelings of narcissistic bliss.

An addict misuses ATMs in a compulsive manner. An addict also abuses ATMs in a habitual and obligatory manner. An addicts resorts to the misuse and abuse of ATMs because they provide an illusory experience of temporary relief from emotional suffering, which has become chronic and unbearable.

An addict is attracted, in part, to these ATMs because they have a "placebo effect." (For an explanation of the placebo effect see, for example, H. Brody, 2000; Harrington, 1997; and Winter, 1998.) However, the placebo effect does not mean, as is commonly yet mistakenly believed, that no real or actual effect takes place. On the contrary, it implies that the effect in question, although real, could not possibly have been achieved solely on the basis of the inherent properties of the agent employed.

In the case of addiction, the placebo effect takes the form of antidepressant or antianxiety relief from psychic pain. An addict desperately needs such relief for the mediating effect of fantasy and mood. Relief does not occur, therefore, primarily as a result of the purely biochemical, physiological, or behavioral effect(s) of a particular ATM.

For example, heroin acts as a central nervous system (CNS) depressant, or, in the language of drug addicts, a "downer." Yet, heroin addicts always speak of getting "high" on heroin. It is a paradox, therefore, that a heroin addict experiences this particular drug as if it were a CNS stimulant.

This apparent paradox is explained, to some degree, by the placebo effect of heroin as mediated by fantasy and mood. A heroin addict, who shoots up or snorts the drug, subjectively experiences its psychoactive effect on the basis of a subjective sense of serene obliviousness and nirvanic tranquility. The fantasy and mood provide, therefore, an antidepressant (psychoactive) effect. Such a psychoactive effect helps to account for the fact that a heroin addict gets "high" on a "downer." The paradoxical effect of heroin is a good example of the Alice in wonderland or surreal quality inherent in all addictions—up is down and down is up.

The phenomenological perspective of our model gives us a view of the ATM–based mobilization of self-hypnotic fantasies and trance-like moods. Such artificial mobilization involves two interrelated acts. First, it entails the literal and actual use of a particular ATM (or combination of ATMs)—such as alcohol, food, drugs, gambling, or sex—as well as all the corresponding activities so integral to the addictive experience. This process consists of the unnatural means—that is, a biochemical, physiological, or behavioral pathway—by which addictive fantasies and accompanying moods are artificially mobilized.

We consider the entire sequence an addict engages in as part of obtaining or acquiring a particular addictive agent for a second process that characterizes the addictive experience. For instance, in the case of many types of drug abuse, all of the unusual and exotic paraphernalia and strange rituals which typically characterize the securing, preparation, and use of the drug are viewed from the perspective of our model as part and parcel of the ATM. The ritualistic nature of the activities surrounding an addict's abuse of ATMs helps to account for the incredible role these agents play in altering consciousness or subjective awareness.

As a defining aspect of addiction, dissociative anesthetization involves an artificial *flip-flopping* of self-state fantasies. The self-state of an addict flip-flops from one organized around nightmarish visions and moods of narcissistic mortification to one organized around beatific visions and moods of narcissistic bliss. This artificial and psychopathological process is referred to as *addictive self-state flip-flopping*; it is contrasted to normal and healthy *self-state switching*.

On the one hand, the former is brief and short term in terms of duration, whereas the latter is more extended and long term, albeit not permanent. On the other hand, as far as concerns affect the former is only partial, whereas the latter is substantial.

The self-state fantasy flip-flopping of addiction is erratic, topsy-turvy, and reflects the absence or faultiness of psychic structure and function. Self-state switching is, in contrast, self-limiting, self-correcting, and is a manifestation of the healthy presence of psychic structure and functioning.

The difference between these two psychic processes may be thought of as follows: Self-state flip-flopping may be compared to a person who changes his or her mind at the drop of a hat, so to speak, and, as a result, is said to be constantly changing on every issue. Self-state switching is analogous to a person who changes his or her mind, or switches position, only in response, however, to convincing evidence that justifies such a shift.

The notion of an inherent dynamic (that is, *dialectical bipolarity*) that underlies the interaction between fantasy and mood is implicit in the concept of changing self-state, whether as part of a psychic process, which is normal and healthy, or as part of a psychopathological process such as addiction. Thus, a positive or hoped-for fantasy vision ushers in a pleasant mood, and together they counteract a negative or dreaded fantasy vision and accompanying unpleasant mood. Yet, the opposite can, and often does, occur.

The natural ability on the part of a person to spontaneously switch from a dreaded (fantasy) vision with corresponding painful mood to a hopeful (fantasy) vision with accompanying pleasurable mood without, however, resorting to artificial (addictive) means, is a cardinal sign of mental health. In contradistinction, the need on the part of an addict for artificial means to flip-flop from one self-state fantasy to its opposite is an indication of mental illness.

Moreover, there is also an *extopsychic* or environmental dimension to addiction equally critical in understanding its phenomenological nature. This dimension revolves around a pathological disturbance in the relationship between the self and the selfobject milieu. An addict does not use things and activities, which are the nonhuman (in contrast to the human) constituents of the selfobject milieu, in a healthy and adaptive manner. Rather, an addict abuses (or misuses) them. In the process, an addict imagines these items as magical agents of illusory control (that is, ersatz selfobjects or ATMs).

According to our model of addiction, these external (or extopsychic versus endopsychic) things and activities may come to serve for an addict as ATMs. Our proposed model contrasts these ATMs with other things and activities that function as what Kohut (1977b) characterized as "nonhuman selfobjects" (p. 55). We have argued that such nonhuman selfobjects may be reconceptualized as transitional selfobjects. Transitional selfobjects may assume the form of typical things and activities, or they may be mutated into pathological versions of these entities. However, both transitional selfobjects and ATMs may be said to exist for an individual as fixtures in a "narcissistic universe."

ATMs are *ersatz selfobjects* and, as such, are distinguished from genuine yet nonhuman or *transitional selfobjects*. Despite functioning as ersatz selfobjects, ATMs do partake of some of the essential qualities of authentic and, in this instance, transitional selfobjects. Unconsciously, an addict fantasizes these nonhuman things and activities as being semi-human in nature; as a result, they are imbued by an addict with capacities normally emanating only from real selfobjects. (See Adler, 1989a,b; 1990 who explores the nature, role, and function of transitional phenomena, transitional objects, and the selfobject in the context of his conceptualization of narcissistic and borderline conditions as existing along a psychopathological continuum. His work is particularly relevant and important for our study in that Adler blends the Winnicottian and British object relations concept of the transitional object with the Kohutian notion of the selfobject.)

An addict has an unconscious experience of these entities and activities as providing antidepressant, antianxiety, pacifying, humanizing, and antipanic relief from many forms of emotional pain. In this sense, therefore, ATMs serve as ersatz selfobjects which, by definition, provide merely *selfobject-like* functions. The improper use or misuse of ATMs enslaves an addict and seriously interferes with already weakened psychological functioning.

In contrast to ATMs, transitional selfobjects function for a person almost like an artificial limb or prosthesis. In this capacity, such a thing (or an equivalent activity) serves for an individual as a mechanical contraption or device connected to the body. As such, it is gradually experienced by a person as if it were a natural part of the body. As an addition to the physical self, it becomes a functional part of the person that may be used to enhance performance.

Wearing eyeglasses is a good example of an everyday thing that could be compared to the functioning of a transitional selfobject. A person who in early childhood develops a problem with normal vision establishes, at a relatively young age, a purely utilitarian connection to eyeglasses. Thus, eyeglasses greatly enhance the visual functioning of the child who without them would be unable to see properly.

In an analogous fashion, a toddler adopts certain things and activities as parts of the self. These entities may evolve into transitional selfobjects, and as such function for a person as the psychological equivalent of eyeglasses. Eventually, an eyeglasses wearer experiences them as a totally natural and normal part of everyday life. In a fashion similar to the use of eyeglasses, the use by a toddler of a transitional selfobject (thing or activity) functions in daily life in an adaptive manner.

In the case of a child who has developed a serious problem with sight, all kinds of basic activities such as reading and writing (to say nothing of simply navigating effectively in the environment) are compromised. However, as soon as such a child is fitted with the right pair of lenses all such normal activities can be resumed and development can proceed. By analogy, the same process occurs in the case of a toddler, who discovers and learns the proper use of things and activities in their capacity to function as transitional selfobjects.

Hence, just as the wearing of eyeglasses helps a child to see, so too does the use of transitional selfobjects improve the psychological functioning of a child. By successfully using a transitional selfobject as an external part (or add-on) of the self, a child compensates for a congenital or developmental weakness in psychological structure and functioning. In essence, a child makes up for what is missing or faulty by creating a utilitarian relationship to a semi-human thing or a nonhuman activity, either of which may provide selfobject functions.

In focusing on the environmental dimension of the phenomenon of addiction, our self-psychological model makes a crucial distinction: it distinguishes among a "psychology of use" or a "use psychology." and the more traditional wish and need psychoanalytic psychologies on the one hand, and the more recent relational viewpoint on the other. Both traditional and relational psychologies are based primarily on a perspective that focuses on the individual in relation to either internal, psychic processes or external, interpersonal interactions.

Our self-psychological theory of use enables psychoanalysts to devote more attention to the unconscious use (or, in the case of addiction, abuse) of things and activities in the environment. (Psychoanalytic theorists whose work adumbrates and anticipates our notion of a use psychology include Bromberg, 1995, Coen, 1992, Eigen, 2004 [1981]; Hanly, 1992; McCarthy, 2000; Newman, 1984; Slochower, 1994; and Winnicott, 1969, 1971 [1969].)

Our fantasy-based model of addiction offers what amounts to a psychoanalytic point of view on the nonhuman world of things and activities. In normal development, a special class of these nonhuman entities undergoes an unconscious process of anthropomorphization. As part of such a process, a toddler imagines that these things and activities possess human qualities, that is, they take on a humanoid and android quality (see Abrams & Neubauer, 1976). Later in life, certain individuals (e.g., addicts) unduly depend on a now mutated version of these once healthy transitional selfobjects. In a mutated form, these ersatz selfobjects function for an addict as magical agents of illusory control. An addict fantasizes them as invested with magical powers because of their psychoactive effects. This is, in essence, the crux of the Narcissus complex, which consists of fantasies of being a megalomaniacal self and as being endowed with magical control.

There is a distinct advantage, from the vantage point of our work, to viewing addiction as based, in part, on an unconscious defense mechanism of self-deception (as distinct from self-delusion). As such, it might be thought of as falling in the same category of unconscious defense as A. Freud's (1966 [1936]) classically-conceived "denial in fantasy." According to Freud (1966 [1936]), denial in fantasy works as follows: "The child's ego refuses to become aware of some disagreeable reality. First of all it turns its back on it, denies it, and in imagination reverses the unwelcome facts" (pp. 79–80).

Moreover, Freud continued:

> If the transformation is successful and through the fantasies which the child constructs he becomes insensible of the reality in question, the ego is saved anxiety and has no need to resort to defensive measures against its instinctual impulses and to the formation of neurosis. (p. 80)

A. Freud (1966 [1936]) emphasized: "This mechanism belongs to a normal phase in the development of the infantile ego, but, if it recurs in later life, it indicates an advanced stage of mental disease" (p. 80). From the perspective of our study, addiction does indeed represent such "an advanced stage of mental disease." However, rather than being based on "denial in fantasy," addiction involves "actualization in fantasy" (see Ogden, 1982, pp. 168–170 on "actualization fantasies") or "acting in" rather than "acting out."

With "actualization in fantasy," the mental landscape of an individual is altered addictively by the mobilization of powerful visual images, which are otherwise latent. There is also concomitant biochemical activity in key areas of the brain. In fact, the psychic mobilization of a potent fantasy, or psychoactive fantasy type, within the unconscious mind may literally affect neuroanatomical structures in the brain and vice versa. (See Ostow, 1954, 1955, 1967, for one of the first, and still pioneering, psychoanalytic explorations of the interrelation, interconnection, and interaction of unconscious fantasy and neuroanatomical structures in the brain such as the frontal and temporal lobes.)

Actualization in fantasy involves, therefore, a radical reshaping of an individual's mental terrain. Throughout life, the mental content of the mind, like the neuroanatomical structures of the brain, retains a certain degree of psychological plasticity. As a result, much of the mental content of the unconscious mind may undergo an alteration in which it is changed into a phantasmagorical form. The plasticity of the ideational contours of the unconscious mind accounts for an addict's ability to evoke fantasy scenarios, the impact of which drastically reshapes the psychological boundaries of the mental landscape.

In this regard, some ATMs truly might be called "designer drugs." Metaphorically, an addict might be portrayed as a mad interior designer or as an insane landscaper of the mental terrain. In the context of this metaphor, an addict may be depicted as a madman who has become carried away by the allure of the tools at hand. This is another way in which we deem an addict as under the influence of a fantasy of being a megalomaniacal self endowed with magical control, that is, as someone who artificially alters a subjective sense of the reality of the self and the world. There is voluminous literature on the topic of an individual's (ab)use of addictive agents such as drugs and alcohol for the unconscious purpose of psychoactively altering the meaning of subjective experience. A representative sample of this extensive and ever-increasing body of work dates back to and continues with the following: Babor et al., 1975;

Bell & Trethowan, 1962; Chessick, 1960; Freed, 1978; Galanter, 1976; Guttman & Maclay, 1936; Haertzen & Hooks, 1969; Hendin, 1975; Hendin et al., 1981; Hill et al., 1974; Johanson & Ujlenhuth, 1981; Klee, 1963; Lasaga et al., 1955; Levy, 1925; McAuliffe & Gordon, 1974; Meerlo, 1952; Mirin et al., 1976; Pihl et al., 1979; Savage, 1955; R.K. Siegel, 1989; J. Silverman, 1968; Smith & Beecher, 1962; Tamerin et al., 1974; Tokar et al., 1973; Vannicelli, 1972; Warren & Raynes, 1972.

However, there is a major drawback to the addictive redesigning of a particular psychological terrain—inevitably an addict only succeeds in creating what amounts to an illusory domain. Such a realm of make-believe necessitates constant deceit, deception, and duplicity on the part of an addict, all of which are required by an addict's desperate attempt to deny the truth of being addicted. Eventually, an addict creates a shadowy netherland of half-truths, making it difficult for an addict to know the difference between fact and fiction. A world of make-believe is a crucial aspect of an addict's double (and secret) life as a Narcissus in a wonderland.

We conclude this introduction to our psychoanalytic phenomenology of addiction with a brief discussion of the interrelated issues of megalomania and control. As noted (see Chapter 1), we borrow our concept of megalomania from Freud's original analysis of the case of Schreber. (For references to the concept of megalomania in this case, see, for example, Jones, 1955; Rochlin, 1973; and Niederland, 1974.) With the exception of Freud, only a few psychoanalysts have given credence to megalomania as a central force in unconscious mental life, and especially, in the world of fantasy. (See, for example, Abraham, 1927; Bergler, 1957; Bion, 1965; Chasseguet-Smigerl, 1985; Eigen, 2004 [1986]; Evans, 1975; Ferenczi, 1926, 1952, 1955 [1930]; E. Jones, 1974 [1913]; M. Klein, 1975 [1957]; Menninger, 1940; Muensterberger, 1994; Nunberg, 1955; A. Reich, 1960; and Steiner, 1999.)

However, many psychoanalysts in this select group have tended to follow in Freud's footsteps. Consequently, they view megalomania primarily as a libidinal or erotic over-evaluation of the ego leading to psychosis and schizophrenia. In contrast, and on the basis of our study of addiction, we seek to demonstrate that megalomania is a phase-appropriate form of archaic narcissism. As such, it must be viewed as separate and distinct from either grandiosity or omnipotence. In other words, from our self-psychological point of view megalomania cannot simply be subsumed by either grandiosity or omnipotence.

Beginning with Ferenczi, a number of the early psychoanalysts construed megalomania as a form of psychological or unconscious control over things and activities. For instance, Menninger (1940; see also Nunberg, 1955) links megalomania with the anal phase of psychosexual development and the phenomenon of sphincter control of the feces. Unconsciously, Menninger seems to be saying the following: a person suffering from megalomania fantasizes that it is possible to exercise a form of magical (sphincter) control over the world of things and activities as fecal material writ large.

In this regard, such a person operates on the basis of an unconscious (anal) fantasy according to which things and activities in the environment are equated with feces. Moreover, and as part of such an unconscious fantasy, these entities are fantasized by such a person as being like feces. Hence, they are imagined as being subject to the same kind of sphincter control as is fantasized by a child during early development. And finally, this unconscious (anal) fantasy consists of the illusion that these "fecal equivalents" are endowed with magical qualities similar to those imagined by a child to be inherent to fecal material.

There is another and related type of thought, both within and outside of psychoanalysis, that deals explicitly with the issue of psychological (or unconscious) control. In the non-psychoanalytic literature (see, for example, Alper, 1996; Baumeister, Heatherton, & Tice, 1994; Vanderlinden & Vandereycken, 1997; Viorst, 1998; Wegner, 2002; and Whiteside, 1998) the concept of control appears most often in the context of addiction, where it is viewed in terms of such phenomena as "loss of control," "locus of control," and "poor impulse control." In the psychoanalytic literature, the concept of control is rarely, if ever, mentioned. (For exceptions, see Eigen, 1979; Furman, 1998; and A. Goldberg, 1988.)

However, in several instances, the idea of control is focused on and discussed in relation to addiction. For example, Volkan (1976; see also Volkan, 1973) takes up the issue of magical forms of control over the psychotherapist and psychotherapy in his description of the case of Margaret, who was "addicted to pills" (p. 225). Good (1995) specifically discusses drug addiction in terms of a narcissistic fantasy of magical control. Or, to take another instance, Levens (1995) bases her entire analytic approach to understanding and treating eating disorders on the central concept of "magical control of the body" (see also Pines, 1993). Yet, none of these psychoanalytic authors in their respective discussions of addiction specifically connect forms of magical control to megalomania.

Our study of what Rado (1933, pp. 17) and Bergler (1957, pp. 23, pp. 28, pp. 30, pp. 32, pp. 40–41, pp. 43, pp. 57) long ago referred to as the megalomania of addiction represents our attempt at providing a self-psychological explanation of this phenomenon. Rather than focusing on the issue of libido and psychosexuality, we explain addictive (in contrast to psychotic) megalomania in terms of the narcissistic illusion of magical control. Nonetheless, we are indebted to the pioneering work of other psychoanalysts such as Ferenczi, Menninger, Nunberg, Volkan, Eigen, Good, and Levens for our self-psychological conceptualization of addiction. We have borrowed from the works of these psychoanalysts in our view of addiction as a form of megalomania involving the narcissistic illusion of control over magical agents capable of radically altering the laws of human nature as well as those governing the natural world.

ETIOLOGY AND PATHOGENESIS

As part of our proposed model, we have incorporated an etiological component in order to focus on the pathogenic origins and course of addiction. From this perspective, we seek to answer the crucial question: *When* does addiction begin and *where* are its pathways? In answering this query, we examine the developmental context of an unconscious, psychic process—originally referred to as "intersubjective absorption"—which occurs between two persons with differently organized subjectivities. More specifically, this unconscious process refers to the means by which a child and a parent(s) share in and are absorbed by a common or joint fantasy. As part of such a shared, or "intersubjective," fantasy a child experiences caretakers, things, and activities as functional parts (either human or nonhuman) of the self, that is, as selfobjects.

To make our work more accessible to a larger audience, we have reconceptualized the process we had originally termed intersubjective absorption. Now we view this process as entailing what we call a narcissistic exchange, of which intersubjective absorption is only one aspect. In a developmental context (in contrast to a psychotherapeutic context) such an exchange process unfolds as follows.

To begin with, a child exchanges or trades the narcissistic functioning of parents, as archaic yet human selfobjects, for the transitional and nonhuman selfobject functioning of things and activities. In this regard, the role of a parental selfobject consists of an ability to provide psychological functions and, more specifically, what Kohut (1977b) describes as "remedial action" (p. 277).

These archaic selfobject functions involve a child's experience of a parent as providing remedial relief from emotional distress. These functions may entail, for instance: (1) the mirroring of archaic grandiosity that generates an antidepressant lift or boost; (2) the idealization and merger with an omnipotent/omniscient figure that produces antianxiety relief in the form of tranquilization and sedation; (3) the joining at the psychic hip with a twin or alterego that facilitates a humanizing or shame-relieving reprise from a sense of self-consciousness, alienation, estrangement, or a sense of being inhuman; or, (4) the use of a thing or activity as a transitional selfobject over which there is an imaginary experience of the self as being megalomaniacal and as possessing magical control that, in turn, serves as an antidote to panicky feelings of having lost control and of being out of control.

In the initial phase of the narcissistic exchange process, a child exchanges or trades the human selfobject functioning of parents—who together make up an emotional unit and an all-purpose remedy for all ills—for the nonhuman selfobject functioning of magically endowed things and activities. It must be stressed that a narcissistic investment and exchange on the part of a child takes place primarily on an unconscious level of fantasy and imagination. In a developmental context, an instance of intersubjective absorption consists of a parent's ability to empathize with a child's phase-appropriate need to endow things and activities with magical qualities, and simultaneously to experience being in absolute control of these entities. Thus, child and parent join together in complementary rather than equivalent ways in the narcissistic exchange or transfer of human for nonhuman selfobject functions.

As part of such an unconscious process, a child anthropomorphizes things and activities and endows them with semi-human qualities (see Abrams & Neubauer, 1976). A child establishes these things and activities as transitional selfobjects, and thus imbues them with the capacity to provide "remedial action."

The movie *Castaway* is a wonderful cinematic example of the process by which a person endows a transitional selfobject with the capacity of "remediation." In this film, the character "Chuck Noland" (played by Tom Hanks) creates a purely illusory relationship with a volleyball. Both Chuck and the volleyball are washed ashore on a deserted island in the aftermath of a plane crash that leaves Chuck as the sole (human) survivor.

Chuck paints a human face on the volleyball, names it "Wilson," and endows it in his imagination with magical qualities. Wilson, as a magically endowed and semi-human entity (that is, a transitional selfobject), helps Chuck to hold onto his sanity. He averts slipping into total madness and insanity.

Instead, he keeps his wits about him despite being alone for an extended period of time with Wilson as his only (imaginary) companion. At the end of the movie, Chuck, who has survived psychologically due to his remedial relationship with Wilson, is finally rescued.

Let us review briefly the first and second phases of the narcissistic exchange process. Initially, an infant, and later a child, *invests* a parent as an archaic yet human selfobject with a certain *amount* of narcissistic credit. At this initial stage, an infant or child is narcissistically invested in a parent as a human selfobject. Later, and as a toddler, a child exchanges, trades, or *transfers* the narcissistic stake in a parental selfobject to a thing or activity. The latter is subsequently endowed by a toddler with the magic powers of parents. Such a nonhuman or transitional selfobject then becomes for a toddler a temporary depository for the narcissistic credit originally invested in parental selfobjects.

In the same developmental context, a toddler experiences such special things and activities as narcissistic commodities or currencies. Different things and activities may function narcissistically as such commodities depending on circumstance, situation, and the specific selfobject needs of a particular child. Empathic parents do not interfere with a child's natural (and phase-appropriate) tendency to make-believe special items or practices have magical qualities.

In addition, they go along with (share) a child's need to pretend these transitional selfobjects can be controlled in such a way that a child feels in possession of the magical powers of these entities. As noted, the illusion of such megalomaniacal control serves for a child as an antidote to panicky feelings of having lost control and of being out of control.

Parents, who empathize with a child's phase-appropriate need to entertain these megalomaniacal fantasies, also understand that sometimes a child needs to imagine an existence in a world of magic, make-believe, and illusion. In such an imaginary world, a child plays fancifully with things and engages in activities with little or no regard for the realities and practicalities of the adult world.

A third phase of the narcissistic exchange process completes this utilitarian transaction. In this phase, a child *divests* part of the narcissistic stock deposited in things and activities and *reinvests* it back to parents. However, a child now experiences parents as more mature yet still human selfobjects. Nonetheless, this narcissistic reinvestment is, under normal conditions, only partial.

Throughout life, even a healthy person retains a normal degree of narcissistic investment in things and activities, which continue to serve as commodities or currencies. In their psychological role as transitional selfobjects, a person experiences things and activities as parts of the self that extend and expand an individual's functional capacities. A youngster who carries over into adulthood a capacity for using transitional selfobjects can realize inherent potentialities that might otherwise go unrealized.

However, during the second and critical phase of the narcissistic exchange process some children become narcissistically *over-invested* in certain things and activities almost to the total exclusion of other people. Instead of functioning as bona fide (narcissistic) commodities, these entities serve for such a child rather as bogus or counterfeit currencies. And, just as counterfeit money undermines and subverts the healthy functioning of an economy, so too do these bogus (narcissistic) curren-cies interfere with healthy exchanges or transactions between the self of a person and the selfobject milieu.

Usually, such a situation occurs because of profound empathic failures (or even antipathy) on the part of parents in their functional capacity as selfobjects. In certain children, a tendency emerges in which they depend too much on things and activities. Such children use these entities in an attempt to fill a void left by parents who are either very unempathic or grossly antipathetic.

Consequently, under these adverse circumstances such a youngster may become developmentally arrested in his or her capacity for transi-tional selfobject usage. A developmental arrest in a child's ability to use things and activities as transitional selfobjects (that is, transitional selfobject usage) constitutes what Kohut (1977b) described as one of the "crystalli-zation points for later psychopathology" (p. 74), such as addiction.

As indicated, a parent may go well beyond simply failing to empathize with a child's phase-appropriate need to treat the nonhuman as human, and vice versa. Instead, a parent may respond with gross antipathy toward a child. We define antipathy (that is, the opposite or antithesis of empathy) as an extreme form of revulsion and repugnance that reduces the self of the individual to a nonhuman or subhuman status. (For a discussion of antipathy in a developmental context see Major and Miller, 1984; see also, Miliora, 2000.)

A child who has experienced the antipathy and megalomaniacal mistreatment of parents may, unfortunately, create a maladaptive fantasy of the self. Such a child fantasizes the self as a robotic machine or automaton and lacks most of the essential qualities of being human, including those of possessing genuine thoughts and feelings. A child who is organized unconsciously in terms of a fantasy of the self as subhuman fails to achieve a developmental milestone of major significance, that is, to develop a sense of being fully or almost fully human.

A youngster who imagines himself or herself as a subhuman entity or as a mechanical thing may be subject, later in life, to a number of narcissistic behavior disorders including addiction and sociopathy, or, in some cases, even to psychopathy. In all of these disorders, a person treats both the self and others as subhuman things. And, in the case of addiction, such megalomaniacal fantasies underlie a person's belief that things and activities can completely take over the role and function of others. (See Steiner, 1999, who makes a very important differentiation between "megalomanic psychopathic manifestations" and a "heroic self." His distinction is very similar to our demarcation between immature (and developmentally arrested) fantasies of a megalomaniacal self as wielding magical control in contrast to a mature sense of a self based on having gained a capacity for mastery.)

We are suggesting, therefore, that an addict is organized unconsciously in accordance with megalomaniacal fantasies of the self (that is, a wizard-like being who is capable of directing talisman-like agents of magical control) as something that can be repaired or fixed like a broken toy. In this regard, an addict selects ATMs like alcohol, drugs, food, gambling, and sex as if they were imaginary tools such as glue, cement, or tape. An addict imagines that such mending materials may be used to piece together the self as if it were a broken item. In this regard, an addict mistakenly believes that ATMs can be used to hold together a self suffering from severe narcissistic damage.

A child uses other people as well as other things and activities as selfobjects, thus making it possible for normal and healthy development and psychological formation of the self. In the context of the narcissistic exchange process, transitional selfobject usage is essential to this overall development. Moreover, the role of nonhuman selfobjects (things and activities) in the evolving structuralization of self-experience is especially crucial during the toddler years. (For a related discussion of this point in terms of Winnicott's notion of the transitional object, see Mahler, Pine, & Bergman, 1975; see also Furman, 1992.)

A toddler may be viewed, chronologically and psychologically, as standing between the developmental stage of infancy and adolescence. On physical and psychological levels, a toddler extends and deepens an infant's earlier relationship with the nonhuman environment of self-object things and activities. In so doing, a toddler develops a utilitarian and practical attitude toward the use of these entities.

In healthy development, these agents serve a vital role as mediators of a toddler's selfobject relationship to parental caretakers. Thus, transitional selfobjects serve for a toddler as psychological *intermediaries* between the human and nonhuman worlds. The psychological status of transitional selfobjects as mediators or intermediaries accounts, in part, for the fact that a toddler endows these nonhuman things and activities with their semi-human qualities.

Transitional selfobjects function as *semi-human intermediaries* that help a toddler to move psychically back and forth between the world of other human beings and that of nonhuman things and activities. A toddler, in the process of using transitional selfobjects, moves psychically between these different worlds of the human and nonhuman; this constitutes the achievement of a developmental milestone of great psychological significance.

Let us outline the developmental sequence of the narcissistic exchange process. Initially, a child creates a fantasy world in which other people are endowed with the capacity to function as archaic yet human selfobjects (phase I). Subsequently, a child imbues other non-human things and activities as selfobjects with a similar functional capacity (phase II). And finally, an older child reinvests in other people this capacity to function as selfobjects. Now, however, these people serve as more mature and human selfobjects (phase III).

Whether human or nonhuman, all of these selfobjects serve developmentally for a child as necessary yet auxiliary regulators of self-esteem and modulators of mood. From a developmental perspective, all of these humans and nonhuman selfobjects are psychologically necessary because without them a child could not effectively regulate self-esteem nor modulate mood.

It may be said that viewed empathically from the perspective of a toddler, he or she learns an important developmental lesson. A special class of nonhuman things and activities may function for a toddler as transitional selfobjects. In this capacity, these entities become semi-human conduits or intermediaries. As such, they serve as a means by which a child may engage in fantasy play and games which, in turn, facilitate the developmental transformation of megalomania. (For a discussion of the adaptive use of fantasy play and games in childhood see, Paley, 1984, 1988, 1990; see also, Clark, 1995; Morrison, 1988; Sawyer, 1997; Stewart, 2001.) In addition, such selfobject activity mitigates against a psychological inevitability constituted by the typical emotional ups-and-downs of childhood.

Later in life, some individuals, for example, addicts, have come to depend too much on the misuse of things and activities. These entities have devolved functionally from transitional selfobjects into ATMs. Individuals such as addicts misuse these ATMs as a means of indulging in childhood fantasies, the psychoactive effects of which allows for simultaneous dissociation and anesthetization. (This is the basis for our original concept of dissociation.)

The preceding observations serve as the basis for our self-psychological explanation for the etiological origins of addiction. From our self-psychological perspective, we view addiction as a pathological form of *self-indulgence*. Such self-absorption revolves around the reliving of archaic narcissistic fantasies and the re-experiencing of accompanying moods of narcissistic bliss. As a result of the combined effect of these psychic events, inevitably an addict is distracted from solving the very real yet often painful problems of adulthood.

Yet, perhaps paradoxically, both transitional selfobjects and ATMs may be experienced subjectively by an individual, or in this case an addict, as responsive and hence as empathic to underlying needs. Several factors help to explain how a person subjectively experiences such seemingly nonhuman things and activities as being empathic. First, a person often fantasizes such things and activities as imbued with semi-human qualities and characteristics. As part of an unconscious process of animation, a person anthropomorphizes them. Hence, they take on qualities of being humanoid and android. Therefore, a person may imagine such things and activities as being empathic regardless of whether or not they function as transitional selfobjects or ATMs.

Self-psychologically speaking, such an *instrumental form of empathy* is consistent with a psychoanalytic understanding of empathy. From a self-psychological perspective, empathy is viewed in terms of the subjective experience of being responded to in an understanding way. Perhaps from the viewpoint of an addict this accounts for the belief that a bottle of booze is an alcoholic's best friend, and the only "one" that truly understands a drunkard. Likewise, an alcoholic often entertains the illusion of being closer emotionally to a bottle of booze than to any other person.

Anyone who is somewhat unfamiliar with addiction and the intimate connection that may exist between an addict and an ATM understandably may doubt the existence of such an almost semi-human relationship. Reproduced below is a so-called "Eulogy to Excessive Food and Cigarettes," written by an addict as an exercise during a stay at an addiction rehabilitation facility. This eulogy accurately describes the typical addict's semi-human connection to ATMs. The eulogy proceeds as follows:

> Good-bye old friends. We've been together a long time, but now we must part. As much as I have loved you, food—you have robbed me of my past, and cigarettes—you will steal my future from me if I continue to have a relationship with you. Through the years, you've calmed me down when nothing else could and made me believe that I was happy. How soothing you were after a day of frustration at work or while I was studying for an exam. So many presentations and strategic plans were created with your support. I never would have made it through some of those stressful times without you. How much easier it was for me to confront a friend or deal with a potential or actual conflict when I had spent time with you prior to the event. I loved you so much I was willing to sacrifice everything for you. There were those evenings and holidays when I made excuses for turning down invitations so that I could be with you alone. Our relationship was exclusive. The goals that I could have chosen for myself were shunted aside so that we could continue our intense involvement. With me, you always came first. As people started to become non-smokers at work, I risked becoming unfashionable so that I would not have to sever my ties with you, cigarettes. We traveled throughout the world together. Whatever city I was in, I selected the restaurants that would offer the most beautiful setting and sumptuous presentation of you. You were a constant provider of "highs," comfort, relaxation and extreme happiness/elation. I will always love you and keep fond memories of you because our relationship was too intense for me and it became destructive. I cannot grow and be all that I was meant to be with you in my life. It is not your fault. You presented yourself in a very alluring manner and I could not handle it. Cigarettes, I need to leave you because no one as yet has figured out how to make you safe. Good-bye, my friends. May you go and rest in peace.

This eulogy speaks for itself; the sentiments expressed by this individual in this farewell epitomize the feelings of a typical addict toward a prized possession, that is, an ATM.

Let us return to the topic of empathy. It may be said that an empathic failure occurs in the current context for the following reason. A person feels unempathized with because of a lack of responsiveness on the part of a thing or activity.

Such an entity may be viewed as more-or-less responsive to the ministrations and manipulations of the user or participant. This kind of *utilitarian responsiveness is indicative of an instrumental empathy.* An individual can, and often does, react with narcissistic rage to what is experienced as an unempathic response on the part of a human self-object (that is, an empathic failure). Similarly, a person may become narcissistically enraged in reaction to a lack of utilitarian responsiveness and instrumental empathy on the part of things and activities as transitional selfobjects.

For example, many people, who are regular users of personal computers ("PCs"), undoubtedly know all too well the extreme frustration and even rage which may occur in reaction to an unresponsive PC. The user experiences it subjectively as failing to respond empathically to commands. It is as if the PC-user imagined that the computer is semi-human, and thus could and should respond empathically to instructions. Makers of both PCs and software programs, who are aware of and sensitive to the frustrations of PC-users are constantly striving to create ever more "user friendly" (that is, empathic) products.

There is a second factor helping to explain how a person may experience things and activities as empathic transitional selfobjects. It involves the functional capacity (similar to that possessed by human selfobjects) of certain agents to activate latent fantasies of an archaic and narcissistic nature. Empathy, in our self-psychological sense, denotes the capacity of either a transitional or an ersatz selfobject to mobilize archaic narcissistic fantasies (or self-state fantasies) and accompanying moods of narcissistic bliss. Our self-psychological view of empathy is truly psychoanalytic in that it stresses the importance and role of unconscious fantasy. (See, for example, I. Miller, 1972; and Beres & Arlow, 1974 for two early and still important discussions of the relation between empathy and fantasy.)

However, from our vantage point, it is important to emphasize a crucial distinction. Certain individuals may have a subjective experience of some magically endowed things and activities as being empathically attuned. Nonetheless, they are never experienced under normal circumstances—regardless of whether they function on a more archaic or a more mature level—as equally empathic as human selfobjects. On the contrary, it is already evidence of the warning signs of the possibility of a particular child developing a narcissistic behavior disorder in the future, if this youngster continues to experience the nonhuman world of things and activities as more empathic (or not being unempathic or antipathetic) than other human beings.

Anyone may have an unconscious experience of either transitional or ersatz selfobjects as empathic; however, there are objective differences that distinguish the former from the latter. There are at least four objective criteria that are critical in distinguishing between genuine and ersatz selfobjects. First, real selfobjects are *transformative* in that they contribute to the unconscious process of psychic structure-building as manifested in the enhancement of the psychological functioning of the self. On the contrary, pseudo selfobjects are *deformative* in interfering with the unconscious process of transmuting internalization and in leading to a developmental arrest in the psychological functioning of the self.

Second, bona fide selfobjects are *evolutionary* in advancing from archaic through transitional to mature forms and functions. In contrast, bogus selfobjects are *devolutionary* in remaining stunted at more primitive levels of functioning. Third, true selfobjects are *generative* in creating new and developmentally more advanced psychological structures and functions. In contradistinction, pseudo selfobjects are *degenerative* in eroding psychic structures and destroying the healthy psychological functioning of these structures.

Thus, ersatz selfobjects or ATMs only mimic the functioning of a transitional selfobject. The latter has utilitarian value as a practical extension of the self. ATMs serve as gimmicks and, as such, add nothing of psychological value to the self.

And fourth, authentic selfobjects are *rehabilitative* in serving as healthy means of psychologically restoring the self to normal functioning. In contrast, ersatz selfobjects are *debilitative* in serving only to weaken the functional capacities of the self.

The pathogenesis of addiction involves an abnormal process which we term *addictivization*. Certain normal activities and healthy things undergo, as part of such a psychopathological process, a mutation. As a result, they cease functioning as transitional selfobjects and instead malfunction as ATMs.

Addictivization constitutes a self-psychological equivalent to the classical psychoanalytic concepts of sexualization and eroticization. These notions were originally developed within classical psychoanalysis to account for the symptomatic or characterological expression of uncon-scious and neurotic conflicts. According to the classical formulation, unconsciously a person sexualizes some thing or activity which, under normal conditions, is totally nonerotic in nature and function.

Regrettably, in our opinion, some classical psychoanalysts employ the concepts of sexualization and eroticization in their attempt to explain addiction. In contradistinction, we argue that addiction is not based in conflicted disturbances of a psychosexual nature; rather it is based in developmental arrests and corresponding deficits, which result in nar-cissistic disturbances.

However, despite the important phenomenological and etiological differences between addiction and other neurotic as well as psychotic conditions, there are also important similarities. For example, we make in our proposed model of addiction an implicit connection between addiction and sexual fetishism. This link is based on a parallel that exists between the use by a neurotic of fetishistic things and activities to achieve sexual potency and the (ab)use by an addict of ATMs to maintain some semblance of narcissistic equilibrium.

An important equivalency may be found between fetishism and addiction in that both involve the obligatory use of specific things and activities. The fetishist must use, by definition, a particular array of things as well as engage in a set routine (compulsive activity or ritual) in order to arouse the sexual fantasies. These erotic illusions are necessary in order for the fetishist to function sexually and achieve orgasm. Likewise, an addict must use certain things or engage in particular activities in order to activate narcissistic fantasies of illusory control in order to experience even a semblance of psychological intactness.

In this regard, then, fetishism, perversion, and addiction all may be distinguished from other forms of psychopathology. Essentially, the latter involve a disturbance within the personality itself, whereas the former entail a disturbance between a person and the environment. And, more specifically, fetishism, perversion, and addiction all are based on a dis-turbance in the (ab)use of oneself or other persons, things, and activities.

Such (ab)use is primarily sexual or narcissistic in nature rather than being practical and empirical in nature. In other words, in these three narcissistic behavior disorders there is a psychopathological disturbance based on *using* rather than on *relating*. This is the basis in our proposed model for the important distinction we make between a *psychoanalytic psychology of use* and other psychoanalytic psychologies of wish, need, and relation.

The underlying (theoretical) connection that exists between fetishism and addiction allows us to use our fantasy-based model to equate the sexual phenomena of masturbation and orgasm to addiction in the following manner. We view ATMs as masturbatory and orgasmic-like equivalents. As such, they facilitate the activation of the narcissistic fantasies and moods that are so central to the addictive state of mind. We believe we are justified, therefore, in construing addictivization as involving the narcissistic equivalent of masturbation and orgasm (that is, narcissistic bliss).

An important analogy may be made between a masturbator and an addict. A masturbator reaches orgasm not merely on the basis of the physical stimulation of the genitals. On the contrary, the successful act of masturbation requires the arousal of a specific set of sexual fantasies. Similarly, an addict does not achieve an orgasmic-like physiological reaction simply by (ab)using certain things or activities. Of equal if not greater importance, an addict must mobilize archaic narcissistic fantasies and moods in order to achieve an addictive state of mind (that is, addictive metamorphosis or phantasmagorical transmogrification). Thus, fantasy and mood are the critical intervening variables for both the masturbator and the addict. Fantasy and mood are the desired end; whereas physical or behavioral activity are the necessary means to this end.

TYPOLOGY

We employ our proposed model to view an addict from several different yet interrelated typological vantage points. Contrary to the view of some, (see, for example, Krystal & Raskin, 1970), we construe an addict as an example of the "fantasy-prone personality" (see, for example, Lynn & Rhue, 1988; Pekala et al., 2000; Rauschenberger & Lynn, 2003; Ring, 1990; Wilson & Barber, 1983). Using the technique of the experimental laboratory, academic psychologists (see, for example, Barrett, 1996; Council et al., 1996; Hilgard, 1965, 1970, 1974; Lynn et al., 1996; Rader et al., 1996; Tellegen & Atkinson, 1974) have spent years studying the phenomenon of absorption in fantasy. These same researchers have linked such absorption in fantasy with a proneness to both dissociation and hypnotizability.

More recently, academic psychologists (see, for example, Bartholomew, et al. 1991; Lynn & Rhue, 1988; Powers, 1991; Wilson and Barber, 1981, 1983) have discovered that among so-called "fantasy-prone persons" there are individuals who are particularly inclined toward an unusually (and, perhaps in some cases even pathologically) high degree of absorption in fantasy. An addict evidences, as a type of fantasy-prone person, a tendency toward preoccupation with phantasmagorical visions; such a proclivity is consistent with a pathological absorption in fantasy. In this sense, then, an addict may be said to be a "fantasy junkie." (Again, see the characters from the movie *Requiem for a Dream*.)

We propound, as part of our typology, the idea of there being an "addictive character." This is a type of character pathology that we have modeled after Freud's original character types. At various phases in some of his early writings (see, for example, Freud), Freud alludes to several types of character pathology. These include that of the hysteric, phobic, obsessive-compulsive, and psychopathic. Freud (1961 [1928]) anticipates our notion of an addictive character in a later essay on Dostoevsky, and more specifically regarding the latter's addiction to gambling, in referring to Dostoevsky as an "instinctual character" (p. 179).

Freud originally conceives of his typology of different character types as organized on the basis of two factors. These consist of pathological fixation points at specific stages of psychosexual development as well as very specific and unconscious fantasies. For example, Freud (1955 [1919]) analyzes in an essay entitled, "A Child Is Being Beaten," character tendencies of a sadomasochistic nature in terms of unconscious "beating-phantasies" (p. 179).

Extrapolating self-psychologically from Freud, we conceptualize an addictive character as a person who is organized unconsciously on the basis of a developmental arrest at the stage of transitional selfobject usage. Such an arrest derives from an archaic narcissistic fantasy of being a megalomaniacal self (that is, as possessing absolute and total) control over magically-endowed things and activities.

We view addiction typologically as a narcissistic *behavior* disorder. In this context, addictive behavior serves for a particular individual as an emergency measure. Such a person feels compelled to prop up a sense of self, which he or she experiences unconsciously as on the verge of narcissistic decompensation. However, such conduct on the part of such an individual has little or no capacity for structure-building of a substantial and enduring nature.

Our self-psychological view of addiction incorporates Kohut's distinction between a narcissistic personality disorder and a narcissistic behavior disorder (see, Kohut, 1977b, p. 193; see also, Goldberg, 1995, 2000). This distinction provides self psychology with its own unique diagnostic and typological niche within which to locate addiction.

(For the moment, we leave aside such complicated diagnostic issues as "dual diagnosis" see, for example, Anthenell & Schucket, 1993; Cocores, 1994; Daley, Moss, & Campbell, 1987; Gold & Slaby, 1991; Kaye et al., 2004; Lesieur & Blume, 1993; Miller, 1993; J. R. Miller, 1994; Modesto-Lowe & Kranzler, 1999; Myrick et al., 2004; Ortman, 1997; Penk et al., 2000 and Petry, 2005.) And, of even greater import, the distinction on Kohut's part is based on his realization that substantial differences exist between narcissistic personality and narcissistic behavior disorders. Moreover, for a self-psychological therapist who is attempting to empathically understand and treat an addicted patient, these typological differences have clinical import.

On the one hand, the so-called narcissistic sector of the personality (namely, that part of the personality organized primarily in terms of regulating self-esteem through establishing and maintaining a functional relationship with others as selfobjects) is typically damaged and disturbed in the case of a narcissistic personality disorder without, however, necessarily eventuating in a pervasive disturbance in behavior. In this instance, a person who is narcissistically disturbed subjectively experiences others as archaic selfobjects; such a person lacks a well-developed capacity to relate to others as separate and independent selves with their own individual needs, interests, and goals.

On the other hand, the psychological disturbance frequently extends in the case of a narcissistic behavior disorder far beyond the realms of experience and thought to the domains of action and deed. In this instance, an individual who suffers from a narcissistic behavior disorder (including an addict, a fetishistic pervert, as well as a sociopath and a psychopath) is unable to hold himself or herself together psychologically by relating functionally to others as archaic selfobjects. For such an individual, the unconscious process of fantasizing another person as an extension of the self is not sufficient. Instead, an individual who suffers from a narcissistic behavior disorder must (ab)use others in such a way that they serve as nonhuman or semi-human functionaries. For such a person the sole purpose of this behavior is avoiding narcissistic mortification and insuring narcissistic bliss.

Moreover, behavior (and not simply experience) becomes in the case of addiction subverted from its normal purpose, which is to facilitate adaptation to the environment. Instead, behavior becomes pathologically distorted for purposes that are purely narcissistic in nature and that entail the misappropriation and misuse of the environment. Such narcissistic behavior is part of a desperate yet futile attempt on the part of an addict to satisfy morbid cravings, which ultimately cannot be satisfied.

It follows that behavior, in the context of addiction, loses all or most of its adaptive and practical value. Rather, it becomes valuable to an addict only insofar as it meets needs of an addictive nature. In this sense, behavior becomes for an addict a physical medium for the expression of fantasies of being a megalomaniacal self and as wielding magical control.

Furthermore, the problem in the case of a narcissistic behavior disorder is not limited to a misuse of others as if they were nothing more than human extensions of the self. The problem extends to the abuse or misuse, by an addict, for example, of another person as if he or she were not even human; others lose not only an essential selfhood but a basic humanness as well. For an addict, they become, at best, semi-human parts of the self.

In addition, an addict may simultaneously mistreat humans as if they were things and misuse things as if they were human! We return here to the "wonderland" of addiction. An addict who, like Alice, is lost in a surreal world, turns humans into things and changes things into creatures with humanoid and android qualities. This is true for other persons whom an addict literally mistreats (rather than figuratively experiences and relates to) as if things.

The same is true for the way an addict mistreats (him)self or her(self). In this regard, an addict misappropriates his or her own self (and not only others) as if it were nothing more than a non-living and mechanical thing lacking in basic humanness. In essence, an addict metamorphizes or transmogrifies into a figurine that is like a humanoid or android.

As distinct from the narcissistic personality disorder, the narcissistic behavior disorder involves a far-reaching extension of the nature of the psychopathology of the self. The psychic disturbance in the narcissistic personality disorder extends only as far as *relating* narcissistically to others, however, strictly on a mental rather than on a behavioral basis. Thus, an individual who suffers from a narcissistic personality disorder relates to another in a way that consists entirely of a narcissistic experience of that person as an extension or part of the self. In other words, this type of narcissistic disturbance is completely mental in nature; it does not entail any kind of behavior or action involving the (ab)use of the other for purely narcissistic purposes.

The disturbance in the narcissistic behavior disorder extends much further to the pathological mistreatment of other people (and things) in a way that has a direct effect on them. People become the unwitting victims of a narcissistic rip-off in which they are abused by the perpetrator merely as props and accouterments. We may speak here of a far more severe form of *psychological usurpation*: other persons are mistreated by a person with a narcissistic behavior disorder in a way that actually deprives them of selfhood and humanness. For example, a sex addict abuses other people as if they were erotic playthings, toys, or gadgets with no more humanity or selfhood than a dildo.

We have explored previously uncharted psychological territory by following and elaborating on Kohut's distinction between narcissistic personality disorder and the narcissistic behavior disorder. We believe that approaching addiction as a narcissistic behavior disorder allows us as self psychologists to plumb here for unexpected depth dimensions of the unconscious mind. At these deeper, psychic depths of the unconscious, other human beings exist for an addict as nothing more than things located in a "narcissistic universe" (Kohut, 1978d, pp. 651, 834). As such, they are used and then are discarded, disposed of, or recycled as if they were nothing more than a ballpoint pen or a plastic bottle. For an addict, other people as well as (one)self have become disposable or reusable items with little or no intrinsic value beyond the purely narcissistic. The existence of other people or the status of things and activities as ATMs is another aspect of addictive metamorphosis or phantasmagorical transmogrification.

Our proposed typology of addiction rests on two notions: (1) the idea of the narcissistic behavior disorder as a distinct form of self-pathology, and (2) Kohut's (1977b) original concept of the "bipolar self." We have taken Kohut's concept as the basis for our *bipolar self typology of addiction*. This typology covers a spectrum of different yet interrelated types of addict ranging from the unipolar to the bipolar, each with its own subtypes (that is, respectively subtypes I and II).

Let us provide the reader with a brief description of these four subtypes of addict. There are two subtypes of addict with a unipolar diagnosis. An addict with the diagnosis of unipolar, subtype I (see, for example, the cases of Teddy and Mary in Chapter 4) suffers from narcissistic damage in only *one* of the major poles of self-experience (that is, grandiosity, omnipotence, alterego, and megalomania). Such an addict craves archaic mirroring, idealization, twinship, or control in order to combat painful emotions such as a depressed sense of emptiness, depletion anxiety, shame, disintegration anxiety, panic, rage, and loneliness. An addict with a diagnosis of the unipolar, subtype II (see, for example, the cases of Joe and JoAnn in Chapter 5) suffers from narcissistic damage primarily in one pole of the self with some minor or secondary damage in another pole. However, addicts with a diagnosis of unipolar, whether subtype I or II, typically abuse only one kind of ATM.

There are two subtypes of addict with a bipolar diagnosis. An addict with the diagnosis of bipolar, subtypes I and II (see, respectively, the cases of Travis and Errol in Chapter 6) suffers from narcissistic damage in two or more of the major poles of self-experience. Such an addict has archaic needs for a variety of selfobject functions (namely, mirroring, idealization, twinship, and control) to combat pronounced, and sometimes violent, mood swings. An addict with the bipolar diagnosis always abuses several ATMs at once or in rapid succession. The presence of psychotic symptoms of either a latent or florid nature is the basis for our typological and diagnostic distinction between addicts with bipolar, subtype II versus those with subtype I.

All of our typological distinctions have a direct bearing on treatment. A psychotherapist who employs our typology as a means of making a differential diagnosis can tailor psychotherapy to suit the specific transference needs of a particular addict. For instance, a psychotherapist who has made the diagnosis of the unipolar type of addiction ought to be prepared to facilitate a selfobject transference with a *singular* focus on primarily one (and secondarily only on another) area of narcissistic damage. Or, to take a second instance, a psychotherapist who has arrived at a diagnosis of the bipolar type of addiction is positioned to facilitate a selfobject transference with a *dual* focus on two or more areas of narcissistic damage.

Our self-psychological typology of addiction makes it possible, moreover, to synthesize some of the exciting new psychiatric work being done on bipolar (mood) disorder (see, for example, Akiskal, 1996; Angst & Cassano, 2005; Barondex, 1998; Berk & Seetel, 2005; Brondolo & Mas, 2001; Deitz, 1995; Goldberg, 2004; Goldberg & Harrow, 1999; Goodwin & Jamison, 1990; Himmelhoch, 2003; Jones, Sellwood, & McGovern, 2005; Katzow et al., 2003; Mackin & Young, 2004; Maj et al. 1999, 2003; Mas, 2003; Mitchell & Malhi, 2004; Mondimore, 1999; Newman et al., 2002; Sacks & Reis, 2003; Sonne & Brady 1999, 2002; Tohen & Zarate, 1999; Whybrow, 1997 and Winokur, 1991). Such a synthetic perspective allows us to view many addicted patients as suffering from some type of bipolar disturbance regardless of the thing or activity to which a particular person is addicted. The bipolar self typology of addiction enables us to illuminate important points of commonality between such otherwise disparate fields as self psychology and biological psychiatry.

Our typology of addiction serves, therefore, as a prime example of both the possibility and feasibility of synthesizing psychoanalysis with biological psychiatry. On the one hand, the former may be viewed as emphasizing unconscious mental processes such as fantasizing and psychic structures such as fantasy. On the other hand, the latter stresses biochemical processes such as neurotransmission between cells within neuroanatomical structures such as the frontal and temporal lobes of the brain.

We have combined self psychology and biological psychiatry to create a unique "bioself-psychological" perspective (see Miliora & Ulman, 1996b) that facilitates a multidimensional focus on the dialectical bipolarity of fantasy and mood. Such a vantage point allows us to better understand the significant extent to which both fantasy and mood are part of a complex set of psychobiological processes.

Indeed, our synthetic version of the bipolar self represents a good example of the advantages to be gained by combining biological psychiatry with psychoanalysis and, in this particular instance, self psychology. (Such a synthesis constitutes a theoretical perspective with a bifocal view of the person as a psychobiological being whose experience of selfhood is determined by both a brain and a mind.) (For recent work consistent with this viewpoint see Eccles, 1994; Feinberg, 2001; Kircher & David, 2003 and Schore, 1994, 2003a,b.)

THERAPEUTICS

We focus attention, employing the therapeutic component of our proposed model, on the fantasy-promoting nature of the psychoanalytic setting as well as the "therapeutic action" taking place therein. The fantasy-promoting quality of psychoanalytic psychotherapy is well-suited to treating a fantasy-prone patient such as an addict. It is an ideal (clinical) milieu within which an addicted patient may introspect about otherwise vague and hazy fantasies. An addicted patient may gain, based on such introspection, a better empathic understanding of the nature and role of these archaic narcissistic fantasies.

In general, we approach psychoanalytic psychotherapy with an addicted patient on the basis of what Ulman and Stolorow (1985) originally conceived of as the "transference–countertransference neurosis." These authors set out to "clarify how the *developmentally arrested psychological structures* of both the patient and the analyst interact to codetermine a specific intersubjective field" (p. 39, emphasis added). In the particular treatment case presented by these authors, this

> intersubjective field was structured on the one hand by the patient's extreme sensitivity and responsiveness to any sign of disturbance in the analyst's sense of well-being and on the other hand by the analyst's need for responses from the patient that would enhance his self-esteem. (p. 39).

The authors argue that the case "illustrates how *the analyst may use the patient as a particular type of selfobject and how the patient may feel compelled to fulfill this function*" (p. 38, emphasis added). They concluded that "transference and countertransference continually shape one another in a specific pattern of reciprocal mutual influence" (p. 39).

Ulman and his subsequent co-workers (see, for example, Miliora & Ulman 1996a,b; Ulman & Brothers, 1987, 1988 and Ulman & Paul 1989, 1990, 1992) take the concept of the transference–countertransference neurosis and refine it as well as apply it to a variety of different clinical populations. For instance, Ulman and Brothers (1987)—in their work with trauma survivors of incest, rape, and combat—refine and sharpen the clinical concept of the transference–countertransference neurosis to focus specifically on "selfobject fantasies" of patient and psychotherapist alike. These authors have advanced the concept of the transference–countertransference neurosis beyond that of Ulman and Stolorow.

The latter authors view it as based on "developmentally arrested psychological structures" of both patient and psychotherapist. Ulman and Brothers note that "in keeping with the theory of intersubjectivity, we found that a patient's *selfobject fantasy of the therapist* may conflict with *an unanalyzed selfobject fantasy of the therapist about the patient*" (p. 180, emphasis added). They indicate that the "simultaneous presence of competing and conflicting *selfobject transference and countertransference fantasies*" (p. 180) creates a version of the transference–countertransference neurosis.

These authors point out that in the "intersubjective context unconsciously organized by the transference–countertransference neurosis, the therapist experiences the patient as providing selfobject functions of mirroring, idealization, or twinship (alterego)" (p. 180). They warn that this "tends to interfere with the patient's selfobject transference fantasy of the therapist as providing these same selfobject functions" (p. 180). However, Ulman and Brothers conclude that "if empathically understood and analyzed, the transference–countertransference neurosis *is invaluable in reconstructing and working through the unconscious meaning of trauma*" (p. 180).

We develop further the fantasy-based nature of the transference–countertransference neurosis in our previous work—that is, the "addiction paper trilogy"—with addicted patients. We (Ulman & Paul, 1990) note that at times "a patient's transference fantasy evokes in the therapist an empathic response whereby the therapist recognizes and accepts the patient's need to experience the therapist as a selfobject" (p. 176). However, in other instances, we indicate "a patient's transference fantasy if not met by empathic understanding by the therapist" (p. 136). Rather, we state, "as a result of the therapist's countertransference fantasy, it elicits an unempathic response from the therapist" (p. 136). We caution:

> Unanalyzed countertransference fantasies of the patient as an archaic selfobject may strengthen the patient's resistance to forming an archaic selfobject transference, they may disrupt an already established selfobject transference. (p. 136).

However, in line with the earlier work of Ulman and Brothers, we discovered that the transference–countertransference neurosis "if empathically understood and analyzed ... is invaluable in reconstructing and working through the unconscious meaning" (Ulman & Brothers, 1987, p. 180) of addictive fantasies.

Finally, Miliora and Ulman utilize the concept of the transference–countertransference neurosis in their psychoanalytic work with panic-disordered patients. They (Miliora & Ulman, 1996a,b) report that the "analyst may react countertransferentially to being treated by the panic-disordered patient *as a superabsorbent sponge or receptacle* that contains disturbing emotions and disorganizing stimuli" (p. 232, emphasis added). "Such a dynamic," which these authors cite as an example of the transference–countertransference neurosis, "can seriously undermine the effectiveness of treatment" (p. 232). In such instances of the transference–countertransference neurosis, Miliora and Ulman indicate that the "patient experiences the analyst as failing to function as a containing presence, that is, an empathic failure has occurred, and a panic attack may ensue" (p. 233).

We take the concept of the transference–countertransference neurosis in the intersubjective context of our current work, and refine and deepen it even further. We follow Blum's (1986, 1988) lead and return to Freud's (1959 [1908a]) original notion of the "shared fantasy" as a basis for our self-psychological refinement of the transference–countertransference neurosis. We conceive of this intersubjective phenomenon as organized unconsciously according to selfobject fantasies shared alike by patient and psychotherapist (see Bonovitz, 2004; LaFarge, 2004; Smith, 2004).

We discover in the context of our psychoanalytic work with addicted patients that such patients are similar to the panic-disordered patient. Both of these types of patients fantasize and use a psychotherapist as an inanimate thing or nonhuman selfobject, that is, as something like a "superabsorbent sponge or receptacle." In certain instances, a psychotherapist can facilitate the psychotherapy with an addicted patient by empathically sharing in such transitional selfobject fantasies.

However, as Ulman and several of his co-workers (see Ulman & Brothers, 1987, 1988 and Ulman & Stolorow, 1985) realize, a potential danger exists in adopting such a stance. For example, a psychotherapist who unconsciously and uncritically shares with a patient in these powerful fantasies may come under the influence of a countertransference involving the abuse of a patient. In so doing, a psychotherapist may seriously impede the progress, if not the viability, of psychotherapy. We provide examples of such instances in our psychoanalytic psychotherapy case histories.

Our self-psychological approach to psychotherapy is based more specifically on the operation of the narcissistic exchange process as it unfolds within treatment. As we originally conceive it, we describe the psychoanalytic therapy of an addicted patient in terms of the therapeutic process of intersubjective absorption. Such a clinical process does, indeed, occur and is an integral feature of our self-psychological approach to psychotherapy. However, by itself it does not adequately capture the essential therapeutic action of our treatment approach.

In essence, in treating an addicted patient we reverse the psychological sequence that unfolds as part of the developmental pattern constituted by the narcissistic exchange process. However, it is first necessary, in order to initiate this therapeutic process, for a psychotherapist to help an addicted patient to gradually wean off the pathological dependence on the selfobject-like functioning of ATMs such as alcohol, drugs, food, gambling, and sex.

The narcissistic exchange process cannot unfold properly unless a patient has first achieved a significant degree of abstinence, sobriety, solvency, etc. No narcissistic interchange between ATMs and the psychotherapy is possible as long as an addicted patient continues to rely primarily on the selfobject-like functions of things and activities. We are, therefore, strong advocates of using such 12-step programs as Alcoholics Anonymous (AA), Overeaters Anonymous (OA), Debtors Anonymous (DA), Gamblers Anonymous (GA), Sex and Love Addicts Anonymous (SLAA) and Sexual Compulsives Anonymous (SCA) as adjuncts to the therapy. (See Finley, 2004 for support of our position.) Or, in extreme cases we utilize addiction rehabilitation centers ("rehabs") in order to achieve remission of the active phase of an addiction.

We believe that cessation of addiction as an ongoing and hence active disorder is preliminary and preparatory to the therapeutic stages of the narcissistic exchange process. These stages consist of: (1) initiating and completing the swapping of the narcissistic functioning of ATMs for the selfobject functioning of psychotherapy; and (2) analyzing and working through the utilitarian nature of the transitional selfobject transference and, in turn, making psychotherapy and psychotherapists less nonhuman and more human.

In the first stage of this psychoanalytic process a psychotherapist helps an addicted patient to *transfer* to the psychotherapy his or her narcissistic investment in ATMs. In so doing, a psychotherapist becomes a healthy replacement for an ATM and gradually takes over its self-object-like functioning. In this sense, then, an addicted patient uses a psychotherapist as a fiduciary in that a psychotherapist is *entrusted* with psychological functions of a precious and invaluable nature.

An addicted patient, in using a psychotherapist as a transitional or semi-human thing and activity, is unconsciously entertaining a megalo-maniacal fantasy about possessing a magical capacity to control both psychotherapy and psychotherapist. A psychotherapist, by allowing a patient to indulge and become absorbed intersubjectively in these fantasies of being a megalomaniacal self, is actually harnessing their potential for therapeutic purposes. In this sense then, a psychotherapist enters into the megalomaniacal realm of the Narcissus complex of an addicted patient.

Ideally, a psychotherapist ought not interfere with an addicted patient's legitimate need to undergo a transference version of the addictive state of mind within the psychoanalytic therapy. On the contrary, a psychotherapist ought to understand that an addicted patient must, for a time, entertain the illusion that a psychotherapist is a thing and that the psychotherapy is an activity, both of which may be magically controlled by an addicted patient as part of a "narcissistic universe." The pejorative connotation of being "controlling" is, we maintain, really nothing other than an addicted patient giving expression to megalomaniacal illusions, which have been developmentally arrested.

At this point in the psychotherapy, an addict fantasizes or imagines the psychotherapist as a transference version of a transitional selfobject (thing or activity). An addicted patient unconsciously experiences a psychotherapist as a narcissistic commodity or currency with a bonafide status. As such, a psychotherapist is something or other that is endowed transferentially by an addicted patient with a magical quality. Such a transference experience entails for an addicted patient the provision of actual selfobject functions including, for example, antidepressant mirroring, antianxiety or pacifying idealization, shame-relieving twinship, or anti-panic control. In sum, an addicted patient exchanges the faulty selfobject-like functioning of ATMs for the effective selfobject functioning of a psychotherapist (and psychotherapy).

A psychotherapist, as part of taking over for the faulty selfobject-like functioning of ATMs, clinically induces what R.F. Sterba (1934) calls "therapeutic dissociation." We contend that such a state of mind is created psychoanalytically in such a way that an addicted patient relives fantasies of being a megalomaniacal self and as endowed with magical control and re-experiences moods of narcissistic bliss in a therapeutic as opposed to an addictive fashion. Such an altered state of consciousness may eventually supersede and supplant an addicted patient's dependence on an addictive state of mind.

Therapeutic dissociation takes place on a cognitive as well as an affective-sensorial level. On the cognitive level, it involves the creation and sharing of a transference fantasy on the part of patient and psychotherapist alike. Such an intersubjective or shared fantasy allows a patient to use both psychotherapist and psychotherapy in a fanciful fashion. Such fantasy-play is consistent with illusions of magical control over a "narcissistic universe."

In the context of the analytic activation of such a fantasy of a megalomaniacal self, an addicted patient can utilize the therapy to provide "psychopharmacotherapeutic" (F. Mas, 2000, personal communication) relief (for instance, antidepressant stimulation or antianxiety tranquilization and sedation) from various forms of emotional distress.

In the process, an addicted patient undergoes a cognitive alteration of consciousness that entails a therapeutic form of dissociation.

Typically, at this phase in the treatment an addicted patient turns the psychotherapy and psychotherapist into an entity that functions as an imaginary *dispensary*. As such, the psychotherapy becomes a thing-like activity (that is, a transitional selfobject) that dispenses self-object functions in the form of specific forms of psychopharmacotherapeutic relief (see Kohut, 1977b, pp. 270–80 on the "psychotropic influence" of certain social or cultural selfobjects).

On an affective-sensorial level, therapeutic dissociation consists of the psychotherapy serving figuratively as a clinical sponge that soaks up and absorbs the overflow of painful emotions. In this sense, a psychotherapist functions as a sponge and exists, therefore, on a self-object level as both an imaginary thing and activity. In other words, a psychotherapist functions for an addicted patient as a sponge-like entity, or transitional selfobject, that actively soaks up any excess of painful feelings and sensations.

If a psychotherapist succeeds in assisting an addicted patient in making a narcissistic exchange, then it is possible to proceed self-psychologically with the next stage of the psychotherapeutic process. In this second and final stage, a psychotherapist aids an addicted patient in experiencing him or her as more than a mere semi-human thing or activity. In so doing, a psychotherapist enables an addicted patient to proceed therapeutically through a previously arrested phase of development.

This phase consists developmentally of a child partially divesting specially endowed things and activities of a certain portion of their narcissistic stock as transitional selfobjects. Following this narcissistic divestiture, a child reinvests this selfobject functioning in parents, however now experienced as more mature, human selfobjects. Psychotherapeutically, the successful completion of this phase of the narcissistic exchange process is accomplished as an addicted patient treats a psychotherapist as a more fully human selfobject, and one which has been reinvested with narcissistic capital.

The analysis and working through of a utilitarian quality of the transference constitutes an essential aspect of the second stage of the psychotherapy with an addicted patient. This feature of the psychotherapy occurs, initially at least, in the context of a patient treating a psychotherapist as what Isakower referred to as "the analyzing instrument" (see Isakower, 1992 [1957]; see also Balter et al., 1980; and Solomon 1992). At this therapeutic stage, a psychotherapist serves as a more-or-less impersonal and semi-human source of information and feedback.

Such data are generated, as far as a patient is concerned, by mechanical means, that is, as if a psychotherapist is some kind of "smart machine." At this point at least, a patient does not experience the psychotherapy primarily in human terms and, thus, as involving a dialogue between two persons. Instead, an addicted patient experiences the psychotherapy as an exchange or transaction between a human being and an instrument that is totally controlled by the individual who possesses and uses it.

In this context, a patient has an illusion that psychotherapy involves a transaction in which a psychotherapist is fantasized or imagined as functioning like a computer. A computer has semi-human qualities insofar as it can metaphorically "speak" and "think." Yet, it is still a machine which is controlled and directed by the PC user. An addicted patient uses a psychotherapist as an analyzing instrument in much the same way that a PC user employs a computer.

Technologically sophisticated instruments and machines such as computers provide invaluable services in performing incredibly complex processes that significantly enhance the performance of the user. A psychotherapist serves for an addicted patient in the selfobject capacity as an analyzing instrument. As such, a psychotherapist enables an addicted patient to entertain fantasies of being a megalomaniacal self and as capable of magically controlling processes that seem to emanate from a humanoid entity. In a paradoxical twist, however, the more an addict patient fantasizes being in control of the psychotherapy, the easier it becomes to relinquish this illusion in exchange for actual mastery.

In this regard, then, both patient and therapist create and share in a transference fantasy of psychotherapy as a thing and activity that functions as a transitional selfobject. A psychotherapist empathically joins in such an intersubjective fantasy in the interest of facilitating therapeutic progress. This does not mean, however, that a psychotherapist believes in the fantasy in the same way as does a patient. A psychotherapist facilitates the emergence and tries not to interfere with the unfolding of such a selfobject transference fantasy. A psychotherapist understands empathically that initially a patient needs to entertain such phantasmagorical illusions without, however, being challenged.

Although occurring in different ways, both patient and psychotherapist become absorbed intersubjectively in a shared fantasy. This is the essence of an intersubjective fantasy. And, in sharing and becoming absorbed in a fantasy of psychotherapy as a nonhuman or transitional selfobject, patient and psychotherapist alike create a psychoanalytic version of "virtual reality" (see Friedman, 2005; Heim, 1993; Pesce, 2000 and Schell, 2000) for their respective discussions of the intermingling of fact and fiction in the creation of virtual reality). Such a psychoanalytic version of a virtual reality gradually replaces the surreal and unreal quality of an addict's existence as a Narcissus in Wonderland.

Yet, an addicted patient inevitably experiences a psychotherapist as unempathic (that is, an empathic failure has occurred) during the second stage of the therapeutic process. A patient may experience a psychotherapist as failing to perform in a manner consistent with transference fantasies, which have gone unnoticed and hence unanalyzed. Ironically, a psychotherapist helps to meet a patient's growing need to experience the former as a more human and less nonhuman presence in addressing rather than by simply redressing empathic failures.

At this critical juncture, a transaction occurs in which there is a narcissistic exchange on the part of an addicted patient of the nonhuman or semi-human functioning of a psychotherapist and psychotherapy (as respectively selfobject thing and activity, that is, as transitional selfobject), for a psychotherapist's emerging status as a more human (selfobject) presence.

We cannot emphasize enough that the narcissistic exchange process as it occurs in the context of an ongoing psychotherapy is based on a genuine, two-way trade. In such an exchange both patient and psychotherapist benefit alike in a mutual and reciprocal fashion. A patient benefits narcissistically from trading in the faulty selfobject-like functioning of an ATM for the vastly superior, selfobject functioning of a psychotherapist. A psychotherapist gains narcissistic satisfaction from serving as a transitional selfobject. In the process a psychotherapist experiences a patient's relief from psychic pain based on the psychopharmacotherapeutic effect(s) or the transitional selfobject transferences.

However, all addicted patients are notorious as con artists and, as such, are adept at perpetrating what amounts to a narcissistic rip-off. Under these countertherapeutic circumstances, no genuine exchange process occurs between the selfobject-like functioning of an ATM and the selfobject functioning of a psychotherapist. Instead, an addicted patient simply takes advantage of a psychotherapist's potential availability as a transitional selfobject without, however, necessarily giving up dependence on an ATM.

This is a classic example of every addicted patient's fantasy of "wanting to have your cake and eat it too." A psychotherapist who allows an addicted patient to succeed in such a narcissistic rip-off has colluded countertransferentially with a patient in seriously compromising the effectiveness of the psychotherapy. Under these circumstances, it is not uncommon for a psychotherapist who has been duped and conned by an addicted patient to have selfobject countertransference reactions ranging from narcissistic rage and antipathy to shame.

Moreover, a psychotherapist may succumb to several other selfobject countertransference reactions that typically occur in the course of using the self-psychological technique of the narcissistic exchange. One such problem may involve a countertransference resistance on the part of a psychotherapist to sharing and becoming absorbed intersubjectively in a patient's transference fantasy of a megalomaniacal self as possessing control of the therapy. The countertransference resistance on the part of a psychotherapist to sharing such a fantasy may interfere with an addicted patient's initial need to experience psychotherapy as nothing more than a narcissistic trade-off.

In this instance, a psychotherapist fails countertransferentially to empathize with an addicted patient's need to use the former in a fiduciary fashion. Instead, a psychotherapist countertransferentially adopts a critical and judgmental attitude, one that may be all too human for an addicted patient.

A second countertransference reaction may involve a psychotherapist who over-identifies rather than empathizes with a transference fantasy of an addicted patient. In this instance, a psychotherapist may all too easily lose himself or herself in such a fantasy. As a result, a psychotherapist does not properly analyze the Narcissus complex. Instead, a psychotherapist joins, at least temporarily, in a selfobject countertransference fantasy of megalomaniacal control. In other words, a psychotherapist follows his or her patient into the wonderland of the Narcissus complex.

In this context, a psychotherapist, and especially one with a prior history of addiction, is prone to a particular countertransference reaction: such a psychotherapist attempts unconsciously to turn a patient into *something* rather than someone. A psychotherapist imagines a patient as something that can be controlled to provide the former with needed relief from psychic pain. As a result, a psychotherapist mistreats a patient by misusing him or her for purely narcissistic and self-centered purposes. Under the influence as selfobject countertransference fantasy of megalomaniacal control of a patient, a psychotherapist undergoes a form of dissociation and anesthetization from emotional ailments.

METHODOLOGY

Before describing our psychoanalytic methodology for the study of addiction, we must first discuss, albeit briefly, a more general methodological issue concerning the examination of fantasy. We are puzzled by the fact that, from a methodological perspective, there is so little in the psychoanalytic literature dealing explicitly with what could be construed of as a clinical means for the study of unconsciowus fantasy. The relative absence of such literature is even more confusing given that Freud himself created psychoanalysis as both a method for illuminating and technique for transforming pathogenic fantasies. (See Lear, 1990 and Hughes, 1994, for discussions of the critical role of fantasy in Freud's early thinking and case studies. See also Edelson, 1988 and Miliora & Ulman, 1996a for arguments concerning the primacy of fantasy for the entire psychoanalytic enterprise.) Hence, we are dumbfounded and frankly distressed that so little attention has been paid by psychoanalysts to developing a specific clinical method for studying unconscious fantasy as it appears naturally and spontaneously in the therapeutic setting of the psychoanalytic consulting room.

There are those, however, who have created ingenious ways for studying fantasy in a testing or laboratory setting. For example, Murray (1981 [1935, 1936]) devised the now famous Thematic Apperception Test (TAT) as a clinical means of pulling and eliciting for fantasies from respondents. Murray's work still stands as a pioneering breakthrough in the development of a scientific method for the study of fantasy. In addition, both Fisher (1954, 1956, 1957, 1960, 1988; see also Shevrin, 2003 for an edited collection of Fisher's articles) and Silverman (1978/79, 1979, 1983) as well as Silverman and Weinberger (1985) and Silverman et al. (1982, 1984) have employed experimental means for the subliminal activation of a number of unconscious fantasies.

Yet despite these exciting advances in the development of non-clinical means of evoking and studying unconscious fantasy, clinical psychoanalysis has failed, in our opinion, to keep pace with these innovative methodologies. However, the study of addiction, which, we believe, is essentially fantasy-based in nature, provides us with a perfect opportunity to design and implement a psychoanalytic methodology that is capable of furthering the scientific study of unconscious fantasy. (For non-clinical studies of the role of fantasy in addiction, see Kalin & McClelland, 1965; Kalin, McClelland, & Kahn, 1972; Segal, Huba, & Suger, 1980 and Wilsnack, 1974.)

There are a number of excellent discussions about the general methodological problems involved in the study of addiction (see, for example, Apsler, 1978; Gambino & Shaffer, 1979; Spotts & Shontz, 1976, 1982, 1983). However, few, if any, of these discussions focus specifically on the psychoanalytic study of addiction. This is surprising because addiction, which entails a hypnoid or dissociated state of mind, is an ideal phenomenon and process for study within the psychoanalytic setting. (See J. Silverman, 1968, who although non-psychoanalytic in orientation, focuses on methodological issues involved in the clinical study of altered states of consciousness.)

The addiction literature contains two early and, for our purposes, important exceptions to the otherwise glaring absence of discussions about the methodological problems involved in the psychoanalytic study of addiction. In the early 1930s, Bromberg and Schilder (1933) published a paper that reports on psychoanalytically oriented research that these clinicians conducted on alcoholic hallucinosis. These researchers discuss eleven cases of this psychopathological condition. These cases are presented by these authors as being *representative* of a much larger group of patients, whom they studied using a psychoanalytic approach to collecting and analyzing clinical data.

Bromberg and Schilder do not employ psychoanalytic psychotherapy as a setting for their research. However, they do devote clinical attention to unconscious fantasy as it emerges and alters consciousness in the form of alcoholic hallucinosis. More specifically, these authors collect and analyze data indicative of what they interpret as latent castration and dismembering fantasies, fantasies that emerge in the context of alcoholically induced hallucinations.

Bromberg and Schilder's study of alcoholism, by analyzing fantasies underlying hallucinatory states, represents an early version of a psychoanalytic research methodology by which to examine the addictive process. Such a psychopathological process creates an addictive state of mind on the basis of the intrusion into conscious awareness of unconscious fantasies. This psychopathological alteration of consciousness occurs, we maintain, as a result of the dissociative triggering of archaic narcissistic fantasy and the anesthetizing activation of moods of narcissistic bliss.

From a methodological perspective, it is a logical step, therefore, to use psychoanalytic psychotherapy as a research setting within which to clinically induce similar dissociative states. It is possible from within the psychotherapeutic setting for clinicians to conduct psychoanalytic research on alterations in consciousness that typically occur as part of an addictive state of mind.

In a methodological spirit similar to that of Bromberg and Schilder, Chessick (1960) employs a research methodology that is explicitly psychoanalytic in his study of addiction. Chessick focuses his attention on analyzing the unconscious fantasies that he believes to be determinative of drug addiction. He even goes so far as to advocate the use of early memories and dreams as an indirect yet valid method of reconstructing the nature of these fantasies of which his research subjects are otherwise amnestic.

Chessick makes an important advance in advocating the use of such a psychoanalytic technique as part of his research on the development of a psychoanalytic methodology for the study of addiction. He illuminates addictive fantasies by using genetic reconstruction, a clinical technique more commonly employed in psychoanalytic psychotherapy for the recovery of forgotten childhood memories. We find it even more fascinating that he discovers that "fantasies of omnipotence" dominate "the mental life of the addict" (p. 549).

Chessick's methodological advance is of particular relevance to the self-psychological model of addiction that we propose in our study. We have expanded upon Chessick's early efforts in our use of the psychoanalytic transference as still another legitimate (clinical) means of interpreting the unconscious meaning of addictive fantasies. The transference experience of an addicted patient replicates a version of the dissociation and anesthetization attendant to phantasmagorical metamorphosis. Such alterations of consciousness are crucial to understanding and treating addiction, even though an addict is often amnestic about the details of these mind and mood altering episodes. (See Krystal & Raskin, 1970, for an earlier psychoanalytic account of what we have referred to previously as dissociative anesthetization and its importance to the addictive state of mind.)

The defensive nature of hypnoid states that occur in the context of addiction creates an amnestic veil. As a result of such amnesia, an addict is unaware of the influence of unconscious fantasy because it is shrouded in darkness. Such an amnestic veil is similar to that which arises in the case of trauma occurring in early childhood. In other words, "blacking out," which is so characteristic of addictive metamorphosis, obscures the psychic presence of unconscious fantasy.

It is possible, however, for a psychoanalytic researcher to raise this amnestic veil. The raising of such an amnestic veil occurs in the context of analyzing the (selfobject) transference as it becomes a clinical medium for capturing addictive fantasies, the nature of which are otherwise fleeting and vague. Our use of the selfobject transference is based on one of Kohut's major discoveries; he found that the transference is primarily narcissistic in nature rather than being sexual or erotic for certain patients—and, especially those such as addicts, who suffer from a narcissistic behavior disorder. These patients do not imagine the psychotherapist as a love object toward whom the patient relates on the basis of early psychosexual desires and wishes.

Instead, such a patient treats the psychotherapist in a utilitarian fashion as a nonhuman thing or activity. A patient uses a psychotherapist as part of a transitional selfobject transference that is based on atavistic fantasies from the past. These archaic narcissistic fantasies (and accompanying moods of narcissistic bliss) are also the basis for an addictive state of mind.

In addition to the general literature already cited on the methodology of studying addiction, the work of Hendin and associates (Hendin, 1975; Hendin, Gaylin, & Carr, 1965; Hendin, Haas, Singer, Ellner, & Ulman, 1987 and Hendin, Pollinger, Ulman, & Carr, 1981) is particularly significant for the current discussion. In a research setting, Hendin et al. employ standard psychoanalytic techniques such as transference reactions, dream analysis, and free association (or trend of associations) for the purpose of data gathering and analysis. Moreover, these psychoanalytic researchers utilize the unstructured flow of the clinical interview as part of their research protocol.

These authors combine these psychoanalytic techniques with interviewing techniques of a more standard nature including structured questionnaires as well as a battery of psychological tests. They combine all of these research instruments for the specific purpose of studying addiction. The psychoanalytic research methodology we use in our study is, in part, an outgrowth of the earlier work of Hendin et al.

Our study also owes a great deal to the "applied psychoanalytic research method of vicarious introspection" developed by Ulman and Brothers (1988) in their previous study of posttraumatic stress disorder (PTSD) in survivors of incest, rape, and combat. Building methodologically on Kohut's self-psychological concept of vicarious introspection,

Ulman and Brothers immerse themselves empathically in the subjective experience of the trauma survivor as both research subject and patient. In this context, Ulman and Brothers conduct a research project involving psychoanalytic psychotherapy of a long-term and intensive nature with representative cases of PTSD in survivors of incest, rape, and combat. This research project serves as a self psychological means of understanding and treating trauma survivors.

We employ a similar methodological rationale in our current study. We employ the self-psychological method of vicarious introspection as the basis for psychoanalytic psychotherapy with representative cases of the major forms of addictions including alcoholism, drug abuse, eating disorders, as well as compulsive gambling, and sex. This method allows us to become empathically immersed in the unconscious fantasy lives of our addicted patients.

The subjective frame of reference, that is, the subjectivity of these addicted patients, constitutes the primary basis from which we formulate our self-psychological explanation of addiction as well as devise specific techniques for its treatment. In addiction, our own and prior histories of addiction serve as another source and means of gaining empathic access to as well as understanding and explaining the unconscious meaning of the addictive fantasies of our patients. And, more specifically, we discovered that our addicted patients imbue their addictive fantasies with a specific unconscious meaning centering on illusions of megalomaniacal control over magically-endowed (that is, psychoactive) things and activities, or ATMs.

The cases selected for long-term and intensive treatment as well as the smaller subset of cases actually presented are all representative of a much larger patient population of addicts whom the authors have treated and continue to treat in psychoanalytic psychotherapy. (For a more detailed discussion of the representative nature of our six case studies, see Chapter 4.) Spotts and Shontz (1976, 1982, 1983) developed the representative case method in the course of their study of the lifestyles of nine American cocaine users. Subsequently, it has been employed by Hendin et al. (1981, 1987), and still later by Ulman and Brothers (1987, 1988).

All of our treatment case studies that we present in detail as part of our present study are representative of our larger patient population in several ways. They are representative in that they illustrate, in a clear and graphic nature, the underlying presence and meaning of the unconscious fantasy lives of the vast majority of our addicted patients. These cases are also representative in that these particular patients are engaged clinically in a way that is typical of the addicted patient in psychoanalytic psychotherapy.

Thus, we have selected cases for study and presentation that are not simply random; rather they are representative of those addicted patients who tend to seek psychoanalytic psychotherapy in a private practice setting. In this regard, the case presentations are especially relevant and useful for the psychoanalytic psychotherapist in private practice. Finally, we intend the psychotherapy case histories to help those psychotherapists who encounter serious problems in their attempts to work psychoanalytically with a population of addicted patients.

Chapter 3

The Theoretical Origins of a Self-Psychological Model of Addiction

PART I: AN OVERVIEW OF
THE ADDICTION LITERATURE

Introduction

This chapter is divided into two parts. The first section consists of an overview of the general literature in the addiction field. We devote special attention to those works particularly relevant for our study.

In this initial section, we aid the reader in locating our study, both conceptually and historically, in the vast body of the psychoanalytic and nonanalytic literature on addiction. Our review of this enormous and constantly increasing literature must be discriminating and selective, focusing only on those works that make a specific contribution to our perspective.

In the second section of this chapter, we piece together and review Kohut's scattered writings on addiction. We weave this material together as a basis for a discussion of points of convergence and divergence between Kohut's thinking and our own.

Our review of the general addiction literature proceeds along two heuristic axes: (1) a *modular axis* that parallels our model in moving from the phenomenological and etiological as well as pathogenic components through the typological to the therapeutic; and (2) an *historical axis* that moves from psychoanalytic schools of thought beginning with the classical, continuing with the ego-psychological and object relational, and concluding with the self-psychological.

Reviewing the selected works along these two heuristic axes enables us to scrutinize specific samples of this literature. We focus on those works that view addiction as based essentially on a narcissistic disturbance in the domain of self-experience. We are especially interested in those studies that support our contention that such a disturbance centers on psychic experience organized in accordance with the unconscious meaning of archaic narcissistic fantasies. In particular, we analyze literature that is either explicitly self-psychological or is implicitly self-psychological friendly or compatible. In addition, this literature has made a significant contribution to the addiction field. Although we focus primarily on psychoanalytic literature, in certain instances we do cite and discuss literature from outside a strict psychoanalytic point of view.

We also examine, in the course of our review, a number of critical, theoretical issues. For example, in reviewing the literature on the phenomenology of addiction, we discuss the related issues of psychopathology and personality. To take another instance, in the analysis of the literature on etiology and pathogenesis, we pursue the topic of an important connection.

We have found a link among masturbation, fetishism, perversion, and addiction, and especially as this linkage points to a common pathogenic root connecting all of these psychic phenomenon. And, to cite a third example, in going over the literature on the typology of addiction, we delve into the topic of diagnostic classification as it relates to addiction and, more specifically, as it concerns the issues of what are referred to as "dual diagnosis" and/or "comorbidity."

In our review we cite examples from the addiction field that are based on examinations of the five main forms of addiction. We attempt to demonstrate in our overview of the literature that within the psychoanalytic subfield of addiction studies there is a fast-emerging self-psychological model. The primary focus of this model is on narcissism, which is viewed as being central to understanding and treating addiction.

In the second part of this chapter, we tie together Kohut's somewhat random thoughts on addiction. These scattered ideas appear throughout the corpus of his considerable self-psychological writings. In piecing together this material, we also place Kohut in a specific historical context.

In particular, we situate Kohut in a way that sheds light on the connection between his thinking on addiction and the thought of other famous psychoanalytic theorists such as Aichhorn and Eissler, both of whom wrote on related topics. We hope, in carefully reconstructing Kohut's thinking on addiction, to indicate clearly that a self-psychological model, which has taken hold rapidly in the addiction field, has solid roots in Kohut's brief yet crucial comments.

Phenomenology

We locate our thinking on the psychoanalytic phenomenology of addiction in the following historical and conceptual context. As regards the classical school of psychoanalysis, our view derives, in part, from the thinking of such pioneers in the addiction field as Bergler (1942, 1957), Rado (1926, 1933, 1957, 1963, 1969), and Simmel (1948). All of these theorists make important contributions to our phenomenological perspective addiction to drugs, alcohol, or gambling. We are especially indebted to Rado. He is the first and only psychoanalytic theorist to make the crucial distinction between psychotic and addictive megalomania.

We also trace our thinking to the ego-psychological and object relational works of thinkers like Milkman et al. (1973, 1977, 1982, 1987), Silber (1970, 1974), Wieder & Kaplan (1969, 1974) as well as Hopper (1995) and Rosenfeld (1959, 1964). This group of authors is particularly important to our position because of their attention to the crucial role of fantasy in the phenomenology of addiction.

Several other thinkers, most notably Wurmser (1968, 1970, 1974a,b, 1978, 1980) as well as Khantzian (1999) and Khantzian et al. (1974, 1975, 1978, 1980, 1983, 1985, 1987, 1990) have synthesized in a fashion that is crucial to our viewpoint the ego-psychological and object relational perspectives with an implicit self-psychological framework. In particular, Wurmser and Khantzian lay the groundwork for our thinking on the narcissistic disturbances in self-experience as being central to the phenomenology of addiction.

In addition, a series of theorists including Adams (1978), Dodes (1984, 1988, 1995, 1996, 2002), Eber (1981), Goodman (1993, 1996a,b, 1998), Krueger (1989, 1997, 2000, 2002), J.P. Martin (1992) and Sands (1989, 1991, 1994) make explicit self-psychological, or self-psychological friendly, and compatible contributions to an ever-evolving self-psychological perspective on the phenomenology of addiction. Adams and Dodes focus on narcissistic disturbances in the self-experience of the drug and alcohol addict, respectively; Krueger, Sands, and Martin take up this same issue in regard to eating disorders; Eber and Goodman adopt this perspective in the context of their respective discussions of compulsive sexual disorders; and Krueger uses this vantage point in his psychoanalytic study of addictive spending and shopping.

Our study both builds on and adds to this growing and impressive body of psychoanalytic work. We seek to understand the role of disturbances in narcissism in the phenomenology of all five of the main forms of addiction.

Finally, several nonanalytic theorists make significant contributions to our thinking on the phenomenology of addiction. To cite only the most important, we mention Carnes (1983, 1991), Jacobs (1987, 1988, 1989), Kalin, McClelland, & Kahn (1965), McClelland, Davis, Kalin, & Wanner (1972), and Peele (1980, 1982, 1985). These thinkers describe different yet equally significant aspects of the phenomenology of addiction. McClelland et al. are pioneers in the use of psychological tests as an empirical means of studying the relationship between fantasy and alcoholic drinking and, by implication, other forms of addiction. Peele argues persuasively in favor of an experiential view of the phenomenology of addiction; thus, according to Peele, an addict becomes habituated to a particular kind of experience. We contend, following Peele, that an addict is best viewed as a fantasy junkie who is habituated to the use of artificial means of inducing experience, which is of a purely illusory and totally unreal nature.

Jacobs, in his work on compulsive or pathological gambling, provides empirical evidence supporting another of our central contentions. (See Grant & Potenza et al., 2004; and Petry, 2005 for recent studies of compulsive or addictive gambling.) He amasses data indicating that addiction—rather than being based on a repressive mechanism as was first posited by classical and neoclassical psychoanalytic theorists—derives instead from a dissociative process.

And last, Carnes is a pioneer in the study of addictive forms of sex, which, he believes, originate in the compulsive need to act out pathogenic fantasies. The work of Carnes is especially germane to our psychoanalytic view of the phenomenology of addiction. It lends itself to our notion that an addict is driven unconsciously to play and live out fantasies, the function of which is of an archaic and narcissistic nature (that is, shoring up a fragile sense of self). In other words, these fantasies function unconsciously to provide an addict with an illusory experience of, for example, an exhibitionistic display of grandiosity, merging with an idealized and omnipotent presence, having a twinship with an alterego, or having megalomaniacal control of magically endowed things and activities.

There are a number of recent psychiatric studies that focus on the phenomenological relationship between addiction and general psychopathology. Those of particular relevance to our thinking include, for instance, Allen and Frances (1986), Brehm and Khantzian (1992), Flores (2004), McGrath, Nunes, and Quitken (2000), Meyer (1986), and Richards (1993).

More specifically, there is a considerable psychiatric literature pointing to the phenomenological presence of the so-called "addictive personality." Of particular relevance to our own position on this still controversial notion are the works of Barnes (1979), Brill et al. (1971), Chein et al. (1964), Felix (1944), Fischer (1973), Gendreau and Gendreau (1970), Henriques et al. (1972), Jacobs (1972), Kolb (1925), Lang (1983), Lester et al. (1976), McLellan et al. (1981), Nakken (1988), Platt (1975), Sharoff (1969), Skinner et al. (1974), Torda (1968), Zwerling and Rosenbaum (1959). However, there are also a number of well-known works critical of the concept of the addictive personality. These include, for example, Craig (1979a,b), Sutherland et al. (1950), and Syme (1957).

Yet, despite these critiques, we maintain, along with many others, that there is, indeed, a particular type of psychopathology with phenomenological features peculiar to and determinative of addiction. In fact, Kohut (1978f [1976]) refers specifically to the "addiction-prone personality" (p. 350). From our self-psychological perspective we refer to this phenomenon as the "addictive character." We distinguish as a type of character psychopathology the addictive character from the so-called "addictive personality." The former as distinct from the latter is organized unconsciously on the basis of a megalomaniacal fantasy of magical control.

Despite the dubious scientific status of the so-called addictive personality, the literature on this phenomenon does refer to a notion important to our self-psychological view of the phenomenology of addiction. This idea concerns what is termed the "fantasy-proneness" of the addictive personality. We return later to this crucial topic as we proceed with our overview of the literature relevant to our thinking on the typology of addiction. It is sufficient to state, for the purposes of the current discussion, that our self-psychological study constitutes an addition to the already considerable body of work pointing to the existence of an addictive personality, or what we prefer to call an addictive character.

Etiology and Pathogenesis

A relatively small number of psychoanalytic studies exist from which to draw our self-psychological explanation of the etiological origins and pathogenic origins of addiction. However, we have taken advantage of the few such existing works in formulating our thinking about the etiology and pathogenesis of addiction. These works include the early and classical studies of Glover (1932, 1933, 1956 [1928]), the ego-psychological perspective of Valliant & Milofsky (1982a,b) as well as (Valliant et al. (1970, 1978, 1983, 1995), the combined ego-psychological and object relational vantage points of Wurmser (1968, 1970, 1974a,b, 1977, 1978, 1980, 1995) as well as Meissner (1980), and finally the viewpoints of Khantzian (1999) and Goodman (1998). The ideas of these authors are most relevant to our thinking for the following reason: they all focus on the etiological and pathogenic origins of addiction in narcissistic disturbances of self-experience.

Several other nonpsychoanalytic studies, in addition to these psychoanalytic works, are important to our thinking on the etiology and pathogenesis of addiction. These date back to Chassell (1938), continue with Pearson and Little (1969), and include the more recent work of Lettieri (1989), Shedler and Block (1990), Striegel-Moore (1993), and Polivy and Otterman (1993).

Notwithstanding the paltry nature of psychoanalytic work on the pathogenic roots of addiction, there is a body of psychoanalytic work dating back to Freud that is particularly germane to our etiological viewpoint. This work focuses on the important interconnections thought to exist among masturbation, fetishism, perversion, and addiction. In addition to Freud, other well-known and classical psychoanalysts such as Simmel (1920, 1948) as well as Rado (1926, 1933, 1957, 1963, 1969) comment on the significant interrelationship they believe exists among these psychic phenomena.

There is a notion, which is implicit in the thought of all of these classical psychoanalysts, concerning the centrality of masturbation as a basic and original model for later means of fantasy arousal. This idea is crucial to a psychoanalytic explanation of the etiological roots that fetishism, perversion, and addiction are thought to have in common. For example, S. Freud (1961 [1928]) suggests that compulsive and habitual masturbation in childhood might be legitimately construed as the original form of addiction.

Classical psychoanalysts speculate that excessive masturbation in childhood lays down powerful, unconscious memories, which later in life come into play in the development of addiction. These childhood memories constitute, according to classical psychoanalysts, the unconscious motivation on the part of so-called perverts for the use of masturbatory equivalents such as fetishistic and perverse (sadomasochistic) sexual activity or compulsive behavior, all of which are thought to be in the service of arousing powerful erotic, and hence potentially addictive, fantasies.

Following the lead of classical psychoanalysts, a later group of ego-psychological and object relational psychoanalysts, including Arlow (1953), Bonime (1969), Laufer (1976), I. Miller (1969), Nydes (1950), Rice (1985/6), and Werner & Levin (1967), subsequently discusses the central role of disturbances in masturbatory activity and fantasizing, both of which are normal occurrences in childhood, as the analogue for later psychopathological forms of symptom formation. More explicitly, Latendresse (1968) connects masturbation with addiction.

Moreover, and again in line with the thinking of early classical psychoanalysts, a number of later ego psychologists, including Bak (1953, 1968, 1974), Dickes (1963, 1978), Greenacre (1955a,b, 1961, 1969, 1970), Katan (1960), and Sperling (1963), pursue and establish, to varying degrees, a connection among fetishism, perversion, and addiction. Bach and Schwartz (1972) use a self-psychological approach in analyzing the Marquis de Sade's perverse and sadomasochistic fantasies. And somewhat more recently, Bach (1994) adopts a similar train of thought on the centrality of narcissistic disturbances in perversion. In addition, from a self-psychological perspective, Stolorow and Grand (1973) as well as Goldberg (1975, 1995) and his adherents (Goldberg, 2000) address the issues of perverse activity and fantasy.

Another important aspect of this entire subject involves the use (or, more accurately, misuse or abuse) of particular things and activities for the purpose of mobilizing atavistic fantasies, which are either perverse or addictive in nature. The use of things and activities for these purposes entails a number of issues relevant to our view of the etiology and pathogenesis of addiction. For example, there is the possibility that a person's connection or attachment to the world of things and activities is neither as simple nor as straightforward as is often and commonly assumed.

Psychoanalytically speaking, we follow Abraham (1927 [1920], Ferenczi (1956 [1913]) and Freud (1953 [1913]), all of whom argue that a child's animistic view of the world may, in certain cases, be largely carried over into adulthood. As a result, the otherwise inanimate world of things and activities becomes unconsciously animated for certain adults. Such a process of unconscious animation (that is, the phenomenon of anthropomorphism) accounts, in part, we believe, for an addict's phantasmagorical treatment of things and activities as if they were almost human.

In addition, a series of psychoanalysts, including Bion (1965, 1967), Bradlow (1973), Searles (1960), and Tausk (1948 [1919]), discuss, in different yet interrelated ways, a person's unconscious connection to and interaction with the nonhuman world. For instance, Bradlow undertakes a psychoanalytic exploration of the way in which for some people fantasy confabulates the world of the human with that of the nonhuman, and vice versa.

We propose what amounts to a "psychoanalytic *use* psychology" (in contrast to the more traditional as well as contemporary psychoanalytic *relational* psychologies) as part of our etiological explanation of the pathogenesis of addiction. In the process, we continue an important yet still somewhat obscure line of thinking among psychoanalysis, one that dates back to Winnicott (1969, 1971 [1969], 1975 [1951], 1989 [1959]). Beginning with Winnicott, a number of psychoanalysts discuss the topic of a person's unconscious *use of an object* as distinct from a psychoanalytic focus on an individual's unconscious *relationship to an object*.

Among those psychoanalysts who take up this line of thought, and whose work is important to our perspective, are Abrams and Neubauer (1975, 1976), Bromberg (1995), Coen (1992), Eigen (2004 [1981]), Hanly (1992), McCarthy (2000), Newman (1984, 1999), Pines (1993), Searles (1960), Slochower (1994), Sugarman and Kurash (1981), Winnicott (1969, 1971 [1969]). All of these authors have made important contributions to a psychoanalytic use psychology. Moreover, some of these authors, for example, Sugarman and Kurash, examine the specific concept of use as part of explaining addictive eating disorders (e.g., bulimia).

The fact that the normal unfolding of the capacity to use an object may become seriously disturbed and derailed is the basis for a central proposition of our etiological explanation of the pathogenesis of addiction.

We maintain that the stunting of transitional selfobject usage leads, later in life, to a pathological dependence on things and activities. These phenomena have become mutated versions of transitional selfobjects, that is, addictive trigger mechanisms (ATMs).

We must point out, however, that an important methodological issue may arise as a result of our even suggesting that a disturbance in a person's capacity to use objects is etiologically significant to explaining the pathogenesis of addiction. This methodological issue concerns the validity of the psychoanalytic technique of what is referred to as "genetic reconstruction."

For instance, Valliant (1983) questions the methodological reliability of using the technique of genetic reconstruction as a legitimate means of arriving at conclusions about the etiology of addiction. Valliant argues that methodologically it is unsound to rely on psychoanalytically reconstructed and retrospective data concerning, for example, the unconscious fantasy life of an individual as it is supposed to have existed in early childhood. On the contrary, he insists that it is only sound to rely methodologically on prospective data that is gathered and analyzed on a longitudinal (as opposed to a retrospective) basis.

However, Valliant's criticism notwithstanding, we still adhere to a time-honored tradition within psychoanalysis that consists of using genetic reconstruction as a clinically useful means of recovering early childhood events and experiences. Such phenomena have long ago been covered over psychically by a veil of infantile amnesia. More specifically, we build on the self-psychological work of A. Ornstein (1983) as well as Ulman and Brothers (1987, 1988).

These authors make a case for the value of using genetic reconstructions in the psychoanalytic process of recovering archaic self-states. For instance, Ulman and Brothers demonstrate the following: in order to understand the unconscious meaning of trauma (incest, rape, and combat) it is necessary to genetically reconstruct archaic narcissistic fantasies that have been psychologically shattered and, as a result, have undergone faulty forms of restoration. Similarly, we apply these same psychoanalytic techniques in gathering clinical data about our addicted patients' early life history and, more specifically, as regards narcissistic disturbances in the use of transitional selfobject(s). We contend that our psychoanalytic methodology, which relies on genetic reconstruction, has explanatory value for an understanding of the etiology and pathogenesis of addiction.

Typology

We employ Kohut's model of the bipolar self as the basis for our self-psychological typology of addiction. We argue that our addicted patients may be divided into different subtypes depending on the exact nature and extent of the psychic damage to various "poles" of the self. These "poles" constitute pivotal domains of self-experience that are psychically organized in accordance with the unconscious meaning of emotion-laden fantasies. Our "bipolar self typology of addiction" incorporates a focus on underlying cognitive and affective disturbances in crucial narcissistic sectors of the personality.

We owe a debt of gratitude for our typological view of addiction to the classical psychoanalytic work of Bergler, the ego-psychological studies of Glover, and the object relational contribution of Rosenfeld. More specifically, Rosenfeld pays particular attention to the unconscious fantasies that he believes are the basis for various addictive attempts at self-cure for painful states of manic depression. More recently, Wurmser and Khantzian make significant theoretical advances in establishing a psychoanalytic typology of addiction that incorporates Kohut's findings on the psychology of the self.

Our proposed bipolar self typology of addiction harkens back to the works of Glover and Rosenfeld, whose respective typologies are based on an underlying mood disorder of a manic-depressive type. According to Glover and Rosenfeld, drug addicts and alcoholics suffer from a manic-depressive disorder that is expressed symptomatically in the form of an addiction. Glover and Rosenfeld believe that addicts abuse a variety of addictive substances in a desperate, yet futile, attempt to modulate extreme states of emotional ups-and-downs. Addicts, from the perspective of these psychoanalysts, are viewed as either clinically (or subclinically) depressed and/or prone to mania. According to these authors, addicts are so mood disordered that they are compelled to abuse various substances to achieve some type of antidepressive and/or antimanic lessening of psychic dysphoria.

The pioneering work of Glover and Rosenfeld on the extent to which an addict selectively chooses different psychoactive substances paved the way for later psychoanalytic formulations. These include Wieder and Kaplan as well as Milkman and Frosch on the "drug of choice" hypothesis and Khantzian on the self-medication hypothesis. The hypotheses of these authors are crucial to reestablishing a specifically psychoanalytic typology of addiction and, in particular, one that includes our own self-psychological contribution.

Our bipolar self typology of addiction is indebted to the work of earlier psychoanalysts such as Bergler, Glover, and Rosenfeld, all of whom write respectively about pathological gambling, alcohol, and drug addictions. Our typological formulation also finds its theoretical origins in more recent work on what in biological psychiatry is now referred to as bipolar mood disorder or bipolar spectrum disorder. (See Chapter 9, where we incorporate the more recent findings of biological psychiatry concerning bipolar spectrum disorders as part of formulating an advanced version of our current typology in the form of a "bioself-psychological typology of addiction.") It is also based, in part, on nonanalytic studies on the relation between fantasy, fantasy-proneness, and addiction.

A growing body of empirical work in biological psychiatry is emerging on the significant relationship between various mood or affective disorders, and especially bipolar disorders (or what was originally conceived of and referred to as manic depression), and addiction. (See Goodwin and Jamison, 1990, for an excellent and comprehensive review of this literature.)

This work dates back to Behar et al. (1984), Bruch (1977), Dunner et al. (1979), Fox (1967), Piran et al. (1985), Quitkin et al. (1972), Robbins (1974), Schuckit (1983), Weissman et al. (1977), Woodruff et al. (1973), Woody et al. (1979), continues with Ciolino (1991), Lydiard et al. (1992), Pandina (1992), Hasin et al. (1996), Sonne and Brady (1999, 2002), Tohen and Zarate (1999) and culminates, more recently, with Abaronovich et al. (2002), Brady and Sinha (2005), Brook (2004), Brown (2005), Cassidy et al. (2001), Charney (2004), DelBello and Strakowski (2003), Dougherty et al. (2005), Evans and Sullivan (2001), Geppert and Minkoff (2004), Greenfield (2003), Havassy et al. (2004), Kaye et al. (2004), McKowen et al. (2005), Myrick et al. (2004), Perugi and Akiskal (2002), Stunkard et al. (2004), Swann (2005), Weiss (2003), Westermeyer (2003), Wilens (2004), and Ziedonis and Krejci (2003). In addition, there is the psychoanalytic study by Weil (1992) on developmentally based disturbances in affect regulation and addiction.

Finally, a number of explicitly self-psychological works (see, for example, Basch (1975, 1976); Lichtenberg (1989); Socarides & Stolorow (1984/ 5); see also, Schore (1994, 2003a,b) were published on affect regulation and dysregulation, which are relevant for our bipolar self-typology of addiction.

The works of Deitz (1995) and Galatzer-Levy (1988) on, respectively, bipolar mood disorder and manic-depression are especially significant for our work. Galatzer-Levy is particularly relevant because he analyzes the specific role of unconscious fantasy in disordered self-states that are manic-depressive or bipolar in nature.

An important body of nonanalytic work exists on the connection between fantasy and addiction. These empirical studies date back to Kalin and McClelland (1965), Kalin et al. (1972), and Wilsnack (1974) on the fantasy-based nature of alcoholic drinking in young men and women and continue with the work of Segal et al. (1973, 1974, 1980) on the equally fantasy-based nature of drug abuse.

The more current studies of various empirically-oriented psychologists—including Bartholomew et al. (1991), Brennis (1996), Lynn and Rhue (1988), Lynn et al. (1988), Powers (1991), Rauschenberger and Lynn (2003), and Wilson and Barber (1983)—on the phenomenon of "fantasy-proneness" in some personalities and in certain personality disorders has obvious significance for our bipolar self typology of addiction. We believe, as do McClelland et al., Wilsnack, and Segal et al., that addicts are in general fantasy-prone and, in fact, are fantasy junkies. The recent work of Milkman and Sunderwirth (1987) provides additional empirical support for our contention regarding the centrality of fantasy in what we refer to as the addictive character.

A number of recent studies have appeared on the typology of addiction (see, for example, Bohn & Meyer, 1994 and Meyer, 1989). The clinical importance of the various addictions as legitimate and specific *types* of diagnostic classification can also be seen in the central place given to them in *DSM-III* (1980), *DSM-III-R* (1987), *DSM-IV* (1994), and most recently in *DSM-IV-TR* (2000). (See Frosch, 1990, for a psychoanalytically oriented discussion on "The Addictions" in the context of the *DSMs*.) (See also Kushner et al., 1999, for discussions on the relationship between addiction and other specific disorders as classified according to *DSM* diagnostic categories.)

Furthermore, the issue of the diagnostic classification of the addictions is addressed in several new works, such as Goodman. In addition, several studies take up the related topics of dual diagnosis in addiction (see, for example, Clark, 2001; Cocores, 1994; Compton et al., 2000; Franken & Hendriks, 2001; Kadden et al., 1995; Landry, 1994; McGrath et al., 2000; Myrick et al., 2004; Norris & Extein, 1991; Penk et al., 2000; Randall et al., 2001; Ruiz et al., 2002; and Richards, 1993) and comorbidity in the addictions (see, for example, Kushner et al., 1999; Modesto-Lowe

& Kranzler, 1999; Petrakis et al., 2002; Scheller-Gilkey et al., 2002; Shivani et al., 2002; Skodol et al., 1999; Spencer et al., 2002; Tonneatto et al., 2000; Tucker & Westermeyer, 1990; Wang & Patten, 2002).

Of greater import for our position, Goldsmith (1993) propounds a self-psychological perspective on the issue of the diagnostic classification (and treatment) of alcohol and drug addictions. We add our bipolar self typology of addiction to Goldsmith's work as part of a self-psychological argument in favor of a psychoanalytic classification of addiction as a subtype of narcissistic behavior disorder (see Kohut, 1977b).

The psychiatric (as opposed to psychoanalytic) nature of the *DSM-IV* (1994) and *DSM-IV-TR* (2000) diagnostic classifications notwithstanding, we maintain the following: addictions may be categorized from our self-psychological perspective as dual diagnostic and comorbid disturbances, which may be classified according to the *DSMs* as falling on both axis I and axis II. We justify an axis I diagnosis because of what we, along with many other addiction specialists, view as an underlying affective or (bipolar) mood disorder common to the addictions. Likewise, we believe an axis II diagnosis is warranted because of what we, again in concert with numerous other authorities, consider to be an underlying narcissistic disturbance typical of the addictions. (See LaBrussa, 1994; and Maxman & Ward, 1994, for discussions of the diagnostic use of *DSM-IV* in relation to addictions.)

Clearly, increasing significance is given by many specialists to the addictive disorders as diagnostic classifications legitimate in their own right. Yet, despite this trend, several recent self-psychologically friendly and compatible studies on the psychoanalytic classification of character disorders (e.g., Josephs, 1992) and psychoanalytic diagnosis in general (e.g., McWilliams, 1994) fail to include addiction as a major type of characterological disturbance. We view our bipolar self typology as our attempt to redress what we contend is a serious shortcoming in this literature. Moreover, our addiction typology, with its emphasis on fantasy, constitutes an addition to the emerging self-psychological literature on fantasy (see, for example, Lachmann & Lachmann, 1995; Lage & Nathan, 1991; Lenoff, 1998; A. Ornstein, 1983, 1992, 1995a; Shane & Shane, 1990; Silverman & Gruenthal, 1993; Stolorow & Atwood 1989; Ulman & Brothers, 1987, 1988; Tolpin, 1974; and Zonis, 1991; see also Lachmann & Beebe, 1989, for a critique of some of this recent work, and especially that of Silverman (1978/9, 1979, 1983) as well as Silverman et al., 1984, 1985).

Therapeutics

Until very recently, there have been few studies on psychoanalytic techniques designed and developed specifically for the treatment of an addicted patient. In the course of discussing the treatment of a particular addicted patient, certain authors offer advice on psychoanalytic techniques of a general rather than specific nature that may be useful in treating addiction. For instance, Gehrie (1990), Geist (1989), Goodsitt (1983, 1985), Krueger (1988, 1997), M.I. Miller (1991), Rozen (1993), and Sands (1989, 1991, 1994) address this topic to varying degrees in the context of their respective discussions on food addictions and eating disorders. Similarly, Dodes (1984, 1988, 1990, 1995, 1996, 2002), Dodes and Khantzian (1991), Gustafson (1976), Levin (1987), and Silber (1970, 1974) take up the topic of the psychoanalytic treatment of the alcoholic patient.

In fact, several of those authors formulate treatment approaches that are self-psychological in nature. Similarly, Adams (1978), Gossop (2003), Hopper (1995), Rosenfeld (1959, 1964), and Wurmser (1978), pursue the general issue of the psychoanalytic treatment of the drug addict. Also, Carnes (1983, 1991), Eber (1981), Goodman (1998), J.D. Levin (1998), Myers (1994, 1995), A. Ornstein (1995b), and Segal (1963) write about using psychotherapy with the sex addict. And, finally, there is Bergler's (1957) work on the psychoanalytic treatment of the patient addicted to gambling.

However, few of these authors formulate a psychoanalytic approach to treating an addicted patient that is specific to this particular population. In other words, few of these psychoanalysts are systematic and comprehensive in spelling out the details of new clinical techniques designed specifically to conduct successful psychoanalytic psychotherapy with addicted patients. And, although Kohut offers a number of innovative suggestions in this regard, his recommendations have remained, until very recently, ignored. Moreover, his suggestions do not constitute anything even remotely approximating a well-developed approach to a self-psychological psychotherapy of an addicted patient.

Now, however, an emerging and burgeoning literature has been and is continuing to appear on different psychoanalytic approaches—including self-psychological—to the psychotherapy of patients who suffer from at least one or more of the five major forms of addiction. Examples of this ever-increasing body of work include the following authors: Barth (2001), Boris (1988), Bromberg (2001), Ceaser (1988), Cohen (1991), Davis (1990), Dennis and Sansone (1990),

Dodes and Khantzian (1991), Frances et al. (1988, 1994), Gonzalez (1988), Goodman (1993, 1996a,b), Imhof (1991, 1995), B. Johnson (1999), Kaufman (1994), Kearney-Cooke (1990), Khantzian (1995), Khantzian and Schneider (1986), Khantzian et al. (1990, 1995), Lerner (1990), Levens (1995), J.D. Levin (1998, 2001), Liebeskind (1991), Liebowitz (1991), Loose (2002), Mark and Faude (1997), May (1991), Murphy and Khantzian (1995), Myers (1995), A. Ornstein (1995b), Phillips (2001), Richards (1993), Rosenthal and Rugle (1994), Rugle and Rosenthal (1994), Sands (1991), Sansone and Johnson (1995), Siegel (1991), A. Smaldino (1991), C. Smaldino (1991), Spence (1988), Steiner-Adair (1990), Stern (1990), Strober (1990), Sugar-man (1990), Swift (1990), Tobin (1993), Walant (1995), Woody et al. (1989, 1994), Wooley (1990), Wurmser (1995), and Zerbe (1993). From this impressive list of psychoanalytic authors and researchers we want to distinguish the following for focusing on narcissism and the self as crucial in treating all major forms of addiction; they are Khantzian, Wurmser, Dodes, Liebowitz, Sands, B. Johnson, Sugarman, Goodman, J.D. Levin, A. Ornstein, Barth, and Strober.

We base our treatment approach on the psychoanalytic concept of the "transference–countertransference neurosis" as originally developed by Ulman and Stolorow (1985), and subsequently applied by Ulman and several coworkers (see, Miliora and Ulman, 1996a,b; Ulman and Brothers 1987, 1988; and Ulman and Paul, 1989, 1990, 1992) to the self-psychological psychotherapy of a variety of disorders. In applying this intersubjective notion to our psychotherapeutic work with addicted patients, we further refine it in the form of the idea of a shared or intersubjective fantasy.

Moreover, the idea of a transference–countertransference neurosis is itself part of a trend within psychoanalysis to renew attention to the omnipresence and usefulness of counter-transference. This trend is exemplified by the recent work of Jacobs (1991), Natterson (1991) and Tansey and Burke (1989). Natterson is particularly significant for our current discussion because of his attention to the work of Ulman and Stolorow on intersubjectivity and, more specifically, to the intersubjective basis of the transference–countertransference neurosis.

In our work with addicted patients, we are furthering the applicability of the psychoanalytic concept of the transference–countertransference neurosis, with its emphasis on the role of fantasy. In the process, we are adding to a line of thinking within psychoanalysis regarding the extent to which the analytic setting is essentially phantasmagorical in nature. This line of psychoanalytic thought includes the work of Arlow (1991, [1977]), Bacal (1990), Blum (1986, 1988), Chasseguet-Smirgel and Goyena (1993), Lichtenberg (1989), Loewald (1960, 1975), Modell (1976), A. Ornstein (1992, 1995a), Shane and Shane (1990), Silverman et al. (1978/9, 1979, 1984), and Volkan (1973).

In addition, we posit that the psychoanalytic psychotherapy of addicted patients involves a transitional selfobject or "utilitarian transference." In the context of this transference, a patient fantasizes unconsciously about controlling the psychotherapist and psychotherapy as, respectively, a nonhuman (or semi-human) thing and an impersonal activity. In this regard, we are both building on the psychoanalytic literature on the transitional or nonhuman dimension of psychoanalytic psychotherapy. This literature includes the works of Coppolillo (1967), Dickes (1963, 1978), Greenacre (1969), Kafka (1969), Kaminer (1978), McDougall (1985), Renik (1992), Searles (1960, 1979 [1976]), Volkan (1973), Volkan and Kavanaugh (1978), and Winnicott (1969, 1975 [1951]).

A psychoanalytic literature also exists on the specific concept of the *use of the psychoanalyst* in contrast to the more traditional focus on the *relationship with the psychoanalyst*. Examples of this literature include Coen (1992), Cooper and Adler (1990), Modell (1976), Newman (1984), Slochower (1994), as well as Adler and Rhine (1988). (See also Pines, 1993.) Our notions of the narcissistic exchange process and the utilitarian nature of the selfobject transference represent our self-psychological additions to the literature on the "use of an object" in the context of psychoanalytic psychotherapy. Our notions also harken back to Isakower's idea of the "analytic instrument" (see, for example, Balter et al. 1980; and Solomon, 1992).

Finally, we derive our idea of therapeutic dissociation, which is a central aspect of psychoanalytic psychotherapy with an addicted patient, from Sterba's (1934) original idea. Sterba advanced the idea of what he calls "therapeutic dissociation" in the midst of the hotly contested debate in the early 1930s concerning what exactly was therapeutic about psychoanalysis. Unfortunately, however, Sterba's notion was overshadowed and eclipsed by Strachey's (1934) ideas on what he refers to as the "mutative interpretation." (See Bergmann & Hartman, 1976, for a useful overview of this analytic literature.) We put forth our notion of therapeutic dissociation, in the context of the psychoanalytic psychotherapy of addicted patients, as a self-psychological contribution to the resurrection and reinvigoration of Sterba's thinking on this crucial topic.

PART II: KOHUT ON ADDICTION

Introduction

Although Kohut does not write extensively on addiction, a careful examination of his work reveals among his writings some scattered ideas of considerable relevance for our discussion. In piecing together these otherwise disparate notions, we discern a particular line of thought indicative of Kohut's self-psychological views on both the nature and psychotherapy of addiction. The illumination of Kohut's views on addiction enables us to highlight some important points of similarity as well as difference between his and our own thinking.

Although relatively unknown at the time to self psychologists, Kohut's insights into addiction were well known to a generation of psychoanalytic researchers on addiction. This awareness helps to explain his selection to write the preface to a 1977 National Institute of Drug Abuse (NIDA) monograph entitled *Psychodynamics of Drug Dependence* (Kohut, 1977a). This volume includes contributions from prominent psychoanalysts in the addiction field, such as Khantzian, Wieder, Wurmser, Krystal, Kaplan, as well as Milkman and Frosch. The influence of Kohut's thinking on addiction is present, to varying degrees, in the thoughts of all of these authors.

In his preface to the 1977 NIDA monograph, Kohut expresses a belief in the extraordinary "explanatory power of the new psychology of the self ... with regard ... to the addictions" (p. vii). However, there is an historical paradox regarding Kohut's proclamation. His self-psychological ideas clearly influenced many preeminent psychoanalysts in the field of addiction studies. Yet, it is only recently that an explicitly self-psychological literature on addiction has begun to emerge. Only within the last decade or so have self psychologists really started to grasp what Kohut foresaw years ago regarding the potential of the psychology of the self for understanding and treating addiction. We consider our own work on addiction as a contribution to the further fruition of Kohut's vision.

Phenomenology, Etiology, and Pathogenesis

Kohut's first thoughts on addiction deal specifically with its phenomenological nature. These ideas appear in Kohut's seminal 1959 paper

"Introspection, Empathy, and Psychoanalysis" (1978b [1959]). He states, "the phenomenon of dependence must be viewed still differently in *analysands with insufficient psychological structure*" (p. 227, emphasis added). He continues:

> Some addicts, for example, *have not acquired the capacity to soothe themselves or to go to sleep. They have not been able to transform early experiences of being soothed or of being put to sleep into an endopsychic faculty (structure).* (pp. 224–25, emphasis added)

He adds, "these addicts therefore have to rely on drugs, not as a substitute for object relations but as a *substitute for psychological structure*" (p. 225, emphasis added).

Several important ideas are embedded in the above passages. Primary among them is the notion that an addict does not suffer from a disturbance in object relations, like, for example, a typical neurotic. On the contrary, an addict suffers from a narcissistic disturbance constituted by inadequate or insufficient psychological structure. Furthermore, such a disturbance expresses itself symptomatically in an incapacity to perform essential psychological functions.

The lack of adequate psychological structure and a concomitant difficulty in psychological functioning distinguish addiction phenomenologically as, in essence, narcissistic in nature. In this sense, therefore, it is different phenomenologically from neurotic forms of psychopathology. In the latter, and in contrast to the former, narcissistic structure is more sufficient and narcissistic functioning is more adequate, although both may be somewhat disturbed.

Kohut also makes a very important etiological point. He (Kohut, 1978b [1959]) noted that an addict has been unable to "transform early experiences of being soothed or of being put to sleep into an endopsychic faculty (structure)" (p. 225). Here, he hints at a key self-psychological idea concerning the etiology and pathogenesis of addiction: namely, that addiction may be viewed as involving a developmental arrest in the essential process of transmuting internalization. As a result, selfobject experience is not transformed, that is, it is not psychologically broken down and reassembled in the form of self-structure and function.

Before leaving the passage quoted above (Kohut, 1978b [1959], p. 227), we point out the following. Kohut refers to "analysands with insufficient psychological structure" in the context of his early thoughts on the phenomenology as well as etiology and pathogenesis of addiction. He seems to be suggesting that he himself had actually psychoanalyzed patients suffering from addiction. In fact, in his discussion of Thomas Szasz's now well-known paper "The Role of the Counterphobic Mechanism in Addiction" (1958), Kohut (1978a [1956]) indicates that he did indeed psychoanalyze one addicted patient over "many years" (p. 203). In the same context, he even alludes to the notion of magical control (that is, megalomania) as crucial to understanding the nature of addiction (Kohut, 1978a [1956], p. 202).

Moreover, in discussing his thoughts on psychotherapy with an addicted patient, Kohut (1978b [1959], p. 225) reveals that he may have originally discovered the clinical phenomenon he would later term the selfobject transference in the context of his psychoanalysis of an addicted patient. In this regard, Kohut's thoughts on addiction are particularly relevant for the fields of addiction studies and self psychology.

For example, we base our self-psychological approach to psychotherapy of addiction on the Narcissus complex. In so doing, we have discovered a hitherto hidden dimension of the selfobject transference, namely that which involves the nonhuman rather than the human. We believe that this nonhuman dimension is central to all three of Kohut's selfobject transferences.

The mirroring selfobject transference involves the fantasized use by a patient of a psychotherapist as a nonhuman thing in the form of a mirror that reflects back to a patient a desired image of himself or herself. The idealizing selfobject transference entails the imaginary use by a patient of a psychotherapist as a demigod and, therefore, as only a semi-human being endowed with superhuman powers and knowledge. And, the twinship or alter ego transference (see Kohut, 1984, pp. 195–96, for a discussion of this view of the twinship selfobject) revolves around a patient's fantasized use of a psychotherapist as a "genie" or supernatural creature, the very existence of which constitutes a magical facsimile of the self. From our vantage point, we envision the functioning of the psychotherapist, in all three of these selfobject transferences, as involving an extension of the otherwise human boundaries of the self to the domain of the semi-human and nonhuman.

In a 1970 paper entitled "Narcissism as a Resistance and as a Driving Force in Psychoanalysis," Kohut flirts with the notion of dissociation in relation to addiction. In the case of narcissistic disorders, Kohut argues that "narcissistic structures remained fixated in their development" (1978c [1970], p. 556). As a result, he maintains: "In their archaic form they were either repressed or *split off* from the other parts of the psyche" (p. 556). He continues: "In the latter case they can strongly dominate the patients' behavior from time to time, for example, in the form of *addictionlike praise-seeking or addictionlike search for idealized selfobjects*" (p. 556, emphasis added).

In this passage, Kohut refers to those archaic psychic presences that are "split off" or dissociated in the form of a vertical split (or tear) from the rest of the psyche. Kohut contrasts the vertical split, which achieves expression psychopathologically in the form of dissociation, from the horizontal split, which gains expression psychopathologically in the form of repression. In the former, a person's self is itself torn apart as a result of a *dissociative split* between juxtaposed and competing versions of an individual's self-image or self-presentation. In the latter, a person's self remains more or less intact, although the individual is deprived of knowledge of psychic material of an emotionally charged nature due to a *repressive barrier* dividing consciousness. Based on Kohut's distinction, we may view addiction as involving a dissociative split rather than a repressive barrier.

In this sense, therefore, we speak of an addict as a character with a split personality, which we distinguish from multiple personality disorder (MPD) or what is now referred to as dissociative identity disorder (DID). We differentiate a split character disorder, like an addict, from MPD or DID in which separate and distinct selves ("alters") are severed psychically from the "host" personality. Yet, despite making a clear distinction between these two disorders (that is, addictions and MPD or DID), we nonetheless envision them as two points that exist diagnostically along a phenomenological continuum of pathological dissociation.

From a psychoanalytic perspective, we may construe an addict as a character (see Bollas, 1992 and Johnson, 1994, for a discussion of the psychoanalytic conceptualization of being a character) who is made up of two poorly integrated selves—an addicted self and a nonaddicted self—both of which reside and co-exist psychologically in the same personality. (For a self-psychological argument regarding the centrality of the vertical, as opposed to the horizontal, split in narcissistic behavior disorders, see Goldberg, 1995, 2000.) Over time, as an addiction worsens and causes further deterioration in character structure, an addicted self takes over more and more of the personality, eventually becoming the predominant part-self of the personality.

In the context of our model, Kohut's brief remarks serve as a catalyst for some further thoughts. An addict, rather than mending the vertical split in the self, only serves to exacerbate an already preexisting potential for the dissociative splitting up of the personality. An addict who relives fantasies and re-experiences feelings and sensations from the past further rips and shreds the already weakened psychic fabric that is barely holding together the personality.

An addict searches frantically and desperately for authentic selfobjects to provide emotional relief from psychic pain; tragically, however, an addict finds only poor *imitations* or faulty facsimiles. These addictive things and activities (that is, ATMs) cannot provide the genuine relief an addict so urgently craves. As a result, an addict is doomed to an endless search for an authentic selfobject, which will forever elude him or her. In this regard, then, an addict is truly representative of what Kohut (1977b) calls "Tragic Man," (p. 206) whom he distinguishes from "Guilty Man" (p. 206).

The Kohut Seminars (edited by Elson), although published in 1987, were originally delivered by Kohut in the late 1960s at the Mental Health Clinic of the University of Chicago (see Elson, 1987, p. ix). In one of these lectures, entitled "Addictive Need for an Admiring Other in Regulation of Self-Esteem," Kohut describes an important phenomenological feature of addiction, namely, its quality of urgency. Kohut noted that addiction "has a *nondescript urgency* to it that is ... encountered ... whether *addiction to a drug, to people, to food, to alcohol, to masturbation or to perverse pursuits*" (p. 113, emphasis added). He continues, "one finds a variety of features, but there is an unnamable quality that an addiction has, *a quality of urgency, a no-delay-tolerating quality*, wiping out all differentiation" (p. 119, emphasis added). Further, he adds: "It is the *urgency* of the aim, *the urgency of the fulfillment as if some void had to be filled* (p. 119, emphasis added).

Kohut returns to the urgent or "no-delay-tolerating quality" of addiction in an important series of passages from a 1980 piece, co-authored with M. Tolpin, on a self-psychological understanding of early development. Together they (Tolpin & Kohut, 1980) point out that the

> thoughts and activities of the child who manifests the phenomenon to which we referred as *forced thought and action* have a specific driven quality, which, like the manifestations subsumed under the heading of sexualization, is *akin to addiction* and, as concerns sexualization, is often *the precursor to true addictions later in life.* (pp. 438–39, emphasis added)

They elaborate:

> This specific experiential feature gives us empathic access to the primary meaning of these symptoms. *Like all addictions, it is meant*

to do away with a defect in the self, to cover it, or to fill it, via frantic, forever repeated activity. (p. 431, emphasis added)

In this same context, Tolpin and Kohut (1980) refer to a child's "forced thought and action" as "pseudo-obsessional psychic activities" (p. 439). Implicitly, therefore, they link obsessive-compulsive disturbances with addiction through the mechanism of "forced thought and action." In other words, we may interpret Tolpin and Kohut as directing our attention to an implicit idea, the explicit meaning of which is as follows: obsessive-compulsivity and addiction are both symptomatic expressions of forced thought and forced action.

In this regard, we may look at addictions as both obsessive and compulsive. An addict experiences himself or herself as forced to think about, that is, to be obsessed with, mental imagery of a blissful state of pleasure in which all pain disappears. An addict also experiences himself or herself as compelled to use particular things and activities that he or she imagines as being conducive to achieving a pleasurable state of Nirvana. We have denoted such things and activities, therefore, as addictive trigger mechanisms, or ATMs.

The implicit connection Tolpin and Kohut make between obsessive compulsivity and addiction is the subject of study by others (see, for example, Anthony & Hollander, 1993; DeCaria & Hollander, 1993; and Hollander, 1991). For our purposes, however, the importance of this connection lies primarily in Tolpin and Kohut's notion of "forced thought and action," and especially as it relates to our self-psychological understanding of addiction. We contend that all addictions may be construed as being based, in part, on the psychological mechanism of "forced thought and action."

Addictions are characterized, therefore, by forced thought in that a type of obligatory and mandatory fantasizing is involved. We view this type of fantasizing as a mode of thought that is unnatural and pathological because it originates in artificial or addictive rather than natural processes. An addict forces such fantasizing rather than simply allowing it to occur in a natural and spontaneous way.

In line with Tolpin and Kohut's notion, fantasizing is a type of "forced thought" to the degree to which pressure arises as a result of two psychological imperatives: (1) the need to counteract and neutralize pain that is overwhelming and unbearable; and (2) the desire for pleasure that is incredible, irresistible, and fantastic. In this sense, then, we contend that fantasizing is forced to the extent to which it is motivated unconsciously by the need to balance a narcissistic equilibrium that is experienced by a person (an addict) as constantly on the brink of disruption.

As a type of forced thought, addictive fantasizing is distinct and different from other and more natural kinds of thinking or thought processes. The former is forced in being stereotypic, preservative, and repetitive. It is completely lacking in creativity and originality, and instead is quite unimaginative and stilted. The latter, in contrast, is not encumbered by demands of an archaic narcissistic nature, and, hence is free and spontaneous. It can go in either of two directions—that of logical thought or that of creative and imaginative thought.

We maintain that addictions are also characterized by "forced action" in that behavior becomes habitual and ritualistic. From our perspective, all addictions entail, therefore, the forced or obligatory use (abuse) of certain things and the compulsive engagement in particular activities. The use by an addict of these agents and pursuit of these activities may appear to an outside observer as being completely irrational. In the case of addiction, however, an addict subverts (rather than perverts) the normal purpose of action as a means of pursuing a rational goal or obtaining a realistic objective. Instead, an addict acts blindly and willfully with little or no regard for the self-destructive consequences of behavior. In this regard, an addict may be said to be willfully self-destructive.

From our vantage point, addictions may be viewed as based on "forced thought and action" in two ways: (1) an addict is preoccupied, absorbed, and obsessed on a cognitive level, or on the level of thought, with fantastic images of an imaginary state of Nirvana; and, (2) an addict is compelled on the behavioral level, or on the level of overt action, to use things and engage in pursuits that are imagined as ushering in such a blissful state.

In these two regards, then, we interpret "forced thought and action" as meaning that an addict enters into a self-induced and hypnotic-like trance. In such a dissociated state, phantasmagorical imagery and associated affects emanating from deep within the unconscious mind pervade and take over an addict's consciousness and subjectivity. In other words, an addict is in an addictive state of mind.

In 1977, with the publication of *The Restoration of the Self*, Kohut (1977b) writes again about the "structural void in the self" of an addict. He states:

> It is the structural *void in the self* that the addict tried to fill—whether by sexual activity or by oral ingestion. And the structural void cannot

be filled any better by oral ingestion than by other forms of addictive behavior. It is the lack of self-esteem of *the unmirrored self*, the uncertainty about the very existence of the self, the dreadful feeling of the fragmentation of the self that the addict tries to counteract by his addictive behavior. (p. 197, footnote 11, emphasis added)

An important idea is implicit in the above passage. This concerns the notion that the "structural void in the self," as expressed in the "unmirrored self," occurs in the context of a failing or faulty selfobject milieu. Our study maintains that such a developmental deficit arises because of a breakdown in a narcissistic exchange process whereby a person swaps human and nonhuman selfobject functioning.

In some cases, such as that which takes place in the addictive character, an individual remains pathologically dependent on psychoactive things and activities as the only means of regulating self-esteem. And, in the case of an addict, as Kohut (1977a) stresses: "Whatever the chemical nature of the substance that is employed, however frequently repeated its consumption ... *no psychic structure is built, the deficit in the self remains*" (p. vii, emphasis added).

In effect, therefore, Kohut contends that an addict suffers from a developmental arrest in the structuralization of self-experience as precipitated by an unempathic (or antipathic) selfobject milieu. This contention on the part of Kohut is central to his thoughts on the etiology and pathogenesis of addiction. For example, in his preface to a 1976 German study of addiction, *Der Falsche Wegzum Selbst, Studien zur DrogenKarrien* (written by vom Scheidt; see Kohut 1978f [1976]), Kohut compares addiction to digestion. More specifically, he suggests that an addict's abuse of drugs may be compared to the malfunctioning of the physiological process whereby food is digested and absorbed. He (Kohut, 1978f [1976]) states:

It is as if a person with a wide-open gastric fistula were trying to still his hunger through eating. He may obtain pleasurable taste sensations by his frantic ingestion of food, but since the food does not enter the part of the digestive system that *absorbs* it into the organism, he continues to starve. (p. 847, emphasis added)

Later, in a similar statement Kohut made in a 1981 interview with Strozier, Kohut contrasts this dysfunctional process of psychological malabsorption with the normal and healthy process of psychic absorption. Speaking in terms of "biological analogies," Kohut (1985) indicates:

we need foreign protein in order to build up our own protein. The essence of our biological equipment is the protein molecule.... The body apparently cannot build up protein molecules. It needs foreign protein, which it then takes apart into its constituent amino acids, and then reassembles these amino acids again to form its own protein.... *This is a good analogy for transmuting internalization.* (p. 483, emphasis added)

There is an important supposition behind the comparison Kohut invokes between the process of psychic structure building via transmuting internalization and the digestive absorption of food and the buildup of protein. He supposes that an empathic selfobject milieu, which is sensitive and responsive, provides a person with requisite narcissistic supplies (that is, essential psychic nutriments and emotional sustenance). In keeping with this presupposition, Kohut (1977a) observed that

it will be of crucial importance to ascertain the fact that a child could find neither confirmation of his own worthwhileness nor a target for a merger with the idealized strength of the parent and that he, therefore, remained deprived of the opportunity for the gradual transformation of these *external sources of narcissistic sustenance into endopsychic resources.* (p. ix, emphasis added)

The above contention on the part of Kohut has direct relevance for a self-psychological perspective on the etiology and pathogenesis of the "addiction-prone personality" (Kohut, 1978e [1976], p. 350), or what we refer to as the addictive character. As a result of a particular type of emotional deprivation, a child becomes too emotionally dependent on these "external sources of narcissistic sustenance" (that is, things and activities). Etiologically speaking, such psychological overdependence on the part of a child becomes the basis, later in life, for a vulnerability to addiction. This is the etiological origin of the pathogenesis of the "addiction-prone personality" or addictive character. From our point of view, certain things and activities are likely to devolve, later in life, into ATMs. At this latter state of life, these ATMs become for an addict nothing more than emotional props with little or no psychological substance.

Kohut (1977a) argues, in his prefatory comments to the NIDA monograph on drug dependence, that an "addict ... craves the drug because the drug seems to be capable of *curing the central defect in his self.* It becomes for him the *substitute for a selfobject*" (p. vii, emphasis added). He (Kohut, 1977a) goes on to state that the addict "by ingesting the drug *symbolically compels the mirroring selfobject to soothe him, to accept him"* (p. vii, emphasis added). "Or," he adds, "he symbolically *compels the idealized selfobject to submit to his merging into it and thus partaking in its magical power"* (p. vii, emphasis added).

In these passages, Kohut makes a number of other points relevant to our phenomenological understanding of addiction. First, he implies that addiction is an attempt at self-cure that goes awry. From our self-psychological viewpoint, we see addiction as a form of faulty self-cure because it involves the *use* of a "substitute for a selfobject," that is, what we term an ersatz selfobject or ATM. It does not entail, therefore, the use of a genuine selfobject.

Second, Kohut suggests in these passages that an addict imagines that it is actually possible to "symbolically compel" a drug, as a "substitute for a selfobject," to become part of a magic act by providing mirroring and idealizing functions. It appears that, according to Kohut, an addict believes that a drug, which is a mere facsimile of the real thing, is, in fact, the real thing.

We build on Kohut's notion of symbolic compulsion as a basis for our thinking on addictive fantasies of a megalomaniacal nature. An addict, as an unwitting captive of these fantasies, believes mistakenly (that is, is self-deceived) that he or she can perform a feat of magic. Such an act of magic on the part of an addict involves the illusion of being able to turn a drug as a "substitute for a selfobject" into an authentic selfobject.

In this regard, it is almost as if an addict is an adherent of the ancient art of alchemy, whereby the alchemist in an act of magic turns ordinary metals into gold. Such acts of magic were part of a larger practice of alchemy that included the use of panaceas and elixirs. An addict is a modern-day alchemist who is organized psychically in accordance with a fantasy of being a megalomaniacal self and as endowed with magical control. As such, an addict imagines the following: it is possible to make-up for the absence or faultiness of a real selfobject by magically or "symbolically compelling" certain things (e.g., drugs) or particular activities (e.g., eating) to take the place of these missing or faulty parts of the self.

An addict experiences a degree of emotional relief from psychic pain in the course of using these things or engaging in these activities. An addict is then under the spell that an experience which is purely illusory (that is, imaginary) in nature is indicative of an actual capacity to control and cancel out psychic pain. An addict, on the basis of this illusion, imbues these things and activities with what Kohut calls a "magical power."

An addict then believes mistakenly that he or she can control and manipulate these entities and agents so as to possess the "magical power" imagined as emanating from them. It is in this sense, therefore, that an addict, as a modern-day alchemist, is under the influence of megalomaniacal fantasies of possessing an imaginary capacity to manipulate magical agents of illusory control.

As a third point of relevance, Kohut indicates that different substitute or alternative selfobjects perform different psychological functions. (In the context of our model of addiction we refer to this as the "selfobject-like" functions of addictive trigger mechanisms, or ATMs.) In this sense, Kohut maintains that selfobject replacements, which perform mirroring-like functions, provide one kind of emotional respite. In contrast, he proposes that those which serve as alternatives for idealizing selfobjects provide a different kind of psychological relief.

In this regard, Kohut seems to be hinting at what we denote as the *psychoactive specificity* of particular ATMs. According to this notion, a special class of things and activities may serve for an addict as ATMs. These ATMs are, in turn, *(ab)used* compulsively by addicts for specific purposes depending on their different psychoactive effects.

As concerns addiction, this amounts to a self-psychological reformulation of the concept well-known in addiction literature as the "drug of choice" hypothesis. Certain authors hypothesize that addicts use different drugs depending on the need for specific psychoactive relief as provided by a purely psychoactive (as opposed to psychopharmacological) effect (Milkman & Frosch, 1973, 1977). For example, one addict may abuse a particular ATM to gain a modicum of antianxiety relief from feeling tense and nervous; whereas another addict may abuse a completely different ATM to achieve a degree of antidepressant respite from feeling down, despairing, and hopeless.

In *The Restoration of the Self*, Kohut (1977b) makes what, for our purposes, is a crucial, albeit largely ignored, distinction. He distinguishes between a "human selfobject" and a "nonhuman selfobject" (p. 56). This distinction serves as a crucial point of departure for our notion of the transitional selfobject.

We contend that an individual may experience a nonhuman thing or activity as possessing human qualities and characteristics. Such subjective experience on the part of a person helps to account for the selfobject-like functioning of these things or activities. This psychic process of unconscious condensation (similar to that which occurs in dreams) amounts to a form of anthropomorphism, or imaginary animation. A child or an adult may imagine certain things and activities as if they were semi-human. These humanoid entities and android agents exist in a transitional or intermediary realm of experience. This domain of subjective experience is located psychologically somewhere between the arena of the purely human and that of the totally nonhuman.

Kohut distinguishes between nonhuman and human selfobjects in the course of discussing the case of "Mr. U.," a patient who suffers from a "fetishistic perversion." Within psychoanalysis there is a well-established link—based on common phenomenology and etiology—among fetishism, perversion, and addiction. It is a psychoanalytic axiom that all three disorders involve a psychopathological disturbance between the person and the human as well as nonhuman surround.

Kohut employs his analysis of Mr. U.'s fetishistic perversion—which involves the compulsive use of various women's undergarments to achieve sexual arousal and potency—as the basis for an important theoretical extrapolation. Kohut roots fetishism etiologically in an arrest in psychological development at a phase involving the *use* of the nonhuman selfobject. In our study, we extrapolate from Kohut's explanation of the etiology and pathogenesis of fetishism and apply it to that of addiction.

Support for our extrapolation is to be found in Kohut's own connection of fetishism with addiction. For example, Kohut (1977b), in discussing the etiological origins of Mr. U.'s fetishistic perversion, comments on the *"quasi-addictive use* made of his body's erogenic zones—*with or without the aid of accompanying fantasies which became the crystallization points for later psychopathology"* (p. 74, emphasis added. See also Kohut's lecture at the Chicago Psychoanalytic Institute on January 7, 1972 [Tolpin and Tolpin, 1996, p. 2] in which he connects perversion and addiction).

If Kohut is correct and fetishism is a quasi-addiction, then certainly there is some justification for an extrapolation from his explanation of the etiology and pathogenesis of fetishism to that of addiction. Moreover, we read Kohut's reference to the "quasi-addictive use" of parts or areas of the body as an allusion to the notion that the (mis)use of things or activities is critical in explaining the etiology and pathogenesis of fetishism. By implication, the same may be said to be true for addiction.

In the above quoted material, Kohut makes another reference of great import for our study. He refers to the presence of fantasies in the context of the "quasi-addictive" or fetishistic use of things and activities, and, in this instance, parts or areas of the body. Kohut implies that sexual fantasies of an obligatory nature are stimulated by the fetishistic use of things and activities.

By analogy, and in line with Kohut's thinking, we contend that narcissistic fantasies of a repetitive nature are activated by a person in the context of the addictive (ab)use of things and activities. We further interpret Kohut as inferring that the use of external things and activities serves as an artificial means of generating archaic narcissistic fantasies, which are highly addictive in nature. Once having been generated, these fantasies then constitute, according to Kohut, the "crystallization point for later psychopathology" including fetishism and, by implication, addiction.

Kohut (1977b), in an earlier discussion of the etiological roots of Mr. U.'s fetishistic perversion, observes: "From the traumatic unpredictability of his mother he had retreated early to the soothing touch of certain tissues (such as nylon stockings, nylon underwear) which were readily available in his childhood home" (pp. 55–56). Kohut continues: "They were reliable and they constituted a *distillate of maternal goodness and response*" (p. 56, emphasis added). This notion of what amounts to *psychological distillation* is the means by which Kohut accounts for the imbuing of inanimate objects with human qualities and, therefore, with the capacity to function as (nonhuman) selfobjects.

In the physical process of distillation a liquid is heated and evaporates into a vapor or mist. Then it condenses and is collected in a purified form as a distillate. By analogy, the following unconscious process may be said to occur during the first developmental phase of the narcissistic exchange process. In the unconscious mind of a child, the essential selfobject functioning of a human caretaker is psychologically distilled, that is, mentally condensed (fused) with a nonhuman thing or activity.

Consequently, this agent becomes for a child a magically endowed entity that is capable of functioning as a transitional selfobject. Unconsciously, a child condenses and incorporates (psychologically distills) into a special plaything a parent's capacity to function as selfobject. As a result, it is now endowed in the child's imagination with magical powers originally derived from a parent.

A future addict, like a fetishist, becomes emotionally stuck, so to speak. As a result, a child who has a proclivity toward becoming an addict is unable to re-invest other people with the psychological capacity to function as selfobjects. Instead, nonhuman things and activities remain, later in life for an addict and a fetishist (as well as for a pervert), the essential means of regulating self-esteem and modulating mood.

As Kohut stresses (1977b) in the case of Mr. U.:

> He used to simultaneously touch certain soft selfobject surrogates (the silky rim of a blanket) and stroke his own skin (the lobe of his ear) and hair, thus creating a psychological situation of merger with a *nonhuman selfobject* that he totally controlled and thereby deprived himself of the opportunity to experience the structure building optimal failures of a *human selfobject*. (p. 56, emphasis added)

This quote clearly demonstrates that Kohut recognizes the presence of "nonhuman selfobjects" as well as "human selfobjects." He is equally clear about the psychological superiority of the latter over the former.

Further evidence of Kohut's recognition of the existence and functioning of nonhuman selfobjects is to be found in his discussion of cultural selfobjects. Kohut (1984) insists: "*Culture, in other words, can indeed function as a selfobject* ... whether it is via a multiplicity of diverse functions or through the personified embodiment of a single cultural hero-ideal such as, in the case of most psychoanalysts, the idealized image of Freud" (p. 203, emphasis added). (See Kohut, 1985, for a further elaboration of his notion of cultural selfobjects.) Kohut (1977b) even implies that cultural or social selfobjects may have a "psychotropic influence" (p. 277) on the functioning of the self. (We return in our discussion of the therapeutic component of our model to Kohut's notion of the psychotropic effect of the nonhuman selfobject.)

Typology

There are several ideas of relevance regarding the issue of typology in Kohut's various writings on addiction. In his prefaces to vom Scheidt's study on drug addiction and his introduction to the NIDA monograph on addiction, Kohut refers to what he calls the "addiction-prone personality" (Kohut, 1977a, 1978f [1976]). Apparently, Kohut believes, as was common at that time among many experts in the addiction field, that some persons are psychologically (and perhaps even genetically) predisposed to addiction. It is possible, in part, to explain the predisposition of the so-called addiction-prone personality, or addictive character, on the basis of the etiological roots of addiction. From the vantage point of our self-psychological perspective, we propose the following etiological explanation of the pathogenesis of addiction: if a particular individual becomes arrested at the phase of development that is organized primarily around the use of nonhuman selfobjects, then such a person is highly prone (albeit not destined) to abuse some nonhuman thing or activity (an ATM) as part of arousing addictive fantasies.

Kohut addresses another issue of relevance concerning his very critical distinction between narcissistic personality disorder and narcissistic behavior disorder. Kohut originally makes this distinction in several places in *The Restoration of the Self* (1977b). He first mentions it in the course of his description of the case of "Mr. M." (p. 51). He develops it further in the context of his discussion of the various types of "disorders of the self" (p. 92).

In this latter context, Kohut distinguishes narcissistic personality disorder from narcissistic behavior disorder in terms of Ferenczi's (1955 [1930]) distinction between autoplastic and alloplastic adaptations. The former involves a change in the organism's relation to (or use of) the environment. In a modification of Ferenczi's distinction, Kohut (1977b) views narcissistic behavior disorders as entailing "alloplastic symptoms" (p. 193). However, Kohut is not clear on the basis of Ferenczi's original distinction between "autoplastic" and "alloplastic symptoms" about how he intends to distinguish narcissistic personality disorder from narcissistic behavior disorder.

For the purpose of our study, however, both Ferenczi's and Kohut's distinctions may be understood as follows. On the one hand, narcissistic personality disorder is rooted in a disturbance *in relating* to others as selfobjects; a person finds it difficult to relate to others in a way that effectively takes advantage of their functioning as selfobjects. On the other hand, narcissistic behavior disorder is determined by a disturbance *in using* other persons, things, and activities as selfobjects; a person has problems in *utilizing* other people, things, and activities as selfobjects. Addiction may be thought to arise, therefore, in an addict's failure to use things and activities properly as nonhuman selfobjects; instead an addict misuses and abuses certain entities and agents in the course of turning them into ATMs.

In the context of our study, we consider a narcissistic behavior disorder to be a more severe form of psychopathology than a narcissistic personality disorder. This position is consistent with and follows from Kohut. Kohut (1977b, pp. 194–99) juxtaposes two of his cases, "Mr. I." and "Mr. M.," in terms of the severity of their respective narcissistic disorders. He describes Mr. I. as a Don Juan character who suffers from a narcissistic behavior disorder as manifested symptomatically in sexual promiscuity and sadism.

In contrast, he diagnoses Mr. M. as a narcissistic personality disorder. And, unlike Mr. I., who exhibits an overt behavioral disorder, Mr. M.'s disorder is limited and confined strictly to the mental (in contrast to behavioral) realm.

Mr. I. acts out his sadistic fantasies toward women on a literal and behavioral level, whereas Mr. M. only engages in mental acts involving sadistic sexual scenarios in which he envisions himself mistreating women. Mr. I. needs the behavioral enactment of the sadistic fantasy to satisfy his morbid craving for narcissistic pleasure. Mr. M., in contrast, is content to merely entertain sexually sadistic fantasies without, however, the need to enact them behaviorally.

According to Kohut (1977b), Mr. M. restricts his narcissistic disorder to the purely mental realm because he has psychic structures of a sufficient and compensating nature with which to moderate his actions. By comparison, Mr. I. lacks the psychic structure necessary to curb his sadistic sexual fantasies. As a result, he feels compelled to act out them in desperate, yet ultimately futile, attempts to defend his fragile narcissistic equilibrium. Mr. I., in behaviorally acting out his fantasies, constitutes a defensive structure that is, according to Kohut, inferior to Mr. M.'s compensatory structure.

Of the two men, Kohut maintains that the "demands made by the diseased self were more intense, more urgent, more primitive in Mr. I.'s case, than in Mr. M.'s" (p. 195). In working psychoanalytically with Mr. I., Kohut believes that eventually it would be necessary to interpret to the patient that "his attempt to raise his self-esteem with the aid of his defensive promiscuity is like the attempt of a man with a wide-open gastric fistula to still his ravenous hunger by frantic eating" (p. 197).

In a related sense, Kohut (1977a) insists: "It is the structural void in the self that the addict tries to fill—whether by sexual activity or by oral ingestion" (p. 197, footnote 11). In this same context, he states that the "structural void cannot be filled any better beyond ingestion than by other forms of addictive behavior" (p. 197, footnote 11).

Returning again to the case of Mr. I., Kohut indicates that "it is the very inefficiency of the defensive maneuvers that explains why they are so incessantly pursued" (p. 297). Kohut argues, therefore, that a narcissistic behavior disorder, such as Mr. I.'s sexual addiction, is more severe than is a narcissistic personality disorder such as Mr. M.'s sexual obsession.

The former involves a "defensive maneuver" or structures, whereas the latter entails compensatory structures.

According to Kohut, a defensive structure merely covers over a primary defect in the self; whereas a compensatory structure overcomes the primary defect in the self by creating what amounts to an alternative or substitute pathway for continued development. Moreover, a defensive structure is, Kohut contends, developmentally static and hence does not undergo any progressive alteration; a compensatory structure is, Kohut asserts, developmentally dynamic and does undergo progressive modification.

The difference between the two types of psychic structure may be viewed as follows. A defensive structure is analogous to a toupee or hairpiece a man uses to cover and hide a bald spot. In contrast, a compensatory structure is analogous to a man growing a beard or mustache as a substitute for balding. Using a hairpiece is a totally artificial gimmick that is intended to create an illusion of actually having a full or near-full head of hair. Growing a beard and mustache is a natural and nonartificial way to compensate for balding, without resorting to a magic trick of merely appearing to have hair.

In addition, it is entirely possible and quite normal for a man to grow fuller and thicker facial hair, whereas nothing natural can be done to a toupee that has no organic roots in the scalp. From our perspective, we compare a toupee or hairpiece, in the context of addiction, to an ATM that fosters fantasy and weakens the self; whereas we liken a beard and a mustache to a transitional selfobject that is real and strengthens the self. (We leave aside the question of the defensive versus the compensatory nature of the case of resorting to hair follicle implants as a means of growing a fuller head of hair, and hence the analogy of this tactic in the context of addiction to an ATM versus a transitional selfobject.)

In light of this discussion, we understand the cases of Mr. I. and Mr. M. in the following manner. Mr. M. establishes an archaic selfobject relationship that allows him to develop and strengthen one sector of his self to compensate for another and weaker sector. Mr. I. fails to achieve this degree of psychic rehabilitation or restoration. Instead, he uses a faulty gimmick—sadistic sexual enactments—as a wobbly prop that consistently breaks down, thus necessitating a vicious cycle of repeating the same addictive behavior.

Before proceeding, however, we must place Kohut's distinction between narcissistic personality and behavior disorders within an appropriate historical and psychoanalytic context. We believe that Kohut arrives at his distinction, at least in part, on the basis of both personal and professional experiences with August Aichhorn, his first psychoanalyst and a psychoanalytic mentor. Aichhorn is well known as a pioneer in the development of a psychoanalytic theory and approach to psychotherapy with juvenile delinquents, who, like addicts, are a very difficult to treat type of patient.

One of Aichhorn's major advances in psychoanalytic thinking—and one particularly relevant for self psychology and our work—concerns his discovery of a narcissistic disturbance, which he believes is central to juvenile delinquency. Aichhorn adopts an implicit position according to which juvenile delinquency may be conceived of as a narcissistic behavior disorder. Also, Aichhorn implies that the narcissistic core lying at the center of juvenile delinquency consists of particular unconscious fantasies, fantasies that we describe as archaic narcissistic fantasies.

For example, Aichhorn (1964) writes the following about one of his juvenile delinquents:

> The child continued to live, in his *imagination*, the joyful life which he had experienced in his grandmother's house, and locked himself more and more in this *imaginary world* as the reality became less and less pleasurable. (pp. 64–65, emphasis added)

Aichhorn continues: "On the other hand, the practical demands of everyday life required that he give up his *fantasy*, that he push it out of consciousness" (p. 65, emphasis added). He concludes: "Yet it remained powerful enough to make him a misfit in his environment" (p. 65).

In a later context, Aichhorn returns to the centrality of fantasy (and, we suggest archaic narcissistic fantasy) to understanding the narcissistic nature of juvenile delinquency. As regards this type of disturbed youth, he (Aichhorn, 1964) observes:

> It happens often that the child withdraws his interest from the outer world and *devotes it entirely to fantasies*, which will then emerge as daydreams. An exceedingly large number of children yield willingly to *pleasurable imaginings*, or, on the contrary, are plagued against their will by *frightful phantasms* and terrifying visions. They are often unable to ward off their daydreams even while sitting in the classroom and they do not follow their lessons at school. (p. 204, emphasis added)

Aichhorn adds that "these children are already too much *absorbed*, not in the teacher's lessons, *but in their own fantasies*" (pp. 204–5, emphasis added).

In these brief passages, Aichhorn alludes to the idea that there are both "pleasurable imaginings" and "frightful phantasms." Our notion of the Janus-faced quality of archaic narcissistic fantasies—namely, the existence of both a positive or hoped for as well as a negative or dreaded version of the same fantasy and the flip-flopping versus the switching of these fantasies in a, respectively, bipolar or dialectical fashion—is based, in part, on Aichhorn's thinking.

Moreover, Kohut takes up Aichhorn's notion of absorption in fantasy. For example, Kohut (1977b) speaks about "absorption through fantasy formation" (p. 32). This notion of absorption in fantasy is central to our concept of "intersubjective absorption," which is really just another way of describing a joint absorption in shared fantasy on the part of two members of a relationship.

In addition, Aichhorn is an early advocate of the use of psychoanalytic empathy (see, for example, Aichhorn, 1964, pp. 127–140). He is also a pioneer in the development of the "narcissistic transference" (see, for example, Aichhorn, 1964, pp. 174–191).

All of these ideas make it clear that Kohut is heavily influenced by Aichhorn's thinking, especially as regards a separate and distinct type of narcissistic behavior disorder of which delinquency and addiction are two subtypes—with perversion as a third. From our vantage point, the difference between these three subtypes of narcissistic behavior disorder may be stated as follows: a delinquent *acts out* archaic narcissistic fantasies on the environment; an addict as well as a so-called pervert or fetishist uses (or misuses and abuses) things and activities in the environment as part of *activating* and reliving these fantasies.

In other words, it may be said that a delinquent, addict, and pervert all perceive the environment narcissistically (see Kohut, 1978d [1972], pp. 644, 645; 1978e [1976], p. 834) as nonhuman parts or extensions of the self, that is, as part of the "selfobject environment" (Kohut, 1977b, p. 247). Thus, it is possible to conceive of the difference among the three as follows: a delinquent *acts out* fantasies on a narcissistically perceived environment, whereas an addict and a pervert *act within* fantasies of a narcissistically perceived environment.

The fact that Kohut is influenced by Aichhorn's thinking in the ways in which we suggest is apparent in examining the early work of Eissler, another of Aichhorn's psychoanalytic prodigies, and once a close colleague and contemporary of Kohut. In a 1950 paper entitled, "Ego-Psychological Implications of the Psychoanalytic Treatment of Delinquents," Eissler advances a number of Aichhorn's ideas. He pursues these ideas in a way very similar to some of Kohut's efforts in this same regard. This similarity provides, we assert, further support to our contention that Kohut's thinking about narcissistic behavior disorder is influenced by Aichhorn.

The early work of Eissler on delinquency is also important in our assertion that addiction is essentially a narcissistic phenomenon, a contention supported by Kohut's thinking as well. As with Aichhorn, and later with Kohut, Eissler believes that delinquency is, at its core, basically symptomatic of a profound disturbance in the narcissistic sector of the personality. More specifically, Eissler indicates that a delinquent cannot transform archaic illusions (fantasies) of being omnipotent into a more mature and realistic view of himself or herself.

For instance, Eissler (1950) observes: "The delinquent's pathology seems to be focused around the conversion of the primary feeling of omnipotence" (p. 106). Furthermore, he notes: "The psychopathology centering around the maintenance of a feeling of omnipotence, however, is, I think, a constant factor in delinquent patients" (p. 107). He concludes regarding the delinquent "that the trauma, a series of traumata, which have initiated the severe pathology of their ego structure, must have occurred at a time when the child's early feelings of omnipotence were one of its main tools in dealing with reality" (p. 104).

Eissler also indicates: "From the observation of children it is known that during a certain phase the child not only feels himself omnipotent, but really attributes such powers to persons of his environment, to animals, *or even to inanimate objects*" (p. 104, emphasis added). We believe that a child's attribution of such omnipotent powers to "inanimate objects" occurs in the context of a phase-appropriate expression of megalomania, which eventuates, under normal circumstances, in the creation of what Kohut terms a *"nonhuman* selfobject" (1977b, p. 56), or what we call a "transitional selfobject." A failure on the part of parents to empathize with a child's need to attribute magical powers to nonhuman things and activities, which are imagined as being totally under a child's control, may lead, later in life, to a dependency on ATMs.

In a number of his cases Eissler explicitly connects addiction with delinquency. For example, several of Eissler's patients are both addicted and delinquent. The notion that both delinquency and addiction are different yet interrelated types of narcissistic (behavior) disorder is implicit in Eissler's case histories.

We return to Aichhorn's and Eissler's thinking on the psychoanalytic psychotherapy of the delinquent, as a type of patient with a narcissistic behavior disorder, in our discussion of Kohut's self-psychological approach to working psychotherapeutically with an addicted patient.

A final topic of typological relevance concerns Kohut's concept of the bipolar self. Inexplicably, like his distinction between narcissistic personality disorder and narcissistic behavior disorder, this notion has received relatively little attention within (or, for that matter, outside of) self psychology. Despite its centrality to the argument Kohut propounds in *The Restoration of the Self*, it has not been developed within the self-psychological literature, where we found only two exceptions—a discussion by Kohut and Wolf (1978) and a brief reference by P. H. Ornstein (1981).

Yet, from the perspective of our study, the concept of the bipolar self is of enormous relevance to our typology of addiction. However, Kohut's thoughts on the bipolar self do not relate specifically to his thinking on addiction. Nonetheless, we have already addressed it earlier in this chapter as part of our general description of our bipolar self typology of addiction. (See also Chapter 2 for a discussion of the topic of Kohut's conceptualization of the bipolar self and its relevance for our typology of addiction.)

Therapeutics

Kohut's first, albeit indirect, reference to treating addiction may be found in his 1956 discussion of Szaz's classic paper, "The Role of the Counterphobic Mechanism in Addiction." Here, Kohut (1978a [1956], p. 203) refers to his own clinical experience with addiction, which, at that time, consisted in the long-term analysis of one case. This reference is of more than passing historical interest. In his subsequent 1959 paper, "Introspection, Empathy, and Psychoanalysis," Kohut makes several comments about the psychoanalytic treatment of an addicted patient. At the time, these statements by Kohut represented major and far-reaching modifications of the classical, psychoanalytic approach to psychotherapy.

Kohut (1978b [1959]) indicates that if addicted "patients are in psychotherapy, they may be said to become *addicted to the psychotherapy or to the psychotherapeutic process*" (p. 224, emphasis added). In 1959, the notion, as advanced by Kohut, of a psychoanalytic patient becoming "addicted" to the psychotherapeutic process constituted a radical and controversial shift in psychoanalytic thinking about the treatment of an addicted patient. Kohut advocates an alteration in the way psychotherapists view the psychoanalysis of addiction in this paper published in 1959. It is not too far-fetched to speculate, therefore, about the possibility that Kohut made this clinical advance in the course of his earlier psychoanalysis of an addicted patient.

The psychoanalysis of this same addicted patient may, moreover, have served as the clinical context in which Kohut (1978b [1959]) realizes that: "Addiction must not, however, be confused with transference: *the therapist is not a screen for the projection of existing psychological structure; he is a substitute for it*" (p. 225, emphasis added). This clinical stance, perhaps derived from Kohut's psychoanalysis of an addicted patient, is based on an implicit notion: namely, that transference ought not to be limited, as classically advocated, to the unconscious projection on the part of a patient of preexisting psychological structure onto a psychotherapist as a so-called blank screen.

We may understand Kohut as implying that the concept of transference must be broadened to include the possibility that a psychotherapist can function as a substitute for such psychic structure. We believe that this position presages Kohut's later concept of the selfobject transference.

It is all the more likely, given the historically important connection between Kohut and Aichhorn, that Kohut, in his early psychoanalytic work with an addicted patient, may have had his first clinical inkling about the nature and function of what he would later term the selfobject transference. Aichhorn, in the course of his pioneering work with juvenile delinquents, recognized the importance of the "narcissistic transference" (Aichhorn, 1964, pp. 174–91). In the context of his work with this type of "youthful impostor" (p. 176), Aichhorn realizes that for the most part such a youngster "had failed to develop any object-libidinal relationship to our person" (p. 175).

Aichhorn points out that such an adolescent patient "had a peculiar psychic structure which makes him well-nigh incapable of forming object-libidinal relations of any kind" (p. 175). Aichhorn concludes, therefore, that such a youngster does not develop the typical and expected object-oriented transference. In arriving at this clinical observation, Aichhorn raises serious doubts about the "analyzability" of such a patient using standard psychoanalytic techniques.

However, Aichhorn, rather than abandoning the psychoanalytic psychotherapy of the juvenile delinquent, persists. And, in persevering, he departs radically from what were at that time accepted psychoanalytic techniques. Based on a delinquent's "peculiar psychic structure," Aichhorn stipulates: "When we meet the type of juvenile delinquent described, then we do not attempt to establish an object-libidinal relationship at all" (p. 190). Instead, Aichhorn recommends that psychoanalysts

> behave from the beginning in a manner which incites the youngster to let his own narcissistic libido flow over to our person, so as ultimately to create that dependence of his total personality upon us, a situation parallel to the ego's dependency upon its ego ideal. (p. 181)

To this recommendation Aichhorn (1964) adds: "We want to take over more and more of his narcissistic libido, we intend to substitute ourselves for his ego ideal, so as to deprive him entirely of his critical faculty" (p. 183).

The work of Aichhorn on a modified psychoanalytic approach to treating juvenile delinquents is revealing and relevant to the current discussion for at least two reasons. First, it is readily apparent that Aichhorn, in distinguishing between an "object-libidinal" transference and a "narcissistic transference," sets the stage for Kohut's later "discovery" and development of the concept of the selfobject transference.

And second, there is the fact that Aichhorn distinguishes between these two types of transferences on the basis of his psychoanalysis of delinquents. This adds further weight to our contention that Kohut, in all likelihood, followed Aichhorn's radical thinking in the course of his psychoanalysis of an addicted patient. The addicted patient psychoanalyzed by Kohut is similar to Aichhorn's delinquent patient; both suffer from a similar "peculiar psychic structure" (that is, a narcissistic disturbance or self disorder), which precludes the possibility of establishing and maintaining a transference based on an "object-libidinal relationship."

Kohut is well aware of Aichhorn's seminal work (see, for example, Kohut, 1971, pp. 161–64). Perhaps it is no accident, therefore, that early in his psychoanalytic psychotherapy with an addicted patient Kohut pursues Aichhorn's idea of a narcissistic transference (in contrast to an object transference). In a related manner, Kohut believes that an addict suffers from a type of narcissistic disturbance very similar in kind to that of a delinquent. It follows that Kohut might well have expected addicts to manifest the same type of narcissistic transference as did delinquents.

Aichhorn may have also influenced Kohut's early understanding of psychoanalytic empathy. In describing his psychoanalysis of an addicted patient, Kohut (1978b [1959]) exclaims: "His dependency cannot be analyzed or reduced by insight, *it must be recognized and acknowledged*" (p. 225, emphasis added). The classical approach to psychoanalysis emphasizes insight as a means of eliminating desires and fantasies, which were thought by traditional Freudians to be infantile in nature.

In the above quote, Kohut argues, by contrast, for psychoanalysts to accept and tolerate narcissistic strivings directed by a patient to a psychotherapist. According to Kohut, these archaic strivings, which originate in early childhood, are carried over, in certain cases, into adulthood.

In fact, in the same discussion of this addicted patient, Kohut (1978b [1959]) implies as much. He observes that

> it is a clinical experience that the major psychoanalytic task in such instances is the analysis of the denial of the real need, *the patient must first learn to replace a set of unconscious grandiose fantasies* that are kept up with the aid of social isolation by the, for him, painful acceptance of the reality of being dependent. (p. 225, emphasis added)

Kohut advances the idea of a psychoanalyst empathizing with a patient's childhood strivings appearing as "unconscious grandiose fantasies," rather than rejecting them as infantile and therefore as pathological. The position advocated by Kohut is seriously at odds with the then prevailing approach to the practice of psychoanalysis. It is, however, consistent with the spirit of Aichhorn's psychotherapeutic advances, which, interestingly enough, are also apparent in the early work of Eissler. But, unlike Kohut, who advances psychoanalysis beyond its classical confines, Eissler steadfastly resists such improvements and instead adheres to a classical form of Freudian psychoanalysis.

Eissler, despite his later role as an ardent and dogmatic proponent of classical Freudian technique, is in his early work on delinquency still under the influence of Aichhorn's nontraditional thinking. In this earlier context, he advocates an approach much like Kohut's. At that time, both Eissler and Kohut depart, in a number of important ways, from standard psychoanalytic techniques.

According to Eissler (1950), in the psychotherapy of a delinquent, many of whom are also addicted, it is necessary that the patient "has experienced the analyst as an omnipotent being" (p. 99). He notes that the psychoanalyst has to "act temporarily like an omnipotent being" (p. 99). Furthermore, he believes that a "positive transference" with such a patient is possible "only after the patient had temporarily accepted the analyst as an omnipotent but benign being" (p. 103).

Eissler maintains that in order to conduct such a psychoanalysis it is necessary for the psychoanalyst to "*identify by empathy* with the open aggression, the stealing, lying, and embezzlement" (p. 121, emphasis added) of a delinquent patient. In other words, he, like Kohut, implies that a psychoanalyst has to "identify by empathy" (that is, to share uncritically and nonjudgementally) with a patient's archaically grandiose fantasies and omnipotent illusions of both self and other.

Of course, it is equally possible that a psychoanalyst may succumb unconsciously to a counter-transference as a result of over-identifying (rather than empathizing) with such a patient's fantasies and illusions. Or contrarily, a psychoanalyst may fall prey to a form of countertransference resistance, thus being unable to identify (and empathize) with such a patient. As Eissler (1950) points out, the difficulty of such empathy by identification is "one of the reasons why the treatment of so many delinquents is doomed to failure" (p. 121). In an analogous fashion, we contend that we are not overstepping our bounds to say the same of "so many" addicts.

Similarly, Kohut (see Elson, 1987, pp. 126–27) later implies the following: An addicted patient can only replace archaic narcissistic fantasies if a psychotherapist gives emotionally of himself or herself in a real and genuine fashion. More specially, according to Kohut, a psychotherapist must be capable of empathizing with a patient's legitimate, yet previously unmet, need for selfobject functions.

In such a way, Kohut claims that a psychotherapist in relation to a patient "sets up the type of situation that ... repeats the childhood situation by fulfilling for them the function that they cannot fulfill for themselves" (pp. 126–27). In the same vein, a psychotherapist gradually enables patients to provide these functions for themselves, or "to do for their own" (p. 127). He adds: "In other words, you allow them to *build up structure*" (p. 127, emphasis added).

Finally, in *The Restoration of the Self*, Kohut (1977b) makes two points important to the psychotherapeutic approach that we advocate in our study. In Kohut's discussion of the case of "Mr. U.," he maintains that the (selfobject) transference could be understood psychoanalytically as indicative of the "existence of earlier (prefetishistic) substitutes for the unreliable selfobject ... [or] selfobject surrogates" (p. 56). In the case of Mr. U., these "selfobject surrogates" consist, according to Kohut, of specific nonhuman things (and activities), or what we term transitional selfobjects. Later, in the same discussion of the case of Mr. U., Kohut noted that the "transference itself, however, never *reinstated the earliest preoccupation with soothing selfobjects* for sufficiently long periods" (p. 57, emphasis added). Once again, the "soothing selfobjects" are, in our terminology, nonhuman or transitional in nature.

Kohut indicates clearly the following in both of the above quoted passages. It is possible for a psychotherapist to reinstate with a patient an early childhood "preoccupation" with nonhuman and not simply human selfobjects. We interpret Kohut, therefore, as anticipating our notion of the transitional selfobject transference.

There is a psychodynamic logic behind our interpretation of Kohut. A similar unconscious dynamic connects fetishism and addiction, both of which Kohut categorizes as subtypes of narcissistic behavior disorder. It is perfectly legitimate, we believe, to extrapolate from the concept of a nonhuman (transitional) selfobject transference, as is implicit in Kohut's description of his psychoanalysis of fetishism, to the psychoanalysis of addiction.

Part II

The Addiction Paper Trilogy Revisited—The Narcissus Complex

INTRODUCTION

Those psychoanalytic authors who present clinical vignettes in support of their ideas about addiction are, with several exceptions, few in number. (See J. W. Adams, 1978, and J. D. Levin, 1987, for exceptions to this general pattern.) Moreover, those authors who present detailed case histories rather than vignettes are rarer still. Our psychoanalytic psychotherapy cases, all six of which have been completed, constitute, therefore, a major advance in the methodology of presenting psycho-analytic data in support of theoretical ideas about addiction.

We present these representative cases as evidence in support of our main contention, namely that all addictions are manifestations of a distinct type of narcissistic behavior disorder and, moreover, are expressed characterologically in the form of the Narcissus complex. Furthermore, we envision from our self-psychological perspective all addictions as atavistic illusions of being a megalomaniacal self and as wielding control over a "narcissistically perceived reality" (Kohut, 1978d [1972], p. 644).

Based on the unconscious principle of the dialectical bipolarity of fantasy and moods, we argue that addicts are "fantasy-junkies" and "control freaks" whose fantasy lives flip-flop erratically from one archaic self-state to another. In particular, this psychic flip-flopping moves in the following manner: an addict induces a self-hypnotic trance (i.e., the hypnoid defense) within himself or herself that flips unconscious subjective experience from one characterized by an excruciatingly painful mood of narcissistic mortification (reflective of a sense of being out of and having lost control) to one characterized by a mood of narcissistic bliss (indicative of a temporary and fleeting feeling of rapture).

We provide the clinical details of our six psychotherapy cases to illustrate the major points of our self-psychological model of addiction. In summary, we have contended that all addictions: (1) are symptomatic expressions of megalomania gone awry in the form of the Narcissus complex and as expressed in the addictive character; (2) consist of a psychopathological abuse of nonhuman things and activities serving as addictive trigger mechanisms (ATMs) to the virtual exclusion of the healthy use of others as selfobjects; (3) involve a type of self-hypnosis or hypnoid defense induced by addictive metamorphosis or phantasmagorical transmogrification; (4) reveal that vertical splits (that is, dissociation in contrast to repression) have deprived a person of any semblance of a sense of a cohesive and unitary version of self, and instead have left an individual with a disturbing sense of self as uncohesive, disunified, and as broken up into splintered or split parts (that is, "part-selves"); and, (5) entail a significant degree of antipathy toward self and others as expressed in self-destructiveness and violence.

The organizational format of the following chapters is as follows. We divide the six psychoanalytic psychotherapy cases into two sections, an overview and a commentary. The overview section consists of a description of the case as it was originally conducted during the early period of our thinking about the nature of addiction and the best approach to its treatment. The commentary section involves a discussion of the case as it continued to unfold following our original description (see Ulman & Paul, 1989, 1990, 1992) and in line with advances in our theorizing. We organize the psychoanalytic material contained within each of these two sections in such a way as to conform with the order of our model; thus we proceed in each section from phenomenology, etiology and pathogenesis, through typology to treatment.

Proceeding in each case from the overview to the commentary section allows us to do justice to the evolving nature of both our theory of addiction and psychotherapeutic approach. For instance, we can follow the natural progression from our intersubjective absorption hypothesis, as we originally conceived it, to our current conceptualization of the narcissistic exchange process.

Or, to take another example, we can follow the changes we have made in our thinking about the best way to view a typology of addiction. At first, we constructed a typology of addiction that consisted of different types of addictive personality disorder. Recently, we have revised our original conceptualization in the form of notions of bipolar self-psychological and bioself-psychological typologies of addiction. We view these latter conceptualizations as each based on different types (and subtypes) of an addictive character who is organized unconsciously on the basis of a fantasy of being a megalomaniacal self and as empowered with illusory control over magically endowed agents that transport an addict to a private wonderland.

We can also outline the progress in our thinking about dissociation as it occurs in the context of addiction. Our thoughts on this topic evolved from an idea of dissociative anesthesia to that of a notion about self-hypnosis, or the hypnoid defense, as the latter occurs in the form of an addictive state of mind that we refer to as addictive metamorphosis or phantasmagorical transmogrification.

In addition, we can observe the shift that has taken place in our view of the nature and function of the selfobject transference of an addicted patient. We can pinpoint how we moved from a standard self-psychological view of the selfobject transference as involving mirroring, idealization, and twinship to a more intersubjective perspective of the selfobject transference as a shared or intersubjective fantasy.

And, most importantly, we can chart the course that led us to our psychoanalytic rediscovery of an old form of archaic narcissism—that is, megalomania. We discover that a specific version of megalomania (that is, a narcissistic notion of illusory control over psychoactive, and hence, magically endowed agents) is an especially powerful fantasy in the unconscious mind of an addict, so all-encompassing in fact that it determines the nature and function of addiction. We learn, therefore, that at the deepest level of unconscious experience an addict is megalomaniacal in that he or she is a fantasy junkie and control freak.

We divide our six representative case histories into three pairs, with a detailed discussion of each of these two cases in the next three chapters. We present our two earliest and first cases—the cases of "Teddy" and "Mary"—in Chapter 4. In Chapter 5, we discuss the cases of "Joe" and "JoAnn," the so-called middle cases that appeared originally in the second of our addiction paper trilogy. And finally, we describe in Chapter 6 the most recent of our six cases, "Travis" and "Errol."

We decided to divide the cases in the above manner for the following reason: Presenting all six of these cases in one extremely long chapter would prove to be very unwieldy and cumbersome; the details of each of the cases might become blurred and confused in the mind of the reader. Instead, we hope that by dividing the cases into three pairs (to separate and demarcate them) each case will stand on its own merits. And in the process, we seek to highlight the representative aspects of each of these six cases, thus providing the reader with graphic illustrations of our overall population of addicted patients.

We provide the reader with a final Summary and Conclusion before ending this second part of our study and proceeding from our presentation and discussion of our six representative case histories. We summarize the cases so that the reader, having already gone over the details of each case, may more easily put together the pieces from all of these cases in order to form a more unified and cohesive picture of the cases as a whole. In other words, we hope that our summary will enable the reader to avoid being overwhelmed and confused by the sheer wealth of clinical material and, in the process, come to see clearly the forest for the trees.

We organize our final conclusion section on the basis of the four components of our self-psychological model, namely, phenomenology, etiology and pathogenesis, typology, and therapeutics. We attempt to bring together the insights we have gained concerning these four components of our model as these advances in our thinking about addiction and its treatment evolved naturally during the course of our in-depth work with our various addicted patients. By bringing together our various conclusions, we intend to assist the reader in deciding about the applicability of our model and the explanatory power of its findings.

There are a number of methodological issues we need to raise as part of an introduction to our approach of presenting representative case histories. First, one or the other of the two co-authors personally conducted the six psychotherapy cases in either psychoanalysis or psychoanalytic psychotherapy. Consequently, we do not, as is often the case, use the patients of supervisees or colleagues. Instead, we use our own cases, even though this entailed exposing many of our own blunders, mistakes, and errors. In the interest of allowing the reader to witness firsthand our personal struggles, both in understanding and in working with these difficult to treat patients, we decide to put into full view all of our false starts, wrong turns in the bend, as well as dead ends. We grew a lot from our mistakes, and we want to share with the reader the very important lessons we learned along our psychoanalytic journey. The fact that we completed each of these cases on the average of 15 years ago has given us the advantage of the passage of time, and with it the perspective of hindsight. From this vantage point, we have reflected on the pros and cons of various conceptualizations and interventions.

Second, the frequency of the psychotherapy sessions with these addicted patients ranged from one to three or four times per week and continued over a period of time varying from 4 to 15 years. As noted, all six of the cases have been terminated and, therefore, provide a psychoanalytic depth to the clinical material, which is essential in constructing our model. Individual psychotherapy is the primary treatment modality we used in working with our patients. However, in several of the cases (namely, Teddy, JoAnn, and Travis) we tried at various times a combination of individual and group psychotherapy. Yet, our focus in the ensuing presentations is based exclusively on the psychoanalytic data derived from the individual psychotherapies; our psychoanalytic conclusions are not derived, therefore, from our patients' experiences either in group psychotherapy or in the combination of individual and group psychotherapy.

Third, there are unavoidable limitations in representative cases. In other words, we could not avoid an inevitable degree of homogeneity and the stereotypical as regards matters of age, sex, socioeconomic, ethnic, and religious background. For example, all of the men and women making up our representative sample come from either middle or working class backgrounds and range in ages from early 20s to mid-40s. Moreover, all our patients are white and heterosexual. Our sample of cases is representative of a significant segment of the addicted patient population typically encountered by psychotherapists in a private practice setting.

However, these patients are not representative of another important segment of this same private practice population consisting of men and women of age, color, and different sexual orientation (that is, gay men and women). And, our patients seek psychoanalytic therapy for their respective addictive disorders, whereas many other addicts either do not seek such psychotherapy or receive psychotherapy in institutional rather than in private practice settings.

In addition, our six representative cases fall along stereotypical gender lines: thus, all the men are alcoholics, drug abusers, compulsive gamblers, or sex addicts; whereas all the women are eating disordered.

Clearly, this somewhat artificial division does not accurately represent the vast array of addicted patients, such as, for instance, a female addicted patient suffering from alcoholism, drug abuse, compulsive gambling and sex. Or, to take another example, it does not represent the now ever-increasing number of male addicted patients suffering from an eating disorder.

Yet, despite the unavoidable limitations of our representative patient sample, we believe that our self-psychological model is applicable to the entire range of addicted patients seeking help from psychoanalytic psychotherapists in a private practice setting. However, we make no claim about the applicability of our model to the more socioeconomically disadvantaged and often minority patient who seeks treatment for addiction outside the requisite clinical confines of the psychoanalytic consulting room.

Fourth, the order in which we discuss these six cases follows their original presentation (see Ulman & Paul, 1989, 1990, 1992). Such an order of presentation allows us to capture the increasing clinical complexity of the cases as we encountered them. For example, Teddy, Mary, Joe, and JoAnn are representative of the addicted patient suffering from a single form of addiction, whether alcoholism or some form of eating disorder. In contrast, Travis and Errol are representative of the poly-addicted patient.

It is a clinical axiom that the psychotherapeutic prognosis is usually better for an addicted patient who suffers from only one form of addiction in contrast to a patient who suffers from more than one, whether it be in a serial or crossover fashion. Together, the cases of Travis and Errol illustrate graphically that working clinically with the multiply addicted (and/or dual diagnosis patient) constitutes an extreme psychotherapeutic challenge, as well as a perilous psychoanalytic journey for a psychotherapist.

And fifth, we wrote the case histories following a self-psychological methodology based on an empathic-introspective point of view. Such a perspective places the patient's subjective experience of their own unconscious at the center of the narrative. The clinical data we employ in writing these case histories is derived psychoanalytically from a lengthy and in-depth immersion in the unconscious experience of our patients. Employing this empathic vantage point enabled us to introspectively make vicarious contact with the unconscious fantasy lives of our patients. We describe in detail the results of our psychoanalytic exploration of this otherwise private and hidden realm of experience. As part of the story of the psychotherapy of each of our patients, we try as much as possible to provide a clear and distinct voice for the unconscious of each of our patients. In the process, we hope to allow the respective patient's unconscious to speak to the reader.

By way of introducing our patients to the reader, we offer a brief preview of the histories of our six psychotherapy cases. Teddy, a male, alcoholic, was in his early 30s when he began treatment and in his mid-40s when he originally terminated his therapy. (He subsequently returns to psychotherapy, following an approximately 5-year hiatus. He remains in therapy during this second round for only a year.) Teddy is in psychotherapy for approximately 16 years of which the original 10 years are spent with one of the co-authors. Prior to returning to his first psychotherapist (that is, one of the co-authors), Teddy spent another 5 years with a female psychotherapist to whom he was transferred for further psychotherapy.

However, our description of Teddy's psychotherapy is based primarily on the 10-year period of his psychotherapy with one of the authors. (We add a postscript to the report of Teddy's case history that provides additional information and further corroboration of some of our main points.) Early in this original 10-year period of his overall psychotherapy, Teddy is hospitalized for alcohol detoxification and rehabilitation. His first hospitalization is followed by a second for further inpatient rehabilitation; together, these two hospitalizations result in a 1-year break in the course of his psychotherapy.

At the beginning of psychotherapy, Teddy is in a tempestuous and failing marriage. He works for his father as a salesman in a business his father owns and operates with a partner. The case of Teddy highlights several key issues: (1) it demonstrates that Teddy's use of sports and being an athlete serves as a transitional selfobject activity that helpes to repair a narcissistic rupture in the self–selfobject matrix constituted by a father–son relationship; (2) it illustrates that Teddy unconsciously fantasizes about psychotherapy as a pedagogic-like activity functioning in his imagination as a transitional selfobject replacement for alcohol, the latter of which served previously as an ersatz selfobject or ATM; and, (3) it points to the presence in Teddy of a latent yet poorly developed capacity for transitional selfobject usage, the psychotherapeutic activation of which proves to be instrumental in the successful remission of his alcoholism.

Mary, a single, 28-year-old young woman, suffers from an addictive eating disorder with bulimic symptoms of bingeing and purging. She is seen in psychoanalytic psychotherapy on a twice weekly basis for over approximately 4 years. The case of Mary reveals the deleterious effects of an unempathic and, at times, antipathetic family environment on the normal development of a healthy sense of self. Likewise, it offers graphic evidence of the adverse consequences of such an atmosphere on a child's ability to utilize the human surround as a psychologically nourishing selfobject milieu. Lacking in such narcissistic nourishment, Mary resorts instead to an addictive abuse of food, eating, and laxatives as her only alternative means of barely sustaining a purely phantasmagorical version of a self as being megalomaniacal.

Moreover, the case of Mary highlights what can go wrong in the psychoanalytic psychotherapy of an addicted patient if a psychotherapist succumbs narcissistically to an intense and powerful countertransference. As a result of a particular kind of narcissistic countertransference, the psychotherapist in this case misses an opportunity to facilitate the replication in psychotherapy of an early childhood version of a specific variety of transitional selfobject activity.

Joe, a 40-year old, married, Vietnam combat veteran, has a long history of alcoholism, depression, and attempted suicide, all of which forces him on numerous occasions to seek hospitalization. Joe, like Teddy and Mary, grows up in a family environment that is unempathic and antipathetic to his fledgling attempts at creating a healthy sense of himself as a human being. Joe is treated callously by his father who is himself quite megalomaniacal. His father behaves toward Joe as if Joe is nothing more than a thing and, more specifically, a piece of wooden furniture.

Yet, despite the grossly inadequate nature of the empathy (or, more precisely, the antipathy) in Joe's early family environment, he, like Teddy, succeeds in establishing a transitional selfobject connection to his father. In contrast to Teddy, however, Joe uses woodworking and becomes handy with carpentry tools as an unconscious means of organizing himself in relation to his father. As becomes evident, Joe and the psychotherapist recreate a fantasy-based version of the woodworking as a symbolic mode of transitional selfobject activity. And, in so doing, they create the intersubjective context within which Joe manages to work through a mortifying fantasy of himself as a worthless and disposable thing. He replaces this dreadful fantasy vision of himself as subhuman or nonhuman with a sense of himself as more fully human.

JoAnn, a young woman in her mid-20s who works as a fashion designer, suffers, like Mary, from an addictive eating disorder with bulimic symptoms. In addition, she is addicted to exercise. She is in psychoanalytic psychotherapy for 6 years with session frequency ranging from one to three times per week. We move psychoanalytically in the case of JoAnn to a much deeper level of the unconscious than was possible with Mary. We reach a level of the unconscious wherein JoAnn experiences herself primarily in terms of a grossly distorted and deformed body image. As evidenced by intense self-loathing and self-hatred, JoAnn is narcissistically enraged with herself. In her antipathy toward herself, she illustrates the self-destructiveness of addictive megalomania gone awry.

In addition, the case of JoAnn clarifies the often overlooked role of a woman's father in the etiology and pathogenesis of an eating disorder. Together, JoAnn and the psychotherapist create an intersubjective field in which the disturbance in JoAnn's interaction with her father re-emerges as an eroticized version of the transference–countertransference neurosis. Fortunately, the psychotherapist empathically understands the unconscious meaning of this intersubjective configuration, which otherwise could seriously undermine the psychoanalysis. Consequently, he proceeds with the psychotherapy to a successful termination. JoAnn and the psychotherapist analyze and work through a complex set of unconscious fantasies, some of which are psychosomatic in nature and manifest themselves psychophysiologically in JoAnn's bulimic symptoms as well as her symptoms of an addiction to exercise. Another subset of these unconscious fantasies appears behaviorally in the non-verbal dimension of the psychotherapeutic dialogue.

Travis, a 42-year-old, married, middle-class benefits counselor, leads what amounts to a truly double life. In one version of his life, he is a husband and father. In the other version of his life, he is a sociopathic addict with a long history of drug abuse, violence, and compulsive sex. Perhaps more clearly than any of our other cases, Travis exemplifies the nature of the splintering of the self and the resulting presence of split selves (or part-selves of which a self as being megalomaniacal is one) as constituents of the addictive character. The case of Travis also makes clear the different ways in which the dissociative split in the psyche functions in addiction in contrast to multiple personality disorder (MPD) or dissociative identity disorder (DID).

During the 10-year period of Travis's psychoanalytic psychotherapy, the transference–countertransference neurosis takes on a uniquely addictive cast. Eventually, the unconscious appeal of both drugs and violence expresses itself for Travis and the psychotherapist in the form of a shared or intersubjective fantasy of the psychotherapy as an "analytic instrument" (Isakower, 1992 [1957]).

As in the case of Teddy, we add a postscript to the case of Travis, who contacts his psychotherapist several years after his termination. We summarize the information gathered during this one-time contact in the interest of further illuminating the all too often lethal and deadly nature of some forms of addiction.

And finally, Errol, a foreign-born, computer salesman from a working-class background, is in his mid-30s when he begins his 10-year psychoanalytic psychotherapy for a poly-addiction to gambling and sex. The case of Errol points to the etiological significance of the "addict-family" (Chein et al., 1964) in the pathogenesis of addiction. It demonstrates that the future addict, or "addiction-prone personality" (Chein et al., 1964), may grow up in a family milieu woefully lacking in the presence of other persons who are capable of serving as caregivers and who are, therefore, able to function as selfobjects.

The environment of Errol's early family life, with the faulty nature or total absence of others as providers of necessary selfobject functions, creates a psychological void. Errol attempts unconsciously to fill this vacuum with nonhuman things and activities, all of which constitute psychopathological precursors to his subsequent addiction to gambling and sex.

Like the case of Travis, Errol constitutes another instance of the complex nature of dissociation in the context of addiction. In a fashion similar to Travis, Errol expresses his form of psychopathological dissociation in both addiction and a vertical split in his sense of self (that is, the presence of a fantasy of being a megalomaniacal self). However, unlike Travis, who is an example of an addict with a split or part-self disorder, Errol is an example of an addict with what is termed in the psychoanalytic literature as an "as if" personality (Deutsch, 1965 [1942]); see also Bartemeier, 1954; Feldman, 1962; Kaywin, 1968; Ross, 1967; and J. Weiss, 1966).

Also as occurred with Travis, the transference–countertransference neurosis in the case of Errol takes on a distinctly addictive quality. In this intersubjective context, patient and psychotherapist alike are caught up in unconscious fantasies about gambling and sex as magically endowed things and activities. The attempt on the part of patient and psychotherapist to work through this intersubjective enmeshment is determinative of both the relative success and failure of this psychotherapy.

Chapter 4

The First of the Addiction Paper Trilogy: The Cases of Teddy and Mary

TEDDY

Overview

When first seen, Teddy, a young man in his early 30s, has been drinking alcoholically for at least 12 years. Married for 5 years, he admits rather nonchalantly to verbal and physical abuse of his wife. An employee of his father, he complains bitterly that his father looks down on him and constantly belittles him in front of others.

Teddy laments that he grew up feeling incompetent and like a nincompoop. It quickly becomes apparent that in Teddy's early life only his mother makes him feel good about himself for simply being himself. Tragically, Teddy's mother dies of brain cancer when he is only 19 years old. Teddy dates the onset of his alcoholic drinking to the trauma of his mother's death.

Early in psychotherapy, Teddy reports a recurring dream of sucking pleasurably at his mother's breast. Teddy and the psychotherapist understand the dream-fantasy of drinking his mother's milk as a symbolic expression of Teddy's addictive fantasy about alcohol; in his imagination it serves as a magic elixir, that is, the unconscious equivalent of his mother's milk.

In our original conceptualization, we described the functioning of alcohol as if it were a genuine selfobject. At this early period in our thinking, we had not yet made an important theoretical distinction in either a developmental or psychotherapeutic context. We had yet to distinguish between the healthy functioning of transitional selfobject things and activities versus the unhealthy operation of ersatz selfobjects such as ATMs.

Despite the obvious pleasure that Teddy associates with his dream-fantasy of the maternal breast, he resists tenaciously the emergence of an equivalent fantasy in the transference. Apparently, Teddy dreads re-experiencing the traumatic loss in the transference of a maternal presence who once sustained him. It seems that he prefers to continue to drink alcoholically rather than risk the repetition of a catastrophic (maternal) loss in the transference.

Initially, the psychotherapist fails to understand and, hence, to analyze the resistance to the transference; the successful analysis of the resistance might have allowed Teddy to give up the selfobject-like function of alcohol for the selfobject provisions of psychotherapy. No doubt, the psychotherapist's difficulty in analyzing the resistance to the transference contributes to Teddy's continued alcoholic drinking. This difficulty also is a factor in the eventual necessity for Teddy to undergo several inpatient hospitalizations for detoxification and rehabilitation.

Teddy spends almost a year in two well-known facilities for addiction rehabilitation. Upon discharge from the second of these rehabilitation facilities, he attends regular Alcoholics Anonymous (AA) meetings, which he continues until one year later when he resumes psychotherapy.

Upon returning to psychotherapy, and now abstinent from alcohol for more than a year, Teddy takes advantage for the first time of the opportunities afforded him by psychoanalytic psychotherapy. He and the psychotherapist successfully analyze his resistance to using the psychotherapy as a replacement for alcohol. Together, they come to understand that his resistance is based on his unconscious dread of being re-traumatized (see A. Ornstein, 1974, 1991, on the "dread to repeat").

Teddy deepens his emotional connection to the entire psychotherapeutic process; he utilizes the psychotherapy as a means of replacing (rather than simply substituting) for alcohol and the unconscious selfobject-like function it serves in his life. Although Teddy and the psychotherapist overcome the resistance to the transference, they do not grasp, at this time, the deeper, unconscious meaning of his recurrent dream-fantasy of sucking at his mother's breast.

As co-determined by Teddy and the psychotherapist, the inter-subjective field is organized unconsciously in terms of a very specific transference–countertransference neurosis: Teddy has a powerful transference need for both a warm mother and good father; the psy-chotherapist has an equally strong countertransference tendency toward enacting the role of the *paterfamilias*. It is no accident, therefore, that Teddy and the psychotherapist organize themselves intersubjectively in accordance with these latter two overlapping fantasies.

Teddy uses his psychotherapy sessions to perform a number of pedagogic-like activities such as using a dictionary to look up the meaning of words that he can neither pronounce nor spell. He also talks extensively with the psychotherapist about self psychology and addiction. Teddy reads books recommended by the psychotherapist and attends lectures and workshops given by the therapist. In the process, Teddy becomes not only a patient but a devoted pupil of the psychotherapist.

Teddy employs this transference fantasy of mentorship to maintain his abstinence, obtains some sobriety, and creates a personal life with more meaning and substance. He and his wife divorce; Teddy then begins the long overdue process of learning how to take care of himself and live on his own. He also trades in his former barroom drinking buddies for some healthier and real friends. In addition, he starts to assert himself more forcefully with his father, who consistently mistreats and disrespects him as if he were a nonentity. For instance, he demands and receives praise and a raise from his father for his vastly improved performance at work.

The psychotherapist is aware that he is functioning transferentially for Teddy as an idealized selfobject presence that enables Teddy to resume an arrested developmental process. Developmentally, Teddy's psychological growth became arrested as a result of his father's early failure to function as a paternal selfobject as well as the loss of his mother and her functioning as a maternal selfobject. Countertransferen-tially, the psychotherapist is very comfortable in the transference role that Teddy assigns to him as the idealized paternal figure who embodies the unconscious fantasy of "father knows best." However, the psychotherapist does not empathically understand the unconscious meaning of Teddy's transference fantasy of himself as "father knows best," especially as Teddy equates it unconsciously with the function of alcohol. Moreover, the psychotherapist fails to grasp the importance of the unconscious connection that Teddy makes between this transference fantasy and the dream-fantasy of sucking pleasurably at his mother's breast.

At this psychotherapeutic juncture, the psychotherapist's own subjectivity pushes him countertransferentially in the direction of an idealization, however, from afar. As a result, Teddy is inhibited in forming an emotionally intimate merger with the psychotherapist. Transferentially, Teddy is more than willing to comply with the psychotherapist's countertransference requirement. Unconsciously, he is prepared to play the part of the attentive student who maintains a respectful distance from his admired teacher.

However, gradually and over time, the psychotherapist grasps and analyzes the unconscious meaning of this transference–countertransference neurosis. In this regard, there is a further unfolding of the psychoanalytic process of what we originally referred to as intersubjective absorption. Intersubjectively, the psychotherapy increasingly absorbs the selfobject-like functioning of alcohol. As a result, Teddy undergoes a psychotherapeutic transformation in which he takes over more of the genuine selfobject functions of the psychotherapy.

With the psychotherapist's help, Teddy improves his vocabulary, spelling, pronunciation, and overall intellectual functioning; he becomes much better educated and more informed. He feels better about himself and no longer sees himself through his father's eyes as either a nincompoop who knows nothing, or as a nitwit who can do nothing right. He internalizes and transmutes the power of the psychotherapist as an idealized selfobject and creates a brand new image of himself as someone who is intelligent and competent. In essence, he has built up bit by bit new psychic structures as evidenced empirically by the acquisition of increased functional capacities. (See M. Tolpin, 1971, on the notion of transmuting internalization as involving the gradual acquisition of new psychic structures.)

Commentary

From a phenomenological perspective, we can look back at our original understanding of the role that alcohol plays in Teddy's fantasy life and see that we had only a rudimentary grasp of the unconscious functions it served. First, we did not distinguish adequately between the bogus nature of the selfobject-like operation of alcohol as an ATM and the genuine functioning of the psychotherapy as a pedagogical form of transitional selfobject activity.

And second, we did not understand properly the dialectical movement of the fantasies and moods that so affected Teddy as part of his alcohol-induced (addictive) metamorphosis. In an alcohol stupor, Teddy undergoes a phantasmagorical transmogrification; in the midst of this artificially induced hypnoid trance (that is, the hypnoid defense) he alters his state of mind in such a way as to feel free temporarily from the otherwise constant pain of narcissistic mortification.

Without alcohol, Teddy is haunted by narcissistically mortifying fantasies and plagued by anxious and panic-ridden moods. In reflecting on these self-states, Teddy describes himself in terms that reveal that he feels totally lacking in the psychological wherewithal necessary to hold together both himself and his world. He seems to feel cut off from a source of psychic strength that would sustain him in the absence of his own ability to maintain himself. His anxiety level and panic at what apparently he subjectively experiences as impending fragmentation propel him into nightly drinking bouts at a series of his favorite neighborhood bars.

Safely ensconced on a bar stool with a coterie of his regular drinking buddies, Teddy is a prime example of the barroom pundit who feels himself to be in the company of like-minded cronies. In the presence of these imaginary experts, Teddy fantasizes himself as engaging effortlessly in brilliant discourse on all variety of serious topics. Teddy whiles away the evening, drinking, absorbed in garrulous gab about nonsense, all the while imagining himself at some intellectual gathering rather than the reality of being at a local tavern. It is as if Teddy is living out a scene from Eugene O'Neill's play *The Iceman Cometh* (1967 [1946]).

As the night progresses, and Teddy becomes ever more intoxicated, he loses all of his insecurities about his verbal and intellectual skills. He undergoes an addictive metamorphosis of sorts in which he imagines that he miraculously changes from a guy who is painfully shy and self-conscious into a fellow with the gift of gab and possessing a prodigious intellect. In a drunken stupor, Teddy pontificates about everything under the sun as he competes with other barroom pundits for center stage. For Teddy, holding court on a nightly basis at the neighborhood bar becomes a fantasized substitute for real and actual achievement.

Teddy, upon arriving home late at night after an evening of carousing with his drinking buddies, is greeted at the door by his wife. Understandably, she is not appreciative of nor impressed by his drunken recounting of his imaginary intellectual feats. As far as Teddy is concerned, his wife is disparaging and ridiculing of him. He reacts narcissistically with rage and, at times, with verbal abuse and physical violence. In this sense, therefore, he is acting as "rageaholic" (see Clancy, 1996, for a discussion of rageaholism addiction).

At these moments, Teddy, who is still under the influence of his megalomaniacal fantasies, indicates that he imagines his wife as if she were a mere stick figure. As such, he feels that he could ignore her completely, or failing that, he could simply remove her from the scene as if she is a prop he no longer needs. The next morning, following one of his typical "rageaholic" outbursts, Teddy is consumed with self-pity, remorse, and regret. He apologizes profusely to his wife, making empty promises to stop drinking and reform his ways.

In the course of abusing alcohol, Teddy undergoes phantasmagorical transmogrification in which he flip-flops from a narcissistically mortifying state to a narcissistically blissful state. As part of this addictive state of mind, Teddy flips subjectively from the pain of experiencing himself as an idiot, who is at the mercy of his father's ire, to the euphoric pleasure attendant to the imaginary experience of himself as a genius.

Alcohol allows Teddy to transport himself in his own imagination into a self-created and private wonderland. As part of the Narcissus complex, Teddy is bedazzled by the brilliance of his own keen intellect as he imagines it being reflected back to him in the admiring gazes of his barroom cronies. In other words, the barroom becomes for Teddy the site of his wonderland and alcohol is the magic elixir that endows him with a superhuman ability to cure all his ills and solve all his problems.

Teddy abuses alcohol with megalomaniacal abandon. Inducing an addictive state of self-hypnosis allows Teddy to entertain wild fantasies about existing in a surreal world. He no longer feels compelled to see himself through his father's eyes as demeaned, belittled, and as some kind of cretin; instead Teddy imagines that he has been transformed into someone who is as smart as a whip and instantaneously knows all the right answers. For Teddy alcohol is like a magic wand over which he has complete control. And, with a flip of his wrist, the wand gives him instantaneous control over all of his intellectual faculties.

In our earlier discussion of this case, we did not delve very deeply into the etiological roots and psychogenic pathway roots of Teddy's alcoholism. However, it is clear in hindsight that Teddy resumed in the transference a line of selfobject development organized primarily on the basis of his aborted relationship with his father. (See Wolf, 1980, on the idea of a selfobject line of development.) In our previous description, we emphasized the paternal and idealizing dimension of the selfobject transference without, however, fully exploring Teddy's early relationship with his father. In addition, we neglected altogether to examine the maternal and mirroring aspects of the selfobject transference.

We also lacked clarity about the psychoactive specificity of particular addictive trigger mechanisms (ATMs), and, in this case, alcohol. Consequently, we attempted to explain the antidepressant effect of alcohol on the basis of an idealizing fantasy rather than in terms of a mirroring fantasy. The latter provides an addict with a narscissistic illusion of being lifted emotionally from depression. In contrast, an idealizing fantasy provides an addict with an illusory experience of antianxiety pacification, tranquilization, and sedation.

Moreover, some ATMs (e.g., cocaine) have one specific psychoactive effect resulting from an antidepressant stimulation of mood. Other ATMs (e.g., alcohol) can have both an antianxiety and antidepressant effect. The combined psychoactive effect of alcohol helps to explain, in part, our original confusion about the different ways in which alcohol affects Teddy's unconscious fantasy life.

Looking back on the case of Teddy from the perspective of our current model makes it possible for us to present a more in-depth description of the roles played by both Teddy's father and mother, roles which we believe set Teddy inexorably on a pathogenic course leading eventually to alcoholism.

We can trace back the etiological roots of the breakdown of the narcissistic exchange process to Teddy's unsatisfactory relationship with his father. Unfortunately, Teddy could not use the extremely circumscribed and limited nature of his interaction with his father as a selfobject. Their relationship was based almost exclusively on Teddy's status as a baseball player, which enables his father to imagine him as a chip off the old block. (See La Farge, 2004, for a discussion of the reciprocal and mutual roles of parent and child in the unconscious process of "the imaginer and the imagined.")

In listening to Teddy, it is clear that his father is vicariously reliving the glory of his own past through Teddy's exploits as an athlete. The intersubjective field created by this developmental context interferes with rather than facilitates Teddy's ability to advance from phase I to phase II of the narcissistic exchange process.

Whatever emotional sustenance Teddy receives from his father depends totally on his ability to provide his father with narcissistic gratification. His father was an academic All-American athlete at an Ivy League college. When Teddy is born, his father has every expectation that his son will follow in his footsteps. Teddy remembers that, even as a child, his father started teaching him how to catch, throw, and hit a baseball.

Teddy recalls that throughout most of his childhood and adolescence he interacts with his father primarily on the basis of his willingness to participate in organized baseball activities. Obviously, baseball serves for Teddy as more than just an athletic activity; it provides him with the only means available to him to have some kind of relationship to his father. As such, it functions for Teddy as a transitional selfobject and intermediary connecting him psychologically (and intersubjectively) to his father.

Unconsciously, Teddy experiences himself as a nonhuman artifact that his father controls on the basis of the latter's own narcissistic agenda. Failing to match or duplicate his father's athletic prowess leaves Teddy feeling bereft and adrift. Outside of his accomplishments on the baseball diamond, Teddy feels that he is of little use or value to his father. Already imperiled narcissistically, Teddy falls apart totally at the age of 19 with the death of his mother. He feels useless, drops out of college, gives up a potential career as a semi-pro or professional baseball player, and loses all purpose and direction in life.

In forgoing baseball, Teddy loses his only meaningful, emotional connection to his father. Teddy suffers this figurative loss at exactly the same time at which he literally lost his mother. He lacks, therefore, the presence in his life of both idealized and mirroring selfobjects.

In the absence of human selfobjects, Teddy reverts back to the world of the nonhuman. In particular, he retreats into a fantasy world of things and activities that serve in his imagination as agents of magical control over his emotional life. Teddy becomes, in essence, a fantasy junkie and control freak. He substitutes an imaginary world, where he is in complete control, for the real world, where he feels useless and out of control. In a fashion analogous to Alice, who slips through the rabbit hole into Wonderland, Teddy passes through the swinging doors of the bar into his own version of a wonderland (see Sugerman, 1989, on the advent of the period of "sex, drugs, and rock 'n roll" in the 1960s and 1970s).

The barroom becomes for Teddy his only alternative to the baseball field. Ensconced happily in the barroom as his new playground, Teddy imagines himself as once again connected to both power and greatness. In an intoxicated state of mind, he experiences a simultaneous sense of pacification, tranquilization, and sedation as well as stimulation and inflation. Yet, no sooner has the alcohol worn off than Teddy finds himself tormented by painful feelings of inadequacy, impotence, and incompetence, thus necessitating still another round of drinking.

Earlier in his life, Teddy successfully masters the tools of his trade—that is, a baseball, a bat, and a mitt—as a means of achieving some semblance of a sense of self. These things and activities serve as transitional seltobjects that help Teddy to organize himself subjectively. In describing his days on the baseball field, Teddy recalls with fond memories that he was filled with fantasies of unlimited power and glory. If Teddy continued to successfully pursue his baseball career, it might have been possible for him to turn his fantasies into realities. Instead, Teddy settles for an unrealized fantasy of himself as a pro ball player, who competes in major league stadiums while his mother and father watch admiringly in the stands and dazzles them with one amazing play after another.

Sipping his drink on the barstool and lost in his own pleasurable reverie, Teddy manages to forget temporarily about all his woes and ills. Suddenly, he was no longer the abysmal failure he imagines himself to be for failing to follow in his father's footsteps both athletically and professionally. In an alcoholic stupor, Teddy entertains himself with narcissistic illusions of success in all areas of his life. In a drunken fugue state, he becomes the son whom he imagines his father had always wanted and whom his mother always worshipped while she was still alive. With drink in hand, Teddy is the supreme and almighty ruler of his own imaginary universe.

Before completing our discussion of the etiology and pathogenesis of Teddy's alcoholism, we must stress that Teddy's father mistreats him in a megalomaniacal manner throughout most of Teddy's life. At best, his father misuses Teddy as a narcissistic extension of himself, that is, a narcissistic artifact designed to embellish his father's own illusions of greatness. At worst, his father controls Teddy and abuses him as a nonentity with few, if any, redeeming qualities.

Off the baseball field, and later as his father's employee, Teddy learns unconsciously from his father to (mis)treat himself in an abusive and megalomaniacal manner. In his unconscious mind, Teddy imagines himself as little more than a functionary and commodity with mere semi-human status. In a self-destructive fashion typical of addicts,

Teddy abuses alcohol with little regard or concern for its deleterious (psychological and physical) consequences. At the lowest point in his addictive drinking (his "bottom" in the parlance of "recovery" from addiction), Teddy has so abused alcohol as to turn his life into a shambles.

Based on our bipolar self typology of addiction, we now diagnose Teddy as unipolar, subtype I. Although Teddy evidences some clinical signs of an empty, depleted depression, his major self disorder consists of disintegration anxiety stemming from a failed paternal idealization. We find symptomatic evidence of Teddy's tendency for fragmentation in his proclivity toward disintegration anxiety and his tendency toward panic and narcissistic rage.

Clearly, anxiety is for Teddy the presenting problem for which he sought psychotherapy. Thus, as evidenced by the need for an archaic idealization, we make an empathic inference that Teddy suffered extensive damage in the narcissistic pole of omnipotence as opposed to the narcissistic pole of grandiosity. Prior to his mother's death, she provided Teddy with a good basis for mirroring and a resulting capacity to keep himself from sinking too deeply into depression.

Massively arrested in his narcissistic capacity to use idealized selfobjects as antianxiety and pacifying agents, Teddy vainly seeks these same functions in alcohol. In this regard, Teddy is typical of those addicts who suffer from a unipolar type of self disorder. Characteristically, an addict with this type of disorder usually abuses only one ersatz selfobject rather than several ATMs at once. In contrast, addicts who suffer from the bipolar type of self disorder simultaneously abuse a number of different addictive things and activities.

Notwithstanding his mother's early mirroring presence, Teddy's father was almost completely oblivious to him off the baseball field. Hypercritical of him as an employee, his father evidences little empathy for Teddy and his plight; rather than appreciating Teddy's need for him to function as an idealized presence, and especially to compensate for the loss of his mother, Teddy's father becomes even more antipathetic toward him.

The fragile sense of male grandiosity on Teddy's part could not sustain him narcissistically in the total absence of his father as an idealized paternal figure with whom he could merge-in-fantasy as a male role model. Teddy is adrift in a sea of antipathy and self-hatred. Metaphorically speaking, he grabs onto drinking as a life preserver, only to find himself, paradoxically, drowning in an ocean of alcohol.

We believe that alcohol is on an unconscious fantasy level especially appealing for Teddy. As a thing, alcohol becomes a substitute for the previous and earlier functioning of a glove, a ball, and a bat, all of which previously serve as transitional selfobjects. And, as an activity, barroom drinking competes, albeit as a distant second, to the activity of mastering the skills of being a baseball player. Teddy is forced to give up his dream of becoming a gifted and admired athlete, and instead swaps stories with his drinking buddies about his former life as an up-and-coming sports hero. Teddy exists in the bottle, so to speak, where memories of the past and an anticipated future become poor substitutes for present and real accomplishments.

From our current self-psychological point of view, we see the psychotherapy of Teddy in a new and clearer light. In our original conceptualization, we viewed the psychotherapy as having proceeded on the basis of a psychoanalytic process we then called intersubjective absorption. We described the workings of this process as unfolding in the context of a particular transference–countertransference neurosis. In our early thinking, we did not go deep enough psychoanalytically into the unconscious fantasy psychodynamics that formed the core of the psychotherapy.

Looking back from the vantage point of our current model, we reconceptualize the psychotherapeutic process in terms of a narcissistic exchange process that is utilitarian in nature. As part of such a process, we discovered a megalomaniacal fantasy at the center of the transference of our addicted patients. As part of such a transference fantasy, an addicted patient imagines having illusory control over the psychotherapist as a (transitional selfobject) thing as well as the psychotherapy as a (transitional selfobject) activity.

Employing empathy, a psychotherapist shares such an intersubjective fantasy with an addicted patient. A patient uses the transference in a utilitarian fashion that allows for therapeutic dissociation based on psychopharmacotherapeutic relief. The transference-based reduction and/or cessation of psychic distress is based on it serving for an addicted patient as an agent of magical control, thus replacing the previous function of ATMs.

In applying the therapeutic component of our new model to the case of Teddy, we realize that the pedagogical nature of the psychotherapy—as manifested both within the sessions and in the extra-analytic setting of lectures and workshops—serves for Teddy as a transitional selfobject activity. In our original description, we made only passing mention of the clinical material relevant to this entire aspect of the psychotherapy. The therapist allows Teddy to use him as if he were a semi-human thing, and, in this instance, a talking dictionary. Teddy asks and the psychotherapist complies with his wish to use the dictionary as a means of increasing his vocabulary and enhancing his pronunciation. In this intersubjective context, the psychotherapist and dictionary blend for Teddy into one semi-human thing.

The psychotherapist also permits Teddy to take advantage of his knowledge and expertise in self psychology. In this sense, then, the complex and multifaceted nature of the pedagogical interaction between Teddy and the psychotherapist is essential to the eventual positive outcome of the psychotherapy. From a self-psychological perspective, the psychotherapist provides Teddy with the selfobject experience he has sought so doggedly yet vainly through his drinking.

Teddy and the psychotherapist participate intersubjectively in a shared fantasy that is a psychoanalytic replica of the positive vision of Teddy as a baseball player previously shared by Teddy and his father. By sharing in such intersubjective fantasy with the psychotherapist, Teddy resumes his aborted development at the stage of transitional selfobject usage.

However, there are at least two crucial differences between the early developmental and later psychotherapeutic versions of this shared or intersubjective fantasy. First, the intersubjective fantasy that Teddy and the psychotherapist share together in its psychoanalytic version is organized unconsciously on the basis of intellectual rather than athletic prowess. As a result, it has a much greater capacity for being transformed. Teddy's athletic abilities have waned as he grows older; however, his intellectual and cognitive capacities are still raw yet intact, and thus capable of further development. The psychotherapy taps into these potentials and helps Teddy organize himself on the basis of this new intersubjective matrix in terms of what he knows rather than what he does.

In the process, the psychotherapy provides Teddy with a much needed fantasy experience of being a megalomaniacal self and as wielding magical control over both the psychotherapist and the psycho-therapy. In the context of the psychoanalytic setting, Teddy's transference fantasy of illusory control is essential to his sense of overall emotional well-being. In gaining such relief, Teddy successfully exchanges alcohol for psychotherapy; the latter functions for him as a genuine, albeit nonhuman, selfobject. As an instance of the placebo effect, it provides him with psychopharmacotherapeutic relief from emotional distress.

In essence, this psychotherapeutic experience serves as a selfobject replacement for alcohol, which functioned not as a psychotropic and medicinal agent, but rather as a psychoactive and addictive substance. The transference fantasy of illusory control enables Teddy to have a necessary experience of therapeutic dissociation. However, this experience was quite different from the dissociative anesthetization that accompanies his addictive metamorphosis; it is palliative rather than addictive.

We have come now to a much better psychoanalytic understanding of the deeper, unconscious meaning of Teddy's recurring dream of sucking pleasurably at his mother's breast. In our original description of this dream, we focused on the more manifest meaning of the dream: that is, the obvious symbolic connection Teddy makes in his unconscious mind between the image of drinking his mother's milk as it flows from her breast and imbibing alcohol as it pours from the bottle.

At the present time, however, we believe that we failed to appreciate a much deeper and latent meaning to the dream. The selfobject transference has a decidedly paternal and idealizing quality to it. In this sense, therefore, it seems to us now that Teddy's dream-fantasy of nursing at his mother's breast may be interpreted as a symbolic equivalent to sitting at his father's knee and imbibing intellectual nourishment.

While growing up, Teddy was deprived by his father of having such an idealizing selfobject experience. Consequently, he depicts such a fantasized selfobject experience with the only unconscious imagery available to him, that is, a nursing experience. In sitting transferentially at the psychotherapist's knee, Teddy is soaking up wisdom and providing himself with "food for thought." In addition, his psychotherapeutic experience of himself, unlike his alcohol-fueled and static fantasy of himself as a (barroom) pundit, is based on a dynamic fantasy with great potential for transformation. Gradually and over time, Teddy with the help of the psychotherapist transforms this fantasy into a psychological reality as evidenced by his increased cognitive functioning and enhanced intellectual growth.

During his first round of psychotherapy Teddy remains with the male psychotherapist for a total of 10 years. (Teddy was in psychotherapy for only 4 years at the time of our original case write-up.) During the latter period of this 10-year span, we learned much of what we incorporate into our current model. However, the psychotherapist realizes that after 10 years in the same psychotherapy a change is necessary.

The psychotherapist concludes that Teddy has gone as far psychoanalytically as is possible with a male psychotherapist and, more specifically, with one whose subjectivity is organized unconsciously in terms of his own grandiosity. Prior to this point, the grandeur on the part of the psychotherapist dovetails nicely (that is, creates an intersubjective conjunction) with Teddy's need for the idealized presence of an omnipotent and omniscient father figure.

The psychotherapist discusses with Teddy the possibility of switching psychotherapists and proceeding in his psychotherapy with a female psychotherapist. Together, they decide that a woman rather than a man would have a much better chance of replicating a psychoanalytic version of Teddy's (mirroring selfobject) relationship with his mother. Hence, she, instead of a male psychotherapist, may be better able to help Teddy to work through the traumatic loss of his mother.

The latter phase of the psychotherapy with the original, male psychotherapist is very difficult for Teddy. It means that he has to face the reality that the psychotherapist is actually a human being with thoughts and feelings of his own. In addition, it implies that the psychotherapist is an agent that Teddy did not necessarily control in the manner in which he had always imagined.

Teddy is hard-pressed during this phase of psychotherapy; however, he manages to give up both his narcissistic illusions of the psychotherapist as a semi-human thing and of the psychotherapy as an activity totally under his control. Concomitantly, he makes considerable progress in his business career as well as his personal relationships, both of which are clear evidence of substantial psychic growth. He learns to operate in the business world in a fashion more commensurate with his functioning within psychotherapy, the latter being modeled itself after his earlier sports activities as a baseball player.

Now, and in contrast to the past, Teddy uses his intellect and his social skills as valuable tools and assets. He makes considerable strides in completing phase II of the narcissistic exchange process, (that is, in moving psychotherapeutically through the stage of transitional selfobject usage) and, in the process, proceeded into phase III.

Teddy remains in psychotherapy for approximately 5 more years with his new, female psychotherapist. He establishes and maintains a healthy, long-term relationship with a woman, an interpersonal achievement that previously has eluded him throughout the entire 10-year period of the first round of psychotherapy with his male psychotherapist. Teddy remains abstinent and sober throughout this long period of time, thus further substantiating the success of his two psychoanalytic psychotherapies. Of equal importance, Teddy's long-term abstinence and sobriety attest to the efficacy of our self-psychological approach to working psychotherapeutically with addicted patients.

Postscript

A number of years (approximately 10) after he formally terminates with his male psychotherapist (that is, a period of 20 years after he first began psychotherapy), Teddy briefly re-enters psychotherapy. This psychotherapy, which lasts for only about a year, is in and of itself quite unremarkable. Yet, this relatively brief period of time notwithstanding, this second round of psychotherapy with the male psychotherapist provides some further information that is worth reporting and discussing. First, despite the now very long passage of time since he first entered psychotherapy, Teddy is still sober and abstinent from alcohol. If nothing else, this fact alone lends additional credence to the viability of our self-psychological and intersubjective approach to psychoanalytic psychotherapy with an addicted patient.

Second, Teddy establishes and maintains a serious and long-term relationship with a woman with whom he is still living. This latter achievement attests, no doubt, to the value of his psychotherapy with the female psychotherapist. And third, for both diagnostic and psychopharmacological purposes, Teddy undergoes a complete battery of psychological testing—testing that is quite revealing and relevant for our purposes.

In discussing the results of Teddy's intellectual test scores, the testing psychologist reports:

> His performance abilities are much lower than his ability to dream [that is, fantasize] and conceptualize ideas. It is apparent that this would create much anxiety, frustration, and fear of failure once he is confronted with making a dream [i.e., fantasy] into a reality. His dream [i.e., fantasy] standards are high and his practical ability to deliver is far lower. (Inserted material added.)

Here, we have independent psychological test evidence that is supportive of one of our main assertions: namely, Teddy is representative of addicts in being a fantasy junkie.

Consistent with our contention that addicts are fantasy junkies who are lost in their own private version of Alice's Wonderland, the testing psychologist concludes that many of Teddy's personality traits "cloud his ability to perceive reality clearly despite the absence of a formal disturbance in reality testing."

From our perspective, we interpret this conclusion as indicative of the fact that Teddy suffers from an addictive rather than a psychotic disturbance in his relation to reality (that is, a "disturbance in reality testing"). From our vantage point, this is the crucial distinction between addictive and psychotic forms of megalomania.

Teddy is an addict and is not a psychotic. A psychotic suffers from a formal thought disorder as evidenced symptomatically, for example, in megalomaniacal *delusions*, such as those Freud (1958 [1911]) reports of Schreber. As part of such delusions, Schreber imagines himself, according to Freud, as the handmaiden of God, and hence, as close to being God. Teddy, in contrast, and as an addict, suffers from an inability to adequately distinguish and properly differentiate between fantasy and reality as evidenced characterologically in the megalomaniacal narcissistic illusion of a self as being megalomaniacal.

In the context of such archaic narcissistic fantasies, he imagines that he is in charge of psychoactive agents of magical control that allow him to entertain the illusion that he rules over his emotions and his emotional affairs. And, prior to his three rounds of psychotherapy, Teddy, as a prime example of the addictive character and Kohut's (1977a, p. 132) "Tragic Man," does not come remotely close to controlling his emotional life. Instead, Teddy is unable to manage his emotional life (that is, it has become unmanageable) and has lost even a semblance of control over it.

MARY

Overview

The case of Mary, a 28-year-old, depressed, bulimic, and laxative-abusing addicted patient, exemplifies several themes. Like the case of Teddy, it illustrates: (1) the powerful nature of an addicted patient's resistance to forming a selfobject transference; and (2) the ubiquitous presence in the psychoanalytic psychotherapy of many addicted patients of the transference–countertransference neurosis. However, in marked contrast to the psychotherapist in the case of Teddy, the psychotherapist in the case of Mary fails to successfully analyze and work through the unconscious fantasies determining this particular version of the transference–countertransference neurosis.

In the early phase of the psychotherapy, Mary presents herself in a timid and frightened manner. She speaks about herself in a particularly disparaging and contemptuous fashion. She constantly refers to herself in the most self-derogatory and self-loathing language. Consistent with her antipathy, she characterizes herself as worthless and as filled with filthy, dirty, and repulsive feelings.

Mary's presentation of herself as gross and disgusting constitutes an early resistance to a mirroring selfobject transference. Rather than exhibiting her archaic grandiose self for mirroring, Mary imagines herself as having to expose herself as "ungrandiose," and thereby as being not entitled to mirroring. The psychotherapist analyzes the narcissistically mortifying fantasy that determines Mary's unconscious resistance to the transference. In the process, he creates an intersubjective context in which Mary experiences the psychotherapy as gradually taking over (that is, absorbing) the selfobject—like functions derived previously from her abuse of food and laxatives.

The psychotherapist facilitates Mary's establishment of a selfobject transference fantasy in which she imagines herself as mirrored for her grandness. This selfobject experience provides her with a healthy alternative to the bulimia and laxative abuse. It also helps to alleviate her depressive sense of emptiness and depletion.

The psychotherapist communicates his empathy for Mary's narcissistically mortifying vision of herself in which she feels required and compelled to expose herself as despicable. In this empathic context, the psychotherapist points out to Mary that she is consumed by an unconscious dread of recreating a painful experience from the past with her mother. He explains to Mary that she assumes that he, like her mother, could neither tolerate her sense of greatness nor accept the exuberant mood that accompanies such a positive vision of herself.

The psychotherapist successfully counteracts Mary's unconscious attempt to re-enact the pathological psychodynamics that structured her early relationship with her mother. This earlier and pathogenic interaction led Mary to organize herself unconsciously in accordance with a mortifying fantasy of herself as despicable and repulsive. As such a loathsome thing, she feels exposed in all her defectiveness before her critical and disapproving mother.

Mary fills up addictively on food as her only way of counteracting this dreadful fantasy and its accompanying depressed mood. Then, she immediately lightens her load, both literally and figuratively, by purging with laxatives. By addictive means she induces a hypnotic-like fugue (i.e., the hypnoid defense) in which she feels artificially stimulated and lifted from her depressed mood.

Mary and the psychotherapist manage to maintain a transference fantasy of mirrored grandiosity. Using her selfobject experience within the transference, Mary fills up and lifts her spirits psychotherapeutically rather than gorging addictively on food and then as if by magic cleansing herself by abusing laxatives. She feels buoyed and far less weighted down by the heaviness of her depression. In this regard, the psychotherapy assumes the form of an intersubjective field, which serves as a symbolic medium or a virtual reality for absorbing the selfobject-like and antidepressant functioning of the bulimia and laxative abuse. (See Heim, 1993; Pesce, 2000; and Schell, 2000, on the concept of virtual reality as a realm for the expression of symbolic and magical thinking.)

Unfortunately, several factors combine to undermine Mary's progress. First, the psychotherapist takes a 3-week summer vacation; upon his return Mary has gone into a real tailspin. She complains bitterly about feeling abandoned and forsaken. She is quite enraged; yet she is unable to express her outrage directly. Instead, she suffers silently, but simmering all the while.

Second, the psychotherapist is quite distracted upon his return by his wife's prolonged and serious illness. His wife became and remained bedridden for a number of months. Under these difficult circumstances, he is required to assume many of her duties in caring for their children and maintaining the household.

The psychotherapist feels overwhelmed and is very anxious about his ability to manage his practice and family all at once. He is depressed about his situation and worries that he lacks the psychological where-withal to cope with everything. In this sense, the psychotherapist is experiencing a moderate degree of depression with symptoms of emptiness and depletion anxiety (that is, feelings of not having or being enough).

Together, Mary and the psychotherapist unconsciously enact their respective roles or parts in the transference–countertransference neurosis. On the one hand, Mary laments the loss of the psychotherapist as a figure in the transference whose attentiveness fills her with joy as she lights up his face with her mere presence. In the absence of this uplifting experience, she describes feeling exactly as she had when she was actively bulimic. In addition, she dreads relapsing.

On the other hand, the psychotherapist reacts countertransferentially with a further drop in his already sagging self-esteem to Mary's upset about losing him as her mirroring selfobject. He feels unable to rise emotionally above his low and quickly plummeting self-worth. On the contrary, he feels incredibly needy and turns unconsciously to Mary as his own mirroring selfobject and antidepressant agent. As an agent by which to inflate his grandiosity, he imagines that she will provide him with a desperately needed sense of relief from his own empty depression and depletion anxiety. In imagining Mary as his mirroring selfobject, the psychotherapist further disrupts her transference fantasy of him as her mirroring selfobject.

Then, adding insult to injury, the psychotherapist introduces the idea of using a tape recorder as part of the psychotherapy sessions. He explains to Mary that he wants to tape the sessions so as to study, and hence, better digest the material. In hindsight, it seems clear, however, that Mary does not accept his explanation.

Instead, Mary experiences the presence of a tape recorder in her sessions as grossly unempathic and as still another narcissistic blow. For Mary, the psychotherapist's use of a tape recorder is a further indication of his self-absorption and lack of empathy. In other words, for Mary it is an empathic failure. And, unfortunately, the psychotherapist does not adequately address or redress this failure in empathy.

The appearance on the scene of a boyfriend is a final factor in the premature demise of the psychotherapy. Paradoxically, and as a result of the initial benefits of the psychotherapy, Mary became involved romantically and sexually with a young man. In retrospect, it is apparent that his interest in her and attention serves selfobject functions similar to those previously provided by the psychotherapist.

Mary reports that she rejoices in her relationship with her boyfriend whose love, she says, really raises her spirits. In contrast, she speaks painfully of having lost her trust in the psychotherapist as well as her confidence in his ability to function for her as he has in the past. Feeling as she does, Mary chooses to leave psychotherapy rather than attempt to work through the serious empathic failure that has disrupted and ruptured the selfobject transference.

Commentary

Phenomenologically, we now view Mary's bulimia and laxative abuse as part of an addictive metamorphosis. As part of her addictive state of mind, she flip-flops from a dreadful and mortifying fantasy state to a blissful and rapturous fantasy state. She abuses food and laxatives as

ATMs, which temporarily relieve her of feelings of worthlessness, emptiness, and depletion. She describes her sense of satiation and subsequent evacuation in a way that suggests the presence of psychoactive fantasy tapes. Apparently, in the context of bingeing and purging, Mary imagines herself as lifting herself magically above her depression and anxiety.

The combination of food and laxatives serves for Mary, however poorly and addictively, as a desperately needed source of antidepressant and antianxiety relief. In typical bulimic fashion, Mary abuses food because of its power to satiate and thus relieve both depression and anxiety. In addition, the laxatives provide Mary with an illusory experience in which she feels freed magically of all her disgusting and repulsive feelings. In the midst of her binge–purge cycle, Mary undergoes an addictive metamorphosis triggered by grandiose fantasies and accompanying moods of uplifting ecstasy.

As part of her Narcissus complex, Mary flip-flops from a mortifying fantasy state of herself as ungrandiose and hence as unmirrorable to a blissful fantasy state of herself as possessed of bountiful grandeur. In such an addictive state of mind, Mary's mood also changes dramatically; it flip-flops from one of despair to one of exuberance.

The narcissistic illusion on Mary's part of well-being is triggered by an addictive transmogrification that finds its deepest unconscious roots in a fantasy of being a megalomaniacal self and as capable of magically controlling all her emotions as well as those of others. In recounting her episodes of bingeing and purging, Mary uses language and imagery that clearly convey her illusory belief that these behaviors endow her with magical powers. So endowed, she imagines that she is capable of radically altering her basic state of being, that is, her psychic reality. Under the influence of this addictive spell, she fantasizes herself as the supreme ruler of (rather than as the victim of) her emotional worlds. In this context, she speaks in an almost reverential tone of her abuse of food and laxatives.

In contrast, Mary experiences the rough and tumble world of human relations quite differently. Mary's descriptions of her interactions with others indicates that she has not yet reached a stage of development in which it is possible for her to relate to others as fully human. Instead, she remains arrested developmentally at a stage in which she treats everyone, including herself, as a semi-human thing or part of a nonhuman activity. The arena of human affairs makes it difficult for Mary to entertain her fantasies of being a megalomaniacal self and illusions of controlling her emotional affairs.

As an example of her difficulty in conducting normal human inter-actions, Mary relates that she has trouble as a saleswoman in dealing with finicky customers. Mary finds it hard to follow the old sales adage that the "customer is always right." This motto runs counter to her unconscious desire to exercise her megalomaniacal domination over others as if they are mannequins or dummies.

Mary frequently reacts to particularly persnickety customers by becoming incensed (narcissistically enraged) at what she experiences as their audacity. Thereafter, she immediately becomes consumed by feel-ings of shame and self-loathing. Mary explains that she hates herself for losing control of her temper in reaction to demanding customers whose reactions she could neither control nor tolerate. In this regard, the normal interaction between Mary and her customers interferes with and disrupts her fantasy of herself as being megalomaniacal.

Mary has little tolerance or patience for the whims of others; she exclaims that she much prefers food and laxatives to people—the former seem to her to do her bidding, whereas the latter exercise wills of their own. Unfortunately, we had not yet discovered in treating Mary the significance of megalomania in understanding addiction. This contributes to the psychotherapist's difficulty in empathically grasping the unconscious meaning of Mary's fantasy of being a megalomaniacal self as magically controlling the emotional nature of her psychotherapy.

A prime example of this pattern of empathic failure involves the psychotherapist's insistence on using the tape recorder during the latter part of the psychotherapy. The psychotherapist fails to realize that Mary might experience the psychotherapist as asserting emotional control over her as a result of his using the recorder to tape the sessions. He does not appreciate that such an action on his part might destroy her narcis-sistic illusion of complete control over the nature of the emotional interactions between her and the psychotherapist. The psychotherapist fails, therefore, to understand the imperative need on Mary's part to entertain the illusion that she, rather than the psychotherapist, is in charge of her psychotherapy.

In such an unempathic environment, Mary acts out her megaloma-niacal need for total control by impulsively and abruptly ending psy-chotherapy. The psychotherapist is completely bewildered and at a loss as to the reason that motivates Mary unconsciously to leave psychother-apy. Lacking in an empathic understanding of the threat to Mary's megalomaniacal illusion of magical control, the psychotherapist feels compelled to sit by idly when Mary seemingly without reason drops out of treatment.

In our original case report, we do not pay enough attention to the topic of etiology and pathogenesis. However, we do know some of the important details of Mary's early life, and, more specifically, we have pertinent information concerning the nature of her interaction with her mother. These facts shed some light on the etiological origins and psychogenic course of her eating disorder.

For instance, we know that Mary's mother teaches her as a little girl to sew, hem, and to do needlepoint. We believe that Mary's involvement with her mother in these activities is indicative of her passing developmentally from phase I to phase II of the narcissistic exchange process. She uses needle and thread as transitional selfobject things and sewing as a transitional selfobject activity, which together instills within her an early sense of her own grandness and competence.

However, Mary is unable to move developmentally from phase II to phase III of the narcissistic exchange process. She relates in excruciating detail how her mother (mis)treats her as if she were a professional seamstress rather than as a little girl trying to have fun as she learned to sew. According to Mary, her mother becomes enraged if Mary fails to pay strict attention to her mother's elaborate sewing instructions. Any sign of the slightest distraction on Mary's part is justification for a harsh rebuke from her mother.

Furthermore, Mary describes sitting motionless for hours as her mother uses (and more accurately *misuses*) her for the purposes of creating "cute, little" outfits for Mary to wear. It is obvious from Mary's description that she feels like a mannequin, who serves no other purpose for her mother than to function as a mock-up dummy. In recalling these experiences, Mary laments that she felt reduced in her status as a human to being only semi-human at best.

Based on these painful and early memories, we arrive at the following empathic inference: Mary is treated narcissistically (that is, megalomaniacal) by her mother as an extension or part of herself rather than as a little girl in her own right. In this context, her mother makes Mary feel like she is nothing more than an (narcissistic) artifact or functionary.

In this intersubjective setting, Mary comes to share unconsciously in her mother's megalomaniacal fantasy of her as a thing-like entity rather than as a human being. Mary becomes an adult who is far more comfortable with the nonhuman in dramatic contrast to the human.

Mary's preference for the nonhuman is indicative of her inability to progress developmentally to phase III of the narcissistic exchange process. She is unable to make this crucial developmental leap because her mother is emotionally unavailable to her as a human selfobject whom Mary feels would respond emotionally to her assertion of control. The lack of empathy, if not outright antipathy, on the part of Mary's mother toward her prevents Mary from psychically re-investing narcissistic capital in her relationship with her mother as well as, later in life, other human beings.

Instead, her mother imagines that Mary is emotionally under her control as part of her megalomaniacalal fantasy of Mary as a nonhuman entity. Under the spell of this narcissistic illusion, Mary's mother imagines that Mary is tied to her as if by a psychic cord, and hence is under emotional control. She seems to have little empathy for Mary's feelings or desires regarding emotional control over herself (and her body), let alone exercising emotional control over her mother. Unconsciously, Mary incorporates her mother's antipathetic attitude toward her and comes, later in life, to treat both herself and others in a similar antipathetic fashion.

Mary has a distinct recollection, both as a child and as an adolescent, that her mother treats her as if she is a sensitive piece of equipment or an apparatus by which her mother attempts to control their emotional interaction. More specifically, as Mary grows up she imagines that she operates for her mother as if she is an emotional Geiger counter or thermostat. She recalls that if the situation gets too hot emotionally between the two of them—meaning that Mary gets too excited and overwrought (that is, is experienced by her mother as being out of control)—her mother treats Mary like she is a Geiger counter that needs to be turned off or a thermostat that needs to be adjusted.

In this sense, therefore, Mary does not even function for her mother as a human selfobject; rather, she serves as *something* that is merely selfobject-like. In this unempathic and antipathetic environment, Mary grows up imagining herself as if she is a semi-human entity whose electrical impulses and mechanical stirrings are emotionally too hot to handle. Thus, her mother (mis)treats Mary throughout her formative years *as if* she is something less than human. As a result, Mary grows to experience herself as semi-human and as an automaton that is controlled in its reactions by someone else.

Mary carries over her mother's megalomaniacal attitude toward her own emotional life. However, Mary even goes one step further than her mother in turning herself by addictive means into an imaginary gadget by which to control all emotionality. Forsaking other people, Mary seeks refuge instead in food and laxatives. In a fashion similar to her mother, Mary (mis)treats herself as if she is nothing more than a mechanical apparatus. Imagining herself as a machine, Mary fuels herself with food and gives herself a regular cleaning with laxatives to remove all the dirt and grime.

We now diagnose Mary, in terms of our self-psychological typology, as unipolar, subtype I. The psychic epicenter of Mary's emotional upset is located in the area of her depressive sense of herself as devoid of anything good inside of her. In this regard, Mary worries incessantly about lacking in basic goodness. She is organized unconsciously in accordance with a mortifying fantasy of herself as being totally disgusting inside.

Mary abuses food and laxatives in an unsuccessful attempt to counteract her dreadful sense of herself. In food and the laxatives, Mary discovers substances that simultaneously alleviate her depressive sense of emptiness and anxious feelings of depletion. Gorging on food provides her with an illusionary sense of being filled with goodies. And, as soon as she feels disgusted about having stuffed herself with food, she purges with laxatives, and, in her imagination, magically cleanses herself of her repulsive feelings.

From a typological point of view, it seems abundantly clear that the basic damage to Mary's sense of self takes place in terms of the narcissistic pole involving mirrored grandiosity. We do not know much about Mary's father and her relationship with him. Mary's father remained a mystery figure throughout the somewhat and relatively abbreviated and aborted psychotherapy.

Nonetheless, we suspect that Mary established some selfobject pathway organized compensatorily around her father. Such an avenue enabled her to experience some degree of merger with an idealized and omnipotent paternal figure. We base our speculation on two factors.

First, we do not find any significant clinical evidence of serious damage to the pole of the self organized unconsciously on the basis of merger with an idealized and omnipotent selfobject. If there were such damage, we would expect to see more clinical evidence in Mary of either a mixed state or true bipolarity. On the contrary, although Mary does evidence some signs of anxiety, it is of a purely depletion (rather than disintegration) type, as is often found in an empty/depleted depression.

Second, in the early part of the psychotherapy, Mary uses the psychotherapist as a conduit by which to return to the world of human beings. Her return is signaled later in the psychotherapy by her ability to engage in a successful relationship with her boyfriend. We believe that the psychotherapist serves in some way as a selfobject stand-in for her otherwise shadowy father. In establishing a relationship with her boyfriend, Mary takes full advantage of her interaction with the psychotherapist, whom she imagines as a somewhat disembodied paternal presence.

However, Mary does not pass psychotherapeutically through phase II of the narcissistic exchange process. Instead, she leap-frogs over this phase, and, in so doing, jumps into a relationship with her boyfriend. Hence, Mary bypasses the psychotherapist as a fully human selfobject in preference for her boyfriend.

As regards the psychotherapy, we now have a much better understanding of the unconscious forces that organize the transference–countertransference neurosis. We also appreciate the way in which this intersubjective configuration simultaneously interferes with the narcissistic exchange process and leads to the premature cessation of the psychotherapy. At this time, the psychotherapist does not possess our current understanding of the significance of both megalomania and the intersubjective nature of the narcissistic exchange process. Nonetheless, he still helps Mary to swap food and laxatives for psychotherapy.

Early in the psychotherapy, the psychotherapist concentrates on working through Mary's unconscious resistance to the transference. His success in this endeavor makes it easier for Mary to imagine herself as exercising emotional control over the psychotherapy. A megalomaniacal illusion of magical control allows Mary to give up her dependence on food and laxatives. It also helps her to replace these psychoactive agents with reliance on the psychopharmacotherapeutic effects of the psychotherapy as performed by the ministrations of the psychotherapist.

Imagining herself as in emotional control also makes it possible for Mary to experience herself as mirrored by the therapist for her grandeur. The combination of the megalomania and grandiosity provides Mary with the psychopharmacotherapeutic effect that she so desperately needed. More specifically, the selfobject transference fantasy of magical control enables Mary to generate a particular psychopharmacotherapeutic effect in the form of a dual antidepressant boost and antianxiety calming. Together, these psychopharmacotherapeutic effects create the clinical conditions under which Mary experiences a necessary therapeutic dissociation from her emotional pain.

Mary makes a major psychic shift in replacing food and laxatives with the therapeutic action of the psychotherapy. Mary relinquishes her illusion of addictive substances as agents of magical control over her emotional world. Mary is no longer dependent on these ATMs, and thus can take utilitarian advantage of the psychotherapeutic process. In so doing, she enters therapeutically into phase II of the narcissistic exchange process.

Unfortunately, the psychotherapy breaks down before Mary can successfully complete the second phase of this process. The tape recorder symbolizes for Mary that she is once again being forced to submit emotionally to the megalomaniacal control of another. In retrospect, we now contend that Mary fantasizes transferentially that she is being maltreated and abused by the psychotherapist as she had been by her mother in the past.

Mary believes that the therapist is more interested in the tape recorder and taping the sessions than he is in Mary and her feelings. From her subjective perspective, Mary feels reduced to the status of a contraption manipulated by and at the disposal of another. In the past, she felt like her mother's Geiger counter or thermostat; now she feels like an accoutrement in relation to the psychotherapist's recording equipment.

Nonetheless, the psychotherapeutic conditions were still present by which the psychotherapist could have attempted to replicate Mary's utilitarian involvement with the transitional selfobject activities of sewing and needlepoint. Psychotherapeutically, it could have been possible for the psychotherapist to involve Mary in some symbolic activity by which to generate an intersubjective fantasy shared by Mary and the psychotherapist. For instance, Mary and the psychotherapist could have joined together in a symbolic activity analogous in unconscious meaning to the pedagogical activity shared by Teddy and his psychotherapist.

In the case of Mary, the psychotherapist countertransferentially placed his own narcissistic needs and desires above those of his patient. Unknowingly, he has replicated, therefore, the pathogenic psychodynamics of Mary's deleterious interaction with her mother. The psychotherapist is too preoccupied by his own personal concerns; consequently, he fails to consider adequately the potential psychological damage he might inflict on Mary and her psychotherapy by introducing the use of a tape recorder.

Countertransferentially, the psychotherapist is too self-absorbed, and, in this sense, is lost in a state of his own dissociative anesthesia. As he entertains megalomaniacal illusions of exercising magical control over Mary and her emotions, he becomes benignly oblivious to her subjective state. In this intersubjective setting, Mary comes to experience the psychotherapist like her mother. She feels that he requires her to monitor her feelings closely like a Geiger counter or thermostat, and thereby keep them safely under control.

In the end, Mary refuses to submit to a countertransference replication of her mother's megalomaniacal stance toward her. She gathers her courage and saves herself from the ordeal of being enslaved and reduced once again to the nonhuman status of an automaton. In the final analysis, her exit from psychotherapy must be seen as an act of bravery and self-preservation.

Chapter 5

The Second of the Addiction Paper Trilogy: The Cases of Joe and JoAnn

JOE

Overview

The case of Joe, a 40-year-old alcoholic, Vietnam combat veteran, revolves around a transference–countertransference neurosis organized unconsciously on the basis of idealization and omniscience. Since his return from Vietnam, Joe has been drinking alcoholically and has made several serious suicide attempts. He blames himself for the death of a buddy who bled to death in a foxhole, where Joe felt compelled to leave him in order to save his own life as he retreated from the enemy.

After returning from Vietnam, Joe has been haunted by the statement that a medic made to him regarding the death of his buddy. Upon returning to the foxhole in the aftermath of the firefight, Joe and a medic found the body of his buddy. The medic said to Joe: "If someone had been with this man to stop the bleeding ... he would have lived!" Joe interpreted the medic's statement as a severe rebuke and as an admonishment of him for his decision to retreat and save himself. Thereafter, he has been filled with an all-consuming shame about what he took as incontrovertible proof of his cowardice.

In the post-Vietnam years, Joe started drinking alcoholically, apparently in the false hope of dousing the burning sense of shame he feels about his cowardice. He describes himself disparagingly as a despicable coward who had lost his courage in battle. He explains that he became so overwhelmed by fear and terror during the fateful firefight that he fled rather than confront the enemy and possibly risk his own life.

Joe is adamant in insisting that he disgraced all those who fought with honor during the war. As far as he is concerned, he declares, he is a "worthless piece of junk" who "should be dumped at the local scrap yard." In other words, apparently Joe feels like a broken and useless item that does not deserve to exist any longer. However, it is unclear whether Joe wants to kill himself outright or just slowly drink himself to death. This is an example of the way in which addiction may be viewed as a form of suicide.

Joe suffers from all of the typical symptoms of posttraumatic stress disorder (PTSD), including recurrent traumatic nightmares. In a particularly disturbing nightmare, Joe relives the scene in which the medic rebukes and admonishes him for abandoning his wounded buddy. Joe notes that he always awakes from this nightmare filled with searing self-hatred. And, his self-loathing spurs his drinking bouts as well as suicide attempts. It seems that Joe imagines that he is atoning for his sin of cowardice by doing away with himself.

Initially, Joe encountered the therapist during a routine discharge session at a Veterans health care system facility, where Joe was hospitalized for alcoholism, depression, as well as for having made several suicide attempts. His most recent hospitalization is only one of many similar hospitalizations and alcohol detoxifications that Joe has undergone in the postwar period. The psychotherapist who was working at that time as a staff psychologist in the outpatient clinic of the Veterans health care system had been assigned to set up aftercare planning with Joe.

During their initial discharge session, the psychotherapist says that he suspects that Joe is deeply troubled by something that took place during combat. Joe is flabbergasted by what he takes as the psychotherapist's ability to "read my mind." Without hesitation, Joe immediately sets up a regular psychotherapy appointment with the psychotherapist. Joe remains in psychotherapy with the psychotherapist for several years.

Early in the psychotherapeutic relationship, Joe presents the psychotherapist with a handsome gift as a token of his gratitude. He gives the psychotherapist a personalized, wooden plaque on which he spells out in beautifully carved out letters the psychotherapist's first and last names. According to Joe, the plaque is meant to express the high regard in which he holds the psychotherapist, whom he imagines as having so quickly read his mind.

Joe explains that his belief in the psychotherapist's ability to read his mind makes it easier for him to describe the incident in which he abandons his buddy, who as a result bleeds to death. Relieved of this tremendous burden, Joe feels spared the excruciating ordeal of having to expose himself before the psychotherapist as a loathsome coward. The psychotherapist accepted the plaque without, however, grasping fully that it signals, both literally and figuratively, the psychotherapeutic unfolding of the narcissistic exchange process.

Joe's unconscious fantasy of the psychotherapist's omniscience (that is, his mind reading ability) is the basis for an idealizing selfobject transference. Empathically, the psychotherapist understands that Joe desperately needs the selfobject experience based on this transference fantasy. The psychotherapist believes that the transference fantasy could become the psychoanalytic means by which Joe could eventually give up alcohol. The psychotherapist thinks that Joe might experience the selfobject merger with him, a personal presence that he clearly idealized as omniscient, as powerful enough to replace and take over (that is, intersubjectively absorb) the antianxiety and pacifying functions of alcohol (an addictive trigger mechanism, or ATM). The psychotherapist anticipates Joe might feel better about himself in the context of the idealizing transference, and thus hopefully feel less like doing away with himself.

And, fortunately, the hopes of the psychotherapist are realized. Indeed, Joe does give up alcohol and maintains his abstinence for 10 months. This is the longest span of time Joe has not abused alcohol. In the afterglow of his newly established abstinence, Joe displays himself proudly before the psychotherapist, whom he desperately wants to impress with the fortitude of his courage in stopping his abuse of alcohol. The pride in his accomplishment helps, he proclaims, to compensate for the intense pain he still experiences in connection to the feeling that he acted in a cowardly and despicable fashion during combat.

During the 10-month period of abstinence from alcohol, Joe and the psychotherapist talk a lot about his early life prior to Vietnam. Joe tells the psychotherapist that his mother had died during childbirth and that he was raised by his father and a stepmother. Although not especially close to either of his parents, Joe indicates that he developed some meaningful emotional contact with his father through a shared interest in woodworking. As a young child, and later as an adolescent, Joe spends hours and hours with his father, literally at his father's knee, in the woodworking shop learning all about the craft. Joe recalls with great fondness how his father teaches him to use all the different hand and power tools essential to woodworking.

For the most part, the memories of the time that Joe spent with his father in the woodworking shop are extremely pleasant. He and his father do not talk much about anything really personal; however, they do spend a great deal of time going over the various ins-and-outs of woodworking.

The description by Joe of himself in this setting suggests to the psychotherapist that Joe has merged-in-fantasy with his father whom he idealizes as a master craftsman. According to Joe, he is absolutely convinced that his father knows all there is to know about woodworking. In essence, Joe idealizes his father as omniscient and all-knowing in general, and especially as regards woodworking.

A particularly painful yet revealing memory stands out, however, for Joe about those years with his father in the woodworking shop. As a youngster, Joe accidentally cut one of his fingers while using a power tool. His finger is bleeding profusely and Joe's father rushes him to a nearby hospital emergency room.

In recounting the event, Joe remembers distinctly that his father seriously considers two alternatives: the first is that of having the finger surgically repaired, the second is that of having it amputated. Joe recalls that his father weighs the two options based partially on the relative cost of each. In the end, his father decides to have Joe's finger operated on rather than having it cut off. It goes without saying that Joe wants to save his finger; however, he indicates that he would have acquiesced without question had his father decided to have his finger amputated.

As interpreted by Joe and the psychotherapist, the unconscious meaning of this incident reveals that Joe takes his belief that "father knows best" quite literally. He is willing to lose his finger rather than question his father's right to decide his fate. Apparently, Joe is prepared to make a physical sacrifice of a valued part of his body as the cost of deferring unquestioningly to his father's authority. It went without saying that for Joe his father, whom he idealizes as omniscient, has the requisite knowledge necessary to decide for him all matters, even those involving whether he keeps or loses his own finger.

The psychotherapist understands Joe's selfobject fantasy of his omniscience as a transference manifestation of Joe's archaic idealization of his father. Joe imagines that both his father and the psychotherapist are all-knowing, and, hence, in Joe's mind they automatically know the right answer to every question. Joe firmly believes that his mission in life is simply to follow their decisions unquestioningly. In the process, however, he deprives himself of the opportunity of developing his own decision-making capacity. As a result, he neither trusts nor has confidence in those few decisions—for instance, the one involving his war buddy—he is forced to make for himself.

The psychotherapist helps Joe to appreciate why the medic's condemnation of his decision to leave his wounded buddy behind has been so devastating for Joe. The psychotherapist explains to Joe that he has ended up second-guessing himself because of his basic mistrust and lack of confidence in his own judgment. The psychotherapist points out to Joe that in all probability he would have died along with his buddy had he stayed behind in the foxhole.

The medic had presumed that Joe could have kept himself alive in the foxhole to tend to his wounded buddy. Instinctively, Joe flees from the foxhole, assuming that fleeing is his only means of surviving. Literally staring death in the face, Joe decides that his first duty is to save himself rather than to risk his own life in a heroic, yet perhaps foolhardy and futile, effort to save his wounded buddy. The psychotherapist tells Joe that unfortunately sometimes combat requires that one decide to save oneself at the expense of a buddy.

Joe is amazed at the psychotherapist's seemingly fantastic ability to read new meaning into the past. On his own, Joe has never questioned the logic of the medic's position. On the contrary, he has always assumed, without hesitation, that the medic was justified in condemning him. Now, he takes over as his own the psychotherapist's new and quite different reading of his fateful decision. Gradually, he reports, he begins to feel relieved of the emotionally crushing burden of shouldering alone the weighty secret of his supposed cowardice.

Despite this major psychotherapeutic breakthrough, events conspired to undermine Joe's considerable progress. Without any warning and with no apparent provocation, Joe's wife leaves him, taking their children with her. Apparently, Joe's wife has gotten fed up with his seeming obliviousness to the emotional well-being of his family. She has complained for years, according to Joe, about the constant moves to ever more rural and remote areas, where Joe seeks to find refuge from the constant pressure of socializing with others.

Joe explains that being around other people only serves to intensify his already painful feeling of cowardice; being in the company of others makes him feel even more like some kind of low-life creature who is barely human. He prefers isolating himself in his woodworking shop, where he feels more comfortable. Alone in the safe confines of his own space, Joe can entertain pleasant daydreams about the "good ole days" before his buddy died in combat.

Joe's imperative need to isolate himself from everyone, including his own family, also complicates his business dealings. No sooner has Joe established himself as a skilled craftsman in a new locale than does he quickly find himself besieged by customers seeking his woodworking services. Emotionally, Joe cannot handle the constant human contact necessitated by interaction with his customers. Seeking refuge, he impulsively closes his shop and retreats as he did in combat to spare himself.

Naturally, by closing down his shop, Joe loses many potential customers, thus considerably reducing his income. And, of course, the loss of earnings adversely affects his ability to serve as the family breadwinner. He knows that his wife has been severely disappointed in him; he imagines that the psychotherapist too shares her disapproval of him.

From a psychoanalytic perspective, the psychotherapist explores with Joe the unconscious meaning behind his conviction that the psychotherapist harbors a secret disappointment in Joe as a result of his failure as a successful wage earner. Together, they talk about the possible connection between Joe's mistaken belief about the psychotherapist and the incident in which he allows his father to decide about the fate of his injured finger. It seems that Joe has thought unconsciously that the psychotherapist is just like his father: thus, the psychotherapist, like his father, requires of Joe a sacrifice of a valuable part of himself (in this instance his own decision-making capacity) as the steep price for continued approval from a male authority figure.

The psychotherapist points out, however, that there is a critical difference between the present and the past. He notes that the sacrifice for Joe in the present psychotherapeutic context concerns the loss for him of face with the psychotherapist following the departure of Joe's wife, who sees him as a failure both as a businessman and as a wage earner. Apparently, Joe worries that the psychotherapist shares his wife's low opinion of him and feels threatened that the psychotherapist would cut off approval as Joe's father had seriously considered cutting off his finger.

The psychotherapist also connects the medic's reprimand in the past with Joe's current dread of the psychotherapist's disapproval. It seems that Joe mistakenly assumes that the psychotherapist like the medic would question as selfish and cowardly his decision to spare himself at the expense of his family. The psychotherapist empathically understands that Joe believes that he is perceived by others as lacking in bravery and always acting in a cowardly fashion.

The psychotherapist dates back to the early finger injury to Joe's chronic lack of trust in his own judgment about his physical and emotional welfare. The memory of this incident reveals the following: Joe defers unquestioningly to the judgment of an authority figure, even to the point of sacrificing a valuable part of himself. As a result, Joe seems to fail to appreciate the courage he displayed in subsequent situations (for example, his war buddy). In a split second, he was forced to make a life-and-death decision about saving himself at the expense of his buddy. Rather than trusting in the wisdom of choice, Joe has succumbed to second guessing and condemning himself.

In this context, it is easy to understand why Joe falls into a deep depression after his wife takes their children and leaves him. Almost immediately, Joe once again second-guesses himself and quickly resumes his alcoholic drinking. The psychotherapist, who is shaken and unnerved by Joe's drinking relapse, fears another alcohol-induced suicide attempt.

Somewhat panic-stricken, the psychotherapist tries in vain to counteract the criticisms Joe's wife has leveled against him. He offers Joe what amounts to faint praise and hollow platitudes. Joe responds by complaining bitterly that the psychotherapist fails grossly to appreciate that Joe is truly a "worthless piece of junk"—both as a husband and as a father.

The psychotherapist sympathetically reassures Joe, however, countertransferentially more out of concern for himself than out of empathy for Joe. Understandably, the psychotherapist has panicked because of the very real possibility that Joe might make another, and perhaps this time fatal, suicide attempt. Unfortunately, the psychotherapist's countertransference sympathy (rather than empathy) has the unintended (and opposite) effect of undermining Joe's transference fantasy of the psychotherapist as omniscient. Rather than reassuring and comforting Joe, the psychotherapist unwittingly causes Joe to lose faith in the psychotherapist's ability to grasp his true essence as a selfish coward. Imagining that the therapist has lost sight of his lack of bravery, Joe feels compelled to expose himself once more before the psychotherapist (and the world) in all his despicable cowardliness.

Following still another hospitalization, Joe and the psychotherapist gradually work through this version of a transference–countertransference neurosis. Jointly, they realize that Joe has reacted to his wife's condemnation of him in exactly the same way as he responded to the medic's reprimand. In Joe's opinion, his wife and the medic are totally justified in their unempathic and even antipathetic condemnation of him.

Having just lost his family, the last response that Joe needs from the psychotherapist is his unempathic sympathy. Paradoxically, Joe desperately needs the psychotherapist to communicate his empathy with Joe's own self-condemnation and antipathy toward himself. In a seemingly ironic twist, had the psychotherapist been more empathic and less sympathetic then Joe might have felt spared the emotionally weighty burden of bearing alone the pain of his sense of himself as a lowly coward.

As the psychotherapist successfully redresses his empathic failure, Joe feels freed of shouldering all of the emotional weight stemming from his shameful sense of cowardliness. He adopts a less critical and antipathetic stance toward himself for having unavoidably contributed to losing his family. Acknowledging his serious limitations as a husband and father, he recognizes that, nonetheless, despite these shortcomings, he attempts to provide for his family—both financially and emotionally—to the best of his ability, limited though that may be.

In the absence of the psychotherapist as an all-knowing figure, Joe returns to the narcissistic bliss of an alcohol-induced state of addictive metamorphosis in which he feels simultaneously calmed and taken out of his misery. At the time, the psychotherapist conceives of alcohol as an ATM, which serves as a psychoactive agent that Joe endows in his unconscious mind as a magical elixir and possessed of antianxiety powers. In this phantasmagorical capacity, alcohol triggers a hypnoid and trance-like state in which Joe experiences both tranquilization and sedation.

The psychotherapist helps Joe to re-establish his (selfobject) fantasy of the psychotherapist as omniscient, which once again enables Joe to give up his reliance on the psychoactive effects of alcohol. For Joe, the re-emergence of the psychotherapist in the transference as an idealized and all-knowing presence serves as a replacement for alcohol, taking over its psychoactive functioning. In a sense, Joe's narcissistic illusion of the psychotherapist as an amazing mind reader frees him transferentially from the need to condemn and loathe himself. In this regard, the psychotherapy provides Joe with psychopharmacotherapeutic relief, which is far more effective than alcohol for his misery and suffering.

Joe reports a dream that he and the psychotherapist interpret as symbolic of his renewed (selfobject) bond with the psychotherapist. In the dream, Joe walks down a street with his combat buddy as they kid with one another and enjoy each other's company. On the level of dream–fantasy, Joe has brought his combat buddy back to life, however, now transferentially in the person of the psychotherapist. In re-evaluating his fateful decision, Joe has finally begun to appreciate the wisdom and courage that he exhibited in deciding to save himself.

Commentary

Now we have a better understanding of the phenomenology of alcohol as it functions in Joe's unconscious fantasy life. Originally, we discussed alcohol on the basis of its capacity to function as a magical substance that Joe unconsciously fantasizes as an idealized agent endowed with antianxiety powers of tranquilization and sedation. We now surmise that Joe imagines himself as a megalomaniacal self and as possessing control over a magical elixir, the imbibing of which induces a state of dissociation and anesthetization. We viewed alcohol in this regard as an ATM, which for Joe has a powerful dissociating and anesthetizing effect.

As a result of its psychoactive effect on the brain, alcohol activates unconscious fantasies that provide Joe with an illusory experience of merger with an idealized and omniscient presence. On the basis of this archaic narcissistic fantasy, Joe feels joined by a force greater than himself. Joe is no longer mortified, under the influence of such an intoxicating fantasy, by his own cowardice; instead, he is phantasmagorically transmogrified in his own imagination into a superhero of larger-than-life proportions. This fantasy of himself as being a megalomaniacal self that wields magical control is the crux of the Narcissus complex in the case of Joe.

In the language of our current model, we construe alcohol as serving for Joe a number of selfobject-like functions. In abusing alcohol, we believe that Joe undergoes an addictive metamorphosis in which he imagines himself as merged with magalomanical forces over which he exercises magical control. Weeping and sobbing as part of his alcohol-induced stupor, Joe conjures up idyllic scenes in which he is once again in the presence of his beloved combat buddy. And, in the past, Joe and his buddy did indeed share many good times together. For instance, they often spent time drinking and carousing while on "R & R," that is, a brief respite from battle in the form of some rest and relaxation.

In contrast to alcohol, we realize that Joe's buddy serves a number of important and genuine selfobject functions for him. Like his father, Joe looks up to his buddy as an all-knowing and protective figure. In this regard, Joe's buddy serves as an idealized selfobject for Joe in whose presence Joe imagines himself as merged-in-fantasy with the omniscient. Joe feels as part of this phantasmagorical self-state possessed of a courage and strength he otherwise feels he lacks. Joe's buddy inspired within him the courage to face the horrors of war.

Seeing his buddy lying mortally wounded in the foxhole shook Joe and forced him to rely on his own judgment. Without his buddy, Joe feels compelled to make a snap decision about a life-and-death matter. Thereafter, Joe, who lacks confidence in his own decision-making abilities, tortures himself relentlessly by second-guessing himself.

Joe's sense of himself as a coward is shame-based; he feels that without his buddy he lacks the courage and fortitude necessary to face the enemy single-handedly. Before his buddy is mortally wounded, Joe has both shared in and borrowed courage from his buddy. Joe employs his buddy's courage as if it is a loan on the basis of which he emboldens himself to face the enemy. In essence, Joe participates in a narcissistic exchange with his buddy: Joe provides his buddy with idealization and admiration, and, in exchange, Joe borrows courage from his buddy.

In the midst of a phantasmagorical transmogrification, Joe conjures up the imaginary presence of his buddy. By merging-in-fantasy with his buddy, Joe experiences himself as reunited, once again, with the psychic presence that instills within him the courage necessary for bravery. In this sense, the use of alcohol on Joe's part gives new meaning to the old adage about finding false courage in a whiskey bottle. However, alcohol does not fill Joe directly with false courage; rather, as a result of its psychoactivity, it allows Joe to entertain a fantasy of possessing his buddy's fighting spirit. This is an example of the placebo effect in that alcohol serves as an agent, the psychoactive effect of which activates a fantasy that produces the desired result.

In the absence of his addictive fantasies, Joe feels tortured by a diametrically opposed and mortifying fantasy of himself as a coward. For Joe, many ordinary situations and typical interactions confront him with the daunting task of standing his ground against an enemy force in the face of which he imagines himself as being totally overmatched. Believing he lacks the requisite courage necessary to successfully defend himself, he retreats quickly into an alcohol-induced fantasy world. In his own private version of wonderland, he imagines himself as a megalomaniacal self that allied temporarily, at least, with the strength and courage of his buddy. This is another instance of the Narcissus complex in the case of Joe.

In a state of alcohol-induced intoxication, Joe unconsciously fantasizes that he has found the courage necessary to face down the threat of an imaginary enemy. This addictive fantasy helps Joe to counteract his painful sense of shame and the dreadful anxiety about being exposed as a coward. In addition, the experience for Joe of being more courageous, even if purely illusory, enables him to feel more human and less like some low-life and subhuman creature.

In this regard, Joe abuses alcohol because it has the psychoactive power to induce cherished fantasies of being reunited with his buddy. (This is an instance of the placebo effect of alcohol.) These narcissistic illusions provide Joe with a twinship-like function in the form of helping him to feel more human (that is, humanization). Thus, in the midst of his drunken reverie, Joe is under the illusion that the imaginary presence of his buddy bestows upon him an otherwise missing degree of humanness. Here, we see the symbolic meaning of the axiom that the whiskey bottle is the alcoholic's best friend.

In his alcoholic delirium, Joe flip-flops from a mortifying vision of himself as a coward to a blissful vision of himself as a courageous hero. However, as is true of all addictive fantasy flip-flopping, these self-deceptive states are whimsical, and hence narcissistically flimsy. Joe drinks more and more alcohol as he is caught up in a vicious and addictive cycle; he flip-flops temporarily from one fantasy state to the other, without, however, any chance of ever achieving substantial psychic change.

Joe catapults himself, without realizing it, into an addictive wonderland in which he entertains the megalomaniacal illusion of magical control over his entire emotional world. In this regard, he imagines himself as megalomaniacal. His megalomaniacal attitude is reflected in his treatment of his family. He treats his wife and children as if they are things with no thoughts or feeling of their own. He moves them about from one place to the next, all the while evidencing little regard for the emotional impact of these constant moves on his family.

In fact, Joe became a phantasmagorical version of a megalomaniacal self under the influence of alcohol. As such, he loses all normal empathy for those closest to him. He simply expects his wife and children to follow him without asking any questions or raising any objections. Consequently, he is quite shocked when his wife seemingly leaves him out of the blue. The psychotherapist and Joe work long and hard to disabuse him of his megalomaniacal attitude toward his wife and children. Only then is Joe able to appreciate fully the part that he played in the loss of his family.

We can now pinpoint the etiological origins of Joe's alcoholism in the problematic relationship with his father. The involvement on Joe's part with his father was organized almost exclusively in terms of woodworking. Over time, Joe experiences hand and power tools as well as the craft of woodworking as transitional selfobjects, which serve as nonhuman intermediaries between himself and his father.

As such, these things and this activity make a narcissistic exchange process possible between Joe and his father. For his part, Joe receives narcissistic supplies and sustenance from his father, who helps him master the craft of woodworking. Joe becomes more skillful and competent as a woodworker, which strengthens him narcissistically by increasing psychic structure and function. Joe structures himself psychically around a sense of himself as a skilled woodworker which, in turn, helps him to function better in the real world. In exchange for his part in this narcissistic process, Joe's father gets a willing apprentice and an obedient supplicant.

We maintain that Joe becomes arrested developmentally at the second phase of the narcissistic exchange process. His father is much too distant and aloof emotionally to facilitate a deep human connection with Joe. His father keeps his emotional distance from Joe, and thus interferes seriously with Joe's narcissistic reinvestment in his relationship with his father (that is, phase III of the narcissistic exchange process). Joe might base such a psychic reinvestment on the symbolic currency of woodworking. On the contrary, Joe remains too invested narcissistically in the use of things and activities.

Over time, Joe's narcissistic over-investment in the use of the nonhuman world of things and activities serves as a pathogenic basis for the addictive abuse of alcohol. Yet, despite his alcoholism, Joe maintains his ability to use woodworking as a transitional selfobject.

However, he has difficulty investing narcissistically in his relationship with other people. Joe has little use for people unless they function narcissistically for him as archaic selfobjects, and sometimes only as mere things with semi-human status.

In this sense, Joe re-creates his father's narcissistic attitude toward him (as a child) in his stance toward others. Under the best of circumstances, Joe's father relates to Joe as an archaic selfobject, which he experiences as extending and expanding his own narcissistic boundaries.

He teaches Joe to become just like himself, a skilled woodworking craftsman.

Through woodworking, Joe's father confers on him a strong sense of being merged with an idealized paternal figure. In addition, woodworking serves for Joe as a basis for a twinship experience with his father in which Joe imagines himself as a chip off the old block, both literally and figuratively.

However, Joe's father (mis)treats him under the worst of circumstances, megalomaniacally as if he is just another piece of wood he controls as he sees fit. For example, Joe's father responds to Joe and the injury to his finger almost as if his son is nonhuman and *nothing* more than a woodworking tool that is broken and needs either to be fixed or discarded. In his father's mind, the crucial question to be answered concerns the relative cost to him of fixing or discarding the broken item. Joe not only learns the craft of woodworking from his father; unfortunately, he also learns to treat himself and others megalomaniacally, almost as if everyone, including himself, are nonhuman things.

Our typological diagnosis of Joe is based on advances in our thinking. There seems to be little doubt that in the intersubjective context of his relationship with his father Joe suffers narcissistic damage. His father facilitates Joe's idealization of him as a gifted craftsman whose skills Joe wants to emulate. However, Joe is forced to idealize his father from afar, and thus he misses the selfobject experience of merger with the omniscient. Perhaps, in imbibing alcohol, Joe is trying to revive a previously missing selfobject experience of the warm glow that emanates from being merged with a paternal source of supreme knowledge and strength.

Moreover, the faulty twinship experience between Joe and his father is limited to Joe feeling human solely on the basis of how well or poorly he emulates his father as a skilled craftsman. Joe never develops a sense of himself as being fully human solely on the basis of just being himself. And, later in combat Joe imagines he had lost all claim to his essential humanness because he had failed to perform in a manner consistent with the military credo of bravery under fire.

Thus far, we stress the limited nature of Joe's relationship with his father and its damaging impact on Joe's capacity for healthy idealization and twinship. However, we believe that the absence of his biological mother throughout his life has a seriously deleterious effect on Joe's sense of grandiosity. He misses the opportunity to experience his mother as a selfobject that could mirror his archaic grandiosity.

The presence of Joe's father and his stepmother does not adequately compensate for the tragic loss of his mother. Joe sequesters his archaic grandiosity, which then remains split off unconsciously as part of a vertical (dissociative) split in the self (that is, as a part-self). As a result of this dissociation, Joe's unconscious sense of his own grandiosity, as a result of this dissociation, fails to undergo the narcissistic transformation that normally occurs in healthy development.

In his adult life, Joe always sees himself as lacking in courage, which, in his mind, is a prerequisite for feeling grand about himself. Lacking a sense of his own courage and grandness, Joe feels compelled to borrow it from others or, later, from a whiskey bottle. Perhaps if his mother had lived, Joe might have developed a better and more realistic sense of his own courage in the face of adversity. Armed with a strong belief in his own courage, Joe might have been better able to withstand the narcissistically devastating criticism of others, such as the medic and then his wife.

In sum and on closer scrutiny, Joe evidences *major* damage to the narcissistic pole of omnipotence with some *minor* damage to the other narcissistic poles of grandiosity and twinship. Based on this pattern of narcissistic damage to the bipolar self, we diagnose Joe as unipolar, subtype II. In contrast to Teddy and Mary (see Chapter 4), whom we diagnose as unipolar, subtype I, Joe suffers from a mixed state. In such a mixed state, he suffers from varying degrees of anxiety (of the disintegration kind) and depression as well as shame, loneliness, and narcissistic rage (that is turned on the self in the form of antipathy).

Paradoxically, Joe abuses alcohol both to pacify and fuel his narcissistic rage. In this latter capacity, it becomes a self-destructive means of addictive suicide. In this regard, Joe abuses alcohol in order to fuel his narcissistic rage, which he then turns on himself. From a self-psychological perspective, (addictive) suicide is the ultimate and most self-destructive expression of narcissistic rage.

From our current psychoanalytic perspective, we now recognize many subtle yet profound aspects of the psychotherapy we missed previously. In line with our current thinking, we view Joe's gift of a wooden plaque to the psychotherapist as follows: On an unconscious level, Joe gives this gift in the hopes of completing a narcissistic transaction: the gift is a symbolic gesture on Joe's part, which signifies his idealization of the psychotherapist from whom he expects to be rewarded with a boost in his fortitude and stamina. Thus, Joe is repeating with the psychotherapist the same kind of narcissistic exchange that he transacted previously with his father and his buddy.

At the time of our original report, the psychotherapist has no way of empathically understanding the deeper, unconscious meaning behind Joe's gesture of gratitude. However, proceeding intuitively, he gives Joe the opportunity to entertain a transference fantasy in which he imagines that he succeeds in striking a bargain or deal with the psychotherapist concerning his megalomaniacal need to entertain the illusion of control of the psychotherapy (that is, a fantasy of being a megalomaniacal self). Fantasizing that the psychotherapist could read his mind allows Joe to imagine himself as being known so completely that he no longer needs to harbor alone the shameful secret of his supposed cowardice.

Joe imagines himself as being a megalomaniacal self who exercises emotional control over the psychotherapist in such a way as to free himself from the painful necessity of subjecting himself to further self-scrutiny. Joe has a selfobject transference fantasy that the psychotherapist knows everything almost as if by magic and without having to be told. As far as Joe is concerned, the psychotherapist knows about his allegedly dishonorable acts of cowardice without ever having to confess them. Believing transferentially in the psychotherapist's omniscience frees Joe from the extremely embarrassing prospect of exposing himself before the psychotherapist as a despicable coward. In magically unburdening himself of the mortifying secret of his cowardice, Joe feels that he has at last found a semblance of the bliss that has so eluded him since the death of his buddy.

In an intuitive fashion, the psychotherapist empathically shares Joe's selfobject fantasy of him as omniscient. In so doing, the psychotherapist makes it possible for Joe to use him in a fashion consistent with his need to experience himself unconsciously as being a megalomaniacal self with control over the therapy. As noted, Joe envisions the gift of the plaque and the psychotherapist's acceptance of it as signaling the beginning of a (symbolic) process of (narcissistic) exchange that would unfold between them. As part of this process, Joe imagines that he would honor and pay homage to the psychotherapist, who he anticipates would return the favor by lending him the courage to face life more bravely than before and, most importantly, without having to resort to alcohol.

In the early phase of the therapy, Joe feels himself redeemed in the eyes of the psychotherapist. The psychotherapist praises Joe lavishly for exhibiting courage in deciding to give up alcohol. Joe is fortified by the psychotherapist's admiration of his courageous decision in a way that far exceeds any illusion of strength fostered by alcohol. In other words, Joe and the psychotherapist together share a sense of Joe's courageous fight against alcoholism.

Joe makes a narcissistic investment on a symbolic level in the psychotherapy that equals an earlier and similar investment in woodworking. Joe learns from the psychotherapist to use the tools of psychotherapy just as he learned from his father to use woodworking tools. In retrospect, it now seems clear to us that Joe models his use of the psychotherapist and psychotherapy on his early experience with his father in the woodworking shop. As Joe works through his narcissistic transference fantasy he gives up an illusion of a megalomaniacal self and of magical control for the reality of better management (that is, mastery) of himself and his affairs. And, in sharp contrast to the blissful and unconscious experience of himself as a megalomaniacal self as fostered by alcohol, the psychotherapy serves a truly utilitarian purpose in helping Joe to master the skills of everyday living.

Actual and long-lasting emotional relief constitutes an especially valuable aspect of Joe's psychotherapy experience. Alcohol provided Joe with a purely temporary and only partial cessation of pain. In contradistinction, psychotherapy provides him with a level of psychopharmacotherapeutic relief previously unmatched by alcohol. Gradually, as his selfobject transference fantasy unfolds, Joe begins to build up his self-esteem. Similarly, he develops healthier and more adaptive means of regulating his moods. During the 10 months of his initial abstinence, Joe is much less subject to painful episodes of demoralizing shame, self-loathing, and antipathy.

The fact that Joe relapses, however, threatens to end all of his progress. The inability on Joe's part to maintain his abstinence and sobriety throws him as well as the psychotherapist into a real emotional crisis. Once again, Joe is consumed with shame and self-hatred.

All the countertransference attempts on the part of the psychotherapist to reassure Joe, with the intention of lifting his spirits, have the exact opposite effect. The sympathetic reassurance offered by the psychotherapist worsens Joe's already fragile state of mind. Only the psychotherapist's eventual recognition of his empathic failure leads to a renewal of the psychopharmacotherapeutic effect of the selfobject transference fantasy as being a megalomaniacal self. Reinvigorated by the selfobject functioning of the transference, Joe manages to give up alcohol for a second time in favor of psychotherapy.

In the latter part of the psychotherapy, Joe increasingly takes over the transitional selfobject functioning of both the psychotherapist and the psychotherapy. He appreciates that he actually displayed tremendous courage despite the prospect of losing his buddy in saving himself and in following his instincts for survival. He realizes that true acts of courage are almost always based on difficult decisions and a willingness to make tremendous sacrifice. In this instance, Joe acts courageously in deciding to go it alone in combat without the presence of his buddy to sustain him.

In the present, Joe decides to confront and ultimately to overcome the enemy in the form of alcohol. In the end, Joe learns an important lesson from psychotherapy: namely, that courage and bravery often consist of deciding to save oneself to fight another day. He learns that there is real wisdom in deciding to make a tactical retreat in order to avoid a strategic surrender.

JOANN

Overview

The case of JoAnn, an attractive young woman in her mid-20s who works as a fashion designer, serves as another example (see, the case of Mary in Chapter 4) of our self-psychological understanding and approach to the psychotherapy of an addict with an eating disorder. Like Mary, JoAnn is a chronic and severe bulimic, bingeing and purging on an almost daily basis. However, unlike Mary, who abuses laxatives as a means of purging, JoAnn abuses physical exercise and jogging as her preferred way of purging. In this sense, she is also addicted to exercising (that is, she is an exercise addict).

Moreover, the case of JoAnn differs from that of Mary in two other important respects. First, and in contrast to Mary, the psychotherapy of JoAnn is organized unconsciously in terms of the psychodynamics of a transference–countertransference neurosis, which is based primarily on JoAnn's early and disturbed relationship with her father. In this regard, the case is unusual in the psychoanalytic literature on eating disorders. This body of literature over-emphasizes, in our opinion, the destructive role of the mother–daughter relationship almost to the virtual exclusion of the father–daughter relationship.

Second, the self-psychological psychotherapy survives in the case of JoAnn and concludes with positive results, notwithstanding several serious empathic failures. This case contrasts, therefore, to that of Mary that ends prematurely due to serious and unaddressed empathic failures on the part of the psychotherapist.

JoAnn enters psychotherapy, which lasts approximately 6 years and is conducted on a three and then twice a week basis, complaining of depressive feelings of emptiness and anxious feelings of depletion. Almost immediately, it was apparent to the psychotherapist that JoAnn suffered from bulimia nervosa in addition to an empty/depleted depression. She backdates the onset of her eating disorder to her teenage years; she laments that it had worsened steadily over the ensuing years.

At the point when JoAnn begins psychotherapy, her bingeing and purging takes up almost all of her spare time. She obsesses about food, eating, her body, and exercise; she is also engaged in other compulsive and ritualized activities that are associated with her morbid obsessions.

Furthermore, JoAnn evidences a serious disturbance in her body image (that is, body dysmorphia). Although quite attractive, JoAnn imagines she is ungainly and unseemly; she hates her body and her appearance with an intensity and fury that is startling. In this regard, she is consumed by a fierce antipathy toward herself, which exemplifies narcissistic rage in an addicted patient.

In addition to the narcissistically mortifying nature of her self-loathing, JoAnn suffers from intensely painful states of shame and panic. No sooner has she gone on an eating binge than she immediately panics. She becomes overwhelmed with shame and self-disgust. Her shame and panic result in long hours of tortuous exercise, conducted both in the gym and in marathon jogging excursions. Any failure on JoAnn's part to workout strictly in accordance with her rigorous exercise program precipitates further episodes of panic, which we distinguish from anxiety attacks. (See Miliora & Ulman, 1996a, for a discussion of this subtle yet profound distinction.)

In a fashion typical of the addictive cycle, JoAnn's relentless and unmerciful assault on her body by nonstop exercising results in her becoming famished and feeling compelled to indulge in still another gluttonous eating binge. In sum, JoAnn evidences an antipathetic disregard of her own physical well-being that illustrates dramatically the willful self-destructiveness of megalomania gone awry.

The psychotherapy with JoAnn is marked from the beginning, and especially in its early stages, by a willfulness and defiance on her part that is paralleled and equaled by a stubbornness and unbending rigidity on the part of the psychotherapist. For example, the psychotherapist presses JoAnn to seriously consider joining Overeaters Anonymous (OA) in an early attempt to break through the vicious cycle of her bingeing and purging. He believes clinically that some degree of abstinence is absolutely essential in order to transfer the selfobject-like functions of the bingeing and purging from the bulimia to the psychotherapy.

However, JoAnn experiences the psychotherapist's strong recommendation to join OA as an arbitrary and dictatorial command from a male authority figure. Predictably, she responds with rageful defiance—she absolutely refuses to join OA. Instead, she insists that she can single-handedly control her problems involving food, eating, and her weight. The adamant refusal on JoAnn's part to join OA leaves the psychotherapist feeling thwarted in his attempt to assert some degree of control over the course of her recovery from her addiction.

During the next several months, JoAnn and the psychotherapist engage in an intense power struggle and battle of wills over the issue of JoAnn joining OA. Both JoAnn and the psychotherapist dig in their heels and, as a result, become equally intransigent and unyielding. During this early phase of the psychotherapy, the psychotherapist has little understanding or insight into the unconscious psychodynamic underlying this tug-of-war.

At the time, the psychotherapist is caught up unconsciously in his own Narcissus complex, which takes the form of countertransference fantasies of himself as being a megalomaniacal self who wields magical control. Consequently, he experiences JoAnn's refusal to join OA as a provocative act of defiance that signifies to him that she is totally out of control. He is so dominated by his countertransference fantasy of being right and in control that he is totally unable to empathize with JoAnn's archaic wishes to assert her own free will and imagine herself as being in complete control. The psychotherapist fails to empathize with and, in fact, becomes antipathetic toward JoAnn's legitimate need to conduct her psychotherapy according to her own narcissistic agenda, or in accordance with her Narcissus complex.

At this psychotherapeutic juncture, the psychotherapist is locked into a seemingly countertherapeutic power struggle with JoAnn. Paradoxically, however, he learns a lot in the midst of this battle of wills about her early life and, particularly, about her relationship with her father.

Beginning when JoAnn was a toddler and continuing thereafter as a young girl, JoAnn reveals that she had a very physically robust relationship with her father. JoAnn and her father engage regularly in a variety of playful games, including wrestling and roughhousing. In this context, she describes how they develop their own private and nonverbal body language as well as an informal pantomime, all of which serve as a means of communicating and playacting with each other.

JoAnn remembers these early years with great fondness and as a period of her life she still relishes as one of her most enjoyable. She loved all the physical contact with her father as afforded her by the games and play. With enormous pride and great joy, she refers to these early years of her childhood as truly blissful; she recalls that she felt as if she held a special place in her father's heart. Her childhood memories of being the "apple of my father's eye" are, we believe, her version of a fantasy of narcissistic bliss.

However, during puberty and with the onset of her sexual maturation, everything changed, according to JoAnn. Without any warning or explanation from her father, he suddenly withdraws from her, ceasing to have any physical contact with her. The joys and pleasures afforded her by their early physical contact stop entirely. She bemoans that her relationship with her father became unpleasant, distant, and strained. She decries that she and her father switch from having almost nonstop and carefree physical contact to having almost no physical interaction.

Moreover, the quality of their emotional relationship changes dramatically, and, JoAnn indicates, went from bad to worse. During this period, JoAnn describes her father as becoming a domineering bully, which is in marked contrast to his previous role as a physical playmate. He no longer engaged with JoAnn in the pure fun of their earlier physical relationship; instead he seeks, she states emphatically, to control her every physical movement and action.

JoAnn's father becomes, she recounts, especially controlling (megalomaniacal) as regards her relationship to food and eating. The family meal at dinner becomes the site for a nightly battle royal between JoAnn and her father over her eating habits. Her father demands that she finish every morsel on her plate before leaving the dinner table. Her unwillingness and refusal to follow her father's dictates results, she stresses, in "Mexican-style" standoffs between the two of them. They sit for long periods at the dinner table glaring angrily at one another.

JoAnn's father often sends her upstairs to her bedroom without any dinner. Later, in the middle of the night when everyone in the family is sound asleep, JoAnn sneaks downstairs and raids the refrigerator. The disturbed relationship with her father constitutes an intersubjective context in which eating becomes for JoAnn an angry form of rebellion and a symbolic act of asserting illusory control.

JoAnn recalls that later, as a teenager, her father needs to control her every move as well as her whereabouts with boys. He absolutely forbids her from going out with boys and literally attempts to imprison her within her bedroom. JoAnn emphasizes that her father is desperate to prevent her from having any unsupervised contact with boys because he fears that she would engage in sexual hanky-panky.

However, JoAnn easily circumvents her father's tyrannical rule by sneaking out of her bedroom window at night. Once free and on her own, she has secret rendezvous with a series of teenage boyfriends. In this context, sex, like food and eating, becomes for JoAnn another forbidden fruit, so to speak, which she consumes and indulges in clandestinely.

Throughout her latter childhood and teenage years, JoAnn and her father engage in knock-down, drag-out verbal brawls. They hurl one invective and vituperative remark after another at each other, thus employing words as if they are physical blows and punches. JoAnn remembers distinctly that her father curses at her, calling her a "goddamned pain in the ass." According to JoAnn, the playful and innocent nature of their earlier physical interaction degenerates into an antagonistic war of words.

JoAnn and her father no longer interact playfully with one another through the physical medium of their games and roughhousing; instead they interact hostilely and belligerently with one another through the linguistic medium of their verbal behavior. In essence, it seems that JoAnn and her father lose the ability to *use* the physical language of the body and face or, more specifically, body language and pantomime as nonverbal means of interacting positively with each other. Instead, as their only alternative, they become verbally abusive toward one another.

In the terminology of our current model, JoAnn and her father conduct a narcissistic transaction by which physical behavior is exchanged for verbal behavior. Unfortunately for JoAnn, the exchange results in her being shortchanged narcissistically. JoAnn is deprived of the presence of an admiring and appreciative paternal figure with whom she could enjoy the physical pleasures of her body and the sensual delights of her budding sexuality. On the contrary, JoAnn feels compelled to forfeit this pleasurable experience for the painful experience of doing battle with her father.

Locked into this intersubjective configuration, JoAnn develops a grossly distorted sense of her "self" as a physical and sexual being. She becomes a megalomaniacal self in the form of being a control freak and a fantasy junkie, both of which contribute significantly to her becoming addicted and eating disordered. She treats her body in much the same fashion as did her father, that is, as if it is a nonhuman thing that can be controlled with little regard for its natural and healthy functioning.

Like her father, JoAnn feels that if her body seems to be out of control, then she is completely justified in subjecting it to extreme punishment and abuse. She fails to develop a sense of her body as a living, breathing part of herself, which is a physical extension of her selfhood. Instead it remains a foreign and strange thing from which she feels alienated and estranged.

Eventually, the psychotherapist catches on to the fact that his struggle with JoAnn over OA is not really about the issue of joining or not joining this 12-step program. He realizes that the power struggle has assumed the form of a transference–countertransference neurosis and, in the process, has become a countertherapeutic replication of JoAnn's interaction with her father over food, eating, and her body. In this intersubjective context, JoAnn and the psychotherapist are playing out the unconscious transference and countertransference roles of rebellious daughter and megalomaniacal father.

Gradually, the psychotherapist gains a better empathic understanding of the unconscious psychodynamics of this intersubjective configuration. As a result, he decenters from his own subjectivity and his countertransference enactment of a fantasy of a megalomaniacal self in the form of being a control freak. This is a countertransference version of the Narcissus complex. In so doing, he backs off his insistence of JoAnn joining OA.

Without further interference from the psychotherapist, JoAnn proceeds on the basis of her own free will, and attempts to gain abstinence in her own way. JoAnn is responding transferentially to the psychotherapist's newfound empathy and consequent hands-off approach. She evidences a greater *willingness* (rather than her prior *willfulness*) to use the psychotherapy to better manage her eating and exercising.

In working through this dimension of the transference–countertransference neurosis, JoAnn and the psychotherapist establish a new intersubjective matrix. Together, they create a psychoanalytic medium through which the ersatz selfobject functions of bingeing and purging are being absorbed intersubjectively and exchanged narcissistically for the genuine selfobject provisions of the psychotherapy.

As this phase of intersubjective absorption, or the unconscious process of narcissistic exchange, progresses, JoAnn uses the psychotherapy increasingly as a means of counteracting both her depressive feeling of emptiness and her anxious feeling of depletion. The absorption within the psychotherapy of the psychoactive effects of bingeing and purging reveals their antidepressive and antianxiety (selfobject—like) functions. The ingestion of food on JoAnn's part and almost instantaneous elimination of most of its fat and caloric content through exercise is an unconscious expression of a psychosomatic fantasy about eating and elimination.

The psychosomatic nature of JoAnn's binge/purge cycle is understood empathically by the psychotherapist as a set of paradoxical actions and reactions. On the one hand, JoAnn fills up on food and, as part of satiation, experiences a simultaneous antidepressant stimulation and antianxiety tranquilization. Together, the psychoactive effects of satiation both dissociate and anesthetize JoAnn. Thus, JoAnn enters into an addictive state of mind, which we refer to variously as an addictive metamorphosis or phantasmagorical transmogrification.

On the other hand, JoAnn immediately panics about gaining weight and becoming fat, having rapaciously satiated herself on food. The panic JoAnn experiences, in turn, precipitates the urge to perform a feat of magical control by purging and hence cleansing herself.

Moreover, the binge/purge symptoms of JoAnn's bulimia represent a hypomanic (that is, a milder form of full-blown mania) and unconscious attempt at defending herself against a chronic sense of emptiness and depletion. However, the defensive nature of JoAnn's bingeing ultimately exacerbated rather than alleviated her depression, thus requiring her to engage in further hypomanic purging. And, paradoxically, her hypomanic purging necessitated yet another round of antidepressive bingeing, thus repeating the addictive cycle.

Instinctively, JoAnn takes advantage of the natural psychoactive effect of satiation. On the basis of psychoactive illusions produced by satiation, it has a capacity to produce an antidepressive illusion of being emotionally filled up as well as an antianxiety illusion of storing up emotional supplies. JoAnn underwent an addictive alteration of consciousness (that is, triggered an addictive metamorphosis).

In such an addictive state of mind, she feels relieved of her chronic and painful sense of inadequacy and defectiveness. Immediately thereafter, however, JoAnn is overwhelmed by shame and panic in reaction to having overeaten. She conjures up another addictive fantasy that she could undo any real or imagined weight gain by excessive exercising and jogging. This represents a version of a fantasy of being a megalo-maniacal self.

In this regard, therefore, purging (like bingeing) took on a mega-lomaniacal meaning because it allows JoAnn to imagine that she has complete control over food and eating. However, unlike bingeing, which produces a simultaneous (antidepressive) stimulation and (antianxiety) tranquilization, purging provides dual shame relieving and antipanic effects. In essence, JoAnn takes advantage of the hypomania inherent in the purging to counteract the shame and panic that plague her as a result of bingeing.

There is still another twist to the binge/purge cycle: in the context of her bulimia JoAnn is plagued by the dreadful and narcissistically mortifying fantasy that she had completely lost control of the entire process of food intake. As a punishment for her imaginary loss of control, she masochistically inflicts pain on herself by subjecting her body to a self-destructive regimen of excessive exercise. The Spartan-like nature of her exercise program expresses her narcissistic rage over what she imagines as her body's mortifying faults, shortcomings, and failures to perform in perfect accordance with the narcissistic illusion of being a megalomaniacal self and as possessing magical control.

As part of such a fantasy of being a megalomaniacal self and as endowed with magical control, JoAnn fantasizes that her body is machine-like and, therefore, should always be in tip-top running condition. On the one hand, her fantasies of megalomaniacal self have shame reducing and antipanic effects. On the other hand, however, the inevi-table disturbance of this fragile and unstable fantasy of her body as a high-performance engine results in her once again feeling ashamed, embarrassed, and panicky.

In summary, JoAnn diverts (and consequently subverts) the normal and healthy functioning of physical movement as a transitional selfobject activity. She converts it into an unhealthy and pathological ATM. In the context of an ersatz selfobject experience, she entertains megalomaniacal fantasies of absolute control over her body and its physical and physi-ological functions. JoAnn exemplifies the Narcissus complex of an addict suffering from an eating disorder, and, more specifically, bulimia. The fantasies of narcissistic bliss are part of a hypnoid state of phantasma-gorical transmogrification. In this fugue-like state of rapture, JoAnn temporarily counteracts the shameful and panicky feelings associated with the narcissistically mortifying fantasy of having lost control of her body.

The psychotherapist came to understand the intersubjective absorption of the psychoactive functions of bingeing and purging as occurring initially in the context of a mirroring selfobject transference. As a result of peer supervision, the psychotherapist worked through his countertransference antipathy. This antipathetic attitude was expressed in his attempt to entertain fantasies of himself as being a megalomaniacal self who has magical control over JoAnn and her addiction recovery. By becoming more empathic and less antipathetic toward JoAnn, the psychotherapist helps her to experience herself as admired transferentially for her grand display of "self-control."

From our self-psychological perspective, the idea of "self-control" is itself an illusion; actually, it refers to a megalomaniacal fantasy rather than to a real psychological capacity. The concept of self-control implies that it is possible to control one's thoughts and feelings, all supposedly on the basis of totally self-generated or automatic means.

However, we maintain that such a form of so-called self-control is a psychological impossibility. It is possible to *manage* (rather than control) one's personal life by organizing one's thoughts and directing one's actions. And, furthermore, this entire psychological process occurs (or fails to occur) exclusively in the context of a selfobject matrix or intersubjective milieu. Hence, the process of learning how to manage (rather than control) one's emotions and emotional affairs does not take place in a selfobject or intersubjective vacuum. It is always necessary, therefore, to use other people, things, and activities as selfobjects that enable one to gain self-management and for psychological mastery over oneself. (See Goldberg 1988; for a very different self-psychological perspective on the concept of "self-control.")

As originally conceived, we viewed the mirroring transference fantasy as providing JoAnn with a healthy alternative to her self-destructive bulimia. Increasingly, JoAnn had given up her exclusive reliance on the abuse of food and exercise as expressions of a fantasy of being a megalomaniacal self and, therefore, relying on faulty means of attempting to regulate her self-esteem. Now, she depends more on the selfobject functioning of the psychotherapy to provide these same self-regulatory capacities.

Following several years of progress and near-total cessation of her bulimia, JoAnn reports a pivotal dream that becomes the *intersubjective frame of reference* for understanding much of the ensuing analysis. (See Ulman, 1987, 1988, for a discussion of the concept of the intersubjective frame of reference in dream interpretation.) In this dream, JoAnn and the psychotherapist are standing together in a kitchen full of food. JoAnn makes tentative, albeit unmistakable, sexual advances toward the psychotherapist, who responds enthusiastically and encouragingly.

The dream heralds a new yet potentially dangerous struggle into which JoAnn and the psychotherapist plunge. In the past, they struggled for illusory control of the psychotherapy primarily in terms of defining the (unconscious) meaning of her physical abuse of food and her body. Now, they contend for illusory control over the psychotherapeutic process as a symbolic activity that defines the (unconscious) meaning of her sexuality, especially as it relates to her eating disorder. In both of these instances, the psychotherapeutic struggle is waged simultaneously through verbal and nonverbal means alike. These different lingos give both linguistic and behavioral expression to JoAnn's psychosomatic fantasies about the unconscious meaning of her physicality as well as her sexuality and sensuality.

During this difficult phase of the psychotherapy, JoAnn has repetitive sexual fantasies about the psychotherapist. She fantasizes explicit erotic situations, leaving little room for the imagination. However, JoAnn is quite shy and reserved, and thus finds it extremely difficult to talk openly about her sexual fantasies. JoAnn is flooded with shame and humiliation in those rare instances in which she initially and yet haltingly describes some of the details of her sexual fantasies.

Yet, despite these difficulties, JoAnn and the psychotherapist work hard psychoanalytically to explore the unconscious meaning of this emotional material. At first, JoAnn hesitates to put into words the images of her sexual fantasies. Apparently, JoAnn imagines that if she dares to speak the words, then she is literally engaging in the action.

However, JoAnn has a demeanor including facial expressions, body language, and tone of voice, all of which reveal the unconscious meaning of her sexual fantasies. Behaviorally, JoAnn is performing an erotic pantomime using body language that serves nonverbally to give motoric and sensorial expression to her sexual fantasies. Her erotic pantomime includes a variety of quite flirtatious physical gestures, movements, facial expressions, and tone of voice.

For example, she crosses and uncrosses her legs, buttons and unbuttons the top snap of her blouse, speaks in a low and sultry voice, runs her hand through her hair, and smiles furtively. Apparently, she is using the physical language of her body as part of an erotic pantomime, which she intends unconsciously to communicate by nonverbal means a sexual and sensuous message.

And her erotic pantomime has the intended effect of sexually arousing the psychotherapist, who fights to maintain empathic contact with JoAnn. In this intersubjective context, he tries not to lose himself countertransferentially in sexual reverie and overstimulation. He has to remind himself constantly that JoAnn is enacting some kind of sexual fantasy, the unconscious meaning of which is not, however, nearly as blatant as is its physical enactment.

At first, the psychotherapist is confused and taken aback by the sudden and seemingly inexplicable appearance of what might be construed as either an erotic or sexual transference. On the one hand, he ponders whether it is a genuine erotic transference, indicative of the emergence of long-repressed memories or incestuous fantasies JoAnn associates with her father. On the other hand, he wonders whether it is an attempt on JoAnn's part to sexualize the transference as an unconscious means of completing some developmentally arrested process. Regardless, the psychotherapist is unclear in his own mind about the unconscious connection JoAnn makes regarding her erotic or sexual transference and her eating disorder.

Interpreting JoAnn's dream illuminates the unconscious connection that she makes between sex and food and eating. In the dream, she envisions her sexual encounter with the psychotherapist as taking place in a kitchen full of food. This is interpreted by the psychotherapist as indicating that JoAnn is consumed by a powerful sexual appetite. It is empathically inferred, therefore, that she wants to devour the psychotherapist as if he is a tender morsel of food.

The psychotherapist, in continuing to work psychoanalytically with JoAnn's sexual dream and fantasies, gains further empathic understanding of the unconscious association JoAnn makes between food and eating, and sex. JoAnn reveals that as a teenager and young adult she was quite active sexually in addition to being bulimic. In fact, by her own estimation she was somewhat sexually promiscuous. Apparently, she gave free reign to her fantasies of being a megalomaniacal self by treating her body like a nonhuman plaything that she could abuse either in bulimic bingeing and purging or in promiscuous and risky sex.

In the developmental context of her fantasy scenarios, JoAnn imagines that she, rather than her father, is in total control of her bodily functions regarding food, eating, and sex. In reminiscing about her childhood and adolescence, she indicates that she had decided that if she could not be the "apple of my father's eye," then she would become "rotten to the core" and a real "pain in his ass." In arriving at this unconscious decision, JoAnn is determined to live out a narcissistically mortifying fantasy of herself as a rotten apple lying at the bottom of the barrel.

JoAnn has become in her unconscious mind a mortifying (fantasy) version of her former blissful self as the apple of her father's eye. As seen through her father's eyes, she feels she has lost the earlier vision of herself as a delicious and tasty apple. In essence, JoAnn comes to picture herself as a spoiled and unappetizing apple, that is, a thing that makes both her and her father sick to the stomach.

Thus, as the psychotherapist devotes closer psychoanalytic scrutiny to JoAnn's sexual dream and fantasies, they reveal her transference need to become once again the apple of her father's eye. She wants the psychotherapist to be as ravenously consumed by sexual hunger for her as she is for him. Imaging herself as part of the dream embracing one another, JoAnn describes a fantasy scene in which she and the psycho-therapist share the delight and rapture of narcissistic bliss as they devour each other in a tryst that fulfills their unbridled sexual appetites. And the erotic countertransference response on the part of the psychother-apist, as revealed in JoAnn's dream, indicates that he shares uncon-sciously in this intersubjective fantasy.

The fact that JoAnn imagines that she shares the (intersubjective) fantasy allows her to increasingly use the psychotherapy as a symbolic arena in which she gives both verbal and nonverbal expression to her sexual imaginings. However, the psychotherapist, unlike JoAnn's father, permits her to entertain the illusion that she, and not he, controls the (psychotherapeutic) process by which she feeds herself narcissistically.

In resuming her arrested psychosexual development, she transforms her megalomaniacal sense of illusory control over her body as well as its physiological and sexual functioning (that is, a fantasy of being a megalomaniacal self) into a mature sense of herself as a physical being. She recognizes, in the context of her newly developed sense of herself, that she does not possess unlimited ability to control her body as regards both its physiological and sexual functioning. As a result, she better appreciates the more healthy yet limited ways in which her body can function and serve her legitimate narcissistic needs.

With the help of the psychotherapist, JoAnn passes through a previously arrested phase of her psychosexual development. In the process, she reverses the pathogenic history of her relationship with her father—she goes from being "rotten to the core" and a "pain in the ass" to becoming once again the apple of her father's/psychotherapist's eyes.

In proceeding psychotherapeutically along this developmental path, JoAnn frees both her gastrointestinal and sexual functioning from serving purely psychopathological purposes. In the past, these functions were subverted narcissistically to serve in JoAnn's self-destructive (and addictive) misuse of her body. In a paradoxical attempt to maintain some semblance of selfhood, she abuses her body addictively with little regard for the self-destructive consequences.

Commentary

Further commentary on this case consists of a closer psychoanalytic examination of a two-way (intersubjective) process: in the first way, JoAnn uses or, in some instances, misuses the psychotherapy; whereas, in the second way the psychotherapist responds (sometimes antipathetically while in other instances empathically) to JoAnn's deployment of the psychotherapy.

For purely heuristic purposes, we divide our continuing discussion of this case into two parts. In the early phase of the psychotherapy, JoAnn and the psychotherapist are caught up intersubjectively in JoAnn's use of verbal behavior as a linguistic means of re-creating a charged emotional atmosphere. This ambience captures the pleasurable as well as the painful aspects of her physical relationship with her father. And in the middle to latter phases of the psychotherapy, JoAnn and the psychotherapist are swept up in her use of visual imagery as well as verbal and nonverbal behavior, which all serve as unconscious means of giving symbolic expression to her sexual appetites.

In the first phase of the treatment, JoAnn use of the psychotherapy as a symbolic means for a narcissistic exchange of selfobject-like functioning of bingeing and purging for the selfobject functioning of the psychotherapist. In the second phase of the treatment, JoAnn employs the psychotherapy as a means of completing her psychosexual development as a woman. She completes this development in the form of exchanging the narcissistic functioning of sex for the selfobject functioning of the psychotherapist. Thus, in both phases of the psychotherapy, JoAnn and the psychotherapist unwittingly replicate various aspects of

JoAnn's interaction with her father as it determines the unconscious meaning of her eating disorder and her sexuality.

JoAnn and the psychotherapist are entangled for some time in a countertherapeutic version of her adversarial interaction with her father. They fight over the issue of her joining OA, and thereby become ensnared in a battle of wills. This struggle is characteristic of the power struggle that transpired between JoAnn and her father. In the past, she struggled with her father to wrest (the illusion of) control from him of her own body as well as its physiological and sexual functioning; in the present, JoAnn asserts her will against the psychotherapist as part of exerting illusory control over her own psychotherapy.

In the context of this developmental setting, JoAnn's father becomes quite antipathetic toward her. In an unempathic fashion, he frustrates her normal and phase-appropriate need to experience herself unconsciously on basis of a fantasy of being a megalomaniacal self and as empowered with magical control of her body and her bodily functions. In this regard, he drives JoAnn into a psychopathological misuse and subsequent abuse of ATMs in the form of food and eating. Apparently, JoAnn feels that if she can not experience a healthy mastery over her own body, then she will resort to unhealthy (and illusory) control over her body.

In an example of "identification with the aggressor" (A. Freud, 1966 [1936]), JoAnn internalizes her father's megalomaniacal attitude toward her body and its normal physiological functions. JoAnn does not treat her body as a corporeal extension of herself and as a medium for physically expressing herself; rather, she misuses and abuses it as a prop in the enactment of her fantasies of megalomaniacal self and of exercising magical control over herself as a nonhuman entity. The physical functioning of JoAnn's body fails to serve for her as a transitional and, therefore, selfobject thing and activity; instead, for JoAnn both physicality and physiology become narcissistically subverted (rather than sexually perverted) from their normal and healthy functioning.

The megalomaniacal abuse of JoAnn's body and its physiological functioning is at the heart of a self disorder we now diagnose as unipolar, subtype II. JoAnn suffers serious damage primarily in the area of grandiosity and secondarily in the area of omnipotence. Consequently, JoAnn finds it extremely difficult to regulate her moods. Her inability to modulate her moods is evidenced by tendencies toward a variety of psychopathological affect states including depression, anxiety, mania, panic, and rage. JoAnn has difficulty in establishing a healthy ability to make normal adjustments in her moods.

In this regard, JoAnn creates what might be termed a psychosomatic fantasy about the (unconscious) meaning of eating food that subverts the normal function of this physiological process. (See Taylor, 1987, for a recent discussion of the unconscious communication between psyche and soma.) Based on her fantasy, JoAnn no longer envisions the natural act of eating food as a simple means of obtaining nourishment; instead this act takes on for JoAnn the unconscious meaning of a mechanism of illusory control. As such, it constitutes for JoAnn an ersatz selfobject. Thus, it substitutes for the healthy use of her body as a transitional selfobject thing. JoAnn attempts, therefore, to substitute a psychosomatic method of regulating her moods for the missing selfobject psychological means.

The proneness on JoAnn's part to experience severe shame, rage, and panic attests to the underlying presence of megalomania as central to her (bipolar) self disorder. The degree of her untransformed megalomania predisposes her to an unhealthy dependence on the misuse of things and abuse of activities as if they are semi-human. As part of her Narcissus complex, JoAnn is unable to transform her fantasy of herself as being a megalomaniacal self; consequently, she mistreats all human beings, especially herself, as if they are nonhuman entities over which she imagines exercising total and unchallenged control.

JoAnn and the psychotherapist successfully work through an early and almost fatal impasse in the psychotherapy. Subsequently, they open up a psychotherapeutic pathway for JoAnn to resume a hitherto arrested developmental process. In the context of the psychotherapy, JoAnn uses verbal behavior as if it is an actual physical activity. She does so in an effort to restore the transitional selfobject functioning of her physical relationship with her father. It is ironic, therefore, that the otherwise unhealthy power struggle engulfing both JoAnn and the psychotherapist becomes a valuable psychoanalytic medium for psychic healing. JoAnn recaptures through the psychotherapy the healthy use of body language as a transitional selfobject activity.

JoAnn exchanges the selfobject-like functioning and psychoactive effects of bingeing and purging for the selfobject functioning and psychopharmacotherapeutic effect of the psychotherapy. She no longer feels compelled to ragefully gorge herself on food as a symbolic means of eating her words, and, in the process, indulging in the psychosomatic fantasy of controlling the emotional intensity of her angry thoughts and outbursts.

In the past, JoAnn experienced a set of extremely contradictory feelings stemming from the psychosomatic fantasy involving food, eating, and her own narcissistic rage. On the one hand, she feels her rage is eating her up and she is likewise eating herself up with her own rage. This combination of feelings expresses JoAnn's narcissistic rage over her imagined failure to exercise unlimited (megalomaniacal) control over her body and its functioning. In this instance, narcissistic rage is a disintegration product. It is reflective of a narcissistic disturbance in JoAnn's psychosomatic fantasy of illusory control over the physiological process of ingesting, digesting, and eliminating food.

On the other hand, JoAnn often feels like she is feeding on her own (narcissistic) rage. She indulges her rage in angry and self-destructive bingeing. Then, as part of purging, she imagines that she magically has dissipated the narcissistic rage into thin air. In such a manner, JoAnn entertains the narcissistic illusion of being a megalomaniacal self and as magically controlling everything that enters and exits her body. In this latter instance, the narcissistic rage JoAnn experiences is indicative of a faulty attempt at self-restoration.

In gaining a measure of abstinence, JoAnn makes the first of two major and significant narcissistic exchanges: she imagines that she has total control over the psychotherapeutic process. And, as a result, she replaces the narcissistically subverted functioning of her body and its psychophysiology for the transitional selfobject functioning of verbal behavior. The latter constitutes a "functional equivalent[s]" (Adler & Goleman, 1969) of physical activity. Following this narcissistic exchange, JoAnn is far less prone to shame reactions as well as rage and panic attacks.

In the second phase of the psychotherapy, it seems that JoAnn is transferentially playing out a sexual fantasy. This transference fantasy could be analyzed on a manifest level as involving the seductive captivation of the psychotherapist. However, on a deeper, latent level, the dream implies that she is using physicality—as expressed in the form of sexuality and sensuality—in the *service of the self.*

Within the psychotherapy session, the expressive (sensually and erotically) nature of her sexual pantomime constitutes a nonverbal body language. Such lingo gives sensorial and motoric voice to an archaic narcissistic fantasy of a self as megalomaniacal and, hence, as having control over the psychotherapist as a captive audience. As depicted in her dream, JoAnn imagines herself as having (transferentially) satisfied her erotic appetites by sexually consuming the psychotherapist.

In the intersubjective context of the psychotherapy, JoAnn uses her prior skill of playing with pantomime in a very creative and useful manner. Ultimately, she uses the nonverbal language of pantomime in the service of playing out a fantasy and creating a mood extremely conducive to the psychotherapy. In this regard, the use of pantomime on JoAnn's part serves as a transitional selfobject activity. As such, it provides a psychopharmacotherapeutic effect essential to inducing a therapeutic dissociation. This psychotherapeutically altered state of consciousness is, however, quite distinct from and vastly superior to the hypnotic state associated with her addictive bingeing and purging.

The sensorial and sensual nature of JoAnn's sexual pantomime allows her to experience an even more intensified version of an earlier therapeutic dissociation. She is enraptured transferentially by the blissful nature of her fantasized sexual conquest of and control over the psychotherapist. The imaginary version of a sexual encounter with the psychotherapist gives unconscious expression to JoAnn's megalomaniacal need to control (by seduction) the psychotherapist.

We stated that JoAnn's transference is conceptualized originally as providing mirroring selfobject functions. Currently, however, we construe it as serving transitional selfobject functions as well. We interpret the manifest content of her dream and associations to the kitchen full of food—that is, a site for her sexual encounter with the psychotherapist—as revealing that JoAnn does not imagine the psychotherapist as a sexual partner of equal status to herself.

On the contrary, JoAnn imagines him as her own personal sex toy, a semi-human playmate that she controls like food and eating. Eventually, the psychotherapist responds empathically (rather than sexually) to JoAnn's desire to imagine him as her sexual plaything. He facilitates, therefore, the further emergence and ultimate psychotherapeutic transformation of JoAnn's fantasy of being a megalomaniacal self.

Upon closer psychoanalytic scrutiny, we interpret the sexual dream as indicating that JoAnn feels fed and nourished narcissistically by the psychotherapist's empathic response to her real and imaginary erotic overtures. JoAnn succeeds in exchanging the literal consumption of large amounts of food, which serve as a symbolic substitute for her insatiable sexual appetites, for the figurative consumption of the narcissistic nourishment as provided by the psychotherapist's empathic functioning as a selfobject.

In the presence of the psychotherapist JoAnn experiences herself as more freely and fully sexual. In this intersubjective context, she becomes less alienated and estranged from her own body and better able to inhabit it physically. In the process, she becomes more emotionally invested in her own physical well-being and more protective of her body and its functioning. JoAnn is enabled by investing greater emotional value in herself as a physical being to feel less enraged at, ashamed of, and panicked by her own corporeality.

JoAnn incorporates her sexuality more completely into her body-self and feels simultaneously more healthy narcissistic pleasure in her own self-image. JoAnn is no longer plagued by the disturbing and extremely unrealistic vision of herself as ugly and grotesque. In place of this (narcissistically) mortifying fantasy she creates a more pleasant and realistic picture of her physically attractive appearance. In this regard, she begins the long overdue process of mastering (rather than attempting to control) the corporeal domain of her being.

In the past, a narcissistic subversion occurred in the normal functioning of both her body and the physiological processes involved in ingestion and digestion. In marked contrast to the past, JoAnn now uses her body and physical activity in a healthy fashion and as part of establishing her femininity. She is completing, therefore, the second of the two major narcissistic exchanges: she swaps the crass pleasure of her crude, sexual appetites for the sublime delight of physical mastery over her own body.

Together, JoAnn and the psychotherapist shared an intersubjective fantasy of her as an alluring temptress and creature who possessed an array of powerful passions and sexual desires. In sharing this intersubjective fantasy, they are able to redefine the unconscious meaning of JoAnn's femininity and legitimate status as a sexual being. JoAnn no longer needs to entertain the illusion of megalomaniacal control over her body because she feels more secure in mastering her own femininity. She exchanges a dissociated state of disembodiment for a healthy sense of physical inhabitation.

JoAnn learns to inhabit her own body, and, in the process, masters its use for healthy physical and sexual purposes. As part of this process, she comes to feel more fully human. Likewise, she no longer experiences the psychotherapist in the same impersonal fashion and as merely a captive audience whose response she orchestrates and manipulates. Instead, she experiences the psychotherapist in a more personal manner as a genuine human being with his own spontaneous, emotional reactions. In this sense, she enters into phase III of the narcissistic exchange process.

Within the intersubjective context of the psychotherapy, JoAnn and the psychotherapist create a sense of herself as a physical being with real corporeal existence. Now that her body is free of psychopathological interference, she can allow it to perform its normal physical functions. Rather than ravaging and torturing her body as something unwanted, JoAnn learns to appreciate and value her own body. At long last it assumes its rightful place as a legitimate source of pleasure and as a physical means of gaining mastery over herself.

Chapter 6

The Third of the Addiction Paper Trilogy: The Cases of Travis and Errol

TRAVIS

Overview

Travis, a 42-year-old, white, middle-class male, is married (with one young daughter) and works as a benefits counselor for veterans. He entered psychoanalytic psychotherapy, which varied from twice to three times a week, complaining of debilitating anxiety and depression. His demeanor is that of a solemn, morose, and distraught middle-aged man. On first impression, he seems rather typical of a man going through a midlife crisis.

However, as psychotherapy progresses, a strikingly different picture emerges of Travis. Rather than being a typical, middle-class, middle-aged man afflicted with a midlife crisis, Travis is, in fact, a drug addict with a long history of violent crime dating back to his adolescence. Indeed, he is a deeply disturbed man who is addicted to drugs, and, more specifically, to a street drug called "speedballs" (a highly addictive combination of liquefied heroin and cocaine injected intravenously with a needle and syringe.)

Drug addiction and antisocial behavior, however, are not his only problems. In addition, Travis suffers from sexual and romantic obsessions. In this regard, he has been involved in numerous extramarital affairs and one night stands. In other words, he is also a sex addict.

Moreover, Travis is consumed with violent fantasies as well as addicted to sexual and romantic fantasies. And, he has a maniacal fascination with powerful handguns, in particular, a .357 Magnum revolver. This is his favorite weapon and the one he used in the commission of armed robbery and stickups. Moreover, he has not hesitated in the past to use his gun. He admits that in all probability he has seriously wounded and perhaps even killed others during the commission of previous violent crimes. On several occasions, he fired his revolver at others while robbing them at gunpoint or in the midst of defending himself during drug deals gone bad. Despite having a substantial history of antisocial and psychopathic behavior, Travis managed somehow to avoid getting caught or being arrested for any of his criminal activities.

In conducting psychotherapy with a patient such as Travis, the psychotherapist faces a serious moral and ethical dilemma. On the one hand, if he tells Travis that it is his professional duty to inform law enforcement authorities about the nature of Travis's current as well as any future criminal activity, then Travis will no doubt immediately leave treatment. On the other hand, if the psychotherapist does not notify the appropriate authorities, then he at least has a chance of keeping Travis in treatment. If he succeeds in the latter, then he can help Travis stop his violent criminal behavior and, in the process, protect the public from a dangerous criminal. However, the psychotherapist, in choosing to follow this second and controversial option, is at risk in colluding with Travis and contributing to his victimization of innocent men and women.

In the face of this dilemma, the psychotherapist makes the following abundantly clear to Travis. The psychotherapist will continue the psychotherapy with Travis only if the latter understands that any further violent criminal activity involving the possibility of physical harm to others will result in the immediate termination of the psychotherapy. Travis readily agrees to this controversial, and some might say wrongheaded and foolhardy, "therapeutic pact."

Fortunately, to the best of the psychotherapist's knowledge Travis never again physically threatens or harms others in the course of his involvement in illegal activities. In this regard, Travis makes a dramatic shift in the nature of his criminal behavior. He shifts from more psychopathic to more purely sociopathic crimes (for example, drug dealing) in which although he does violate the law he nonetheless gives up violence as a principal means of securing money to support his drug habit.

In essence, Travis lives what amounted to a dual existence or double life: by day he lives the life of an unassuming and humble bureaucrat whose existence bore no connection to sex, drugs, and rock 'n roll; whereas, by night he exists as a wild and crazed mad man whose very being is determined by sex, drugs, and rock 'n roll.

And, of equal importance for Travis, his daytime self seems to be split from his nighttime self. In view of this dissociative split in his self-experience, which consists of two separate "part-selves," each with a distinct existence, we believe that Travis is especially illustrative of the addictive character. The extent of the vertical split in Travis's character structure is graphically representative of the kind of dissociation commonly found in the addictive character.

Shortly after beginning psychotherapy, Travis describes his childhood and adolescence as an only child growing up in a typical urban setting. His father is a lawyer who works for a large bureaucratic agency, while his mother is a housewife and homemaker. Travis emphasizes that he was raised in a very chaotic, disturbed, and, at times, violent environment at home.

Travis's father is a rageful alcoholic (that is, an alcoholic and a rageaholic), who often attacks and beats both Travis and his mother. Travis remembers many instances in which he feared for the lives of both himself and his mother. He recalls cowering in his bed at night as his father and mother fought. During these terrifying episodes, he often wonders whether he and his mother would survive through the night.

The scary and frightening picture that Travis paints of his father notwithstanding, he insists that his father is not all bad. Travis's father, like many alcoholics (and rageaholics), has a split or dual personality; he is, in Travis's words, a "Dr. Jekyll and Mr. Hyde." In his Dr. Jekyll persona, his father could be quite engaging and extremely personable. Travis stresses that his father is very intelligent, well-educated, and literate, possessing a broad range of erudite interests and intellectual pursuits. There were many books around the house, and Travis always enjoyed talking with his father about a variety of serious topics. However, Travis bemoans that his father's alcoholism and violent temper (that is, rageaholism) prevent him from forming an emotionally intimate relationship with his father. On the contrary, he laments that he constantly felt distant and apart from his father.

Travis expresses pity and sorrow for his mother especially in connection with the mistreatment she received at the hand of his father. Despite a certain degree of sympathy for his mother, Travis evidences little respect for her and her ordeal. Instead, he describes her as a rather pathetic woman, who has been browbeaten, intimidated, and cowed by his father. With scorn and derision, he labels her as pitiful and as having meekly allowed herself to be brutally subjugated or controlled by her husband.

Travis resents that his mother had been unable to stand up both for herself and him against his father. She failed, according to Travis, to spare him from his father's Hyde-like wild rantings and violent ravings (that is, his rageaholism). In Travis's opinion, she was relegated by his father to nothing more than a doormat and whipping post. The attitude Travis has toward his mother indicates that he has come to share his father's antipathy toward her.

In the context of this family atmosphere—characterized as it was by a lack of empathy and show of antipathy—Travis reveals that as a child he retreated into his own fantasyland. As a youngster, one of his favorite toys is a tripod-mounted machine gun that fires rubber bullets. He spends hours and hours playing with his toy machine gun, lost in fanciful reverie and reassuring daydream.

As part of his play fantasies, Travis notes that he often imagines he is John Wayne and that he, like his matinee idol, is fighting the enemy and is proving victorious over them. According to Travis, his make-believe games of being John Wayne always involve fantasy scenarios in which he is locked in hand-to-hand combat with the enemy whom he vanquishes with his toy machine gun. Travis readily accepts the psychotherapist's inference that the imaginary enemy he pretends to kill is a symbolic stand-in for his father.

Travis's childhood recollections suggest that as a youngster he has a very vivid, active, and fertile imagination. Apparently, Travis retreats to his fantasy world as a safe refuge to which he flees regularly as an escape from his antipathetic home environment. Instead, he seeks solace in his play fantasies.

Pathogenic evidence exists, therefore, that at a relatively early age Travis is well on his way to coming under the influence of the Narcissus complex. In a similar vein, his fantasy world allows him to entertain a fantasy of being a megalomaniacal self who magically controls his own emotions as well as the emotional affairs of his family. This fantasy of megalomaniacal self compensates somewhat for his sense of having no emotional control in the context of his family affairs.

As an adolescent, Travis escapes from his family to a life on the streets with his teenage peers. Travis's street life is typical of that day and era: he begins using alcohol and drugs as well as getting into trouble with his pals. Sometimes, his brawls include a variety of dangerous weapons, including brass knuckles and switchblades. Moreover, Travis starts his life as a career criminal by committing petty crimes and engaging in antisocial acts of vandalism.

Travis does not complete high school and go on to college, thus failing to follow in his father's footsteps. Instead, he drops out of high school and enlists in the military. He spends a number of years in the service, where he learns how to use high-powered firearms; while in the service he also manages to get his high school equivalency degree.

Following his discharge from the military, Travis marries, has a child, and quickly becomes addicted to speedballs. Without much forethought or planning, he soon drifts into a life of violent criminal activity. He uses the money he garners from his crimes to support a drug habit that is becoming increasingly severe and expensive.

During this same period, Travis also becomes involved in numerous sexual liaisons with a variety of women. Some of these women are prostitutes and fellow junkies he associated with at "shooting galleries," that is, the back alleys and abandoned buildings where he shoots up his drugs. These are purely sexual encounters with little or no emotional meaning or genuine romantic overtones. In the lingo of the street, Travis refers to these brief sexual rendezvous as "scoring," thus leaving little doubt about the unconscious connection for him between fornicating with these women and injecting drugs.

Travis's descriptions of his interactions with these women implies that for him they exist as mere *sexual playthings*, lacking in any independent and separate status as persons in their own right. In Travis's mind, their sole purpose is to serve as disposable items he can discard after being used just like the disposable needle and syringe he throws away after injecting drugs.

Furthermore, and in a fashion analogous to speedballs, women appear to function for Travis as addictive trigger mechanisms (ATMs) that catapult him into an extremely pleasurable fantasyland. In this addictive wonderland, Travis imagines himself as a sexual potentate who fulfills his every emotional whim by controlling everyone and everything; that is, he is under the influence of being a megalomaniacal self and as wielding magical control fantasies at the core of the Narcissus complex. (We return in the case of Errol to the issue of sex addiction and its influence on transference–countertransference neurosis.)

In fact, Travis makes it abundantly clear that he experiences orgasms and orgasm-like highs using both sex and drugs. In certain respects, however, his drug high is even more intense and, hence, addictive than is the high he experiences from sex. The combination of intravenously injected heroin and cocaine (speedballs) provides Travis with what he describes as a Nirvanic state of bliss and oblivion.

In such an addictive state, he nods off into a drug-induced stupor. In such a trance-like state, Travis explains that he feels no pain and imagines himself floating, as if suspended in midair, in a carefree zone of peacefulness and tranquility.

Apparently, speedballs serve for Travis as an ATM that produces a hypnoid state (that is, the hypnoid defense) in which he feels magically free of all the emotional pain emanating from his daily life. As the drugs rush through his veins and travel into his brain, he feels simultaneously stimulated, tranquilized, sedated, and pacified. In our terminology, Travis abuses drugs as ersatz selfobjects that provide psychoactive effects, the subjective nature of which Travis experiences like an antidepressant, antianxiety, and de-aggressiver.

Travis has a complex ritual surrounding the securing, preparation, and injection of his drugs. Obtaining the drugs, or "copping dope," is followed by the employment of the "works." These drug paraphernalia consist of the spoon and matches he uses as a "cooker" with which to liquefy the heroin and cocaine as well as the needle, syringe, and elastic strap with which to inject the drug.

Travis, like most junkies of the past and present, is extremely careless in his use of needles and often shares contaminated or "dirty" needles with other junkies who frequent the same "shooting gallery." (We return in the Postscript section to this crucial matter.) In listening to Travis describe in detail his drug-use rituals the psychotherapist becomes aware of the symbolic function served by the paraphernalia or "works" he employs in preparing and injecting the drugs. Travis speaks about the drug paraphernalia and the ritualized use of these items as if he is describing the erotic foreplay that precedes sexual intercourse.

The relationship between Travis and the opposite sex is not limited, however, to impersonal and emotionless couplings. On a number of occasions, Travis becomes quite emotionally involved and romantically obsessed with several of the women with whom he has sexual relations. In these instances, Travis thinks about nothing other than his latest romantic conguest.

Travis, in a fashion characteristic of a sex (and love) addict, spends a good part of every day lost in daydreams and reverie about his most recent romantic fantasy about a particular woman. In such an addictive state of mind, Travis has little thought, concern, or worry about either his wife or daughter. He can think only of the woman about whom he entertains romantic fantasies.

As part of his romantic reverie, he is desperate to spend every free moment with the latest object of his infatuation, regardless of the possible damaging consequences to his marriage and family life. Moreover, his romantic addiction with a specific woman also seriously inteferes with his commitment to psychotherapy. In fact, in one specific instance, it contributes to his temporarily dropping out of psychotherapy. Indeed, in all of these instances, it is apparent that Travis is a captive of his own Narcissus complex.

These women exist for Travis only through his own imagination and solely as creatures of pleasure. As such, these women are no more real for Travis than are actresses who act as characters in a movie. The women who inhabit Travis's fantasyland serve as mere semi-human props whose utility is based exclusively on the roles they play in Travis's latest sexual extravaganza.

We divide psychotherapy with Travis into two different phases: (1) in the first and early phase, Travis and the psychotherapist struggle valiantly to help him to achieve a modicum of abstinence from drugs and sex as well as a complete and total cessation of all criminal activity; and, (2) in the second and latter phases—marked by Travis's return to psychotherapy after a 1 year absence and following a near-fatal drug overdose—Travis and the psychotherapist resumed the goal of establishing and maintaining abstinence from all addictive and sociopathic behavior as part of their psychotherapeutic work together.

Upon entering psychotherapy, Travis describes himself as being totally "strung out" on drugs and at the end of his rope. He is hopelessly addicted to speedballs, involved in procuring money to support his drug habit by committing violent crime, and habituated to treating women as sexual playthings. He pleads with the psychotherapist to take him on as a patient despite the serious nature of his addictions and what he knows is his poor prognosis.

As a benefits counselor, he explains that he heard the psychotherapist make a professional presentation on treating violent and drug-addicted patients. He went to great lengths to lavish praise on the psychotherapist in the hopes of persuading the latter to see him in psychotherapy.

Initially, the psychotherapist recognizes the spontaneous presence of Travis's idealizing selfobject transference. Travis unconsciously desires to align himself transferentially with the psychotherapist whom he imagines as an ally strong enough to combat and counteract the powerful hold over him by drugs, violence, and sex. As if by magic, Travis fantasizes that close proximity to an all-powerful ally will permit him to absorb his ally's (namely, the psychotherapist's) strength, willpower, and fortitude.

In the initial stages of the psychotherapy, the psychotherapist has two very powerful countertransference reactions to Travis's transference. On the one hand, he is flattered and somewhat narcissistically seduced by the intensity of Travis's archaic idealization. It is extremely difficult for the psychotherapist to completely resist the alluring temptation of being so archaically idealized. The psychotherapist's own fantasies of (archaic) grandiosity are reactivated countertransferentially by the unconscious pull of Travis's transference fantasy of being merged with an idealized and omnipotent presence.

At first, however, the (intersubjective) fantasy shared by Travis and the psychotherapist of the latter as a demigod proves to be extremely beneficial for the psychotherapy. Travis latches transferentially onto the psychotherapist like a drowning man grasping a life preserver. Travis holds onto a fantasied image of the psychotherapist as a megalomaniacal figure endowed with magical powers. Apparently, Travis believes that such a fantastic presence is his only means of getting off drugs and stopping his criminal career.

Conceptualized in the language of our original theory of intersubjective absorption, we infer the following: the idealizing selfobject transference has become a psychotherapeutic medium for absorbing some of the selfobject-like functions of speedballs, which provide psychoactive relief from dysphoric moods of depression, anxiety, and rage. It appears, therefore, that Travis is beginning to transform the psychotherapist and the psychotherapy into a transitional selfobject thing and an activity, which replace drugs, sex, and violence.

On the other hand, the psychotherapist also has a countertransferential reaction to the fantasy allure of Travis's drug addiction. The psychotherapist himself has a prior history of substance (alcohol and marijuana) abuse. As a result, he reacts countertransferentially with his own addictive fantasies in response to Travis's nonstop talk in session after session about the intense pleasures of getting high on drugs.

In addition to speaking constantly about drugs in his sessions, Travis also reports many drug dreams. For example, "I'm at a party. I impulsively eat heroin and then I snort it. I feel a warm glow pass over my body." In response, the psychotherapist finds himself actually dreaming of once again getting stoned on marijuana. (We return in the Commentary section to another aspect of the psychotherapist's countertransference, namely, his reaction to Travis's use of weapons and the fantasy appeal of violence.)

The psychotherapist, as part of his countertransference reaction to drugs, becomes quite antipathetic toward Travis's plight and fight against drug addiction. The psychotherapist adopts a countertransferentially defensive stance based on an unconscious reaction formation: he plays out the role of the strict disciplinarian who has little time or patience for Travis's frequent relapses and never-ending series of excuses and rationalizations.

Under these intersubjective circumstances, it is hard for the psychotherapist to have much empathy (or sympathy) for Travis and the unconscious meaning of his valiant struggle to overcome his drug addiction. Instead, the psychotherapist succumbs to countertransference antipathy.

Every time Travis relapses, he claims to have had an epiphany about the supposed reasons for his latest "slip." In reaction, the psychotherapist launches into an even more impassioned and stern lecture about the dangers to Travis of continued drug abuse. In hindsight, it seems that the psychotherapist is seeking to warn not only Travis but himself of the dangers of drug abuse.

As part of a transference–countertransference neurosis, the psychotherapist adopts a defensive posture based on an unempathic over-identification with Travis. The psychotherapist is himself so tempted yet distressed countertransferentially by the personal allure of getting high and stoned on drugs that in fantasy he imagines himself as identical to Travis. In this intersubjective context, the psychotherapist attempts, albeit unsuccessfully, to force onto Travis his own solution to drug addiction. As a result, he seeks to compel Travis to cease and desist from all use of drugs.

Blinded by his own countertransference antipathy, the psychotherapist fails to empathize with a bona fide aspect of Travis's own attempt at introspection as a means of understanding the underlying reasons contributing to his relapses. With considerable sarcasm, the psychotherapist ridicules Travis's myriad explanations for his relapses as nothing more than defensive rationalizations without serious intellectual merit. He openly communicates to Travis his antipathy for what he construes to be the melodramatic and hyperbolic nature of Travis's supposed revelations.

At this point in the psychotherapy, Travis reports a dream (the details of which are not relevant) that, if properly interpreted, might have revealed the unconscious meaning of his fight against drug addiction. In retrospect, it is clear from the manifest content and his associations to the dream that Travis has quite a mythological and Odyssean view of himself. In associating to this dream, Travis reminisces about his childhood and his make-believe games in which he imagines himself in the role of John Wayne who shoots his (toy) machine gun to kill enemy soldiers.

Unfortunately, the psychotherapist fails to empathize with Travis and to understand that he is seeking, however obliquely, to accomplish two simultaneous objectives. First, he wants to impress the psychotherapist with his intellectual acumen and prowess; second, he seeks to enlist the psychotherapist as a brother-in-arms in his struggle against drugs. Travis imagines this battle as a titanic clash between himself and drugs: he casts himself as Odysseus and the drugs as the Sirens, who are tempting him as an alluring nemesis.

In a similar vein, the psychotherapist fails to appreciate that transferentially Travis fantasizes himself as both an Odyssean hero and a Greek tragedian. In the latter capacity, he casts the psychotherapist in the role of the Greek chorus. Due to countertransference, the psychotherapist has missed the mirroring and twinship dimensions of the selfobject transference. They elude him because he is too caught up countertransferentially in Travis's archaic idealization of him.

Over time, both the unanalyzed countertransference reaction and over-identification of Travis on the part of the psychotherapist contribute to a breakdown in the psychotherapeutic process of intersubjective absorption, or what we now refer to as the narcissistic exchange process. The idealizing selfobject transference (intersubjectively) absorbs some of the selfobject-like functions of drugs (namely, antianxiety and pacifying). As evidence for this assertion, Travis reports that he is, in fact, far less anxious and prone to mania and violence.

However, the respective antidepressant (mirroring) and humanizing (twinship) selfobject-like functions of speedballs are not absorbed into the selfobject transference. Consequently, drugs continue to have a psychoactive effect on Travis. They provide him with an antidepressant stimulation and a humanizing illusion of being connected to and joined with others.

Then, all of a sudden, and rather unexpectedly, Travis drops out of psychotherapy. He is still getting high on speedballs and supporting his expensive drug habit by illegal (yet nonviolent) means. And, Travis is, at this particular juncture in the psychotherapy, so romantically and sexually addicted to a woman as to have lost all interest in further treatment.

Travis returns to therapy after approximately a one-year absence and shortly after a near-fatal overdose on drugs. Once again, and as was the case in the past, Travis, upon returning to therapy, bestows the psychotherapist with great accolades and compliments. Now, however, and in contrast to the past, Travis is pleading for a second chance.

By the time the psychotherapist agrees to take Travis back into psychotherapy, he has participated in peer supervision of the case with his co-author and colleague. Together, they analyze his countertransference antipathy as it expresses itself both in the form of a defensive reaction formation and over-identification. They recognize that it blinds the psychotherapist to several critical dimensions of the selfobject transference. The psychotherapist, in the second psychotherapeutic go-around with Travis and following peer supervision, adopts a less defensive and more empathic stance toward Travis and his addiction.

However, in order to avoid another, and perhaps fatal, overdose, the psychotherapist and Travis develop a special means of enhancing the potency of the psychotherapy as a selfobject replacement for drugs. They work out the following arrangement: Travis agrees to call the psychotherapist and leave a message on his answering machine before he "scores" or "cops dope" again.

In addition, Travis also commits himself as part of this agreement to talking with the psychotherapist in person prior to injecting drugs again. The period between the time Travis leaves a message on the answering machine and the moment Travis actually speaks with the psychotherapist constitutes a psychotherapeutic "time out." During this "breather," Travis has a chance to rethink and hopefully change his mind about getting high on drugs.

Thereafter, both the telephone and answering machine become integral and semi-human components of the psychotherapy. Adhering strictly to the agreement, Travis leaves long messages on the answering machine about a variety of topics. In talking in sessions with Travis, it is evident to the psychotherapist that Travis has concocted a transference fantasy of the psychotherapist as a semi-human thing, the megalomaniacal presence of which inhabits the telephone and answering machine, thus animating them and bringing them to life.

Travis emphasizes that he feels like he possesses magical control over the psychotherapist (that is, he imagines himself as being a megalomaniacal self) whose voice he hears on the answering machine as he leaves messages at all times of the day and night. As he listens to the psychotherapist's voice and begins his messages, Travis says he pictures the psychotherapist as a disembodied presence in his life that he summons up and controls as he sees fit. Travis speaks about leaving his messages in terms remarkably similar to those he uses in talking about drugs.

According to Travis, the act of leaving a message helps him to stop shooting up drugs because it feels to him like he is injecting himself with a psychotherapeutic (psychopharmacotherapeutic) dose of contact with the psychotherapist. Unlike the face-to-face sessions, the impersonal and rather anonymous nature of this contact allows Travis, he explains, to express himself emotionally to the psychotherapist in ways in which he otherwise feels too inhibited.

As the second round of the psychotherapy progresses, Travis is more connected to and more reliant upon the psychotherapist's telephone and answering machine than to the psychotherapist himself. By dealing with Travis's many drug-related emergencies on the telephone, Travis and the psychotherapist develop a selfobject bond that gradually replaces both his connection to drugs and involvement in illegal activity to support his drug habit. During the next several years of the psychotherapy, they spend hours and hours interacting with each other through the telecommunication medium created by the combination of the telephone and the answering machine.

We make the empathic inference, therefore, that the psychotherapist functions as a transitional selfobject thing existing in Travis's imagination as a disembodied yet semi-human presence. The psychotherapist, who exists for Travis as an inhabitant of the telecommunication devices, is now an imaginary servant who is at Travis's beck and call (that is, whom Travis imagines he controls as part of a fantasy of being a megalomaniacal self). In addition, the very act of using these telecommunication devices, with their inherent impersonal and anonymous interaction, serves for Travis as a transitional selfobject activity.

In the course of their face-to-face sessions, Travis and the psychotherapist speak more openly and candidly about the significance of the telephone and the answering machine. In this context, Travis associates his semi-human connection to the psychotherapist via telecommunication devices to intimate attachments he had made throughout his life to such nonhuman things. These entities include his toy machine gun, his .357 Magnum revolver, and his drug paraphernalia.

Together, Travis and the psychotherapist have quite inadvertently stumbled upon a psychotherapeutic arrangement of major significance. This arrangement enables Travis to make a selfobject connection with the psychotherapist that rivals and eventually supersedes the one he has made previously to inanimate things and activities.

Travis explains that the telecommunication devices provide him with a psychotherapeutic experience that surpasses the one he experiences on drugs and in the past through violence. It tranquilizes and sedates him like speedballs, thus providing him with a psychopharmacotherapeutic effect (namely, antianxiety and pacification) that is powerful enough to replace the purely psychoactive effect of drugs. Moreover, the psychotherapeutic experience provides Travis with a much needed narcissistic illusion of being a megalomaniacal self and as empowered with magical control over the psychotherapy. This allows him to imagine himself as simultaneously admired and allied.

Travis conjures up, via telecommunications, an imaginary state of affairs in which he fantasizes himself as a larger-than-life character of Odyssean proportions. In this imaginary role, he imagines himself as engaged in a heroic battle against a deadly enemy, with the psychotherapist in the background as the admiring audience and Greek chorus. In addition, Travis feels himself empowered by an alliance with the psychotherapist as a brother-in-arms in his fight to overcome his addiction.

Travis progresses over the next couple of years considerably in the psychotherapy. He establishes and maintains abstinence from all forms of addiction—drugs and sex—as well as ceases all antisocial and criminal behavior. Of equal importance, Travis also develops a less semi-human and hence more human connection to the psychotherapist. The nature, content, and associations to a series of dreams that Travis reports at this juncture reveal a great deal about the unconscious meaning of his deepening connection to the psychotherapist.

In one of these dreams, Travis notes:

> I'm in a room talking with a male friend about the difficulty in
> establishing a daily exercise program despite its health benefits. As
> I'm talking, I notice that the door is open. Standing outside in a
> crowded shopping mall is a naked man with a clip board. I'm struck
> by the fact that the man doesn't seem to be bothered at all about
> being naked in the middle of a crowd of people; instead, he seems
> very relaxed and at ease. I also notice that the man has a big cock.
> I think to myself (in the dream) that I wish that I had a big cock
> like the naked man.

There are many fascinating aspects of this dream, all of which are
interpreted at length by Travis and the psychotherapist. However, for
the purposes of the present discussion, there are several features that
are most relevant. Both the manifest content of the dream and Travis's
associations reveal that he unconsciously connects the naked man with
the psychotherapist.

Apparently, Travis internalizes the psychotherapist as a more human
presence whom he is in the process of transmuting into a phallically
endowed figure worthy of emulation. He admires the psychotherapist
as someone he imagines as unabashed and uninhibitedly displaying his
phallic endowment and prowess. He wants to possess these phallic
qualities too. The psychotherapy becomes a symbolic arena in which
Travis imagines himself as "strutting his stuff" and "showing off" his new
found sense of potency.

In the past, Travis says he needed a nonstop string of sexual
conquests, drugs, a weapon, and a willingness to use it, all in order to
feel secure about his masculinity. Now, he states, he has progressed to
a point of maturity at which he recognizes that these things are all merely
props, and not the real thing. True manhood resides, Travis exclaims, in
a secure sense of one's own inner psychic strength and fortitude.

In a second dream from this series, Travis indicated:

> You and I are standing together in a bathroom and are pissing in
> urinals. As we're pissing, I look down at a mirror located in-between
> the two urinals. I can see our cocks. I notice that yours is larger than
> mine, but I say to myself that mine is big enough.

Again, although there are a number of interesting aspects to the
dream, our current focus concerns one in particular. Together, Travis
and the psychotherapist interpret the dream as indicating that Travis
continues to evolve in his unconscious sense of himself as a man. As

part of this unconscious process, he internalizes the psychotherapist as a phallic ideal by which to measure himself and his progress. Based on the dream and its interpretation, it appears that unconsciously Travis internalizes and transmutes, or intersubjectively absorbs, enough of the psychotherapist's powerful presence to feel secure and "big enough."

Commentary

There are several dimensions of this case that require further commentary. However, there is one underlying and unconscious psychodynamic that needs to be further illuminated in order to pull together these strands. In our preceding discussion, we emphasize a particular dimension of the transference–countertransference neurosis, which we believe is central to understanding the case: namely, the intersubjective fantasy shared by Travis and the psychotherapist about the unconscious meaning and function of drugs. We stress that Travis and the psychotherapist share not only a fantasy but a history of drug abuse as well. This shared history creates countertransference problems for the psychotherapist, which initially interferes with his ability to conduct the psychotherapy.

However, the psychotherapist and Travis share still something else in common: both have a history of antisocial and criminal activities. During much of the early phases of the psychotherapy, Travis is actively engaged in antisocial and criminal behavior related to his drug addiction. The psychotherapist also has a past that includes an alcohol and drug abuse history as well as a record of juvenile delinquency.

As a teenager, the psychotherapist had an antisocial history, which included disciplinary problems at school, associating with known vagrants and felons, possessing and using a dangerous weapon (a switchblade knife), committing vandalism, engaging in shoplifting, and destroying public property. In this regard, he was involved in a number of incidents that were brought to the attention of school officials and law enforcement authorities. In several of these situations, he was arrested and charged as a juvenile. Eventually, he appeared before a judge in juvenile court and was placed on a year's probation. The judge made it abundantly clear to all concerned (that is, the then teenaged psychotherapist and his parents, both of whom were lawyers) that another appearance in juvenile court would automatically result in being sentenced to reform school.

We now believe that the psychotherapist's prior history of juvenile delinquency shapes his subjectivity in the context of the psychotherapy with Travis in a particular fashion: it plays an important role in structuring a critical intersubjective dimension of the transference–countertransference neurosis. Together, Travis and the psychotherapist share an intersubjective fantasy of the unconscious appeal of violence, which is integral to the analysis of Travis's Narcissus complex.

In addition to a shared history of antisocial and criminal activity, based, no doubt, on a similar pattern of enacting violent fantasies, Travis and the psychotherapist also share a number of other developmental similarities. Both were raised in middle or upper middle-class families; both have fathers who are lawyers and are real intellectuals. As boys and youngsters, both are quite estranged and alienated from their respective fathers, each of whom is distant and aloof from his respective adolescent son.

By turning to the streets and teenage peers, Travis and the psychotherapist also respond similarly to the alienation and estrangement they experience in their similar relationships with their fathers. In the course of their respective adolescences, both Travis and the psychotherapist are exposed to and subsequently become involved in the use, and eventual abuse of addictive substances, including alcohol and especially drugs. Both also share similar tendencies toward violent sociopathy (and, in the case of Travis, psychopathy).

There can be little doubt that their similar problems in fashioning an emotionally sustaining relationship with their respective fathers seriously interferes in their ability to transmutingly internalize their fathers as idealized paternal imagos. As a result, they develop a limited capacity to regulate themselves emotionally, and especially to steer their aggression in a productive direction. We empathically infer that both unconsciously attempt to utilize their aggression to shore up a flimsy, phallic narcissism and accompanying fragile sense of masculinity.

There is an impressive body of literature that documents the important connection between drug addiction and sociopathy as well as psychopathy (see, for example, Cadoret et al., 1984; Chein et al., 1964; Forrest, 1994; Lindner, 1946; Menninger, 1938; Schucket, 1973; Valliant, 1975; Wurmser, 1978; Wurmser & Spiro, 1969; and Yochelson & Samenow, 1986). From our self-psychological perspective, however, megalomania constitutes a significant link between these two types of narcissistic behavior disorder. In the instances of both drug addiction and sociopathy (and particularly in psychopathy), the addict and/or sociopath (psychopathy) has a very narcissistically disturbed view of the human surround.

For these types of individuals, other people either do not exist as humans at all or they exist only as semi-human things. As such, other people have very little narcissistic value for the addict or sociopath (or psychopath) beyond the purely practical value that they possess as a means to achieving a particular end. A sociopathic (or psychopathic) addict, like Travis and the psychotherapist as a teenager, is governed by fantasies of being a megalomaniacal self controlling the fate of others. Hence, this type of individual personifies an addict as the consummate fantasy junkie and control freak.

Lost in a wonderland of narcissistic illusion, an addict imagines that other people are mere stick figures or doll-like replicas of real human beings. Having so dehumanized others, a sociopathic (or psychopathic) addict treats or mistreats them with little or no regard for the harm or damage inflicted on them. It is a foolhardy person, indeed, who attempts to thwart a sociopathic (or psychopathic) addict's need for a megalo-maniacal illusion of ultimate control. Such resistance often results in a narcissistic rage reaction on the part of this type of addict, who then may strike out with a blind and violent fury.

Any action on the part of another person, which unduly interferes with the personal agenda of a sociopathic (or psychopathic) addict, is typically experienced by the addict as a narcissistic injury that precipitates some type of (antisocial) response. In the midst of such narcissistic rage, a sociopathic (or psychopathic) addict may find himself or herself consumed by violent fantasies of utter destruction. These *narcissistic rage fantasies* on the part of this type of addict fuel a wrath that subsides only with the subjugation or annihilation of the unwitting offender.

From a typological perspective, we view Travis as an addictive character who suffers from a self-disorder of the bipolar (in contrast to unipolar), subtype I with a predominance of narcissistic rage of a sociopathic and psychopathic nature. In the case of Travis, the absence of a maternal mirroring presence in combination with the presence of an alcoholic and violent father produced massive psychic damage in all major (narcissistic) areas of Travis's sense of self.

Unlike most of our other patients, Travis had resorted in the past to violence against others as one of his preferred ways of attempting to hold himself together narcissistically. The psychic fuel for Travis's nar-cissistic rages is violent and megalomaniacal fantasies of annihilating and obliterating others. In the context of past criminal acts of a violent nature, Travis evidenced an antipathetic indifference toward the well-being of others. From our self-psychological perspective, such callousness is truly diagnostic of sociopathy and psychopathy.

In this respect, Travis's experience of violence at the hands of his father, who is himself quite megalomaniacal, also contributes significantly to a serious narcissistic disturbance in Travis's sense of his own humanness. Travis has a history of abusing and violently mistreating others as well as himself. Everyone, including himself, exists in Travis's imagination as if they are at best semi-human and at worst nonhuman things. The disturbed sense of Travis's humanness is reflected in his antipathetic disregard for his own physical and emotional well-being.

We believe that Travis is typical of many dissociated patients who suffer early, and sometimes irreparable, damage to their ability to create a whole (or, integrated and unified) sense of self. Early in life, the selfobject milieu of these patients is so unempathic and antipathetic as to preclude such a developmental achievement. And, the narcissistic damage in these patients leads to dissociative splits (that is, vertical splits) in the self. Such vertical splits are evidenced by parts of the self (or part-selves) that remain developmentally unintegrated and untransformed.

However, an addicted patient like Travis, in contradistinction to a typical multiple personality disorder (MPD) or dissociative identity disorder (DID) patient, does not undergo spontaneous forms of dissociation as expressed in the guise of multiple selves or "alters." Rather, a patient such as Travis ends up in a dissociated or hypnoid state as a defensive by-product of the addictive process. In such a hypnoid state, psychic parts or fragments of an addict's self, which are otherwise vertically split off, gain access to and take over consciousness in the form of archaic narcissistic fantasies. An addicted patient such as Travis is different in some significant respects from the MPD or DID patient. However, in other respects, we think it is perfectly legitimate to place all of these patients on a phenomenological continuum of pathological dissociation.

In the early phases of the psychotherapy, Travis reported in great detail about his past robberies and stickups. And, in response, the psychotherapist was distressed to find himself having violent dreams of once again fighting with and attacking other people with dangerous weapons. In retrospect, it seemed clear that the psychotherapist's own prior history of violent and antisocial behavior was stirred up by Travis and his emotionally charged recounting of his criminal activities. The psychotherapist found the countertransference fantasy appeal of violence too strong to resist, or at least on the unconscious level of dream-fantasy. The psychotherapist found himself unable countertransferentially to resist the allure of dreaming about a fantasy of being a megalomaniacal self and as empowered with magical control over others resulting from the use (or, more accurately, the misuse) of violence and weapons.

Earlier in our discussion of the case of Travis, we describe the reaction formation which characterizes the psychotherapist's counter-transference response to Travis's continued abuse of speedballs. We now suggest that the psychotherapist is also caught up countertransfer-entially by the unconscious (that is, fantasy) appeal of violence. The psychotherapist, as a result of sharing with Travis megalomaniacal fantasies of violent control, joined Travis as an imaginary partner-in-crime. The countertransference pull of his own fantasies of being a megalomaniacal self handicapped the psychotherapist in his ability to interpret the unconscious meaning of violence for Travis.

In this instance, the psychotherapist was unaware initially that he shares with Travis the fantasy appeal of violence. The lack of awareness on the part of the psychotherapist helped to create a trans-ference–countertransference psychodynamic that seriously interfered with the narcissistic exchange process. It hindered Travis's ability to make the narcissistic swap of the psychoactive effects of criminal behav-ior for the psychopharmacotherapeutic effects of the psychotherapy. The psychotherapist had difficulty in establishing himself for Travis as a transference presence that invites and facilitates such an exchange, and with it, the absorption of the narcissistic functioning of illegal activity.

Travis and the psychotherapist shared an unconscious intersubjective fantasy of antisocial behavior that made them imaginary partners-in-crime rather than brothers-in-arms. In the latter capacity, it would have been possible for them to ally themselves in a joint fight against a common enemy, namely, the violent and ultimately self-destructive life of a junkie. Instead, they shared the (intersubjective) fantasy of being partners-in-crime. This served only to exacerbate rather than ameliorate Travis's underlying proclivity toward sociopathy (and, in the past, psychopathy). (See Gole-man, January 15, 1995; Bob Herbert, April 22, 1999; and Kershaw, Novem-ber 7, 2003 for reports in the popular press [*New York Times*] on the connections among addiction, violence, fantasy, and control.)

A growing consensus is emerging among influential circles within both the academic and scientific communities about the truly addictive nature of violence. We contend that violence is addictive, in part, because of its arousal of fantasies of being a megalomaniacal self who wields violence as a means of magical control. Certain narcissistically disturbed individuals experience exhilaration and intoxication under the influence of the fantasy of being a megalomaniacal self who treats other people as if they were disposable items.

It is our contention that such an individual, for example, a socio-pathic (or psychopathic) addict, is arrested at the developmental stage of the toddler, who, at times, may treat people like they were things, and vice versa. As part of the Narcissus complex, certain toddlers, and later a sociopathic (or psychopathic) addict, may be highly prone to violent temper tantrums. In such blind rages, such an addict may attack or treat other people or property on the basis of the sudden breakdown of distinctions, which we normally make, between the human and the nonhuman as well as between the ownership and the usurpation of property.

If the psychotherapist was less drawn into and distracted by the shared fantasy of being a partner-in-crime with Travis, then Travis might have become more easily (intersubjectively) absorbed in a shared fantasy of being a brother-in-arms with the psychotherapist. Such an intersub-jective context might have served as a clinical medium facilitating the narcissistic exchange of "sex, drugs, and rock 'n roll" for psychotherapy.

Based on such a psychotherapeutic transaction, Travis might have become fortified narcissistically enough to withstand the inevitable crash that ensues from withdrawing from his illusions of living the high life and similar fantasies of traveling in the fast lane. The failure to complete this stage of the narcissistic exchange process left Travis with little or no recourse other than to continue his secret, subterranean existence as a fantasy junkie addicted to a life of crime.

Following his return to psychotherapy, Travis and the psychother-apist together made a fortuitous discovery regarding the transitional selfobject functioning of the telephone and answering machine. This serendipitous finding served as the basis for creating the psychothera-peutic ambiance necessary for Travis to imagine himself as a brother-in-arms with the psychotherapist.

Over the telephone and in his long messages on the answering machine, Travis chronicled the details of his battle to overcome his addiction to "sex, drugs, and rock 'n roll." Perhaps, for Travis the more impersonal nature of such communication facilitated a previously missing dimension to the psychotherapeutic dialogue. Travis exchanged the narcissistic functioning of drugs, his ATMs—that is, the drug works, sex, and the .357 Magnum revolver—for the narcissistic functioning of the telephone and the answering machine. For Travis, these latter entities proved to be more valuable as utilitarian instruments.

The two dreams, which Travis reported during this latter phase of the psychotherapy, take on a new and additional meaning when we place them in the context of the narcissistic exchange process. We now make an interpretation of a latent and deeper meaning of these dreams, which suggests a fantasy shared by Travis and the psychotherapist of the psychotherapy as a phallic tool and weapon, that is, an "analytic instrument" (Isakower, 1992 [1957]). In view of their similar early histories and common developmental psychopathologies, it is not so surprising that Travis and the psychotherapist might share an unconscious (intersubjective) fantasy of the psychotherapy as a symbolic phallus, which they imagine that they jointly possess and control.

Our current re-interpretation of the latent content of these two dreams points in this direction. Travis wished unconsciously to share in what he imagined as the psychotherapist's cockiness, that is, the latter's self-assurance and self-confidence. Apparently, Travis detected what he considered to be the psychotherapist's sense of himself as being phallically well-endowed. (This is a form of narcissistic rather than sexual endowment, that is, phallic narcissism.) Travis conceived of such a phallic endowment as an invaluable weapon in his battle against drugs. (See, for example, Edgcumbe & Burgner, 1975; Forman, 1981; Meissner, 1985; and Rothstein, 1984a,b for a more classically psychoanalytic perspective.) These more Freudian authors might view both Travis and the psychotherapist as "phallic-narcissistic characters" who share a fantasy of the psychotherapy as a phallic weapon. In contrast to our self-psychological perspective, the more classically oriented view emphasizes the purely defensive and regressive nature of such a shared fantasy, without, however, giving sufficient attention to its more adaptive and progressive features.

We concur with what these more traditional psychoanalysts might argue is a fantasy shared by Travis and the psychotherapist of the psychotherapy as a powerful weapon or instrument. However, we view this shared or intersubjective fantasy as having more adaptive, and hence psychotherapeutic, potential.

On the basis of such a jointly held fantasy, Travis experienced both the psychotherapy and himself as endowed with enough phallic prowess to succeed in the battle against his addiction. Sharing in such an intersubjective fantasy allowed Travis to imagine himself as a megalomaniacal self who exercises magical control of *something* even more powerful than the tools of his trade (that is, drug works and, in the past, weapons). The narcissistic illusion of being a megalomaniacal self and as endowed with control over the psychotherapy as an "analytic instrument" enabled Travis to gradually exchange drugs, sex, and violence as ATMs for the analytic instruments as constituted by the telephone and the answering machine.

The semi-human nature of these telecommunication devices was crucial to the eventual success of the narcissistic exchange. Fortunately, it was not necessary for Travis to make an immediate swap of the psychotherapist as a personal and human presence for drugs, sex, and violence. Had such been the case, then, in all likelihood, Travis would not have been able to complete the trade inherent in the narcissistic exchange process.

Postscript

A number of years passed since Travis successfully terminated his psychoanalytic psychotherapy. He recontacted the psychotherapist with the tragic yet predictable news that he had recently tested positive for the HIV virus. All the years of sharing dirty needles as part of his intravenous drug use had finally caught up with Travis.

The ultimately self-destructive and suicidal nature of Travis's fantasy of being a megalomaniacal self is all too apparent in light of his testing positive for HIV. Unfortunately, Travis would eventually pay the ultimate price, namely his life, for indulging himself addictively in the megalomaniacal fantasy of specific things and activities (ATMs) as agents to entertain the illusion of magical control over his psychological universe.

Soon after learning of Travis testing HIV-positive, the psychotherapist had a dream that he too is similarly infected. Knowing full-well that he is not, in fact, HIV-positive, the psychotherapist realized that his dream reflects a resurgence of his old over-identification with Travis. Just as he had shared with Travis in the latter's fantasies about drugs and violence, so too the psychotherapist imagined he shared with Travis in a fate worse than death. Despite all the years that had elapsed since Travis was in psychotherapy, the psychotherapist still shared a fantasy with Travis of dying together as the cost of having been partners-in-crime.

ERROL

Overview

Errol, a 36-year-old, foreign-born computer salesman, began his approximately 10-year psychotherapy complaining of a variety of symptoms including severe anxiousness, agitation, and depression. He was referred to the psychotherapist by our patient Teddy (Chapter 4), who is his sponsor in Alcoholics Anonymous (AA). At the start of his psychotherapy, Errol was briefly abstinent from alcohol; however, he is still an active gambling and sex addict. (Aside from two early and relatively minor relapses, Errol remained abstinent from alcohol throughout his psychotherapy.)

In the past, Errol gambled addictively by betting excessively on racehorses at the track; in the present, he speculates on the stock market, and, more specifically, he bets on whether the market will move up or down on a given day. Errol is sexually addicted to prostitutes, massage parlors, peep shows, as well as to masturbating compulsively.

We dub our patient Errol on the basis of specific masturbation fantasies. In his masturbatory fantasy scenarios he imagines himself as being similar to the film star Errol Flynn. Like the movie matinee idol, our patient Errol is debonair, quite handsome, and possesses a European flair as exemplified by a taste for fine wines, expensive clothes, and beautiful women. In appearance, he strikes a swashbuckling pose reminiscent of Errol Flynn as a pirate in a poster from one of his early action-adventure movies.

In the initial phase of the psychotherapy, we gain the following picture of Errol's early life. He grew up in a major European capital as one of three children. (He immigrated to the United States several years before he began psychotherapy.) Early in psychotherapy, Errol reveals that as a youngster he devised a rather unique and very unusual method of masturbation: he stuck his penis into the nozzle of a vacuum cleaner, turned on the machine, and reached orgasm through the sucking and vibrating motion of the nozzle rubbing against his erect penis.

The psychotherapist explores in some psychoanalytic depth Errol's highly unusual yet innovative form of masturbation; the psychotherapist reconstructs a line of development in the evolution of the content and function of Errol's masturbatory fantasies. They evolve from a childhood version as poorly articulated, ill-formed, and vague imagery to a stereotypical version in adolescence and adulthood. In this latter version, Errol fantasizes himself as an Errol Flynn-like figure surrounded by a bevy of adoring young women. Errol envisions them all as enthralled and captivated by his phallic endowment and orgasmic prowess.

This more fully evolved masturbatory fantasy is organized unconsciously on the basis of an archaically grandiose image of Errol as a sexual stud, whom women find both overpowering and irresistible. In the context of his Narcissus complex, he fantasizes himself as being a megalomaniacal self who is surrounded by an audience of adoring young women, all of whom function for him as imaginary selfobject mirrors reflecting back the brilliance of his phallic narcissism. (See Lenoff, 1998, for a discussion of "phantasy selfobjects.")

As activated by masturbation, the phantasmagorical image Errol conjures up of himself contrasts sharply with the painful reality of his existence as a child and teenager. He portrays these early and adolescent years as extremely bleak, foreboding, and morose. As a child, Errol describes himself as existing in a world almost devoid of any contact with other human beings. He relates he has little involvement or connection to either his parents or two siblings, a brother and sister. During his childhood and youth, he spends most of his time alone. He is absorbed narcissistically in solitary activities, including masturbation with a vacuum cleaner.

The youthful selfobject milieu in which Errol grows up is extremely impoverished and without the presence of healthy connections to other human beings. During this period, he experiences himself as a freak of nature without any close relationships to other family members or any friends. Existing as a self-proclaimed oddball, Errol says he imagines himself as different from everyone else and as lacking in a basic and essential humanness. Experiencing himself as a psychological pariah, Errol fantasizes himself as existing in his own lonely habitat, a domain he is convinced is cut off by an unbridgeable gulf from the rest of the world.

The somewhat autistic and schizoid world of Errol's youth places severe emotional limits on his existence. His emotionally meaningful contacts are limited to inanimate things and activities. These nonhuman entities substitute poorly and inadequately for missing and absent selfobject connections to other human beings.

It is no wonder, then, that Errol resorts to the use (or abuse) of a vacuum cleaner—it serves as a mechanical way of generating masturbatory fantasies by means of which Errol transports himself magically to a private wonderland, the pleasurable and narcissistic illusions of which temporarily supplant the otherwise painful reality confronting him. In essence, Errol grows up organized unconsciously in accordance with a mortifying narcissistic fantasy of himself as an alien being. As such an inhuman creature, Errol's only experience of himself as even somewhat human occurs in the midst of the narcissistic bliss of masturbation.

Gradually, it becomes more obvious to the psychotherapist that a very important yet unconscious connection exists for Errol between the compulsive masturbation of his youth and his later addiction as an adult to gambling and sex. In his younger years, Errol escapes regularly into a masturbatory-induced fantasy world. In his youthful version of this wonderland, he imagines himself as no longer alone, ignored, and inhuman; instead, he metamorphizes into a sexual superman who possesses extraordinary erotic powers that enable him to cast a spell over females.

As part of this version of his lifelong masturbatory fantasy scenario, these young women willingly became his sexual slaves. As an adult, he plays out these psychoactive fantasy tapes, with their psychoactive (that is, antidepressant and humanizing) effects, in the form of his addiction to gambling and sex. Errol re-experiences as an adult the narcissistic pleasures of his youth through addictively reliving these fantasies of being a megalomaniacal self.

As a sex addict, Errol abuses women in the course of (mis)treating them as his personal property and sexual playthings. In this regard, Errol, like Travis, entertains himself with fantasies of himself as being a megalomaniacal self who, as a sexual potentate, rules over and controls a harem of exotic beauties.

Similarly, and in the midst of his addiction to gambling, Errol imagines himself as at first a slick handicap bettor, who always picks the winning horse at the race track, and later as a financial wizard, who is a mastermind of the ups and downs of the stock market. (See Grant & Potenza (eds.), 2004; and Petry, 2005 for recent studies on compulsive or addictive gambling.) Long ago, Freud (1961 [1928], p. 272) argued that masturbation is the root of all subsequent forms of addiction. In line with Freud's early contention, the therapist views Errol's childhood masturbation as the basis for his later addiction to both sex and gambling. These latter two forms of addiction are intended unconsciously by Errol to serve as "fantasy fixes" that will remedy the painful reality of his day-to-day living.

Early in psychotherapy, Errol reports a dream the interpretation of which depicts in symbolic form his subjectivity, especially as reflects both in his depressing memories of his youth and his morose accounts of his current existence. In the dream: "I am walking *alone* down the street. There are no other people around. I'm just surrounded by tall skyscrapers. I'm panicked because there is no one else around."

Errol comments on the dream-fantasy of himself standing alone and panic-stricken amidst the concrete, steel, and glass of the towering buildings. He associates this image to his lifelong sense of himself as a being whose main connection is to the nonhuman world of things and activities. Later in the psychotherapy, the significance of Errol's sense of panic in the dream becomes much clearer.

When the psychotherapist asks Errol to free associate to the "tall buildings," Errol mentions they remind him of his penis as it becomes erect during masturbation. He says he feels at least somewhat human and alive in the midst of masturbating. Otherwise, he indicates he experiences himself as at best a subhuman being who wanders alone as an alien among the massive and imposing buildings of the big city. In this regard, he refers to himself as a creature much like the Elephant Man, that is, a deformed freak of nature with barely human features.

At this point in his life, Errol lives by himself in a sparsely furnished one bedroom apartment. Besides the customers he deals with as a computer salesman, Errol manages to make some human contact through anonymous sex. He engages in this sexual activity on an almost nightly basis with street hookers or other prostitutes in massage parlors and peep shows. Errol also has a fleeting experience of human contact during the hours and hours he spends at his stockbroker's office. In this setting, he stands with other speculators staring transfixed and spellbound (or, more specifically, in a hypnoid and altered state of consciousness) at the terminal of the electronic ticker tape.

Errol has a very active fantasy life, one he enacts on a regular basis. For example, he admits he often goes to bars, masquerading as an important foreign dignitary living here in the United States. As part of his charade, Errol picks up various women and "beds them for the night" (that is, has sex with them). Sometimes, he continues to play act his make-believe role for days and even weeks. This is an example of a fantasy of being a megalomaniacal self, that is, a fantasy junkie and control freak.

Many of the women whom he picks up and cons are quite well-to-do. Bamboozled by Errol, they entertain him at their summer and winter homes, introducing him to many of their socially and financially prominent friends. Errol stays in character throughout the entire episode and pretends to be a European of aristocratic heritage.

A large body of psychoanalytic literature exists (see, for example, Bartemeier, 1954; Feldman, 1962; Katan, 1958; Kaywin, 1968; Martin, 1988; Ross, 1967; Sherwood & Cohen, 1994; Weiss, 1966) that describes a psychological disorder originally labeled by Deutsch (1965 [1942]) as the "as if" personality. Deutsch asserts that such a person suffers from a severe form of dissociative disturbance she refers to as "depersonalization" (p. 263).

According to Deutsch, in such a depersonalized state a person's sense of self is psychopathologically disturbed, making it extremely difficult for an individual to distinguish between fantasy and reality. Consequently, this type of disturbed person tends to substitute especially "[n]arcissistic fantasies" (p. 268) for the reality of actual relationships, and, in the process, becomes a mere by-product of his or her own imagination. Such individuals can live out much of their lives on an "as if" basis, that is, involved in acting the part of a make-believe character whom they have invented in their own minds. In this sense, then, such a person's existence is based more on fantasy than reality. (For several recent studies of such personalities, see J. Martin, 1988, on William Faulkner; and Sloan, 1996, on Jerzy Kosinski; Carrere, 2000; and Finstad, 2001, on Natalie Wood.)

Errol falls clearly into the category of the "as if" personality. His self-absorption in and acting out of his grandiose fantasy of himself as the European aristocrat is evidence of the severe nature of the dissociative disturbance in his sense of the psychological reality of his self. In this regard, we locate Errol (like Travis) on a phenomenological continuum of pathological dissociation. The case of Errol makes clear that an individual may suffer simultaneously from both an "as if" personality disorder and an addictive disorder.

Both Errol and Travis are addicts whose level of dissociation is extreme enough to make it clear that addiction shares in some of the same characteristics and unconscious psychodynamics as other disorders such as DID or the "as if" personality. Persons who suffer from these disorders are involved in a narcissistic (in contrast to a psychotic) retreat from reality into a fantasy world. In such an imaginary domain they are cut off from healthy contact with other people and events. The difference between an individual who suffers from DID or the "as if" personality and a person who is addicted is as follows: the former concocts fantastic visions of their personal existence, whereas the latter conjures up addictive fantasies about the magical qualities of things and activities.

As the psychotherapy progresses, Errol repeatedly asks his psychotherapist the same rhetorical question: "So, what do you think?" Errol immediately poses this question every time he makes what he believes is a particularly dazzling observation.

Initially, the psychotherapist is puzzled by the meaning and function of Errol's query. However, he surmises that Errol intends unconsciously for the inquiry to be purely rhetorical. Thus, Errol does not really desire or expect the psychotherapist to provide an actual answer to his question. Rather, he wants the psychotherapist simply to confirm and agree with his latest and greatest insight. Indeed, Errol desires for the psychotherapist to respond admiringly and to be in total agreement with him. From our self-psychological perspective, we infer that Errol wishes unconsciously to be mirrored and twinned by the psychotherapist as a transference selfobject.

The psychotherapist responds empathically to Errol's transference fantasy of being mirrored and twinned by a selfobject. In so doing, the psychotherapist initiates the therapeutic process, which we originally referred to as intersubjective absorption (see Ulman & Paul, 1989). More specifically, the psychotherapist facilitates a narcissistic exchange, on Errol's part, of the psychoactive (antidepressant and humanizing) functions of gambling and sex for the psychopharmacotherapeutic effect of the psychotherapy.

Errol and the psychotherapist incorporate Errol's rhetorical question as an ongoing part of the psychotherapeutic dialogue. Errol often poses it in his lengthy and elaborate messages, many of which he leaves on the psychotherapist's telephone answering machine.

At this point in the evolution of our work with addicted patients, we already had discovered the selfobject function of this telecommunication device in treating Travis. Thus, we employed it in a similar fashion in the psychotherapy with Errol. In working with Errol, the telephone answering machine serves a function similar in the psychotherapy of Travis.

It allows Errol to establish a selfobject connection with the psychotherapist that is very impersonal and anonymous in nature. And, in a manner similar to Travis, Errol indicates that he really enjoys the free access and illusion of control that are part of a fantasy of being a megalomaniacal self in which he imagines himself magically summoning up the psychotherapist. He imagines, he says, that the psychotherapist is almost like a genie in a bottle.

In this regard, we are reminded of Kohut's (1984) description of the fantasy-based nature of twinship. In Kohut's original discussion, he describes a psychoanalytic situation in which a patient recovers a child-hood memory involving a fantasy of possessing and controlling a "genie in the bottle" (p. 195). Having replicated a version of this fantasy in the transference, she imagines that Kohut functions for her in a fashion analogous to that of her genie.

With the aid of the telephone answering machine, Errol creates a phantasmagorical twin and alter ego, which he imagines as answering him with an approving nod of consent to Errol's every question. Having asked his question—whether in session or over the phone—Errol simply proceeds as if the psychotherapist has answered in complete agreement with him. Such agreement is based unconsciously for Errol on the fact that he and the psychotherapist share an identical opinion. Apparently, Errol believes he and the psychotherapist see eye-to-eye on all matters. In sharing such an intersubjective fantasy with Errol, the psychotherapist facilitates a twinship dimension to the selfobject transference.

Based on his childhood relationship to a nonhuman thing (namely, the vacuum cleaner) Errol, like Travis, makes a vital connection to the semi-human telephone answering machine. In the past, the vacuum cleaner functioned for Errol as a pre-addictive thing, which we distin-guish from a pre-fetishistic object. In the present, the telecommunication device, unlike the vacuum cleaner, functions as a healthy entity rather than as a psychopathological thing. In this latter capacity, the telephone answering machine is part of a transitional selfobject fantasy, which is in the service of the psychotherapy.

The psychotherapist manages to achieve an early psychotherapeutic objective in shifting the psychoactive (that is, antidepressant and human-izing) effects of Errol's addictions away from his ATMs (or, ersatz selfobjects) and toward the psychotherapy. However, this psychothera-peutic shift is only partial. During this period of the psychotherapy, Errol abstains from gambling for approximately six to ten months; however, he has very little success in achieving the same kind of abstinence from sex.

Yet, despite the only partial nature of his recovery from both of his addictions, Errol still makes some major strides in improving his life. He marries (for the second time) and begins to set up a home and have a family. Now, as a family man, Errol speaks openly about wanting to emulate the psychotherapist, who he knows has recently moved his own family to a well-to-do suburb outside of the city. (He has knowledge of this fact because he began seeing the psychotherapist in the city and now Errol sees him in his new home office.)

However, Errol is unsuccessful in his attempt to buy a home in the same community as that of the psychotherapist. In deep despair, Errol plunges emotionally into an empty, depleted depression. He complains bitterly of feeling once again like a complete failure who does not belong to the human race. The psychotherapist makes a valiant effort to help Errol overcome this emotional setback. Yet, despite the psychotherapist's most well-meaning intentions, Errol relapses on gambling and continues to be addicted to sex.

In the midst of this addictive relapse, Errol reports the following dream: "I'm with a group of people and we're all gambling. Everyone is winning. We're all happy and excited." In associating to the dream, Errol leaves little doubt about its unconscious meaning: it symbolically reflects his fantasy of being a megalomaniacal self who abuses gambling as an activity of magical control that miraculously reverses the emotional woes of his financial misfortune.

As part of his addictive fantasy, Errol imagines himself as undergoing a metamorphosis. In this dream, he is transmogrified from a lonely loser, without any friends or acquaintances, into a "winner among winners," who is surrounded by his pals and cronies. As an ersatz selfobject or ATM, gambling enables Errol to come under the influence of the addictive fantasy. It provides him simultaneously with the illusion of being connected to and "twinned" by other people (that is, humanization) as well as being uplifted and relieved of a depressive sense of inadequacy and incompetence (that is, mirrored).

The sudden and dramatic nature of Errol's gambling relapse necessitates that the psychotherapist analyze further the unconscious psychodynamics of the transference–countertransference neurosis. (In the Commentary section, we return to a discussion of the unconscious forces contributing to Errol's failure to achieve long-lasting abstinence from his sex addiction.) In the course of peer supervision with his colleague and co-author, the psychotherapist revisits and reviews his own past in regard to a prior addiction to gambling.

As a young man, the psychotherapist was quite an habitué of the racetrack. He whiled away many pleasurable hours at the track poring over the racing forms, traded tips on "sure" winners with other bettors, and waged considerable sums of money. In fact, the psychotherapist garnered quite a reputation among his close friends as an expert on racehorse betting.

Rarely, if ever, did he go to the track alone. Instead, he was almost always accompanied by a buddy, who treated him to a lavish meal in exchange for betting tips. The narcissistic nature of this exchange is transacted, however, in the context of an addiction rather than as part of a transitional selfobject activity. The narcissistic currency in this exchange is bogus, therefore, and does not evolve functionally into an adaptive form of psychological structure.

At the time of Errol's relapse, the psychotherapist is under considerable financial pressures as a result of purchasing an expensive, new home. During sessions with Errol, the psychotherapist finds himself drifting off into reveries about winning the lottery. In this intersubjective context, the psychotherapist has difficulty empathizing with Errol's tales of financial woe. Instead, the psychotherapist fantasizes about finding some magic solution to his own emotional and monetary troubles. The psychotherapist escapes unconsciously into his own gambling fantasies about winning a jackpot.

In addition, the psychotherapist becomes further self-absorbed and distracted in the midst of his own addictive reverie. He entertains various financial scenarios involving the best way to invest his imaginary fortune. The psychotherapist imagines scenarios in which he invests his money in the stock market, where he makes a financial killing and raises the capital necessary to eliminate all the unanticipated expenses of owning a new home.

Like Errol, the psychotherapist is fascinated by the stock market as well as other investment opportunities, which are more speculative and risky in nature. In contrast to Errol, however, the psychotherapist is much more circumspect and ultimately successful in his financial transactions on the stock market and with other investments.

Nonetheless, the psychotherapist becomes lost in his own wonderland and, consequently, loses empathic contact with Errol's mortifying fantasy of himself as an abysmal failure and subhuman being. The self-absorption on the part of the psychotherapist interferes, therefore, with the psychotherapeutic process of intersubjective absorption (or narcissistic exchange).

Imagining himself as an instant millionaire, the psychotherapist escapes (dissociates) temporarily in fantasy from his otherwise narcissistically mortifying fantasies of financial ruin. Lost in daydream, he concocts fantastic images of himself "rolling in dough" and freed as if by magic from all of his economic pressures. In the context of his Narcissus complex, the psychotherapist imagines scenes in which he is a megalomaniacal self who commands the attention of his friends, all of whom flock around him in amazement at his unbelievable luck.

The psychotherapist's fanciful reveries are a classic example of a common gambling fantasy, namely, the fantasy of "Lady Luck" As part of such an addictive fantasy, a gambler imagines Lady Luck smiling down and bestowing upon him or her a fabulous fortune that solves all problems in one fell swoop. From our self-psychological vantage point, we believe that this gambling fantasy of "Lady Luck" is narcissistic at its core. More specifically, it incorporates a phantasmagorical image of the gambler, who as a result of transmogrification merges with a maternal presence imagined as being both idealized and omnipotent.

The narcissistic pull of the psychotherapist's countertransference fantasy interacts with the narcissistic power of Errol's transference fantasy; together these archaic narcissistic fantasies structure the intersubjective field and create a particular form of the transference–countertransference neurosis. From our intersubjective perspective, we believe that the psychotherapist's gambling fantasy competes and interferes with Errol's fantasy of the psychotherapy as a selfobject, thus impeding the replacement of the ATM gambling by that of the therapy.

As part of the transference–countertransference neurosis, the psychotherapist becomes quite impatient and frustrated with Errol. He has little tolerance countertransferentially for Errol and his pain over failing to join the psychotherapist as a neighbor and, in the process, having realized his twinship fantasy. The intolerance on the part of the psychotherapist fuels a narcissistic rage reaction in which the psychotherapist experiences considerable antipathy toward Errol. And, this antipathy contributes countertransferentially to Errol's relapse.

In this particular instance, the fact that Errol and the psychotherapist share a gambling fantasy creates an "intersubjective disconjunction" (Atwood & Stolorow, 1984, pp. 47–55). The psychotherapist is so narcissistically consumed by his own gambling fantasy that he disrupts the psychotherapeutic process of intersubjective absorption. This, in turn, interferes with Errol's unconscious takeover of the psychoactive effects of his addiction to gambling.

Following continued peer supervision, the psychotherapist succeeds in working through his own countertransference fantasy and the resulting antipathy. Thus, once again he becomes empathically available as a selfobject to Errol in the transference. The psychotherapist addresses and redresses the empathic failure that upset Errol's selfobject fantasy. Introspecting about his recent lapse into gambling reverie, the psychotherapist empathizes more effectively with Errol's fantasy scenario of narcissistic bliss as a result of "hitting it big."

With the selfobject bond restored, Errol feels comfortable and secure enough to rely on the psychotherapy once again instead of gambling as a means of regulating his self-esteem. Subsequently, Errol re-establishes his abstinence from gambling and remains abstinent for a considerable period of time.

Commentary

The focus of our overview of Errol's case is on the nature and effect of a fantasy he shares with the psychotherapist concerning the unconscious meaning of addictive gambling. Initially, this shared fantasy facilitated the intersubjective absorption or narcissistic exchange of the psychoactive effects (that is, mirroring/antidepressant and twinship/humanizing effects) of gambling as an ATM. Sharing this fantasy with the psychotherapist enabled them to create the intersubjective conditions necessary for Errol to experience psychotherapy as a selfobject replacement for gambling.

However, this same shared fantasy of gambling created, later in the psychotherapy, a different set of intersubjective conditions. And, under these more countertherapeutic circumstances, the fact that Errol and the psychotherapist shared this fantasy temporarily breaks down the process of intersubjective absorption or the narcissistic exchange process.

This shared fantasy of gambling was organized unconsciously on the basis of a psychotherapeutically-induced experience of twinship that allowed Errol to imagine the psychotherapist as his alterego. This twinship experience helped Errol to feel more like a human being and less like the Elephant Man. The humanizing effect of this twinship fantasy was critical to alleviating Errol's painful sense of himself as a freak of nature. Based on his transference fantasy, Errol imagined himself as being in a state of narcissistic bliss, which temporarily counteracted his excruciating sense of narcissistic mortification.

In a similar vein, his mood shifted dramatically from one of alienation and estrangement to one of camaraderie and solidarity. This dramatic improvement in Errol's self-image and accompanying affect exemplified both the phenomenon of the dialectical bipolarity of fantasy and mood as well as that of therapeutic dissociation.

In our initial review of the case, we did not adequately address a number of key factors, which we can now more clearly illuminate by applying our current model. From our phenomenological perspective, the most important aspect of the case concerns the Narcissus complex and megalomania. A distinct megalomaniacal quality is inherent in Errol's gambling and sex addictions.

Prior to beginning psychotherapy, Errol spends most of his free time caught up in gambling fantasies and lost in fanciful daydreams. As he strutted around his stockbroker's office, he was self-absorbed in psychoactive fantasy tapes in which he imagines himself as being like the movie character "Gekko," played by Michael Douglas in the film *Wall Street*. This cinematic figure is a clear example of a fantasized version of being a megalomaniacal self who excercises magical control over his vast financial empire. As he pranced around, he conjured up phantasmagorical images of himself as one of an elite group of financial tycoons, all of whom control vast fortunes and unlimited funds. Unfortunately, Errol acted out these addictive fantasies, thus borrowing and wagering large sums of money that he can ill afford to lose. Although he made a decent salary as a computer salesman, he betted addictively on risky stock tips, which had little chance of paying off.

Over the years, Errol deteriorated in his gambling addiction from wagering wildly on horses at the race track to betting maniacally on stock market options. And, the extravagant and compulsive nature of Errol's betting on the stock market classified it diagnostically as a gambling addiction. (See Miliora, 1997, for a self-psychological view of gambling.) He invested money in the market in a truly uncontrolled manner that is consistent with megalomaniacal self-destructiveness. In contrast, the psychotherapist managed his money in the stock market and his other investments in a judicious and prudent manner. Thus, whereas Errol lost large sums of money, the psychotherapist increased his wealth considerably.

Yet, despite the clearly uncontrolled nature of Errol's wagering on stocks and options, he nonetheless imagined himself as in complete control of his betting. This is, therefore, the central paradox or irony that defines the essence of addictive megalomania. An addict imagines himself or herself on the basis of a fantasy of being a megalomaniacal self and as being in possession of and having magical control over specially endowed things or activities; however, actually an addict loses control over an ATM, or psychoactive agent of illusory control, and is really out of control. In essence, an addict loses the ability to manage effectively his or her own emotional affairs. The unmanageability of an addict's life makes it ultimately impossible for an addict to be the master of his or her own fate.

The magnitude and intensity of addictive megalomania in the case of Errol is also apparent in his sexual compulsivity. Errol, like Travis, treated women as his personal property; they were his sexual playthings over which he imagined himself as a megalomaniacal self who exercises magical control over them. However, Errol, unlike Travis, evidenced a sadomasochism that is central to his sexual addiction.

Women existed for Errol on an unconscious fantasy level as nothing more than erotic toys. As such, these women retained in Errol's imagination the status of his personal property. Errol abused these women sexually in the context of his addiction to prostitutes, massage parlors, and peep shows. This sexual abuse reflected tremendous contempt and disregard on Errol's part for the essential humanity of these women.

We maintain that the sexual abuse to which Errol subjected these women is indicative of his psychopathological hatred or antipathy toward women, a disregard that is diagnostic of a type of sociopathy. In further substantiating our diagnosis of sociopathy, we point to the fact that Errol, prior to immigrating to America, was sentenced as a young adult to serve time in prison for crimes he committed to support his gambling addiction to racehorse betting.

We contend that Errol, like Travis, is sociopathic to the degree to which his addictive megalomania rendered him oblivious and indifferent to the suffering he inflicted on others or to the deleterious effects of his actions on others. In this regard, his sociopathy was fueled by narcissistic rage fantasies or rageaholism. (In the Typology part of this section, we return to the topic of Errol's narcissistic rage and its relation to his addictions.)

Errol, in addition to being addicted to the sexual abuse of women, also is addicted to compulsive masturbation. When not procuring street hookers or other prostitutes at massage parlors and peep shows, Errol masturbated constantly and compulsively day and night. Errol admitted that as an adult his masturbatory fantasies are sadomasochistic in nature.

In these fantasies, Errol imagined that women are forced against their will to service him sexually. Many of his masturbatory fantasies were quite stereotypical; however, at a deeper, unconscious level they consisted of thinly veiled rape and torture scenarios.

We maintain that the underlying violence of Errol's masturbatory fantasies attests to the sociopathy that is so much a part of Errol's narcissistic rage fantasies and megalomania. Fueling the rage and megalomania is essential as a trigger for Errol to enter into a state of addictive metamorphosis.

In a self-hypnotic trance, Errol enacts fantasies of himself as being megalomaniacal that degenerate from abuse of himself to abuse of others. Dissociated and anesthetized, Errol deceives himself into believing that neither he nor the women he abuses suffer any serious or lasting damage as a result of his destructive behavior. This self-deception is a classical example of addictive denial. (See Kearney, 1996, for a discussion of the role of denial in addiction.)

We can say much more about the psychogenic course of Errol's addictions. To begin with, we need to point out that Errol grows up under the conditions of the classic "addict family" (Chein et al., 1964, p. 274). Both of his parents are themselves addicted. His mother is addicted to Valium and amphetamines, whereas his father is an alcoholic and in all probability a sex addict.

While Errol is still a youngster, his father works as a ladies hairdresser. According to Errol, his father has numerous affairs with various female customers. It is also worth noting from a pathogenic perspective that both of Errol's two siblings end up as addicts: his sister is eating disordered and bulimic, whereas his brother is a heroin addict who eventually dies of AIDS.

Living with two addicted parents, Errol exists in an extremely barren selfobject environment, which, in all likelihood, contributes pathogenically to his becoming an addict himself. Listening to Errol talk about his early family milieu leaves little doubt in the psychotherapist's mind concerning the empathically impoverished and antipathetic nature of his early surround.

Errol describes both of his parents as being utterly unavailable to him as emotional caregivers. As the youngest of his siblings, Errol often finds himself alone with his parents and lacking in any peer support from either his older brother or sister. His mother is, as Errol recounts, lost in her own drug-induced stupor. She wanders about the house aimlessly, muttering incoherently and unintelligibly to herself. And, typically by the time his father arrives home late at night, Errol is already asleep. On those rare occasions when his father is around in the evening, he is, Errol remembers, often "plastered" and prone to flying into wild, alcoholic rages (that is, alcohol-fueled rageaholism).

In any event, Errol bemoans the fact that his parents are too self-absorbed and distracted to pay much attention to him or, alas, even notice his presence. The description Errol gives of his parents leaves the clear impression in the psychotherapist's mind that they are not only unempathic but antipathetic toward him. Apparently, they make him feel unwelcome in his own home, as if he is an inconvenience and *something* that is a real nuisance.

It follows from an etiological point of view that Errol's parents mistreat him in a megalomaniacal fashion because they are themselves addicted. (See the case of Megworth in Chapter 8 for a firsthand account of the megalomania of two addicted parents.) Errol comes to regard himself as nothing more than a thing or item, which seems to have little intrinsic value to his parents and, in fact, is superfluous to them. His subjective sense of himself as something almost nonhuman leaves Errol with an indelible psychological scar. This emotional scarring contributes significantly to his mortifying fantasy of himself as a psychologically deformed creature like the Elephant Man.

In the antipathetic environment of the home in which Errol grows up, he became pathologically dependent upon nonhuman things and activities and, more specifically, comes to depend inordinately on masturbating with the vacuum cleaner. Unlike many of our other patients, for example, Teddy or Joe, Errol finds no emotional way back to a meaningful connection with his (human) selfobject milieu. In this context, Errol is bereft of selfobject connections to other family members and, consequently, becomes pathologically over-attached to the selfobject-like functioning of a vacuum cleaner.

Moreover, Errol was unlike Teddy or Joe in that he is unable to rely on transitional selfobject activities (that is, respectively baseball and woodworking) as a means of compensating for the empathic failure of his (human) selfobject surround. In contrast, the vacuum cleaner functions in a fashion quite distinct from the functioning of the things that are part and parcel of the activities of baseball and woodworking.

Unlike these things, the vacuum cleaner is not destined to evolve psychologically into *something* useful to Errol's future development. In his imagination, Errol does not endow this machine with any personal qualities, which may have imbued it with a semi-human status. The vacuum cleaner, which Errol fails to anthropomorphize, becomes for him a pre-addictive (and selfobject-like) thing rather than a transitional selfobject.

From an empathic perspective, the psychotherapist views Errol's compulsive masturbation as the solitary activity of a lonely child desperately attempting to survive in a home environment grossly unempathic and antipathetic. We believe his masturbation is a symptom of a mild to moderate form of childhood autism. Bettelheim (1955, 1967) long ago documented the connection between autism in children and megalomania; in line with this work we see Errol's masturbation as megalomaniacal.

From this vantage point, it is seen as an attempt on Errol's part to create his own megalomaniacal fantasy world. As such, it constitutes an alternative for Errol to the emotional atmosphere of his home, one which is characterized by starkness and bleakness. Later, Errol repeats this same pattern of fantasy enactment in the form of acting "as if" he is a European aristocrat.

The autistic quality of Errol's masturbation points to its narcissistic nature and, hence, to the relevance of a self-psychological perspective. In the selfobject context of an unempathic milieu, the psychotherapist envisions Errol's masturbation as serving primarily narcissistic (rather than autoerotic and hence sexual) purposes. It represents an attempt on Errol's part to shore up a fragile sense of self that is extremely underdeveloped and vulnerable to narcissistic decompensation.

The psychotherapist views Errol's childhood masturbation as autistic and, therefore, as narcissistic and not autoerotic. This viewpoint helps to account, in part, for the fact that Errol becomes an addict rather than a pervert. Unlike a pervert, who needs a fetishistic object in order to function sexually, Errol is an addict who needs an ATM to function narcissistically.

Errol has no difficulty performing sexually and achieving orgasm by a wide variety of exotic means. In this regard, he evidences none of the rigidity and inflexibility of a pervert, who achieves orgasm only through a sexual ritual involving erotic props and gadgets.

Lacking any viable means as a child of reconnecting with his (human) selfobject surround, Errol exists in a schizoid world he constructs totally out of his own imagination and fantasies of being a megalomaniacal self. The cognitive style of a person like Errol may be characterized, therefore, as solipsistic (that is, self-referential, idiosyncratic, and insular). It prevents Errol from passing successfully from phase II to phase III of the narcissistic exchange process.

There is a scarcity in Errol's early environment of genuine narcissistic currency. Consequently, it is difficult, if not impossible, for him to conduct a meaningful and profitable exchange between the selfobject worlds of the human and nonhuman. As a result of being narcissistically bankrupt early in life, Errol never recuperate from this dire state of selfobject impoverishment. Instead, he is destined to trade in bogus narcissistic currency as evidenced by his addiction to gambling and sex.

We employ the typological component of our model in order to shed new light on a number of significant features of Errol's addictive character. Among our psychoanalytic psychotherapy cases, Errol is the most representative example of an addict whom we would diagnose as suffering from a self disorder of the bipolar, subtype II. The description of Errol's early childhood and adolescence makes it clear that he suffered severe psychic damage to all of the major sectors of the domain of his self-experience. His selfobject milieu fails empathically to mirror his grandiosity, to allow for merger with parental figures idealized as omnipotent (and omniscient), or to provide for twinship with an alter ego.

In addition, Errol has scant opportunity to pass successfully through the narcissistic exchange process. In the context of his Narcissus complex, he is unable to use as transitional selfobjects the things and activities he finds in his nonhuman environment. Similarly, he cannot transform his fantasies of being a megalomaniacal self and as endowed with magical control into a mature sense of mastery. The latter would have enabled Errol to master (rather than attempt to control) his emotions and his emotional affairs.

Panic and narcissistic rage are prominent features of Errol's bipolar, subtype II self disorder. In typical bipolar fashion, Errol fluctuates in his moods with rapid cycling from hypomania and mania to depression. In addition, he often panics and becomes narcissistically enraged.

Underlying these dysphoric affect states is a serious and chronic disturbance in his fantasy of being megalomaniacal and as exercising magical control over both his imaginary financial empire and harem. Even the slightest narcissistic disturbance in Errol's megalomaniacal fantasy of magical control sends him into a panic and rage. It is as if his narcissistic thermostat is permanently out of whack, thus making it almost impossible for him to regulate his emotional temperature with any degree of regularity. In other words, Errol runs emotionally hot and cold.

Panicked and enraged, Errol experiences himself emotionally as having lost control of himself. In these dysphoric states, he resorts to desperate measures to quell the terror of feeling like he is out of control.

However, Errol in turning to gambling and sex finds them futile to quiet himself down. As soon as Errol escapes to a narcissistic state of blissful euphoria, then he plunges back into a narcissistically mortifying state of panic and rage.

In fact, Errol becomes so panicked and enraged that he strikes out emotionally at anyone and everyone in his immediate vicinity, including co-workers, strangers, and his wife. It really does not matter to Errol whom he strikes out at; all that counts to him is that someone other than himself is to blame for his extreme discomfort and that someone else is going to pay for his dysphoria. In this respect, Errol is typical of the so-called rageaholic now so often described in addiction recovery literature.

In this dysphoric state, Errol's sense of himself becomes so disorganized and chaotic that he decompensates psychologically to a psychotic level of functioning. He is so overwhelmed by panic and rage that he slips into a psychotic state in which everything becomes surreal and unreal. These psychotic episodes occur with such regularity and intensity that they constitute an underlying baseline of his overall personality functioning. In other words, Errol is latently and sometimes manifestly psychotic.

The extreme nature of Errol's panic and rage tax the psychotherapy (and psychotherapist) to its limit. The psychotherapist attempts to utilize the mirroring and twinship dimensions of the selfobject transference in combination with the idealizing and pacifying dimension. However, the selfobject transference, in all its various manifestations, proves to be insufficient to alleviate Errol's psychotic levels of panic and rage.

As a result, the psychotherapist decides to refer Errol for a psychiatric and pharmacological evaluation. This results in Errol being placed on a psychotropic drug regimen of mood stabilizers and antipsychotic medication. Such a combination of psychotropic medications is typical for individuals such as Errol who suffer from bipolar spectrum disorder with psychotic features. Fortunately, Errol responds relatively well to his drug regimen and, consequently, he continues on it throughout the remainder of his psychotherapy. (In the Treatment part of this section, we return to the clinical rationale for combining psychoanalytic psychotherapy with psychopharmacotherapy.)

A review of the clinical aspects of the case of Errol consists of a description of the psychotherapy as it was conducted through a period lasting for approximately five years. At this still early point in the development of our thinking, we base our self-psychological ideas about psychotherapy of an addicted patient on the notion of intersubjective absorption. We conceptualize the clinical course of the treatment primarily in terms of the psychotherapeutic process of intersubjective absorption as well as the notion of the transference–countertransference neurosis. More specifically, we describe our relative psychotherapeutic success in utilizing intersubjective absorption as a clinical process by which to take over the psychoactive effects (that is, mirroring/antidepressant and twinship/humanizing) of gambling.

We point out that the gambling fantasy, which Errol and the psychotherapist share together, generates a powerful psychic vortex that structures the intersubjective field. An intersubjective configuration is organized unconsciously between Errol and the psychotherapist in terms of a shared (twinship) fantasy. Initially, this intersubjective fantasy facilitates, then interfers, and finally solidifies the psychotherapeutic action of a transitional selfobject transference.

Errol has a megalomaniacal fantasy of both the psychotherapist and the psychotherapy as being like the vacuum cleaner, that is, as *something* that he controls on the basis of emotional whim, or metaphorically speaking by the flip of a switch. However, Errol uses the narcissistic illusion of controlling the psychotherapy for constructive purposes in contrast to his masturbatory *misuse* of the vacuum cleaner for addictive purposes.

In our overview of this case, we leave off at the point at which Errol re-establishes his abstinence from gambling. At the psychotherapist's insistence, Errol joins Gamblers Anonymous (GA), which proves to be critical to his continued success in maintaining his abstinence. He attends GA meetings on a regular basis, gets a sponsor, and works the steps. In other words, he is fully engaged in the program.

In our self-psychological psychotherapy with an addicted patient we do not find any inherent conflict between the utilization of 12-step programs (that is, peer groups designed to assist an individual in recovering from an addiction) and psychoanalytic psychotherapy. We (Ulman & Paul, 1989) refer to the "auxiliary selfobject function" of 12-step programs, which we believe is often essential to the successful psychotherapy of addicted patients. Throughout the last 4 years of his 10-year psychotherapy, Errol remains abstinent from gambling, in part, because of his involvement in GA.

In addition, Errol, during the middle phase of the psychotherapy, marries and starts to raise a family. The ability on Errol's part to succeed in marriage and as a family man is due, in large measure, to an improvement in his finances. He amasses considerable sums because he stopped squandering all his money on addictive gambling.

We contend that Errol's success in life is also due to his identification-in-fantasy with the psychotherapist as a twin and as an alterego who serves for Errol as a male role model. In essence, Errol models himself unconsciously after the psychotherapist, an unconscious process which is integral in helping Errol overcome his gambling addiction.

For example, as the psychotherapy progresses, Errol takes up jogging and tennis, activities he knows the psychotherapist enjoyed. We maintain that these activities serve transitional selfobject functions and are created, like some fantasies, in the intersubjective context of the psychotherapy.

Errol, unlike our other addicted patients such as Teddy or Joe, does not develop much of a healthy selfobject connection to the nonhuman world of things and activities. He needs, therefore, for the psychotherapist to exercise "active empathy" (Ulman & Paul, 1992), that is, to provide Errol on a literal level with examples of normal activities and things that can function for him as transitional selfobjects.

As Errol increasingly develops these capacities, he is better able to use the psychotherapy as a healthy alternative to gambling. The psychopharmacotherapeutic effect of the psychotherapy (that is, the antidepressant effect of mirroring and the humanizing effect of twinship) replaces the purely psychoactive and addictive effects of the gambling. As a result, the intensity of the therapeutic dissociation proves to be powerful enough to counteract the dissociative and anesthetic effects of Errol's addictive gambling.

It seems clear to us that for Errol the psychotherapy serves as a utilitarian alternative to the gambling. It allows him to imagine himself as magically in control of a process even more useful than gambling in helping him to alleviate his painful distress. Errol uses the transitional selfobject transference unconsciously as a means of partially modifying and transforming his fantasy of being a megalomaniacal self and as possessing illusory control into a healthy sense of adaptive mastery of his emotional world. As part of resolving his Narcissus complex, Errol exchanges the faulty narcissistic functioning of gambling as an ersatz selfobject for the utilitarian functioning of the psychotherapy as a transitional selfobject.

The narcissistic exchange process is, therefore, quite successful as regards gambling; however, it is not nearly as efficacious as concerns Errol's sex addiction. It is important to point out that Errol's sex addiction is obscured clinically during the early years of the therapy (and, more specifically, the first through the fifth years) by the overwhelming magnitude of his gambling addiction.

It is only in the latter phases of the psychotherapy, and following his cessation from gambling, that his addiction to sex takes center stage in both his life and in the psychotherapy. Errol, in a fashion typical of many addicts, simply substitutes his addiction to sex for his gambling addiction. This is an example of a cross-over addiction.

As the psychotherapy focuses increasingly on Errol's sex addiction, it becomes evident to the psychotherapist that helping Errol to gain abstinence from his sex addiction will prove far more difficult than was the case with gambling. It is at this juncture that the psychotherapist makes his referral of Errol for medication.

There is a growing body of literature (see, for example, Adelman, 1993; Beitman, 1991; Cabaniss, 1998; Carroll, 2001; Goldhamer, 1993; Grilo, 2001; Hausner, 1993, Jamison, 1991; Kahn, 1993; Kantor, 1993; Karasu, 1993; Milrod & Busch, 1998; Nevins, 1993; Powell, 2001; Roose & Johannet, 1998; Rubin, 2001; Sammons, 2001; Sandberg, 1998; Weiss, 2003; Wylie & Wylie, 1993; Wyman & Rittenberg, 1992; Yager, 1991; see also the pioneering work in this area of Ostow, 1954, 1955, 1962, 1979, 1992) that documents the efficacy of combining psychoanalytic psycho-therapy and psychopharmacotherapy, especially in the case of working with difficult to treat patients, such as the addict. The overall effect of the psychopharmacotherapy helps to reduce Errol's rapid and often unpredictable mood swings from mania and depression and vice versa. It also proves helpful in defusing the explosive nature of Errol's rage reactions.

However, even the combined effects of the psychopharmacother-apy and psychotherapy prove to be somewhat ineffective in containing the panic reaction that is so central to Errol's addictive megalomania and especially to his addiction to sex. (See Miliora & Ulman, 1996b, for a bioself-psychological understanding and approach to treating panic disorder.)

Belatedly, the psychotherapist comes to the realization that there is a second, unconscious fantasy shared on an intersubjective basis by Errol and the psychotherapist. And, it structured the intersubjective field in a fashion that seriously compromises the effectiveness of the psycho-therapy in ameliorating Errol's addiction to sex. Unconsciously, Errol and his psychotherapist share a megalomaniacal fantasy of both gam-bling and sex addiction. And, in the case of the latter addiction, they share an intersubjective fantasy stemming from compulsive masturbation. The therapist is himself addicted to masturbation during a brief period of the psychotherapy.

We want to focus on this relatively limited period of Errol's psychotherapy to dramatize the serious difficulties that can arise in treating an addicted patient in the case of a psychotherapist who is similarly addicted. However, in focusing on this specific period of the psychotherapy, we do not want to mislead the reader into arriving at the false conclusion that the psychotherapist remained addicted to masturbation throughout any sustained phase of the psychotherapy. On the contrary, he overcame his addiction to masturbation, in part, as a result of the benefits of his own (and second) psychoanalysis. Except for a relatively short period of time, the psychotherapist remained abstinent from compulsive masturbation.

However, despite the abstinence of the psychotherapist, the damage was already done, so to speak. Unfortunately, Errol remained actively addicted to sex, with the exception of only a few, intermittent periods of abstinence, throughout the latter part of the psychotherapy.

We also do not want to misrepresent a major difference that distinguishes the respective addictions to sex of Errol and the psychotherapist. Unlike Errol, the psychotherapist is not involved in abusing women who are trapped and virtual slaves of the sex industry.

Moreover, the psychotherapist does not share with Errol a proclivity for certain types of masturbatory fantasy. As already stressed, the masturbatory fantasies that arouse Errol sexually are latently sadomasochistic in nature. Errol acts out the sadomasochistic content of his masturbatory fantasies in the course of procuring and abusing women whom he encounters in the course of his travels in the sordid world of the sex industry. The enactment of masturbatory fantasies on Errol's part serves as a partial outlet for his intense narcissistic rage, which is reflective of his underlying hatred and antipathy toward women.

In sharp contrast, the psychotherapist entertained masturbation fantasies that were nonviolent and romantic in nature. In these fantasies, he imagines himself making love to anonymous women, all of whom he pictures as voluptuous and bountiful goddesses. In this crucial regard, the psychotherapist is quite distinct from Errol, who resorts to compulsive masturbation in a vain attempt to gain a twisted sense of being more human. In contradistinction, the psychotherapist lost himself in masturbatory fantasies in an addictive effort to intensify his otherwise latently archaic grandiosity.

The psychotherapist suffers from an empty depression accompanied by painful and disorganizing depletion anxiety. During this specific period of Errol's psychotherapy, the psychotherapist found himself irresistibly drawn to masturbation. It was for him a surefire means of achieving psychoactive relief from the pain of narcissistically mortifying fantasies of not being enough or having enough. The psychotherapist imagines in the context of these dreadful fantasies that he has lost all emotional control of himself and his affairs.

Clear and distinct differences exist, therefore, between Errol and the psychotherapist regarding both the content and function of their respective sexual addictions. Yet, despite these differences, Errol and the psychotherapist do share an unconscious fantasy that is addictive in nature: they share a megalomaniacal illusion of themselves as sexual supermen. And, unfortunately, the psychotherapist does not analyze this shared fantasy during this period of the psychotherapy. His empathic failure seriously undermines the effectiveness of the psychotherapy in helping Errol to overcome his sex addiction.

These masturbatory fantasies, as shared intersubjectively by Errol and the psychotherapist, are narcissistic in nature in that they are both megalomaniacal and somewhat autistic. Errol and the psychotherapist share a megalomaniacal fantasy of masturbation as a magical activity that miraculously transports them to their own respective fantasy worlds. Once in their masturbatory wonderlands, they imagine themselves as sexual potentates unrivaled in their megalomaniacal control over their harems. To varying degrees, both Errol and the psychotherapist remain during these magical interludes autistically removed from the painful realities of their individual lives; instead they enjoy the narcissistic pleasures of their respective and fantasized Shangri-las (see, for example, Pleig, 1997).

Several features of the transference–countertransference neurosis during this period of the psychotherapy indicate that it is organized unconsciously on the basis of a shared fantasy of sex as an ATM, or, psychoactive agent of magical control. First, and most obviously, the psychotherapist found himself vicariously living out his own addictive fantasies of sexual conquest through Errol's "sexploits" or "sexcapades." In this regard, the psychotherapist is, at times, psychotherapeutically too passive. He fails countertransferentially to empathically confront Errol about what the psychotherapist somewhat naively imagines as Errol's exciting adventures in the squalor of the sex industry. (See Adler & Buie, 1991 and Buie & Adler, 1991 on the uses and misuses of confrontation in psychotherapy.)

236 The Self Psychology of Addiction and Its Treatment

At other times, however, the psychotherapist became annoyed and frustrated with Errol. Feeling quite antipathetic toward Errol, the psychotherapist ragefully reprimands him for engaging in addictive and potentially self-destructive activities.

In these instances, the psychotherapist is caught up in a "countertransference resistance" (Racker, 1968), or what we term countertransference passivity. (See S. Brody, 1964, for a classical analysis of the unconscious nature of psychopathological passivity.) The psychotherapist retreats countertransferentially into a very passive stance in the face of Errol's active addiction to sex. In other words, the countertransference passivity of the psychotherapist expresses itself in two forms of antipathetic reaction: either inactivity or hostility (that is, he is "passiveaggressive").

The failure on the psychotherapist's part to empathically confront the nature and meaning of Errol's sex addiction points to the deleterious effects of an "intersubjective disjunction" (Atwood and Stolorow, 1984, pp. 47–55). The addictive sexual behavior on the part of Errol is evidence of an extremely overt form of narcissism. His behavior is brazen and shameless; whereas his attitude is unrepentant. In a fashion typical of the sociopath, he shows almost no embarrassment, self-consciousness, or remorse about his active involvement in the grimy world of prostitutes, massage parlors, and peep shows.

In marked contrast, the addictive sexual behavior of the psychotherapist is reflective of an extremely covert form of narcissism. His behavior is decidedly secretive; whereas his attitude is trepidatious. The psychotherapist was unlike Errol, who seems relatively unconcerned about the unsavory nature of his sex addiction. The therapist is very self-conscious and worries about being viewed, or deemed by others, as a sexual deviant.

The intersubjective disjunction occurs in the context of the differences in narcissistic style (see S. M. Johnson, 1987, on different styles of narcissism) that characterize Errol's versus the psychotherapist's addiction to sex. On the one hand, the narcissistic style of Errol necessitates that he become increasingly more active and exhibitionistic in his sex addiction. On the other hand, the narcissistic style of the psychotherapist dictates that he become progressively more passive and voyeuristic in response to Errol's blatant exhibitionism. Thus, the narcissistic attitude of Errol toward the world is characterized by an aggressiveness and flamboyance, whereas the narcissistic attitude of the psychotherapist toward life is marked by passiveness, avoidance, and shyness.

There is, however, a second yet less obvious feature of the addictive fantasy of sex as shared unconsciously by Errol and the psychotherapist. The psychotherapist "identifies-in-fantasy" with Errol as an erotic hero whom he imagined engaging in amazing sexual adventures. In this regard, the psychotherapist joins Errol as an imaginary third party to these sexual peccadilloes. Thus, the psychotherapist, during the specific psychotherapy sessions currently under consideration, entertains day-dreams or reveries of a *ménage à trois*.

In these imaginary scenes he passively watches as Errol actively ravishes a series of exotic women. For instance, the psychotherapist concocts one such *ménage à trois* fantasy in the midst of his being titillated by Errol, who makes sexual jokes of a ribald nature.

We know from Freud 1953 [1905] that there is an important connection between humor and the unconscious. And, there can be little doubt that the risqué humor shared by Errol and the psychotherapist is reflective of a jointly held narcissistic illusion about sex. Moreover, the addictive fantasy, which Errol and the psychotherapist share intersubjectively, is determinative unconsciously of a crucial dimension of the transference–countertransference neurosis.

Or, to take another example of the psychotherapist's *ménage à trois* fantasies, on occasion Errol brings into session with him photographs of a sexually explicit nature. These pictures, which Errol cut from European tabloids, show semi-nude women posing in provocative positions. Errol shares these trashy news photos with the psychotherapist, who, due to narcissistic countertransference, is too passive and does not effectively interpret or analyze the latent meaning of these exchanges.

The psychotherapist fails, therefore, to facilitate a psychotherapeutic process of narcissistic exchange; instead he participates unintentionally as an imaginary third party or passive voyeur in Errol's open and active display (both verbally and visually) of his sexual addiction. The transference–countertransference neurosis consists intersubjectively of the following scenarios: the psychotherapist enacts the role of the passive voyeur, and thus becomes the unwitting counterpart to Errol, who plays the role of the active exhibitionist.

Furthermore, we believe that there is a strong homoerotic component to the transference–countertransference neurosis. We argue that it is homoerotic rather than homosexual because it is primarily narcissistic rather than relational (or object-oriented) in nature. In these particular sessions, the psychotherapist literally sits by as he passively listens to Errol actively describe the details of his sexual encounters.

In this intersubjective context, the psychotherapist fantasizes himself unconsciously as a voyeur watching as Errol exhibits his extraordinary sexual prowess. Temporarily, the psychotherapist dissociates and anesthetizes himself, albeit at Errol's expense. However, the psychotherapist, as part of these countertransference fantasies, never imagines any direct sexual involvement with Errol or, for that matter, with the women.

On the contrary, he imagines himself in a purely passive and voyeuristic position, which is quite distinct from envisioning himself as actively joining Errol in the lovemaking scenarios. In this context, the psychotherapist enters into a dissociated mental state in which he imagines himself as if he is a patron who views, without participating in, a live sex show.

The *ménage à trois* fantasies of the psychotherapist are homoerotic in another sense. The therapist is involved unconsciously with Errol in a symbolic form of mutual masturbation. On the one hand, Errol is symbolically engaging the psychotherapist in symbolic forms of masturbation as he recounts sexually arousing and ribald stories.

On the other hand, the psychotherapist is engaging Errol in symbolic forms of masturbation by responding too passively to his erotically charged accounts. In a sense, therefore, he allows Errol to "get off" narcissistically on recounting his own sexual exploits. In this sense, Errol and the psychotherapist are engaging each other unconsciously in symbolic forms of masturbation by giving one another the metaphoric glad hand.

It is imperative that we distinguish two different ways in which a psychotherapist may share an addictive fantasy with an addicted patient. In the first instance, it is psychotherapeutically beneficial to share such a fantasy with a patient. This is true to the extent to which a psychotherapist becomes self-conscious and self-aware of its unconscious organizing effect on the psychotherapist's own subjectivity.

Such intersubjective sharing may lead to a heightening of a psychotherapist's empathic grasp of the unconscious meaning and function of an addictive fantasy for a particular patient. In this respect, we employ the term *sharing* to mean the empathic acceptance and ability to participate vicariously in such a fantasy through what Kohut (1971) originally termed "vicarious introspection" (p. 219).

However, as concerns the second instance, it is countertherapeutic to the degree to which a psychotherapist shares a patient's fantasy in a nonintrospective and, hence, unempathic or antipathetic fashion. Such unself-aware sharing on the part of a psychotherapist tends to remain unconscious, and is thus uncritical and unself-reflective. For example, the psychotherapist, in the case of Errol, played out Errol's fantasies during the specific period of the psychotherapy currently under scrutiny rather than empathizing with them by introspection.

Some psychotherapists who work with addicted patients are especially drawn into a countertransference over-identification with their addicted patient, and hence too easily come under the influence of a shared addictive fantasy. The powerful psychoactive effect of such an addictive fantasy attests to the absolute necessity for such psychotherapists to be especially wary of their own countertransference tendencies to join a patient in addictive fantasizing and/or behavior.

In summary, we hope that our unorthodox, and perhaps controversial, candor and frankness about the countertransference difficulties encountered by this particular psychotherapist in working clinically with Errol's sex addiction will serve as a warning to other psychotherapists. Psychotherapists who treat an addicted patient must work through their own addictive fantasies. As psychotherapists, we learned this lesson the hard way from our respective psychotherapies with Travis and Errol.

SUMMARY AND CONCLUSION

Summary

We want to provide the reader with a review and summary of the six treatment case studies before proceeding with our conclusions about the Narcissus complex and its expression in the addictive character.

Teddy

The case of Teddy demonstrates the need, in working self-psychologically with an addicted patient, for psychotherapeutic aids or "auxiliary selfobjects" such as hospitalization, which includes detoxification and rehabilitation, as well as a 12-step program. Overcoming an initial resistance to the transference—a not uncommon phenomenon in psychoanalytic psychotherapy with addicted patients—ushers in the emergence of a distinct version of the transitional selfobject transference.

Teddy had an unconscious fantasy of the psychotherapy as an academic or scholastic activity in which he imagined the psychotherapist as a wise, if not omniscient, mentor and himself as the star pupil. We refer to this particular selfobject fantasy as pedagogic in nature. We document how and why this fantasy enabled Teddy to (narcissistically) exchange the psychoactive (antianxiety and pacifying) functions of alcohol for the psychopharmacotherapeutic effect of the psychotherapy. The latter was generated by the power of a transference fantasy of the psychotherapy as a transitional selfobject.

We indicate from an intersubjective perspective that the psychotherapist shared with Teddy the latter's megalomaniacal fantasy of the psychotherapy as a symbolic activity and thing. This intersubjective fantasy replicated for Teddy the transitional selfobject functioning of playing sports. As a youngster, and later as an adolescent, Teddy made unconscious use of baseball as a transitional selfobject activity. He also employed the "tools of the trade" (that is, a ball, a bat, and a glove) as transitional selfobject things.

Teddy's attempt to master the skills of baseball provided him with a desperately needed opportunity to interact emotionally with a father who was otherwise aloof and highly critical. Baseball, as a transitional selfobject phenomenon, served unconsciously for Teddy as a nonhuman or semi-human intermediary through which he could connect emotionally with his father. Baseball functioned as an (transitional selfobject) activity that enabled Teddy to interact emotionally with his father and thus to develop psychologically, albeit in an arrested fashion.

The analysis of Teddy's transference allows us to reconstruct the psychogenic nature of the intersubjective field as it is co-determined by a father–son relationship. As a 19-year-old, Teddy experienced the traumatic loss of his mother due to brain cancer. Unfortunately for Teddy, we discovered that the death of his mother precipitated the breakdown of his relationship with his father. As a result, that relationship ceased to provide for Teddy both human and non-human selfobject functions.

The narcissistically traumatic combination of the simultaneous loss of both Teddy's mother and father as selfobjects set the stage for his subsequent pattern of alcoholic drinking. Teddy was left emotionally bereft of the selfobject functioning of his parents. In their absence, he turned in desperation to an imaginary relationship with the bottle (that is, alcohol).

Following the narcissistically traumatic loss of the selfobject functioning of his parents, Teddy apparently experienced himself as lost in a world seemingly devoid of any meaningful emotional connection to other people. As an angry drunk (that is, as a rageaholic), Teddy grew increasingly rageful and antipathetic toward himself and others. We find evidence of this dysfunctional pattern both in his self-destructive drinking as well as in his violent behavior toward his wife. It seems safe to say that Teddy was consumed with narcissistic rage, antipathy, and addictive cravings, all of which followed on the heels of the dual traumas of the literal loss of his mother and the figurative loss of his father.

Ten years of psychoanalytic psychotherapy between Teddy and his male psychotherapist reveals a specific version of the transference–countertransference neurosis. It is structured by the intersubjective field as it was co-determined unconsciously by patient and psychotherapist alike. In particular, the psychotherapist empathically shares Teddy's megalomaniacal fantasy version of the psychotherapy as a pedagogic-like activity.

The psychotherapist accepts, therefore, that he exists for Teddy as a semi-human thing and that the psychotherapy serves as a symbolic activity. He empathetically understands that Teddy needs to indulge in the fantasy of himself as megalomaniacal, and thus of controlling both the psychotherapist and the psychotherapy. Allowing Teddy to indulge transferentially in a megalomaniacal fantasy of himself as empowered with magical control is for Teddy an initial counterbalance and eventually a replacement for indulgence in alcoholic drinking.

We diagnose Teddy in terms of our bipolar self typology of addiction as an addict of the unipolar, subtype I. Teddy suffered major narcissistic damage in his capacity to idealize an omnipotent (and omniscient) paternal figure. As a result, he sought megalomaniacally to control (disintegration) anxiety and (narcissistic) rage through the addictive abuse of alcohol, which served as an ATM with psychoactive (and more specifically antianxiety, antipanic, and pacifying) effects.

Gradually, Teddy worked through the megalomaniacal nature of his transference fantasy and simultaneously replaced his need for the psychoactive effects of alcohol with his own capacity to regulate his fluctuations in mood. Of equal importance, he came eventually to experience both himself and the psychotherapist as more fully human.

Mary

Mary, like Teddy, resisted unconsciously the establishment of a (transitional) selfobject transference. Mary dreaded the repetition in the transference of the narcissistic trauma that she suffered early in her life at the hands of her mother. Based on this mortifying dread, Mary resisted the unconscious pull toward a transference experience in which she entertained a fantasy of herself as megalomaniacal in that she exercised magical control over the psychotherapy and the psychotherapist.

As the psychotherapist analyzed the dread behind the resistance to the transference, he learned about the unconscious meaning of Mary's early and narcissistically traumatic experience with her mother: She experienced her mother as exerting megalomaniacal control over her emotional life and treating her like an automaton. As a semi-human thing, Mary transmogrified herself into the perfectly behaved, good little girl. In this role, Mary's every thought and emotion were programmed by her mother as if by remote control. In this developmental setting Mary imagined herself as a narcissistic functionary who carried out her mother's every order.

Mary created, in the context of the megalomaniacal (mis)treatment by her mother, an unconscious fantasy of herself as a machine-like automaton. As part of her Narcissus complex, she imagined that she was a mechanical device—that is, an emotional Geiger counter or thermostat—that her mother controlled by turning Mary on or off at her mother's emotional discretion.

Mary suffered from an addictive eating disorder in which she abused food and laxatives. The physiological process of ingestion, digestion, and elimination are narcissistically *subverted* from their normal bodily functions. Instead, Mary misused the physiology of her own body in a futile effort to gain megalomaniacal and illusory control over her own emotional life.

The pathogenic nature of Mary's early narcissistic interaction with her mother was evident in the antipathy (self-hatred and self-loathing) she experienced toward herself, and especially toward the natural functioning and normal physiological processes of her own body.

We classify Mary typologically as another example of an addict of the unipolar, subtype I. Mary suffered narcissistic damage to the extent to which she was prevented by her mother from using (and controlling) the latter as a mirroring selfobject. In the absence of a selfobject milieu empathic to her narcissistic needs, Mary turned instead to fantasies of being a megalomaniacal self and as wielding control of her own body.

As part of the transference–countertransference neurosis, the psychotherapist recreated an unconscious version of Mary's disastrous relationship with her mother. Determined to pursue his own narcissistic agenda, the psychotherapist introduced and used a tape recorder in Mary's sessions. Mary experienced the psychotherapy, in the intersubjective context of this breach of empathy, as *something* that the psychotherapist controlled rather than as a (psychotherapeutic) process that she controlled.

The narcissistic illusion of being a megalomaniacal self who exercises such magical control was crucial for Mary's recovery from bulimia. Deprived by the psychotherapist of this selfobject experience, Mary fled the psychotherapy in order to pursue her relationship with her boyfriend.

In the case of Teddy, the psychotherapy was organized unconsciously on the basis of his prior use of baseball as a transitional selfobject. Unfortunately, a psychotherapeutic process with a similar unconscious organizing effect did not occur in the case of Mary. Rather, in this case, the psychotherapist was unable to build successfully upon Mary's earlier use of sewing as a transitional selfobject activity.

It would have been necessary for Mary to imagine herself as playing out the equivalent role in the transference to that which she played in childhood as the seamstress. In the event of such an experience, then perhaps Mary and the psychotherapist might have shared a fantasy of the psychotherapy as a transitional selfobject activity, which was the functional equivalent to sewing. It was possible that such an intersubjective fantasy might have become a critical psychotherapeutic medium through which Mary could have given up the addictive, albeit antidepressant, effect of bingeing and purging. She might have been then able to replace the psychoactive effects of her ATMs with the genuine psychopharmacotherapeutic effects of the psychotherapy.

Joe

The case of Joe, another male alcoholic, was similar in some ways to that of Teddy. Joe resumed, in the intersubjective field of the psychotherapy, his psychological development as it was arrested at the stage of transitional selfobject usage. Joe was traumatized narcissistically by his antipathetic father who, behaving megalomaniacally, mistreated Joe as if he was an inanimate thing.

We diagnose Joe in terms of our bipolar self typology as an addict of the unipolar, subtype II. Joe managed in the presence of an idealized paternal figure to develop psychologically in a somewhat normal and healthy fashion. However, Joe, following combat in Vietnam and the loss of an idealized paternal figure (namely, his war buddy) narcissistically fell apart and as a result went to pieces. Joe also suffered as part of a self disorder with mixed features from depletion anxiety and shame-based antipathy toward himself.

The wooden plaque that Joe gave to the psychotherapist as a gift at the beginning of psychotherapy was a symbol and harbinger of the later success of the narcissistic exchange process. Joe developed a transference fantasy that allowed him to take over the transitional selfobject functions of the psychotherapy. In this regard, Joe modelled his experience of psychotherapy after his earlier experience of wood-working as a transitional selfobject activity.

Joe used his newly-acquired, psychological capacities as a healthy replacement for alcohol. In the process, he created a subjective sense of his own inherent humanness. Thus, he succeeded in effectively counteracting his previous suicidal desire to dispose of himself as an irreparably broken and useless thing.

Following several serious lapses in empathy, the psychotherapist finally managed to empathize with Joe's antipathy toward himself and his narcissistic rage (that is, his rageaholism) as it expressed itself in his alcoholic drinking and suicidality. The successful restoration of Joe's transferential sense of the psychotherapist's omniscience was crucial. It permitted Joe to feel known by the psychotherapist at such a deep level that he was unburdened of his own antipathetic self-consciousness, and hence free to become a better version of himself.

JoAnn

In the case of JoAnn, in contrast to the case of Mary, we gain a much deeper, empathic understanding of the unconscious dimension of an addictive eating disorder. The case of JoAnn was organized unconsciously by a transference–countertransference neurosis, the analysis of which illuminated the megalomaniacal underpinning of her relationship with her father. JoAnn abused her body in the process of eating and exercising as a psychophysiological means of symbolically expressing the unconscious (narcissistic) meaning of both her preoedipal and oedipal experiences with her father.

From our self-psychological vantage point, we see JoAnn as reversing an unhealthy (developmental) process by which she went from a blissful experience of herself as the apple of her father's eye to a mortifying sense of herself as a real thorn in his side. In other words, in the intersubjective context of her interaction with the psychotherapist,

JoAnn went from being an exasperating and frustrating presence to being the apple of the psychotherapist's eye.

JoAnn and the psychotherapist shared and enjoyed an intersubjective fantasy, which achieved expression in a nonverbal language of body movements, facial expressions, and physical gestures. JoAnn and the psychotherapist were able through this psychotherapeutic version of pantomime to communicate unconsciously just as JoAnn had done in the past with her father in the nonverbal medium of play.

The use of language (verbal and nonverbal) became a transitional selfobject activity of enormous psychotherapeutic import. JoAnn was enraptured by the narcissistic bliss and erotic ecstasy of a shared fantasy. She was so enthralled that she experienced a degree of therapeutic dissociation sufficient enough in its psychopharmacotherapeutic intensity to relieve her of her dysphoric moods. In the past, JoAnn sought in vain to magically control her dysphoria through a combination of bulimic bingeing and purging.

In terms of our addiction typology, we classify JoAnn as another representative of an addict of the unipolar, subtype II. She suffered narcissistic damage in her capacity to feel both mirrored by and merged with males as human selfobjects. Crippled in her ability to modulate panic and narcissistic rage, JoAnn was often consumed by shame and antipathy toward her own body and its normal physiological functioning.

The psychotherapist responded empathically by allowing JoAnn to entertain the fantasy of herself as being megalomaniacal in her mistaken illusory belief that she magically controls the psychotherapy. His empathic response proved to be instrumental in helping JoAnn to repair the narcissistic damage she had suffered at the hands of her father. With the onset of her budding sexuality, her father had lost empathic contact with JoAnn; and, in fact, had retreated emotionally from her and adopted a very antipathetic attitude toward her.

JoAnn was successful in working through the erotic dimension of the transference–countertransference as she entered belatedly into her own womanhood. At the same time, she felt the enlivening force of a sense of her own humanness. In this respect, she experienced herself and the psychotherapist with less antipathy and with greater empathy. She no longer had a sense of herself and the psychotherapist as one-dimensional stick figures, the two of whom she imagined as being locked into mortal combat over illusory control of the psychotherapy. Instead, she developed a gradual, more realistic, and healthy sense of the two of them as multifaceted human beings who, together, functioned as partners in a joint endeavor.

Travis

The case of Travis illustrates the sometimes significant connection that may be said to exist between addiction and other psychopathological disorders in which dissociation plays a major role. It was almost as if Travis existed as two very different and quite distinct people: by day he was a respected veterans benefits counselor, a husband, and a father; by night he was a drug-crazed and violent criminal, who also had a sordid passion for sexual liaisons with a variety of women whom he had encountered in the darkness of his nocturnal existence. In this sense, therefore, Travis exemplified Robert Louis Stevenson's *Dr. Jekyll and Mr. Hyde*.

Like that fictional character, Travis concocted a potent combination of drugs (speedballs), which he injected intravenously as a psychoactive means of triggering his addictive metamorphosis. Travis shot up with speedballs and secured sex with a variety of prostitutes as part of inducing a hypnotic-like trance. In such an altered state of mind, Travis came under the spell of megalomaniacal fantasies, which were at the unconscious core of his Narcissus complex.

In this defensively altered and hypnoid state (i.e., the hypnoid defense), Travis dissociated and anesthetized himself as he fell under the influence of a powerful set of fantasies and moods that took over his mind. He gave free rein to a violent form of megalomania damaging to others as well as to himself. The level of Travis's narcissistic rage (that is, rageaholism) and antipathy toward others reached truly sociopathic, and even psychopathic, proportions. Eventually, it culminated in an addictive form of suicide (that is, an overdose).

From a typological perspective, we consider Travis to be illustrative of an addict of the bipolar, subtype I. He suffered severe narcissistic damage to all major sectors of the sense of the self. Consequently, he was prone to various forms of dysphoria, including an empty and depleted depression, disintegration anxiety, panic, and narcissistic rage. Travis engaged in the addictive abuse of speedballs and sex as ATMs. His need for two different kinds of ATMs was a testament to the truly bipolar nature of his self disorder. His moods swung rapidly between depression and mania. The violent nature of Travis's narcissistic rage was exacerbated, no doubt, by the underlying bipolar nature of his major mood disorder.

The intersubjective context of a transference–countertransference neurosis served as a clinical setting in which Travis and the psychotherapist shared a fantasy about the phantasmagorical appeal of drugs and violence. The unconscious appeal of the latter was based for both Travis and the psychotherapist on the fantasy of violence as a godlike or megalomaniacal form of control over the life and death of others.

With the help of peer supervision, the psychotherapist finally understood the power of the unconscious appeal of violent fantasies and was better able to help Travis work through a (transitional selfobject) transference fantasy of the psychotherapy as at first a powerful weapon and then as an "analytic instrument." This allowed Travis to recover from his poly-addiction to drugs, violence, and women. And, in the process, he overcame the legacy of a childhood organized unconsciously in accordance with the Narcissus complex. As part of such an unconscious complex, Travis retreated to a blissful fantasy world as his only refuge and means of escaping from the mortifying reality of his early home life.

Errol

Perhaps more than any of our other representative cases, our patient Errol points to the existence of a family milieu (that is, the "addict family") in which a child confronts an environment in which there is a complete absence of usable selfobjects, either human or nonhuman. In such an antipathetic and selfobjectless setting, a child (in this case, Errol) has difficulty anthropomorphizing and animating the world of nonhuman things and activities. Consequently, Errol did not learn how to create and use transitional selfobjects as intermediaries between himself and others as human selfobjects.

In this respect, therefore, Errol was unlike many of our other patients, almost all of whom managed somehow to proceed from the first to the second stages of the narcissistic exchange process. In sharp contrast, Errol became arrested developmentally at an almost autistic level of megalomania.

In an environment devoid of usable selfobjects, Errol turned instead to the masturbatory misuse of a vacuum cleaner, which served as a precursor to his later sexual addiction. The misuse (that is, the compulsive masturbation) on Errol's part of the vacuum cleaner was indicative of the process of addictivization: he substituted nonhuman things for human beings in a futile attempt to create some kind of sustaining selfobject milieu. Later in life, Errol continued this addictive pattern by abusing gambling and sex.

Errol, like Travis, is exemplary of the truly bipolar type of addict, who suffers from a severe mood disorder (that is, falls diagnostically within the bipolar spectrum disorder). As is often typical of such an addict, Errol cycled rapidly between extreme moods of depression and mania. As part of such rapid cycling, Errol also suffered from an overwhelming panic that reaches psychotic proportions. The presence in the case of Errol of a latent psychosis constituted the diagnostic means by which we distinguish him as an addict of the bipolar, subtype II.

The case of Errol also demonstrates graphically the double-edged nature of the transference–countertransference neurosis. The ways in which Errol and the psychotherapist shared fantasies of gambling and sex (as ATMs) works both for and against the psychotherapy. The psychotherapist employed a 12-step program such as GA as an "auxiliary selfobject" as well as augmented the psychotherapy with psychophar-macotherapy.

In so doing, the psychotherapist helped Errol to establish and eventually to maintain abstinence from his gambling addiction. Unfor-tunately, however, these same types of therapeutic interventions did not prove powerful enough to augment the psychotherapy in such a fashion as to enable Errol to overcome his addiction to compulsive sex.

The case of Errol serves as a good example of the kind of serious problems that can arise in those instances in which a psychotherapist has unresolved addictive problems. Such addictive countertransference interferes with effective psychotherapy of an actively addicted patient like Errol. Although the psychotherapist rather quickly resolved his own addictive problem, he nonetheless experienced considerable antipathy toward Errol.

Paradoxically, the countertransference antipathy on the part of the psychotherapist toward Errol expressed itself in a countertherapeutic passivity. The empathic failure by the psychotherapist to confront Errol about his addiction to sex prevented Errol from using the psychotherapy as a selfobject replacement for masturbation and other forms of compulsive sex. As a result, he remained actively addicted to sex throughout most of the psychotherapy.

Conclusion

The progression in which we discuss our concluding points follows the usual order of our model: thus, we begin with phenomenology, move through etiology and pathogenesis, follow with typology, and end with therapeutics.

Phenomenology

Our six representative cases provide significant psychoanalytic data in support of our main phenomenological point regarding the megalomaniacal nature of all addictions. All of our addicts, as the cases illustrate, suffer from the Narcissus complex in being fantasy junkies and control freaks. A person with such narcissistic disturbance may be prone to imagine being a megalomaniacal self and as possessing a kind of magical control over a special class of things and activities. These entities have specific psychoactive effects which, in turn, provide an addict with a narcissistic illusion of being a megalomaniacal self by means of which to magically control his or her emotions and emotional affairs.

The issue of control has special relevance as regards addictive (versus psychotic) megalomania. There is a body of empirical literature (see, for example, Keller, 1972; Distefano et al., 1972; Paredes et al., 1973; Oziel & Obitz, 1975; Plumb et al., 1975; Obitz & Swanson, 1976) on addiction that refers to phenomena described variously as the "locus of control" and the "loss of control."

We contend that a connection may be made between these empirical observations concerning an addict's perception of control, as originating or emanating from the external environment, and our psychoanalytic inferences regarding megalomaniacal or magical control. In essence, both perspectives (that is, empirical and psychoanalytic) suggest that an addict believes erroneously that control of one's emotional life can be exercised at will by possessing and using certain entities located externally to oneself. Paradoxically, an addict ends up losing control over the very things (and activities) mistakenly thought (by an addict) to be doing one's bidding.

We are suggesting, therefore, that addicts suffer a similar fate to that which befalls Mickey Mouse in Walt Disney's "Sorcerer's Apprentice." Addicts, like Mickey, come under the influence of a fantasy of being a megalomaniacal self according to which they imagine themselves as masters of their own personal universes. On the contrary, in actuality they have lost control of themselves and their emotional world.

The empirical conceptions of the relation between control and addiction dovetail well with our psychoanalytic ideas. An addict discovers that certain things and activities have a powerful and psychoactive effect on the brain. We describe this as the psychoactive specificity of ATMs. For an addict, this power endows these entities with the status of means of magical control.

We maintain that an addict is convinced that ultimate control resides in the use (abuse) of these ATMs. An addict imbues these entities as mind- and mood-altering agents with a phantasmagorical meaning that supplants the meaning of reality. Such dramatic alterations of consciousness on the part of an addict foster the illusion of having actually changed the reality of one's emotional existence.

However, in an ironic and tragic twist of fate, an addict falls victim to a vicious cycle: the more an addict seeks to control the uncontrollable, the more control is lost, and consequently the more an addict feels out of control. In this sense, then, our cases illustrate the principle of the dialectical bipolarity of fantasy and mood; they offer graphic evidence of the degree to which an addict flip-flops between a narcissistically mortifying fantasy of being out of control to a narcissistically blissful fantasy of being in control. An addict who is engulfed in a topsy-turvy psychic whirlwind is swept up by a disorganizing combination of affects such as panic and rage. The madness (insanity) of addiction is based, in part, on an addict oscillating psychically between narcissistic illusions of control and loss of control and being out of control.

Our cases also reveal another aspect of the insanity of addiction that consists of extreme narcissistic rage and antipathy. An addict goes insane, so to speak, because of rampant swings between the narcissistic illusions of control and loss of control. An addict treats everyone—including him/herself as well as others—in a truly megalomaniacal fashion: for an addict all human beings are merely means to an end rather than ends in themselves. Likewise, the personal existence of an addict takes on an insane quality in that it becomes reduced for an addict to the issue of whether one is in control or out of control.

An addict becomes, as part of the Narcissus complex, totally dependent on the psychoactive effects of specific things and activities. These ATMs make it possible for an addict to undergo a form of self-hypnosis, which is characterized by trance-like and fugue-like states. In certain instances (e.g., Travis) the degree of dissociation attendant to such a defensively altered and hypnoid state eventuates in the appearance of a dissociated version of the self. Such a part-self may be quite at odds with the ordinary version of the self. In particular, we suggest that addicts (e.g., Travis and Errol) suffer from serious vertical splits in the structure of self-experience.

Etiology and Pathogenesis

Our six treatment case histories point to an important correlation between addiction and trauma. (See Chapter 10 for a more extensive discussion of the interrelationship between addiction and trauma.) Normally, the selfobject milieu of the average family is empathic enough to meet a child's phase-appropriate megalomaniacal need to anthropomorphize and hence to animate the otherwise inanimate. Such a typical form of anthropomorphization is the basis for a child's ability to create transitional selfobjects.

As the by-products of the child's imagination, these magical agents of illusory control serve as intermediaries between the worlds of the human and that of the nonhuman. These entities enable the child to pass successfully from phase II to phase III of the narcissistic exchange process, and thereby progress developmentally beyond the stage of transitional selfobject usage. However, all of our cases involve a developmental form of narcissistic trauma, which grossly distorts and aborts this normal process.

A close examination of the histories of our six future addicts indicates that the normal empathy of the average family is, in their cases, extremely faulty or entirely missing. Instead, our future addicts grow up in a family milieu that is, to varying degrees, either unempathic or antipathetic. Regardless, such a selfobject milieu becomes the developmental context in which a future addict starts down the pathogenic pathway leading eventually to a preoccupation with (ab)using things and activities as a means of magically controlling the world of emotions.

Such an illusion of a megalomaniacal self is the basis later in life for an addict to depend on specific things and activities as an unconscious means of activating psychoactive fantasy tapes. The tendency of a future addict, whether during adolescence or adulthood, is to addictivize (rather than sexualize) things and activities, which then heightens the chances of psychopathological dependency on ATMs. The tendency of a future addict to subvert (rather than pervert) the healthy (selfobject) functioning of things and activities in the nonhuman surround constitutes one of the most serious calamities in the breakdown of the narcissistic exchange process.

Several of our cases (e.g., Errol) demonstrate that the unempathic or antipathetic environment of an "addict family" may be so severe as to deprive a child of usable selfobjects. In such an inhospitable environment, parents mistreat, misuse, and abuse a child as if he or she is a narcissistic artifact lacking in essential humanness. Correspondingly, the unconscious self-experience of a child may become organized in terms of a narcissistic fantasy of being a lifeless automaton that exists in a selfobjectless void. Such a selfobjectless environment forces a child to take a fateful turn in development: such a child becomes inordinately reliant on things and activities as poor substitutes for missing selfobjects.

Moreover, such a child grows up in a way that weakens rather than strengthens the development of a normal sense of being fully human. This sense of humanness instills in a child a feeling of being entitled to the normal expression of healthy sexuality and aggression. Instead, in the case of a future addict, a child has an unconscious experience of sexuality and aggression as foreign and alien forces, which must be controlled in order to be exploited and manipulated. Thus, empathic failures (that is, narcissistic traumas) occurring at a preoedipal phase of development, and especially those resulting in difficulties in the use of transitional selfobjects, may seriously interfere with a child's capacity to utilize things and activities as part of the oedipal process of integrating sex and aggression into the self (e.g., JoAnn).

Typology

The typological division of our six cases attests to the many advantages to be derived from the diagnostic classification of our addicted patient population into four distinct yet interrelated subtypes, all of which exist along a unipolar–bipolar continuum. (See Chapter 9 for an elaboration and refinement of our bipolar self typology of addiction.) Our typology rests on our psychoanalytic discovery that there is a type of character psychopathology—the addictive character—epitomized by a narcissistic behavior disorder (that is, the Narcissus complex) with megalomaniacal features. Regardless of subtype, all our addicted patients are megalomaniacal in that they misuse and abuse things and activities as magical agents of illusory control.

Such ATMs, or ersatz selfobjects, possess few, if any, inherent qualities—other than a specific psychoactive effect(s) of a highly addictive nature—that would allow an individual to use them as authentic selfobjects. An addict indulges in a fantasy of being a megalomaniacal self and as possessing of magical control over the emotional foundation of selfhood. An addict, by resorting to the abuse of these mind and mood altering agents, indulges in a fantasy of a megalomaniacal self and as endowed with of illusory control over the psychic world of thoughts and feelings. The addictive process serves for an addict as an artificial means of manipulating the sense of the psychic reality of the self; however, it does not entail any real or substantive change in the nature of the self.

In the course of presenting our six cases, we provide one or more illustrative examples of each of the four subtypes of addicted patient. As evidenced by the abuse of a single thing or activity, an addicted patient with the unipolar, subtype I or II diagnosis suffers from narcissistic damage in one (and not two or more) major pole of self-experience. The basis for the diagnosis of the first of these subtypes of addicted patient (e.g., Teddy and Mary) rests on evidence of a psychological disorder characterized by anxiety, depression, shame, loneliness, panic, and/or narcissistic rage. An addict who suffers from such painful feelings experiences dysphoric moods, which include an empty/depleted depression, fragmentation, estrangement and alienation, as well as panic and/or narcissistic rage states.

An addicted patient with the unipolar, subtype I diagnosis presents clinically as follows: there is a diagnostic picture uniform in nature, namely, there is a clear instance of either anxiety or depression rather than both. Although either anxiety or depression may be primary in these cases, there is always the possibility of the secondary presence of panic and/or narcissistic rage.

The second of these subtypes of addicted patient (e.g., Joe and JoAnn) is subject to a mood disorder that is truly mixed in nature, that is, it involves in varying degrees a mixture of both anxiety and depression. An addict who suffers from a mood disorder with such mixed features may experience to a lesser degree other painful feelings such as loneliness, panic, and/or narcissistic rage or rageaholism. In contradistinction to the unipolar subtype I of addict, an addicted patient with the diagnosis of unipolar, subtype II suffers major damage to one of the narcissistic poles of the self with only minor damage to a second pole.

An addicted patient with the bipolar, subtype I or II diagnosis suffers from significant damage in two or more of the narcissistic sectors of self-experience. The bipolar nature of this kind of narcissistic damage is apparent in an addict's abuse of two or more ATMs.

In addition to the abuse on the part of an addict of several different kinds of ATMs (or more specifically, those providing different psychoactive effects), there are two key features that distinguish the bipolar from the unipolar type of addicted patient. First, there is the presence in the truly bipolar addict of either hypomania or mania, which is quite distinct clinically from anxiety. And second, this type of bipolar addict tends to cycle in mood, with varying extents of rapidity, from a manic state to a depressive state and vice versa. However, in a manner similar to a unipolar type of addicted patient, a bipolar type of addicted patient may also suffer from various other painful effects including loneliness, panic, and/or narcissistic rage.

The crucial diagnostic criteria that distinguish the bipolar I from the bipolar II subtype of addicted patient involve the presence (in either latent or florid form) of psychotic features. For example, we make a typological (and diagnostic) distinction between Travis and Errol on the basis of the presence in the latter case of a latent and eventually florid psychosis.

Demonstrating the utility of our typology of addiction allows us to make a very important point, namely, concerning the clinical value of combining Kohut's concept of the bipolar self with the concept of bipolarity currently in use in biological psychiatry and the neurosciences. Juxtaposing these otherwise distinct conceptions of bipolarity enables us to make a unique self-psychological contribution to the synthesis of psychoanalysis and biological psychiatry. It is indeed paradoxical that perhaps more than any other idea currently in vogue within psycho-analysis, Kohut's discarded notion of the bipolar self is particularly well-suited to aiding in the integration of psychoanalysis, biological psychiatry, and the neurosciences. Employing the concept of bipolarity permits us to bridge the wide chasm still separating these three disci-plines. In bridging this gap, we hope to make a convincing case for the relevance of Kohut's concept of the bipolar self, and, in the process, to renew interest in it within as well as outside of self psychology.

Therapeutics

For purely heuristic purposes, we divide our concluding comments about psychotherapy into a set of two interrelated categories, namely, the clinical and the psychoanalytic. The clinical category includes conclu-sions drawn from the cases regarding the more practical aspects of conducting psychoanalytic psychotherapy with an addicted patient. The psychoanalytic category consists of conclusions deduced from the cases concerning the deeper and more unconscious aspects of the psycho-therapy.

Regarding the clinical or technical aspects of the psychotherapy, we learned a lot about the common difficulties typically encountered by psychotherapists who work with an addicted patient. We found that it is absolutely necessary at instances of acute crisis to hospitalize an actively addicted patient. In certain cases (e.g., Teddy and Joe), such hospitalization is necessary in order to achieve detoxification and rehabilitation. In other cases (see, for instance, Joe), hospitalization is required as part of stabilizing an addicted patient suffering from another disorder of a potentially life-threatening nature, such as suicide.

We also discovered that there is great value to employing 12-step programs as "auxiliary selfobjects" by which to significantly augment the psychotherapy. In some cases (e.g., Teddy and Errol), 12-step programs like AA and GA proved to be instrumental to a particular patient in recovering from addiction. However, in other cases (e.g., JoAnn), the attempt to employ a 12-step program such as OA proved to be ill-advised and ultimately countertherapeutic. Based, therefore, on the widely divergent reactions of our different patients, we learned an important lesson about the use of 12-step programs: namely, the decision as to whether to use these self-help and peer groups must be made on a case-by-case basis rather than in an across-the-board fashion.

We also came to appreciate the clinical importance of the augmentation of the psychotherapy of certain addicted patients (see, for example, Errol) with psychopharmacotherapy. In many instances, the successful use of psychotropic medication(s) determines whether or not a private practitioner can work psychoanalytically with a particular addicted patient, especially one diagnosed as a bipolar, subtype I or II.

Our cases do not adequately illustrate the actual extent to which effective psychopharmacotherapy is often essential to psychoanalytic psychotherapy with a wide range of addicted patient. (See the case of Byron in Chapter 9 for further evidence of the value of combining psychotherapy with psychopharmacotherapy.) However, the various diagnostic distinctions of our bipolar self typology of addiction—with its emphasis on different types of affective and mood disorder—enables a psychotherapist to make a more reliable clinical diagnosis, which, in turn, justifies the use of psychotropic medication in conjunction with psychotherapy.

Another, and purely serendipitous, finding concerns our discovery of the psychotherapeutic value of using the telephone and the answering machine as part(s) of treating an addicted patient. In several of our cases (e.g., Travis and Errol), the use of these two communication devices was instrumental to the relative success of the respective psychotherapies. These electronic devices allowed for a degree of anonymity in a patient's communication to a psychotherapist, which is crucial to enhancing a patient's unconscious fantasy of the psychotherapy as an impersonal transaction.

Other psychoanalysts with a self-psychological orientation (see, for example, Lindon, 1988) have commented previously on the value of using the telephone in conducting a psychoanalysis; our own experiences in working psychoanalytically with our addicted patients lend further credence to this finding. There is, however, from our self-psychological point of view, one especially crucial aspect of our having incorporated the use by our addicted patients of the telephone and answering machine as integral parts of the psychotherapy. This concerns the extent to which these telecommunication devices facilitate and enhance an addicted patient's transference fantasy of himself or herself as a megalomaniacal being with magical control over the psychotherapist. These devices allow an addicted patient to fantasize that he or she has the psychotherapist at their beck and call.

Moreover, we became cognizant of the importance of peer supervision to psychoanalytic work with an addicted patient. In several of our cases (e.g., Travis and Errol), employing peer supervision was critical to helping the treating psychotherapist in working through problems resulting from narcissistic countertransference.

In the absence of peer supervision, it is unlikely that the psychotherapist in question could have proceeded without further and even more seriously jeopardizing the psychotherapy. Our experience convinces us that peer supervision should be employed whenever possible in working psychotherapeutically with an addicted patient, a patient who so often stirs up narcissistic countertransference in a psychotherapist.

Our concluding point about the clinical aspects of psychotherapy concerns the issue of outcome. Although the actual number of case reports in these chapters is relatively small, these six cases are representative of a much larger and more clinically significant number, that is, a figure totaling approximately 120. This figure reflects the total number of cases of addicted patients seen in long-term, psychoanalytic psychotherapy between the co-authors over a 20-year period.

Although this figure may seem rather high, upon closer scrutiny it breaks down as follows: this figure, as split between the co-authors, amounts to 60 cases a year per co-author; and, divided over the 20-year period, the 60 case number averages three long-term psychotherapy cases per year. Three cases per year is not an unusually high number for each of the co-authors to have treated in psychoanalytic psychotherapy in any given year over this 20-year period, especially in view of the fact that during this span of time each of the co-authors has become a specialist in working psychoanalytically with a wide variety of addicted patient.

The percentages obtained for our representative cases are, therefore, indicative of (although not equal to) our overall outcome averages. Our averages are as follows: there is one premature drop out from psychotherapy (the case of Mary) for a percentage of approximately 16.5; there are four long-term and full recoveries from various addictions (the cases of Teddy, Joe, JoAnn, and Travis) for a percentage of approximately 66.75; and there is one partial or incomplete recovery (the case of Errol) for a percentage of 16.5. Leaving aside the case of Errol, our outcome percentage for full recovery is still quite respectable at 66.75%. We believe that our ratio of success to failure (that is, approximately 2:3 to 1:3) compares favorably to the outcome percentages of any psychoanalytic (or, for that matter, any nonpsychoanalytic) approach of which we are aware.

The main psychoanalytic conclusion derived from our cases concerns the inherently intersubjective nature of our self-psychological approach to psychotherapy with an addicted patient. A great deal has been written about intersubjectivity from a self-psychological perspective (see, for example, Atwood & Stolorow, 1984; Orange, Atwood, & Stolorow, 1997; Stolorow & Atwood, 1992; and Stolorow, Brandschaft, & Atwood, 1987). These authors maintain that intersubjectivity is based on a *two-person psychology*.

However, a close examination of the case material in this literature reveals a somewhat inexplicable failure on the part of these authors to adequately account for the necessarily *two-way nature* of psychoanalytic psychotherapy conducted according to the principles of intersubjectivity. Although claiming to be intersubjective, these authors consistently sidestep the inherently two-way nature of a patient–therapist dyad. Rather, they prefer to focus most of their psychoanalytic attention on reconstructing the intersubjective field as it is inferred to have existed between parent and child.

We contend that the failure on the part of these authors to pay sufficient attention to the presence of countertransference on the part of the psychotherapist constitutes a serious shortcoming. It makes it difficult, if not impossible, for them to illuminate the full contours of the intersubjective field as it emerges within the psychoanalytic relationship.

All of our cases, in marked contrast, offer graphic evidence of the two-way nature of truly intersubjective psychotherapy in the form of the transference–countertransference neurosis. We conducted and discuss each of our cases on the basis of a clear recognition of the omnipresence of some form of transference–countertransference neurosis. In other words, we do not retreat like some other authors from the unavoidably messy nature of the here-and-now of psychoanalytic psychotherapy to the relatively neat and tidy nature of a long ago and distant past.

More specifically, our cases highlight the megalomaniacal nature of the transference–countertransference neurosis as it emerges (both verbally and nonverbally) within the intersubjective field as it is co-determined by addicted patient and psychotherapist alike. We demonstrate the double-edged quality of the transference–countertransference neurosis—sometimes it facilitates the psychotherapeutic work, whereas at other times it obstructs and impedes progress. The psychotherapist's ability to recognize the presence and understand the meaning of the transference–countertransference neurosis is the key factor determining whether or not this intersubjective configuration moves the psychotherapy forward or backward.

In working psychoanalytically with an addicted patient, the ability of a psychotherapist to make use of the transference–countertransference neurosis is based on an empathic understanding of the need to share megalomaniacal fantasies about the psychotherapy as a thing or activity. On the one hand, a psychotherapist who has succeeded in working through such fantasies (that is, is more conscious of their presence) can empathically grasp the unconscious meaning of similar fantasies in an addicted patient. By initially sharing these cherished fantasies with a patient in an uncritical and non-judgmental fashion, a psychotherapist creates a therapeutic ambiance in which these narcissistic illusions can be subjected to more rigorous scrutiny at later phases of the psychotherapy.

On the other hand, a psychotherapist who has failed to work through such fantasies is more likely to share them on the basis of an unconscious over-identification with a patient. Such a countertransference over-identification on the part of a psychotherapist may seriously jeopardize the psychotherapy (e.g., Travis and Errol). With a psychotherapist who shares in an unself-aware fashion, such an unconscious fantasy with an addicted patient is in danger of unwittingly jeopardizing the psychotherapy. This proclivity tends to occur more often in the instance of a psychotherapist who has unresolved and latent addictive tendencies, or in one who is actively addicted during the course of working with an addicted patient.

In regard to the psychoanalytic psychotherapy of an addicted patient, we believe that there is no more serious impediment to effective treatment than that of a psychotherapist who is also actively addicted. Our own clinical experiences as well as that of supervisees and colleagues convinces us of the following point: namely, that actual or potential addiction is, without a doubt, the most underreported and little discussed problem confronting psychoanalytic psychotherapists who work intensively with addicted patients.

In many of our cases, we also see that antipathy plays a crucial role in psychotherapy for patient and psychotherapist alike. Most of our (representative) patients have serious difficulty with antipathy toward themselves and others. However, we also document that antipathy is not the sole province of an addicted patient.

On the contrary, the therapist may also succumb in certain instances to countertransference antipathy in the form of negative attitudes and reactions toward an addicted patient. Such responses assume many countertransference guises including reaction formation, narcissistic rage, as well as overactivity and passivity. Clearly, these antipathetic responses interfere with a psychotherapist's capacity for empathy, and must, there-fore, be analyzed and worked through.

Finally, our psychotherapeutic experience with addicted patients constitutes a body of psychoanalytic evidence that documents the pres-ence and effect of a new kind of selfobject transference, namely, the transitional selfobject transference. This selfobject transference is based on a patient's unconscious fantasy of the psychotherapist and/or psy-chotherapy as respectively a magically-endowed thing or activity, either of which a patient imagines being able to control at will.

We refer to a selfobject transference as megalomaniacal because it is organized unconsciously on the basis of a narcissistic illusion of magical control. And, furthermore, the selfobject transference fantasy of being a megalomaniacal self and being gifted with magical control serves three interrelated purposes: (1) it constitutes the psychotherapeutic medium that absorbs (intersubjectively) the psychoactive effects of ATMs (that is, continues the developmentally thwarted means for the unfolding of the process of narcissistic exchange); (2) it facilitates a narcissistic exchange process; and (3) it generates a psychopharmacotherapeutic effect in the form of therapeutic dissociation.

Part III

An In-Depth View and Expanded Version of a Self-Psychological Model of Addiction

Chapter 7

A Psychoanalytic Phenomenology of Addiction

PART A: THE HISTORICAL CONTEXT

Introduction

Before describing the details of our view of the phenomenology of addiction, we first locate our perspective in a specific historical context. We do so with a review of the work of a number of key theorists in the addiction field. We trace the origins of our position back to the ideas of Rado and Simmel—two of the earliest psychoanalytic theorists on addiction. We continue with an examination of the thinking of Wieder and Kaplan as well as that of Milkman. Finally, we conclude with a discussion on the thought of Krystal, a thinker whose work constitutes a cornerstone of modern psychoanalytic thinking on addiction.

Of course, in reviewing these various authors, we focus on those aspects of their work that are most germane to our view of the phenomenology of addiction. In particular, we feature aspects of their thought touching on the following topics: the fantasy-based nature of addiction as a narcissistic disorder; the dynamic interaction between fantasy and mood; dissociative anesthesia, or addictive metamorphosis and phantasmagorical transmogrification; the psychoactive specificity of addictive trigger mechanisms (ATMs); and the idea of a use psychology. In discussing these topics, we outline a psychoanalytic phenomenology of addiction that lends support to our overall position. Our discussion also serves as an introduction to a more in-depth and extensive discourse on our thinking about the phenomenology of addiction.

Sandor Rado

The work of Sandor Rado, an early psychoanalytic pioneer in the study of addiction, spans a remarkable 40-year period from the 1920s to the 1960s. Rado is one of the founders, along with Abram Kardiner, of the adaptational school in psychoanalysis. Rado had a special interest in drug abuse and, more specifically, narcotic addiction. In addition, he is one of the first psychoanalytic theorists to devote attention to the narcissistic nature of addiction, which he argues is essentially a psychological (rather than biological) phenomenon and disorder.

In his early writings on narcotic addiction, or what he called "pharmacothymia," Rado maintains that it is based on a narcissistic disturbance of the ego. He (Rado, 1933) states:

> We discover that ... the ego is now maintaining its self-regard by means of an *artificial technique*. This step involved an alteration in the individual's entire mode of life; it means a change from the "realistic regime" to a "pharmacothymic regime" of the ego. (p. 9, emphasis added)

He continues:

> A pharmacothymic therefore, may be defined as an individual who has betaken himself to this type of regime; the ensuing consequences make up the scope of the manifestations of pharmacothymia. (p. 9)

He concludes: "In other words, this illness is a *narcissistic disorder*, a destruction through *artificial means* of the natural ego organization" (p. 9, emphasis added).

In defining addiction as a "narcissistic disorder," Rado argues that it involves a basic psychopathological and "artificial means" of "maintaining self-regard," which eventuates in the "destruction ... of the natural ego organization" (p. 9). From our perspective, the "artificial means" of "maintaining self-regard" encompasses the abuse of ATMs, which, in turn, leads to an addictive state of mind.

In pursuing his idea that addiction is a "narcissistic disorder," Rado (1933) notes: "It is as though the distress and pettiness of the ego had been only a nightmare; for it now seems that the ego is after all, the *omnipotent giant it had always fundamentally thought it was*"

(p. 8, emphasis added). Here, and in line with our self-psychological position, Rado describes the archaically narcissistic nature of addiction, which he links to the "pharmacogenic" effect of narcotic drugs. He (Rado, 1933) indicates: "In the *pharmacogenic elation* the ego regains its *original narcissistic stature*" (p. 8, emphasis added).

These passages make evident the extent to which Rado describes the phenomenology of addiction in terms that parallel our own. This similarity is especially clear as regards the notions of dialectical bipolarity, dissociative anesthesia or addictive metamorphosis, and psychoactive specificity. As early as 1933, Rado writes about "pharmacothymia," a condition he defines as a drug-induced "sharp rise in self-regard and the elevation of the mood—that is to say, elation" (pp. 5–6). Rado argues that in so describing pharmacothymia he is

> not so much referring to the possible discomfort due to symptoms from individual origins as to the *inevitable alteration of mood*. The emotional situation which obtained in the initial depression has again returned, but exacerbated, evidently by new factors. *The elation had augmented the ego to gigantic dimensions and had almost eliminated reality*; now first the reverse state appears, sharpened by contrast. *The ego is shrunken* and reality appears exaggerated in its dimension. (pp. 8–9, emphasis added)

Rado adds: "What the pain of the *pharmacogenic depression* gives birth to is, with the rigorous psychological consistency, the *craving for elation*" (p. 9, emphasis added). These passages make clear the following: Rado's description of pharmacothymia is completely consistent with our self-psychological description of the dynamic interaction of fantasy and mood in a dialectical and bipolar fashion. Implicit in Rado's description is his view of pharmacothymia as inherently both dialectical and bipolar. It is dialectical because the depressive mood that accompanies it usually leads to a "craving for elation." It is typical for this "craving for elation" to subside and diminish, eventuating in a depressive crash in mood. Thus, pharmacothymia involves an emotional dialectic of erratic, uncontrolled, and often violent mood swings. The latter trap an addict in a vicious cycle of emotional highs and lows. Moreover, pharmacothymia is bipolar because it involves the presence of two different moods, which oscillate and vacillate as the polar opposites of one another.

Moreover, we interpret Rado's description of pharmacothymia as alluding to the dialectical bipolarity of fantasy and mood. For example, Rado describes pharmacothymic elation as augmenting the "ego to gigantic dimensions," whereby it almost eclipses reality. We understand his description as an allusion to the notion of a grandiose fantasy and accompanying mood of narcissistic bliss. The combined presence of particular fantasies and moods in the unconscious mind of an addict is the means by which an addict becomes lost in an imaginary world. It is in such a wonderland of crass pleasures that an addict escapes temporarily from the often painful reality of day-to-day living.

Or, to take another example, Rado describes the depressive phase of pharmacothymia as entailing a severe shrinking of the ego. From the perspective of our study, we maintain that his description may be read as referring to the polar opposite of a grandiose fantasy: namely, the negative or dreaded fantasy version of a mortifying existence as a reduced or lesser being, that is, a fantasy of the self as "ungrandiose."

Rado connects pharmacothymia, therefore, with disturbances in archaic narcissism. For example, he (Rado, 1933) states: "What the pharmacothymic regime bestowed upon the ego, was, however, a *valueless inflation of narcissism*" (p. 13, emphasis added). Or, similarly, he observed: "The elation has *reactivated his narcissistic belief in his invulnerability*" (p. 13, emphasis added).

In one of his last papers on addiction, Rado (1969) comments that the "'magic' of narcotic drugs lies in the *direct biochemical action on the brain*, in their bypassing the prerequisite adaptive effort, and performance" (p. 264, emphasis added). Here, we find Rado referring to what we describe as the varying pathways or routes by which different ATMs activate and intensify various fantasies and moods.

In his early writing on addiction, Rado describes a phenomenon that parallels our concept of the psychoactive specificity of ATMs—an essential feature of dissociative anesthetization or addictive metamorphosis. He indicates that drugs may have either an "analgesic (sedative, hypnotic)" or a "stimulating effect" (p. 397). Rado's statement, made in 1926, is particularly prescient in anticipating ideas that are later crucial to psychoanalytic thinking on addiction. For instance, he adumbrates the well-known "drug of choice" hypothesis, first introduced by Wieder and Kaplan, and later elaborated on by Milkman and Frosch. According to this hypothesis, addicts choose and select different drugs on the basis of the specific and differing psychoactive effects of the substance. More specifically, the two above mentioned sets of authors hypothesizes that some addicts are drawn more to drugs that provide an antidepressant effect, whereas other addicts are attracted to drugs that engender an antianxiety effect.

From our own self-psychological perspective, we envision what Rado envisions as the "analgesic (sedative, hypnotic) effect" in terms of the antianxiety effect of certain ATMs (that is, tranquilization, sedation, pacification, and containment). These entities provide an addict with an imaginary experience of: (1) merger with *something* fantasized as omnipotent or, (2) containment by *something* fantasized as a mirror with which to frame grandiosity. Likewise, we construe what Rado describes as the "stimulating effect" of drugs as involving an antidepressant effect provided by specific ATMs (that is, inflating, uplifting, buoying, or boosting). These things or activities engender in an addict an imaginary experience of being mirrored by the use (abuse) of *something* special.

Rado notes that drugs can have either an "analgesic (sedating, hypnotic) effect" or a "stimulating effect." In this sense, Rado seems to be aware that psychic pain can occur either because of too much or too little feeling. In other words, psychic pain may be of two different sorts—emotional hyperactivity or emotional hypoactivity. Moreover, Rado (1933) stresses that drugs both diminish psychic pain as well as increase psychic pleasure. Together, these drug-induced states (that is, an addictive state of mind) involve what he terms the "pharmacogenic pleasure-effect." Disorders, such as an addiction as well as a fetishism or a perversion, simultaneously engender paradoxical psychoactive effects. They both diminish pain and increase pleasure. This dual action lends to these disorders an extremely corrosive effect on the character structures. Such psychological corrosion accounts, in part, for the fact that these disorders are so difficult to treat psychotherapeutically.

Along similar lines, Rado (1933) points out: "*Benumbed by ... illusion,* the ego's adherence to the pharmacothymic regime is strengthened all the more" (p. 13, emphasis added). We read Rado in this statement as hinting at the dissociating and anesthetizing effects of addiction. In other words, the ego is benumbed or anesthetized as part of pharmacothymia. In the terminology of our model, we state that an addict has a sense of self that is determined unconsciously by the dissociative effect of illusion and fantasy.

Rado (1933) continues his discussion of the narcissistic nature of addiction by asking the following rhetorical question: "Did not the ego obtain a tremendous real satisfaction by mere *wishing,* i.e., without effort, as only that narcissistic image can?" (p. 8, emphasis added). We, like Rado, believe that an essential feature of addiction, as a narcissistic disorder, entails "wishing," imagining, or fantasizing." More specifically, we maintain that addiction involves conjuring up imaginary visions that are hypnotic in nature. It is in this later sense that we refer to addicts as fantasy junkies. Speaking metaphorically, addicts may be thought of as consuming large quantities of the junk food of the mind, which like all junk food is lacking in nutritional value.

We find support in Rado for our central contention that addiction activates and intensifies fantasies of great narcissistic pleasure. He (Rado, 1933) asserts that the *"pharmacogenic pleasure instigates a rich fantasy life"* (p. 11, emphasis added) by discharging the *"libidinal tension associated with these fantasies"* (p. 12, emphasis added). In terms of psychoanalytic theory, Rado adheres in this context to a classical notion of libido. He explains the power of these fantasies, which are activated by addictive means, in terms of the Freudian concept of hypercathexis. Following modern psychoanalytic thinking, we adopt a more sophisticated position, namely that there is a dramatic alteration in the case of the abuse of ATMs of brain chemistry, neuroanatomical functioning, and psychophysiology. In addition, there is a parallel process involving the unconscious activation of fantasy and intensification of pleasurable mood.

In a subsequent 1957 paper, Rado picks up the theme of the narcissistic nature of addiction. Moreover, at this latter stage in his thinking, he anticipates more clearly our self-psychological position. Rado (1957) argues that there are several different versions of the self—a "tested self," a "primordial self," and a "desired self." He states that the "grown organism lives under a more or less realistic system of self-government presided over by an adjusted though lovingly retouched self-image called the *tested self*" (p. 166, emphasis added). "This image," he continues, "derives from and inherits the organizing functions of the *primordial self*, the secret aim-image of its most deeply repressed aspirations" (p. 166, emphasis added).

In a still later 1969 book, Rado insists that the *"core of the human being is so illusional* that what we admire enough to learn appears to be only what we already know" (p. 122, emphasis added). Thus, Rado argues that the primordial self, which gives rise to the desired self, is, at its center, illusional. His argument is similar to our contention that at its core the archaic self is phantasmagorical.

Rado hints also at the self-psychological notion of the selfobject. He contends that from the vantage point of the primordial self the "infant views his parents, upon whose ministrations he depends for his survival, as deputies who exercise his magic powers for him" (p. 106). According to Rado the young organism's first image of itself is of proprioceptive (kinesthetic) origin. Enchanted by its ability to move, it attributes unlimited power to its intentional actions and *pictures itself as an omnipotent being.* This self-image constitutes the representation of the total organism at psychodynamic levels and presides over the integration of its behavior we call it the *primordial self.* (pp. 165–66, emphasis added)

Later in 1969, Rado adds that the "parent is considered omnipotent only as a proxy because he is the almighty agent of the really almighty self" (p. 129). In addition, he asserts that the "parents are considered omnipotent not for the sake of their own glory but for the egoistic reasons of the baby" (p. 120).

The discussion by Rado of the self, in its various forms and in relation to parental "deputies" or proxies, sets the stage for a further description of the narcissistic nature of addiction as a disorder of the self. He (Rado, 1957) suggests: "If in the adaptive struggle for existence self-government fails, the organism may seek to strengthen its tested self with regressively revived features of his primordial self" (p. 166). However, he continues, "such repair work is bound to miscarry, since the resulting *aggrandized self-image* can only undermine realistic self-government" (p. 166, emphasis added).

Rado regards addictions as just such a form of miscarried repair. In the case of the "intoxicated patient," he insists that a "sudden change from pain to pleasure, from inhibition to facilitation has proved to him by the full weight of an actual experience that after all, he is the *omnipotent giant* he had always fundamentally thought he was" (p. 166, emphasis added). He suggests that it might be tempting to "view the *patient's grandiose picture of himself as harmless illusion* bound to collapse as soon as the wave of elation subsides" (p. 166, emphasis added).

However, Rado warns that such an assumption is mistaken. On the contrary, Rado contends that an addicted patient's "situation is worse than before: he feels he must *recapture yesterday's grandeur* by taking another dose. Thus the craving for elation develops" (p. 166, emphasis added).

The notion of recapturing "yesterday's grandeur" corresponds to a critical aspect of Rado's thinking on the narcissistic nature of addiction. He maintains that at its phenomenological center addiction is a narcissistic disturbance of megalomaniacal proportions. Rado (1933) compares addictive megalomania to schizophrenic or psychotic megalomania; he claims that both are "manifestations of *narcissistic regression*" (p. 17, emphasis added). Rado states that the two forms of megalomania are "based upon a regression to the '*original narcissistic stature*' of the ego" (p. 10, emphasis added).

In his 1957 essay, Rado returns to the idea of addictive megalomania. He indicates that the "interdependent phenomenon of elation and craving for elation show that the patient's *grandiose idea operates with delusional strength*" (p. 166, emphasis added). He adds that the "patient's image of himself as an *omnipotent and indestructible giant* must be clinically described as a thinly veiled *narcotic delusion of grandeur* rooted in the drug which has produced the intoxicating pleasure-effect for him" (p. 166, emphasis added). Thus, an addict suffers from a narcissistic disturbance in self-experience, which is evidenced, according to Rado, by the symptom of megalomaniacal delusions of grandeur. We refer to this as the fantasy of the megalomaniacal self as possessing magical control.

Before concluding our review of Rado, we need to briefly examine some early as well as some more recent psychoanalytic thinking on megalomania.

Freud (1953 [1913]), (see Eigen (2004 [1986]) for a discussion of Freud's view on megalomania), Jones (1974 [1913]), Ferenezi (1956 [1913]) and continuing with M. Klein (1975 [1950, 1952, 1955, 1957]), Nunberg (1955), A. Reich (1960), and Chassequet-Smirgel (1985) all discuss megalomania, although not referring specifically to addiction. More recently, Eigen (2004 [1986]), Green (1986), and Steiner (1999) as well as a number of other psychoanalytic authors have focused on megalomania in relation to schizophrenia and psychosis. For example, Bergler (1957) roots addictive gambling in what he refers to variously as a gambler's "megalomaniacal attitude" (p. 23), his "childlike megalomania" (p. 28), or "infantile megalomania" (p. 32), or his "original megalomaniacal glory" (p. 41), Rado and Bergler are two of the few psychoanalysts to connect megalomania explicitly and primarily with addiction.

However, for the purposes of the present discussion, the significance of the thinking on megalomania of various psychoanalytic theorists from Freud to Eigen lies in the very important connection that they all make between it and narcissism. To varying degrees, all these authors describe megalomania as a severe form of psychopathological disturbance in the psychic realm of archaic or infantile narcissism. According to these psychoanalysts, the schizophrenic or psychotic person suffers from an extremely over-inflated and aggrandized self-image; that is, these persons are megalomaniacal about their own importance and power. Such megalomaniacs over-value themselves and their own significance to the degree to that they lose touch with reality. In essence, the megalomaniac is psychotic because fantasies of grandeur reach delusional proportions.

For example, Freud (1911) analyzes Schreber as suffering from megalomaniacal delusions of grandeur in which he fantasizes himself as chosen to be the personal handmaiden of the Lord. Yet, according to Freud, Schreber simultaneously imagines himself as picked out by God for individual persecution. M. Klein (1975 [1950, 1952, 1955, 1957]), in her analysis of psychotic children, makes explicit what is implicit in Freud. As evidenced both by Schreber and certain psychotic children, she argues that paranoid psychosis is based, in large measure, on what she called "megalomaniacal phantasies" of delusional grandeur. Both A. Reich (1960) and Chasseguet-Smirgel (1985) take up Klein's idea of the megalomaniacal fantasy. They link it to disturbances in archaic or infantile forms of narcissism. In fact, both of these latter psychoanalysts discuss megalomania in terms respectively of "narcissistic fantasy" and "narcissistic phantasies."

However, despite the importance of megalomania to understanding archaic narcissism and psychopathological disturbances in this central realm of the psyche, Kohut and other self psychologists ignore it almost completely. Perhaps Kohut steers away from including megalomania as one of the major forms of archaic narcissism because it is viewed psychoanalytically in terms of Freud's original distinction between primary and secondary narcissism. Kohut wishes to avoid this distinction, which is so central to Freud's libido theory, because he (Kohut) wants to place narcissism on a separate developmental line, a track distinct from that of object love. He refuses to view narcissism as it is traditionally conceptualized in classical psychoanalysis. On the basis of this conceptualization, narcissism is seen as simply an early stage of object love which, later in life, is expressed regressively only in psychopathological conditions.

Kohut, by circumventing Freud's distinction between primary and secondary narcissism, substitutes for megalomania notions of archaic forms of grandiosity and omnipotence. This substitution is now generally accepted in self psychology. However, in our opinion, it fails to capture the in-depth nature and true role of megalomania in such severe narcissistic disorders of the self such as those occurring in psychosis and addiction.

Furthermore, as we demonstrate below, it is possible to reconceptualize megalomania self-psychologically in a way that does not rely on the distinction between primary and secondary narcissism. Likewise, such a self-psychological reconceptualization of megalomania need not be grounded in libido theory. Therefore, we ought not view megalomania when it appears in adulthood as, by definition, a fixation point and a form of pathological narcissism.

In returning to Rado's idea of addictive megalomania (in contrast to psychotic megalomania), we incorporate, for the first time, the concept of megalomania as part of self psychology. In so doing, we hope to make a valuable contribution to both self psychology and the addiction field. The description of addictive megalomania by Rado contains the implicit notion that an addict becomes over-inflated on a psychopathological basis because of an illusion of possessing magical psychic powers. An addict imagines these powers as emanating from the use (ab)use of narcotic drugs. An addict is under a spell involving a magical belief of possessing supernatural powers. For example, Rado (1933) states that "a magical movement of the hand introduces a magical substance and behold, pain and suffering are exorcised, the sense of misery disappears and the body is suffused by waves of pleasure" (pp. 7–8).

The (mistaken and illusory) belief on the part of an addict in possessing these powers of magical control is so enthralling and hypnotic that it ushers in an alteration in an addict's subjective sense of that which is real and that which is unreal. In other words, an addict who undergoes such an alteration has difficulty in distinguishing between the real and the unreal. Instead, an addict escapes to a surreal world in which a fantasy of being a megalomaniacal self and as empowered with magical control is experienced unconsciously as a subjective reality.

We use Rado's conception of addictive megalomania as the basis for a central point of our entire argument. We point out that in the context of addiction megalomania is manifested in the form of fantasies of possessing uncanny powers, which are thought of by an addict as deriving from the use of magically endowed things and activities. An addict is megalomaniacal in our sense, therefore, on the basis of the following belief.

An addict imagines that human nature and, more specifically, the very nature of psychic life, can be magically controlled by the mere use of a particular substance (for example, alcohol, drugs, or food), or by simply engaging in a specific activity (for instance, gambling or sex). In this regard, an addict is a Narcissus lost in a wonderland of megalomaniacal proportions; fantasies of being a megalomaniacal self and as exercising magical control constitute, therefore, a dimension of unconscious mental life that we term the Narcissus complex.

Grandiose and omnipotent fantasies typically arise in the context of a functional relationship to human selfobjects that provide mirroring or idealization. In contrast, we argue that megalomaniacal fantasies emerge in the context of a solely utilitarian connection to and use of nonhuman (transitional) selfobjects. A grandiose fantasy involves an unconscious experience of the self as great, wonderful, outstanding, extraordinary, or superb (namely, a greater being) in relation to another person, who functions purely as a mirroring selfobject. An omnipotent fantasy entails an unconscious experience of the self as merged with an all-powerful and all-knowing being, who functions as an idealized selfobject. A twinship fantasy concerns an unconscious experience of the self as replicated by an identical double, who functions as an alterego by which it is possible to duplicate the thoughts and feelings of the self. A megalomaniacal fantasy revolves around an unconscious experience of the self as a demigod, who is capable of controlling the psychic world of thought and emotion through the (ab)use of an array of extraordinary things and activities, which function either as healthy transitional self- objects or unhealthy ATMs.

In summary, one is grandiose or omnipotent primarily in relation to the world of human beings, whereas one is megalomaniacal mainly in connection to the world of nonhuman things and activities. Thus, it is *who* one stands in relation to that is critical in the case of grandiose, omnipotent, or twinship fantasies; whereas it is *what* and *how* something is used or abused that is crucial in the case of megalomaniacal fantasies.

However, we are not implying that grandiose, omnipotent, or twinship fantasies are strictly the by-products of interactions between the self and the human milieu any more than that megalomaniacal fantasies arise only in connection to transactions between the self and the nonhuman environ. Rather, we want only to emphasize that, unlike grandiose, omnipotent, and twinship fantasies, megalomaniacal fantasies capture a unique quality of the unconscious meaning of the intersection or interconnection between the self and the nonhuman surround. Similarly, we want to stress that megalomaniacal fantasies in the case of addiction are primary, whereas other archaic narcissistic fantasies are secondary.

We believe that megalomaniacal fantasies are similar to grandiose, omnipotent, and twinship fantasies in that all of them are phase-appropriate in the normal development of healthy narcissism. Megalomaniacal fantasies occur typically during the toddler period of childhood. During this stage, a toddler fantasizes about being a wizard or sorcerer who controls all sorts of things and activities that are imagined by a child as the functional equivalent of a magic wand. (See, for example, Chasseguet-Smirgel, 1985, p. 122, who described the megalomaniacal nature of normal childhood inventiveness.)

In dramatic contrast, a toddler who becomes developmentally stunted or arrested at this stage of transitional selfobject usage fails to transform fantasies of a megalomaniacal self as endowed with magical control into normal psychic structure and functioning. In a desperately futile attempt to regulate self-esteem and modulate mood, such a child becomes pathologically dependent for self-regulation on inanimate things and activities as parts of the nonhuman surround.

Such a child often develops into an adult who is unconsciously organized in accordance with megalomaniacal fantasies. As a result, such an individual is prone to breakdown, later in life, with narcissistic disorders such as addiction.

Let us give a prime example of such megalomaniacal fantasies in addiction. We cite the example in which an addict indiscriminately mixes and matches the human with the nonhuman, or the animate with the inanimate, to form semi-human creations and inventions. There could be nothing more megalomaniacal than an addict's alchemistic metamorphizing of things and activities into humanoid entities and, vice versa, engaging in the transmogrification of human beings into android agents. As a Narcissus lost in a surreal wonderland, an addict is the megalomaniac *par excellence.*

A cornerstone of our central contention concerns the notion that an addict is organized unconsciously in terms of megalomaniacal fantasies about the self-metamorphizing power of such things as alcohol, drugs, and food as well as such activities as eating, gambling, and sex. Let us return to our earlier distinction between narcissistic personality and narcissistic behavior disorders. We now envision the difference as follows.

We distinguish these two related yet distinct disorders on the basis of the predominance of a particular type of archaic narcissistic fantasy. On the one hand, the narcissistic personality disorder is based mainly on grandiose, omnipotent, and twinship fantasies of a self in relation to another person(s); one, however, who is imagined by an individual as a human selfobject. On the other hand, the narcissistic behavior disorder rests essentially on megalomaniacal fantasies of things and activities. An addict imagines these entities as, for example, ersatz selfobjects by which it is possible to exercise a magical control over the emotional state of the self. In addiction, our notion of megalomania contains an implicit connotation whereby there is a cognitive disturbance of thought and an affective disturbance of mood. As such, our notion of a fantasy of being a megalomaniacal self fits in neatly with our idea of the bipolar self-typology of addiction. (See Chapter 9 for a full discussion of this concept.)

Ernest Simmel

In addition to Rado, Ernest Simmel is another of the early pioneers in the development of a psychoanalytic phenomenology of addiction. And, like Rado, he makes a number of important contributions relevant to our position on phenomenology. First, although not referring directly to megalomania, Simmel nonetheless alludes to it in the context of his discussion of alcohol addiction, or what he terms "dipsomania." Simmel employs this once popular term in an allusion to the alcoholic's irresistible urge, craving, and insatiable thirst for alcohol. The alcoholic is, in this sense, dipsomaniacal or megalomaniacal in the pursuit and use of alcohol.

Furthermore, Simmel, again like Rado, directly links addiction with psychosis. In a footnote, Simmel (1948) observes: "Of all the addictions, the alcoholic addict shows most clearly that the *addicted ego tends to realize the same unconscious regressive psychological strivings as the psychotic ego*, an indication that an addiction may be a last defense against psychosis" (p. 22, footnote 9, emphasis added).

We contend that one of the major "unconscious regressive psychological strivings" linking addiction with psychosis is megalomania. We maintain megalomania is, therefore, a common denominator by which to make a connection between addiction and psychosis. This linkage has important implications for understanding these severe forms of psychopathology.

An addict is megalomaniacal because he or she abuses or misuses things and activities for the sole purpose of artificially altering consciousness and mood. In a sense, then, an addict may be thought of as making a last ditch attempt to stave off a psychological breakdown into psychosis. An addict clings tenaciously to things and activities that are experienced as endowed with the narcissistic illusion of magical control. In the process, an addict holds, however precariously, to some semblance of a normal sense of the reality of the self in relation to the external world.

In contrast, a psychotic, having lost even a tenuous hold on this sense of reality, has all but broken with it. As part of such a break, a

psychotic retreats into a self-made and megalomaniacal world of delusions and hallucinations. In contrast to megalomania in addiction, in
psychosis it is a sign of an often irreversible break with reality; in this
context it is not, therefore, indicative of a last and desperate attempt to
hold onto some, however limited, contact with reality. Paradoxically, an
addict, unlike a psychotic, sustains some tenuous connection to a
consensually validated view of reality, including that of human nature.

An addict does so under the influence of a megalomaniacal illusion
that certain psychoactive things and activities permit one to magically
control the psychic reality of thought and emotion. However, this fantasy
of a megalomaniacal self and as wielding magical control over the
psychological laws governing human nature on the part of an addict
inevitably fails. Then, an addict is more vulnerable to a break with reality
of a degree more typical of a psychotic.

In a fashion similar to Rado, Simmel conceptualizes addiction as
based largely on fantasy. For example, he (Simmel, 1948) states that the
"addict thus acts out his *pregenital masturbatory fantasies* by returning
in effect to his mother as her baby to be nursed and taken care of"
(p. 18, emphasis added). Or, later, and in a similar vein, he notes that
the "*pregenital masturbatory fantasies* which these addicts strive to
satisfy are what I once called 'reciprocal autoeroticism'" (pp. 19–20,
emphasis added). Simmel explains that these pregenital or autoerotic
masturbatory fantasies entail the "various erogenous zones of the body
[serving] to satisfy each other for want of satisfaction from the mother"
(pp. 19–20). He continues that these were "wishful fantasies of urinating
or defecating into one's own mouth" (pp. 19–20).

Simmel describes a Nirvanic fantasy of a return to the womb and
a prenatal existence as an unconscious factor that is central to alcohol
addiction. He (Simmel, 1948) claims that an alcohol addict has an
unconscious fantasy of imbibing the mother and, in the process,
"becomes one with her and thus approximates psychologically a return
to her womb" (p. 21). Moreover, Simmel contends that the "alcoholic
drinks himself into oblivion, the mental state of prenatal Nirvana: emergence from this utopia is a rebirth with mother in attendance ready with
milk to nurse him back to life" (pp. 21–22).

Clearly, Simmel views addiction as based largely on unconscious
fantasy—that of pregenital or autoerotic masturbatory fantasies and that
of Nirvanic fantasies of return to the womb and prenatal existence. These
addictive fantasies involve what we construe as forms of archaic narcissism. The masturbatory fantasies of the genital or autoerotic type entail

a purely narcissistic involvement with and use of the body as a means of attempting to satisfy basic needs.

Such a reliance on the body, which is rooted in archaic narcissism, stands in dramatic contrast to an otherwise normal dependence and reliance on the mother as a need-satisfying (self)object. By implication, Simmel argues that a person who is prone later in life to alcoholic addiction turns the body and its various erogenous zones into a thing. As such, it has been used already in early childhood as part of a narcissistic activity.

Similarly, the Nirvanic fantasy encompasses an even more archaic form of narcissism. In this fantasy, an alcoholic imagines returning to the womb, thus transcending the psychic reality of human and corporeal existence. As part of such a fantasy, an alcoholic fantasizes an existence as a prenatal self, receiving nourishment and supplies without the slightest effort. Such a Nirvanic fantasy is archaically narcissistic in reversing the normal relationship between self and environment.

Under normal circumstances, a sense of self is dependent, to a large extent, on the ability of an individual to adapt successfully to the environment. In so doing, an individual provides himself or herself with psychological nourishment and emotional sustenance. However, such an adaptation entails an essential requirement: it requires the unconscious transformation (via transmuting internalization) of archaic narcissism into healthy forms of self-assertion, self-actualization, and self-realization.

Under the psychic influence of a Nirvanic fantasy, however, an alcoholic inverts and reverses this normal situation. Instead of having to adapt to the environment as part of psychological survival, an alcoholic imagines being transported by magic back to the womb. Here, the environment and, more specifically, the womb are adjusted to suit the needs of the prenatal self. It is the height of archaic narcissism on the part of an alcoholic to fantasize a state in which everything is supplied miraculously to oneself solely on the basis of existing as a pure physical being. In this regard, we believe that the addictive fantasy of a return to a Nirvanic existence in the womb is based on the following: an alcoholic indulges in a megalomaniacal illusion of magical control whereby an ATM (in the form of alcohol) functions as the equivalent of the umbilical cord.

Simmel also describes as central to alcohol addiction a process that touches on the issues of dialectical bipolarity and psychoactive specificity. He (Simmel, 1948) asserts that the "wish to bring about the alcoholic elation, has become a compulsion because it is dominated by and has been elaborated upon by the process of the unconscious" (p. 11). We interpret Simmel as implying, in this passage, the following: there is an unconscious "wish" or fantasy with an accompanying mood of elation, which together are activated and heightened by compulsive drinking. There is, in other words, an unconscious dynamic by which fantasy and mood interact dialectically to produce an addictive state of mind.

In addition, according to Simmel, there is an inherent bipolarity to this unconscious dynamic. Simmel indicates: "All addictions, and especially alcoholic addiction, are protectors against depression" (p. 10). Furthermore, he insists that the "psychoanalytic process has succeeded in unmasking alcoholic elation as a defense against depression" (p. 21). Simmel also points out that there is an "identity between depression and elation of the alcoholic" (p. 25).

We read Simmel as suggesting that despite appearing to be moods that are polar opposites, alcoholic elation and depression are really two sides of the same emotional coin, so to speak. In the addictive cycle, elation may override depression temporarily only to be superceded by it. These extreme and polar opposite moods are bipolar in nature; they also follow repetitively from and upon one another in a vicious cycle.

Finally, Simmel (1948) connects the pleasurable affective state of "alcoholic elation" to an "artificial pharmacotoxic" (p. 7) condition. He suggests that the "ego finds a way of denying painful reality by re-establishing the infantile pleasure principle ... through *artificial pharmacotoxic elation*" (p. 7, emphasis added). The notion of an "artificial pharmacotoxic elation" is similar to Rado's pharmacothymia and is related to our notions of addictive metamorphosis and psychoactive specificity. Moreover, and perhaps most importantly, Simmel hints at Rado's idea of addictive megalomania by suggesting that an alcoholic replaces a painful psychic reality with an artificially-induced pleasurable psychic reality.

Simmel is very clear that the pharmacotoxic or psychoactive effect of alcohol is important yet not decisive. Instead, he argues that what is ultimately critical is the unconscious, psychogenic effect. He insists that the "biochemical effect of alcohol is not the decisive factor for its use but the *psychological effect which the ego derives from it*" (p. 8, emphasis added). We construe as the psychoactive specificity of what Simmel described as the "psychological effect which the ego derives" from alcohol is, from our perspective, its psychoactive specificity. Alcohol generates addictive fantasies and moods, which have an antidepressive effect, and which are characteristic of an addictive state of mind (that is, addictive metamorphosis and phantasmagorical transmogrification).

Wieder and Kaplan

Wieder and Kaplan (1969) propose a neo-classical (that is, ego-psychological and object relational) psychoanalytic phenomenology of drug addiction. Their proposal is especially relevant to our current discussion. In particular, these authors develop the now well-known "drug of choice" hypothesis—a notion commonly, albeit erroneously, attributed to Milkman and Frosch. In fact, the latter two authors elaborate on rather than originate the idea.

More importantly for our purposes, however, Wieder and Kaplan touch on a number of issues germane to our phenomenological conception of addiction: namely, they conceptualize it as based on fantasy and, more specifically, archaic narcissistic fantasy. They also allude to notions similar to that of the dialectical bipolarity of fantasy and affect, dissociative anesthesia (or addictive transmogrification), ATMs, and psychoactive specificity.

The view of addiction as fantasy-based is evident throughout the work of Wieder and Kaplan. For example, they state: "*Ubiquitous childhood and adolescent fantasies expressing the work for magic potions of diverse effects* contribute to some early disturbances and food fads" (p. 401, emphasis added). Similarly, they observe:

> *Conscious fantasies about drugs* are invariably present during times of illusion, emotional distress, and development crisis. *The wish for instant, magical chemical influence on the brain or body is then ubiquitous.* (p. 401, emphasis added)

In arriving at a fantasy-based view of addiction, Wieder and Kaplan illuminate the dialectical and bipolar nature of the dynamic interaction between fantasy and mood. On the one hand, they point out that the "pharmacologic effect facilitates the *fantasy fulfillment of wishes for union, and fusion* with lost or yearned for objects" (p. 404, emphasis added). In a similar vein, they indicate that an essential aspect of the drug experience involves a *"feeling of blissful satiation conducive to hypercathecting fantasies of omnipotence, magical-wish fulfillment, and self-sufficiency"* (p. 404, emphasis added).

In both of these passages, Wieder and Kaplan highlight the archaically narcissistic nature of drug-induced fantasies and the mood of bliss that accompanies them. Similarly, they note that one of their drug-addicted patient's "realistic activity was a *living out of denial in fantasy*, for as a con man who persuaded others to accept his falsehoods as truth, he momentarily realized his *narcissistic omnipotence*" (p. 427, emphasis added).

Wieder and Kaplan are also cognizant of the polar opposite or flip side of such fantasies. For instance, they maintain that a lessening of "aggressive cathexis of object representations and diminished aggression against objects *reduce the anxiety stemming from annihilation fantasies* and projected aggression" (p. 420, emphasis added). Or, they indicate that "*fantasies threatening abandonment and destruction* ... renew the search for the drug" (p. 430, emphasis added).

These psychoanalytic observations indicate that Wieder and Kaplan believe the pharmacogenic effect of drugs simultaneously produce blissful fantasies and defend against mortifying fantasies of "annihilation," "abandonment," and "destruction." Moreover, they suggest that drug-induced fantasies of narcissistic bliss significantly reduce anxiety and aggression.

Wieder and Kaplan center their psychoanalytic phenomenology of addiction on a notion they call the "pharmacogenic effect" of drugs. According to these authors, this pharmacogenic effect is based on the "*physiological concomitant* ... which stimulate fantasies ... or are secondarily incorporated into them" (p. 400, emphasis added). They explain that this effect

> represents a diffuse, direct and indirect alteration in cellular physiology and biochemistry, where ultimate psychic expression appears as a modification of the energy equilibrium of the personality structure or as *cathectic shifts*. (p. 400, emphasis added)

Wieder and Kaplan distinguish between transitional objects, which are normal and healthy, and pharmacogenic "correctives" or "prostheses," which are abnormal and pathological. They connect transitional objects to addiction in that "their magical relief-giving qualities ... also contribute to the concept of 'drugs'" (p. 401). Later, Wieder and Kaplan indicate that those persons who are archaically organized on a psychic level "rely on drugs ... to shore up, and *supply controls* and gratifications which adequate structuralization provides unaided" (p. 428, emphasis added). In this same context, they argue that drugs "act as an energic modifier and redistributor, and as a *structural prosthesis*" (p. 428, emphasis added).

We incorporate their notion of drugs as "structural prosthesis" in our concept of ATMs. As such, these ATMs serve as "structural prosthesis" or gimmicks, which only mimic the functioning of authentic (transitional) selfobjects.

We build on Wieder and Kaplan's concept of "pharmacogenic effect" and "prosthesis" in constructing our notion of an ATM-based state of dissociative anesthesia, or addictive metamorphosis. In a manner similar to Wieder and Kaplan, we maintain that an addict employs things and activities as ATMs because they enable an addict to entertain megalomaniacal fantasies of magical control. These psychoactive agents affect sensitive areas of the brain. On the level of unconscious experience, the neurological and biochemical activity of the brain of an addict is experienced mentally by an addict in the form of highly pleasurable fantasies of narcissistic bliss.

We discard the antiquated libido theory of neo-classical psychoanalysis. Therefore, we eschew an understanding of the "pharmacogenic effect" in terms of "cathectic shifts" in psychic energy or libido. Rather, we understand the pharmacogenic effect on the basis of dissociated reliving of fantasized self-states and an anesthetized re-experiencing of moods of narcissistic bliss, both of which originate in childhood. However, we completely concur with Wieder and Kaplan regarding the "physiological concomitant" as well as biochemical and behavioral correlates of the pharmacogenic effect. Such correlates are equivalent, in our model, to dissociative anesthesia or phantasmagorical transmogrification.

We follow Wieder and Kaplan's work on the pharmacogenic effect in viewing addictive metamorphosis as entailing an artificial process by which an addict is able to generate blissful states of narcissistic fantasy and mood. However, again diverging from the libido theory of neo-classical psychoanalysis, we envision these affective and sensorial changes in terms of the self-induced alteration on the part of an addict of the subjective experience of one's physical self or being. (See Lichtenberg, 1978, for an early, self-psychological discussion of the "body self" and its relation to the mental self.) The ability of an addict to create subjective changes in physicality corresponds to a parallel capacity to affect unconscious modifications in the mental self as expressed in the addictive state of mind.

Early in their work, Wieder and Kaplan mention that they "view ... states of intoxication as, *chemically-induced regressed ego states*"

(p. 403, emphasis added). They connect these regressive ego states to "specific developmental phases of early childhood" (p. 420). They rely on the developmental theory of Margaret Mahler (see, for example, Mahler et al., 1975).

Employing a Mahlerian perspective, they make specific comparisons between an "LSD state ... with the autistic phase in the sense that LSD produces a toxic psychosis the phenomenology of which resembles 'cracking the autistic shell'" (p. 429). Moreover, they observe that the "dreamy lethargy, the blissful satiation, and the fantasies of omnipotence, experienced while 'on the nod' with opiates, have similarities with narcissistic regressive phenomenon of the symbiotic state" (pp. 428–29). In addition, they contend that the "effects of amphetamines are reminiscent of the 'practicing period' of the separation-individuation phase" (p. 429).

Wieder and Kaplan explain that in all cases the "drug choices were governed by internally consistent psychodynamic pharmacogenic reason" (p. 416). Wieder and Kaplan make a comparison between states based on the use of different drugs and states arising in particular phases of development. Their comparison is important to one of our central contentions.

It lends support to our claim that dissociative anesthesia, that is, the addictive state of mind, involves the dissociated reliving of fantasies and an anesthetized re-experiencing of moods from various periods in early development. However, unlike Wieder and Kaplan, we argue that a person who experiences an addictive reliving of fantasies and re-experiencing of moods suffers from an arrest in the developmental unfolding of healthy narcissism. In this sense, therefore, we do not envision such an individual as a fixation at particular psychosexual stages of early development.

We incorporate Wieder and Kaplan's ideas on the particularities of developmental failures in early life and the "drug of choice" hypothesis into our understanding of the psychoactive specificity of ATMs. For example, we deem some addicts as more likely to be drawn to abusing CNS depressants in an effort to combat disintegration and hypomanic anxiety. These ATMs provide idealized selfobject-like (psychoactive) functions in the form of tranquilization, sedation, pacification, and containment.

An addict depends on these agents because of an underlying developmental failure in the capacity for idealizing parental figures as omnipotent (and omniscient). In such a case, there is a serious disturbance in the sector of an addict's self-experience as it is organized unconsciously on the basis of idealization of omnipotent figures. Consequently, certain persons are prone, later in life, to abuse antianxiety agents, which gradually plunge them into an addictive quagmire.

Or, to take another example, we believe that other addicts are more likely to be attracted to the abuse of central nervous system (CNS) stimulants in an attempt to offset an empty and depleted depression. These ATMs provide mirroring selfobject-like (psychoactive) functions in the form of stimulation, exhilaration, and excitement. An addict relies on these entities because of a developmental failure in the capacity to experience grand exhibitionism before a mirroring (that is, admiring and awestruck) audience. In these instances, there is a severe disturbance in the sector of an addict's self-experience as it is organized unconsciously in terms of grandiose exhibitionism. Hence, some of these persons will, later in life, abuse antidepressant agents, which eventually trap them in a form of addictive quicksand.

Finally, we do not concur with Wieder and Kaplan regarding their contention that the addictive state of mind is completely regressive and pathological; instead, we construe it as, in part, a faulty attempt at self-restoration. In other words, from our self-psychological perspective an addict is not so much regressing unconsciously to early stages of psychosexual development, but rather remains developmentally arrested at states of archaic narcissism. An addict fails to develop beyond these atavistic and fantasy-based self-states. Similarly, an addict lacks the psychic structure and functioning that results from the actualization in real life of some version of these archaic fantasies. Thus, an addict is forced, later in life, to substitute faulty and pathological means by which to attempt to achieve what would otherwise be healthy forms of regulating self-esteem and modulating mood.

Harvey Milkman

The work of Harvey Milkman, who began writing about addiction with Frosch in the 1970s and continued in the 1980s with Sunderwirth, is another major influence on our thinking. Milkman is cited in *The New York Times* by Daniel Goleman (1992) as one of those researchers "stretching the boundaries of addiction." His thinking is especially significant to our position on the centrality of fantasy to a psychoanalytic understanding of the phenomenon of addiction.

In a 1973 article, written with Frosch on heroin and amphetamine abusers, Milkman notes that the "high level of artistic and political aspirations witnessed in our subjects appear to be *later developmental derivations of ... infantile fantasies of omnipotence* [sic] (p. 248, emphasis added). Here, in this early reference, Milkman reveals his keen appreciation of the importance of fantasy and, more specifically, archaic narcissistic fantasy, to an understanding of addiction.

However, Milkman does not fully develop his thoughts on the important extent to which addiction is a fantasy-based phenomenon until the publication in 1987 of *Craving for Ecstasy: The Consciousness and Chemistry of Escape* (written with Sunderwirth). Milkman argues that addictions may be thought of as involving "three pleasure planes" (p. 45), which he describes as those of "relaxation, excitement, and fantasy: *these are the underpinnings of human compulsion*" (p. xiv, emphasis added).

In a similar vein, he indicates that persons "repeatedly pursue these avenues of experience as *antidotes for psychic pain*" (p. 18, emphasis added). Moreover, according to Milkman, these "preferred styles of coping—*satiation, arousal, and fantasy*—seem to have their origins in the first years of life" (p. 18, emphasis added). Milkman continues:

Childhood experiences combined with genetic predisposition are the foundations of adult compulsion. The drug group of choice—depressants, stimulants, and hallucinogens—is the one that best fits the individual's characteristic way of coping with stress or feelings of unworthiness. (p. 18)

He emphasizes: *"People do not become addicted to drugs or mood altering activities as such, but rather to the satiation, arousal, or fantasy experience that can be achieved through them"* (p. 18, emphasis added).

In essence, we collapse Milkman's "three distinct types of well-being," "antidotes to psychic pain," or "preferred styles of coping" into one—namely, fantasy. We construe, therefore, the addictive fantasy as providing an experience of narcissistic bliss in the form of antianxiety, relaxation or satiation as well as antidepressant excitement or arousal. Based on the self-psychological concept of twinship, we also include a third type of psychoactive and addictive fantasy, which relieves shame and diminishes painful self-consciousness. Such a twinship fantasy produces an experience of unself-consciousness. Such a subjective sense is based on an illusion of being one with others, whom an addict imagines as doubles or alter egos. We refer to this as the humanizing effect of the twinship fantasy.

We also build on Milkman's implicit notion of "antidotes to psychic pain"—antidotes that may be of a healthy or unhealthy variety. We refer to the healthy variety as a transitional selfobject and to the unhealthy kind as an ersatz selfobject, or an ATM. We differentiate between things and activities as healthy transitional selfobjects versus unhealthy ATMs on the basis of the following distinction: the former have an inherent or acquired capacity to undergo transformation, whereas the latter tend toward deformation.

In addition, Milkman is quite clear that persons become addicted to an experience; they are not addicted to a thing or activity. This crucial distinction is the basis for our contention that an addict becomes psychopathologically dependent on the unconscious replaying of a particular fantasy tape, with a specific psychoactive effect(s). An addict depends only to a secondary degree on a particular thing or activity, which triggers a mind and mood altering subjective experience. In other words, fantasy (and mood) is primary to the addictive state of mind, whereas the things and activities, or agents, are secondary.

In this regard, Milkman is explicit and emphatic about the centrality of dependence on fantasy to understanding the phenomenon of addiction. For example, he writes about the "addiction to fantasy" on numerous occasions (see, for example, pp. 147, 150, 154, 155) as well as about "fantasy addicts" (p. 155). In this connection, we borrow from Milkman in referring to addicts as fantasy junkies. Along these same lines, Milkman refers to an addict as a "compulsive fantasticator" (p. 124), and similarly describes addiction as a type of "compulsive fantastication" (p. 141). Milkman goes so far as to refer to a "biochemical addiction to fantasy" (p. 154).

We derive our notion of the addictive thing or activity (that is, the ATM), in part, from the work of Milkman. For instance, he refers to using various entities and agents as a form of "patching the self from without" (p. 120). As an example of such "patching," he points out that "TV addicts are tranquilizing themselves with visual Valium" (p. xiv). The concept of abusing TV watching as a form of "visual Valium" parallels one of our major contentions. We contend that a wide variety of things or activities (ATMs) may be abused for the purpose of inducing addictive states of mind characterized by a specific psychoactive effect, for example, antianxiety tranquilization or antidepressant stimulation.

Milkman also makes a very important distinction between unhealthy fantasy, such as those involved in addiction, and healthy or "creative" fantasy, of which there are two varieties. First, the receptive fantasy, according to Milkman, involves the "concentration on thoughts or pictures that have been produced by others, for example, watching television, reading a novel, or visiting a black-light poster display" (p. 122).

Second, Milkman describes an active fantasy that entails the "production of images and thoughts that emerge spontaneously from one's own psyche" (p. 122). We combine Milkman's concepts of the receptive and active fantasy in our notion of the intersubjective fantasy, especially as regards its formation and expression in the contexts of both development and psychotherapy.

Milkman specifies that the active fantasy "may be highly representational and reality oriented" (p. 122). According to Milkman, a person who entertains such a fantasy may visualize "how to approach his or her employer, or they may be highly abstract and unrealistic, such as imagining the creation or destruction of the universe" (p. 122). In this connection, he claims that "fantasy images exist on a continuum ranging from realistic to abstract" (p. 122). Milkman asserts:

> Like food, fantasy has great potential for abuse because it is vital to survival. Adaptive in providing a solution or reprieve from conflict or stress, fantasy may also destroy by compromising one's ability to perceive and react effectively to objective reality. This outcome is most likely when, *as with cocaine, imagination is colored by intoxication.* Culturally influenced fantasy without drugs may be used as an adaptive coping mechanism. In excess, however, the process of mental excursion may provide endogenous intoxication and lead to drastic consequences for the individual. (pp. 138–39, emphasis added)

In addition, Milkman describes a third type of fantasy he calls "interactive." Such a fantasy, he maintains, arises in the context of the interaction between the individual and the inanimate or nonhuman environment. As an example of this type of "interactive fantasy" (Milkman & Sunderwirth, 1987, p. 143), he cites that which occurs as a basic feature of playing the popular game *Dungeons and Dragons*. Such games generate interactive fantasies in which the respective players take on what Milkman (and Sunderwirth) term a "fantasy identity" (p. 143).

This idea of the interactive fantasy serves as a basis for our conception of a fantasy that arises in conjunction with a person's healthy use of transitional selfobjects. We contrast this type of fantasy from those that an individual generates on the basis of the unhealthy abuse of ersatz selfobjects.

We follow Milkman in our understanding of the nature of fantasy as regards both its central role in addiction and the way in which it may range from the normal to the abnormal. There is an inherent dualism fundamental to the very nature of fantasy. Such a dualism is reflected in the way in which fantasy expresses itself in an adaptive or maladaptive fashion. It also manifests itself in a positive and pleasurable manner (that is, blissful) or in a negative and painful fashion (that is, mortifying).

In arguing for a conception of addiction as fantasy-based, Milkman also discusses the neuroanatomical and biochemical basis for what he terms "addiction to fantasy." We incorporate his discussion as part of our view of the phenomenology of addiction and, more specifically, as concerns addictive metamorphosis and psychoactive specificity.

Milkman notes in his early work with Sunderwirth that those "compelled by fantasy enjoy activation of the right hemisphere of their cerebral cortex" (p. xv). (See Ostow, 1954, 1955, for one of the first and pioneering psychoanalytic studies of the neuroanatomy of unconscious fantasy.) In referring to the neuroanatomy of fantasy activity as "right hemisphere thinking," Milkman indicates that the biochemical correlate of such thought may involve the "conversion of the brain's own indole or phenylethylamine compounds into hallucinogenic variations of these chemicals" (p. 19). He also points out that "rapid neurotransmission in the dopaminergic pathways in the neocortex is related to fantasy" (p. 152).

Milkman emphasizes, however, that the self-induced stimulation of the "neocortex in order to produce *altered states of consciousness* must somehow be rewarded by a desired feeling, or else there would be little reason for reproducing such imagery" (p. 154, emphasis added). He states, moreover, that the "center of positive and negative emotion is the limbic system which has neuronal connections that extend into the neocortex" (p. 154). As a result, he contends: "Self-imagery in the neocortex is translated into the desired emotional state through neuronal pathways to the limbic system" (p. 154).

Milkman maintains that such "self-induced activities or experiences can bring about the release of endogenous chemicals (norepinephrine, if the desirable experience is arousal; or endorphins, if the desired experience is satisfaction)" (p. 154). He claims that following the "release of these endogenous substances" an imbalance is created as part of the "accompanying change in neurotransmission, which is then countered by enzymatic changes in the brain" (p. 154). An addict, according to Milkman, "must engage in more frequent and more intense episodes of *self-stimulated fantasy* in order to achieve the desired level of *fantasy reward* (p. 154, emphasis added). He concludes, therefore, that "various fantasy addicts may be associated with arousal or satiation states, depending on the type of limbic stimulation desired" (p. 154).

Henry Krystal

The work of Krystal, which is germane to our current discussion, spans four decades (1960–1990). As such, it constitutes a body of psychoanalytic thought on the topic of addiction that is one of the most extensive and significant in the field. It is not an exaggeration to state that Krystal is one of the modern founders of psychoanalytic thinking on the phenomenology of addiction. We trace the evolution of Krystal's ideas through four decades, focusing specifically on those aspects of his thought that are particularly relevant to our thinking about addiction as a fantasy-based phenomenon.

Addiction as a Fantasy-Based Phenomenon

At different times throughout his writings, Krystal stresses the central role of fantasy (or its absence in a healthy form) as an unconscious determinant of addiction. However, it is necessary to point out that his understanding of the fantasy-based nature of addiction undergoes a major shift in emphasis. In the first phase of his thinking, he conceives of addiction as involving a complex and interactive set of fantasies, which are all varieties of what he (Krystal, 1978) refers to as an "addictive fantasy" (p. 219). In the second phase of his thought, he shifts to a view of addiction as entailing an alexithymic arrest in the developmental capacity for fantasy-making, the latter of which he thinks of as both creative and adaptive in nature. This change in emphasis notwithstanding, Krystal continues to stress the importance of fantasy and arrests in the capacity for fantasizing as critical to understanding the phenomenon of addiction.

Krystal first discusses the important role of fantasy in addiction in an early work with Raskin entitled *Drug Dependence: Aspects of Ego Functions*. He (Krystal & Raskin, 1970) observes that "alcohol and drug dependent persons ... seem to be unable to give up or change libidinal positions, but tend to try *to preserve the relations in phantasy through repression*" (p. 41, emphasis added). Krystal, like Simmel, claims that what he subsequently calls the "addictive fantasy" is based on a "wish ... to obtain a state of Nirvana through fusion with the drug as an object substitute" (p. 48). Krystal believes that an addict uses alcohol or drugs as an unconscious means of fantasizing a state of fusion between "his self-representation and his benign object representation" (p. 68). According to Krystal, a drug or alcohol is endowed in the unconscious mind of an addict with all the positive and caretaking qualities of the mother.

Moreover, Krystal contends that an addict, by symbolically "taking in" the good mother in the form of alcohol or drugs, has a fantasy experience of an "introjection of the transubstantiation of the object" (p. 69). Krystal argues that a revealing analogy may be drawn between the Christian sacrament and the unconscious fantasy of an addict. In the Eucharist the "body and blood of Christ materialize in the sacrament" (p. 48).

In a similar fashion, Krystal maintains that an addict by ingesting alcohol and drugs imagines the good mother as having been absorbed by magic into the very core of the self. In the process, an addict experiences an enhanced sense of power, well-being, and security. In this regard, Krystal asserts that an addict uses the "drug as a *transubstantiation*, a constantly repetitive validation of the existence of the object, and the possibility of the fulfillment of [the] *fantasy of introjection*" (p. 48, emphasis added). In terms similar to our own, Krystal envisions an addict as a modern-day alchemist who, using a form of black magic, turns alcohol or drugs into the good mother. In this capacity as an alchemist, an addict is also a megalomaniac.

However, Krystal insists that there is a tragic aspect to the entire scenario of the addictive fantasy. Typically, the ego is impoverished in the case of addiction and, as a result, an addict "indulges in delusional attempts toward repair and self-sustenance by taking in of 'concrete' object-substitutes which are experienced as the transubstantiation of the object" (p. 71). Krystal adds that the "object-substitute, dependent producing drug, and object relations become endowed with ambivalent transferences and must fail just as the original object (mother) was experienced as failing during the crucial stages" (p. 71) of the early childhood of an addict.

Thus, the mother, or her "object-representation's present transference 'materialization'" (p. 66) as fantasized unconsciously by the addict in the form of alcohol or drugs, cannot provide the desired state of Nirvanic bliss or "infantile satiation-fusion" (p. 58). As a result, an addict, Krystal indicates, is "unable to achieve a *fantasy fusion between his self-representation and his benign object representation* (p. 68, emphasis added), and is "thus caught in a double bind" (p. 69).

According to Krystal, this "double bind" entails a constant disappointment with the object-representation "because it fails to fulfill the yearnings for fusion and Nirvana" (p. 69). Yet, "at the same time," Krystal observes, an addict "must cling to the object and cannot tolerate separation" (p. 69). Krystal maintains, therefore, that there is "the need for the repetition" of the fantasy experience of the "introjection of the transubstantiation of the object" (p. 69).

Krystal characterizes this entire process of addiction as involving the "primitization" (p. 104) of the fantasies "that underlie the foundations of the personality." (p. 104). Thus, Krystal contends that addiction entails a psychopathological process whereby fantasy is permanently reduced to its most primitive form. As a result, it is less useful as a vehicle for adaptation; moreover, in the context of addiction it becomes more and more primitive and maladaptive.

In two later 1970s contributions, Krystal pursues his ideas on the relation between fantasy and addiction. The first, published as part of a National Institute of Drug Abuse (NIDA) monograph (with a preface by Kohut), is entitled "Self- and Object-Representation in Alcoholism and Other Drug Dependence: Implications for Therapy" (1977). In this piece, Krystal further expounds on his view of the complex nature of the unconscious dynamics involved in the addictive fantasy.

Krystal (1977) argues in casting his ideas on this topic in a developmental rather than clinical framework that "in order to survive, some drug-dependent individuals had to repress their rage and destructive wishes toward their natural love object" (p. 96). He goes on: "This manifests itself in a rigid 'walling off' of the maternal love object representation, especially with an idealization of it, and attribution of most of life-supports and nurturing functions to it" (p. 96). Krystal concludes: "By doing this, the patient manages (in his fantasy) to protect the core object from his fantasized destructive process and assume that someone *out there* loved him and would take care of him" (p. 96).

Later, Krystal (1978a) relates that "in our work as adult analysts, it is clear that *we are sharing with the patient a reconstruction of his original fantasies regarding his mother and her messages to him*" (p. 228, emphasis added). In the same essay, he notes that these psychoanalytic reconstructions are possible because such fantasies "make their appearance in the transference in the analysis of alcoholics and other drug dependent individuals" (p. 231).

In these passages, Krystal alludes to a notion of fantasy that is similar to our concept of the dialectical bipolarity of unconscious fantasy. Krystal pursues the idea that the addictive fantasy is based on the dialectical interaction between two polar opposite illusions: on one side is the illusion of the destruction of the "maternal love object representation," whereas on the other side is the illusion of the hoped or wished for protection of this psychic version of the caring mother.

However, unlike our self-psychological point of view, Krystal envisions the early origins of the "addictive fantasy" as follows: it lies developmentally in a psychopathologically ambivalent object relationship between the infant and mother. Such an internal object relationship involves an excess of destructive aggression necessitating a dissociative split between object-representation and self-representation.

Krystal elaborates on this line of thinking in the second of his 1970s contributions, entitled "Self-representation and the Capacity for Self-Care" (1978a). In this essay, Krystal refers to Glover's early work on alcohol addiction. In this regard, Krystal argues that an alcoholic inevitably finds it almost impossible to give up drinking because alcohol has become a magical and powerful elixir that "*contains the symbolic expression of the fantasy of taking in the love object*" (p. 214, emphasis added).

Krystal implies that such "internalization-of-maternal-functions ... is one of *the most important fantasies of mankind* and as such represents important analytic material" (p. 239, emphasis added). In essence, according to Krystal, the addictive fantasy is about the "internalization-of-material-functions." However, Krystal stresses that the fantasy of having taken in a maternal capacity for caring amounts to nothing more than an illusory panacea. (See Krystal, 1978a, for a critique of Kohut's concept of transmuting internalization, especially as regards its applicability to explaining addiction. Krystal criticizes Kohut for raising the notion of transmuting internalization to the level of a theoretical postulate. According to Krystal, this Kohutian notion is not an actual psychological process, but is, on the contrary, a mere "introjection fantasy" [p. 233].)

Yet even as an illusion, the addictive fantasy has a powerful effect on subjective experience. Krystal (1978a) explains that the forceful psychological action of the "addictive fantasy" is based, in part, on the "placebo effect" (p. 215). Krystal insists that an addict under the influence of the addictive fantasy is "able to exercise his hitherto inhibited function, but he denies his part in it, and attributes the activity to the pill" (p. 215).

According to Krystal, the "ingestion of the pill represents a ritual, or symbolic act, through which one gains access to a function which otherwise remains blocked" (p. 215). Krystal (1978a, p. 219) indicates that the addictive fantasy of taking in the "maternal love object" or the "benign introject" enables an addict to subjectively experience the mother as providing care and making him or her feel good. Of course, this is all an illusion; and thus, once the imaginary experience that stems from the addictive fantasy wanes, an addict is still lacking in a capacity for genuine and healthy self-care. An addict is, therefore, compelled to repeat the entire scenario of the addictive fantasy in order to once more undergo an imaginary experience of being cared for by the good mother.

Krystal considers "what prevents the patient from 'internalizing' these functions, and indeed, *whether the model of taking in such functions from without is a reflection of the patient's fantasy* or whether, in fact, functions are 'taken over' from parental and later transference objects" (p. 216, emphasis added). In his consideration of this issue, Krystal responds that there exists a "ubiquitous" fantasy that involves a "universal blocking of our autonomously controlled parts of the body" (p. 227). These autonomous functions "have been blocked by a fantasy" (p. 226). Krystal emphasizes· "That is why we may conclude that substance dependent ... patients ... experience their self-caring functions as reserved for the maternal object representation and psychically 'walled-off'—inaccessible to them" (p. 226).

Earlier in this same article, Krystal contends that this "normal inhibition of the exercise of volition over autonomic or affective aspects of ourselves is like any conversion paralysis, *the symbolic representation of a fantasy*" (p. 221, emphasis added). According to Krystal, this "*fantasy, however, pertains not to our genital or phallic conflicts, but to the vital functions*" (pp. 221–22, emphasis added).

In this regard, Krystal suggests that the "longing to regain alienated parts of oneself is the real meaning behind *fantasies of fusion with the good mother* so clearly discernible in drug-dependent individuals" (p. 231, emphasis added). Krystal adds that "when the substance-dependent patient tries to regain his alienated functions by swallowing the symbol of the object-representation to whom he attributed these powers, he is confronted with his *infantile fantasies* that caused him the problems originally" (p. 233, emphasis added). Krystal believes that such an "'introjection fantasy' is a form of partial union of the self-representation and object-representation, at which most people arrive at the end of mourning" (p. 233, emphasis added).

Earlier, Krystal notes: "It is because the needed functions are experienced as part of the object-representation that in the ritual of reclaiming them by the *fantasy* of devouring or 'introjecting' the object is symbolically acted out" (p. 222). However, Krystal adds: "The frightening and 'sickening' aspects of introjected objects suggest the problem of ambivalence toward the object-representation is what prevents them from fulfilling the *cannibalistically tinged fantasies*" (p. 238, emphasis added).

Krystal distinguishes his view of "unconscious fantasy" from that of classical psychoanalysis. The latter emphasizes fantasy as an unconscious means of giving symbolic expression to psychosexual and aggressive drives. In this sense, therefore, it would appear that Krystal is hinting at an unconscious domain of psychic life the nature of which is more basic and fundamental than that of psychosexuality and aggression. We refer to this as the realm of archaic narcissistic fantasy. In fact, later in this same essay Krystal (1978a) terms this the "fantasy of self-care" (p. 240).

In describing the nature of this fantasy, Krystal states that "we can observe that the symbolic representation of the child's need goes hand in hand with his ability to experience his narcissistic omnipotence in terms of fulfillment of his wishes" (p. 240). He continues by pointing out the "availability of a *good selfobject* not only permits the grandiosity of the child to unfold appropriately but also permits the feeling that it is proper for him to 'take care of himself'" (p. 240, emphasis added). "In other words," Krystal insists that "*the infantile omnipotence permits the fantasy of self-care when the actual capacity for it is nil*" (p. 240, emphasis added).

Krystal makes an argument that is, in our opinion, implicitly self psychological in nature, and hence especially pertinent to our position. He contends that a child's archaic grandiosity and infantile omnipotence unfold naturally and "appropriately" in the presence of the "good selfobject." Such unfolding is manifested in the functioning of the "fantasy of self-care."

The presence and functioning of this fantasy allow a child to experience himself or herself subjectively as providing self-care, whereas it is clear from an objective perspective that a child cannot, at this time, provide much in the way of actual self-care. However, a child relinquishes this fantasy-based experience of self-care in the process of gradually developing the actual means and wherewithal to care for oneself.

Krystal asserts that the development of the actual capacity for self-care is a means of replacing the fantasy of self-care. This development takes place, Krystal maintains, through the mental construction of the maternal object-representation. However, Krystal believes that in the course of this developmental process "there is a fatal tendency to confuse the suppliers with the experience of gratification" (p. 241). Moreover, he claims: "To lose sight and control of one's authorship of all of his experience of gratifying, affective and life-preserving functions, and to attribute these to the object-representation, sets the stage for future prescription of their use" (p. 241). In a similar vein, he insists that there is an "*infantile fantasy that one's vital functions were part of the object-representation* and that the taking over of these would imply an introjection of the maternal object representation which was prohibited" (p. 228, emphasis added).

We contend that Krystal believes there are two critical failures or arrests in development in the case of addiction. Moreover, both of these breakdowns involve, and are based on, two types of developmental arrest in "infantile fantasy." Later in life, these arrests in development lead to the creation of the addictive fantasy.

The first arrest in development entails the failure to adequately create and utilize the "fantasy of self care." Transforming this fantasy enables an individual to develop the capacity for actual self-care. The second developmental arrest revolves around an attempt at compensating for the absence of the fantasy of self-care. In such an instance, a person creates an alternative fantasy of being cared for by the mother.

Krystal asserts that a mother normally cares for her offspring first as an infant and then as a child. However, according to Krystal, it is a child's subjective experience of being cared for rather than the actual fact of being cared for that is critical in developing the capacity to care for the self. The addictive fantasy of taking in the "benign introject" effectively bypasses the ubiquitous fantasy, which otherwise walls off caring functions.

In summary, it can be said that Krystal conceives of addiction as follows: it involves the fantasy of taking in the mother in order to be able to temporarily entertain the illusion of actually being cared for by her. As Krystal observes: "When it is necessary to 'baby' one's self, *the unconscious fantasy* may become manifest that the 'benign introject' is doing it, or lending the permission to do it" (p. 241, emphasis added). Thus, Krystal concludes that addiction is based on a circular kind of thinking, which is a feature of unconscious fantasizing. This unconscious system of fantasy thought entails a form of denial. There is a denial of the reality that early maternal caretaking simply facilitates the development rather than the creation *de novo* of the inborn capacity for self-care. Such a capacity is rooted in maturational processes of both a biological and psychological nature.

The Dynamic Interaction of Fantasy and Mood

As early as in his 1966 piece entitled "Withdrawal from Drugs," Krystal explores an essential feature of the phenomenology of addiction. We describe this aspect as the dialectical and bipolar nature of the dynamic interaction of fantasy and mood. In this early contribution, Krystal (1966) indicates that a drug addict is plagued with unconscious conflicts involving "cannibalistic" fantasies and "primitive aggression," all of which are "experienced as terribly dangerous" (p. 301). Krystal states: "*These fantasies* and conflicts were there all through the period of addiction. The resulting feelings break through in the drug-escape reaction, after having been partially blocked by the drug" (p. 301, emphasis added).

These statements are indicative of Krystal's belief, which he had long held, that a dialectical dynamic underlies addiction. He notes that dreaded fantasies and affects are offset by the drug experience. He implies that some positive and countervailing psychic constellation temporarily overtakes conscious awareness, and hence overrides the negatively-toned psychic constellation.

Krystal (1966) divides fantasy and mood into "three aspects or components" (p. 301). According to Krystal, these three aspects consist of the "physiological or expressive aspect of affects;" the "idea of it is another," for instance, "'I am in danger' in anxiety, and 'all is lost and hopeless' in depression" and finally, the "intrapsychic conflict and underlying ideational contents which have developed into the above ideas" (p. 301).

In this context, Krystal refers to the meaning of medication as prescribed for an addicted patient by a psychiatrist. Krystal points out that "where tranquilizers are used on a supportive basis, without any interpretations attempted, *the physician counters the patient's fantasy of abandonment by offering new hope*, a new form of this 'milk of human kindness'—in the form of a new medication" (p. 302, emphasis added). In this regard, Krystal describes what amounts to a dynamic interaction between fantasy and mood in determining the unconscious meaning of (prescribed) drugs.

According to Krystal, a patient may experience receiving medication unconsciously in the form of a hopeful fantasy of being cared for and attached. A positively-toned fantasy counteracts, therefore, the polar opposite and dreaded fantasy of "abandonment." Such a dialectical bipolarity is relevant for understanding the unconscious dynamics and meaning of prescribed medications as well as illicit drugs.

In the 1970 publication *Drug Dependence*, (co-authored with Raskin), Krystal observes: "A drug, food, or even idea, in *the phantasies of borrowing, acquiring, or 'introjecting,' can be applied to relieve or counteract unpleasant states or affects*" (p. 47, emphasis added). In this brief observation, Krystal hints again at the notion of the dialectical bipolarity of fantasy and mood as essential to the unconscious dynamics underlying disorders such as addiction. In addition, the description by Krystal of "phantasies of borrowing, acquiring, or 'introjecting,'" is an allusion, we believe, to the megalomaniacal quality of what we would term *utilitarian fantasies*.

An addict activates a particular atavistic self-state by the use of particular psychoactive things and activities. Such an archaic self-state is organized unconsciously in accordance with narcissistic fantasies and accompanying moods of narcissistic bliss. An addict is under the influence of megalomaniacal fantasies about the powers of certain psychoactive things and activities that empower an addict with magical control of psychic reality. In fact, we contend that the megalomaniacal aspect of these utilitarian fantasies is the crucial and defining characteristic of what Krystal terms the addictive fantasy.

In this book, Krystal also writes about the nature of the affective dimension of the dialectical bipolarity that underlies the addictive fantasy. He states: "However, in many drug dependent persons we find an affect, combining depression and anxiety, a disturbance in which the de-differentiation of anxiety and depression takes place or a state in which differentiation was never successfully accomplished" (p. 22). He adds that the "affect seemed to approximate the infantile 'total' and somatic distress pattern rather than a clear-cut adult affect pattern" (p. 22).

According to Krystal, a major repression or arrest in the natural unfolding of affect occurs in the case of addiction. As a result, an addict is not capable of subtle, varied, and mature emotional responses; rather an addict can muster only a limited range of feelings as characterized by a polarity of affects. Thus, the emotional repertoire of an addict is extremely narrow; it consists of polar opposite and crude feelings on either end of an emotional spectrum.

For example, an addict vacillates, in our language, between emotional states characterized by narcissistic mortification and narcissistic bliss. For an addict, narcissistic affect states, which are more subtle, refined, and developmentally advanced, are either totally absent or poorly formed.

"The normal development of affects" proceeds, according to Krystal (1978a), "in the direction of their desomatization and differentiation" as well as the "progressive development of differentiated affective responses, modulated in their intensity, with increasing vocalization, verbalization, and symbolization" (p. 242). Occurring in tandem with the development of affects is a similar process regarding cognition. Krystal describes this as involving the "development of reflective self-awareness, and the use of symbols and *fantasy for progressive intrapsychic structure formation*" (p. 242, emphasis added).

In contrast, a drug addict, for instance, fails to undergo a natural process involving the normal unfolding of fantasy and affect. Instead, this process has gone awry for an addict. Krystal (1978a) contends: "Alcoholics and drug addicts are among those people who have a great inhibition in carrying out a multitude of 'mothering' or self-comforting functions" (p. 223).

Krystal continues: "In studying their difficulties, we gain a chance to observe that we are dealing with an intrapsychic block which prevents them from the consciously exercised use of these functions" (p. 223). As a result, Krystal believes, "such a person loses his capacity to take care of himself, to attend to his needs, to 'baby' or nurse himself when tired, ill, or hurt narcissistically" (p. 224). In essence, Krystal maintains that the "affect tolerance" of an addict is "impaired because they do not feel free to exercise the kind of comforting, gratifying care that a mother gives to a distressed child" (p. 224).

One of Krystal's major findings concerns "an inhibition in the substance-dependent patient's ability to take care of themselves physically and emotionally, in the literal sense of the word" (p. 224). Krystal observes that in "regard to the inhibition in self-caring functions, we have to deal with the *fantasies that underlie the distortions in self and object representations*" (p. 243, emphasis added). In an earlier passage, Krystal describes these fantasy-based "distortions" as characterized by "barriers within one's self-representation, with which the most basic life-maintaining functions and affective functions are experienced as outside the self-representation, and as part of the object representation" (p. 222).

As noted, Krystal believes that this "barrier" consists of a fantasy that effectively blocks off the maternal caring functions from free and uninhibited use. In this regard, Krystal asserts that "substance-dependent ... patients ... experience their self-caring functions as reserved for the maternal object representations, and psychologically 'walled off—inaccessible to them" (p. 226).

At the end of this 1978 article entitled "Self Representation and the Capacity for Self Care," Krystal suggests that "alexithymia" is a form of "disturbance in affectivity ... and symbolization" (p. 243), which is relevant to understanding the failure of fantasy and affect to unfold naturally in a developmental process. He characterizes alexithymia in terms of an "operational thinking." According to Krystal, such a form of thinking manifests itself in a serious and psychopathological "impoverishment of imagination, and a blocking of drive oriented cognition" (p. 243).

With the introduction of the concept of alexithymia as crucial to understanding addiction, Krystal initiates the second phase of his thinking on fantasy and addiction. He shifts his focus from the presence of the addictive fantasy to the absence of creative fantasy. In a 1979 article entitled "Alexithymia and Psychotherapy," Krystal emphasizes that the "operative thinking" characteristic of alexithymia involves "a marked impairment in [the] capacity for creativity, *especially in regard to drive gratification fantasy*" (p. 19, emphasis added).

As a type of alexithymic, an addict is unable, Krystal maintains, to develop a rich and varied fantasy life. Instead, an addict becomes a captive of primitive fantasies of catastrophic doom. Krystal describes these fantasies as involving the "danger of helplessness" and the "dread[ed] expectation of the return of ... psychic trauma" (p. 27). Such a fantasy, Krystal argues, results in a "disturbance of affect handling" as expressed in the belief that "emotions 'belong to,' or emanate from the object, and that the subject is not permitted to *control* them" (p. 27).

Addiction involves as a form of alexithymia, a serious disturbance in the dialectical interaction of fantasy and affect. As such, it is based on both a cognitive and affective disorder. The cognitive disorder is based on thinking and thought processes that are "operative" in that they are "deprived of drive implementation, and *gratification-directed fantasy* and [are] dominated by banal chronologically oriented 'facts'" (p. 29, emphasis added).

Such an "operational" mode of thinking leads to a corresponding disturbance in affect and sensation in which "emotions are undifferentiated, mostly somatic and poorly verbalized" (p. 29). Krystal (1979) adds: "Affects are not utilized as signals to oneself, and patients cannot tell how they feel. The 'expressive,' i.e., physiological, aspects of emotions manifest themselves as troublesome sensations or psychosomatic illnesses" (p. 29).

Krystal elaborates further on the alexithymic nature of addiction. He (Krystal, 1983) points out: "There is a *blocking of the wish-fulfillment fantasy making*, a function necessary to the formation of the neurotic defenses" (p. 599, emphasis added). In addition, he writes that this "general diminution of the capacity for wish fulfillment fantasies" (p. 610) occurs "both on a level of the conscious daydream and well as unconscious fantasy" (p. 610).

Subsequently, Krystal (1988) contends that the normal capacity by which a person engages in "wish-fulfillment fantasy making" depends on the ability of a child to "form the transition from the sensory motor functioning to an *illusion of self-gratification* and *through it to a world of fantasy*" (p. 321, emphasis added). According to Krystal, in order for this "transition" to occur "there has to be an attachment to the mother of such power and confidence that the infant can gradually extend the attachment from the nipple to her face, to her sounds, and to other sensory signals to words" (p. 321).

As an alexithymic, an addict fails, Krystal contends, to successfully make this vital transition from the "sensorimotor" to the "world of fantasy." Instead, an addict develops a faulty capacity for "wish fulfillment fantasy making." As a result, Krystal (1982b) maintains, an addict is "missing symbolic structures" (p. 367) necessary for healthy self-repre-sentation. Or, as Krystal (1982b) indicates, there is in the case of alexithymia a "blocking inhibition of wish-fulfillment fantasies pertaining to one's self" (p. 367). Such a blocking is an example of "operative thinking" in the sphere of the self-representation.

Such "operative thinking" also manifests itself in the sphere of the object-representation. In this instance, Krystal (1982b) describes it in terms of a "preoccupation with things at the expense of object relations" (p. 610). Krystal notes that the "combination of *impairment in the capacity for fantasy* and abstract thinking and the lack of affective clues *deprives the patient of the ability to empathize and to be emotionally involved with their significant objects*" (p. 610, emphasis added). Further, he (Krystal, 1982b) indicates that the "*absence of the 'human' quality* contributes to making these patients thought '*operative*' or *thing oriented*" (p. 359, emphasis added).

There is, therefore, an important parallel between Krystal's descrip-tion of operative thinking and some of our ideas. The parallel is as follows: Krystal views operative thinking as characteristic of alexithymia and typical of addiction; in contrast, we describe a pre-addictive stunting, which occurs at the developmental stage of transitional selfobject usage. From our perspective, such developmental stunting, which is typical of addiction, results, later in life, in a dependence on nonhuman things and activities, or ATMs. Thus, there is a commonality between Krystal's conceptualization of addiction and our own; we both envision an addict as "thing oriented."

Krystal relies on Winnicott's notion of the transitional object and describes this phenomenon in terms that are consistent with the psy-choanalytic perspective of object relations. He (Krystal, 1988) states that the "transitional object in infancy is a *kind of auxiliary device by which the illusion of omnipotence is transformed into an acceptable view of the object*—because it provides the illusion of magical control over the object" (p. 325, emphasis added).

According to Krystal (1988): "From the beginning, transitional objects are part of the self-soothing, that is to say, affect modification—

learning to keep one's affects in the range of comfort" (pp. 488). Krystal observed that "transitional objects develop from into-the-mouth-mother substitutes that directly regulate one's physiologic processes, to increasingly more abstract transitional objects and activities" (p. 488).

"Eventually," Krystal (1988) contends, "the benign mental representation becomes so secure that the direct use of a security blanket can be given up" (p. 335). As a result, Krystal posits: "Dreams, *fantasies*, and play can be used to *activate the image of the mother so that self-caring can be carried out*" (p. 335, emphasis added). Krystal (1988) states that the "transitional process becomes the means and facilitator of symbolic representation and *wish-fulfillment fantasy*" (p. 485, emphasis added).

From our perspective, we translate Krystal's thinking into our terminology as follows. Transitional selfobject usage is critical for the development of the mental ability that is necessary in order to play in fantasy or to engage in fanciful play. The capacity for what Kohut (1977b, p. 159) calls a "fantasy game" is essential to psychological development. Krystal (1988) emphasizes that "some people develop enormous blocks about accessing these inner resources and inner structures—*the products of their own imagination* (p. 335, emphasis added). According to Krystal, these same "people can access these inner resources, their own functions, *only in states of modified consciousness in dissociative states ... in a trance*" (p. 335, emphasis added).

In his earlier work with Raskin, Krystal (1970) alludes to an "extreme form of transference" (p. 71) in which the "fantasies involved" manifest themselves as part of "an action undertaken by the object-representation's present transference 'materialization'" (p. 66). Later, in referring to an alcoholic's relation to alcohol, he (Krystal, 1978a) insists that the "'last drop,' however, becomes virtually impossible to give up, because *it contains the symbolic expression of the fantasy of taking in the live object*" (p. 214, emphasis added).

Krystal is of the opinion that there is a serious limitation on the part of the alcoholic in the attempt to symbolically swallow and hold onto the "love object." He points out that the "*external object* which is experienced as containing the indispensable life power that the patient wants to, but cannot, 'internalize' illustrated the basic dilemma dominating his psychic reality" (p. 214, emphasis added).

Apparently, Krystal views certain things and activities (which we call ATMs) as being infused with a phantasmagorical quality. Such an illusory characteristic is based, in part, on the psychoactivity of a certain class of things and activities. Such a psychoactive capacity enables these entities to substitute, however faultily, for a healthier means of self-sustenance and maintenance.

Krystal calls attention to the transformation of omnipotence through the use of transitional objects and the corresponding increase in the capacity for "affect modification." His position closely parallels our self-psychological analysis of a similar process. He also focuses on the derailment of this developmental process and its eventual manifestation in the psychopathological need for addictive substances to "activate the image of the mother so that self-caring can be carried out ... in states of modified consciousness, in dissociative states ... in a trance."

It is clear that Krystal's description anticipates an important aspect of our discussion. He adumbrates our description of the pathological process of dissociative anesthesia or the addictive state of mind whereby an addict (ab)uses ATMs in an addictive fashion in order to activate narcissistic fantasies and heighten moods of narcissistic bliss.

PART B: A PHENOMENOLOGICAL VIEW OF THE UNCONSCIOUS MIND OF AN ADDICT

Introduction

In exploring the phenomenological dimension of addiction, we attempt to answer the following question: What is the nature of addiction as a psychological phenomenon? Posing this question somewhat differently, we ask: Is there a common psychopathology that underlies the major types of addictions and, more specifically, alcoholism, drug abuse, eating disorders, gambling, and sexual compulsivity?

A review of our previous self-psychological writings on addiction indicates that our earlier perspective led us to an *implicit* notion that addiction is a narcissistic phenomenon. Our view is implicit because we did not explicitly state that we conceptualize addiction as a narcissistic phenomenon per se. Nonetheless, our prior conceptualization is totally consistent with our current and explicit point of view that addiction is a narcissistic (behavior) disorder *par excellence*.

Our self-psychological perspective is at variance, however, with much of the early psychoanalytic writing on addiction. Many of the first generation of psychoanalytic theorists who write about addiction follow the lead of Freud and his original adherents. In line with the Freudian position, they view addiction as just another symptomatic expression of a psychosexual disturbance.

However, there is another line of thought that we discern in the history of psychoanalytic writings on addiction. This psychoanalytic thought supports our contention that addiction is best conceptualized as a narcissistic disorder. We have already reviewed this literature (see Part A of this chapter).

Our argument that addiction is a form of narcissistic psychopathology is based on two fundamental tenets of self psychology. First, we conceive of addiction as narcissistic because it involves a serious disturbance in the relationship between the self and the selfobject milieu. This narcissistic disturbance manifests itself pathologically in the following way.

In the course of the normal development of a healthy sense of self, an individual gradually learns to use other people, things, and activities as selfobjects with which to regulate self-esteem and modulate mood. In dramatic contrast, an addiction-prone person fails to complete such normal development with any degree of success. And, as a result, such an individual does not pass through the critical stage of *transitional selfobject usage*. Instead, a future addict becomes developmentally arrested (that is, psychologically stunted) at this stage of transitional selfobject usage.

An addiction-prone person has a tendency, later in life, to abuse a variety of psychoactive entities and agents in a compulsive manner in a desperate yet futile attempt at regulating self-esteem and modulating mood (that is, controlling the nature of psychic reality). This faulty effort at regulation and modulation, which is exogenous (rather than endogenous) in nature, involves a pathological dependence on ATMs. An addict abuses these psychoactive agents as a means of mobilizing otherwise latent fantasies of narcissistic bliss.

The phantasmagorical nature of this addictive state of mind hypnotizes and mesmerizes an addict. Such a hypnotic effect engenders in an addict a sense of being insulated and protected from painful stimuli, whether experienced as originating from within or without.

Second, we maintain that addiction is narcissistic because it entails an unhealthy type of self-absorption. As part of such a psychopathological self-centeredness, an addict exists in a surreal world, or wonderland, consisting of hypnotic fantasies and mesmerizing moods. Together, such self-hypnotic fantasies and moods produce an altered state of consciousness (that is, an addictive state of mind).

We previously referred to this state as dissociative anesthesia, and now refer to it as addictive metamorphosis or phantasmagorical transmogrification. On the one hand, the unconscious mobilization by an addict of such hypnotic fantasies produces a cognitive alteration of the sense of the psychic reality of the self which, in turn, dissociates an addict from disturbing ideation. On the other hand, the mesmerizing mood that accompanies these fantasies anesthetizes an addict. Such anesthetization occurs on the basis of an emotional and sensorial alteration of a basic feeling tone, which is crucial to the sense of the psychic reality of the self.

Dissociative anesthesia, or addictive metamorphosis, is a fugue-like state, which an addict produces on a mental level on the basis of the dialectical interaction of fantasy and mood. In the unconscious mind of an addict, such a psychodynamic creates an alteration of the cognitive, affective, and sensorial dimensions of self-experience. We argue, therefore, that addiction is narcissistic because it involves a self-induced form of hypnotic trance, or an altered state of consciousness. Addiction is, therefore, narcissistic because it entails a form of artificially induced (as opposed to spontaneously occurring) dissociation from the often painful reality of day-to-day experiences of oneself (in relation to the selfobject milieu).

Addictive metamorphosis is simply one example of a psychopathological condition based on an altered state of mind. It temporarily alleviates psychic pain by allowing an addict to escape, in imagination, to a private fantasy world of magical illusion and reverie—however, at an emotional cost of enormous proportions to an addict. As a psychopathological process, phantasmagorical transmogrification entails an abuse of ATMs, which eventually becomes all-consuming.

The compulsive abuse of ATMs by an addict is characterized by a repetitive replaying of stereotypical and psychoactive fantasy tapes. Thus, as psychological tolerance for these addictive fantasies increases, an addict repeats the same fantasy experience over and over again in a frantic effort to maximize pleasure and minimize pain. These fantasies undergo a transmogrification, which is based on the addictive process of pathological repetition, whereby they gradually lose their original potency.

An apt and important comparison may be made in this regard between "videogame junkies" and an addict. A junkie of video game toys like Nintendo or Playstation—involving computer-simulated action complete with special (visual and sound) effects—is so-called because of the habituating effect of the play.

In a similar manner, an addict replays the same or very similar fantasy tapes on the imaginary screen of the unconscious mind. An addict imagines in viewing these fantasy tapes with the mind's eye being engaged in miraculous feats that engender exquisite narcissistic pleasures. We suggest, therefore, that an addict is a *fantasy junkie* exactly as video junkies are habitués of Nintendo or Playstation—both prefer to inhabit an imaginary world rather than to exist in the mundane day-to-day world of ordinary existence.

An addict builds up ever greater degrees of psychological tolerance and, in the process, gradually descends ever deeper into a private fantasyland from which there is no escape. Yet, despite this desperate attempt to escape from the travails of day-to-day living, an addict still finds ordinary existence hard to bear. In the realm of daily living, an addict vacillates erratically in demeanor from activity of a frenzied and frantic nature to lethargy, boredom, and passivity.

Addictive metamorphosis is an essential phenomenological feature of addiction. It is narcissistic in nature because an addict is entrapped in a fugue-like state of pathological self-absorption. In such a state, an addict is engrossed and preoccupied with what is ultimately a futile attempt to satisfy narcissistic cravings, which are ultimately insatiable. It becomes increasingly difficult for an addict to interact with other people in any normal or healthy way or to use things and pursue activities in an adaptive fashion.

Instead, an addict creates a psychic barrier that diminishes emotional contact with the world of daily living. Similarly, and as part of such a psychopathological form of dissociation, an addict loses touch (yet does not completely break) with a sense of reality, at least one consensually validated by others and shared by the vast majority of normal people. On the contrary, an addict becomes a permanent inhabitant of a surreal fantasyland. Existing in such a mental realm, an addict adopts a private logic that is completely solipsistic and, therefore, is at odds with common sense.

Ultimately, addiction is narcissistic because it entails an idiosyncratic version of the world of thought and emotion (that is, the psychic reality of human nature). In discussing narcissistic disorders of the self, Kohut refers to such a profound disturbance in the sense of reality variously as a "narcissistically experienced world" (1966, p. 450), a "narcissistic conception of the world" (1966, p. 451), and an "archaism of the experience of the world" (1971, p. 63).

Addiction as a Narcissistic Disturbance in the Self–Selfobject Matrix

Another principle tenet of self psychology is that the self is the experiential epicenter of the personality. On the level of subjective experience, the self may be sensed, imagined, or fantasized as either a subject, and hence as an "I," or as an object, and thus as a "me." Still another basic self-psychological tenet is that the self (the "I" or the "me") by necessity exists and develops in a psychosocial milieu of other people, some of whom may function unconsciously as extensions or parts of the self. In general, self psychologists contend that without an experience of "you" as part of "me," or as my selfobject, "I" could not exist at all as a self. In other words, "I" would exist in such a case as a self lacking in form, structure, and function.

From the subjective frame of reference of the self, other people may exist as auxiliaries or adjuncts that function as selfobjects. In this context, self psychology posits that "I" experience "you" unconsciously as part of "me." As part of "me," "you" function subjectively for "me" as "my" selfobject. In this sense, "I" imagine or fantasize that "you" are totally and completely under "my" control.

On this level of fantasy, "I" imagine that "I" control "you" in the same way "I" control my arm or "my" leg. From this subjective perspective there is, therefore, a quality of the self-experience of the selfobject that is inherently megalomaniacal.

We do not doubt that the major thrust of Kohut's work focuses on the nature of the relationships he believes exist between the self and the *human* selfobject milieu. We can put this matter in more "experience near" (Kohut, 1977b, p. 245) and less "experience distant" (Kohut, 1977b, p. 245) terms. Kohut is concerned primarily with the relationships that develop between "me" and "you" as regards "you" functioning for "me" as "my" *human* selfobject.

Self psychologists have, for the most part, followed Kohut's lead in focusing almost exclusively on the purely human dimension of the self–selfobject matrix. For instance, Wolf (1980) refers to and describes the development of "selfobject relationships." We can take two other and more recent examples from self psychology. Stolorow and his collaborators (see, for example, Atwood & Stolorow, 1984; Orange, Atwood, & Stolorow, 1997; Stolorow & Atwood, 1992; Stolorow, Brandchaft, & Atwood, 1987) as well as Lichtenberg and his co-workers (see, for example, Lichtenberg, 1989; Lichtenberg, Lachmann, & Fosshage,

1992) view personality primarily, if not exclusively, in terms of the mode of relating between the self and *human* selfobject(s).

However, as noted (see Kohut, 1977b; and Chapter Two), Kohut (1977b, p. 56) makes an important distinction between human and nonhuman selfobjects. By employing this important distinction, we construe the self–selfobject matrix in terms of the *use* made by an individual of certain things and activities as *nonhuman* selfobjects. There is more involved, therefore, in the self–selfobject matrix than a person-as-self relating solely to others-as-selfobjects.

In the context of a typical self–selfobject matrix, an individual may experience others as nonhuman selfobjects that are used in an adaptive fashion. We refer to this as the *mode of using*, which may be either normal or abnormal, and which we distinguish from the *mode of relating*.

Moreover, self psychologists have largely ignored that realm of subjective experience in which an "it" (that is, a thing or an activity) becomes part of "me." On this experiential level, "I" experience "it" functioning as "my" nonhuman selfobject. In addition, in this same subjective domain, "you" may become an "it" and vice versa, that is, "it" becomes a "you."

In this realm of subjective experience, both "you" and "it" may function for "me" as "my" nonhuman selfobjects. Thus, on this level of unconscious experience, "I" can imagine a "you" as an "it," and, vice versa "I" can fantasize an "it" as a "you." Here again, it is apparent that there is a megalomaniacal quality inherent to the subjective experience of the nonhuman world of things and activities.

Let us take an example from the realm of addiction. In the case of sexual compulsivity, a sex addict experiences another person almost as if he or she is an inanimate thing and, more accurately, a sexual *plaything*. In this instance, "I," as a sex addict, have an imaginary experience (that is, fantasize) "you" as if you were an "it." However, for a sex addict "you" as an "it" lack the capacity necessary to function as a nonhuman selfobject. Instead, "you," as an "it," serve only as a sexual plaything, that is, as an ATM.

As the example of sexual addiction illustrates, there are ways, some of which are healthy and others of which are unhealthy, in which "you" may be experienced by "me" as an "it." On the one hand, "I" may experience "you" as an "it" that functions for "me" as a legitimate, transitional selfobject with the inherent capacity for self-transformation. On the other hand, "I" may experience "you" as an "it" that serves "me" only as an ersatz selfobject. Such an ATM lacks the capacity for transforming the self or for evolving itself into advanced forms. True selfobjects are dynamic, whereas bogus selfobjects are static.

However, something different may also occur. For instance, in the case of addictive or compulsive overeating, an addict experiences an "it" (that is, food) as if "it" were a "you." In this context, a compulsive overeater treats food as if it is semi-human; such an addict also imagines that food functions as if it is a human selfobject, whereas it is an ATM. A compulsive overeater, like all addicts, confabulates fantasy and reality. As a result of such confabulation, an addict tends to be constantly disappointed and disillusioned.

Unconscious fantasy activity allows for blending, blurring, and fusing (that is, condensing or confabulating) of human with nonhuman attributes. This unconscious animation makes it possible to create imaginary, android entities or fantasized, humanoid agents. An individual may unconsciously experience all of these imaginary creations as being endowed with and as possessing a mixture of both human and nonhuman characteristics. Certain things and activities (including both transitional selfobjects and ATMs) may have psychoactive effects that are either inherent or acquired. The psychoactive nature of these agents facilitates the process of unconscious condensation in which human qualities are mixed and matched with nonhuman characteristics.

The characters from children's cartoons and comic books are classic examples of the process of unconscious animation by which it is possible to mix and match, via fantasy and imagination, the human with the nonhuman. (See Caruth, 1968 and Widzer, 1977, for two psychoanalytic studies of comic books; see also Merritt and Kaufmann, 1993, for a study of Walt Disney's early attempts at cinematic animation, which include a silent film version of Carroll's *Alice's Adventures in Wonderland* entitled *Alice's Wonderland* as well as Stern, 2003, on the *Wizard of Oz*.) A useful analogy may be drawn, therefore, between the unreal world of cartoons and comic books and the all too real world of addiction.

An addict—as a modern-day Narcissus who is lost in a wonderland—creates a fantasy world remarkably similar to the domain inhabited by characters from cartoons and comic books. Both of these phantasmagorical domains are populated by make-believe creatures, which are created in the respective imaginations of addict and comic book writer (and reader) alike.

The imaginary creations of an addict and comic book writer (and reader) combine in idiosyncratic ways the human with the nonhuman. Thus, humanoid agents may exist in an addict's fantasy or in a writer's imagination. These android entities are more human than nonhuman, and vice versa, they may be more nonhuman than human.

To a significant degree the process of unconscious animation, in which human and nonhuman are condensed or confabulated, occurs in accordance with animistic mental principles originating in early childhood. The imaginary world of cartoons and comic books as well as the fantasy world of an addict are both organized unconsciously, in part, on the basis of the laws of animism by which the realm of the inanimate is magically animated. (See Chapter 8 for a full discussion of the role of animism as well as anthropomorphism in the etiology and pathogenesis of addiction.)

ATM-things and ATM-activities set off powerful mental fantasy tapes. On the basis of these tapes, an addict imagines being in the possession of extraordinary or superhuman powers very similar in nature to those belonging to characters from cartoons and comic books.

Fantasy, in particular archaic narcissistic fantasy, is a common psychological denominator connecting the otherwise disparate worlds of cartoons and comic books with that of addiction. However, fantasy is used in these two domains for very different purposes. Although based largely on fantasy, the make-believe world of cartoons and comic books illustrates that fantasy is often essential to healthy entertainment.

On occasion, writers of comic books may even use fantasy to teach readers how to distinguish between good and bad, right and wrong, as well as to impart some universal truths about such essential issues as justice and injustice, reward and punishment, as well as life and death. (See Fingeroth, 2004, on *Superman on the Couch: What Superheroes Really Tell Us about Ourselves and Our Society.*) In this regard, fantasy has more than mere entertainment value; it also has educational value as a medium for imparting to the reader of cartoons important lessons about the meaning of existence. In this sense, fantasy is progressive to the degree to which it raises (rather than lowers) awareness and, in the process, serves a pedagogical purpose.

In contrast, fantasy is subverted in the world of addiction from fulfilling any progressive purpose. As part of the psychopathological process of addictive metamorphosis, the denigration of fantasy, as a symbolic and imagistic language, leads to its bastardization as a complex medium for self-expression. At such a reduced and crude level of self-articulation, fantasy corrupts healthy entertainment, thus engendering ignorance rather than wisdom. At the same time, it creates atavistic (narcissistic) cravings on the part of an addict for illusory solutions and magic remedies, which actually thwart rather than advance creative problem-solving.

In this sense, fantasy degenerates into a retrogressive (rather than progressive) form of expression. An example of the latter may be found in healthy entertainment, including cartoons and comic books. The difference between these two varying expressions of fantasy can be stated as follows: In its progressive expression, fantasy involves the healthy process of envisioning future possibilities; whereas in its retrogressive expression, fantasy entails the unhealthy longing for an imaginary past which, in all probability, never existed. A fundamental difference exists, therefore, between intemperate and immodest fantasy and temperate and moderate fantasizing.

Narcissistic (or self-state) fantasizing may be viewed as occurring along on a continuum ranging from the archaic to the mature. At the archaic end of this continuum, narcissistic fantasizing is totally unrealistic and impractical, whereas at the mature end of the continuum such fantasizing is characterized by creativity, inventiveness, and innovation. We refer to the former type of fantasy as retrogressive and to the latter kind as progressive.

Moreover, at the archaic end of the continuum fantasizing is static, crude, and idle, whereas at the mature end it is dynamic, elaborate, and adaptive. However, fantasizing is narcissistic at both ends of the continuum to the degree to which it is self-centered and self-absorbing; the difference is that at the archaic end fantasizing takes place in its original and early childhood form, whereas at the mature end it occurs in a transformed and adult form.

Furthermore, a person may engage in one instance in archaically narcissistic fantasizing, while at another moment the same person may become engrossed in more developmentally advanced types of self-state fantasizing. Obviously, an addict is the kind of person who engages primarily in *escapist fantasy*, the intent of which is to avoid unpleasantness by denying, minimizing, or rationalizing the painful nature of real life problems. In contrast, a healthy individual is the type of person who entertains *adaptive fantasy*, which is based on fanciful and playful mental activity, and thus provides amusement, enchantment, and enrichment. (See Kohut 1977b, pp. 159 and 161 on the topic of "fantasy game" and the "remedial attempt enacted in...fantasy game.")

This description makes it clear that a normally rich and varied fantasy life, with all its considerable potential for adaptation, has, in the case of an addict, become developmentally arrested at the level of archaic narcissistic fantasy. (See Mayes & Cohen, 1992, for a psychoanalytic study of the normal development of imagination and fantasy. See also Cobb, 1993 [1977], for a discussion of the vital role of the world of nature in enriching a child's powers of imagination.) From our perspective, an adult who is addicted is pathologically dependent on these atavistic hypnotic fantasies. An addicted person constructs an unconscious character structure that is dominated by archaic narcissistic fantasies.

An addict comes to depend on the illusory effects of these powerful fantasies. These narcissistic illusions create an emotional condition characterized by rapid mood swings from fantasy scenarios of narcissistic mortification to fantasy scenarios of narcissistic bliss, and back and forth. Such a vicious cycle of *self-state fantasy flip-flopping* is still another narcissistic feature of addiction.

Many of our addicted patients report memories that indicate that as children they were treated by parents as if they were a nonhuman, or at best a semi-human, thing lacking feelings and thoughts. Apparently, as children these patients were supposed to function for their parents in a very mechanical, and even robotic, fashion as a nonsentient entity. As children, they were expected by adults to follow parental commands without thinking, almost as if they were automatons.

A child's capacity for experiencing both the self and others as human is grossly distorted and disturbed by being treated by parents in this megalomaniacal fashion. A parent's (or parents') megalomaniacal mistreatment of a youngster during childhood creates the intersubjective context for the emergence, later in life, of various narcissistic behavior disorders. These include addiction, perversion, as well as sociopathy and psychopathy.

The healthy process of selfobject relating, and the equally normal process of selfobject usage, may both become developmentally arrested or stunted. (See Chapter 8 for a complete discussion of developmental stunting at the stage of transitional selfobject usage and the bearing of this developmental arrest on the etiology and pathogenesis of addiction.) In other words, these developmental processes both may go awry. In the case of transitional selfobject usage, things and activities become tools (of the self) employed to augment functioning; developmental stunting at this stage creates the conditions under which these same entities become props, crutches, and gimmicks rather than functional instruments.

We refer to such a faulty gadget as an addictive trigger mechanism, or an ATM. Certain things and activities such as alcohol, food, drugs, gambling, and sex have a psychoactive quality of an inherent or acquired nature that provides the user (and, more specifically, an abuser) with desperately needed yet purely symptomatic relief from emotional distress. These ATMs provide such relief in the form of specific psycho-active effects.

These effects include antianxiety, antidepressant, deaggressive and pacification, shame-relieving or humanization, and anti-panic. The various psychoactive effects of any given ATM (or combination of ATMs) enable an addict to subjectively experience these things or activities as if it (or they) were a true (transitional) selfobject. Thus, an addict has an illusory experience of mirroring, idealization, twinship and "transitioning" (that is, the megalomaniacal fantasy of being in control of one's psychic reality). In the unconscious mind of an addict, the psychoactive effects of ersatz selfobjects or ATMs create an illusory (imaginary) experience that the cognitive, affective, and sensorial nature of psychic reality have changed for the better, when, in fact, nothing has changed on a psychic level except, perhaps, for the worse.

Some entities and agents have psychoactive effects that are benign and beneficial, whereas other things and activities have psychoactive effects that are malignant and deleterious. Determining the difference between these two types of things and activities is based, in part, on two interrelated factors: (1) the underlying, narcissistic makeup of the user; and (2) the amount, type, and frequency of use (or abuse) of a particular thing or activity. Hence, the psychoactive effect, which is beneficial in the case of a transitional selfobject, results from genuine mirroring, idealization, twinship, or transitioning.

As such, it leads to a healthy process whereby psychic structure is built and then functions in accordance with its design. In contrast, the psychoactive effect, which is deleterious in the case of an ersatz selfobject, is a manifestation of a psychopathological process. In such a condition, and as a result of the selfobject-like nature of ATMs, psychic structure is weakened and psychological functioning is reduced.

In addition, ATMs vary considerably in the extent to which a particular thing or activity provides one or more psychoactive effects of a specific nature. We can mention, for example, two possibilities. Both alcohol and food possess an inherent combination of psychoactive properties, the effect(s) of which proves to be very attractive to an addict. An addict is drawn to these substances because they can provide multiple forms of symptomatic relief from various types of painful mood (that is, moods of narcissistic mortification).

In contrast, cocaine, as a central nervous system (CNS) stimulant, is far more limited than are either alcohol or food in the range of its psychoactive effects. Unlike alcohol and food, the cocaine-ATM is capable of providing only one type of symptomatic relief—namely, an antidepressant effect. (Paradoxically, certain cocaine addicts, even when they are no longer experiencing depression, continue to abuse more of this drug. They do so in order to obtain even higher levels of antidepressant effect in the form of a hypomanic "rush," or state of euthymia.)

As mediated unconsciously by fantasy and mood, the psychoactive effect of a specific ATM is produced by biochemical, physiological, or behavioral means and is characterized as its *psychoactive specificity*. It seems that addicts need to artificially mobilize different fantasies and moods depending on different kinds of underlying psychic distress. In addition, they appear to differ in the means by which they prefer to achieve the same desired end. For instance, some addicts prefer a simpler and more direct biochemical route (e.g., the abuse of alcohol or drugs). However, other addicts prefer a somewhat more roundabout route (e.g., the abuse of food and eating). And, still other addicts prefer an even more circuitous pathway (e.g., compulsive gambling and sex).

We can only speculate as to what accounts for this difference among addicts concerning a *preferred psychoactive pathway*. It may have something to do with the different types of physical sensation that arise along these various pathways. It seems, therefore, that different biochemical, physiological, and behavioral pathways produce varied types of sensation. Such sensations may be integral to the mobilization of a desired set of fantasies and moods. Or, conversely, different fantasies and moods may produce various kinds of physical sensation. These sensations are crucial to the specific type of psychoactive effect desired by a particular addict.

In any event, and regardless of the preferred pathway, the specific psychoactivity of any ATM is based on the placebo effect. (For varying and different views on the placebo effect, see Blakeslee, 1998; Brody, 2000; Coleman, 1993; Freeman & Rickels, 1999; Friedman, 2002; Harrington, 1997; Horgan, 1999; Kaptchuk et al., 2002; Kolata, 2001a,b; Noonan & Cowley, 2002; Talbot, 2000; Tuma, 2002; Winter, 1998.)

We conceive of the placebo effect as occurring in the context of addiction because of the unconscious mediating role of fantasy and mood. Together, these phenomena create a specific and psychoactively based alteration of mind and mood. This alteration may be based on antianxiety or antidepressant relief, for example; however, such relief does not result exclusively from the actual biochemical, physiological, or behavioral changes that occur in the context of the use (or abuse) of a particular ATM.

Rather, such antianxiety or antidepressant relief occurs primarily because of the nature of the unconscious fantasy activated and the type and intensity of mood (that is, affect and sensation) aroused. The unconscious mediating role of fantasy and mood accounts in the context of addiction for the psychoactive specificity of a particular ATM.

From our perspective, fantasy and mood serve as unconscious mediators between the thing used or activity engaged in and the resulting psychoactive effect. The effect of ATMs is, therefore, unlike the effectiveness of psychotropic drugs such as Prozac. These drugs typically act directly on the brain without the unconscious mediating role of fantasy and mood. In contrast, the effectiveness of illicit drugs like cocaine depends to a significant degree on the mediating role of fantasy and mood.

In this sense, therefore, we deem addictive substances or activities as placebos, by which we do not mean that they have no actual effect. On the contrary, we maintain that they have an actual effect, however, one which is mediated unconsciously by fantasy and mood rather than by direct action on the brain. In essence, the psychoactivity of ATMs is, in part, an artifact of the mediating role of fantasy and mood. In other words, this is an instance of mind over matter.

Moreover, there can be little doubt that under a specific set of circumstances a particular addict may prefer one type of pathway over another as a means of activating unconscious fantasy and intensifying mood. And, of course, this preference may vary a great deal over time and under different situations.

The psychoactive specificity of ATMs accounts for the abuse by addicts of different things and activities (either alone or in various combinations) to obtain a particular kind of emotional relief. For example, one addict may be drawn to abusing an addictive substance such as alcohol due to a specific type of "narcissistic crisis" (Wurmser, 1978) and because of the powerful yet faulty antianxiety effect of alcohol. The particular psychoactive effect of alcohol enables this type of addict to imagine this substance as if it were almost a human being who provides actual soothing and calming.

Or, to take a second example of a hypothetical nature, another addict may be driven to abuse an addictive substance like cocaine. Unlike the just mentioned addict, this second addict suffers from a different type of "narcissistic crisis." And, in contrast to alcohol, which is a CNS depressant, cocaine is a CNS stimulant. As such, it is capable of generating grandiose fantasies, which have a psychoactive effect of an antidepressant nature.

In a fashion similar to an alcoholic, a cocaine addict undergoes a phantasmagorical transmogrification. Both the cocaine addict and an alcoholic imagine an inanimate substance, albeit a psychoactive drug, as taking on almost human qualities. An addict is misled by such an imaginary experience. An addict believes mistakenly that interaction and contact with other human beings is unnecessary because the drug meets all needs.

In a final example, a third addict may be driven to abusing food because of its unique capacity to provide psychoactive effects of both an antidepressant and antianxiety nature. A compulsive overeater or bulimic may (subjectively) experience a physical process, such as gorging and stuffing oneself with food, as the antidepressant equivalent of filling up psychologically on narcissistic nourishment. However, this experience is purely illusory because the narcissistic supplies provided by compulsive or bulimic overeating are the psychological equivalent of junk food. As a result, and paradoxically, a food addict is unable to feed himself or herself with any healthy narcissistic sustenance.

In addition to the antidepressant effect of food, a compulsive overeater or bulimic may (subjectively) experience it as providing antianxiety tranquilization and sedation as part of satiation. However, for an addict the antianxiety effect of food as expressed in the tranquilization and sedation that accompanies satiation is as faulty as is its antidepressant effect. A compulsive overeater is relieved temporarily and partially of (disintegration) anxiety.

Moreover, such a food addict is flooded and overwhelmed very quickly by poorly modulated anxiety, thus necessitating the resumption of addictive overeating. With the onset of an addictive cycle, a compulsive overeater once again feels compelled to abuse food and eating. Such an addict attempts to complete the ultimately impossible task of physiologically stuffing down unpleasant and painful feelings.

In the context of a psychopathological process of self-absorption, an addict uses (abuses) ATMs as tricky gimmicks. As part of the Narcissus complex, an addict becomes a victim of self-deception which, in some cases, may lead to self-destruction. (Addictive self-destruction entails the psychological obliteration of a healthy sense of the self and the impoverishment of the selfobject milieu; it may or may not result in actual death.) An addict inadvertently plays a magic trick on himself or herself—one that often has disastrous consequences. An addict deceives himself or herself into believing that specific entities and agents (that is, ATMs) that are actually harmful and destructive are really beneficial and helpful.

In this regard, an addict perpetrates a form of self-deception. Having deceived himself or herself, an addict becomes a captive of addictive illusions. In the midst of such an illusory spell, which cannot be so easily broken, an addict exists as a figment of his or her own imagination.

In this sense, an addict lives out a counterfeit existence as a fantasy junkie. It follows that an addict cannot conjure up pleasant, imaginary scenarios without resorting to the use of gadgets. Therefore, addiction may be viewed from our perspective as a form of black magic—one, however, that relies on the use of artificial potions and elixirs that cast psychoactive spells.

An addict traps himself or herself, as a magician gone mad, in a nightmarish world of megalomaniacal fantasies that are generated by the habitual abuse of things and activities. An addict believes incorrectly that these entities are endowed with a capacity for magically controlling psychic reality. So endowed, an addict imagines being in possession of magic wands by which to control mind and mood.

Fantasies of being a megalomaniacal self that underlie addiction consist of the illusion that magically endowed things and activities bestow upon the user the capacity to alter radically the actual nature of human thought and emotion (that is, the psychic reality of human nature). In fact, addiction results only in a purely artificial alteration of mind and mood. As such, it is as fleeting as are the fantasies and moods on which it is based. An addict imagines on the basis of fantasies of being a megalomaniacal self that he or she controls the world of emotions when, in effect, an addict's emotions and emotional affairs have become totally unmanageable. It is an irony of fate that an addict ends up like Mickey Mouse who, in Walt Disney's *Fantasia*, plays the role of the "Sorcerer's Apprentice." Like Mickey, an addict is at the mercy of the very things and activities he or she imagines as doing one's bidding.

Addiction as a Narcissistic Disturbance in Self-Experience

The psychopathological process of addictive metamorphosis is based on an extreme form of self-absorption. An addict is a modern-day version of the Narcissus of early Greek mythology. As such, an addict is lost in the reflecting pool constituted by an addictive wonderland. As a lost soul, an addict removes himself or herself from everyday concerns; as a result, an addict eventually becomes indifferent to everyone and oblivious to everything.

There is, however, a difference between an addict and Narcissus. Unlike Narcissus, an addict is mesmerized by an image of the self as perceived in the reflecting pool of the imagination. Furthermore, an addict does not simply wither away and die as did Narcissus in the Greek myth. Rather, an addict impoverishes himself or herself psychologically, thus fading away slowly into a mere shadow of his or her former self.

As part of addictive metamorphosis, dissociative anesthetization involves an abnormal form of self-absorption, one that must be distinguished from other healthy forms of self-absorption. For example, a person may become absorbed in a hobby, a craft, or a more serious endeavor. Leisurely pastimes as well as more substantive pursuits all may be considered as transitional selfobject activities which, to varying degrees, engender healthy self-absorption. Such absorption is characterized by an introspective self-scrutiny, a vision of future possibilities as well as an exploration of new forms of creative and artistic expression.

Healthy self-absorption entails a concentrated and focused kind of mental activity. Such activity may express itself in the form of leisurely play, serious problem-solving, artistic improvisation and creation, skill improvement and talent development, or the envisioning of new possibilities. Healthy self-absorption also leads to the expansion of consciousness. It is, therefore, in stark contrast to the self-absorption produced by dissociative anesthesia. The latter severely constricts conscious awareness as well as limits introspection and empathy.

Our foregoing discussion makes clear that dissociative anesthesia, which is an essential feature of addictive metamorphosis, alters both the cognitive and the affective realms of mental life. This accounts, in part, for its incredible capacity to alter unconscious experience. However, more is entailed in addictive metamorphosis than adding pleasure as a means of lessening pain, and, in the process, altering conscious awareness.

In the course of examining dissociative anesthetization, we discovered that the unconscious mind is organized, in part, on the basis of a dialectical bipolarity. This principle of mental life is inherent and fundamental to the unconscious organization of experience—both real and imagined. And, it is generated by the unconscious organizing activity of fantasy and mood. We believe that the *dialectical bipolarity of fantasy and mood* is basic to all forms of unconscious mental functioning. Freud (1955 [1920]) discovered this psychological given long ago; however, he described it in terms of, respectively, the repetition compulsion and the pleasure principle. In the context of our model, Freud's ideas about these facets of unconscious mental life are expressive of the dialectical bipolarity of fantasy and mood.

Loosely speaking, we re-interpret the repetition compulsion and the pleasure principle as expressing the following: everyone has an unconscious desire to create pleasant mental scenarios in the form of blissful fantasies. However, according to Freud (1955 [1920]) there exists an opposing yet equally powerful proclivity inherent to unconscious mental life. He calls this the death instinct. Freud hypothesizes that such a drive consists of a tendency to perseverate on painful and unpleasant scenarios of imaginary helplessness, hopelessness, and mortification. This mental proclivity may be viewed as an expression of the repetition compulsion in conjunction with the death instinct.

We reconceptualize Freud's two principles of mental functioning as follows: There is a psychological principle according to which it is possible for a pleasurable fantasy to offset and counteract a painful fantasy. However, the mere creation of a pleasant fantasy offers only a temporary and partial solution to the problem of replacing a negative mind-set with a positive one. In general, it may be stated that unless narcissistic fantasy has undergone sufficient and adequate developmental transformation, then self-state fantasy flip-flopping merely in the unconscious mind of a particular person merely replaces one archaic and unpleasant fantasy with another equally archaic yet pleasant fantasy.

An addict is such a person because he or she suffers from serious defects and deficits in both psychological structure and function. As a result, such an individual remains caught in a cycle of never-ending and repetitive attempts at reversing the unconscious state of the self from one archaic narcissistic organization to another equally archaic condition. An addict cannot transform archaic narcissistic fantasy, on an unconscious level and, as part of this cycle, into more mature psychic structure and evolved psychic function. Such an unconscious transformation and evolution would assume the form of a richer inner world of more sophisticated mental images and more complex emotions.

The developmental transformation of archaic narcissistic fantasy into more substantial types of psychological structure makes it possible for a person to more effectively regulate self-esteem and modulate mood. This, in turn, facilitates an individual's capacity to *switch* rather than merely *flip-flop* from one self-state to another. Such switching involves a person's ability to maintain a positive mind-set with relative ease and for a reasonably sustained period of time.

A Review of Psychoanalytic Literature on the Dynamic Interaction of Fantasy and Mood

We have described our self-psychological view of addiction as a narcissistic phenomenon. Now, we proceed with a review of some relevant psychoanalytic literature. This material addresses and supports our central position, namely, there is an unconscious dynamic that is dialectical and bipolar in nature and is created by the interaction of fantasy and mood. Of equal, if not greater, importance, this literature focuses on the narcissistic aspect of this unconscious dynamic.

None of this literature is explicitly concerned with addiction. However, it is all very relevant to the current discussion. It helps to explicate the meaning of the concept of dialectical bipolarity, a notion of crucial importance to our self-psychological view of the phenomenology of addiction.

The review proceeds with a critical discussion of selected literature that is self-psychological (or self-psychological friendly) in perspective. The review culminates in an assessment of a 1974 article by the self psychologist Paul Tolpin. Inexplicably, despite its import, it has been largely ignored by other self psychologists. We attempt in our review to demonstrate the superiority of the self-psychological viewpoint. More specifically, we seek to show how self psychology can clearly demonstrate that the unconscious dynamic, which is generated by the interaction of fantasy and mood, is essentially narcissistic in nature.

Eigen, Bach and Schwartz, and Tolpin

For the purpose of the current narrative, the otherwise diverse works of Eigen (see, for example, 1979, 1989, 2004 [1980, 1981, 1986, 1991]). Bach and Schwartz (1972), and P. H. Tolpin (1974) can be welded together to create a conceptual bridge. Using such a transverse, it is possible for us to connect the work of these authors to our own self-psychological thinking about dialectical bipolarity. From the perspective of our present study, the works of Eigen, Bach and Schwartz, and Tolpin all may be viewed as moving progressively toward a point of view more explicitly self-psychological.

Eigen advances psychoanalysis toward a theory of the dialectical bipolarity of fantasy and mood. He focuses specifically on the narcissistic dimension of this psychodynamic interaction, Eigen is indebted, therefore, to the classical Freudian tradition within psychoanalysis. However, he follows more closely in the footsteps of Winnicott, Bion, and Lacan, all of whom deviate significantly from a strict Freudian perspective. In addition, in the earlier part of his *oeuvre*, Eigen is influenced by the work of Kohut.

In his paper, "Instinctual Fantasy and Ideal Images," Eigen emphasizes that: "My use of 'drive' is preeminently focused on the role of fantasy as the formation of one's self-image" (p. 62). Later, in *The Psychotic Core* (2004 [1986]), he notes: "From what has been said about Freud's thought, *fantasy is an out-growth of or euphemism for hidden hallucinatory activity*" (p. 51, emphasis added). As articulated by Eigen, we view the phenomenon of fantasy as a by-product or expression of "hallucinatory activity." As such, it is critical to an understanding of the unconscious mental principle, which we characterize as the dialectical bipolarity of fantasy and mood. This principle implies that individuals possess an inherent capacity to envision, with hallucinatory vividness, either *narcissistically blissful fantasies of incredible pleasure* or *narcissistically mortifying fantasies of unbearable pain*.

Eigen recognizes this paradoxical quality of unconscious fantasizing. In an article entitled, "Creativity, Instinctual Fantasy and Ideal Images," he states: "In instances of serious personality impoverishment contact with ideal images can genuinely nourish the ego, build supplies and restore hope, as well as stimulate and support the wish for meaningful work" (p. 91). Then, in reference to the self-psychological thinking of Kohut, he indicates: "Kohut ... has recently emphasized ways in which *ideal images* spontaneously arise in narcissistic transferences and ultimately add to the personality's overall well being and ability to function" (p. 91, emphasis added). It is fair to say that Eigen in this context uses the notion of "ideal images" in ways that anticipate our very similar use of the concept of fantasies of narcissistic bliss.

Moreover, Eigen (1989) is aware of the bipolar or double-sided nature of fantasy. For example, in his discussion of Winnicott, he stresses that Winnicott "pictures the patient caught in a kind of fantasy structure" (p. 607). Eigen continues that according to Winnicott: "In extreme cases the individual can spend the better part of his life trapped in fantasy (recall Winnicott's distinction between the unlived life of fantasy and the lived life of dreaming)" (p. 607).

And, from our perspective, an addict is a "fantasy-trapped individual" (Eigen, 1989). Unwittingly, an addict creates a psychic trap in which he or she flip-flops constantly from one self-state to another. Initially, an addict has mortifying fantasies of a self as a degraded and lesser being. Subsequently, and in a polar opposite self-state, an addict has blissful fantasies of a self as an elevated and greater being.

Among the psychoanalytic theorists under review, Eigen is especially significant to our work for several reasons. First, he is extremely cognizant of the double edged or bipolar nature of fantasy; and, second, he has a keen awareness of the dialectical nature of the interaction between fantasy and mood. For example, in one of his case histories, Eigen (2004 [1982]) postulates: "Above all there is a positive validation of the penis in general even to the point of overstimulation, clearly an attempt to experience some kind of *narcissistic integrity* through the father image" (p. 125, emphasis added). Furthermore, he states: "Work with the phallic fantasy led to repair of certain aspects of [the patient's] self-image and to a genuine gain in potency" (p. 127).

In these two passages, Eigen stresses that a fantasy, or an "ideal image," which is positively toned and pleasant, functions in a restorative fashion. It does so, according to Eigen, by repairing psychic damage to a self. Eigen is sensitive about the psychological value of such fantasies. However, nonetheless, he takes into consideration the presence of contrary psychic forces, ones countervailing in nature.

In fact, he is rather explicit about the clash between what we construe as mortifying fantasies and blissful fantasies. For instance, Eigen emphasizes that the above-mentioned patient's "struggle to constitute valuable ideal experiences" had to be understood in the context of the need to "endure polluting and destructive attacks" (p. 129). This description lends itself to a view of these "attacks" as narcissistically mortifying fantasies of the loss of a phallically endowed sense of self.

Eigen (2004 [1982]) alludes again to what we construe as the principle of the dialectical bipolarity of fantasy and mood. Here, in discussing the case of "F," he maintains: "With F both sides of *dissociated polarities* could be gathered into the transference so that transition from splitting to ambivalence could be made" (p. 376, emphasis added). With great elegance, Eigen describes in this clinical observation the polarity or bipolarity that is inherent in the functioning of different sides of the personality.

Eigen also hints at the critical idea that dissociation is an unconscious process separating and keeping apart polar opposite sides of the personality. Kohut refers to this as the vertical split in the psyche or self. From our perspective, the vertical split involves a dissociative division in self-experience. Such a split is evidenced by a developmental failure on the part of an individual to integrate and synthesize archaic narcissistic fantasies into the mature personality structure.

Remaining unintegrated in the unconscious mind of a particular person, these self-fragments exist, therefore, as separate psychic and emotional presences. During addictive metamorphosis, an addict has an unconscious experience in which the self is imagined in the form of archaic narcissistic fantasies and accompanying moods of narcissistic bliss.

We distinguish the psychopathological resort on the part of an addict to dissociation and anesthetization from the healthy response on the part of a psychotherapy patient to ever greater degrees of intersubjective absorption of an archaically narcissistic fashion. There is a crucial difference between the former (that is, dissociative anesthetization) and the latter (namely, intersubjective absorption). The latter offers an addicted patient with an alternative, and more successful, means by which to reabsorb dissociatively split-off fragments of the self.

An addicted patient who is undergoing self-psychological psychotherapy has an opportunity to absorb through transmuting internalization parts of the self. Such a process of intersubjective absorption stands in stark contrast to an addict's flip-flopping between one form of archaic narcissistic fantasy and another.

Eigen makes the same point in describing the psychotherapeutic process of healing the "dissociative polarities" of F's personality. He contends: "Without such a development, the most far-reaching assimilation of identifications or, in *Kohut's phrase, 'transmuting internalization'* could not adequately occur" (p. 91, emphasis added).

In a 1972 article, "A Dream of the Marquis de Sade: Psychoanalytic Reflections on Narcissistic Trauma, Decompensation, and the Reconstitution of a Delusional Self," Bach and Schwartz come even closer than did Eigen to a self-psychological understanding of the dialectical bipolarity of narcissistic fantasy and mood. As a matter of fact, they are quite explicit about the connection between their ideas and those of Kohut. For example, they (Bach & Schwartz, 1972) indicate: "We relate [our] ideas to current concepts of narcissistic pathology and find them particularly congruent with the formulation advanced by Kohut" (p. 474).

Like Eigen, these authors focus on an unconscious dialectic involving the interaction between what we describe as fantasies of narcissistic bliss and those of narcissistic mortification. For instance, in the case of the Marquis de Sade, they note that the "compensatory use of invulnerable self-images protect the self from the constant threat of its own destruction" (p. 471).

It is relatively easy to translate this statement into our own language. From our perspective, we see de Sade as attempting, however unsuccessfully, to counteract mortifying fantasies of the psychological death of his self with blissful fantasies of invulnerability. In addition, Bach and Schwartz even refer to these imaginary visions, which are in diametrical opposition, as "archaic fantasies" (p. 473), thus further anticipating our work.

In still other significant ways, Bach and Schwartz adumbrate our ideas. They argue that cases like de Sade entail a self–selfobject matrix that has assumed qualities of a purely phantasmagorical nature. In fact, in the case of de Sade it is floridly delusional. In discussing de Sade's psychosis, they maintain that his sexual fantasies, all of which are overtly masochistic and sadistic in nature, are symptomatic manifestations of a failed attempt to (1) "restitute delusionally idealized selfobjects" (p. 474), as well as an unsuccessful effort to (2) "animate a delusional grandiose self" (p. 474).

On the one hand, these authors contend: "Sadistic fantasies here seem to function as attempts to prevent the final dissolution of the delusioned self, to prevent a yielding or submission that is equated with death" (p. 470). On the other hand, they assert: "Masochistic fantasies ... are evoked as the idealized parental imago fades, and represent more and more desperate attempts to experience *its* presence, to submit to *its* power" (p. 470).

From our vantage point, we interpret Bach and Schwartz as follows: They suggest that de Sade is psychotic because he is organized unconsciously in terms of a delusional belief in the power of an idealized selfobject. In other words, narcissistic fantasies of archaic grandiosity and omnipotence, which at a certain stage of development are phase-appropriate, in the case of de Sade assume delusional and hence psychotic proportions. Moreover, de Sade attempts, according to these authors, to hold himself together narcissistically by entertaining a variety of sadistic and masochistic fantasies.

However, de Sade organized himself unconsciously on the basis of a sense of self that is delusional and, hence, extremely fragile and vulnerable. His sadomasochistic fantasies have to be extreme to the degree to which they: (1) imbue him with an illusory sense of his own power, or (2) engender a magical belief, on his part, in the power of the idealized selfobject. In this context, Bach and Schwartz view de Sade's "masochistic fantasies as restitutional attempts to reanimate and cling to idealized imagoes which have been denied and destroyed as their promised omnipotence failed" (p. 471). Similarly, they depict de Sade's sadistic fantasies as a "return to more archaic fantasies of the delusional self whose existence is validated and affirmed through sadism and murder" (p. 471).

Bach and Schwartz characterize de Sade's sadomasochistic fantasies as failed attempts at a sexual reconstitution of self and selfobject. From our viewpoint, de Sade's efforts are futile for the following reason: The dreaded fantasies of mortification are accompanied by narcissistic affects of an intensely painful nature. Consequently, not even the wildly sadomasochistic fantasies of de Sade can counteract the devastating effects of "experiences of self-fragmentation, bodily disruption, and 'death of the self'" (p. 474).

Bach and Schwartz hint at the dialectical and bipolar nature of de Sade's (archaic narcissistic) fantasies. For instance, they interpret de Sade's sadomasochistic and psychopathic novel, *The 120 Days of Sodom*, as an artistic expression of his "narcissistic fantasy that 'a child is being murdered'—my childhood grandiose self is being destroyed—endlessly carried out and just as endlessly denied" (p. 473).

In our terminology, de Sade finds himself trapped psychologically in a vicious cycle. In this trap, he attempts to cancel out dreaded fantasies of mortification with wishful fantasies of bliss. However, these latter fantasies are nullified almost immediately, thus forcing him to repeat the process over and over again.

The work of Bach and Schwartz is a forerunner to our notion of the dialectical bipolarity of fantasy and mood. It also anticipates our self-psychological view of the role of this unconscious dynamic in addiction. In essence, we argue that in modern terminology de Sade is a sex addict extraordinaire. As such, he is obsessed with perverse fantasies of the sadomasochistic abuse of the self and others, all of which he imagines as mere sexual playthings, or ATMs.

As part of his sexual addiction, de Sade also is driven to enact these fantasy scenarios compulsively on both literal and behavioral levels. De Sade is, like all addicts, a fantasy junkie; and like all fantasy junkies he ends up becoming trapped in addictive quicksand. Thus, the harder he tries to escape from the addictive quagmire through wishful fantasies of bliss, the deeper he sinks into the depths of dreaded fantasies of mortification.

Bach and Schwartz provide a psychological portrait of de Sade that highlights the tragic nature of all addictions: an addict cannot use certain things and activities—regardless of how often repeated, how much used, how long abused, or how psychoactive in nature—to provide psychological substance and emotional sustenance. In other words, despite the narcissistic illusions on the part of an addict of possessing powers of magical control, an addict cannot perform the proverbial magic trick of pulling a rabbit out of a hat.

There is a paradox to Tolpin's 1974 article, "On the Regulation of Anxiety: Its Relation to 'The Timelessness of the Unconscious and Its Capacity for Hallucination'." In all probability it is not discussed, nor even cited, in the self psychology literature because it predates his later works, which were more explicitly self-psychological. However, for our purposes, it is extremely important. If there is one work by a self-psychologist, other than Kohut, that is crucial to our thinking it is Tolpin's 1974 paper.

In this essay, Tolpin comes closer than any other self-psychologist to anticipating many of our most important ideas, and especially those concerning the dialectical bipolarity of fantasy and mood. In the work of Tolpin this idea is described as the "hallucinatory wish-fulfillment" capacity of the unconscious mind. On the basis of this notion, Tolpin refers to

> the ... operations of a *specific psychic tendency*, an operation related to the mechanism of hallucinatory wish-fulfillment which to varying degrees is able to affect the regulation of anxiety by calling up from the mind's store of memories, previously experienced and remembered states of gratification. (p. 152)

Tolpin points out that "these memories of gratification-pleasure were then used to counteract actually occurring, or, as yet, only anticipated states of unpleasure" (p. 152).

We can draw an immediate comparison between our notion of dialectical bipolarity and Tolpin's similar yet earlier notion of hallucinatory wish-fulfillment and the regulation of anxiety. We postulate that there is a psychic tendency, which under normal circumstances is automatic and spontaneous, for counterbalancing painful fantasy visions with pleasurable fantasy scenarios. Similarly, Tolpin suggests that there is a "specific psychic tendency" to hallucinate wishes as having been fulfilled as a means of regulating anxiety. We elaborate, in more explicitly self-psychological terms, on the thinking of Tolpin (as well as Eigen).

In support of our comparison, we point out that Tolpin is clear in linking hallucinatory wish-fulfillment with fantasy. For example, he

(Tolpin, 1974) notes that the hallucinatory wish-fulfillment "recreates the experience of satisfaction through action or *fantasy or ... by fantasied action (ideation or thought)*—that is, by hallucination" (p. 154, emphasis added).

There is another important similarity between our thinking and that of Tolpin. He argues, as do we, against pathologizing hallucinatory wish-fulfillment or fantasy by viewing it as solely defensive in nature. Instead, he advocates a view of these processes as adaptational as well. He claims that

> whereas hallucinatory wish-fulfillment ... (*and the partial transformations ... into unconscious or conscious wish-fulfilling fantasies or behavior*) have for the most part been acknowledged, often pejoratively as important escapist psychological mechanisms, not enough attention has been paid to their *pertinence throughout life as mechanisms of positive value* which allow the mind more degree of necessary autonomy from and some degree of control over the dangers of the real world. (p. 157, emphasis added)

Tolpin describes in this passage and in the language of our model the "positive value" inherent to the developmental transformation of both narcissistic fantasy and mood. We assert that the modification of these affect-laden fantasies makes it more possible for an individual to regulate and modulate the typical fluctuations that inevitably occur in self-esteem. According to Tolpin, processes such as hallucinatory wish-fulfillment and fantasizing are not necessarily pathological, defensive, and hence detrimental to psychological functioning. Instead, he contends that they may be crucial to the establishment and maintenance of a steady narcissistic equilibrium.

In elaborating further on the "mechanism of hallucinatory wish-fulfillment," Tolpin indicates that it

> allows the mind the advantage of a certain degree of independence from impinging stress of inimical realties with which it is daily beset and, therefore, gives it more flexibility in its reaction to such stresses by permitting a buffering delay and, under the best of circumstances, the possibility at least of a more adequate and moderate response to disturbing fears and dangers. (p. 152)

In explaining the operation of this mechanism, Tolpin asserts: "Hallucinatory wish-fulfillment *substitutes a positive physiological-ideational experience for a negative or painful one* rather than by simply attempting to squelch it or somehow get rid of it" (p. 156, emphasis added). In this brief observation, Tolpin alludes to the notion of both a psychic dialectic as well as a bipolarity. In line with our concept of dialectical bipolarity, Tolpin believes there is a "specific psychic tendency" to substitute a "positive, physiological-ideational experience for a negative or painful one."

Moreover, Tolpin also pairs physiological-ideational experiences, which are the positive and negative opposites of one another, in a fashion analogous to our juxtaposing of the fantasies of the polar opposite forms of narcissistic bliss and mortification. From our perspective, psychological health means the following: it is relatively easy and automatic for a person to substitute a blissful fantasy of narcissistic pleasure for a mortifying fantasy of narcissistic displeasure without, however, having to resort to artificial and addictive means.

Tolpin further expounds on a notion very similar to what we refer to as the psychic principle of dialectical bipolarity. He stresses that an "affect is countered by an affect, and anxiety is blended with and diluted by pleasure" (p. 160). Moreover, he adds that the

> *balance between these two opposing memory systems* can also lead to increased stabilization of this psychic apparatus through *the modulation of disruptive emotional extremes* which, therefore, favor its continuing cohesiveness and structuralization. (p. 100, emphasis added)

Here, Tolpin emphasizes, as do we, that "balance" and "modulation" are essential to "structuralization."

Furthermore, Tolpin seeks to

> demonstrate ... the powerful effect of some instances of hallucinatory wish-fulfillment ... that were capable of *reversing* an increasingly unpleasurable affect and rebalancing a perturbed psychic equilibrium in the brief span of a psychic moment. (p. 166, emphasis added)

Tolpin describes the psychic power of hallucinatory wish-fulfillment to reverse pain to pleasure. His description is similar to our analysis of the fantasy process by which self-states may be switched (rather than flip-flopped) from negative to positive.

Moreover, Tolpin makes another important point. He indicates that the dialectic of hallucinatory wish-fulfillment extends beyond the specific regulation of anxiety to the general modulation of dysphoric affect or mood. He maintains that pleasurable gratifications that arise in the context of hallucinatory wish-fulfillment are

> homeostatically valuable in that they may *deflect or mitigate the eruption of too great a sense of deprivation or inadequacy,* and thereby reduce the danger of experiencing too intense degrees of *self-dissatisfaction, and of longing, depression, anxiety and rage.* (p. 175, emphasis added)

Here, Tolpin extends the psychic range of hallucinatory wish-fulfillment to cover all these other dysphoric affects. Thus, it is legitimate to compare Tolpin's analysis with our own, especially as regards the dialectical bipolarity of fantasy and mood. We share with Tolpin a notion that is implicit in our own position. This notion suggests that a wide variety of fantasies that are positively toned and pleasurable may "deflect or mitigate" the effect of other fantasies consisting of an equally diverse range of painful affects.

Tolpin, like the present authors, is cognizant of the inevitable drawbacks and shortcomings of such a psychic process. He recognizes the potential pitfalls attendant to an emotional process whereby psychological regulation is based on hallucinatory wish-fulfillment, or what we call the dialectical bipolarity of fantasy and mood. For example, he emphasizes that hallucinatory wish-fulfillment may create a type of enduring illusion or "central organizing fantasy" which

> may remain to a considerable extent an end it itself—*a half-real, half-delusional self-experience, maintained with relatively little alteration of an infantile form,* which colors all of life with a hue of unreality and which thereby limits thought, or action, or understanding to all but those directions that are suited to its undisturbed conservation. (p. 158, emphasis added)

As a result, Tolpin asserts that hallucinatory wish-fulfillment may in certain cases lead to a "life dominated by *unrealistic fantasies, daydreams, and illusions about oneself*" (p. 158, emphasis added).

Tolpin offers an analysis of the dangers of hallucinatory wish-fulfillment as a psychic regulatory mechanism that parallels an important aspect of our thinking. His analysis is analogous to our view that psychological stumbling blocks may arise in childhood. Such pitfalls are a result of a child's developmental failure to transform archaic narcissistic fantasies and accompanying moods into healthy psychic structure. In other words, there is a developmental failure in psychic structure building.

Tolpin provides a clinical vignette that is particularly relevant to our present study. He presents the case of a young man whose abuse of marijuana lead to a "life dominated by unrealistic fantasies, daydreams, and illusions of oneself." We cite this case as a means of further linking Tolpin's work with our own fantasy-based model of addiction and, more specifically, with the phenomenological component of our model.

Tolpin describes this patient ("Case B") as a "single man in his early twenties [who] suffered from symptoms of intense depression, outrage, and angry vindictiveness" (p. 168). Following the use of marijuana, the patient reported a dream of "heightened self-admiration" (p. 168). According to Tolpin, the

> *pharmacological effect* of the marijuana was helpful in allowing the patient to experience enough current pleasure-gratification to overcome his more characteristic chronic moods of unpleasure—anger-anxiety. (p. 169, emphasis added)

Here, Tolpin describes the "pharmacological effect of the marijuana" in terms of "pleasure-gratification," thus implicitly links its function to that of hallucinatory wish-fulfillment. This description is remarkable in anticipating our notion of the arousal of psychoactive fantasy tapes, which occurs as part of phantasmagorical transmogrification.

Tolpin continues his discussion of the patient's drug-induced alteration of his subjective state. He observes: "Now the currently pleasurable experience was able to re-establish its linkage to a powerful early experience of gratification" (p. 169). According to Tolpin, this "early experience of gratification" involved, as revealed in the patient's dream, a combination of "heightened pleasure in his own integrated motor activity and an *early union with an idealized powerful father and an admiring responsive mother*" (p. 169, emphasis added).

Tolpin offers an interpretation of this patient's marijuana-stimulated dream, which accords nicely with our self-psychological understanding of the fantasy-based experiences of our addicted patients. More specifically, this patient's dream reveals a fantasy of merger with a paternal imago who is idealized as omnipotent. It also depicts a grandiose fantasy of an exhibitionistic display of the self before a maternal figure who is imbued with mirroring qualities. As they appear in the dream, these images are similar to those our addicted patients conjure up with hallucinatory vividness through the use of a variety of psychoactive ATMs.

There are important similarities between the patient described by Tolpin and those we have discussed. They all have phantasmagorical experiences that are based on an imaginary self–selfobject matrix. In the realm of imagination, these patients experience narcissistic "pleasure- gratification [overcoming] the more chronic mood of compulsive- anger-anxiety" (p. 169).

Moreover, our addicted patients, like Tolpin's marijuana-smoking patient, lack a healthy capacity for the adaptive use of fantasy or hallucination wish-fulfillment. As a result, they cannot effectively change the unpleasant into the pleasant. Furthermore, these patients cannot use other people, things, or activities as transitional selfobjects by which to supplement the regulation and augment the modulation of inevitable fluctuations in self-esteem.

Instead, our addicted patients, like the one described by Tolpin, must resort to a psychopathological and dysfunctional means of regulating self-esteem. They use or abuse a variety of addictive agents as an artificial means of inducing a phantasmagorical experience of pleasure that, in turn, serves to dissociate and anesthetize.

Tolpin concludes his discussion of the case of patient B with a reference to an "archaic narcissistic transference" (p. 169). He claims that this transference

> enabled [the patient] for a somewhat extended period of time to *mitigate anxiety* of the unmodified loss of not yet separated and indispensable aspects of himself which contributed to a stable self and to his sense of well-being. (p. 169, emphasis added)

It is interesting, and perhaps revealing, that Tolpin uses the same term "mitigate" in both the above context and in an earlier one. In the earlier context, he uses the term "mitigate" to describe the effect of hallucinatory wish-fulfillment gratifications. Similarly, in the above passage, he uses this term in describing what we call the psychopharmacotherapeutic effect of the transitional selfobject transference.

It appears, then, Tolpin entertains the notion that an archaic narcissistic transference can "mitigate anxiety." From our perspective, we interpret Tolpin as implying that the transference may have a psychopharmacotherapeutic and, more specifically, antianxiety effect. In addition, Tolpin also indicates that in mitigating anxiety an archaic narcissistic transference replicates the mitigating effect of hallucinatory wish-fulfillment.

Tolpin hints at a number of ideas relevant to our thinking about "therapeutic dissociation." It is a clinical means by which to replace the dissociating and anesthetizing effects of addictive metamorphosis. In working psychotherapeutically with our addicted patients, we induce psychoanalytically this state of therapeutic dissociation. And, in the process, we enable our patients to undergo a fantasy-based experience of what Tolpin refers to as "not yet separate and indispensable aspects of [the self]." From the vantage point of our psychotherapeutic approach, we believe that such a fantasy-based experience constitutes the psychoanalytic revival of a transitional selfobject transference. An addicted patient gains by means of such a transference, psychotherapeutic relief from chronic, emotional pain. Hence, just as is true in the case of Tolpin's patient, so too do our addicted patients have the following psychotherapeutic experience. Because they have undergone an experience of therapeutic dissociation it is possible for them "for a somewhat extended period of time to mitigate anxiety" as well as other dysphoric affects.

Chapter 8

The Etiology and Pathogenesis of Addiction

INTRODUCTION

The major question we want to answer in this chapter is: *Is there a common etiological basis for the pathogenesis of addiction?* Answering this question necessitates that we allude to a series of debates in the addiction field surrounding the issues of etiology and pathogenesis. For example, there is the debate over the existence of a so-called "addictive personality," that is, a premorbid and preaddictive personality. (In Chapter 9 we return to the concept of what we term the "addictive character" as part of our discussion of the typology of addiction.) To take another instance, there is the debate over whether addiction is a physical disease or a psychological disorder. As part of this topic, there are two other interrelated matters: (1) Is addiction better conceived of as one basic and underlying malady with a variety of psychopathological expressions? or, (2) Is addiction best viewed as several different and essentially unrelated maladies?

And finally, there is the hotly contested issue of the most rigorous methodological way to study addiction so as to better understand its etiological origins and explain its pathogenic course. (See Khantzian, 1987, for a discussion of what he calls the "cause-consequence debate.") One school of thought in the field, and the one to which we subscribe, argues as follows: It holds that it is possible to understand the etiology and pathogenesis of disorders like addiction through employing the traditional psychoanalytic method of genetic reconstruction. According to this position, genetic reconstruction is a reliable methodology of gathering data, and especially data about the nature and workings of the unconscious mind. Hence, the findings based on the use of this method are, according to our position, scientifically valid.

Another, and contrasting, school of thought has been highly critical of this methodological position. (See Valliant 1970, 1978, 1983, 1995; Valliant & Milofsky 1982a,b, as a staunch advocate of this position.) This school contends only longitudinal rather than retrospective studies are methodologically sound enough to yield scientifically valid findings.

A long tradition exists in both the psychoanalytic and non-analytic subfields of addiction regarding the central query of this chapter. There is a vast literature on the etiology and pathogenesis of addiction. It dates back to Freud (1961 [1928]), who first connects addiction etiologically to a pathogenic disturbance in sexuality and, more specifically, to a problem originating in infantile masturbation. Freud argues that addiction in adulthood is the unconscious equivalent of disturbed and excessive masturbation in childhood.

Freud's view has more than mere historical import; until recently it continued to affect the prevailing psychoanalytic position regarding the etiology and pathogenesis of addition. According to this more classical position, addiction is best viewed as originating in a disturbance in the sexual and aggressive drives. Moreover, the classical position conceives of addiction as following a particular pathogenic course, which is based on disturbances in psychosexuality and aggression and is similar to other neurotic disorders.

A more modern psychoanalytic position, and one to which we adhere, views addiction as originating in a narcissistic disturbance at the core of the personality. From this perspective, addiction pursues a pathogenic course quite different from typical neurotic disorders. Consistent with this contemporary point of view, we conceive of addiction as originating in a developmental arrest in the transformation of a particular archaic narcissistic fantasy (that is, a fantasy of being a megalomaniacal self).

This megalomaniac fantasy involves an illusion on the part of an addict of possessing agents of magical control that make it possible to manipulate the forces or laws of human nature in a way that radically alters psychic reality. Such a *fantasy matrix of self and selfobject* amounts to a fantasy of being in control of the psychological forces of psychic reality. As such, an addict imagines himself or herself as a potentate with powers of magical control capable of altering all the laws of nature, especially those of human nature.

From a developmental perspective, a child enters an imaginary world in which the animate and inanimate as well as the human and the nonhuman are all blurred and mixed up. Abraham (1979 [1920]) Ferenczi (1956 [1913]), Freud (1953 [1913]), as well as Piaget (1959, 1962, 1973), and more recently Hanly (1992), all refer to this type of confabulation as the principle of animism.

We describe this phenomenon of the unconscious mind as the process of *animation* we believe is involved in the etiology and pathogenesis of addiction. From our self-psychological vantage point, we envision a psychological arrest in the normal unfolding and transformation of a fantasy of being a megalomaniacal self and as possessing magical control over the laws of human nature that govern psychic reality. This developmental arrest takes place in the intersubjective context constituted by child and parent(s) or other caregivers. From within this particular setting, the narcissistic exchange process breaks down and miscarries.

Stressing the importance of etiology and pathogenesis in understanding a phenomenon as complex and multifaceted as addiction is consistent with the best thinking in the contemporary mental health field. For instance, Maxman and Ward in the second edition of the modern classic, *Essential Psychopathology and Its Treatment* (1994), include an entire chapter on etiology (and pathogenesis). (See Lettieri on "Substance Abuse Etiology" in the 1989 American Psychiatric Association multi-volume work, *Treatment of Psychiatric Disorders*; see also N.S. Miller, 1995 who devotes an entire section of his book, *Addiction Psychiatry*, on the topic of etiology.) Maxman and Ward state: "In general, etiology refers to the *origins* of a disorder, whereas *pathogenesis* refers to all *the mechanisms* that ultimately produce it" (p. 57). These same authors add: "In this chapter, the term *etiology* encompasses pathogenesis and includes everything that has caused the patient's presenting difficulties" (p. 57).

Implicit in this definition is the idea that both etiology and pathogenesis may be equated with causation. We adopt this notion and view of etiology and pathogenesis in terms of causation, referring to the former as the *cause* and the latter as the *course*. Using this terminology, the main question of this chapter might be rephrased simply as: *Is there a common psychological cause that helps to account for the typical course of addiction?*

Let us now preview the remaining section of the chapter. First, we present our self-psychological view on the cause and course of addiction.

We focus specifically on the breakdown and miscarriage of the narcissistic exchange process. We contend that the derailment of this process serves as a developmental context for understanding and explaining how an archaic (that is, untransformed) fantasy of megalomaniac control over the forces of human nature, and hence psychic reality, causes addiction to take its particular pathogenic course.

In particular, we focus on the megalomaniacal process we call *addictivization* (in contrast to sexualization) as critical in accounting for the cause and course of addiction. Many classical as well as self-psychological analysts (for example, Goldberg, 1995; see also Goldberg, 2000) attempt to explain addiction on the basis of sexualization. In contrast, we understand this narcissistic behavior disorder on the basis of the addictivization of things and activities.

We define addictivization as follows: commonplace entities and agents are imbued unconsciously by a child with phantasmagorical powers, thus engendering them in a child's imagination with the status of magical elixirs, potions, or acts. In other words, addictivization involves an unconscious process whereby a child endows ordinary things and activities with extraordinary powers. They assume for a child the form of *manna* from heaven and, as such, a child imagines them as being supernatural.

In defining addictivization, we describe the narcissistic exchange process as leading from use to abuse through misuse. In essence, we view addiction [as rooted etiologically in a megalomaniac process in which a *subversion* (*rather than perversion*) occurs.] The normal transitional selfobject functioning of childhood things and activities is subverted so that they devolve, later in life, into ersatz selfobjects, which then serve as ATMs.

In the second and next part of this chapter, we conduct a selective and critical review of literature directly relevant to our self-psychological view of the origins and course of addiction. We begin with Freud and continue with Glover as well as others who explored the etiology and pathogenesis of fetishism and perversion in relation to addiction. We conclude with [Wurmser, who is representative of the modern view of addiction as stemming from a narcissistic disorder.]

An important methodological point concerns the quantity and quality of the data that are used to arrive at conclusions regarding the origins and course of addiction. In support of our position, we point to our six previously published, and now entirely revised and updated, psychoanalytical psychotherapy case histories, as well as the main author's earlier work on adolescent and adult marijuana abuse (see Hendin et al., 1981, 1987), all of which constitute a significant body of data gathered psychoanalytically from addicts who vary in age and type.

We see from our self-psychological vantage point that the central methodological and evidential issues involve our ability to establish the fantasy-based origins and unfolding of addiction. From this perspective, fantasy neither *causes* addiction nor is it the *consequence* of addiction; rather it is a *basis* for addiction in terms of its origins and its unfolding.

Obviously, one of the best and major means of illuminating such fantasies is by reconstructing the childhood world of patients who are currently in psychoanalytical psychotherapy. Such patients need not be limited to adults; in fact, they may include adolescents and children. And, as the basis for our study we conducted psychoanalytical psychotherapy with adults as well as adolescents and children. Thus, we collected psychoanalytic data from a population of research subjects ranging in age from young children through adolescents to adults.

The collection of this retrospective data is based on what Chein et al. (1964) refer to as "imaginative reconstruction" (p. 252). By means of imaginative reconstruction, or what Margulies (1989) characterizes as "empathic imagination," we have gained empathic access to a patient's unconscious fantasy life. Having made contact with the phantasmagorical realm of experience, a therapist is then in a legitimate position to hypothesize about the etiological origins and pathogenic course of disorders such as addiction.

In support of our position, Pearson and Little (1969) stress:

> No matter what chemical reaction the external agent may induce, *it is knowledge of how its use affects the fantasy life of the addict that is the essential criterion in determining whether or not a state of addiction exists.* (p. 1171, emphasis added)

Beres and Arlow (1974) argue that it is possible by using "analytic empathy...to reconstruct the nature of...fantasy" (p. 29). According to these authors, the psychoanalytic reconstruction of unconscious fantasy, which originates in early childhood and yet is still potentially active later in life (that is, as a "screen phantasy"), allows for the "instant communication of an unconscious fantasy shared in common between therapist and patient" (p. 36). The sharing in the present of fantasy between patient and psychoanalyst may constitute a psychoanalytic reproduction of fantasy as it was originally shared in the past between child and parent. And, more specifically, the sharing of fantasy between patient and psychotherapist constitutes a legitimate means for reconstructing the fantasies of the past as they may serve as the basis for the cause and course of addiction.

We can point to a number of evidentiary sources in support of our methodological position. For instance, there are our original and now entirely revised and updated psychoanalytic psychotherapy studies. There is also the previously published work of the main author on both adolescent and adult chronic marijuana abusers (see Hendin et al., 1981, 1987). These studies, especially the one involving adolescent marijuana abusers, are particularly germane to the issue of the fantasy basis of the cause and course of addiction. The latter study (Hendin et al., 1987) is especially supportive of a number of our current assumptions regarding both of these matters.

Ulman and coworkers find evidence of an underlying narcissistic disturbance in adolescent marijuana abusers that is significant from an etiological perspective in the pathogenesis of drug abuse. These psychoanalytic investigators discovered that marijuana serves for certain youngsters as a "*modifier of disturbing emotions* such as anger, as a *reenforcer of fantasies* of effortless, grandiose success" (p. 104, emphasis added). They point out:

> Fantasies of being destined for a special fate, to become rich, and to excel at a sport they scarcely played were typical of the parody of success, achievement, and confidence marijuana sustained in some of the young men. (p. 104)

Similarly, these researchers realize that the

> young female marijuana abusers, while not usually expecting particular greatness, nevertheless maintained a magical belief that good things would happen to them: college acceptance while flunking out of high school or happiness in love while dating unexpressive or abusive young men. (p. 104)

These authors conclude: "For all these adolescents marijuana helped sustain in an unrealistic way and with self destructive effects, the desire for power, control, achievement, and emotional fullness" (p. 104).

In addition, and perhaps most significantly from a methodological point of view, we refer in support of our position to our case of "Megworth" (or "Meggy"). This case of a child with preaddictive tendencies adds further to the evidential weight of our clinical database.

Having a child in psychotherapy from the age of 4½ to 6 (that is, a child who begins psychotherapy as a toddler) gives us a distinct methodological advantage. It allows us to base our conclusions, in part, about the cause and course of addiction on data about early history gathered directly from a youngster (as opposed to genetic data obtained retrospectively from adults or adolescents). The addition of data derived from the psychotherapy case of Meggy significantly strengthens our methodological position.

In the fourth and final section of this chapter, we present the psychotherapy case history of Meggy in support of our self-psychological view of the cause and course of addiction. We introduce the case with a discussion of psychoanalytic literature on cartoons, comic books, and fairy tales as mediums for expressing and representing certain childhood fantasies of a narcissistic nature. This literature serves as a theoretical backdrop for our extended self-psychological analysis of a classic Walt Disney cartoon as a means of illustrating particular themes relevant to the case of Meggy. In addition, we refer to the case of "Paul," as presented by Bettelheim in his book *Truants from Life* (1955). This case further illustrates the normal pattern of childhood megalomania gone awry.

A SELF-PSYCHOLOGICAL VIEW OF THE ORIGINS AND COURSE OF ADDICTION

The megalomaniacal process of addictivization is crucial to our self-psychological view of the origins and course of addiction. Addictivization is a signal of the breakdown and miscarriage of the normal developmental sequence constituted by the narcissistic exchange process. In normal development, this process unfolds as follows.

A child and, more specifically, a toddler, invests nonhuman things and activities (that is, transitional selfobjects) to such a narcissistic degree that they take over, partially and temporarily, the human selfobject functions originally provided by parents or other caregivers. These transitional selfobject things and activities serve for a toddler as necessary intermediaries or conduits between the human and nonhuman worlds (see Abrams and Neubauer, 1976). In other words, these entities and agents help a toddler to traverse successfully the sometimes psychologically daunting chasm that separates the domains of the human from that of the nonhuman.

As transitional selfobjects, these things and activities are endowed unconsciously by a toddler with such a phantasmagorical aura that they take on a magical quality. A child imagines them as a hybrid combination of the human and the nonhuman, that is, as semi-human. We refer to this unconscious fantasy activity as animation; we connect it with the process of animism previously described by Freud, Ferenczi, Abraham, and Piaget.

We also believe that the unconscious process of animation finds expression on a cultural and creative level in the form of comic books, cartoons, and fairy tales. In all of these mediums, nonhuman things and creatures are endowed through animation with human qualities as part of being brought to life as if by magic. Animism makes it possible for human beings to use fantasy and imagination as a means of bringing to life the inanimate and nonhuman world constituted by things, activities, and creatures. This is a normal and healthy reflection of a phase-appropriate, megalomaniac fantasy of magical control.

The capacity on the part of a person to animate the inanimate significantly enriches one's relationship to the nonhuman world. It makes it possible for an individual to use things and activities from this nonhuman realm *as if* they were extensions of the self. A person incorporates them unconsciously into the realm of self-experience. Once within this realm, an individual experiences them as part of the self.

We return to the topic of animation in our analysis of Disney's "The Sorcerer's Apprentice." For the moment, suffice it to say that a toddler, who cannot animate and bring to life by the magic of imagination an otherwise inanimate realm of things and activities, may suffer a serious developmental arrest. Such an arrest interferes with the capacity for creative imagination and the related use of things and activities as transitional selfobjects.

In contrast, a child may be compelled to escape from an unempathic or antipathic milieu into a make-believe world. This kind of refuge for such a child is at the expense of developing a healthy connection to real people and events. As a result, such a child is predisposed and prone to misuse rather than use things and activities.

This predisposition may, and often does, lead to outright abuse and addiction during adolescence and young adulthood. Psychoanalysts from a variety of theoretical orientations, including the new school of relational psychology, have begun to discuss the issue of *use* in general. However, they do address the topic of misuse, and subsequent abuse, as a basis for addiction (see, for example, Bromberg,

1995; Coen, 1992; Eigen, 1989, [1981], 2004 [1981], [1991]; McCarthy, 2000; Muensterberger, 1994; Newman, 1984, 1998, 1999; Pines, 1993; Searles, 1960; Slochower, 1994; Sugarman & Kurash, 1981; Winnicott, 1969, 1971 [1969]).

The third phase of the narcissistic exchange process ushers in a new leap forward in a child's capacity for the healthy use of things and activities as transitional selfobjects. The older and latency-aged child looks again to human beings as selfobjects. A youngster expects such human selfobjects to perform some, albeit not all, of the narcissistic functions previously provided by semi-human and transitional selfobject things and activities. Even though a child reinvests human beings with a capacity to function once again as selfobjects, this does not preclude the continued and healthy use of things and activities as transitional and nonhuman (or semi-human) selfobjects.

In fact, we insist that later in life the ability on the part of a person to use (rather than misuse or abuse) things and activities is a significant developmental milestone. It signifies the developmental transformation of a fantasy of being a megalomaniacal self and as wielding magical control. We describe such an achievement as that of the capacity for mastery. (See Furman, 1988, for a psychoanalytic study of the development of the capacity of mastery in early childhood.)

From a developmental perspective, it is crucial for a child to achieve mastery over the nonhuman world of transitional selfobject things and activities. It is necessary for a child to establish and maintain a capacity to manage his or her emotions and emotional affairs. From our self-psychological perspective, the third phase of the narcissistic exchange process completes the developmental transformation of fantasies of being a megalomaniacal self and as endowed with magical control over the emotional forces and psychological laws of (human) nature. A person who completes this process has mastery of particular skills and an ability to be the master of one's own emotional world.

This crucial developmental transformation occurs in an intersubjective context. Parents serve for a child as human selfobjects who are empathic to real abilities and promote the development of these skills. Parental empathy with a child's creative potential facilitates the realization of these talents. In contrast, parents may have unconscious fantasies that a particular child possesses imaginary means of control, and, as a result, they foster similar illusions in their child.

The lack of parental empathy seriously interferes with a child's successful completion of the third phase of the narcissistic exchange process. An empathic failure on the part of parents or caregivers at this phase is characterized by a developmental arrest in a child's capacity for transitional selfobject usage. Such a developmental arrest may express itself (symptomatically or characterologically) later in life as a particular psychopathological proclivity. There is a tendency on the part of an individual to abuse things or activities as ersatz selfobjects, or ATMs, at the expense of the healthy use of transitional selfobject.

The entire narcissistic exchange process takes place, we believe, in a specific developmental context determined by the interaction between toddler or child and the environmental milieu. We contend that Kohut (1978d [1972]) has such a context in mind when he uses phrases like an "archaic perception of reality" (p. 643), a "*narcissistically perceived reality*" (p. 644), and "archaic environment" (p. 645), a "narcissistic or prenarcissistic view of the world" (p. 645), an "archaic psychological world" (p. 646), and a "narcissistic universe" (p. 651).

We assert that this narcissistic universe is based unconsciously on fantasies of being a megalomaniacal self and as wielding magical control over everyone and everything. Indeed, Kohut (1978d [1972]) alludes to such fantasies in his reference to the "absolute control over an archaic environment" (p. 645).

We conjecture that Kohut has in mind ideas similar to our notions about fantasies of being a megalomaniacal self in regard to control over things and activities (that is, nonhuman selfobjects). Originally, Kohut (1978d [1972]) refers to a "narcissistic matrix" (p. 652) or the "[m]atrix of archaic narcissism" (p. 655). Subsequently, he (Kohut, 1977b) refers variously to the "child's experience of the relation between the self and the selfobject" (p. 80), "[s]elf/selfobject relations" (p. 83), the "life-sustaining matrix of the empathic responsiveness of the selfobject" (p. 123), and the "changing parental selfobject matrix" (p. 277).

We construe this narcissistic matrix, or self–selfobject matrix, primarily in terms of specific archaic narcissistic fantasies. We suggest that such a matrix is best described as consisting of fantasies of self in relation to or as regards the usage of a selfobject. This is a *narcissistic fantasy matrix*. We are concerned with the effect of this matrix on the cause and course of addiction and, more specifically, with the emergence, unfolding, and gradual transformation of fantasies of being a megalomaniacal self and as possessing magical control. (See Ogden, 1990, pp. 179–81 for an object relations and Winnicottian conception of a similar psychological matrix.)

Within the developmental context of this narcissistic fantasy matrix, a toddler, and later an older child, imagines himself or herself as a master or cosmic ruler of a narcissistic universe. A child who exists experientially in an illusory world as an imaginary potentate entertains unconscious fantasies about possessing a magical control over the environment. A child imagines that it is possible as part of such fantasies to dramatically alter the basic laws of nature, including those governing the normal functioning of the animate and inanimate as well as the human and nonhuman.

Such a fantasy of being a megalomaniacal self fuels a child's belief that it is possible to animate and bring to life the inanimate or nonhuman as semi-human creatures. Things and activities serve for a toddler in this capacity as transitional selfobjects. A child endows them with the capacity to significantly enhance the functioning of the self, and hence to build psychic structure.

In addition, and again as part of a megalomaniacal fantasy, a toddler imagines the domain of the human, including self and selfobject, as possessing mechanical qualities typically associated with nonhuman things and activities. Thus, a child reverses the process of animation, in which the nonhuman is brought to life, and mechanizes the human. We believe that the process of mechanization involves a child fantasizing about the self and caregivers *as if* they were mere contraptions. As such, they function in a child's imagination as extensions or nonhuman parts of the self. In the throes of such a megalomaniacal fantasy, we speculate that a child engages in an unconscious process of phantasmagorical transmogrification whereby human beings are imagined by a child as automatons, humanoids, and/or androids.

As regards megalomania, there is an important intersubjective aspect to the unconscious organization of the narcissistic fantasy matrix of self and selfobject. Ideally, parents and caregivers are empathic to a child's phase-appropriate and megalomaniacal fantasies of being master of the universe or ruler of the cosmos. They allow a toddler to entertain and enjoy a fantasy of magical control over everyone and everything in the immediate surround (that is, the selfobject milieu).

Adult caregivers will also empathize with a child's fantasy of having creatively blended and mixed the human with the nonhuman as well as the animate with the inanimate. They will marvel at and respond empathically to a child's imaginary creations in the form of semi-human creatures. Parents and/or caregivers will delight, therefore, and share with a child in an imaginary world in which the inanimate is animated and the animated is mechanized.

However, conditions for a particular toddler may be, unfortunately, far from ideal. In other words, either a parent fails to empathize and participate in a toddler's megalomaniacal fantasies; or, conversely, a parent overidentifies with and overindulges in these fanciful illusions. Such failures of parental empathy may lead to a developmental arrest at the stage of transitional selfobject usage. We contend that such an arrest in development is, later in life, a crucial etiological basis for some individuals for the pathogenesis of addictions.

We find support for our self-psychological position regarding megalomania and addiction in the work of Blos, a classical psychoanalyst well known for his studies of adolescence. Blos (1963) notes that certain adolescents "will tell you that their fantasies are more real than anything in the outer world" (p. 121). He adds: "They accept, consequently, the outer world only as far as it gives credence to their inner reality; they attach it or they turn away from it as soon as the need gratification it offers ceases to be in immediate and perfect harmony with the need tension they experience" (p. 121). Blos stresses: "This condition is typical of the adolescent user of drugs" (p. 121).

In illuminating the archaically narcissistic nature of this "condition," Blos points out: "In this constellation, then action assumes the quality of *magical gesture* ... it offers a *delusional control over reality*" (pp. 125–26, emphasis added). Furthermore, Blos suggests that this "tendency in conjunction with a narcissistic isolation compounds the well-known *megalomaniacal trend* of the adolescent who uses the external world for his aggrandizement in the same way as the child used the parent for the gratification of his narcissistic needs" (p. 126, emphasis added).

Blos concludes: "In both cases, a supply of inexhaustible riches—*even if only imagined, namely, wished for*—seems to be outside; all that remains to be done is to keep the flow of these *narcissistic supplies steadily flowing toward the self* (p. 126, emphasis added).

In line with Blos, we conceive of addiction as rooted etiologically in a developmental arrest in the phase-appropriate unfolding of a fantasy of being a megalomaniacal self and as empowered with magical control over the laws governing the nature of physical and psychic reality. On the basis of such a fantasy, a youngster imagines the external world—including all the people, things, and activities constituting such a universe—as a private preserve of boundless and limitless "narcissistic supplies flowing toward the self."

From our perspective, there is another problem relevant to the cause and course of addiction. It concerns the mistreatment and misuse by parents or caregivers of a child as a nonhuman thing or as part of an inanimate activity. This problem occurs if parents or caregivers are themselves still organized unconsciously in accordance with their own megalomaniacal fantasies.

In such an instance, an adult caregiver imagines and experiences a child as if he or she is nonhuman or inanimate. An adult turns a child into a mechanical thing or activity. In so doing, a parent interferes or deprives a child of the necessary yet megalomaniacal experience of magical control. Moreover, a parent fosters in a child an unhealthy need and drive to experience, later in life, the self as exercising magical control of the selfobject milieu. We are suggesting, therefore, that such antipathy on the part of a parent fosters in a child a proclivity to perceive and experience the world as a "narcissistic universe."

The psychopathological process of addictivization expresses itself in a developmental arrest characterized by a failure to sufficiently transform a fantasy of being a megalomaniacal self, which, in turn, interferes with the narcissistic exchange process. A child who is prone to addiction later in life maintains an unhealthy over-investment in the narcissistic functioning of things and activities. Such a child fails to re-invest other human beings with a healthy capacity to function narcissistically as mature selfobjects.

We envision such a child as becoming involved in the addictivization of otherwise normal things and healthy activities. Instead of using things and activities in an adaptive fashion, such a toddler misuses them on the basis of an abnormal dependence on their narcissistic functioning. A child may be said in such cases to be in a preaddictive state of mind. These are the early warning signs of the emergence, later in life, of an addictive character.

Based on addictivization, a child begins to manifest an unnatural over-attachment to odd things and peculiar activities. It seems as if a child's very psychological well-being depends on the idiosyncratic functioning of these now magically endowed entities and agents.

In the course of life, addictivization expresses itself in an unconscious process of *acting-in*. The traditional psychoanalytic explanation of addiction relies on the concept of acting out. From our self-psychological perspective, the problem with this explanation is that it implies that there is an unconscious acting out of drive-based fantasies of sex and aggression.

We conceive of addiction differently. We construe it as the unconscious acting-in of a fantasy with powerful psychoactive effects. The value of our conceptualization is that it provides an explanation of addiction stressing the primacy of the self rather than drives. It also adopts an empathic stance in viewing addiction as an addict's attempt, however faulty and dysfunctional, to use the world of things and objects as a selfobject, even if such use really amounts to nothing more than abuse.

Things and activities in the environment serve for an addict as ersatz selfobjects. In this capacity, they engender fantasies of mirrored grandiosity, idealized omnipotence, alter ego twinship, and magical control. These phantasmagorical experiences provide psychoactive relief for an addict.

Such relief may appear in some form of an antidepressant stimulation, antianxiety tranquilization and sedation, anti-shame humanization, antiaggressive pacification, or antipanic organization. An addict as a control freak and fantasy junkie abuses things and activities from the environment in the unconscious process of transporting himself or herself to an imaginary, inner world. It is in this sense that we speak of addiction as a form of unconscious acting-in.

Thus transported to a surreal world, an addict acts as a modern-day alchemist. An addict fantasizes himself or herself as endowed with the powers of magical control equivalent to that of an alchemist. An addict imagines possessing a miraculous power whereby it is possible to turn ordinary things and activities into wondrous elixirs and potions as well as being able to perform magic tricks and feats. Of course, all these unconscious illusions are expressions of a fantasy of being a megalomaniacal self and being capable of controlling the emotional forces of one's life.

A child passes through and completes the second phase of the narcissistic exchange process successfully when the fantasy of megalomaniacal self unfolds normally and develops naturally. Traversing the stage of transitional selfobject usage is crucial to developing mastery in the form of a capacity to manage (rather than control) one's emotions and emotional affairs. A child who fails to get to this stage becomes absorbed psychopathologically by fantasies of being a megalomaniacal self and as endowed with magical control over the forces of nature, especially those of human nature.

In contrast, a youngster who succeeds in completing this stage of development can temper and modulate megalomaniacal illusions. This tempering and modulation occurs as a child learns how to use a wide variety of things and range of activities for healthy narcissistic purposes. A youngster develops real talents and skills by mastering the use of these various transitional selfobjects. These capacities serve narcissistically as healthy replacements for a narcisstic illusion of magical control over an imaginary world of android things and humanoid activities with which to radically alter psychic reality.

Mastery requires of a child a capacity to tolerate the painful frustrations and disappointments that inevitably arise as part of a process of trial and error. A youngster who cannot tolerate the frustration of trial and error is less likely to develop a healthy capacity for mastery. Instead, such a youth is more likely to remain organized unconsciously in accordance with fantasies of being a megalomaniacal self possessing magical control.

However, such fantasies are by definition so archaic because they are especially fragile, vulnerable, and prone to easy disturbance. If a person experiences disruption of a narcissistically blissful fantasy of magical control, then he or she is overwhelmed by a painful and disorganizing sense of panic. These panicky feelings arise from narcissistically mortifying fantasies of being out of control or of having lost control.

We assert that the fantasy of being a megalomaniacal self and as empowered with magical control over a narcissistic universe is behind the so-called locus of control phenomenon, which is purported to be common to all forms of addiction. The fantasy of being a megalomaniacal self and as exercising magical control helps to account for a puzzling paradox of addiction: an addict has the illusion of control, whereas, in actuality, an addict is totally without any control.

In other words, an addict is a captive of a vicious cycle. The more an addict attempts to counteract an underlying panic over loss of control with illusions of absolute control, the more an addict is inevitably disillusioned and more panic-ridden. We are hypothesizing, therefore, that the pathogenesis of addiction is based on an important etiological connection between megalomania and panic. (See Miliora & Ulman, 1996b for a "bioself- psychological" analysis of panic and its correlation with addiction.)

REVIEW OF THE LITERATURE

We seek to achieve three interrelated objectives in our critical and selective review of a body of literature relevant to the issue of the origins and course of addiction. They are as follows: (1) to place our self-psychological view of the etiology and pathogenesis of addiction in a relevant historical context, thus providing a proper setting within which to appreciate our particular perspective; (2) to use our self-psy-chological viewpoint as a conceptual lens through which to view more clearly the work of others who attempt to explain the origins and course of psychopathology in general and addiction in particular; and, (3) to assess the work of others from our self-psychological vantage point as a means of contributing to the discussion of the etiology and patho-genesis of addiction. In essence, our literature review focuses on the fantasy-based nature of psychopathology as a general phenomenon, and specifically on addiction as a particular type of fantasy-based disorder.

The importance of unconscious fantasy to a psychoanalytic under-standing of etiology and pathogenesis can be dated back to Freud and his early writings. Of particular relevance are his works dealing with the classic neurotic disorders such as hysteria, obsession, phobia, and psychopathy. In a series of papers spanning from the mid-1890s to the early 1900s, Freud (1953 [1906], 1955 [1893–1895], 1955 [1909a,b], 1959 [1908a,b]) seeks to establish the etiological and pathogenic significance of unconscious fantasy for neurotic symptom-formation.

Freud, for example, in his 1906 paper, "My Views on the Part Played by Sexuality in the Aetiology of the Neuroses," connects "phantasies" (p. 274) with hysterical symptoms. He states that the former "were transformed directly" (p. 274) into the latter. He adds: "It was only after the introduction of this element of *hysterical phantasies* that the texture of the neurosis and its relation to the patient's life became intelligible" (p. 274, emphasis added).

Freud explains that the "most complicated symptoms are themselves revealed as representing, by means of 'conversion,' phantasies which have a sexual situation as their subject-matter" (p. 278). However, in his 1908b paper, "Creative Writers and Day-dreaming," Freud refers to another major category of fantasy in contrast to those whose "sub-ject-matter" is sexual. In particular, he mentions a type of fantasy he describes as "ambitious wishes...which serve to elevate the subject's personality" (p. 147, emphasis added).

In line with Kohut's early work on fantasy (see Ulman & Brothers, 1988, for a detailed discussion of this topic), we elaborate on Freud's original notion of "ambitious wishes." We describe these ambitious wishes as archaic narcissistic fantasies of the self *in relation to* or *in use of* the selfobject (both human and nonhuman).

Furthermore, we argue that a crucial parallel exists in the patho-genesis of addictive disorders and that of psychosexual fantasies in the pathogenesis of neurotic disorders. From an etiological perspective, the former entail ambitious wishes or megalomaniacal fantasies of magical control over the forces of (human) nature, and hence psychic reality. We refine Freud's (1959 [1908a]) original notion of an unconscious fantasy revolving around "ambitious wishes" (p. 147). We base our study of addiction on this refinement and offer it as a self-psychological contribution to the psychoanalytic literature on addiction.

Freud (1959 [1908a]) believes that the immaturity, unreality, and the archaic nature of fantasy (rather than fantasy itself) are crucial to neurotic and psychotic symptom-formation and psychopathology in general. For instance, he notes:

> If phantasies become over-luxuriant and over-powerful, the conditions are laid for an onset of neurosis or psychoses. *Phantasies, moreover, are the immediate mental precursors of the distressing symptoms complained of by our patients.* Here a broad by-path branches off into pathology. (p. 148, emphasis added)

Freud leaves little doubt about the *causal significance* of "hysterical phantasies" in relation to psychogenic symptom-formation. In his 1959 [1908b] paper, "Hysterical Phantasies and their Relation to Bisexuality," he indicates that

> psychical structures are regularly present in all psycho-neuroses, particularly in hysteria, and that these latter—which are known as *hysterical phantasies—can be seen to have important connections with the causation of neurotic symptoms.* (p. 159, emphasis added)

Freud (1959 [1908b]) stresses:

> *Hysterical symptoms are nothing other than unconscious phantasies brought into view through "conversion"*; and insofar as the symptoms are somatic ones, they are often enough taken from the circle of the same sexual sensations and motor innervations as those which had originally accompanied the phantasy when it was still conscious. (p. 162, emphasis added)

He (Freud, 1959 [1908b]) continues:

> Anyone who studies hysteria, therefore, soon finds his interest turned away from its symptoms to the phantasies from which they proceed. The technique of psycho-analysis enables us in the first place to infer from the symptoms what those unconscious phantasies are and then to make them conscious to the patient. (p. 162)

Consistent with this assertion, Freud (1959 [1908b]) makes a distinction that is crucial for our purposes. He points out:

> We also know of cases—cases which have their practical importance as well—*in which hysterics do not give expression to their phantasies in the form of symptoms but as conscious realizations*, and in that way devise and stage assaults, attacks or acts of sexual aggression. (p. 162, emphasis added)

The "conscious realizations," about which Freud speaks, represent psychopathological alterations of conduct and behavior. Such transmogrifications are similar yet distinct from the symptomatic alterations of mind and body constituted by neurotic disorders such as hysteria, obsession, and phobia. These two types of psychogenic metamorphoses differ primarily as follows: the former expresses unconscious fantasy through the *medium of action*, whereas the latter represents unconscious fantasy through the *medium of thought*.

As we note, Freud (1961 [1928]) returns to this distinction in his 1927 paper on Dostoevsky's gambling addiction. In so doing, Freud provides a rudimentary basis for a fantasy-based theory of the cause and course of addiction. We assert that an important comparison may be drawn between Freud and Kohut. Freud makes a distinction between two types of fantasy-based psychopathology (that is, neurotic and instinctual) analogous to Kohut's distinction between narcissistic personality disorder and narcissistic behavior disorder of which addiction is one major subtype.

However, an important difference exists between hysterical phantasies, which are, according to Freud, converted into neurotic symptoms involving the mind and body, and those which are "acted out" as "conscious realizations." The latter are acted out, so to speak, in the arena of conduct and behavior. In this regard, these realms of experience are disturbed psychopathologically, therefore, to the degree to which they become a medium for acting out unconscious fantasies.

The unconscious mechanism of acting out has become the basis for the psychoanalytic understanding (and treatment) of addictions. In the area of the addictions, it has become the equivalent of conversion in the area of neurotic disorders. From our perspective, however, it is misleading to employ the unconscious mechanism or phenomenon of acting out as the basis for explaining addiction. The adoption of this concept to explain addiction entails a view of this disorder as a discharge phenomenon or a "disintegration product" (Kohut, 1977b, p. 121).

We prefer a self-psychological view of addiction. We see addiction from such a perspective as a desperate yet faulty attempt on the part of an addict to maintain or restore some semblance of a cohesive sense of self. From our vantage point, addiction involves neither acting out nor conversion; rather, it entails induction and acting in.

In addiction, various things and activities serve as ATMs. As such, they are abused behaviorally and physiologically by an addict as part of inducing a powerful, psychoactive fantasy. An addict experiences a subjective alteration of mind and mood as part of such an artificially induced and fantasy-based state of consciousness.

Thus, we prefer to view the act of using (or abusing) things and activities, which possess for an addict an innate or acquired psychoactive power, as the means by which a fantasy achieves unconscious expression. We distinguish this perspective as distinct from that according to which the behavior or action is viewed as the symbolic expression of the fantasy. The thing and activity are, in our opinion, less important than the fantasy.

In his early 1900' papers on etiology and pathogenesis (Freud, 1953 [1905], [1906], 1955 [1893–1895], 1962 [1896a,b], [1898]) lays the groundwork for a fantasy-based theory of the cause and course of addiction. He establishes this foundation by distinguishing between two distinct yet interrelated types of fantasy-based psychopathology. In the first type (that is, neurosis), fantasy manifests itself in a symptomatic alteration of normal mental and physical functioning. Whereas, in the second type (that is, instinctual), fantasy expresses itself in a symptomatic alteration of normal action and behavior.

Freud (1959 [1908b]) suggests that the second and latter type of psychopathology is based on the model of infantile masturbation. He describes the "masturbatory act" as consisting of "two parts" (p. 161). He indicates: "One was the evocation of a phantasy and the other some active behavior for obtaining self-gratification at the height of the phantasy" (p. 161).

Freud concludes that the "assaults, attacks or acts of sexual aggression," which he later refers to as examples of the second type of fantasy-based psychopathology, are nothing other than masturbatory equivalents. According to Freud, these psychopathological actions are equivalent to masturbation for the following reason: they involve the unconscious translation or conversion of childhood masturbatory fantasies into a symptomatic alteration of adult behavior.

Freud returns to this formulation in his analysis of Dostoevsky's gambling addiction. In this context, he hints at what we construe as a description of an addictive type of character. (We return to this topic in Chapter 9 in our discussion of an addiction typology.) Freud (1961 [1928]) describes Dostoevsky as an "instinctual character" (p. 179), whose major problem revolves around his addiction to gambling. We feel it is justified to compare Freud's notion of the "instinctual character" to our concept of an addictive character.

We believe that Freud's (1961 [1928]) idea of an instinctual (or addictive) character is consistent with and follows from his earlier thoughts on character typology. The earlier character types include the hysterical, obsessed, phobic, and psychopathic. Freud never fully develops nor elaborates his ideas on the instinctual (or addictive) character type. Nonetheless, we contend that it can be included legitimately in Freud's overall typology of character psychopathology.

We add an addictive character to Freud's character typology. However, we must distinguish it from some of Freud's other types of character psychopathology. It is unlike the hysterical, obsessed, and phobic, all of which involve a psychopathological alteration of mentation. It is similar to the psychopathic character in entailing a psychopathological modification of action and behavior. In line with Freud's own distinction, we argue that unconscious mental content such as fantasy may intrude into the realm of action and behavior as well as thought (and affect). (See Krueger, 2002, on what he terms "action symptoms" for a distinction which is similar to that of Freud.)

Freud alludes to Dostoevsky's addiction to gambling as a "mania for gambling" (p. 190). In this sense, he links it etiologically to our conception of addiction as megalomaniacal in nature. Freud roots Dostoevsky's gambling addiction in infantile masturbation. Viewing it as a masturbatory equivalent, Freud observes: "The 'vice' of masturbation is replaced by the addiction to gambling; and the emphasis laid upon the passionate activity of the hands betrays this derivation" (p. 193).

Furthermore, Freud concludes:

> If the addiction to gambling, with the unsuccessful struggles to break the habit and the opportunities it affords for self-punishment, is a repetition of the compulsion to masturbate, we shall not be surprised to find that it occupied such a large space in Dostoevsky's life. (p. 194)

This observation by Freud ought to be interpreted, we insist, in light of his previously quoted passages on the fantasy-based nature of masturbation. Interpreting the passage in this context leads, we speculate, to a view of Dostoevsky's gambling addiction as similarly based on fantasy. It appears that Freud conjectures that Dostoevsky gambles addictively as part of an "active behavior" by means of which he evokes an intensely pleasurable fantasy. From an etiological perspective, Freud roots the addiction in a pathogenic fantasy complex, which is organized unconsciously on the basis of infantile sexuality.

Our perspective on all addiction is based in part on Freud's implicit view of Dostoevsky's gambling addiction as fantasy-based. However, unlike Freud, we do not root addictions etiologically in pathogenic (erotic) fantasies. Instead, we locate the etiological origins of addictions in a pathological arrest in the developmental transformation of "ambitious wishes," or archaic (narcissistic) fantasies. From our self-psychological perspective, we consider that fantasies of being a megalomaniacal self that are carried over from childhood into adulthood are a critical unconscious determinant in a pathological course leading to addiction.

Before leaving Freud's thoughts on the nature of (hysterical) fantasies and their etiological relation to neurotic pathogenesis, we must emphasize that he envisions fantasy to be bipolar and dialectical in nature. For instance, he (Freud, 1908b) indicates that

> There are many symptoms where the uncovering of a sexual phantasy (or of a number of phantasies, one of which, the most significant and the earliest, is of sexual nature) is not enough to bring about a resolution of the symptoms. (p. 164)

In order to achieve such resolution, Freud (1959 [1908b]) insists that it is necessary to uncover and analyze "*two* sexual phantasies, of which one has a masculine and the other a feminine character" (p. 164). Freud contends that "one of these phantasies springs from a homosexual impulse" (p. 164). He concludes: "It remains true that a hysterical symptom must necessarily represent a compromise between a libidinal and a repressive impulse; *but it may also represent a union* of two libidinal phantasies of an opposite sexual character" (p. 165, emphasis added).

We submit that Freud is referring in this latter passage to a non-conflict-based view of symptom-formation and pathogenesis. Such a view of etiology and pathogenesis rests on the blending, molding, or "union" of two opposing fantasies. It is not based on the conflict-based clash between two opposing fantasies. We incorporate this Freudian idea into our thinking about the psychodynamic nature of fantasy, that is, its dialectical bipolarity.

From this perspective, we view an addict as flip-flopping unconsciously from a fantasy of narcissistic mortification to a fantasy of narcissistic bliss. Because of the underlying instability of the latter fantasy of narcissistic bliss, an addict is trapped in the nonstop process of fantasy flip-flopping. In contrast to a more traditional and classical psychoanalytic stance, our self-psychological position posits that narcissistic equilibrium and disequilibrium are more important to psychic life than are drive conflict and compromise.

In this regard, we create a self-psychological alternative to a classical psychoanalytic approach. We base such an alternative on our conceptualization of the dialectical bipolarity of archaic narcissistic fantasy. The classical psychoanalytic approach seeks to explain all symptom-formation and psychopathology, including addiction, in terms of a model of psychic conflict.

In contrast, we explain the origins and course of addiction on the basis of a model of psychic deficit. Our deficit model rests on a psychological imperative: namely, that all individuals operate psychologically to establish, maintain, and restore some semblance of narcissistic equilibrium—no matter how unstable and fleeting.

A number of psychoanalysts pursue Freud's preliminary thoughts on the role of fantasy in the etiology and pathogenesis of addiction. Foremost among this group is Edward Glover, the highly regarded British ego psychologist. In the late 1920s and early 1930s, Glover wrote a series of articles on the origins and course of both alcoholism and drug addiction. He also addresses the issue of the interrelationship between addiction and perversion.

In all of his papers, Glover emphasizes the degree to which fantasy is psychically determinative of the psychopathological course taken by both addiction and perversion. For example, in his 1928 article on the etiology of alcoholism, Glover observes: "There is one subjective factor which hinders adequate appreciation of the extent of *phantasy activity* (1956 [1928], p. 83, emphasis added). He continues: "The investigator is apt to describe much of the *drunkard's phantasy life* by calling him an 'inveterate liar'" (p. 83, emphasis added).

Glover insists that the so-called "drunkard's" behavior, including those psychotic-like symptoms such as "alcoholic hallucinosis or delirium tremors" (p. 83) as well as others like "[l]ying, romancing, boasting, obscene wit, illusion, confabulation, hallucination, and delusion, *all are results of overcharged phantasy*" (p. 83, emphasis added). As a result, Glover asserts that, "we must inquire to what extent the *alcoholic's*

overcharge of phantasy life leads to actual gratification in real life
emphasis added).

However, Glover cautions: "But it is not enough to sa   ..at
withdrawal from reality increases or activates phantasy; *it activates
phantasy corresponding to definite layers of psychic development* (p. 83,
emphasis added). And, the layer of "psychic development" that Glover
identifies as crucial to understanding alcoholism is particularly significant to our self-psychological point of view. Glover indicates: "So
between *narcissistic fixation* anxiety and regression, *the ego of the
alcoholic is overcharged with narcissistic libido*" (p. 87, emphasis
added). He adds: "Relations with objects are of course established, *but
the ego hardly dares love anyone who cannot be identified with the self*"
(p. 87, emphasis added).

In the above quoted passages, we believe that Glover hints at the
following idea: the origins and course of alcoholism and, by implication,
other addictions, are based on a developmental arrest at the stage of
archaic narcissism. Such archaic forms of narcissism consist of particular
fantasies. These (unconscious) fantasies involve an imaginary relationship between the "self" and others experienced, however, not as genuine
"objects," but rather as parts or extensions of the self. Glover considers
as "part-objects" what we construe to be selfobjects. And, in the case
of addiction, selfobjects are nonhuman or transitional selfobjects. Moreover, the latter have devolved over time into ATMs.

In Glover's 1932 paper on the etiology of drug addiction there is
further evidence of his emphasis on the importance of narcissism to
understanding addiction. Glover remarks:

> Acceptance of an early polymorphous ego-organization involves some
> recasting of existing rigid descriptive views of narcissism; or at least
> some distinction of the problem of narcissistic *energies* from (a) the
> problem of narcissistic topography, and (b) the clinical problems of
> narcissistic feeling or reaction. (p. 309)

In this passage, Glover hints at a radical notion, namely, that the
study of drug addiction necessitates a new and, for that period, sweeping
revision of the classical psychoanalytic view of narcissism. The psychoanalytic perspective prevalent at that time views narcissism as an early
stage in psychosexual or libidinal development. However, it may become
under adverse circumstances a point of psychopathological fixation.

Implicit in this view is a conceptualization of narcissism based
purely in the energic terms of the libido theory. In contrast, Glover

seems to argue for a different view of narcissism. He appears to be suggesting that narcissism is structured topographically, or layered psychically, along specific and separate developmental lines.

Furthermore, Glover implies that the classical psychoanalytic view of narcissism is seriously limited. According to this perspective, narcissism is based solely on a psychopathological fixation to an early stage in the development of the libido. Glover advocates an expanded clinical vantage point whereby narcissism is conceptualized as consisting of very personal feelings and subjective reactions. We describe such subjectivity in terms of fantasies and moods of narcissistic bliss and/or mortification.

The thoughts on narcissism as advocated by Glover set the stage in various ways, therefore, for Kohut's later ideas. In particular, Glover anticipates Kohut's emphasis on a line of psychic development separate and distinct from that of libido. Although he did not spell it out specifically, Glover probably has in mind the idea that narcissism develops from archaic to mature forms.

From this perspective, which is compatible with self psychology, narcissism in an adult need not be deemed as by definition psychopathological. Rather, it may have undergone healthy transformation, or it may be in a state of developmental arrest. And, even in the latter case, it may still be possible for an archaic form of narcissism to undergo developmental (or psychotherapeutic) transformation, even in adulthood, and within the context of an empathic selfobject milieu.

Subsequently, and in the same 1932 article, Glover asserts: "The main difficulty is that, owing to the confused state of identifications of self and object, *what appears to be a pure object-restitution is condensed on a system of restitution of the self by the object*" (p. 233, emphasis added). Glover adds: "And the whole point about drug addiction is that it represents a phase of development when *primitive part-objects are introjected and absorb psychic energy*" (p. 325, emphasis added).

It is clear from these two statements that Glover focuses specifically on the "self," as distinct from the ego, as well as objects. In so doing, he comes to an important realization. In drug addiction, an addict attempts, according to Glover, to restitute or restore the self by using (abusing) an object (or part-object) rather than vice versa. And, Glover maintains that an addict's attempted self-restitution, regardless of how faulty or ultimately unsuccessful, occurs on the basis of an unconscious introjection and absorption of so-called part objects.

We interpret Glover as implying that addiction may be viewed as based on a narcissistic process of self-absorption. As part of this unconscious process, an addict's sense of self becomes psychopathologically dependent on the incorporation and utilization of part-objects rather than whole objects. These nonhuman part-objects include various addictive drugs and alcohol, all of which an addict treats (or mistreats) and abuses *as if* they were actually human and whole objects. Such treatment on the part of an addict endows these part-objects (in our terms, ATMs) with the capacity to function narcissistically as agents with which to attempt a restitution of the self.

The notion that part-objects play a central role in addiction constitutes a major contribution by Glover to our self-psychological position. On an implicit level, he understands addiction as involving an attempt by the addict to gain megalomaniacal control over the (internal and psychic) object world. As part of such fantasized control, a child (and, in some cases, later in life, an addict) imagines the part as the whole or the nonhuman as human. Moreover, in many important respects Glover's view of the part-object anticipates Kohut's concept of the selfobject. Both the part-object and the selfobject function narcissistically as necessary, albeit imaginary, extensions of the self.

The notion in Glover's writing of "part-objects" also adumbrates our own idea of nonhuman or transitional selfobject things and activities. Glover bases addiction etiologically on the use by an addict of part-objects. His thinking on this topic parallels our own.

Following Glover, we envision addiction as entailing a devolution of healthy transitional selfobject things and activities into psychopathological ATMs. The former are genuine selfobjects that provide developmentally necessary functions, whereas the latter are ersatz selfobjects that provide only psychoactive relief from dysphoria.

Finally, Glover, in his 1933 piece, "The Relation of Perversion-Formation to the Development of Reality-Sense," makes an important connection between the etiology and pathogenesis of perversion with that of addiction. Glover roots both disorders in the "'reality' systems of infants and children [which] are clearly *phantastic*" (p. 488, emphasis added). Moreover, according to Glover, such a phantasmagorical reality system is based in both the case of perversion and addiction on a form of "primitive narcissism" (p. 492).

Glover describes perversion in terms of what he calls a "narcissistic fetich" (p. 501). Such a fetish involves the use by a pervert of "primitive part-objects" (p. 500) rather than "complete objects" (p. 500). Glover explains:

> Indeed I have the impression that one of the most profitable ap-
> proaches to the study of reality-sense lies in the study of fetishism,
> including here *narcissistic fetiches* in which parts of the patient's own
> body or clothes provide sexual gratification. (p. 500, emphasis added)

Glover makes a clinical discovery of major significance regarding the narcissistic (rather than psychosexual) nature of perversion. He equates it both etiologically and pathogenically with addiction. He asserts that both perversion and addiction are narcissistic because they involve the use (or abuse) of part-objects (whether human or nonhuman) instead of whole objects.

Glover realizes that these two disorders are based, in essence, on a narcissistic illusion that the part equals the whole. In our terminology, such an illusion on the part of an addict entails the narcissistic fantasy of a thing or activity as the equivalent of a person. Both an addict and a pervert are unable to establish healthy relations with objects. Instead, they remain arrested developmentally at the stage of using the part as if it were the whole.

Glover indicates, moreover, that in the case of both an addict and a pervert a sense of self remains narcissistically precarious and fragile. Glover maintains that both addiction and perversion, therefore, involve a fundamental problem in the unconscious organization of the sense of self. The position that Glover adopts is quite distinct from that advocated by classical psychoanalysis. He regards addiction and perversion as involving a disturbance in the organization of psychosexuality or the instinctual drives. Thus, in his pioneering work on perversion, Glover helps to pave the way for our self-psychological view of addiction.

A number of other psychoanalysts advance Glover's thinking about narcissism in the etiology and pathogenesis of perversion, fetishism, and addiction. In particular, these psychoanalysts pay special attention to the role of what Glover calls "part-objects" in the origins and unfolding of these disorders. For the most part, however, these psychoanalysts equate Glover's notion of the part-object with Winnicott's later, yet related, concept of the transitional object.

This distinguished group of psychoanalytic investigators includes Stevenson, Greenacre, Katan, Sperling, Dickes, Kafka, Bak, Natterson, Benson, and McDougall. The attempt on the part of these investigators to root fetishism and addiction in a common etiology and pathogenesis has significance for our study that goes beyond merely historical. A careful examination of the literature on fetishism (see, for example, Bak, 1968, 1974; Benson, 1980; Dickes, 1963, 1978; Greenacre, 1955a, 1961, 1969, 1970; Kafka, 1969; Katan, 1960; McDougall, 1985; Natterson, 1976; Sperling, 1963; Stevenson, 1954) reveals, for our purposes, an important line of psychoanalytic thinking.

This line of thought proceeds from Glover's notion of the part-object through Winnicott's concept of the transitional object to Kohut's idea of the selfobject. (See M. Tolpin, 1971, who uses Kohut's notions of trans-muting internalization and a "transitional selfobject" [Kohut, 1971, p. 28] to distinguish a self-psychological position from that of Winnicott on the use by an infant of a nonhuman thing as part of psychic structure-building.)

For example, Benson (1980) is explicit in connecting Winnicott and Kohut as regards their respective and related ideas of the transitional object and the selfobject. Benson describes the former as "narcissistic guardians" (p. 258). He suggests that such things and activities serve important adaptive purposes as concerns psychological development. He notes that the "transitional object represents a selfobject in the transitional zone of experience and from the viewpoint of narcissistic development is instrumental in self-esteem regulation" (p. 258).

Others such as Adler (1985, 1989) and Cooper and Adler (1990) also argue for an integration of the concepts of the Winnicottian transitional object with the Kohutian selfobject. (See also Bacal & Newman, 1990, who argue for a broader and more thorough integration of object relations and self psychology.) Such a position is congruent with our idea of the transitional selfobject. Bacal and Newman (1990), M. Tolpin (1971), and Stolorow and Lachmann (1980) all allude to our notion of the transitional selfobject. Our concept of the transitional selfobject builds on Winnicott's as well as Kohut's thinking. (See Kohut, 1971, who refers to a "transitional selfobject.") More specifically, it reflects their thought on how nonhuman things and activities function for individuals as phantasmagorical extensions or parts of the self.

The psychoanalytic literature on fetishism brings into sharp focus the nature of a psychopathological disturbance, which involves an essentially fantasy-based attachment to and use of nonhuman things and activities. Greenacre (1969) observes that the

> fetishist has developed the capacity to form a strong visual picture of the fetish, or *more frequently a fantasy* in which the fetish plays an important part and which must be sustained firmly or in some way acted out in foreplay to serve in place of the concrete fetish. (p. 161, emphasis added)

In addition, Bak (1968) refers to a "primal fantasy" of the phallic woman, which he believes is critical to the emergence of fetishism.

Other psychoanalysts such as Bradlow (1973), Katan (1960), and Natterson (1976) make similar points. They suggest that a psychopathological disturbance of fantasy-based attachments to nonhuman things and activities also may be expressed in illusions of the self as inanimate or as a part of another person. Katan speaks about "pathological fantasies" in which a person has an unconscious experience of the self *as if* it is an anatomically functioning part of another person. Katan links such psychopathological fantasies to specific fetishisms.

Bradlow describes a fantasy of the self as nonhuman in which there is an unconscious "identification with an inanimate object" (p. 487). He indicates that such fantasies may be translated as follows: "This is really not being experienced (felt) by me, but by someone else. That other person is not human. I am; therefore I have nothing to be anxious about" (p. 488).

According to Bradlow, these fantasies cause a "split" in the ego expressed symptomatically in depersonalization. He even indicates that these fantasies of a "non-human self" are narcissistic in nature. He observes:

> The basic fantasy deals with the sense of not being human which may be expressed in various ways by people in terms of their own fantasies of what it means to be "not human." To be human is to be invulnerable; to feel non-human expresses both *the narcissistic injury and defense against it*, being non-human and consequently, invulnerable. (p. 490, emphasis added)

Finally, Natterson describes three male homosexual patients each of whom has a fantasy of "being a doll, and, on the basis of these fantasies, functioning for the self as a transitional object" (p. 140). He concludes that these doll fantasies function narcissistically for these patients as a means of providing a "desperately needed sense of comfort and relief from anxiety" (p. 140).

Both Bradlow and Natterson refer to the narcissistic function of the respective fantasies which they describe. Other psychoanalytic investigations also make a convincing case for the narcissistic nature and function of a variety of different fetishisms. Greenacre (1961), for instance, focuses on the narcissistic function of what she describes as a pill fetishism. She states: "The fetishistic pills served to protect against the danger of helplessness in sleep rather than directly to promote sleep itself" (p. 196). In this context, she equates the pill fetishism with a "pseudo-addiction" (p. 195). McDougall (1985) also connects the fetishistic use of what she calls the "transitory object" (p. 77) with "narcissistic well-being" (p. 79).

In an earlier work, Kafka (1969) maintains that the body itself may be experienced narcissistically as a transitional object. And, on the basis of such an experience, a person may abuse it in the form of self-mutilation—the latter being an expression of narcissistic rage.

Later, Stolorow and Grand (1973) describe a fetishistic perversion in which the patient has a "fantasy of being crushed against a powerful object, and of having his self-boundaries powerfully ruptured, emphatically dramatized the very existence of those boundaries" (p. 368).

Several other psychoanalysts develop further the idea that certain things, including the body, may function narcissistically by serving as a transitional object. Sugarman and Kurash (1981) suggest that food functions in the case of bulimia in such a narcissistic fashion. They also contend that marijuana serves for borderline adolescents as a transitional object and, as such, provides similar narcissistic functions in the form of self-regulation.

McDougall (1985) comes even closer to our position. She distinguishes between the healthy use of transitional objects and the psychopathological abuse or misuse of transitional objects such as that which occurs in addiction. In fact, she refers to such things and activities as "addictive object[s]" (p. 79).

A number of the psychoanalysts already cited believe that fetishism is a symptomatic expression of a developmental arrest in the normal unfolding of fantasy. For instance, Greenacre views fetishism in terms of what she (Greenacre, 1955a) labels "set fantasies" as the fetishist's limited fantasy life, which she infers is "stereotyped" (p. 193) and used in "repetitive thought imagery" (p. 193). According to Greenacre, such set fantasies are repetitive, and thus serve primarily defensive rather than adaptive purposes. They are not, therefore, "available for intellectual pursuits" (p. 193). Greenacre also anticipates our view of the psychobiological and psychosensorial activation of addictive fantasies. In the context of fetishism, she observes that the fetishistic thing or activity serves as a means for the "psychosensory activation" (p. 193) of specific erotic fantasies.

Several of these psychoanalytic authors speak about these narcissistic fantasies in terms that are similar to our description of megalomania.

Sperling (1963) roots fetishism etiologically in a "fantasy of omnipotent control" (p. 381). She believes:

> *The need for omnipotent control exercised through the fetish*, often shown only in such actions as carrying an amulet or a "magic" pill, serves to counteract the fear of loss of the partobject needed not only for instinctual gratification (pleasure) but as a matter of life and death. (p. 389, emphasis added)

Subsequently, McDougall (1985) notes: "In unconscious fantasy such ways of utilizing external objects as though they were inanimate form part of the infantile belief that one has created by oneself everything that exists" (p. 79). She claims that such unconscious fantasies involve an illusion of the

> malleable others as stand-ins for what should have been in infancy a genuine transitional object—that is, an object that represented the mother but was also regarded by the infant as its own creation. (p. 79)

Our concept of the fantasy of the megalomaniacal self enables us to describe such a normal and phase-appropriate illusion in terms of a vision of being the master of the laws of human nature, and hence the ruler of psychic reality. An understanding of the cause and explanation of the course of disorders such as fetishism and addiction is based, in part, on Kohut's (1978d [1972]) notion of a narcissistically perceived universe. The unconscious experience on the part of a child of a narcissistic universe is based on a fantasy of a megalomaniacal self as wielding magical control over a world constituted by transitional selfobject things and activities. In contrast, an addict's similar yet different fantasy of having magical control over psychic reality on the basis of the (ab)use of ATMs is a psychopathological inversion. That is, in actuality, ATMs control an addict, and not vice versa.

Glover's early work on the cause and course of addiction spurred a series of studies on this topic including those of Chassell (1938), Chein et al. (1964), Knight (1937a,b), Knight and Prout (1951), Pearson and Little (1969), Rado (1957, 1963), and Wurmser (1974a,b).

Of this group, Wurmser is especially relevant to our self-psychological position. He (Wurmser, 1974b) finds the cause of addiction in what he refers to as a "narcissistic crisis" (p. 826). He describes this crisis in terms of

> intense emotions like disillusionment and rage, depression, anxiety, in an actualization of a lifelong massive conflict about omnipotence and grandiosity, meaning and trust. (p. 826)

He asserts: "This actualization inevitably leads to massive emotional disruption and thus to the addictive search" (p. 826).

Wurmser (1974b) even hints at a megalomaniac quality to this "narcissistic crisis." He states: "Drugs provide a sense of *magical domination and manipulation over one's inner life,* analogous to that which science and technique appear to have over the outside" (p. 827, emphasis added).

Regarding addiction, Wurmser (1974b) follows Greenacre's thinking on the impoverishment of fantasy life in fetishism. Wurmser argues that drug addiction, like fetishism, reflects a "general degradation, contraction, or rudimental development of the process of symbolization and, with that, of *the fantasy life*" (p. 827, emphasis added).

According to Wurmser, this type of developmental arrest in the capacity to symbolize and fantasize is best thought of as a "hyposymbolization" (p. 827). He (Wurmser, 1974b) concludes: "Obviously, drugs do not function as a substitute for the lacking symbolization; *nor do most enrich the impoverished fantasy life*" (p. 837, emphasis added).

Wurmser's concept of hyposymbolization supports our argument regarding the role in addiction of narcissistic fantasy and mood. Moreover, an addict suffers, Wurmser asserts, not only from an impoverishment of fantasy life. In addition, an addict experiences a similar impoverishment of emotional life.

The constriction of affects is, Wurmser insists, basically narcissistic in nature. He refers to the emotions of an addict as "archaic" (p. 833). He (Wurmser, 1974b) indicates that an addict's craving for drugs results from an "upsurge of these most disturbing affects" (p. 833). He points out that such a drug-craving "can be equated to a *rapid narcissistic decompensation* and the break through of those *archaic feelings* evoked by a most massive sense of *narcissistic frustration*" (p. 833, emphasis added).

Although not psychoanalytic in a strict sense, Striegel-Moore (1993) alludes to megalomania as crucial to understanding the origins and course of "binge eating." Referring to the "cultural myth of the superwoman" (p. 157), she claims it "embodies the view that a woman can extend her responsibilities from wife and mother to career woman without compromising quality of performance in any of her roles or extolling undue personal sacrifice" (p. 157). She indicates that these "unrealistic expectations have been implicated in the rise of eating disorders, particularly bulimia nervosa" (p. 157).

Striegel-Moore argues that the cultural myth of the superwoman is internalized on an individual level as an ideal of the "woman who has it all: career, family, beauty" (p. 157). Elements of archaic grandiosity and omnipotence are clearly present in this fantasy. However, there is also a megalomaniacal element; it is expressed symptomatically in an exaggerated emphasis on controlling and manipulating body, weight, food, and eating. All of these things and activities may be viewed as expressions of a fantasy of being a megalomaniacal self in which a woman imagines herself as controlling the forces of human nature.

THE CASE OF MEGWORTH ("MEGGY")

We already have suggested that there is an important similarity between the psychic process of animation and the cinematic process of animation. We point out that Freud (1953 [1913]), Ferenczi (1956 [1913]), Abraham (1979 [1920]), and later Piaget (1959) all describe animism as a type of unconscious thought process prevalent among primitive peoples and children alike. We note that Ferenczi, in particular, focuses on the archaically narcissistic nature of animism.

Basing himself on Freud's (1953 [1913]) concepts of the "omnipotence of thought" (p. 90) and "intellectual narcissism" (p. 90), Ferenczi refers to a related notion he describes as the fantasy of omnipotence. According to Ferenczi, this unconscious (narcissistic) fantasy is crucial in the animistic process of endowing the world of inanimate things and activities as well as creatures with human qualities. Animism is part of a phase-appropriate form of megalomania, which enables a child to imagine having brought by magic to life the otherwise inanimate and nonhuman. (See Róheim, 1930, on the connection between animism and magic.)

Belief on the part of a child in the substantiality of animistic creations fosters a megalomaniacal illusion of magical control over everyone and everything in the immediate surround. We contend that a child entertains the unconscious belief that he or she is endowed with supernatural powers. On the basis of this magical thinking (see Fogarty, 2000; Odier, 1956; Róheim, 1955; Serban, 1982; Vyse, 1997), a child imagines that it is possible to populate the world with an assortment of humanoid and android creatures. A child experiences these hybrids as being under his or her spell and as willing to do his or her bidding. In this context, a child feels like a wizard or sorcerer whose magic commands can control everything and everyone.

The phantasmagorical world of a young child is similar, in some sense, to Alice's Wonderland; it also approximates the universe created for children and teenagers in cartoons and comic books. We refer, in passing, to several psychoanalytic studies of cartoons and comic books as well as fairy tales. All of these works emphasize fantasy and myth as crucial to the appeal and meaning of these imaginary adventures and make-believe tales.

Bender and Lourie (1941), in one of the first of these psychoanalytic investigations, describe several children in whose cases comic books play a phantasmagorical role. In the case of "Helen," for example, the "child had misinterpreted and distorted part of the story *to fit her own phantasy life*, disregarding the constructive ending of the plot because she wasn't ready for it" (p. 44, emphasis added). Or, to take another instance, "Kenneth," is endowed with "a rich phantasy life revolving about the saints, heaven and hell. *When he started to read comic books he shifted his phantasies* to include many of the supernatural features in the stories" (pp. 45–46, emphasis added).

In addition, the case of "Tessie" is particularly germane for our purposes. Bender and Lourie point out:

> Even in the taking of medication could be traced the effect of comic book content, with the child expecting to receive from the pills she was given the powers acquired by certain of the comic book characters, such as the Hour Man, who obtained his supernatural powers from a "miracle" pill. (p. 42)

As these cases illustrate, childhood provides a rich fantasy basis for the adult illusion about the magical effects of certain psychoactive things and activities. From our perspective, it is the actual psychoactivity of these agents in combination with their purely phantasmagorical effects that together endow otherwise ordinary entities with their extraordinary capacity to function as ATMs.

Peller (1954), in discussing "Daydreams and Children's Favorite Books," notes that a "child can spin a daydream with such emotional intensity that he will remember it in later years; indeed, he may live his life under its spell" (pp. 415–16). In venturing the following suggestion, Peller observes that

> children are presented with stories at a very early age and the experience of gaining pleasure from something that is past, that is gone, may lead to an increased cathexis of human memories. (p. 46)

She surmises: "If my view is correct, *fantasy here enhances contact with reality*" (p. 416, emphasis added).

Caruth (1968), in her paper "Hercules and Superman: The Modern-day Mythology of the Comic Book," follows Peller's lead regarding the possible adaptive value and function of fantasy in children's storytelling. She makes an important distinction between the "primary process fantasy" (p. 8) and "[s]econdary process fantasies" (p. 8). She posits:

> By primary process fantasy I refer to those fantasies devoid of any possibility of fulfillment in reality because they are dominated by the type of thinking found in dreams and fairy tales, that is, prelogical magical thinking. Secondary process fantasies, on the other hand, adhere to the reality principle and are potentially realizable in reality. (p. 8)

Caruth's distinction supports one of our central contentions, namely, that archaic (narcissistic) fantasy may develop within the context of an empathic selfobject milieu into mature, psychic structures, which function, later in life, in an adaptive fashion. The addictive dependence on the part of an adult on narcissistic fantasy and mood indicates that such a developmental transformation has become arrested and, thus, has failed to unfold. It is almost as if an addict is trapped like Alice in Wonderland, which ultimately becomes more hellish than heavenly.

Widzer (1977), in his article "The Comic-Book Superhero: A Study of the Family Romans Fantasy," focuses on both fantasy and archaic forms of narcissism. He asserts that

> the *self-esteem* of all children and all adults is affected by the *assimilation and adaptation in fantasy*, whether consciously or not, of any idealized self or object shape that is relevant to the individual's own particular conflict or level of integration. (p. 566, emphasis added)

In this passage, Widzer combines the Piagetian notions of assimilation and adaptation with the Freudian concept of (the unconscious) fantasy to form the idea of "assimilation and adaptation in fantasy." Widzer suggests that in employing this idea both children and adults attempt to regulate self-esteem by using fantasy-based visions of self (and object) rather than by employing more realistic visions. Moreover, he indicates that such illusory versions of the self (and object) are modeled after imaginary rather than rational ideals.

Turning his attention to the subject of the hero, Widzer asserts: "The extent to which the individual or group will identify with the hero and the manner in which the identification is utilized are related to the amount of *need for narcissistic gratification* which cannot be provided elsewhere" (p. 567, emphasis added). On the basis of the concept of "assimilation and adaptation in fantasy," Widzer appears in this statement to imply the following: individuals model themselves and base their sense of self on heroic visions that provide "narcissistic gratification" otherwise unavailable.

Such heroic visions often are purely phantasmagorical and have little basis in reality. Widzer points out, for example, that the comic book hero Superman, "serves as a bridge and facilitator between the conflict of the unconscious and those of reality. *Fantasies of omnipotence* remain dominant" (p. 568, emphasis added). Pursuing the theme of fantasies of omnipotence, Widzer describes another comic book super-hero, "The Man Thing," as follows: "Although he acquired his powers by accidental immersion in the swamp, he *omnipotently and narcissistically* injected himself with the chemical that caused the transformation" (p. 597, emphasis added).

We equate Widzer's understanding of the role of fantasies of omnipotence in comic books with fantasies of megalomania in addiction. For instance, an addict is like "The Man Thing" in using an artificial agent or magic potion to induce a metamorphosis, which is intended unconsciously to dramatically alter the nature of his or her very being and existence. Furthermore, an addict, as part of an artificially induced metamorphosis, is similar to "The Man Thing" in becoming an android or humanoid. Both figures assume the form of a hybrid being—half human, half nonhuman—who is endowed with superhuman powers.

However, there is crucial difference between the comic book super-hero and an addict. The former is a fictional character whose metamorphosis is depicted artistically for purely dramatic purposes, whereas the latter is a real-life person whose metamorphosis is self-induced (that is, an autohypnotic defense) for totally addictive purposes. Yet, an addict draws on the same powers of imagination as those utilized by creators of comic book superheroes.

Moreover, an addict imagines that a special category of things and activities (that is, ATMs) function in a similar fashion to Kryptonite for Superman, and thereby endow and addict with similar superhuman powers. An addict mistakenly believes that such purely imaginary powers are, in fact, real. An addict needs to artificially induce a purely phantasmagorical state (that is, phantasmagorical transmogrification) in the desperate hope of finally capturing an ever elusive experience of Nirvana.

Bettelheim (1975) writes about the phantasmagorical quality of the magical thinking that determines the unconscious meaning of fairy tale. More specifically, he describes the magic role of animistic thinking in bringing to life the otherwise inanimate domain of the nonhuman world. Other commentators also examine fairy tales from a psychoanalytic vantage point. (See, for example, Brothers, 1995; Cath and Cath, 1978; Schrieber, 1974). For instance, Schreiber (1974), in analyzing fairy tales from a classical psychoanalytic perspective, argues that the film version of *The Wizard of Oz* serves as a significant screen memory in the life of a particular psychoanalytic patient. Cath and Cath also use the film version of *The Wizard of Oz* as a basis for their analysis of the original fairy tale (see also Stern, 2003). However, unlike Schreiber, these authors adopt a psychoanalytic perspective that is friendly and compatible with self psychology. (See also Brothers, 1995, for an explicitly self-psychological analysis of Pinocchio.)

In analyzing a film version of a contemporary fairy tale, Schreiber as well as Cath and Cath set a methodological precedent for our self-psychological analysis of "The Sorcerer's Apprentice," starring Mickey Mouse in Walt Disney's animated film, *Fantasia*. Furthermore, Schrieber's position regarding *The Wizard of Oz* as a screen memory parallels our view of "The Sorcerer's Apprentice" as a pop culture version of a commonly held "screen phantasy" of childhood megalomania. In support of this position, we present the case of Meggy to illustrate the actual operation of megalomaniacal fantasies in childhood.

It is no accident, we assert, that Disney's animated version of "The Sorcerer's Apprentice," which is now available as part of the video/DVD version of *Fantasia*, has become one of the most popular cartoons ever made. The Disney version is based on Goethe's original poem, "The Sorcerer's Apprentice" (for an English translation of the German, see Roberts et al., 1964), and uses Paul Dukas' musical treatment (as conducted by Leopold Stokowski) of the poem as a film score.

Given the continuing popularity of Disney's "The Sorcerer's Apprentice," it is safe to say that it appears to have captured the popular imagination of the American public. We maintain that it gives artistic expression to the unconscious meaning of the megalomaniacal fantasy of childhood involving magical control over the forces of nature, including, and most importantly, the forces of human nature. It also attests to the inevitable disillusionment, if not shattering, of this narcissistic fantasy. Perhaps, Disney's "Sorcerer" is a cartoon version of the "screen phantasy" of the megalomania all adults experience as young children.

In addition, Mickey Mouse, as the apprentice in Disney's "Sorcerer," is, we suggest, a modern-day version of Carroll's *Alice in Wonderland*. Both characters give dramatic expression to the dangers of indulging in megalomania, and both illustrate the pitfalls that the megalomaniacal addict succumbs to as a Narcissus in a wonderland.

A synopsis of Disney's "Sorcerer": In the opening scene, the Sorcerer performs a magical feat, as Mickey, who is fetching water with buckets, watches mesmerized and spellbound. The Sorcerer completes his magic feat, takes off his cap, and leaves.

Mickey, who is left alone, cannot resist the temptation to put on the Sorcerer's cap and try his own hand at some magic. Wearing the cap endows Mickey with supernatural powers. As his first act of magic, he brings to life a broom. He then shows it how to use the buckets to draw and fetch the water.

Mickey, who is enthralled with his new-found magical powers, sits down proudly to watch as the obedient broom performs its assigned task. Mickey falls asleep and has the following dream: Mickey is in the heavens and is able to control the planets, stars, and, in fact, the entire universe. He makes various heavenly bodies shoot across the sky in dazzling displays of fire and light. In the dream, he imagines himself as in control of the cosmos and as master of the universe.

Mickey awakens from his fantastic dream when he falls out of his chair and lands in a deep pool of water. Mickey, who suddenly realizes that the unresponsive broom has flooded the Sorcerer's abode, panics and attempts to stop the broom from bringing up more water. However, Mickey now loses control of the broom; it pays no attention to his protestations to stop.

In a frenzy, Mickey takes an ax and chops the broom into pieces. However, in a miraculous fashion, each piece of the broom reconstitutes itself in the form of an intact duplicate. Then, armed with a pair of buckets, each of the now hundreds of brooms proceed to draw, fetch, and pour more and more water into the already flooded space.

Mickey finds himself caught in a whirlpool of water and is on the verge of drowning, when the Sorcerer returns and sees the flood. He takes charge quickly, rectifies the situation, and gets everything back in order. Saved by the Sorcerer's intervention, Mickey, in a sheepish manner, resumes his job of drawing and fetching water.

In an earlier publication (see Ulman & Paul, 1992, pp. 120–21), we turned to a brief self-psychological analysis of this cartoon as an allegory on the basis of which we sought to explain the relationship between an addict and ATMs. However, on the basis of the preceding summary, we can now provide a more complete analysis.

From our self-psychological perspective, there is a special quality inherent to Mickey's relation to the Sorcerer. We interpret it as a depiction of the narcissistic fantasy matrix of self and selfobject which forms a critical intersubjective context for the development, or developmental arrest, of childhood megalomania. More specifically, the relationship between Mickey and the Sorcerer depicts in metaphoric fashion the narcissistic exchange process, and how, later in life, it may go awry, leading, in some cases, to a devastating disorder like addiction.

The Sorcerer is obviously an idealized and omnipotent figure to whom Mickey is apprenticed as a novice and potential protégé. In borrowing the Sorcerer's magic cap, Mickey is symbolically and, in the cartoon, literally taking on and taking over his supernatural powers. The entire relationship between Mickey and the Sorcerer is clearly fantasy-based.

Mickey, who exchanges his purely human abilities for the Sorcerer's superhuman powers, transforms magically into a sorcerer himself. And, the cap is the key to the whole exchange process as well as the subsequent metamorphosis Mickey undergoes. The cap endows Mickey with his magic powers by means of which he animates and appears to control what was previously an inanimate broom.

We argue that there is a megalomaniacal quality to Mickey's use of the magic cap and his apparent control over the broom. Mickey, in using the Sorcerer's magic cap, is endowing himself with superhuman powers, which he borrows by donning the Sorcerer's cap.

This is a good example of what we claim is the nature of a child's megalomaniacal fantasy. Because of its connection to and association with parents, a child endows a special thing or activity with imaginary and magical powers. A child exchanges the narcissistic functioning of the parents as human selfobjects for the similar operation of some thing or activity as a transitional selfobject.

And, like the Sorcerer's magic cap, a child fantasizes a transitional selfobject thing or activity as imbued with magic powers. Just as Mickey originally seems to control the broom, a child imagines animating and controlling the nonhuman world on the basis of the unconscious belief that he or she now possesses magical powers.

A close analysis of Mickey's dream should dispel any remaining doubt about the megalomaniacal nature of Mickey's state of mind in the context of wearing the Sorcerer's magic cap. In his dream, Mickey imagines himself as literally the ruler of the cosmos and master of the universe. In other words, he has a megalomaniacal dream-fantasy of himself as magically in control of everything in existence (that is, a fantasy of being a megalomaniacal self and as wielding magical control). In the context of a toddler's early use of things and activities, a child, just like Mickey, is a captive of a phase-appropriate megalomaniacal fantasy of magical control over everyone and everything in sight.

Such phase-appropriate fantasies normally undergo healthy developmental transformation as a child learns, with the parents' help, how to actually master the use of things and activities. Such actual mastery is in stark contrast to a megalomaniacal illusion of magical control. A child who is in the process of exchanging imaginary control for real mastery re-invests parents narcissistically as now mature, human selfobjects. In addition, a child learns to master things and activities as transitional selfobjects. These entities enable a child to develop, in turn, a capacity for modulating thought and tempering mood. Hence, a child learns a management technique for dealing with the nature of psychic reality rather than entertaining the illusion of controlling it.

Mickey's magical use of the broom illustrates, however, that the narcissistic exchange process does not always proceed normally. Sometimes, a child has to contend with the absence of parents as human selfobjects or the presence of depriving or overindulgent parents. In this context, a child may become overinvested in the narcissistic functioning of nonhuman things and activities.

And, in these cases a child, just as is the case with Mickey, experiences a loss of control over these supernatural things and activities. Moreover, a child reacts like Mickey, who, in a state of panic, attacks the broom in a desperate yet ultimately futile attempt to destroy it. Similarly, a child panics and becomes narcissistically enraged at a non-human world of things and activities that are experienced by a child as having gone madly out of control.

Under such adverse circumstances, a child may become developmentally arrested at the stage of transitional selfobject usage. As a result, a child remains organized unconsciously by fantasies of being a megalomaniacal self consisting of narcissistic illusions of magical control over supernaturally endowed things and activities. In a fashion analogous to Mickey, such a child may be overwhelmed by panic and narcissistic rage in the midst of a narcissistic universe that has suddenly become unresponsive to a child's magical thinking. For such a child, things and activities become, like the broom that originally is an ordinary and useful tool, uncontrollable entities that seem to be possessed with minds of their own.

A child whose magical control over these things and activities has become so vital to a sense of well-being is in danger of succumbing to a form of psychopathological self-absorption. In such a self-state, a child becomes attached to these things and activities to the extreme detriment of being able to re-invest narcissistically in human beings as selfobjects.

Instead, a child clings tenaciously to things and activities to the almost virtual exclusion of other human beings. A child who is lost in a private fantasy world of megalomaniacal proportions fails to learn how to master, in an adaptive manner, the use of things and activities. Rather, a pattern of misuse and abuse emerges in childhood that sometimes leads in adolescence to problems of abuse. These difficulties may worsen during young adulthood into full-blown addictions.

It is crucial that the Sorcerer appears in the final scene of the Disney cartoon. All children are like Mickey in that they have a tendency to become self-absorbed by their own megalomaniacal fantasies of magical control over their immediate surround. Only in the presence of empathic parents, who intuitively understand the importance of helping a child to temper and moderate these megalomaniacal fantasies, may a child proceed normally with the narcissistic exchange process.

Unfortunately, some children become in the absence of such empathic parents dependent on the misuse of a variety of potentially psychoactive things and activities. Then, later as adults who are addicted, they imagine ATMs as functioning just like the Sorcerer's magic cap. However, in actuality these ATMs are more like the brooms; that is, they become quite unmanageable and threaten to destroy an addict. It is necessary in such cases for an addict to be in the presence of an empathic psychotherapist, who functions like the Sorcerer, in order to receive the lifesaving help that Mickey gets with the return of the Sorcerer.

Before turning to our discussion of the case of "Meggy," it is important to mention a case from Bettelheim's *Truants from Life* (1955). The case of "Paul" is particularly relevant to our analysis of childhood megalomania. Bettelheim focuses his description of this case on Paul's megalomaniacal attitude toward the world, which involves a kind of confusion in which human and nonhuman are confabulated.

Bettelheim argues that Paul "began to act out not only against inanimate objects but against persons, though the way he treated people often made us wonder whether he ever recognized them as human beings" (p. 70). Furthermore, and on the basis of his megalomania, Paul often imagines himself as a less than human creature who, as a result, is endowed magically with superhuman strength (Bettelheim, 1955,

p. 71). Bettelheim clarifies that the essence of Paul's psychological problem involves a relinquishment of what Bettelheim refers to variously as "megalomaniacal notions about his own power" (p. 84), "megalomaniacal tendencies" (pp. 108, 126), "megalomanic hopes" (p. 124), "megalomanic…phantasies," (p. 126), "megalomanic daydreaming" (p. 132), and "megalomanic reactions" (pp. 136, 137).

Bettelheim distinguishes clearly between forms of childhood megalomania and infantile omnipotence. In the case of Paul, Bettelheim remarks:

> Similar ways of *relinquishing megalomania* have been observed in other children. They parallel the development in infants of a capacity to *give up the belief in their own omnipotence* as they learn to trust their parents and invest all power in them. (p. 109, footnote 27, emphasis added)

Paul tries on the basis of his fantasies of being a megalomaniacal self and as empowered with unlimited magical control over himself as well as his environment and everyone and everything in it. In regard to Paul, Bettelheim observes: "Only as *master of a world* of slaves could his security be assured" (p. 84). (We refer to such "megalomaniacal notions" or "megalomaniacal tendencies" as a fantasy of being a megalomaniacal as master over the forces of nature, and most significantly, over the psychological forces making up the core of one's human nature.)

Apparently, Paul, as a captive of his own fantasy of himself as being megalomaniacal, also imagines himself as possessing a magical power that enables him to metamorphize himself into strange and barely semi-human creatures. Paul enacts his fantasies of being a megalomaniacal self and as possessing magical control of what he clearly experiences as a narcissistically perceived universe. In actuality, however, he really exercises very little control over the things, activities, and people in his environment.

Paul is unable to use his environment as a source of mastery by which to foster a healthy means of managing himself, his emotions, and his emotional affairs. Instead, Paul is without any ultimate means of either external or internal mastery. Bettelheim points out:

> Even this exaggerate method of acquiring self-control was hard to maintain. Again and again Paul went back to his old request that we control him so that he would not have *to master the act of controlling himself.* (p. 84, emphasis added)

Bettelheim implies in this passage that there is a normal progression from megalomaniacal forms of magical control to more mature forms of mastery. Paul learns through interaction with an empathic psychotherapeutic milieu how to exercise a genuine mastery of his environment and himself. Such mastery is in striking contrast to Paul's previous and purely megalomaniacal form of magical control over a narcissistically perceived universe.

Proceeding from Paul to Megworth (or "Meggy" for short), it is obvious that we chose this name in an allusion to megalomania. In focusing on childhood megalomania, we are pursuing a theme that we develop throughout this chapter. In particular, we examine further an idea that we present as central to our analysis of Mickey Mouse in "The Sorcerer's Apprentice."

There is a long tradition, based on the psychoanalysis of children in the field of psychoanalysis, of understanding etiology and pathogenesis. This tradition dates back to Freud's (1955 [1909a]) case history of "Little Hans" and is exemplified by the work of a series of child psychoanalysts such as Melanie Klein and Anna Freud. The early works of Mahler (1949a,b) and E. Sterba (1949) are of particular relevance to the current discussion.

More recently, psychoanalysts have become increasingly aware of the importance of childhood (and adolescent) psychopathology to an understanding of a variety of adult disorders. This is especially germane as regards the etiologic and pathogenic roots of addiction, which, we maintain, lie in a developmental arrest at the stage of transitional selfobject usage. We suggest that this arrest first occurs during the toddler period and re-emerges, following the latency period, in early adolescence with a resurgence of teenage megalomania (see Blos, 1963, on megalomania in adolescence).

The recent interest in childhood psychopathology is evident in a burgeoning literature on this topic. Of particular interest is the body of work that focuses on two specific diagnostic categories referred to as "conduct disorder" and "oppositional defiant disorder" (see *DSM-III-R*, 1987; *DSM-IV*, 1994; and *DSM-IV-TR*, 2000, for a clinical description of these two childhood disorders). The American Psychiatric Association (APA) multi-volume treatment manual, *Treatments of Psychiatric Disorders* (2001), describes these two disorders as "immature personality disorders." The APA treatment manual argues for the inclusion of "narcissistic personality disorders" as one of four subtypes of the immature personality disorder. (The other three subtypes are "oppositional personality disorder," "passive aggressive personality disorder," and "dependent personality disorder.")

The inclusion by the APA of the narcissistic personality disorder as one of the four subtypes of immature personality disorder is of particular significance to our self-psychological argument. The APA treatment manual indicates that children who fall into the narcissistic personality disorder category "failed as toddlers to realize that their parents were imperfect separate individuals with their own interests and to relinquish gradually the illusion of their own grandiosity" (p. 778). The authors of the manual continue:

> Because they believe that they are *omnipotent* and *omniscient*, they deny their weaknesses and lack of knowledge. They cannot bear to make mistakes, are intolerant of frustration, and are enraged by criticism. (p. 779, emphasis added)

The authors of the APA guide conclude:

> Narcissistic children can tolerate neither their own defects nor the less than ideal nature of others, of whom they are hypercritical. They feel entitled to the presence of ideal persons. Consequently, they are easily slighted and attack others as deficient or unfair. (p. 779)

There is no specific mention in the APA treatment manual of megalomania as a characteristic of the childhood narcissistic personality disorder. However, we maintain that such a core trait or characteristic is consistent with the APA description of this disorder. (For an analysis of the trait or characteristic of megalomania in seriously disordered children see Gordon, unpublished.) In placing Meggy in this diagnostic category, we argue that his narcissistic personality disorder—which includes problems with conduct, opposition, and defiance—could become the basis, later in his life, for a narcissistic behavior disorder and, more specifically, an addiction. (See Garner, unpublished, for an analysis of the etiological and pathogenic roots of incest perversion in a case involving a developmental arrest of archaic narcissism.)

We assert that Meggy evidences signs in childhood of becoming an addict later in life. We suggest, therefore, that he exhibited even as a child symptoms of the Narcissus complex, and, likewise, gives expression to a childhood version of Narcissus in wonderland. A childhood illusion of unlimited control over a "narcissistic universe" (Kohut, 1978d [1972]) is a good example of what Shane and Shane (1990) refer to as a "fantasy in the making."

A fantasy of being a megalomaniacal self and as wielding magical control over a world of transitional selfobject things and activities is, we maintain, phase-appropriate during childhood. It should not be considered to be, in and of itself, a sign of serious and early psychopathology. As Caruth (1968) points out, childhood fantasies may remain at the level of primary process and thus, later in life, retain their original archaic quality. Or, according to Caruth, these same fantasies may progress to a secondary process level, and, hence achieve greater cognitive and affective sophistication.

The clinical setting of family therapy with Meggy serves as a psychoanalytic medium in which his fantasy of being a megalomaniacal self emerges. The setting of family therapy also facilitates the uncovering of the problems in the unfolding of the narcissistic exchange process as it broke down in this case.

Meggy, a 4½-year-old toddler, is seen in the context of a family therapy, which lasts approximately a year-and-a-half. His mother and father, who immigrated to this country from England, are in their own concurrent and respective psychotherapies with the authors of this study. Having Meggy's parents simultaneously in psychoanalytic forms of psychotherapy provides the authors with a rare opportunity to gain direct empathic access to deeply unconscious processes and material. This unusual psychotherapeutic situation enables the treating psychotherapists (the authors of this study) to tap into unconscious fantasies that are operating in all members of this family below the surface of consciousness.

We must emphasize that both Meggy's mother and father are themselves actively addicted at the time of the family therapy. His father is a sex addict who watches and uses pornography as part of a ritual of compulsive masturbation. He is also a "rageaholic" (see Clancy, 1996, on anger and addiction) who is prone to violent outbursts including the physical abuse of Meggy's mother. This abuse occurs throughout Meggy's infancy and childhood. Meggy's mother is addicted to alcohol, suffers from an addictive eating disorder, and also is a "rageaholic."

Both parents exhibit clear symptoms of narcissistic behavior disorders in the form of their respective and joint addictions. In this sense, they constitute what Chein et al. (1964, p. 274) call the "addict family." From a research perspective, Meggy's family life is a perfect setting for exploring the etiological and pathogenic roots of addiction. Moreover, from a methodological point of view, Meggy and his parents serve as a "representative case study" of the "addict family." (See Spotts & Shontz,

1976, 1982, 1983, for a discussion and application of the representative case study method to the study of addiction.)

Meggy is a cute, even adorable, little boy. He always dresses in the latest and most fashionable clothes of children as well as adolescents, all of whom are much his senior. In this sense, he is quite precocious. Although initially very shy, Meggy gradually relaxes, feels safer and more secure in the setting of the family therapy, and eventually opens up emotionally. His cognitive development and verbal ability are excellent, and, in fact, he is somewhat precocious in these areas of development. He often brings to the sessions various toys, facsimiles or other plastic versions of his favorite cartoon, comic, and movie characters.

Yet, despite his obvious assets, Meggy reveals early in the context of the family therapy an emotional immaturity indicative of an incipient narcissistic disorder. He seems quite spoiled, self-absorbed, and self-indulgent. It is often difficult during sessions for the psychotherapist to engage him in meaningful, if only brief, conversations on any topic that falls outside his immediate and somewhat limited purview. The psychotherapist has an initial impression of a child already somewhat lost in his own private fantasy world and who, as a result, is noticeably oblivious to the immediate surround of his selfobject milieu.

His parents brought Meggy into family therapy because of a variety of serious problems at home and school (during preschool and kindergarten). At home, Meggy exhibits a number of behavioral and conduct problems, all of which are consistent with the diagnosis of narcissistic personality disorder. Meggy has become increasingly difficult for his parents to handle. His development reflects, we assert, an arrest at the stage of transitional selfobject usage, which is organized unconsciously in terms of a fantasy of being a megalomaniacal self and as exercising magical control.

In addition, Meggy already has developed a chronic problem with sleep (see *DSM-IV*, 1994 and *DSM-IV-TR*, 2000, for a discussion of the diagnosis of sleep disorder). He has violent nightmares of monsters and other scary creatures that are trying to harm him. Consequently, he never sleeps through the night; instead, he enters his parents' bedroom on a regular basis in the middle of the night. He sleeps literally in their bed or on the floor next to them. Meggy's parents are beside themselves because of the constant disruption of their own sleep. They are always on the verge of losing their tempers because they are sleep deprived; and, in view of their own respective fragile narcissistic equilibriums, at other times, they are unable to restrain themselves and fly off the handle with Meggy and at each other.

In addition to a serious sleep disturbance, which includes recurrent nightmares, Meggy also evidences other significant symptoms. He is openly oppositional and defiant in relation to his parents. He refuses to return to and remain in his own bed at night, even if one of his parents stays with him to help him get back to sleep.

He rarely follows his parents' requests or instructions with any degree of cheerfulness. Instead, Meggy engages them in bitter battles of will and power struggles. In this context, he has temper tantrums if he does not get his own way. As a result, any semblance of a normal decorum in the house is completely absent.

According to his parents, Meggy has become an unholy terror and what Mahler (1949a,b) refers to as an "*enfant terrible.*" Meggy is incredibly willful and self-possessed. For example, he once unplugged the telephone jacks in order to interrupt a conversation his mother was having with a teacher about his problems at school. Meggy tells the psychotherapist that he got this idea from watching a movie.

The problems Meggy has at home are not limited, however, to acts directed at his parents. Even at 4½, he already is displaying signs of serious self-destructive and even suicidal behavior. Sometimes, in the midst of a temper tantrum, he punches himself in the arms and legs. He also takes sharp instruments and uses them to scratch and gouge himself. During these episodes, he sobs that he wants to kill himself and to die.

Despite these very serious problems, Meggy could be at other times a joy and pleasure for his parents. He is extremely bright, verbal, and has a wonderful sense of humor. In many ways, he is psychologically older than his chronological age. Due to his parents' serious marital difficulties, each often sought Meggy out as an alternative to being with one another. They misuse him in these instances as a surrogate mate and companion. As a result of having such an adult role foisted prematurely upon him, Meggy is deprived, to a serious extent, of a normal childhood experience of selfhood.

Meggy is also quite creative and artistically gifted. He loves to draw and paint and is always working on some artistic project. In this sense, he takes after his mother, a gifted and successful artist.

Meggy exhibits clear and early signs of creativity in relation to his use of drawing and painting. Yet, he also shows signs of a serious disturbance in his relation to the use of the nonhuman world of things and activities. For example, he is overly attached to a pacifier, which he calls his "Thumbie."

In naming his pacifier "Thumbie," Meggy is evidencing the tendency in children of his age to condense or confabulate, in a megalomaniacal fashion, the human with the nonhuman. For example, he endows his thumb with the qualities and characteristics of a nonhuman (or semi-human) thing. Thus, it is no accident Meggy chooses the name "Thumbie" for his pacifier. Just as parent and caregivers employ a pacifier during infancy for the purpose of soothing and calming an infant, so too do some children of Meggy's age still use their thumbs to serve the same narcissistic function.

"Thumbie" for Meggy is a semi-human thing that serves as a transitional selfobject. It is a humanoid or android entity, which Meggy imbues with both human and nonhuman attributes. "Thumbie," as part of his body, goes everywhere with Meggy. This enhances the magical illusion of control over "Thumbie." He also literally sucks his thumb and rocks endlessly as he alternatively mouths his "Thumbie". Despite all their best efforts, his parents have been unable to stop Meggy from the incessant sucking of his "Thumbie."

Following preschool and upon entering kindergarten, Meggy demonstrates signs of serious behavioral and attitudinal problems. Even at his relatively young age, he develops a "school phobia" (see *DSM-IV*, 1994 and *DSM-IV-TR*, 2000, for a discussion of this diagnostic entity). Consequently, he is unable to go to school and remain there alone without being initially accompanied by one or both of his parents. For Meggy's parents, getting him up in the morning and off to kindergarten turns into a torturous ordeal for them. They are often at their wits end in attempting to get Meggy to school in the morning.

The school phobia from which Meggy suffers may be an early indication of some underlying and latent panic disorder. Such a possibility is supported by the presence of a panic disorder in both parents. (For a discussion of the genetic basis of panic disorder, see D. F. Klein, 1964, 1980, 1981; Klein et al., 1985; see also Bibb & Chambless, 1986; Cox et al., 1989, 1990; Ham & Hope, 2003; Moran, 1986; Mullan et al., 1986; and Smail et al., 1984 on the connection of panic disorder with addictive behaviors.)

Meggy has difficulty relating to his kindergarten peers, with whom he could neither socialize nor engage in typical childhood games and play. In addition, he finds it hard to cooperate with his peers during activities or exercises that require an ability to get along with others. He feels his peers and classmates dislike him. Indeed, he is quite convinced he is distinctly hated. He does not like to share his things with others. Instead, he prefers to be involved in purely solitary activities, which require neither sharing nor cooperating with others.

In fact, Meggy often spent hours, at kindergarten and at home, engaged in various solitary pursuits, including his various artistic projects as well as other forms of self-involved play. He often insists on being totally alone in his own room at home in order to pursue play activities and games. He is remarkably imaginative in his play and games; as a matter of fact, his parents often worry about his self-absorption and total preoccupation with make-believe to the almost total exclusion of involvement with other people. Despite their concerns about the inordinate amount of time Meggy spends alone and by himself, his parents report nothing that might be indicative of any early problem with sex such as excessive touching of his genitalia or actual masturbation.

Meggy's behavior at kindergarten is such a serious problem that it is necessary for his parents to have several teacher-parent conferences. Of even greater concern, Meggy begins to steal things from classmates and from the classroom. He explains that if he develops a particularly keen interest in some item, he feels unable to resist the temptation to take it for himself.

There is little doubt Meggy has his parents wrapped around his little finger. In a fashion that seems quite inappropriate and unhealthy, Meggy seems to dominate and control his parents. Moreover, he runs roughshod over a series of nannies, au pairs, and babysitters. Given his abilities and talents, he is quite engaging and forms very close attachments to several of these young women.

Despite his capacity for attachment and relating, Meggy is nonetheless extremely demanding and insistent about controlling all aspects of his relationship with these young women. It is almost as if he imagines himself as a little prince, who commands these young women as his servants in waiting. Any attempt on the part of these young women to assert a normal and healthy degree of adult supervision over Meggy is met by him with either passive-aggressive resistance or open rebellion. Rather than providing proper adult guidance, these young women are more often than not reduced by Meggy to a subservient status. Having relegated them to such a lowly status, Meggy then expects them to be at his beck and call.

It is clear that neither of Meggy's parents provides him with normal limits or healthy boundaries by which to help him manage his own emotional life and behavior. And, as a result, they cannot help him learn how to exercise his own form of healthy self-regulation. Instead, his parents are unempathically overindulgent, permissive, and lax.

In view of how his parents dote and lavish attention on Meggy, it is completely understandable that he imagines himself as at the center and master of his own narcissistic universe. Being the youngest of three children (that is, the "baby" of the family) further enhances this narcissistic illusion. His position as the youngest also strengthens his already very powerful belief in his inalienable right and ability to control everyone and everything in his immediate surround (that is, his selfobject milieu).

Meggy's problem in dealing with kindergarten and his peers in the classroom is related, in part, to the fact that he is out of his element in this environment. Outside of the home, Meggy finds it difficult, if not impossible, to indulge and enact his fantasy of being a megalomaniacal self and as having magical control. Beyond the confines of home and hearth, Meggy is confronted with the vagaries of life, which seriously interfere with and disturb his narcissistic illusion of being a megalomaniacal self and as being possessed with magical control of all around him.

In addition to being the "baby" of the family, Meggy was a near-miracle birth. Before giving birth to Meggy, his parents had gone unsuccessfully through all of the various medical procedures designed to treat infertility. Finally, they conceived, only to have to abort their first fetus. With the birth of Meggy, his parents, who desperately want a son (their first two children are girls), feel that they are blessed with a godsend.

However, despite their joint joy with his birth, Meggy's parents continue to have major marital difficulties. Married for almost 15 years when Meggy is born, his parents have had a very rocky marriage almost from the start. As noted, both Meggy's parents suffer from severe and chronic addictions and problems in managing their tempers. They fight constantly, have sexual problems in terms of both the frequency and quality of their love-making, and have very poor communication skills. As indicated, their marital discord worsens over the years and, by the time Meggy is born, his parents are literally and figuratively at each other's throats. Shortly after Meggy's birth, the marriage deteriorates to such an extent that his parents briefly separate.

The marital problems continue throughout Meggy's infancy and childhood. He often witnesses his parents' fights, and worse still, is exposed to his father's violence against his mother, as well as a family pet (a cat) to whom Meggy is especially attached. It is obvious that Meggy's parents raise him in a very unhealthy and confusing family environment. On the one hand, he is spoiled, pampered, and overindulged; and yet, on the other hand, he is presented with a model of behavior based on parental "loss of control" and excess.

This is a case in which the parents of a child have problems not only in their marriage but in their own individual and respective lives.

Both parents have long histories of severe psychiatric difficulties, which necessitate years and years of psychoanalytic psychotherapy. However, despite all of these years of individual as well as previous marriage therapy, Meggy's parents until recently have not made much significant progress or improvement, neither as individuals nor as a married couple.

The degree and severity of their individual problems are further substantiated by the extent of psychopharmacological treatment that is necessary for each. Both parents are diagnosed as suffering from a bipolar spectrum disorder and are treated psychopharmacologically in a manner consistent with such a diagnosis. (See *DSM-IV*, 1994 and, *DSM-IV-TR*, 2000, for discussions of this spectrum of major spectrum disorders.) (In Chapter 9, we return to the topic of the interconnection between bipolar spectrum disorder and Kohut's notion of the bipolar self as the basis for a bioself-psychological typology of addiction.) In this regard, Meggy's parents might aptly be referred to as a "bipolar couple." (See Carlson & Sperry, 1998; Fisher, 1999, Lachkar, 1992; and Solomon, 1989 for discussions of this type of disordered marital couple.) In addition, each parent suffers from latent and psychotic thought disorder. Evidence of this disorder of cognition is present in a tangeality of thought, a looseness of associations, and paranoid ideation.

The nature of their respective (as well as joint) psychopharmacological treatment is extremely complicated and fraught with difficulty. Were it not for the skill of their current psychopharmacologists, neither parent would have progressed as much during their recent individual and combined psychoanalytic psychotherapies. Yet, despite the massive psychotropic drug regimen necessary for each parent, and notwithstanding the multifaceted nature of their psychotherapy, it is a constant struggle for their respective psychotherapists to deal with the ups and downs as well as wild fluctuations in mood suffered by Meggy's parents. No sooner has one parent stabilized than the other seems to become completely destabilized and decompensates.

As the preceding description indicates, Meggy, as he grows up, is confronted by a selfobject milieu that reflects his parents' extreme difficulty in empathizing with him. They respond to him alternatively with unempathic overindulgence and pandering to his every whim and then, without warning, react unempathically with narcissistic rage and exasperation. In an unwitting fashion, they create an *"enfant terrible"* who knows no limits or boundaries and has little ability to regulate himself.

Meggy is a child who seemingly lacks the normal ability to regulate self-esteem and modulate mood. His behavior and conduct, both at home and at kindergarten, attest to a serious arrest at the stage of a megalomaniacal fantasy of magical control. It is a paradox that while imagining himself as being in complete control of his immediate surround Meggy is, in actuality, unmanageable regarding his capacity for effective self-regulation.

Despite their best intentions, Meggy's parents fail him empathically in their individual and joint functioning as human selfobjects. By giving in to his every whim, they create in him a capriciousness that we believe is an attitudinal expression of an underlying megalomania. Meggy is a captive of his own fantasy of being a megalomaniacal self and as moving his parents, other caregivers, teachers, and peers around as if they all are chess pieces or checkers on an imaginary game board.

An exemplary of the Narcissus complex, Meggy is lost in his own phantasmagorical self-image as it appears in the mental reflecting pool of his imagination. Ironically, Meggy's megalomaniacal fantasies of magical control eventuate as evidenced both attitudinally and behaviorally in a serious inability to manage either his emotions or emotional affairs.

The extent to which his parents—good intentions aside—empathically fail Meggy in their functional capacity as human selfobjects forces him to become too dependent on his "Thumbie." It apears that in Meggy's unconscious fantasy life this inanimate thing has become endowed with magical qualities and powers emanating from his parents. As such, his "Thumbie" serves initially as a typical transitional selfobject, which helps to supplement for expectable empathic lapses in his human selfobject milieu.

However, given the serious nature of the empathic shortcomings of this selfobject surround, Meggy becomes overinvested in the narcissistic functioning of this "Thumbie." In other words, Meggy passes through the first phase of the narcissistic exchange process; however, he becomes developmentally arrested at the second phase and, as a result, he fails to proceed successfully to the third phase.

Meggy cannot rely sufficiently on his human selfobject milieu. Consequently, he becomes too dependent on the nonhuman selfobject environment. At the same time, his phase-appropriate fantasies of being a megalomaniacal self and as possessing magical control are inordinately intensified. As a result, it seems that Meggy's narcisstic fantasies are already failing to undergo the unconscious process of developmental transformation.

Instead, a split is occurring in which these fantasies are proceeding along two very different pathways. On the one hand, they are becoming dissociatively split off (that is, a vertical split is taking place) and become cut off in his unconscious mind. Having been split off, these archaic (narcissistic) fantasies fuel Meggy's attempt to manipulate his environment. As a result of his defensive attempts at manipulation, Meggy intends unconsciously to ward off an inner and panic-ridden sense of himself as having lost and being out of control. He lacks, therefore, the proper means of using the environment for self-regulation and mastery.

On the other hand, these same fantasies are, in the context of Meggy's adaptive use of transitional selfobject things and activities, undergoing some degree of developmental transformation. It is instructive to contrast his misuse of his "Thumbie" and related compulsive rocking with his adaptive use of pencils, paper, crayons, paints, and brushes, all of which are in the service of his fledgling artistic endeavors. The latter represents a very creative and healthy means of mastery over things and activities.

In learning how to draw, sketch, and paint, Meggy experiences a tempering of his fantasy of being a megamanical self and as endowed with magical control as well as a modulation of his extreme swings in narcissistic mood (that is, flip-flopping from a mood of narcissistic bliss to one of narcissistic mortification). This helps to moderate his phantasmagorical vision of his environment as a "narcissistic universe" over which he reigns supreme and unchallenged.

Meggy is beginning to master the art of composing pictures, thus developing real skills, talents, and abilities. Such actual (rather than imaginary) capacities are a reflection of a budding process of psychic structure-building. In laying these rudimentary building blocks of a solid sense of self, Meggy is establishing some ability to regulate self-esteem, modulate mood, and exercise self-restraint.

Unfortunately, Meggy's parents fail him in their difficulty in empathizing with his true humanness. Instead, they treat him in a typical megalomaniacal fashion, as a little marionette or puppet whose every motion and action they attempt to manipulate by pulling imaginary strings. They dress him in clothes usually worn by older children and teenagers. Caught in open marital warfare, they abdicate almost all normal forms of parental authority and responsibility. In the midst of their bitter and sometimes violent confrontations, they each treat Meggy as if he is just another weapon to be used at their disposal.

In all of these ways, they inevitably instill in Meggy a fantasy of himself as nonhuman or as at best semi-human. Given their common addictive character structure, it is not at all surprising that they are unable to fully appreciate Meggy's need to experience himself as fully human. They experience and treat him as a narcissistic extension of their own inhuman view of themselves.

Under these adverse circumstances, it is little wonder that Meggy treats himself and others as if he and they are poor imitations of real human beings. Perhaps, his narcisstically mortifying fantasy of himself as only partially human helps to account for his lack of self-regard, which results in self-destructiveness. He may imagine that in harming himself he is merely breaking a toy or doll. In abusing others, including himself and his various caregivers, he may be expressing a mistaken, and megalomaniacal, belief: namely, humans are subject to the same laws of nature as those that govern the world of nonhuman things and activities.

In the case of Meggy there is evidence of some progressive movement from primary process to secondary process fantasizing, or from an archaic to mature form of narcissism. However, and regretfully, the psychic balance prior to the family therapy seems to have tipped clearly against Meggy. Consequently, left to his own devices it would be extremely difficult for him to continue to proceed in a healthy direction along the normal pathway leading to a mature form of narcissistic functioning.

Further indication of such a developmental arrest is evident in Meggy's proneness to panic and narcissistic rage. His proneness to panic expresses itself symptomatically in both his school phobia and sleep disturbance (see Koenigsberg et al., 1998, on "nocturnal panic;" see also Miliora & Ulman, 1996a, for a self-psychological approach to understanding and treating panic). His narcissistic rage is clear in his tendency to fly into temper tantrums and in his self-destructive behavior as well as suicidal ideation.

In the beginning of the family therapy, Meggy finds the psychotherapist to be quite an intrusive and annoying presence. He experiences himself as unable to control either the family therapy or the psychotherapist. He is upset and distraught about what he experiences as the psychotherapist's failure to allow him to dictate the terms of the family therapy.

Gradually, however, Meggy feels more empathically understood by the psychotherapist and begins to use him as a transitional selfobject, one which eventually replaces his "Thumbie" and compulsive rocking. It seems that transferentially Meggy experiences the psychotherapist transferentially as a nonhuman or semi-human selfobject. As such, he allows the psychotherapist to slowly take over some of the narcissistic functions previously performed, albeit poorly, by his "Thumbie."

In other words, Meggy is resuming his development by creating within a psychotherapeutic milieu a vitally necessary fantasy matrix of self and selfobject, one that previously was missing. This matrix provides him with the psychological means necessary for establishing some greater degree of self-regulation over himself and further mastery of his environment.

Unlike his parents, the psychotherapist is empathic to Meggy's desperate need for limits and boundaries. Quietly, yet firmly, the psychotherapist structures the family therapy sessions so as to facilitate the illusion for Meggy that he is actually in charge. In psychoanalytically resurrecting a fantasy of being a megalomaniacal self, the psychotherapist allows Meggy to imagine that he controls the psychotherapist-as-thing and the psychotherapy-as-activity.

In addition, the psychotherapist provides Meggy and his parents with very concrete and practical ways of helping Meggy to better regulate his emotions, behavior, and interactions. The psychotherapist assists Meggy's parents with the implementation of these behavioral interventions in Meggy's day-to-day life. In this sense, the psychotherapist is serving in the role and is performing the selfobject functions, which Meggy's parents in the past were unable to assume and exercise.

The psychotherapist is empowering Meggy's parents in their capacity to manage him more successfully. In this clinical setting the psychotherapist is also heightening the appeal of Meggy's parents to him as human selfobjects to whom he can turn reliably to help him in learning greater self-regulation and mastery. In so doing, the psychotherapist is creating the conditions within the home for the resumption and completion of the second and third phases of the narcissistic exchange process. Under these circumstances, Meggy will be in a better position to give up his megalomaniacal belief in his magical control over his world. Instead, he can turn to his parents as trustworthy, dependable, and healthy alternatives to his "Thumbie."

The psychotherapist, in gaining empathic access to the unconscious fantasy life of this child, plays a vital role in effecting a dramatic improvement in Meggy's behavior and attitude. He gives up his "Thumbie," he begins sleeping through the night, is far more responsive to requests from his parents, significantly reduces his tendency for temper tantrums, and in a fashion normal for his age goes to and stays at kindergarten. At the end of the family therapy, Meggy is freer from the psychic grip of his own fantasies of being a megalomaniacal self and related dependence on and misuse of inanimate things and activities. Instead, he is in the process of transforming his magical illusions into real capacities and actual abilities. We can only hope that these changes will result in lasting improvements, improvements capable of protecting Meggy against the addictive fate that befell his parents.

Chapter 9

A Bioself-Psychological Typology of Addiction and Approach to Psychotherapy with an Addicted Patient

INTRODUCTION

In a previous chapter (Chapter 2), we introduce the general outline of our self-psychological typology of addiction. From our self-psychological perspective, we refer to six subtypes of addict ranging from unipolar to bipolar. We also discuss our general thinking about a self-psychological approach to psychoanalytic psychotherapy with an addicted patient (see Chapters 2 and 3). We trace the evolution of our psychotherapeutic approach to working with this especially difficult to treat patient population. This evolution entails adding to our original ideas about intersubjective absorption and the transference-countertransference neurosis with notions of the transitional selfobject transference, dissociative anesthesia (or what we now term addictive metamorphosis or phantasmagorical transmogrification), as well as intersubjective fantasies as shared unconsciously between patient and psychotherapist alike.

In this chapter, we go beyond both our earlier typological and psychotherapeutic conceptualizations. We build on the previous work of Miliora and Ulman (1996a,b; unpublished) and Ulman & Miliora (2000) on a bioself-psychological understanding and treatment of panic disorder and the obsessive-compulsive character. Now, we formulate a corresponding bioself-psychological viewpoint on a typology of and psychotherapy with an addicted patient.

Our bioself-psychological point of view entails a unique integration on both the level of theory and practice. We synthesize Kohut's (1977b, 1978b [1959], 1979; see also Kohut & Wolf, 1978; Tolpin and Kohut, 1980, as well as Lecture 20 [April 11, 1974] as edited by Tolpin & Tolpin, 1996) ideas on the bipolar self with the notion of bipolarity as recently articulated by biologically oriented clinicians (see, for example, Akiskal, 1996; Angst et al., 2003; Belmaker, 2004; Cassano et al., 2004; Dilsaver et al., 1999; Himmelbach, 2003; Jamison, 1991; Katzow et al., 2003; Mackin & Young, 2004; MacKinnon et al., 2002; Maj et al., 1999; Mantere et al., 2004; Martínez-Arán et al., 2004; M. Miller, April and May, 2001; Mitchell & Malhi, 2004). We believe there is a natural point of commonality between these two otherwise disparate frames of reference and conceptualizations. A union between the Kohutian concept of the bipolar self and bipolarity as understood by biological psychiatry constitutes our attempt to contribute to the contemporary movement within the mental health field to combine psychoanalysis with biological psychiatry as well as the neurosciences (see, for example, Brockman, 1998; Cooper, 1993; Cozolino, 2002; Gedo, 1991; Harris, 1998; Kandel, 2005; Kircher & David, 2003; Leeman & Leeman, 2004; F. M., Levin, 1991; M. L. Miller, 1991; Schore, 1994, 2003a,b; Shevrin et al., 1996; D. J. Siegel, 1999; Vaughan, 1997).

We make a case for the notion of what we call the *addictive character*. As we formulate our bioself-psychological perspective on a typology of addiction and its treatment, we distinguish our bioself-psychological conceptualization of an addictive character from the so-called and controversial notion of an addictive personality. This latter theoretical construct is scientifically dubious and, as a result, its status is questionable. Moreover, the notion of an addictive personality is not based on psychoanalytic thinking; rather it rests entirely on nonpsychoanalytic thinking as derived from academic psychology and eclectic theories of personality.

In striking contrast, we construct our idea of an addictive character on a long tradition within psychoanalysis. This legacy stretches back to Freud. He speculates that different types of character may be distinguished on the basis of a particular type of unconscious fantasy. (See S. Freud 1908a,b; 1955 [1909a,b].)

We contend that in the case of an addictive character a particular kind of archaic narcissistic fantasy serves unconsciously to organize the subjectivity of such an individual. More specifically, we have discovered that at the unconscious core of an addictive character lies a fantasy of being a megalomaniacal self and exercising illusory control over the psychological world of human emotions. More to the point, an addictive character fantasizes or imagines having control (that is, being able to manipulate at will) over his or her emotional life through the use (or more specifically, abuse) of a symbolic magic wand. Such an instrument assumes for an addict the form of addictive things and activities, which we label addictive trigger mechanisms (ATMs). An addictive character, who we postulate is organized unconsciously on the basis of such a fantasy of being a megalomaniacal self, is in common parlance a "control freak."

We divide this chapter into four interrelated parts. The first section consists of a selective and critical review of literature relevant to and supportive of our conceptualization of a bioself-psychological typology of addiction. As noted, the concept combines Kohut's idea of the bipolar self with current thinking on the bipolar spectrum disorders within biological psychiatry and the neurosciences. In the second part of this chapter, we introduce a representative case study (which for research purposes we distinguish from a case history) of an addictive character. This particular person is a patient whom we shall name Byron. Byron has been in psychotherapy for a number of years and, as of this writing, remains in long-term psychoanalytic psychotherapy with one of the authors. In the third section of this chapter, we review literature pertinent to our bioself-psychological approach to working psychoanalytically with an addicted patient. In the final section of this chapter, we return to and conclude the presentation of our case study of Byron. In the process, we illustrate techniques of our psychotherapeutic approach.

A BIOSELF-PSYCHOLOGICAL TYPOLOGY OF ADDICTION

Kohut's Concept of the Bipolar Self

Kohut first started formulating his concept of the bipolar self in 1975 during the course of his lectures at the Chicago Institute (see Tolpin & Tolpin, 1996), continues in Chapter Four of *The Restoration of the Self* (1977b), and culminates in his thinking on this topic in a series of papers (see Kohut, 1979; Kohut & Wolf, 1978; and Tolpin & Kohut, 1980). In view of the importance of this conceptualization to Kohut's later and more refined theory of the self, there is surprisingly little attention paid to it in the self-psychological literature. (For exceptions see P. H. Ornstein, 1981; Wallerstein, 1981; Chessick, 1985; and Riker, 1996.) It is almost as if Kohut's notion of the bipolar self has been relegated by self psychologists to a theoretical and clinical scrap heap. We are making an effort to bring back Kohut's idea of the bipolar self into the mainstream of contemporary self-psychological thinking. In so doing, we articulate our conceptualization of a bioself-psychological typology and approach to psychotherapy with an addicted patient.

Kohut, in Lecture 20 (Tolpin & Tolpin, 1996) delivered on April 11, 1975 at the Chicago Psychoanalytic Institute, says that the

> self should be conceptualized as a lifelong tension arc linking two polar sets of experiences: on ones side, a pole of ambitions related to the original grandiosity as it was affirmed by the mirroring selfobject, more often the mother; on the other side, a pole of idealizations, the person's realized goals, which, particularly in the boy though not always, are laid down from the original relationship to the selfobject that is represented by the father and his greatness. (p. 307)

Kohut, later in this same lecture, refers to the "bipolarity of the formation of the self" (p. 317). According to Kohut (Tolpin & Tolpin, 1996)

> it is as if each child has two chances, that if there is a disturbance in the selfobject's mirroring responses, the availability of any idealizable selfobject can make up for the failures in the former experiences. (p. 308)

Kohut continues:

> And the same is true the other way around. If a child turns from a distorted or insufficient mirroring experience toward the idealized selfobject in order to create an especially strong set of ideals and goals and is then disappointed by the idealized selfobject, he may turn back to the mirroring selfobject to attempt to finish or to reinforce the incomplete work of the earlier mirroring phase (p. 308).

Kohut (Tolpin & Tolpin, 1996), in adumbrating our notion of an addictive character, concludes that the "*characterological* end result will, of course, be a different one" (p. 308, emphasis added) depending on which of these "two chances" development affords a particular child.

In Lecture 20, Kohut (Tolpin & Tolpin, 1996) anticipates our idea of an addictive character as a psychological "end result" of a developmental arrest in the "bipolarity of the formation of the self." Here, he describes the case of a patient suffering from "addictionlike homosexual masturbatory activities several times every day" (p. 309). Kohut connects this "addictionlike" activity to a "series of grandiose fantasies related to specific, comparatively accessible memories, preconscious or conscious, concerning this man's relationship to his mother" (p. 310).

Kohut (Tolpin & Tolpin, 1996) observes that at the

> moment of ejaculation, which was always delayed, prolonged with all kinds of *elaborative subsidiary fantasies*, that created feeling suffused not only with sexual pleasure and excitement but with a feeling sense of great strength, triumph, and holiness, as well. (p. 313, emphasis added)

Kohut maintains that this "was the essence of these masturbatory fantasies, which he repeated over and over and over again with a kind of *addictive need*" (p. 313, emphasis added).

In summarizing the analysis of this patient, Kohut indicates:

> Indeed, some independent male self had begun to be formed in the relationship in an idealized father, but this particular self, the true grandiose self of the little boy, had gone into repression, was isolated; and above that horizontal split in the personality was not defensive grandiosity but a depressed feeling, a sense of emptiness, a sense of yearning for something. (p. 315)

According to Kohut, through a "remarkable *synthesis in fantasy*" (p. 313, emphasis added) this "man invented to combine religious symbolism and crude, unconscious selfobject needs along with a subtle rendition of what we mean by transmuting internalization of the idealized object" (p. 313).

In later publications, Kohut continues to link the "bipolarity of the formulation of the self" with what we, following Ulman and Brothers (1988), refer to as an archaic narcissistic fantasy. As part of a refinement in our thinking, we equate this latter idea with the notion of a "self-state fantasy." This notion represents an application of Kohut's (1977b, p. 109) concept of the "self-state dream" to the area of unconscious fantasy. For instance, in *The Restoration of the Self* (1977b), and more specifically in the chapter on the bipolar self, Kohut notes that there is a period during development

> when the several constituents of the nuclear self are acquired (when, for example, the nuclear ambitions are established through the consolidation of the *central grandiose-exhibitionistic fantasies*. (p. 178, emphasis added)

Or, to take another example, Kohut and Wolf (1978), in discussing the bipolar self, state that in many narcissistically disturbed patients the

> creative-productive potential will be diminished because their intense ambitions which had remained tied to unmodified grandiose fantasy will frighten them. (p. 419, emphasis added)

They continue:

> In view of the fact, furthermore, that the selfobject's responses had focused prematurely and unrealistically on *the fantasized performance or the fantasized product of the self* but had failed to respond appropriately to the exhibitionism of the nascent nuclear self of the child as the initiator of the performance and as the shaper of the products, the self will, throughout life, be experienced as separate from its own actions and weak in comparison to them. (p. 419, emphasis added)

Kohut, in his work with Tolpin (Tolpin & Kohut, 1980), offers an explanation of addiction which, for our purposes, is significant. In his joint effort with Tolpin, Kohut attempts to explain addiction on the basis of the notion of "forced thought and action" (p. 438). Kohut (and Tolpin) describes forced thought and action as having a "driven quality which, like the manifestations subsumed under the heading of sexualization, *is akin to addiction*, and, as concerns sexualization, *is often the precursor to true addictions later in life*" (pp. 438–39, emphasis added).

Kohut (Tolpin & Kohut, 1980) continues: "This specific experiential feature gives us empathic access to the primary meaning of these symptoms" (p. 439). He concludes: "Like all addictions, it is meant to do away with a defect in the self, to cover it, or to fill it in a frantic, forever activity" (p. 439).

From our vantage point, we view addictive fantasies of the megalomaniacal illusion of magical control as a type of "forced thought." Moreover, we construe the use (abuse) of magically-endowed things and activities (that is, ATMs) as a kind of "forced action."

THE BIPOLARITY OF BIOLOGICAL PSYCHIATRY

A new era has dawned within psychiatry—biological psychiatry. A scientific revolution is taking place. It consists of medical advances in the techniques for understanding the biological nature of the human brain as it functions or malfunctions, respectively, in mental health or mental illness. Within the context of this revolutionary advance, psychiatry is transforming our old notions of manic-depressive illness as a discrete psychopathological entity.

We currently realize that bipolar illness is a disorder that consists of subtypes falling (and often moving) along a spectrum. As part of this new understanding, biological psychiatrists view bipolar illness as a heterogeneous rather than a homogenous disorder. As such, it varies both as regards different subtypes as well as chronicity and severity.

More recently, biological psychiatrists think of bipolar (spectrum) disorders as originating in genetically based neuroanatomical and biochemical abnormalities in the development and functioning of certain parts of the brain. More specifically, these areas of the brain are crucial to the regulation (or dysregulation) of mood. In particular, we now know that dramatic and often erratic fluctuations in mood may result from the basis of genetic and neuroanatomic abnormalities in brain chemistry.

These radical shifts in mood are evidenced by either depressive lows or manic highs, or sometimes they occur simultaneously in what biological psychiatrists refer to as "mixed states" (see, Mas, 2003). Such extreme emotional lability in an individual is often, although not always, accompanied by psychotic distortions in thinking and thought (that is, a formal thought disorder).

Moreover, such intense swings in mood manifest themselves in what biological psychiatrists term "rapid cycling" (see, for example, Mackin & Young, 2004). Such rapid cycling involves a back and forth change in mood ranging from depressive lows to manic highs. The latter may at times include a euthymic mood of false well-being. The rapid cycling typical of some forms of bipolar disorder may take place literally within minutes, hours, or days. It almost always entails sudden and unexpected swings between depression and mania (or hypomania—a type of disordered mood that does not assume the proportions of full blown mania).

According to the latest edition of the *Diagnostic and Statistical Manual of Mental Disorders* (*DSM-IV-TR*, 2000), which is the current and official guide used by mental health professionals for the purpose of making psychiatric diagnoses, there are two major subtypes of bipolar (spectrum) disorders. (See Spiegel, January 3, 2005 on the central role of Robert Spitzer, M.D. in the evolution and development of *DSM*.) These subtypes are designated in *DSM-IV-TR* as either bipolar type I or bipolar type II, with the former being, in essence, more severe and chronic than the latter. Growing evidence is emerging of still a third and distinct subtype known as bipolar type III (see, for example, Akiskal, 1996). In subtypes of *DSM-IV-TR*, both bipolar I and II disorders are described as manifested in one of at least three distinct fashions: predominantly depressed (see Mitchell & Malhi, 2004) or manic (hypomanic) mood and sometimes both, that is, mixed. This later condition involves both depression and mania (or hypomania), either in a rather static state or a state of rapid cycling.

The work of Whybrow deserves close scrutiny because he focuses on the topics of the "meaning" and the "feeling of control" (p. 170) as crucial to understanding the origins, nature, and course of bipolar disorder. We are especially beholden and indebted to Whybrow for his emphasis on the notion of the "feeling of control." The stress that Whybrow places on control links his thinking to our notion of megalomania.

And, the latter represents our expansion and addition to Kohut's notion of the bipolar self. In the context of our bioself-psychological conceptualization, the work of Whybrow serves, therefore, as a crucial bridge linking the studies on bipolarity by biological psychiatrists and that of Kohut.

According to Whybrow, the "feeling of control" is essential to an in-depth appreciation of the meaning of a series of internal (endopsychic) and external (extopsychic) events. Together, these events often trigger an underlying and latent condition of bipolar illness. Whybrow (1997) observes:

> Ultimately it is the *personal meaning* and significance that we attach to any event, and the *feeling of control* that we have over the situation, that helps determine physiological arousal and how vulnerable we are to stress. (p. 170, emphasis added)

Whybrow contends:

> However, rapidly it became obvious that, rather than the strain of the task itself, it was the *feeling of control* that an individual was able to exert over any situation that determined whether or not physiological arousal occurred. (p. 170)

He concludes: "Rather than the challenge it was the meaning of the challenge that appeared to be critical" (p. 170).

Whybrow presents a case of one of his patients who is especially illustrative of his hypothesis concerning control as being central to bipolar illness. According to Whybrow, this particular patient develops bipolar disorder on the basis of the "personal meaning" of a situation that he experiences as signifying a "loss of control" (p. 185) and as implying that it is "beyond control" (p. 187). Whybrow points out that this patient

> recognizing the *impending loss of control*, experiences escalating levels of subjective distress and an increasing disturbance of the general housekeeping functions of the self—concentrating, sleep, appetite, and so forth. (p. 191, emphasis added)

He continues:

> This pain and disorganization further heightens neural arousal and in an interplay with genetically and developmentally vulnerable neural systems in the amygdala and other limbic regions, initiates the pathway to mania or melancholia (p. 191).

SYNTHESIZING THE VERSIONS OF BIPOLARITY WITHIN SELF PSYCHOLOGY AND BIOLOGICAL PSYCHIATRY

Several reasons justify our effort at fusing a union between the self-psychological and the biological-psychiatric versions of bipolarity. First, we rely on the work of several other self psychologists with psychiatric backgrounds (see Deitz, 1995 and Galatzer-Levy, 1988). Following the work of these self psychologists, we argue as follows: the understanding within biological psychiatry of bipolarity, or bipolar (spectrum) disorder, provides self psychology with a necessary and otherwise missing description of the affective dimension of the bipolar self and disorders in its emotional functioning.

Biological psychiatrists devote considerable attention to depression and mania as well as hypomania as these mood disorders are manifested in bipolar spectrum disorder. We maintain that for a specific person these disturbances in mood accompany disorders of the bipolar self as understood by Kohut. In general, a disturbance in the pole of grandiosity may find expression in either an empty, depleted depression or, in contrast, in over-expansive and over-exuberant mania or hypomania; whereas a disturbance in the pole of omnipotence may appear in either depressive disillusionment and disappointment in the idealized or, in contrast, in manic (or hypomanic) delusions of superhuman physical and/or mental powers.

We maintain that an individual may be subject to specific outcomes resulting from a disturbance in either or both of these poles of the self. These consequences involve an eruption in a person's unconscious mind of archaic narcissistic fantasies (that is, self-state fantasies) and an accompanying disruption of mood. For some people, such deleterious results may lead to a resurgence of being a megalomaniacal self and as wielding illusory and magical control, which were previously vertically split-off. This is especially true for those individuals who are vulnerable to both bipolar spectrum disorder as well as various forms of addiction. (Such persons suffer from comorbid psychiatric and addictive disorders, and thus fall under the rubric of "dual diagnosis." See Chapter 2 for references to the concept of dual diagnosis.)

However, before we pursue this topic, let us make a case for the need on the part of biological psychiatrists as well as neuroscientists to seriously consider a self-psychological understanding of the bipolar self. (See Feinberg, 2001; Feinberg & Keenan, 2004; Kircher & David, 2003; LeDoux, 2002; Meissner, 2003; and Siever, 1997, for views on the self and the brain by neuroscientists, psychiatrists, and psychoanalysts.) As indicated, biological psychiatrists are very strong in being able to explain the origins, nature, and course of disturbances in mood or affect in the bipolar spectrum disorder. Yet they tend, in general, to be quite weak in understanding the unconscious psychodynamics of this disorder as it disturbs and disrupts a person's psychic life.

Kohut's original conceptualization of the bipolar self describes the different poles or vectors of experiences of the self in relation to the selfobject milieu. His description provides biological psychiatrists with a wonderful opportunity to better understand the unconscious psychodynamics of bipolar spectrum disorder. On the one hand, a person who experiences empathic failures in the selfobject mirroring of the fantasized grandiosity of the self may have tendencies to either depression or mania (hypomania) of a bipolar nature. On the other hand, an individual who experiences empathic failures in the selfobject idealization of the fantasized omnipotence/omniscience of the self may have similar proclivities to either depression or mania (hypomania) of a bipolar nature. And finally, someone who experiences empathic failures in both poles of the self is likely to suffer from a bipolar spectrum disorder characterized by mixed states and rapid cycling.

A second reason, as alluded to earlier, warrants our attempt to blend self-psychological and biological-psychiatric versions of bipolarity. This concerns the fact that many individuals suffering from bipolar disorder also develop various forms of addiction. There is a growing awareness among biological psychiatrists of what is termed the comorbidity of bipolar disorder and addiction (see, for example, Angst et al., 2003; Brown, 2005; Swann et al., 2004; Tohen & Zarate, 2005; and Winokur, 2005).

There is also a phenomenon that is described variously as "crossover," "polyaddiction," or "dual diagnosis" in the case of patients with such a dual diagnosis. In the present context, such designations indicate that certain individuals are prone to developing multiple forms of addiction as part of a co-existing bipolar spectrum disorder (see Chapter 3 for a list of citations on this literature).

It is not necessary for our purposes to get involved in a lengthy and detailed discussion of the literature on the comorbidity of bipolar disorder and addiction. Similarly, we need not become too engrossed in exploring the literature on "crossover," "polyaddiction," or "dual diagnosis."

Suffice it to say that the disciplines of self psychology and biological psychiatry need one another. They need each other in order to offer an adequate understanding of these phenomena as well as an effective means of working psychotherapeutically with patients suffering simultaneously from bipolar spectrum and addictive disorders. A synthesis of the self-psychological and biological-psychiatric versions of bipolarity (that is, a bioself-psychological typology of addiction and psychotherapeutic approach) provides these respective disciplines with something each desperately needs: namely, a means of combining psychoanalysis with neuroscientific advances in understanding the functioning of the human brain in both health and illness (see, for example, Panksepp, 1999; Nagera, 2001).

AN ADDICTIVE CHARACTER

In the course of the present discussion of our bioself-psychological typology and approach to psychoanalytic psychotherapy with an addicted patient, we allude to the concept of an addictive character (as distinct from what is now the scientifically dubious notion of an addictive personality). The psychoanalytic literature on different types of character and character psychopathology dates back to Freud and his early followers, continues with later psychoanalytic theorists, and advances into the present.

Freud (1953 [1906], 1955 [1893–1895, 1909a,b], 1959 [1980a,b]), describes a number of different types of character and corresponding forms of character psychopathology including the hysteric, phobic, obsessive, and libidinal. Freud focuses his attention in all of his discussions on different psychosexual and aggressive fantasies, which he discovered psychoanalytically to be an unconscious organizing presence in these various types of neurotic character.

Following in Freud's footsteps, Jones (1974 [1913]) describes what he terms the "God complex." Such a complex determines, according to Jones, a certain kind of character psychopathology. Jones is significant for our purposes because he argues that the "God complex" involves an individual's unconscious identification with God as derived from a "megalomanic phantasy" (p. 244). Jones maintains that this "phantasy is not at all rare, and possibly occurs here and there in all men" (p. 245). He stipulates, however, that there is a "class of men with whom it is much stronger than usual, so that it forms a constant and integral part of their unconscious" (p. 245). We believe that persons with an addictive character represent such a "class of men."

Jones contends that individuals suffering from the "God complex," as a psychopathological expression of an unconscious "megalomanic phantasy," have a distinct characterological make up. He observes that this

> unconscious complex, like any other important one, leaves important traces of its influence on conscious attitudes and reactions and analysis of a number of individuals with whom it is strongly pronounced shows that the character traits thus produced constitute a fairly typical picture, one clear enough to be applicable for diagnostic purposes. (p. 246)

In these observations Jones anticipates our self-psychological perspective concerning an addictive character. The latter is a type of person who suffers from a form of narcissistic psychopathology. Jones states: "In my experience the main foundation of the complex is to be discovered in a colossal *narcissism*, and this I regard as the most typical feature of the personalities in question" (p. 247). He insists that all the "character-traits presently to be described can either be directly derived from narcissism, or else stand in the closest connection with it" (p. 247).

Moreover, Jones observes: "Excessive narcissism leads inevitably to an excessive admiration for and confidence in one's own powers, knowledge, and qualities, both physical and mental" (p. 247).

In addition to Jones, a number of Freud's other early followers make important contributions to a psychoanalytic theory of character and character psychopathology. Among these followers is Abraham, who produces a whole series of important papers on what he describes as character formation (see, for example, Abraham, 1927 [1921, 1924, 1925]). Ferenczi (1926 [1916–17]) adds to this early psychoanalytic literature on character. Glover 1956 [1924, 1925] and W. Reich (1945) are two other major figures in the early psychoanalytic movement whose contributions to a theory of character we must single out for special mention.

In clear anticipation of our concept of an addictive character, Sharoff (1969), an American psychoanalyst, published a paper entitled, "Character Problems and Their Relationship to Drug Abuse." Sharoff proposes in this paper that "individuals with certain types of problems are more apt to abuse one type of drug rather than another" (p. 186). Borrowing from Horney (1937), Sharoff employs his idea of the neurotic "living in imagination" and applies it to what we term an addictive character.

Sharoff indicates that, according to Horney, imagination "changes the neurotic's beliefs and feelings into reality for him" (p. 192). Thus, the neurotic "needs to feel invulnerable, and behold, he is" (p. 192). Likewise, Sharoff points out that an addict "needs to feel he is a great artist, writer, scientist, and he feels this under the use of the drug" (p. 192). And finally, Sharoff anticipates our contention that a megalomaniacal fantasy is the psychic organizer of the unconscious mental life of an addictive character. He suggests that an addict "needs to feel he is not bound by ordinary laws of nature and in his imagination this is so" (p. 192).

We find a basis for our concept of a distinct type of addictive character in contemporary and recent psychoanalytic literature on character. Frosh (1970) speaks about a "psychotic character"; A.M. Cooper (1989) talks about a "narcissistic–masochistic character"; Brenner (1994) writes about a "dissociative character"; and Bernstein (1995) describes a "grandiose character, primary type." All of these psychoanalytic authors believe that these respective character types suffer from a distinct form of psychopathology. Accordingly, they ought to be distinguished from other psychiatric entities for diagnostic, typological, and psychotherapeutic purposes. Each of these different types of character has their own unique form of psychopathology.

From our perspective, the work of Baudry (1983, 1989a,b, 1990, 1999) is of particular importance because of his attention on the role of unconscious fantasy in the psychic determination of character. Baudry (1989a) notes that a "particular fantasy can influence more than one trait—in fact, it can color an entire character" (p. 664). Conversely, Baudry asserts, a "particular trait may be the outcome of more than one unconscious fantasy" (p. 664).

According to Baudry (1989a), a particular type of character develops on the basis of the "acquisition of *persistent unconscious fantasies* which become organized in increasingly complex fashion and shape...traits" (p. 673, emphasis added). We believe that an addictive character develops on the basis of the "acquisition" of a megalomaniacal fantasy. Such an illusion constitutes for an addictive character a persistent unconscious fantasy. It allows an addictive character to imagine that he or she possesses specific things and activities (ATMs) from the immediate selfobject milieu which endow an addict with magical control over the psychological laws governing human nature.

A REPRESENTATIVE CASE STUDY OF AN ADDICTIVE CHARACTER: THE CASE OF BYRON—PART I

Byron, who is representative of an addictive character, fits neatly into our definition of bioself-psychological typology of an addictive character in a number of significant ways. First and foremost, he is representative of the phenomenon of comorbidity, dual diagnosis, crossover addiction, and polyaddiction. He suffers simultaneously from both bipolar spectrum disorder of a mixed type (that is, depression and mania) as well as multiple addictions.

At one time or another during Byron's still ongoing and over 10-year psychoanalytic self-psychological psychotherapy (two or three sessions per week), Byron suffers in a highly unusual and quite remarkable manner from all five of our major forms of addiction (that is, alcoholism, drug abuse, eating disorder, compulsive gambling, and sexual addiction). At various points during his psychotherapy, Byron is multiply addicted (for example, he is addicted simultaneously to more than one thing and/ or activity or ATM); whereas at other times Byron is addicted only to one thing or activity, or ATM. Whether Byron is multiply or singly addicted depends largely on the nature and course of his bipolar spectrum disorder; and, vice versa, the severity and intensity of his bipolar spectrum disorder correlates with the nature and course of his addictions.

The diagnosis of a bipolar spectrum disorder of the mixed type, which includes rapid cycling, is made independently by his self- psychological psychotherapist and his biological psychiatrist. The latter is treating Byron psychopharmacologically with a wide array of psychotropic medications. The psychotherapist, who specializes in a self-psychological and intersubjective approach to psychotherapy with bipolar addicts, or addictive characters, works closely in conjunction with a biological psychiatrist. This particular psychopharmacologist (namely, F. Mas, M.D.) specializes in treating patients who suffer from a condition characterized by the comorbid presence of both bipolar spectrum illness and addictive disorder(s). The collaborative and collegial relationship between these two mental health professionals has been, and continues to be, crucial to working successfully with this very difficult to treat patient.

Yet, despite the successful nature of their joint and collaborative efforts, Byron's dual problems sometimes become quite severe. As a result, on several occasions he requires psychiatric hospitalization. Fortunately, however, these psychiatric hospitalizations are relatively brief and prove to be very effective in stabilizing Byron's bipolar mood disorder. Despite his numerous and severe types of addiction, Byron refuses steadfastly to enter into any rehabilitation facilities.

Another aspect of Byron's case makes it quite unique. This aspect concerns the nature of his referral to the psychotherapist. Byron is referred to the psychotherapist by his father when Byron is in his mid to late 20s. For a number of years, his father himself had been in psychoanalytic psychotherapy with the same psychotherapist.

Prior to this referral, Byron had undergone psychotherapy with a number of other psychotherapists, unfortunately, however, with little or no progress. On the one hand, his father is very pleased with the results of his own psychotherapist; whereas, on the other hand, he is extremely unimpressed and displeased with Byron's lack of success with other psychotherapists. Consequently, Byron's father makes a highly unusual request of the psychotherapist. He asks him to take his son into psychotherapy.

However, before agreeing to see Byron, the psychotherapist makes the following condition a prerequisite for conducting psychotherapy with Byron. To be exact, the psychotherapist makes one point abundantly clear to Byron and his father. The psychotherapist stipulates the following: in the future, while Byron is still undergoing psychotherapy with the psychotherapist, if his father should require further psychotherapy, then it would be necessary for the psychotherapist to refer Byron's father to another and different psychotherapist. Fortunately, Byron's father never needs additional psychotherapy, and hence this stipulation never has to be executed.

The fact that the psychotherapist had had Byron's father in long-term psychoanalytic psychotherapy provides the former with a wealth of psychoanalytic data on Byron's early years and developmental history. This is information that Byron could not himself possibly have provided. These details constitute a veritable gold mine of background history on Byron's childhood, adolescence, and young adulthood.

In this regard, the psychotherapist is also privy to the father's unconscious mental life, especially his fantasies. Thus, the psychotherapist has a rare opportunity. He is able to gain empathic access to both Byron's unconscious fantasy world as well as to the influence of his father's unconscious fantasies on the formation and development of this phantasmagorical universe.

At the time Byron begins his psychotherapy he is single, lives alone, and works in the field of information technology. He has had several brief and disappointing relationships with women and is currently pursuing casual dating. He enters the current psychotherapy with a history of serious episodes of both depression and mania as well as a history of multiple or polyaddiction.

The psychotherapist quickly realizes that Byron is suffering from both bipolar spectrum disorder of the mixed type as well as a pattern of crossover addiction. At this early stage in the psychotherapy, the psychotherapist refers Byron to his psychiatric colleague for a psychopharmacological consultation. He did so in order to combine the psychotherapy with psychopharmacotherapy. As noted, this combination proves to be essential in working self-psychologically with Byron in psychoanalytic psychotherapy. Therefore, it continues unabated into the present.

The psychotherapist is absolutely certain of at least one fact: Byron could not have been able to make the significant progress that to date he has achieved without this combination of psychoanalytic (self-psychological) psychotherapy and psychopharmacotherapy. At this point in his psychotherapy, Byron has achieved long-term abstinence from most of his addictions and his bipolar spectrum disorder is in remission. (For reasons we cannot explain, Byron continues, on an intermittent basis, to be active as regards his sexual addiction.)

The psychotherapy with Byron has been lengthy, intensive, and arduous. However, it allows the psychotherapist to empathically understand the unconscious psychodynamics of Byron's dual disorders (that is, his bipolar spectrum and addictive disorders).

Perhaps most important, Byron manifests in several fashions his megalomania both outside of and within the psychotherapy. First and foremost, he resorts to the addictive abuse of a wide variety of things and activities, or ATMs. We conjecture that for Byron his abuse of these ATMs is intended unconsciously to induce narcissistically blissful fantasies and moods, each constellation of which has specific psychoactive effects. For Byron these fantasies of narcissistic bliss are, in turn, designed unconsciously to combat and offset a countervailing set of fantasies and moods of narcissistic mortification. The addictive nature of this dimension of Byron's megalomania is connected psychodynamically to the onset of panic that broke through emotionally on a regular and ongoing basis.

And second, Byron is megalomaniacal in being a classic control freak. Any aspect of Byron's immediate surround that seems to him to be out of place or out of order is so disturbing and upsetting to him that he feels compelled to respond immediately and decisively.

For example, he feels the need to entertain the illusion that he exercises complete control over the psychotherapist's office. This includes temperature, lighting, sound or noises such as doors slamming in the office suite. In fact, Byron insists on instructing the psychotherapist on the fine points of closing doors in such a way as to eliminate the sound of slamming doors. Byron demands the psychotherapist's complete and undivided attention at all times during the session. He often complains about what he describes as the psychotherapist's fidgetiness. He complains that the psychotherapist's restlessness interferes with his concentration and train of thought. He experiences as a narcissistic injury and as an empathetic failure on the part of psychotherapist any deviation, regardless of how slight and minor, in what Byron deems as the requisite physical setting and appropriate amblence of his psychotherapy sessions. It results in an emphatic demand on Byron's part for the psychotherapist to make an immediate and satisfactory readjustment or rearrangement in whatever is disturbing Byron at any given moment during the session.

For instance, Byron complains on a regular basis that the psychotherapist is too "fidgety" and that he sits in his seat with his knees up, thus blocking Byron's view of the psychotherapist's face. Byron remarks that the psychotherapist's fidgetiness and posture in his seat interfere with Byron's ability to concentrate on what he is saying. Byron also instructs the psychotherapist on how to close the office door in a quiet fashion, instead of what Byron considers to be the loud and irritating fashion in which the psychotherapist closes the door.

Or, to take another example, Byron requests on a fairly regular basis that the psychotherapy sessions be conducted over the phone. The psychotherapist empathically understands this request. He sees it as an attempt on Byron's part to create a transitional selfobject transference fantasy of megalomaniacal control over the psychotherapy. The psychotherapist, empathically understanding Byron's narcissistic need for this transference fantasy, feels that he has a legitimate rationale to agree to Byron's request.

During these "phone sessions," Byron often has music from his radio playing in the background of his apartment. Yet, Byron is disturbed and irritated (that is, narcissistically enraged) by any noise or even static on the telephone line that he believes emanates from the psychotherapist's phone. He actually asks the psychotherapist to check these noises or static in order to reduce or eliminate them. Byron declares that he finds them to be extremely disruptive. He insists that they interfere with his ability to concentrate on what he is discussing.

The psychotherapist is himself perplexed, confused, and a little irritated (that is, narcissistically engaged on a countertransference basis). As a result, he asks Byron about what seems like an apparent contradiction. He quizzes Byron about the seeming paradox constituted by his need for background music despite his total inability to tolerate even the slightest noise emanating from the psychotherapist's phone.

Byron offers the following and illuminating explanation of this paradoxical situation. He explains that he "controls" the background music, and hence finds it not at all disturbing, but rather comforting. In stark contrast, he feels that he has no control over the noises or static which he is convinced originate from the psychotherapist's phone. The latter state of affairs, according to Byron, is totally unacceptable. According to Byron, it makes him feel as if he is "out of control" or has "lost control." This example serves as a graphically illustrative instance of an addictive character acting out a fantasy of being a megalomaniacal self as a control freak.

We have stressed that it is essential for any psychotherapist who works with addicted patients to establish and maintain a transitional selfobject transference fantasy. Consistent with our thinking, the psychotherapist did not attempt to analyze as resistance Byron's requests for total control. Rather, he does his best to comply with Byron's every demand without question and without reservation or hesitation. He does so in the interest of facilitating in Byron's imagination a (transitional selfobject) transference fantasy of control over many aspects of his psychotherapy session.

Even at this early stage of the psychotherapy, the psychotherapist had enough "empathic imagination" (see Margulies, 1989, for a discussion of empathic imagination) to understand the unconscious meaning behind Byron's demands. In his own mind the psychotherapist makes the following empathic inference. He intuits that Byron feels emotionally out of control and as if he has lost control of his inner, psychic world. Thus, he desperately needs to imagine and experience himself in total control of his outer world. Apparently, Byron imagines he can exercise control, however faultily and fleetingly, over the psychotherapy as an external world that will compensate for what he senses as the loss of control over his internal world.

Clearly, Byron has an imperative need to experience himself as in complete control of his immediate surround. It extends, however, far beyond his psychotherapy session to the outside environment. For instance, Byron spends much of his time in these earlier psychotherapy sessions describing in excruciating detail the nature of his torment and suffering due to noises he hears from the apartment above him. He is quite panicked and feels unable to do anything on his own to successfully control and halt what are for him terribly disturbing sounds coming from his neighbor's upstairs apartment.

Byron spends his days and nights in utter terror and in a constant state of panic awaiting the next noise. As a result, he implores the psychotherapist to help him and to intercede on his behalf.

We advocate the following position: A psychotherapist should, in such a situation, do everything in his or her power to allow an addicted patient to fantasize a psychotherapist as a magical instrument over which such a patient imagines having unlimited and unfettered control. Consistent with our policy, this particular psychotherapist did his best to respond empathically to Byron's panicked cry for help.

The psychotherapist makes a recommendation to Byron, in moving clinically to the realm of the extra-analytic. He suggests that Byron enlist his father's assistance in attempting to resolve what has become for Byron a narcissistic crisis of nightmarish and cataclysmic proportions. Fortunately, Byron, with his father's aid, convinces his neighbor to lay down new carpeting, for which Byron's father agrees to pay. Laying down the carpet significantly cuts down on the noise factor about which Byron has been so panicked and annoyed (that is, narcissistically enraged).

Megalomania and fantasies of a megalomaniacal self as being empowered with magical control are, in Byron's case, at the psychic epicenter of an unconscious complex (that is, the Narcisistic complex). This complex consists of a variety of archaic narcissistic fantasies, or self-state fantasies. In a manner that is typical of an addictive character, Byron entertains the following fantasy of being a megalomaniacal self. He imagines himself using (that is, abusing) various mind and mood altering things and activities that enable him to magically control what he otherwise subjectively experiences as his uncontrollable emotional life.

As noted, during the course of his psychoanalytic self-psychological psychotherapy, Byron resorts to the abuse of the major forms of ATMs, namely, alcohol, drugs (marijuana), food, gambling, and sex. Sometimes, he abuses several of these ATMs at once, whereas at other times he abuses a single ATM. The addictive abuse of different ATMs, either in various combinations or one at a time, depends on whether the bipolar spectrum disorder from which Byron suffers is in a more depressed or manic phase, or is in a mixed state.

For example, Byron sometimes abuses an ATM or a combination of ATMs in an attempt to ward off depression. Either singularly or in combination, the ATMs induce in Byron a particular type of hypnoid and dissociated state of mind. In such a state of dissociation, Byron experiences himself on the basis of grandiose fantasies of exhibitionism and accompanying moods of narcissistic bliss. These latter self-state fantasies are characterized by an antidepressant sense of exuberance, excitement, and expansiveness that anesthetizes painful moods of narcissistic mortification.

Or, to take another instance, Byron attempts at other times to fend off mania (or hypomania) by abusing an ATM or ATMs. Again, either singularly or in combination, the ATMs engender in Byron a hypnoid and dissociated state of mind, which is organized unconsciously by omnipotent fantasies of merger with an idealized imago. The latter self-state fantasies are accompanied by moods of narcissistic bliss. These narcissistic moods are characterized by an antimanic sense of calmness, tranquility, and serenity. Once again, these self-state fantasies anaesthetize moods of narcissistic mortification.

To take a third example, Byron abuses in still other instances a combination of antidepressant and antimanic ATMs. He resorts to this particular pattern of addictive abuse for the following reason: Unconsciously, he is attempting to defend against a mixed state in which he often cycles rapidly from depression to mania (or hypomania) and back and forth. In fact, in these mixed states Byron simultaneously experiences a painful combination of both depression and mania.

The psychotherapist pieces together a rather clear picture of Byron's developmental history. He does so through the use of a unique combination of psychoanalytic data. The psychotherapist employs analytic reconstruction as well as the information previously reported to him by the father about the Byron's infancy, childhood, and adolescence. This picture also helps the psychotherapist to gain an empathic understanding of the presence of a system of self-state fantasies, which is narcissistically quite complex and intricate in nature. For Byron, life at home as a child and later as an adolescent, is the psychogenetic setting for a crippling developmental arrest. It interferes with the transformation of archaic narcissistic fantasies into mature psychic structures of self-regulation and self-management. (It should be noted that we do not subscribe to the commonly employed notion of self-control. Rather we adhere to the idea of self-mastery.)

The following picture emerges of Byron's early family life. He is the second of two children; he has an older sister, who, from all reports by Byron and his father, manages to escape rather unscathed from the prevailing family psychopathology. Unfortunately, the same could not be said for Byron for whom the selfobject milieu of the family proves to be quite unempathic if not downright antipathetic. His sister goes on to get married, have children, and hold down a very responsible job. She evidences no signs of bipolar or addictive disorder(s).

As a youngster, Byron's father suffers from, is diagnosed with, and is treated for bipolar disorder of the mixed type. His father is a sweet and well-meaning man; however, his father has his own very serious psychological problems. He struggles to resolve these difficulties throughout Byron's early and later years of growing up in his family.

Consequently, his father is, for the most part, largely unavailable to Byron as an idealizable paternal imago. In other words, Byron lacks a father figure who is capable of engendering in him developmentally phase-appropriate fantasies of omnipotence and omniscience. In the absence of such necessary selfobject fantasies Byron is left in a state of narcissistic vulnerability, which includes moods of mania and hypomania.

In these dysphoric affect states, he feels like he is on the verge of fragmenting or as if he is disintegrating psychologically. In addition,

Byron remains developmentally arrested as regards an intense longing and craving for a selfobject experience of merger with an idealizable male figure whom he can fantasize in his imagination as both omnipotent and omniscient.

During the entire time in which Byron is growing up, his mother suffers from an intractable and refractory depression. Both Byron and his father present a very similar, and almost identical, picture of Byron's mother. She often retreats into her room, pulls down the shades, goes to bed, and spends long periods of time in the dark, alone, inconsolable, and totally removed from normal family life.

Consequently, Byron experiences his mother as completely unavailable to him as a mirroring maternal figure. In the depths of her own depression, she is self-absorbed and preoccupied with her own pain and misery. She is, therefore, unable to facilitate a process whereby Byron imagines himself as grandly exhibiting himself before her as a selfobject that he fantasizes as a mirroring presence.

Kohut (1971, 1977b) describes a mother's role as a mirroring selfobject. According to Kohut, she has a gleam in her eye that reflects back to her child a selfobject experience of being seen as grandiose. As a result of his mother's depression, Byron is deprived of selfobject fantasies of her as an admiring and awestruck audience. Instead, as his mother stares blankly into space she might as well have been dead. It appears that in Byron's unconscious mind she seems to be totally lacking in a capacity to reflect back to him an imaginary image of himself as grandly and proudly exhibiting himself before her as a worshipful audience.

Tragically, Byron's childhood experience of his mother as figuratively dead to the world becomes a literal fact. In his early 20s, Byron's mother dies suddenly and without warning on a commercial airplane that crashes and burns. In response to his mother's unexpected death, Byron exhibits the numbing symptoms typical of posttraumatic stress disorder, or PTSD. (See Ulman & Miliora, 2003, for a discussion of traumatic loss and PTSD.) The numbing symptoms of PTSD further complicate and exacerbate Byron's already preexisting and comorbid bipolar spectrum and addictive disorders.

The absence during Byron's childhood and adolescence of his mother as a mirroring selfobject leaves him narcissistically vulnerable to an empty/depleted depression. In such a depressive state of mind, he experiences himself subjectively as totally lacking in and without the narcissistic supplies necessary for self-sustenance. Furthermore, Byron remains developmentally arrested in another important sense. He is left with an unmet and narcissistic need to experience himself on the basis of grandiose illusions in which he imagines himself as exhibiting himself before a female figure he fantasizes as a mirroring selfobject.

The portrayal of the selfobject milieu that characterizes Byron's childhood and adolescence is quite salient. It points to a bipolar disturbance in two of the narcissistic sectors of the self, that is, grandiosity and idealization. In addition to the bipolar nature of Byron's narcissistic disturbance, there is evidence in Byron's history of still further empathic failure on the part of the selfobject milieu. This failure concerns the area of self-experience that is organized unconsciously in terms of a fantasized or imaginary twinship.

As noted, both Byron's father and mother suffer from serious mood disorders, which together genetically predispose Byron to bipolar spectrum disorder. Moreover, his only sibling is a female considerably older than Byron. In this developmental context, Byron complains of feeling that he is always alone and an outsider in his own family. He lacks the presence of a selfobject twin to provide him with an alterego experience. As a result, Byron constantly senses himself among the other members of his own family as being strange and odd. He says that he feels as if he were not really human.

Based on Byron's description of himself as a child and adolescent, it seems as if he fantasizes himself as less than human, and as at best semi-human. And, in fact, there is a mechanical and robotic quality to Byron's self-presentation. The psychotherapist regularly finds himself in his own countertransference reverie (see Ogden, 1997, on countertransference reverie) in which he imagines Byron as if he is nonhuman and an automaton.

In the absence of genuine twinship experiences, Byron tries unconsciously to induce an addictive state of dissociation in which he could imagine an alterego selfobject experience, however of an ersatz nature. He sought these ersatz selfobject experiences through the abuse of specific ATMs. These ersatz selfobjects (or ATMs) seem to foster in Byron's unconscious mind the illusion of companionship and alikeness to other human beings. His eating disorder is exemplary of such an imaginary experience. Eating is such a social activity that it is often possible to imagine oneself as surrounded by others even when one sits alone and overeats.

From our self-psychological perspective, and in terms of Byron's developmental history, there is ample evidence of extensive narcissistic damage in all sectors of his self-experience. However, from our vantage point, one area of damage stands out above all the others. He rarely if ever experiences any healthy and phase-appropriate ability to entertain a fantasy of being a megalomaniacal self and as possessing of magical control over the transitional selfobject world of nonhuman things and activities. On the contrary, Byron laments that he experiences everything and every activity as if it is at the disposal of some other member of his family.

In the case of Byron, there is a failure in transmuting internalizations. As a result, there is a failure in the normal developmental transformation of the fantasy of being a megalomaniacal self and as exercising magical control into a more mature sense of being able to manage one's emotions and master one's emotional life. Instead, Byron remains developmentally arrested on the basis of this self-state fantasy.

Later in Byron's life, this unconscious fantasy transmogrifies into the unhealthy and abnormal craving for ATMs. These things and activities serve as a narcissistic source by which Byron is able to entertain fantasies of being a megalomaniacal self and as endowed with magical control over his psychic world. In this sense as well, Byron and his developmental history are representative of an addictive character.

And, from our viewpoint, the following fact is particularly fascinating and tantalizing. Namely, despite the presence of severe mood disorder on both the paternal and maternal sides of his family, no other member of Byron's family ever had or has a problem with addiction. On the basis of this fact, it is intriguing to speculate as follows: In the case of Byron, is the extensive and developmentally untransformed nature of his megalomania determinative unconsciously of his addictive character?

THERAPEUTICS

In an earlier chapter (see Chapter 2), we review a body of psychoanalytic literature that serves as a backdrop for our psychotherapeutic approach to treating addicted patients. In this section of the present chapter, we examine a specific corpus of psychoanalytic literature. This body of work is particularly relevant to and supportive of our self-psychological and intersubjective approach to psychotherapy with addicted patients. This is a necessarily selective and critical review of this particularly pertinent literature. Following this review, we return to the case of Byron. In this context, we attempt to provide clinical illustrations of the two cornerstones of our psychotherapeutic approach.

Review of the Literature

Our review of this literature centers on the following topics: narcissism, self psychology, unconscious defense mechanisms (more specifically dissociation), shared fantasies, countertransference, and finally current self-psychological attempts at integrating the findings from the neurosciences with those of psychoanalysis. The latter efforts are germane to our concepts of therapeutic dissociation and the psychopharmacotherapeutic effect of selfobject transference fantasies.

Recently, two authors paid special attention to the topic of narcissism for understanding addiction. Richards (1993), the first of these authors, states that "narcissistic issues...have been linked earlier in this book to the dynamics of denial in addiction and the intrapsychic and object relational aspects of drug use as a mode of self regulation" (p. 283).

Kaufman (1994), the second of these authors, seeks to understand the "narcissistic personality disorder" (p. 77) as a means to treating addicted patients. His discussion of aspects of psychotherapy with this patient population is of particular significance to our approach.

The first aspect is fantasy. Kaufman observes when referring to what he terms "closet narcissists," that they may "present themselves as timid, shy, and ineffective, but [may] reveal themselves later in therapy as having a richly *grandiose fantasy life*" (p. 78, emphasis added). He continues: "*These fantasies may be acted out during intoxication*, particularly on hallucinogens or stimulants" (p. 78, emphasis added).

Kaufman later describes the psychodynamics of the addicted and narcissistic patient in a way which we interpret as anticipating our ideas about addictive metamorphosis or phantasmagorical transmogrification. He maintains these patients "feel they have not lost their blissful unity with their all-giving, mirroring, idealizing mothers" (p. 79). He adds: "Then they must seal themselves off from the reality of the external world, which disputes this illusion; they do this by avoidance, denial, and devaluation of any reality input to the contrary" (p. 79). He concludes: "NPD [narcissistic personality disorder] patients can also *induce this fused bliss artificially* through drug experiences, such as opiod dreaminess, sedative oblivion, or stimulant euphoria" (p. 79, emphasis added).

Kaufman also emphasizes the importance of empathy and provision in psychotherapy with addicted and narcissistic patients. He notes: "An essential aspect of the psychotherapy of SAS [substance abusers] with

NPD is the *provision* of a corrective emotional *empathic experience*, which helps to compensate for their earlier empathic failures" (p. 80, emphasis added).

There are a number of authors who purport to have adopted a self-psychological approach to working psychotherapeutically with addicted patients. J. D. Levin (1987), for example, titles his early work, *Treatment of Alcoholism and Other Addictions: A Self Psychology Approach*. More recently, J. D. Levin (2001) has published a second book on addiction, which he titles *Therapeutic Strategies for Treating Addiction: From Slavery to Freedom*. In this latter treatise, he claims that to a significant degree he relies on Kohutian theory and self-psychological technique.

Levin makes some interesting points in his second book. We applaud the importance he gives to the phenomenon of control, or what we deem as megalomania, in understanding and working psychotherapeutically with addicted patients. For instance, Levin stresses that "addicts have a pathological need for omnipotent control" (p. 92). He elaborates this point with the following insight:

> The drug is simultaneously experienced as an object they believe they can control and coerce into doing their will, *and as an object they believe gives them control of their subjective states and of the environment* (p. 92, emphasis added).

The above insight on the part of Levin is instructive. And, he makes some interesting and perceptive observations about the psychology of an addict and how to proceed with them in psychotherapy. Yet, despite these astute insights, Levin's later book, like his earlier work, is seriously compromised from our self-psychological perspective. Both works are undermined because of his heavy reliance on the notion of "pathological narcissism"—a concept totally anathema and antithetical to self psychology.

The concept of "pathological narcissism" is completely at odds with one of Kohut's major findings. Kohut argues as follows: The psychological phenomenon otherwise referred to within psychoanalysis as "pathological narcissism" has, according to Kohut, no basis in subjective reality, and hence is a misnomer. Both Kohut and self psychology contend, in the strongest possible terms, that narcissism is not by definition "pathological"; rather, it is either archaic or mature. Archaic narcissism, may develop or fail to develop (that is, remain developmentally arrested) into a more mature form.

As is apparent from the subtitle of his first book, Levin claims that he is providing a self-psychological approach to treating addiction. However, he refers constantly throughout his work to "pathological narcissism." Consequently, we wonder how his works can be considered by others to be seriously and genuinely self psychological in nature.

The understanding on Levin's part of narcissism as pathological, as opposed to archaic (and in contrast to mature), seems to us to be more consistent with the psychoanalytic thinking of Kernberg (1975, 1976, 1984). While Kohut was still alive, Kernberg was a major opponent and adversary. Kernberg was, and remains, opposed to all or most of self-psychological thinking about theory and technique.

Furthermore, there is only one instance as far as we know in which Levin presents his work in a *bona fide* self-psychological forum. A number of years ago and under the auspices of a now defunct organization, The Society for the Advancement of Self Psychology (SASP), the authors invited him to speak on the topic of addiction. Frankly, we did not find his presentation to be especially self-psychological in nature. In fact, we found it to be more Kernbergian than Kohutian.

Moreover, and again as far as we are aware, Levin never publishes any of his numerous works on addiction in a collection that is generally recognized as truly self psychological in nature (for example, the series *Progress in Self Psychology*, which consists of selected papers from the Annual International Conference on the Psychology of the Self). We, contend, therefore, that Levin rather than being an authentic self psychologist is, in actuality, a Kernbergian in Kohutian clothing.

In an edited book, Liebowitz (1991) presents a chapter with the title, "Bulimia: A Self Psychological Study." Liebowitz makes clear that she believes that the "person with bulimic symptomology is suffering from an addictive disorder" (p. 96). Her position is consistent with and supports our contention that eating disorders are one of the five major forms of addiction.

Liebowitz suggests that an "approach...that would focus on intrapsychic conflict, on exploring and analyzing defense mechanisms and resistances, or on interpreting drives does not allow for transmuting internalizations and therefore does not strengthen self-structure" (p. 98). She points out that "it has been my experience that when self-structure becomes stronger, the patients' perceptions become more realistic, the need for pathological defenses weakens, and underlying motives and meanings of the defenses and resistances can be explored and analyzed" (p. 99).

Another aspect of the work of Liebowitz is of particular relevance for our psychotherapeutic approach. Liebowitz is sensitive to the issue of control, or what we maintain is the expression of megalomania. She believes that the issue of control is crucial to understanding and working psychotherapeutically with addicted patients such as those who suffer from bulimia. In discussing her self-psychological psychotherapy with these patients, Liebowitz contends that the "binging and vomiting provided a momentary sense, *albeit pseudo*, of cohesiveness and *control of life*" (p. 180, emphasis added).

In a similar vein, she adds that "because they needed so much outside approval and, therefore, shaped their behavior to the much needed other, *they felt controlled and manipulated*" (p. 100, emphasis added). In this sense, Liebowitz shares our view that an addicted patient has an inordinate and psychopathological need to entertain the illusion of control because they feel so controlled as they are growing up. In the case of an addicted patient, we construe Liebowitz as implying that a developmental arrest has occurred in the normal and healthy transformation of megalomania into a capacity for self-management and self-mastery.

Liebowitz is also aware of the importance of facilitating the fantasy of controlling psychotherapy in the unconscious mind of an addicted patient. In this context, she warns that the "greatest pitfall for the therapist is to collude unconsciously in taking controls from the patient" (p. 100). Liebowitz alludes to the flipside of the fantasy coin of megalomaniacal control, that is, the narcissistically mortifying fantasy of being out of control or having lost control. She argues that since the "patients feel no control over their lives, I believe the therapist, as selfobject, has to be flexible enough *to allow these patients to control aspects of the treatment* situation without interpreting these actions as acting-out or resistances" (p. 101, emphasis added).

As an example of the latter, Liebowitz states that in the "case of my patients, *the need to control* was exhibited in a need to change the hour of their sessions from time to time" (p. 101). She readily concedes that when "I could, I allowed for the changes in time and did not interpret" (p. 101).

The work of Sands (1991) represents still another example of a self-psychological approach to treating bulimia. However, for our purposes the emphasis that Sands gives to dissociation and empathy are of particular relevance. Sands (1991) challenges "a central self-psychological belief: Namely, that if one provides an empathic environment and analyzes the patient's fears of retraumatization, the archaic narcissistic needs will be spontaneously mobilized within a selfobject transference" (p. 34). On the contrary, Sands suggests that the "situation is more complicated in the case of eating disorders (or other addictive disorders) in which the archaic needs have been dissociated and then detoured into eating disordered pathology and, as a consequence, are not available to fuel a selfobject transference" (p. 34).

Sands hints at our distinction between transitional selfobjects and ATMs. She believes that at

> some crucial point in development, the individual invents a new, restitutive system by which disordered eating patterns rather than people are used to meet selfobject [sic] needs, because previous attempts with caregivers have brought disappointment, frustration, or even abuse. (p. 35)

As a core facet of an addicted self Sands describes a phenomenon that we term addictive metamorphosis. She explains that as the

> nuclear needs (and the affects surrounding them) are not responded to empathically because they somehow threaten the caregiver's narcissistic equilibrium, they are split off from the total self-structure and may then be organized into a separate section of the personality. (p 39)

She proposes that "when the individual later begins to experiment with bulimia, *the biochemical effects of the binge-purge cycle create an altered state* that serves to reinforce the already existing split in the psyche" (pp. 39–40, emphasis added).

Sands makes a reference to an idea that we consider to be consistent with our prior notion of dissociative anesthesia. She contends that disordered bulimic eating "operates as a defense in that it 'numbs' the painful affects, like rage, surrounding the unmet nuclear needs" (p. 39, emphasis added).

Finally, Sands makes reference to a crucial connection via dissociation between addiction and trauma. This connection is one of the central contentions of our concluding chapter (see Chapter 10). She points out that there is "mounting evidence of a clear relationship between dissociative symptoms and childhood traumas" (p. 40).

A. Ornstein (1995b), in a contribution to a book edited by Dowling titled *The Psychology and Treatment of Addictive Behavior*, tackles the problem of sexual addiction. Two aspects of Ornstein's discussion are crucial to our argument. First, she focuses on the nature and role of fantasy in the sexually addictive behavior of her patients; and second, she examines the crucial role of fantasy in cure via the (selfobject) transference.

Ornstein describes one of her sexually addicted patients. She discerns in her patient a "fantasy that would follow the [sexual] encounter would not be restricted to a desire for sexual intimacy, though the quality of the sexual experience (the level of arousal and strength of orgasm) played an important part in the subsequent fate of the affairs" (p. 106). Rather, she insists that the "most important aspect of the attraction was the way the man would respond to her overtures" (p. 103). Here, Ornstein seems to be alluding to the mirroring selfobject(-like) function of a sexually addictive fantasy.

In a further discussion of this same patient, Ornstein notes that "by masturbating accompanied by fantasies of having intercourse either with Carl, a somewhat older boy, or with her father...she could relieve boredom or depression; they were either enlivening and energizing or soothing and comforting" (p. 106). In other words, and in the language of our model, these addictive masturbatory fantasies provided either an antidepressant selfobject-like boost and/or antianxiety selfobject-like tranquilization and sedation.

Ornstein quotes from her patient who bemoaned her fate. Her patient laments: "It is a fantasy world. I don't feel lively or alive without it...but it also depresses me that this is what I need to make myself feel better" (p. 106).

In chronicling her psychotherapy with this particular patient, Ornstein reports on a series of sexual transference fantasies. All of these illusions seemed to take over the role of the patient's previous addictive sexual fantasies. According to Ornstein, in these transference fantasies, which were manifestly sexual in nature, there is something that is implicit yet very important. It involves a latent selfobject function that provides an experience of being mirrored.

Ornstein suggests that these latently narcissistic transference fantasies, which were of the mirroring selfobject variety, become over time "replaced by fantasies in which I would take care of her as if she were a baby" (p. 106). In this sense, therefore, the latently narcissistic transference fantasies undergo a shift. They change from an initial mirroring selfobject function to a later idealizing selfobject role.

Ornstein presents clinical evidence of transmuting internalization that, she claims, results from the analysis and working through of these selfobject transference fantasies. She relates how her patient "found that she could calm herself with the fantasy that I would tuck her in and wish her good night" (p. 110). Ornstein concludes: "Such experiences in the transference could—retrospectively—best explain her increased ability to regulate her tension states and make the repetition of the symptomatic behavior less necessary" (p. 110).

As presented by Ornstein, the description of her analytic work with her sexually addicted patient is consistent with and supports our approach. From our perspective, we envision Ornstein in her role as psychoanalyst/ psychotherapist as taking over the selfobject-like functions of sex as an ATM. She does so, in our terminology, via a transitional selfobject transference fantasy. This transference fantasy provides genuine (as opposed to ersatz) selfobject functions of both mirroring and idealization.

Gradually, these selfobject functions are, in the language of our approach, intersubjectively absorbed via transmuting internalization. As a result, Ornstein's patient becomes capable on her own of creating new self-structures. Subsequently, these newly created self-structures enable the patient to provide herself with her own narcissistic functions. Again, from our vantage point, we believe that this particular patient, both in the past and in the present context of her sexually addictive behavior, experiences these archaic narcissistic fantasies as providing only an ersatz and illusory selfobject-like function.

In a very recent publication, Seymour (2003) presents a paper on the "Long-term Treatment of an Addictive Personality." He employs an explicitly self-psychological approach to his psychotherapeutic work with a patient suffering from multiple, polyaddictive, or crossover addictions. (See Carmichael et al., 1977; Woodham, 1987; and Gordon, 2002, for studies concerning how to work psychotherapeutically with addicted patients from either an explicitly self-psychological perspective or a self-psychologically friendly viewpoint.) Interestingly, Seymour (2003, p. 340) even links his work with one of our earlier efforts, that is, one of the papers from our addiction trilogy (Ulman & Paul, 1990).

Like Ornstein, Seymour presents a case of a patient who has manifestly sexual transference fantasies. However, Seymour adopts the vantage point of an empathic stance. From this perspective, he understands these manifestly sexual transference fantasies as having a latent (unconscious) meaning narcissistic in nature.

In summarizing his case, Seymour concludes: "She missed her 'old ways' (drinking, cutting herself, bulimia) but used our relationship for self-soothing. She needed to see me as an idealizable selfobject—all that was good in her came from me" (pp. 333–34).

A number of psychoanalytic theorists link together several unconscious defense mechanisms. Such defense mechanisms are understood by these clinicians as assuming the form of resistances. These theorists include denial, minimization, rationalization, intellectualization, and projection as typical of these unconscious defense mechanisms. (See Kaufman, 1994, pp. 47–65 and Landry, 1994, pp. 191–218, and for their respective discussions of these defense mechanisms.)

However, these unconscious defense mechanisms ultimately prove to be unsuccessful. In other words, they fail to protect a person from conscious awareness of the painful realities of emotionally charged states of affairs. According to Kaufman (1994): "Alcohol and drugs are frequently used as substitutes for defense mechanisms" (p. 47). He contends that substances of abuse "prevent more adaptive defenses from being developed and lead to the atrophy of healthier defenses previously utilized" (p. 47).

We read Kaufman as alluding to what we have termed in the past as dissociative anesthesia. For example, he notes, "these substances provide a substitutive homeostasis, or an *anesthetized*/obliterated state in which conflicts are removed from awareness" (p. 47).

Furthermore, and for the purposes of our current discussion, two unconscious defense mechanisms as they are manifested in psychotherapy as resistances are especially noteworthy. The first of these concerns an addicted patient's over-dependence on a particular type of unconscious and addictive fantasy.

We contend that this addictive fantasy is archaically narcissistic in nature. Also, we indicate that such an addictive fantasy generates a pleasurable state of narcissistic bliss. Such a self-state fantasy is intended by an addict to function as an unconscious defense against a painful condition that is associated by an addicted patient with a mood of narcissistic mortification and panic.

Kaufman (1994) views these addictive fantasies as being autistic in nature. According to Kaufman, these so-called autistic fantasies involve the "use of *drug-induced daydreams* as a replacement for effective action or relationships (particularly symbiotic fusion under the influence of narcotics, or ecstatic visions on hallucinogens)" (p. 56, emphasis added). As regards what he connotes as the autistic nature of addictive fantasies, Kaufman concludes: "Excessive reliance on such fantasies makes it all the more difficult to develop the coping skills necessary to obtain reality-based gratification when sober" (p. 56).

The description by Kaufman of the nature and function of autistic fantasies is consistent with and supports one of our central contentions: namely, fantasies of being a megalomaniacal self as in a state of magical control as well as an accompanying mood of narcissistic bliss are part and parcel of phantasmagorical transmogrification.

Dissociation is the other major unconscious defense mechanism and form of resistance relevant for our understanding of addiction. As regards the present discussion, we cite Ferguson's (1990) paper on "Mirroring Processes, Hypnotic Processes, and Multiple Personality" as buttressing our psychotherapeutic approach to working with an addicted patient.

First, Ferguson's work is explicitly self-psychological. He states that "in this paper I am going to approach [multiple personality] from the point of view of the psychology of the self" (p. 417). He (Ferguson, 1990, p. 418) maintains that certain hypnotic techniques may be viewed as analogous to and functioning in a fashion similar to the transference as well as the working through of the transference. The similarity, according to Ferguson, between hypnosis and transference as well as its working through coincides with an important point in our argument.

A central point of our particular psychotherapeutic approach concerns the notion of therapeutic dissociation, which we borrow from R.F. Sterba (1934). We argue (see Chapter 2) that it is crucial for a psychotherapist working with an addicted patient to attempt to facilitate a state of therapeutic dissociation. Such a state enables an addicted patient to replace his or her psychological dependence on the hypnoid defense of addictive metamorphosis with a clinically-induced state of therapeutic dissociation.

Ferguson explains the unconscious psychodynamics that he believes are involved in multiple personality disorder (MPD), or what is now diagnosed as dissociative identity disorder (DID). We correlate his explanation to our description of the unconscious psychodynamics of addiction.

According to Ferguson (1990) the "creation of multiple personalities seems to rely on two psychological devices working in conjunction and under the 'right' conditions" (p. 430). First there is the "power of fantasy to relieve loneliness and emotional deprivation in the form of imaginary companions" (p. 430).

Later in the paper, Ferguson makes the following observation: "Hypnosis, in liberating affect, memory, and *unconscious fantasy*, could very well accelerate the disorder in the borderline patient's already tumultuous internal world" (p. 446, emphasis added). We suggest that the same hypnotic process of "liberating…unconscious fantasy" occurs in the mind of an addict. Such an individual suffers from a narcissistic behavior disorder in which he or she depends on the hypnoid defense of addictive metamorphosis.

And second, Ferguson states, there is the "capacity to use hypnotic processes to ward off anxiety and other unacceptable affects by dissociating them from conscious awareness" (p. 430). We argue that there is a similar process at work in the cases of MPD or DID and addiction. In each of these psychopathological disorders, a person has a proclivity for an over-dependence on fantasy and dissociation as part of a process of self-hypnosis. In the case of addiction, such self-hypnosis assumes the form of addictive metamorphosis or phantasmagorical transmogrification.

Another important parallel exists between Ferguson's description of the development of multiple personality disorder and our discussion of the creation of an addicted self. Ferguson insists that the

> fragility and chronic narcissistic vulnerability of the primary personality necessitates the intensification of the hypnotic defense to the point where it becomes an unconscious reflex mechanisms triggered by cues from both internally and from the environment (p. 430).

Ferguson adds that at "this point the dissociation has become an automatic process and a permanent alter [addicted] self has been created" (p. 430). We hypothesize that in the case of an addict the same "hypnotic defense" or dissociative process has become "automatic."

Ferguson concludes that a "selfobject milieu that is deficient in mirroring responsiveness toward the child that creates a self structure fragile enough that self-hypnosis will be a favored means of defense" (pp. 432–33). We indicate that for a future addict it is not only "mirroring responsiveness" that "is deficient." Rather, the selfobject milieu may be in the case of such a narcissistically vulnerable person lacking in other crucial forms of empathic responsiveness. The selfobject milieu may fail to be empathically responsive to the phase-appropriate need on the part of a youngster to entertaining selfobject fantasies of idealization, twinship, and especially megalomania.

Ferguson concludes his paper with several observations of particular relevance for our notion of therapeutic dissociation. He notes that the "reemphasis on the working through of the mirror transference as the principal instrument of healing in the cases clarifies the role of hypnosis in the treatment process" (p. 447). He continues: "Hypnosis must work in conjunction with and as a basic element in the development of the transference, not as an attempt to short-cut the process" (p. 447). We believe that the therapeutic dissociation, as created by the psychopharmacotherapeutic effect(s) of the transference, is equivalent to the hypnotic aspect of the transference.

We discuss the role of dissociation in working psychotherapeutically with an addicted patient. As part of our discussion, we must address a growing body of literature that documents the phenomenon of countertransference dissociation in the psychoanalyst/therapist. Recently, several pieces have appeared that address this phenomenon as a general therapeutic occurrence. These include Glucksman's (1998) article "Altered States of Consciousness in the Analyst" and Aron and Bushra's (1998) paper "Mutual Regression: Altered States in the Psychoanalytic Situation."

However, a number of contributions among this emerging literature warrant special attention. They address this phenomenon of countertransference dissociation as it occurs in working psychoanalytically with addicted patients. Barth (2001), who works self-psychologically with eating disordered patients, observes:

> I find it useful to remind myself that eating-disordered behavior and dissociation are often, paradoxically, the only ways that a cheat can stay alive with me, and that I have to find a way to tolerate the fluctuations of not only her dissociative activity but also my own in order to be with her. (p. 49)

Anderson (2001) also talks about the role of dissociation within the psychotherapist in working clinically with an eating-disordered patient. Bromberg (2001) likewise speaks about a psychotherapist's dissociation as crucial to successful clinical work with eating disordered patients. He emphasizes that the "therapist's own dissociative processes enter the picture" (p. 77) in the context of such work. He indicates that a "transitional reality has to be constructed in which trust in human relatedness begins to become possible, and thus can happen only through the therapist's surrender to his own dissociated self-experience" (p. 77).

As recounted by Bromberg, his approach to conducting psychoanalytic psychotherapy with an eating disordered patient is especially germane to our self-psychological approach to psychotherapy with an addicted patient. More specifically, Bromberg talks about constructing a "transitional reality" in his psychotherapeutic work with eating disordered patients. In this sense, his thinking is similar to our position. The similarity centers on the importance of a transitional (selfobject) transference or "reality" as crucial to psychoanalytic work with an addicted patient.

In addition, Bromberg emphasizes creating "trust in human relatedness." Here, we understand Bromberg as anticipating one of our central contentions. We contend that in working with an addicted patient it is possible to resume a crucial yet developmentally arrested process. This may occur, however, only if a psychotherapist is able to establish, maintain, analyze, and work through a transitional selfobject transference. This involves helping an addicted patient to progress clinically from depending on transitional selfobject transference fantasies of the psychotherapist as a semi-human thing and the psychotherapy as a nonhuman activity to more mature and fully human interactions and involvements.

We mentioned the concept of countertransference in the context of our exploration of dissociation in both the patient and the psychoanalyst/therapist. Dissociation may occur in both participants in a psychotherapeutic relationship in a fashion that is mutual and reciprocal. Such an occurrence has import for our concept of the transference-countertransference neurosis, especially as it applies to working psychotherapeutically with an addicted patient.

The notion of countertransference in working with addicted patients dates back at least to articles appearing in the early 1960s. For example, Moore (1961) published a paper entitled "Reaction Formation as a Countertransference Phenomenon in the Treatment of Alcoholism." Moore characterizes his position as follows: "Because of renounced infantile cravings, the therapist is angered by the constant seeking of indulgence by the alcoholic patient" (p. 495). He opines that the psychotherapist "may express this directly by rejection of the patient."

Moore elaborates his point by noting that because the "therapist is often made anxious by any awareness of anger at his patients, he may defend himself by establishing a reaction formation in the form of an overly indulgent and permissive attitude toward the alcoholic" (p. 485). According to Moore, such an "attitude is destructive of the patient's chance of recover as it impairs his reality testing and encourages denial of the severity of the drinking problem" (p. 485). Moore indicates that in such a case "the therapist's unconscious hostility ultimately finds its mark" (p. 485).

Leaping forward to the present, we must single out for special mention a number of more recent articles on countertransference in reaction to an addicted patient. For instance, we cite May (1991) because of his attention to the phenomenon of a psychotherapist's fantasies of an addicted patient. In the context of our current discussion, we believe that such a phenomenon is crucial to understanding the phantasmagorical underpinnings of a transference-countertransference neurosis in general and, more specifically, in working psychotherapeutically with an addicted patient.

May mentions "fantasies about our patients" (p. 2) as critical to the "development of tolerance and acceptance of all our patients' reactions" (p. 2). He indicates that as long as these fantasies "are unconscious, they can impede the work of analysis and are viewed as countertransference reactions" (p. 2). On the contrary, he asserts that as "they become conscious, they can become manageable" (p. 2).

May makes it clear that an addicted patient seems "to feel that *the fantasies were realities*" (p. 3, emphasis added). As a result, according to Moore, such addictive fantasies although "inside his mind...sustain him through those times when he wasn't high" (p. 3). In other words, addictive fantasies are not, as we have asserted, only present outside of the psychotherapy session, where an addicted patient actually abuses some thing or activity (that is, an ATM).

On the contrary, we suggest that these addictive fantasies are always present, at least on a latent level, in the unconscious mind of an addict. On a figurative level, it may be said that addicted patients bring these addictive fantasies with them into the psychotherapy session. However, in the context of the psychotherapeutic setting and in contrast to external settings, a psychoanalytic psychotherapist can analyze these addictive fantasies as they are manifested in the form of a transitional selfobject transference.

May also hints at megalomania in speaking about control as a particular countertransference problem in treating an addicted patient. He suggests that "an unconscious wish in the analyst to control the patient" (p. 7) may occur as a result of an addicted patient's tendency toward (self-destructive) acting out. Moreover, May believes that a psychotherapist who is working with such a patient may unconsciously seek "to defend [against] helplessness" [that is, a feeling based on a countertransference fantasy of being out of control or having lost control] with the "wish to control the patient" (p. 7).

In these quoted passages, we interpret May as describing a fantasy of being a megalomaniacal self and as possessing magical control. In the case of addiction we conjecture that such fantasies are the nub of the transference–countertransference neurosis. We agree with May about the importance of the psychotherapist's recognition of the countertransference fantasy of controlling an addicted patient. This kind of introspection on the part of a psychotherapist is crucial, we assert, to understanding and using the transference–countertransference neurosis for psychotherapeutic purposes.

In a fashion similar to that of May as well as that of our own, Kaufman (1994) subscribes to a contemporary view of countertransference. In particular, he adopts a modern perspective on countertransference fantasies as they may occur in the context of treating addicted patients. He states that there is a

> "contemporary view" which...acknowledges the importance of reciprocal cycles of interaction between patient and therapist, and it includes the therapists tuning in to their own unconscious feelings and fantasies about their patients to learn more about aspects of the patients behaviors that are not consciously obvious. (pp. 185–86).

We have conducted a critical and selective review of the literature on countertransference and especially countertransference fantasies. This review segues naturally into an examination of work related to our notion of shared (or intersubjective) fantasies as they may arise between an addicted patient and a psychotherapist. (See Fine, 1983, for a non-psychoanalytic exploration of the phenomenon of shared fantasies as they appear in the context of "role-playing games" such as Dungeons & Dragons.)

Renik (1992), in his article on the "Use of the Analyst as a Fetish," comes very close to our ideas on an addicted patient's use of the therapist as a (transitional selfobject) transference substitute or replacement for an ATM. As regards his discussion, we interpret Renik as anticipating another one of our central points. He adumbrates our thinking about the inevitability (and even necessity) of a transference-countertransference neurosis especially as it is organized unconsciously by intersubjective fantasies of a selfobject nature shared by patient and psychoanalyst/therapist alike. Renik indicates that: "Inasmuch as use of the analyst as a fetish involves idealization of him or her, there is significant temptation for the analyst to be seduced into collusion" (p. 556). "Furthermore," according to Renik, "our theory leads us to expect that we will become very important to our patients, and this can sometimes obscure the necessity to analyze as symptomatic a patient's preoccupation with his or her analyst" (p. 556).

Renik warns that a "patient's use of an analysis as a fetish can evoke countertransference reactions that will dispose the analyst to want to end the treatment prematurely" (p. 562). Or, on the contrary, Renik cautions that the "use of an analyst as a fetish, can evoke countertransference reactions that will dispose the analyst to perpetuate an endless, unanalytic treatment relationship" (p. 562).

A parallel exists between Renik's thinking and that of our own on a patient's use of a psychotherapist. Renik observes that a patient may use an analyst as a fetish, whereas we argue that an addicted patient may use a psychotherapist as a transitional selfobject (thing or activity, which may replace the functioning of an ATM(s).

Grusky (1999) in an article titled, "Conviction and Conversation: The Role of Shared Fantasies about Analysis," examines the "fantasy process that is involved in the development of an identification [on the part of the patient] with the analyst" (p. 404). She suggests that there is a mutual and reciprocal "fantasy process" that takes place between patient and analyst. According to Grusky, an analyst entertains illusions with a specific unconscious meaning. She claims that this meaning may be interpreted as follows: "'I can help you the way my analyst helped me'" (p. 414).

Grusky refers to a "fantasy of an intergenerational chain of identification from patient to analyst [and] analyst to patient" (p. 422). In discussing the nature of such a "shared fantasy," she explains that the

> analyst's conviction about his/her patient's analyzability and psychological capacities is based, in part, on a parallel re-creation of the maternal-paternal or family-like bond that is transferred from the analyst's own personal analysis. (p. 422)

Grusky concludes with the following reflection:

> If the hypothesis proposed at the beginning of the paper connecting the patient's idea that his or her *analyst was also a patient with fantasies of kinship or family relationships* is also evidence of beginning identifications, then it makes sense that a patient would be acutely aware of the analyst's personal sense of conviction. (p. 427, emphasis added)

Grusky elaborates on what she refers to as an "intergenerational fantasy." Such a fantasy is shared, according to Grusky, by patient and psychoanalyst/therapist and involves illusions about their common and similar past histories. Her notion of an intergenerational (or intersubjective) fantasy is of particular relevance for working with an addicted patient.

This is especially true in those instances in which a psychotherapist has a past that involves a history of addiction. Whether or not a psychotherapist shares this very personal information with a patient is beside the point. The fact remains, as Grusky indicates, that unconscious communication between patient and psychoanalyst occurs in general, and more specifically, in the form of shared (intergenerational or inter-subjective) fantasies.

It is not uncommon, therefore, for a particular addicted patient to imagine as part of a transference fantasy that a psychotherapist has been or is similarly addicted. A psychotherapist who is alert and sensitive to such transference fantasies on the part of a patient can use similar countertransference fantasies about a patient's addiction. These countertransference fantasies may be employed by a psychotherapist to interpret the unconscious meaning and empathically understand the selfobject-like function of a patient's addictive fantasies.

The unconscious sharing of addictive fantasies that may occur between an addicted patient and a psychotherapist with a prior history of addiction gives a special quality to the transference–countertransference neurosis as it structures the intersubjective field. This is especially true for those psychotherapists who are in some relatively advanced phase of their own recovery from addiction. They are in a unique position: they can use their own addictive countertransference fantasies as a means of gaining empathic access to a patient's addictive fantasies as they are manifested in the transference.

Therapeutic Dissociation and the Psychopharmacotherapeutic Effect of the Selfobject Transference

A growing literature is appearing on the importance of integrating psychotherapy and pharmacotherapy with addicted patients (see, for example, Carroll, 1996, 2001, and Grilo, 2001). However, from our vantage point, what is most exciting is a small yet significant body of self-psychologically oriented work that tends to support one of our major contentions. This concerns therapeutic dissociation as arising from the psychopharmacotherapeutic effect of the selfobject transference. We maintain that the notion of a psychopharmacotherapeutic effect of the (selfobject) transference is the basis for a bioself-psychological approach to psychotherapy with an addicted patient.

Let us return to the work of Ferguson (1990), which we previously discussed in the context of dissociation. Ferguson suggests that "it is the mirroring responsiveness of the therapist, as it develops in the working through of the mirror transference, that neutralizes the effects of...anxiety" (p. 441). He goes on to suggest that the "quiet mirroring and nonjudgmental acceptance seems to ameliorate the anxiety" (p. 441).

In the above quotes, we read Ferguson as hinting at what we argue is the psychopharmacotherapeutic effect, and more specifically, in this particular instance, the antianxiety effect of selfobject transference fantasies. The latter, in turn, creates a clinical condition which we, following Sterba, term therapeutic dissociation. Such therapeutic dissociation is necessary for an addicted patient to eventually give up a psychopathological dependence on addictive metamorphosis or phantasmagorical transmogrification, that is, entering into an altered or addictive state of mind.

Gedo (1991) is one of the first of a growing number of psychoanalysts who recognize the important implications of recent findings in the neurosciences for psychoanalytic theory and technique (see, for example, Brockman, 1998; Cooper, 1993; F. M. Levin, 1991; L. Miller, 1991; Schore, 1994, 2003a,b; and Vaughan, 1997). From our point of view, however, there are several self-psychological authors who warrant special attention. They attempt to integrate the recent findings of the neurosciences into a model that takes advantage of the strengths of both biological psychiatry and psychoanalysis.

Baker and Baker (1996), for example, advance such a model in their self-psychological work on attention deficit/hyperanxiety disorders (or AD/HD) in adults (see also Palombo, 2001). They refer to their model as being "biopsychosocial" in nature. We maintain that their model is similar to our bioself-psychological model. In the course of "using clinical examples," they "concentrate on the ways that attentional symptoms disrupt efforts of AD/HD patients to find sufficient selfobject experiences throughout the life cycle" (p. 224).

We can employ their description of the "attentional symptoms" of "AD/HD patients" and the disruptive effects of these symptoms on finding "sufficient selfobject experiences through the life cycle." There is a similarly disruptive process that takes place in an addicted patient. Like an AD/HD patient, an addicted patient has difficulty in generating and finding "sufficient selfobject experiences." This latter problem has serious and deleterious ramifications for an addicted patient. It forces an addicted patient to become psychopathologically dependent on ATMs as an alternative, albeit faulty, means of attempting to repair and restore a narcissistically fragile sense of self (see Schore 1994, 2003a,b).

There is a similarity between our findings, based on working with addicts with bipolar (spectrum) disorder, and those of Baker and Baker, who work with AD/HD patients. In treating patients with the AD/HD, Baker and Baker note that there are several ways in which the symptoms interfere with the "development of needed selfobject transferences" (p. 239). First, they "disrupt the intrapsychic processing of a successfully found therapeutic relationship" (p. 239); and, second, "they provoke countertransference problems" (p. 239). Likewise, Baker and Baker (1996) stress that medication "has a powerful salutary effect in both the transference and countertransference" (p. 239). In this context, their position is consistent with our thinking regarding working psychotherapeutically with a bipolar addict.

In two recent and remarkable papers, Wolf et al. (2000, 2001), make major and significant strides in synthesizing the neurosciences and self psychology. Their work provides support for our bioself-psychological model. In discussing a particular patient, these authors (Wolf et al., 2000) point out that what "seemed a key factor to this patient's improvement was the presence of an important person whom he experienced mainly as *nontraumatic* and *empathic*, and who eventually was able to introduce new implicit-procedural patterns" (p. 423). They add that it is possible to understand this process as involving a "down- regulation of old synaptic connections...or...new synaptic connections that modify the emotional intensity of the old connections" (p. 423).

In other words, Wolf et al. (2000, 2001; see also, Leeman & Leeman, 2004), have made, for our purposes, a crucial discovery. They have discovered a link between the (selfobject) transference and its effect as well as it impact on brain function. This supports our notion of the psychopharmacotherapeutic effect of the (selfobject) transference.

THE CASE OF BYRON—PART II

In returning to the representative case of Byron, we divide our discussion of his psychotherapy into two key aspects: (1) the transference-countertransference neurosis as it is organized unconsciously by respective degrees of dissociation on the part of the patient and psychotherapist as well as by intersubjective fantasies of megalomaniacal control as shared unconsciously by patient and psychotherapist alike; and, (2) the replacement of addictive metamorphosis by therapeutic dissociation as it occurs on the basis of the psychopharmacotherapeutic effect(s) of the transitional selfobject transference.

There are two psychodynamics that unconsciously organize the transference–countertransference neurosis as it arises between Byron and the psychotherapist. The first involves the respective degrees to which each of them underwent some form of dissociation. During the course of the psychotherapy, Byron often seems to be lost in both time and space. Throughout the course of the psychotherapy, he regularly drifts into fugue-like states of reverie as he shifts unconsciously from different forms of a transitional selfobject transference.

Sometimes, he seems to be imagining himself as grandly exhibiting himself before the psychotherapist as a mirroring selfobject. In other instances, it appears he senses himself as merged-in-fantasy with the psychotherapist, whom he imagines as omnipotent and omniscient. Apparently, still other times, he experiences himself as the twin of the psychotherapist, whom he fantasizes as an alterego selfobject. And finally, and from our point of view most importantly, at crucial moments he seems to entertain a fantasy of himself as megalomaniacally exercising magical control over the psychotherapist, whom he imagines as his own personal and magical instrument.

The psychotherapist becomes aware, gradually and over time, in all of these instances, that he too is undergoing a reciprocal and mutual form of dissociation. An intersubjective field, co-created by Byron and the psychotherapist takes form in which the psychotherapist has a countertransference experience. It is an inevitable and unavoidable pull of Byron's various transitional selfobject transference fantasies.

The psychotherapist fantasizes himself countertransferentially in the following ways: He imagines himself as the perfect mirror by which to reflect back to Byron his fantasized display of his archaic grandiosity. He entertains the illusion of himself as an idealized creation of Byron's (and his father's) imagination(s). As such a creation, the psychotherapist fantasizes himself countertransferentially as endowed by Byron with superhuman powers of omnipotence and omniscience.

On the basis of Byron's transference idealization of the psychotherapist, the latter experiences a countertransference upsurge and resurgency of his own archaic grandiosity. The psychotherapist entertains unconscious and grandiose countertransference fantasies. Perhaps, these fantasies help to account for his somewhat unorthodox decision to see the son of a former patient (namely, Byron's father) in psychotherapy.

Moreover, the psychotherapist fantasizes himself countertransferentially as Byron's alterego twin. On the basis of this twinship countertransference fantasy, he imagines that he shares with Byron a common experience of the father. In his own imagination, the psychotherapist becomes Byron's imaginary brother, that is, one of two psychotherapeutic sons of a symbolic father. He also envisions himself and Byron as fellow addicts, who, as such, are both fantasy junkies and control freaks.

And lastly, and most crucially, the psychotherapist imagines himself as a magical figure, who is similar to the Sorcerer in Disney's animated cartoon of "The Sorcerer's Apprentice." In this dissociative state of countertransference reverie (see Ogden, 1997, on the phenomenon of countertransference reverie), the psychotherapist has the illusion that he has magical control over Byron. Like Mickey Mouse in "The Sorcerer's Apprentice," Byron serves countertransferentially for the psychotherapist as one of his broom-like minions.

The varying degrees of dissociation, which patient and psychotherapist experience respectively in a similar manner, occur in the shared context of a set of intersubjective fantasies. From our perspective, the most crucial intersubjective fantasy that they share is organized unconsciously around fantasies of being a megalomaniacal self and as having magical control over one another.

Byron imagines, as part of his intersubjective fantasy, that he controls the psychotherapist, who serves in Byron's imagination as a magical instrument of psychotherapeutic relief. In the context of this same intersubjective fantasy, the psychotherapist imagines that he controls Byron, who serves in the psychotherapist's unconscious mind as a psychotherapeutic functionary. In this latter capacity, the psychotherapist fantasizes that Byron is supposed to respond perfectly to the psychotherapist's every clinical ministration and intervention.

The transference–countertransference neurosis is a ubiquitous aspect of the intersubjective context of every psychotherapeutic relationship. We maintain that it is never a question, therefore, of whether or to what degree this intersubjective configuration is present or absent. The only question is: To what extent can a particular psychotherapist gain over time an introspective understanding of the unconscious workings of a specific transference–countertransference neurosis?

Eventually, the psychotherapist does, with the case of Byron, gain such an introspective understanding. His introspective grasp of the unconscious psychodynamics of this intersubjective configuration enable him slowly to use the transference-countertransference neurosis for psychotherapeutic purposes. We contrast the presence of such an understanding to its absence. In the latter instance, a psychotherapist may fall victim to the countertherapeutic effect of the transference-countertransference neurosis. (See the case of Mary in Chapter 4 for an example of such a lack of empathic understanding.)

Fortunately, however, in the case of Byron the psychotherapist does gain insight into the unconscious working of the transference-countertransference neurosis. Consequently, it is possible for this particular psychotherapist to harness its potential for the clinical benefit of Byron. More specifically, the psychotherapist uses this intersubjective configuration as a means of inducing a state of therapeutic dissociation. And, over time, this state of therapeutic dissociation replaces Byron's psychopathological dependence on phantasmagorical transmogrification.

The psychotherapist employs the psychopharmacotherapeutic effects of Byron's various transitional selfobject fantasies. He takes advantage of the antidepressant effect of the mirroring selfobject transference fantasy. This helps him to boost and lift Byron out of his empty/depleted depression.

The psychotherapist also uses the antianxiety effect of the idealizing selfobject transference fantasy. This allows him to provide Byron with an experience of calming and soothing in the form of tranquilization and sedation.

In addition, the psychotherapist exploits the humanizing effect of the alterego twinship transference fantasy. This assists him in counteracting Byron's shameful sense of himself as nonhuman or at best semi-human.

And finally, and most significantly, the psychotherapist puts to good use the antipanic effect of Byron's transference fantasy of himself as megalomaniacally exercising magical control over the psychotherapist. In Byron's imagination, the psychotherapist functions as a magical instrument. In this latter capacity, Byron entertains the illusion of offsetting his panicky experience of himself as having lost control of his immediate selfobject milieu as well as being out of control as regards his emotional life.

Speaking metaphorically, the transference–countertransference neurosis becomes in the hands of the psychotherapist a clinical vehicle for analyzing the hypnoid defense of phantasmagorical transmogrification as it manifests itself both inside and outside of the psychotherapeutic setting. The analysis of this dissociative resistance (that is, the hypnoid defense) goes hand-in-hand, one might say, with the establishment and maintenance of a transitional selfobject transference. Perhaps in a somewhat paradoxical sense, the unfolding of Byron's transitional selfobject transference triggers a countertransference reaction on the part of the psychotherapist. Together, these mutual and reciprocal responses produce a specific version of the transference–countertransference neurosis.

However, the seeming paradox of this situation is only apparent; the basis for resolving it lies in the following fact: It is only possible for the psychotherapist with the appearance of the transference–countertransference neurosis to induce in Byron a clinical state of therapeutic dissociation. The latter occurs as a result of the psychopharmacotherapeutic effects, which accompany the various forms of Byron's transitional selfobject transference fantasies. In summary, the transference–countertransference neurosis becomes the intersubjective context in which Byron replaces addictive metamorphosis with therapeutic dissociation.

Part IV

Findings and Conclusions

Chapter 10

Addiction and Trauma (PTSD)

A REVIEW OF PSYCHOANALYTIC CASE MATERIAL REGARDING ADDICTION AND TRAUMA

We intend to make our final chapter a true culmination of our work, rather than simply a summation of preceding chapters. In the process, we want to illuminate a crucial interrelationship we believe exists between addiction and trauma or posttraumatic stress disorder (PTSD). In the current context, we equate trauma with PTSD. We use the two concepts, therefore, as equivalent and interchangeable.

The connection linking addiction and trauma (or PTSD) is present, for example, in our last case study, Byron (Chapter 9). Byron suffers from PTSD due to the traumatic loss of his mother. Byron did not resort to his addictions purely as a result of PTSD. However, clearly the traumatic loss of his mother exacerbated an already complicated condition of polyaddiction, multiple addiction, or crossover addiction.

We find evidence of the interface between addiction and trauma in all of our cases, either *in status nascendi* or in a fully developed version. These representative case studies include Megworth or "Meggy," Travis, Errol, JoAnn, Joe, Teddy, and Mary. Yet, our concern with the relationship between addiction and PTSD predates our present work. The origins of our current focus on this interconnection date back to the work of Ulman and Brothers (1987, 1988).

Ulman and Brothers present a self-psychological approach to understanding and treating trauma or PTSD. For example, in the case of "Nick," a Vietnam combat veteran, they discern a connection between addiction and PTSD. They report that Nick, in the course of combat in Vietnam, experiences what Volpicelli et al. (1999) refer to as "uncontrollable trauma." Ulman and Brothers analyze the case of Nick in terms of the shattering and faulty restoration of several archaic narcissistic fantasies. One of these unconscious fantasies expresses itself as an illusion that Nick could, as part of his magical thinking, imagine himself as becoming invisible during combat. This fantasy of invisibility enables Nick to imagine himself as being invulnerable, and hence as safely out of harm's way.

Interestingly for our present work, Ulman and Brothers (1988) refer to this fantastic process of magical thinking as a form of "personal metamorphosis" (p. 281). In this regard, they anticipate our current notion of addictive metamorphosis or phantasmagorical transmogrification. Such a dissociative process involves a psychopathological alteration of healthy imagination (see Andresen, 1996; Bosnak, 2003; Britton, 1998; Cobb, 1977; Cohen & MacKeith, 1991; Cornoldi et al., 1996; Currie & Ravenscroft, 2002; Emde et al., 1997; Grapanzano, 2004; Mayes & Cohen, 1992; McGinn, 2004; Modell, 2003; Morrison, 1988; Rescher, 2003; Rodman, 2002; Sartre, 2004 [1940]).

Nick resorts, both during his tour of duty in Vietnam and in the ensuing years following combat, to the addictive abuse of cocaine and marijuana. He does so in an ultimately futile attempt to artificially buttress his otherwise shaky fantasy of invulnerability. From the perspective of our present outlook, we re-interpret the case of Nick as follows: The "uncontrollable trauma" that Nick experiences in combat shatters his megalomaniacal fantasy of magical control. The traumatic shattering of this self-state fantasy leaves Nick panic-ridden. His panicky feelings are based on a sense that he has lost control or is out of control. These latter feelings are an expression of a mood of narcissistic mortification. We speculate that Nick, in a cocaine and marijuana-induced state of dissociation, regains an illusion of himself as once again invulnerable, and hence as back in control.

Based on our current re-interpretation of the case of Nick, the following seems clear. We see fantasy and dissociation as key factors that serve as the mediating variables connecting addiction and trauma. In our current work, these same mediating factors are also present in all of our cases. Like the case of Nick, we understand these eight cases as involving narcissistic trauma as expressed in the shattering/disturbance and faulty restoration of a fantasy of being a megalomaniacal self and as wielding magical control. As a consequence of the traumatic shattering/

disturbance of this fantasy, all eight of our current cases have an unconscious experience of themselves based on the opposite of the self-state fantasy of being in control. In other words, they imagine themselves as having lost control or being out of control. A mood of narcissistic mortification accompanies this dreadful fantasy.

In all eight of our cases, a feeling of panic precipitates an attempt, however faulty, to restore a fantasy of being a megalomaniacal self and as possessing magical control. Seven out of eight of our cases (Meggy being the exception) make faulty attempts at self-restoration by entering unconsciously into a dissociative state of addictive metamorphosis. The individuals in these seven cases seek unconsciously to induce, through the abuse of a wide and diverse variety of things and activities or ATMs, a dissociative state of mind characterized by phantasmagorical transmogrification. In the imaginations of our seven cases, these entities are endowed with a capacity of magical control.

However, in all eight of our cases, the persons in question (adults and child) entertain an especially intoxicating fantasy. They imagine themselves as having regained a megalomaniacal control over their psychic and emotional lives. Thus, all eight of our cases believe implicitly in the old adage that "fantasy becomes reality."

We make an important distinction regarding two different types of trauma that befall our eight cases. All of their traumas are narcissistic *in nature,* that is, the traumas entail the shattering/disturbance and faulty restoration of a fantasy of being a megalomaniacal self and as being empowered with magical control. However, some of the traumas are cumulative or developmental, whereas others are of a severe and shock variety.

On the one hand, Mary, JoAnn, Errol, Travis, and Meggy all suffer from some form of narcissistic trauma that is cumulative or developmental trauma in nature. In these particular cases, the specific type of trauma entails a series of experiences, which together have the shattering or disturbing impact of a minor or moderate degree on the emotional lives of our patients. In certain instances, these episodes first occur in childhood and continue through adolescence into young adulthood.

In some of these cases, the cumulative or developmental (narcissistic) trauma is based on a lack of empathy, or downright antipathy, on the part of the selfobject milieu (that is, parents or caregivers) to a specific, yet phase-appropriate fantasy. This megalomaniacal fantasy involves an imaginary experience of oneself as exercising magical control over the physical laws of nature as well as the psychological laws governing human nature. Or, in other of these cases, caregivers or parents, who make up the selfobject surround, are unempathic and/or antipathetic. They mistreat a child or adolescent in such a way that he or she feels completely at the mercy of or controlled by the whims and caprice of others.

On the other hand, Teddy, Joe, and Byron all experience some form of narcissistic trauma that is shocking and severe. This type of trauma may involve the sudden death and unexpected loss of a loved one (e.g., Teddy and Byron). Or, it may entail the shock trauma Joe experiences during combat in Vietnam. In either instance, this particular type of severe trauma is, literally as well as figuratively, shocking and earth-shattering.

The central thesis of our concluding chapter is as follows: we theorize that three key variables—namely, control (or the loss of control and being out of control), fantasy, and dissociation—serve as mediating factors connecting addiction and trauma. (See Barton, 2005; Director, 2005; Gerzi 2005; Orlandini, 2004, all of whom lend support to our central thesis.) More specifically, we contend that addiction and trauma are interrelated in the following manner. A traumatic experience (or event) shatters/disturbs a person's narcissistically pleasurable fantasy of being a megalomaniacal self and as being endowed with magical control over the psychic world of thoughts and feelings. An addict fosters this unconscious illusion by abusing addictive things or activities. All of these entities exist and are readily available to an addict as part of the immediate surround constituted by the physical universe of things and activities. An ensuing dissociative disorder such as PTSD and/or an addiction(s) results from such a traumatic experience (that is, the shattering/disturbance of a fantasy of being a megalomaniacal self and as wielding magical control).

In an apparent paradox, a traumatized individual who already suffers from the dissociative symptoms of PTSD resorts to still further dissociation in the form of phantasmagorical transmogrification. In such an addictively induced state of dissociation, a trauma survivor regains a narcissistic illusion of being a megalomaniacal self and as exercising magical control as well as an accompanying mood of narcissistic bliss. The state of addictive dissociation (in contrast to traumatic dissociation) is based on an unconscious process of phantasmagorical transmogrification.

This psychic metamorphosis leads to a temporary solution. A painful self-state fantasy and accompanying mood of narcissistic mortification (and, more specifically, a panicked sense of having lost control and a feeling of being out of control) is temporarily replaced in the unconscious mind of the affected individual by a pleasurable self-state fantasy and accompanying mood of narcissistic bliss. This latter fantasy emanates from an illusion of magical control over both the worlds of the psychic and the physical.

A trauma survivor undergoes, as part of addictive metamorphosis, an alteration in the realms of both the psychological (that is, psyche or mind) as well as the physical or corporeal (that is, brain and central nervous system). On the one hand, and as part of phantasmagorical transmogrification, the psyche or mind of a trauma survivor is altered by the unconscious upsurgence of specific archaic narcissistic fantasies or self-state fantasies. On the other hand, the brain and central nervous system are altered, again as part of addictive metamorphosis, by a radical biochemical change. Thus, phantasmagorical transmogrification involves the mind (that is, fantasy) and the brain (that is, biochemistry), each of which may be said to work hand-in-hand in a truly bioself-psychological manner. (See Baladi, 2001; Conlan, 1999; Cozolino, 2002; Eccles, 1994; Feinberg, 2001; Gazzaniga, 1985; Llinás, 2001; Restak, 1991; Siegel, 1999; Siever & Frucht, 1997, on the intimate and intricate relationship between mind and brain and vice versa.)

We divide the remaining sections of our concluding chapter into two parts. The second part concerns our bioself-psychological understanding of the connection between addiction and trauma as mediated by the variables of control, fantasy, and dissociation. In this second section of our concluding chapter, we refer, in passing, to a general body of literature relevant to our bioself-psychological understanding.

However, we focus most of our attention in this section on several articles especially pertinent to our discussion. We discuss the contributions of the following authors: Volpicelli et al. (1999) on "The role of uncontrollable trauma in the development of PTSD and alcohol addiction;" Grosch (1994) on "Narcissism, Shame, Rage, and Addiction"; J. R. Miller (1994, 2002) on "Substance Abuse: The Role of Depression and Trauma—A Case Report" and "Heroin Addiction: The Needle as Transitional Object"; Hopper (1995) on "A Psychoanalytic Theory of 'Drug Addiction': Unconscious Fantasies of Homosexuality, Compulsions and Masturbation within the Context of Traumatogenic Processes"; and Everill et al. (1995), Grave et al. (1996), Pekala et al. (2000), Reto et al. (1996), as well as Gold and Seifer (2002) on dissociation.

We devote the third part of our concluding chapter to a discussion of the technique(s) for working psychotherapeutically with patients who suffer from some type of addiction(s) as well as some form of (narcissistic) trauma. In this last part of our concluding chapter, we cite, *en passant*, literature on what is referred to in the addiction field as dual diagnosis. This body of literature reports on studies on the psychotherapeutic as well as pharmacotherapeutic treatment of patients who suffer from these two interrelated disorders (that is, addiction and trauma). In particular, we pay special attention to those works that focus specifically and exclusively on psychotherapy with "addicted survivors of trauma" (see Evans & Sullivan, 1995).

We turn, in completing this third part of our concluding chapter, to the work of J.R. Miller (1994, 2002) and Hopper (1995) (see also, B. Johnson, 1999). We focus our attention on the respective comments by Miller and Hopper on working psychoanalytically with addicted survivors of trauma. Their contributions warrant a detailed examination because they are explicitly psychoanalytic in nature. In this regard, these studies are distinctly different from the work of other authors. Such researchers deal with the topic of psychotherapy with addicted survivors of trauma. However, they proceed from a more eclectic rather than strictly psychoanalytic orientation.

A BIOSELF-PSYCHOLOGICAL UNDERSTANDING OF THE RELATIONSHIP BETWEEN ADDICTION AND TRAUMA

In recent years, a literature has emerged documenting the empirical and clinical nature between addiction and trauma. This literature dates back to at least the mid-1990s with the appearance in the *PTSD Research Quarterly*; an entire issue (Meisler, Fall 1996) is devoted to the topic of "Trauma, PTSD, and Substance Abuse." This special issue contains an overview by Meisler on this topic, as well as a selective and critical review of recently published articles that address this matter.

A number of other empirically oriented pieces have been published, beginning in the late 1990s and continuing to the present, on this topic. (See, for example, Back et al., 2000; Brady et al., 1998, 2003; Clum et al., 2002; Coffey et al., 1998; Curry, 1999; Donovan et al., 2001; Jacobsen et al., 2003; Knisely et al., 2000; Sonne et al., 2003.) However, for our purposes, the pieces by Grosch (1994), Hopper (1995), J. R. Miller, (1994, 2002), O'Donnell et al. (2004), and Volpicelli et al., (1999) deserve especially close scrutiny.

Volpicelli et al. (1999) emphasize that after "experiencing uncontrollable traumatic events, animals and humans show physiological, behavioral, and emotional symptoms of distress" (p. 258). They report that several authors (see Seligman, 1976) refer to this kind of response as "learned helplessness."

In this vein, Volpicelli et al. point out that the "grouping of symptoms that follow experience with uncontrollable trauma is called 'learned helplessness effects'" (p. 258). They single out Seligman (1975) for being the first researcher to make this observation. They also cite him for having coined the phrase "learned helplessness effects."

According to Volpicelli et al. (1999): "Both PTSD and learned helplessness develop following exposure to negative stressors or uncontrollable events" (p. 258). They indicate that the *"biochemical changes* observed in animals following uncontrollable trauma parallel those changes sometimes seen in humans following uncontrollable traumatic events" (p. 258, emphasis added). We return, later in our discussion of Volpicelli et al. and their recognition of such "biochemical changes," to the import of their observation for our bioself-psychological understanding of the interface between addiction and trauma.

Volpicelli et al. make other observations about the nature of the response to uncontrollable trauma that are relevant for our bioself-psychological perspective. They note that the "model presented ... suggests that uncontrollable trauma in humans and other mammals should lead to a release of endorphins and increased numbing" (p. 259). Moreover, these authors state: "Although exposure to uncontrollable trauma, produces a modest analgesia, it is brief and there is no endorphin withdrawal following the traumatic experience" (p. 259). They specify that in the case of traumatic events "alcohol use can increase endorphin activity" (p. 259).

These authors conclude:

> In this way, drinking can compensate for the endorphin withdrawal that follows a traumatic experience. The endorphin compensation hypothesis (ECH) suggests that when people drink alcohol after traumatic events, the alcohol makes up for the lack of endorphin activity. (pp. 259–60)

The work of Volpicelli et al. contains a number of features of crucial significance for our position. First and foremost, these authors offer a distinct perspective in comparison to many other authors from both psychoanalytic and non-psychoanalytic perspectives (see for example,

Lifton, 1967, 1988; Krystal 1978a,b, 1985; 1988; van der Kolk, 1987; van der Kolk & van der Hart, 1995; Schiraldi, 2000). Unlike these other researchers, Volpicelli et al. have a unique point of view regarding the (unconscious) meaning of traumatic experiences.

Volpicelli et al. conceptualize trauma in a subtle yet profoundly different way than do others. They view it as having a personal meaning based on the trauma survivor experiencing the event as something that is "uncontrollable" rather than its being overwhelming. There is more than a mere semantic difference that distinguishes Volpicelli et al. from other investigators. This difference concerns the meaning of traumatic experience as being defined by the trauma survivor as being uncontrollable rather than being overwhelming.

From our psychoanalytic point of view, there are important implications inherent in the definition offered by Volpicelli of a person mentally processing an experience as being traumatic because it is uncontrollable. It implies that an experience becomes traumatic for a survivor because it has an unconscious meaning that is primarily cognitive in nature. In contrast, and again from our psychoanalytic perspective, defining an experience as traumatic because it is overwhelming suggests that it has an unconscious meaning for a survivor which is, in essence, affective (that is, emotional) in nature.

We do not dispute the importance of affect in defining an experience for a survivor as traumatic. However, from our vantage point, the affective determinant is secondary to the primacy of the cognitive determinant. An emphasis on cognition versus affect supports one of our central contentions. We contend that the unconscious meaning of trauma, and the resulting PTSD, resides for an addicted survivor in an experience that shatters/disturbs "central organizing fantasies" (Nurnberg & Shapiro, 1983) of megalomania and magical control.

We are claiming, therefore, that an event is traumatic because it is experienced unconsciously by an addicted survivor as being uncontrollable. An addicted survivor experiences such an event as uncontrollable on the level of cognition. It is not experienced by an addicted survivor as traumatic primarily because it is emotionally overwhelming. Rather, the feeling on the part of an addicted survivor of being emotionally overwhelmed is a traumatic sequalae that follows the initial and shattering/disturbing experience of being unable to control a particular situation.

This latter cognitive meaning is accompanied for an addicted survivor of trauma by a mood of narcissistic mortification. Thus, a mood of narcissistic mortification is the affective component that accompanies the cognitive component. The latter is characterized by the shattering or disturbance of a fantasy of being a megalomaniacal self and as being endowed with magical control. We extrapolate from the work of Volpicelli et al. as follows: We suggest that for an addicted survivor an experience takes on a traumatic meaning primarily due to the cognitive shattering/disturbance (and subsequent faulty restoration) of unconscious fantasy rather than because of an affective disturbance of the emotions.

In summary, we argue as follows: The connection between addiction and trauma is primarily cognitive and secondarily affective. In this sense, fantasy takes precedence over emotions and mood. In other words, we believe that it is primarily fantasy (rather than affect) which defines for an addict the unconscious meaning of a traumatic experience.

Implicit in the work of Volpicelli et al. (1999) is a focus on the concept of control (that is, looking at trauma as defined by its being uncontrollable) as a crucial mediating factor linking addiction and trauma. However, these authors are important to our position for other reasons as well. They pinpoint the biochemical effects of trauma on the functioning (or malfunctioning) of an individual's brain.

These same authors describe the subsequent necessity and craving for alcohol on the part of an addicted survivor. Alcohol serves for an addicted survivor as a means of combating and offsetting the psychic pain (and, from our perspective, the sense of panic) arising from a mood of narcissistic mortification. We find additional support for our bioself-psychological model in the observations of Volpicelli et al. on the biochemical effects of the "uncontrollable."

We maintain that an addict seeks out particular things and activities (addictive trigger mechanisms, or ATMs) with specific psychoactive effects in an unconscious attempt to alter brain chemistry. Here, we are referring to our notion of psychoactive specificity. An addict has the capacity to alter brain chemistry, however fleetingly and superficially, in a specific fashion.

In particular, an addicted survivor may reverse the biochemical effects of a traumatic experience of the "uncontrollable." The capacity of an addicted survivor to reverse, on a temporary basis, the biochemical after-effects of trauma has dramatic results. It contributes to the unconscious illusion on the part of an addict of having regained control over an emotional life and psychic universe that are experienced as having gone awry (that is, as being out of control).

Grosch (1994) makes a number of points pertinent to our argument. For example, he clarifies that a "narcissistic disturbance refers not to a diagnostic category, but rather to a dimension of psychopathology which cuts across all the traditional nosological entities" (p. 55). Likewise, he continues:

> Thus one would speak of the degree of self-pathology, referring to the degree of structural impairment and vulnerability of the sense of self, the acuteness of the threat of narcissistic decompensation, and the motivational priority or urgency of the narcissistic function in a variety of pathologic states. (p. 55)

Or, to take another instance, he describes addictive "substances, activities, and objects" in terms similar to our notions of ATMs and psychoactive specificity. He argues that these entities "have hedonic and regulatory effect in their own right because of their inherent *triggering* of affects" (p. 61, emphasis added). He observes: "One group of activities *triggers* affects through either *the calming or the stimulation of sensual pleasure*" (p. 61, emphasis added). He adds: "Other activities that become available as *inherent triggers* of affect are risktaking as gambling, the multiple stimulating and calming effects of smoking, and the whole range of effects of drugs, drinking and toxic substance usage" (p. 62, emphasis added).

However, in the present context, Grosch is most relevant as regards his comments about the relationship between fantasy and addiction. He begins his self-psychological discussion of trauma by defining it as essentially narcissistic in nature. He notes that the "utilization and reliance on any age-appropriate means to obtain a selfobject experience that relieves a multitude of possible discomforts are not pathologic in themselves" (p. 62). According to Grosch: "They become pathological when obtaining and preserving the activities, objects, or substances become a central focus of the person's motivation" (p. 62).

As part of this psychopathologic process, Grosch points out that the "sources of discomfort are not then subjected to recognition and a search for solution" (p. 62). Instead, he argues, that the "goal has become to assure the availability of the means to obtain the relief *the addictive demand* is for the activity ... the object...or the substance (cigarettes, alcohol, cocaine)" (p. 62, emphasis added).

In these passages Grosch speculates on the nature of trauma as essentially narcissistic in nature and as having psychopathological sequalae in the form of addiction. His formulation is remarkably compatible with and in line with our own. In the language of our model, we read him as implying the following: There are certain things and activities that, under normal circumstances, are healthy and phase-appropriate as comforters from various forms of psychic discomfort and distress. However, abnormal conditions may arise in which a youngster experiences gross and serious empathic failures, if not outright antipathy, on the part of the selfobject milieu. Under these abnormal circumstances, things and activities undergo a psychopathological process whereby a person addictivizes them (that is, addictive metamorphosis or phantasmagorical transmagnification), and they become, later in life, ATMs.

Grosch indicates: "As long as the person's dominant motivation is to *pursue the fantasy and resist every effort to create doubt about its validity or its compatibility with other goals*, little attention can be given to the actual sources of distress" (p. 62, emphasis added).

Furthermore, he adopts an empathic point of view and observes:

> From the person's point of view, distress arises from the threat to dislodge the belief or *illusion or unconscious fantasy that has become the source of vitalizing experience* he relies on to cope with stress from a variety of sources. (p. 62, emphasis added)

Grosch explains:

> Omnipotence (such as *illusions of indispensability* and indefatigability) and over-idealization…are *fantasy elaborations* used in this way are a means to create *illusory*, but consistently creatable selfobject experiences, however brief and vulnerable. (pp. 62–63, emphasis added)

There is only one yet crucial issue with which we find fault with Grosch in this last passage. We fault Grosch for equating genuine selfobject experiences with "illusory," and hence selfobject-like experiences. From our self-psychological perspective, we go to great lengths to make the following point clear: There is a crucial difference between experiences based on the functioning of genuine versus ersatz selfobject (things and activities). As part of our effort in this context, we spell out the criteria that distinguish genuine from ersatz selfobjects (see Chapter 2).

Finally, Grosch warns that for

> patients whom we are able to help in psychotherapy, a strong desire for sustainable selfobject experiences from more ordinary sources persists alongside of *the addictive search for alternative triggers* recognized to be maladaptive. (p. 63, emphasis added)

J. R. Miller (1994, 2002) supplies us with still further support with which to buttress our position. She begins her 1994 article with several references to a "hopeless fantasy" of mastery over traumatic stressors (pp. 753, 754–55). As part of such a "hopeless fantasy," Miller (2002) describes how heroin addicts fantasize that by "mainlining...they were feeding themselves as mothers would automatically do with their own children" (p. 300). We equate Miller's idea to a "hopeless fantasy" of mastery with our notion of a megalomaniacal fantasy of magical control.

In fact, Miller (1994) even emphasizes the idea of a fantasy of control as crucial to understanding the connection between addiction and trauma. She states: "Thus, under the most extreme, devastating, horrifying conditions, the addict is able to exert a kind of *imaginary internal and external set of controls* which have been developmentally shattered, beginning in infancy" (p. 755, emphasis added).

Here, too, Miller is in line with our thinking. She lends support to our bioself-psychological understanding of the relationship between addiction and trauma. More specifically, she is in agreement with one of our central hypotheses. This concerns the developmental shattering and/or disturbance in the life of a child or adolescent of the phase-appropriate fantasy of megalomaniacal self and of possessing magical control.

Miller (2002) returns, in her most recent paper and in the context of her discussion of heroin addiction, to the idea of the traumatic shattering of fantasy. She observes: "This engenders a constellation of pathology, which *shatters the imagined* original good objects, including a pervasive sense of malignant emptiness, depletion, and a chronic, unbearable loneliness" (p. 299). In this passage, Miller appears, we believe, to be describing a mood of narcissistic mortification, which ensues from a traumatic shattering/disturbance of a fantasy of being a megalomaniacal self and as empowerd with magical control.

Later, in this same paper, Miller adds further weight in favor of our argument. She regards what amounts to a fantasy of control as crucial to understanding the interface between addiction and trauma. She describes a heroin addict as injecting the drug as a magical means by which to allow himself or herself "to conjure an *imaginary constellation* of good objects, *thereby containing the blow of early trauma and taking control of its poison*" (p. 302, emphasis added).

In a "case example," Miller (1994) emphasizes the importance of a phantasmagorical version of control as a crucial linkage connecting addiction and trauma. In the course of discussing this case example, she paraphrases her patient as follows. According to Miller, her patient implies that her addiction, far from being a passive retreat from trauma, is "*an active statement* of her wish [that is, fantasy] to *construct and control* the quality and response to suffering" (p. 759, emphasis added).

Miller stresses the centrality of the concepts of control and fantasy to understanding the interrelationship that exists between addiction and trauma. She also makes several references to dissociation as worthy of mention. For example, she states "substance abuse takes the form of self-medicating, and *dissociating* oneself from enormous psychic pain" (p. 756, emphasis added).

Miller recognizes, as we do, that there is something seemingly paradoxical about the connection between addiction and trauma. This concerns the following fact: trauma assumes a dissociative cast in the form of PTSD symptoms (see Ulman & Brothers, 1987, 1988); yet it nonetheless leads an addict to resort to another kind of dissociation. We have referred to this type of dissociation as addictive metamorphosis or phantasmagorical transmogrification.

We can attempt to explain this apparent paradox in the following manner. Traumatic dissociation results, we contend, from the shattering/ disturbance of an addict's megalomaniacal fantasy of magical control. An addict has no alternative but to attempt unconsciously to restore, however temporarily and faultily, such a self-state fantasy of being a megaloma-niacal self. As part of this ultimately doomed effort, an addict triggers a dissociated state of addictive metamorphosis (that is, abusing ATMs). An addict, in such an altered state of consciousness, imagines once again being a megalomaniacal self and as having regained magical control.

Metaphorically speaking, an addict enters into an addictive state of phantasmagorical transmogrification in an attempt to fight fire with fire. From a psychoanalytic perspective, this effort on the part of an addict is an example of A. Freud's (1966 [1936]) concept of the unconscious defense mechanism of turning passive into active. In this particular instance, traumatic dissociation is passive in nature. In this regard a trauma survivor experiences a hypnoid alteration of consciousness as expressed pathologically in the form of PTSD. An addicted trauma survivor engages in an unconscious process of magical thinking, which takes the form of an illusion of having turned a passive form of disso-ciation into an active form (that is, phantasmagorical transmogrification).

According to Hopper (1995), the core of his theory centers on the idea that "motivation for addition to drugs is based on the need to entertain certain fantasies…that originate within traumatogenic processes" (p. 1121). Hopper expresses little or no doubt about the phantasmagorical nature of addiction. He reports that in his "clinical experience, people who are addicted to drugs are also *and perhaps primarily addicted to fantasies* and compulsions that are associated with and facilitated by using them" (p. 1129, emphasis added). In this passage, Hopper makes it clear in a very explicit fashion that he believes that people are addicted primarily to fantasy.

In a fashion similar to our thinking about psychoactive specificity, Hopper observes that an addict uses various substances to activate different types of unconscious fantasy. Hopper notes:

> The use of "downers" will also be associated with unconscious fantasies of an identification with an 'internal saboteur,' and the use of 'uppers' will also be associated with fantasies of hatred and violence and illicit sexualities. (p. 1125)

In a similar vein, he indicates that by "offering opportunities for excitement and illusions of triumph, taking drugs becomes an anti-depressant action" (p. 1125).

Finally, Hopper contends that there are different "pharmacological properties of the main two different kinds of drugs" (p. 1130). Moreover, he asserts that the difference in the "pharmacological properties of the main two different kinds of drugs" accounts for the difference in the types of fantasies generated by these psychoactive agents. In this sense, he suggests that drugs "with specific pharmacological properties facilitate the production, development, maintenance and *control* of specific fantasies" (p. 1130, emphasis added).

Hopper's theory supports our notion of psychoactive specificity, adding strength to our bioself-psychological model. The following idea is implicit in our notion of psychoactive specificity. We hypothesize that different ATMs generate a particular type of archaic narcissistic fantasy with an accompanying pleasant mood of narcissistic bliss. We speculate that the psychoactive generation of these narcissistic fantasies and moods is part of a psychopathological alteration of brain chemistry, or an addictively induced change in the (dys)functioning of the brain. This is an example of a psychosomatic process in the addiction field. (See Taylor, 1987, for a discussion of the psychic effect of fantasy on the brain as part of the soma.)

We read Hopper as being in agreement with one of our central contentions: namely, addicts are "control freaks." We have already quoted several passages in which Hopper alludes to the idea of control. And, we cite specific material from Hopper regarding the illusion or fantasy of control as being crucial to understanding an addict's use of drugs.

Hopper describes the unconscious motivation of a cocaine addict as an example of an addict's need to feel in control: "Cocaine addicts use their drugs in order to regulate such fantasies in the sense that they try *to control* the scenes [that is, the phantasmagorical scenes], especially their endings" (p. 1131, emphasis added). Moreover, Hopper suggests that the "motivation for the compulsion to enact fantasies is the desire to communicate, to expel and to evacuate painful anxiety, and to attack and *control both internal and external objects*" (p. 1131, emphasis added).

In all of these passages Hopper emphasizes the concept of control as being central to his psychoanalytic understanding of addiction. In this sense, therefore, we maintain that his views are congruent with our bioself-psychological understanding of addiction. He aligns himself with us in understanding addiction as being based, to a significant degree, on what we call a fantasy of being a megalomaniacal self and as exercising magical control.

We find great support in Hopper's writings for our bioself-psychological view of addicts as fantasy junkies and control freaks. However, we part company with Hopper as regards the nature and types of fantasies that determine the unconscious meaning of addiction. In contrast to our self-psychological thinking, Hopper adopts a psychoanalytic line of thinking that stems from British object relations and Kleinian thinking. Consequently, he envisions psychosexual and aggressive fantasies as forming the unconscious bedrock of addiction. In contrast to psychosexual and aggressive fantasies, we place archaic narcissistic fantasies as foundational in determining the unconscious meaning of addiction.

We disagree sharply with Hopper about the nature and type of fantasy that are unconsciously determinative of all addictions. Yet, we do agree with Hopper on one issue. We concur with Hopper that all addictions involve a psychopathological perversion of the essential process of unconscious fantasizing. Under normal and healthy circumstances, fantasy plays an adaptive and constructive role in a person's psychic life. An addict perverts this unconscious function into a maladaptive and destructive role. In this regard, therefore, we, like Hopper, construe addiction as undermining and pathologizing the unconscious mental faculty of imagination.

Finally, Hopper argues in support of our contention that addiction and trauma are integrally linked. He indicates that in "addiction, there is always a history of trauma, and in trauma, there is always a history of 'bad' habits and often a pattern of substance abuse" (p. 1134). He adds: "It is appropriate to think in terms of a 'trauma syndrome that involves addiction, as in terms of an addiction syndrome that involve trauma" (p. 1134).

An impressive literature exists on dissociation as a factor that mediates the connection between addiction and trauma (see, for example, Wilson, 2004; Gershuny et al., 2004; Lightstone, 2004; Talbot et al., 2004; Sartre et al., 2004). This body of work has tended to be, although not exclusively, empirical in nature. This research focuses on bulimia (see, for example, Everill et al., 1995; Grave et al., 1996; and, Reto et al., 1996), substance abuse (see Pekala et al., 2000), and "sexual addiction/compulsivity" (see Gold & Seifer, 2002).

Everill et al. (1995) theorize dissociation as a disturbance in cognition involving an *escape from awareness* (p. 155). These authors regard dissociation as a mediating factor between addiction (that is, bulimia as an addictive eating disorder) and trauma. They state:

> In particular, it is proposed that a temporary cognitive narrowing is experienced during a binge as the bulimic refocuses attention on to the immediate stimulus. This refocusing allows a reduction in negative affect or a general reduction in self-awareness. (p. 155)

Everill et al. hypothesize that "bulimic symptomology will be greater when a history of abuse is reported...and that dissociation will act as a mediating factor in this relationship" (p. 156). Furthermore, they assert that the "'escape from awareness'" model...suggests that this relationship will be particularly strong in the case of bingeing behavior" (p. 156). In addition, they maintain that an "intolerable cognitive state triggers the use of dissociation and a search for tension-reducing behavior, such as bingeing" (p. 153). Finally, they indicate that bingeing may serve a "number of specific functions, including temporary distraction, a filling of emptiness, and numbing of psychic pain" (p. 158).

In that last statement Everill et al. touch on several points especially germane to our position. More specifically, we interpret them as hinting in the language of our model at the notion of addictive metamorphosis. Consistent with our notion, these authors believe that a bulimic uses binges to escape from awareness, and, in the process, creates a dissociated state characterized by distortion and a "numbing of psychic pain."

If we look back at our prior notion of dissociative anesthesia, which is a forerunner to our current concepts of addictive metamorphosis or phantasmagorical transmogrification, we find two central aspects of this idea that are also present in the thinking of Everill et al. First, a parallel exists between their idea of escaping from awareness and our thinking about dissociation. And second, we find a similarity between their thinking about the "numbing of psychic pain" and our thoughts on addictive anesthetization.

We also read Everill et al. as thinking in terms that coincide with our idea about psychoactive specificity. They view a bulimic as employing bingeing as a means of attempting to fill emptiness, thus serving, in the language of our model, as an anti-depressant. The selfobject-like activity of this ATM functions for a bulimic to counteract, however faultily, an empty/depleted depression. Such a psychopathological condition originates from an early selfobject milieu that fails empathically to provide adequate mirroring.

Reto et al. (1996) point out that, in the case of survivors of physical and sexual abuse, dissociation and "bulimia may develop then as a method of continuous effort to remain unaware of the emotional reactions" (p. 63) to the meanings of these traumas (that is, physical and sexual abuse). These authors add that "bulimia itself becomes a dissociative mechanism using obsession with food and weight in addition to bingeing and purging as a primary way of splitting off feelings and memories related to traumatic experiences" (p. 63). They conclude: "Escape through bulimia also may allow the individual to re-experience the affects associated with the trauma while *exerting some control over the event* (p. 63, emphasis added).

We would re-phrase this latter astute statement from the perspective of our model, as follows. We emphasize that the control, which a bulimic imagines exerting over traumatic affect is, of course, illusory. Hence, it is faulty and ultimately fails.

The attempt on the part of a bulimic to exert imaginary control over traumatic experience(s) is futile. This futility helps to account for a crucial fact. Namely, that a bulimic, like all addicts, becomes trapped in a psychopathological cycle from which there appears to be no escape.

In Chapter 1 of our book, this vicious cycle of addictive abuse is referred to as the Narcissus complex. Consequently, an addict resorts to the repeated use (abuse) of ATMs. Such addictive repetition enables an addict to have a narcissistic illusion of magical control over that which remains an "uncontrollable" traumatic experience. We construe the repetitive nature of all addictions as based on an addict's ill-fated and doomed attempt to control the "uncontrollable."

For our purposes, Pekala et al. (2000), in their empirical study "Dissociation as a Function of Child Abuse and Fantasy Proneness in a Substance Abuse Population," reach some interesting and pertinent findings. They state that the "results of the present study support *fantasy proneness as a major variable in the prediction of dissociation with a substance abuse population*" (p. 122, emphasis added). They continue that "fantasy proneness appears to be tapping a construct that is not only exacerbated by child abuse, but may represent a trait, like absorption, a variable related to fantasy proneness...that is *genetically mediated*" (p. 123). In this latter observation, these authors touch on an issue, that is, genetic predisposition, which is relevant to and supportive of our bioself-psychological model.

The need on the part of an addict to alter brain chemistry and, as a concomitant, to alter state of mind or consciousness, is based, we believe, on a specific kind of genetic predisposition. This genetically based proclivity expresses itself in a particular type of irregularity in the functioning of an addict's brain chemistry. There are many articles, both in the popular press and in more scientifically oriented publications, reporting on recent findings by neuroscientists on such irregularities in the brain functioning and brain chemistry of addicts. (See, for example, *The New York Times*, Thursday, July 18, 1996; Brody, *The New York Times*, Tuesday, September 30, 2003; Massing, *The New York Times*, Saturday, June 24, 2000; O'Neil, *The New York Times*, June 24, 2003; and Pantoine, *Brainwork*, January–February, 2003).

Pekala et al. conclude their study by noting that the "data suggest important information for understanding the importance of both fantasy proneness and child abuse in the etiology of dissociative disorders" (p. 125). In sum, they assert that although "causality cannot be determined from this correlational study design, the data suggests *that dissociation...may be as much a function of fantasy proneness*, as of reported child abuse" (p. 125, emphasis added).

At least, according to these authors, there is clearly empirical evidence supporting the idea that the interrelationship between addiction and trauma is mediated by both "fantasy proneness" and dissociation. These same investigators are less clear, however, regarding whether fantasy proneness causes dissociation or vice versa. Regardless, they have no doubts about the mediating influence of fantasy proneness and dissociation on the connection between addiction (and more specifically, substance abuse) and trauma.

Gold and Seifer (2002) in their study, "Dissociation and Sexual Addiction/Compulsivity: A Contextual Approach to Conceptualization and Treatment," arrive at their findings from a more clinical (as opposed to empirical) methodology. Their clinically based findings on dissociation as a mediating factor that links addiction and trauma lend credence to our position. These authors specifically link childhood sexual abuse (CSA) with sexual addiction/compulsivity (SAC) via the mediating effect of dissociation. They state that "the presence of dissociative states" (p. 65) is a defining characteristic of SAC with a history of CSA. These authors describe such "dissociative states" as including

> lack of awareness of salient aspects of SAC patterns, despite repeated execution of these behaviors; poor recollection of SAC incidents even when they are recent; clouded awareness during SAC activity; and a sense that the behavior is occurring automatically and outside of conscious control. (p. 70)

Gold and Seifer discuss dissociation from a developmental perspective. They maintain that it "can be understood as being related to insecure or disorganized attachment due to the lack of consistent availability and responsivity of caretakers" (p. 77). From our self-psychological vantage point, these authors may be interpreted as asserting that an unempathic selfobject milieu is critical in leading to dissociation. Gold and Seifer, in their own words, examine dissociation from the viewpoint of an experience of "growing up in an ineffective family context" (pp. 76–77).

Regarding this context, they argue that there is a

> lack of secure attachment...[which] translates into disconnectedness from others, from one's own emotional experience, and from the immediate present, all of which interfere with the capacities for sexual responsiveness, emotional intimacy, and the integration of these two spheres of capacities. (p. 77)

Gold and Seifer maintain that "dissociative disconnection from the immediacy of sexual experience can be understood as a major reason why SAC persists even though it may actually be sexually and emotionally unsatisfying or even aversive" (p. 77). These authors conclude that because SAC is "carried out in the automatic, experientially detached manner that defines dissociative phenomenon, recollection recognition, and integration of the unsatisfactory nature of SAC is unlikely to occur" (p. 77).

PSYCHOTHERAPY WITH AN ADDICTED SURVIVOR OF TRAUMA

By now, a vast literature has emerged on what is commonly referred to in the mental health field as the patient with a dual diagnosis or comorbid disorders (that is, a psychiatric disorder as well as an addictive disorder). (See volumes edited by Gold & Slaby, 1991; N.S. Miller, 1993, 1994; Westermeyer et al., 2003. See also, Clark, 2001; Compton et al., 2000; de Graaf et al., 2002; Evans & Sullivan, 2001; Finley, 2004; Franken & Hendriks, 2001; Hien et al., 2004; Kushner et al., 1999; Landry et al., 1994; McGrath et al., 2000; Modesto-Lowe & Kranzler, 1999; Mueser et al., 2003; Ortman, 1997; Penk et al., 2000; Petrakis et al., 2002; Randall et al., 2001; Richards, 1993; Ruiz et al., 2002; Scheller-Gilkey et al., 2002; Shivani et al., 2002; Skodol et al., 1999; Spencer et al., 2002; Tonneatto et al., 2000; Tucker & Westermeyer, 1990; Volkow, 2001; Westermeyer et al., 1995.)

This type of patient suffers simultaneously from an addictive disorder as well as another type of psychiatric disorder. According to the noso-logical framework of *DSM-IV-TR* (2000), these patients may suffer from a psychiatric disorder falling diagnostically either on axis I or axis II. It is also possible that such a patient with a dual diagnosis may suffer from both an axis I and axis II disorder in addition to an addictive disorder.

We should mention parenthetically that from the technical vantage point of *DSM-IV-TR* an addictive disorder in and of itself is considered to be an axis I diagnosis. Thus, a patient with a dual diagnosis may suffer hypothetically from two different types of axis I illnesses—an addictive disorder combined with some other type of axis I malady. Examples of the latter type of disturbance might include generalized anxiety disorder (GAD), a major mood disorder like bipolar disorder, or schizoaffective disorder.

We want to stress the following point in the strongest terms possible. To be more precise, we need to emphasize that we are not adopting the position that our patients are dual diagnosis in the strictest and most technical sense of *DSM-IV-TR*. We are not suggesting, therefore, that as defined by *DSM-IV-TR* our patients suffer from an axis I disorder in the form of an addiction and, simultaneously, may be diagnosed as suffering from an axis II disorder in the form of a personality disorder (Clusters A, B, and C).

And, to be even more emphatic, we are not implying that our patients suffer from a narcissistic personality disorder as described in

DSM-IV-TR. On the contrary, the crux of our argument is that from our self-psychological perspective we view all addictions as essentially narcissistic in nature. (See Grosch, 1994, on the essentially narcissistic nature of all addictions.) In other words, we argue that, in essence, all addictions entail an underlying shattering/disturbance and faulty restoration of an archaic narcissistic fantasy of the self as megalomaniacal and, as such, in possession of magical control.

A small yet significant body of work exists on the psychotherapeutic treatment of addicted survivors of trauma (see, for example, Evans & Sullivan, 1995; Howard, 2000; Miller & Guidry, 2001; Najavits, 2002; see also the edited volumes by Ouimette & Brown, 2003; and Schwartz & Cohn, 1996). Of this literature, the contribution of Evans and Sullivan stands out. These authors are pioneers in blazing a trail that links addiction and trauma. In addition, they devise specific approaches tailored to working psychotherapeutically with patients who are both addicted and trauma survivors. They develop a psychotherapeutic approach to treating these patients that incorporates the findings from the fields of both addiction and trauma studies.

We applaud Evans and Sullivan for their groundbreaking work in this long neglected area, namely working psychotherapeutically with addicted survivors of trauma. However, there are two aspects of their approach where we part company with Evans and Sullivan.

The first psychotherapeutic matter about which we take issue concerns the phenomenon (the illusion or fantasy) of control. (See Friedlander, 1988 for a discussion of the origins of this phenomenon in childhood.) As we previously indicate, Evans and Sullivan (1995) subscribe to the so-called phenomenon of "loss of control." This is a notion that is well-known and commonly used in the addiction field. (See Distefano et al., 1972; Fiorentine & Hillhouse, 2003; Good, 1995; Keller, 1972; Moore & Ohtsuka, 1999; Oziel & Obitz, 1975; Obitz & Swanson, 1976; Paredes et al., 1973; Plumb et al., 1975 for various discussions of the so-called phenomenon of "loss of control" in the context of addiction.) Evans and Sullivan (1995) believe that the loss of control phenomenon is crucial to understanding addiction as well as to treating addicts (pp. 71–72).

In this regard, they adopt a purely extrospective stance rather than adhering to an introspective and empathic perspective. On the one hand, a clinician may view a particular addict's behavior from a position that is outside of that person's subjective frame of reference. Based on such an extrospective point of view, it certainly looks to an outside observer as if an addict has, indeed, lost control of a particular addictive behavior or set of behaviors.

However, on the other hand, a clinician may view this same addict's behavior from a position that is within that particular person's subjective frame of reference. A very different picture emerges from such a vantage point of "vicarious introspection" (Kohut, 1971, p. 219, footnote 8). As defined by Kohut (1971), vicarious introspection or empathy involves an "observer who occupies an imaginary point inside the psychic organization of the individual with whose introspection he empathically identifies" (p. 219, footnote 8).

From this vantage point of vicarious introspection, an empathic observer understands that, as employed in the addiction field, an addict does not experience himself or herself as having lost control. In the first place, there is the unconscious defense mechanism of denial, which is commonly accepted by addiction experts as the *sine qua non* of all addictions. Secondly, from our viewpoint, an addict does not experience a so-called "loss of control." Rather, and on the contrary, an addict imagines himself or herself in a manner which is, in fact, the opposite of having lost control.

An addict is under the intoxicating influence of a fantasy of being a megalomaniacal self and as endowed with magical control. As a result, an addict has the unconscious illusion of exercising magical control over the entire world of thoughts and feelings. An addict imagines himself or herself as wielding a magic wand over things and activities (that is, ATMs). With the flick of the wrist, an addict conjures up a narcissistic illusion of having compelled emotions to respond in a fashion dictated by the waving of the magic wand (that is, the abuse of ATMs).

Evans and Sullivan (1995), in describing an addict's behavior in terms of control, state: "Their attempts to keep things *under* control by such acts as lying, scheduling long lunches, and forging checks indicate their increasing desperation *to control what is out of control*" (p. 71, emphasis added). Based on this view, they are ardent proponents of confronting "alcoholics and addicts about their *control issues*" as a "key part of treatment" (p. 71, emphasis added).

We strongly disagree with the approach of Evans and Sullivan (1995) on confrontation. We insist that it is a very bad idea to confront an addicted survivor of trauma about so-called "control issues." Such an approach is likely to be countertherapeutic, especially during the early phases of psychotherapy.

We oppose a psychotherapeutic approach based on adopting a confrontational style with addicted survivors of trauma regarding so-called "control issues." Rather, we advocate an approach that facilitates and allows an addicted survivor of trauma to entertain the following illusion. He or she imagines having magical control over both the psychotherapy and the psychotherapist.

We base our non-confrontational style on an empathic understanding of an addict's unconscious fantasy life. As part of such an imaginary world, an addicted survivor of trauma has a desperate need to experience an illusory sense of magical control, and especially in the intersubjective context of a transitional selfobject transference fantasy. We believe that such a fantasy-based transference experience enables an addicted survivor of trauma to undergo therapeutic dissociation. In a state of therapeutic dissociation, an addicted survivor of trauma may more readily give up a pathological dependence on ATMs. In addition, such a patient finds it easier to resist the urge to drop down the rabbit hole of addictive metamorphosis.

Evans and Sullivan (1995) advocate confronting an addicted survivor of trauma about control issues, thus disregarding the possible counter-therapeutic effects. Such an approach will interfere with or prevent the unfolding of a (transitional selfobject) transference fantasy of a megalo-maniacal self as possessing magical control. And, the latter is an absolute psychotherapeutic necessity for working successfully with addicted survivors of trauma. It enables them to bring their fantasies of being a megalomaniacal self from the outside world to the inside domain of the psychotherapeutic setting. On the basis of a specific type of selfobject transference, a psychotherapist may assist an addicted survivor of trauma in analyzing and working through these unconscious fantasies.

We disagree with Evans and Sullivan (1995) about a second psychotherapeutic issue involving the phenomenon of dissociation. They describe their work with a particular client named "Linda." As part of their description, they make the following observation: "We decided not only that she was highly dissociative but that she was also in a *therapy-induced trance*, trying to work through her trauma but in a dissociated way that her work would never become integrated" (p. 190, emphasis added). They continue: "Our goal, in collaboration with the client, is *to disable the dissociation defense as an automatic response* (p. 191, emphasis added).

From the vantage point of our approach, we find a remarkable paradox embedded in the description by Evans and Sullivan of their psychotherapeutic work with Linda. On the one hand, these authors correctly recognize that Linda is in a "therapy-induced trance," or what we call a state of therapeutic dissociation. Yet, on the other hand, these same authors fail to appreciate the psychotherapeutic value of this state of mind. In fact, in a further discussion of their work with Linda, they proudly report the following fact. They announce that they purposefully and actively interfered with this "therapy-induced trance" in order to break it.

Evans and Sullivan deprive Linda of a vital psychotherapeutic experience without, however, appreciating the potential for countertherapeutic damage. In all likelihood, Linda, in the absence of such an experience, would be unable to relinquish her pathological dependence on addictive metamorphosis. Deprived of a necessary experience of therapeutic dissociation, we believe that Linda would inevitably find it far more difficult, if not impossible, to stop resorting to addictive dissociation (that is, phantasmagorical transmogrification).

Consequently, Linda would be more prone to remain actively addicted. In our opinion, she would continue to be addicted despite the good intentions of her psychotherapist, who, in this particular case, is Evans. This is a classic example of a tragic fact: the road to psychotherapeutic disaster is paved with the good intentions of psychotherapists, who, although well-meaning, engage in countertherapeutic interventions.

Before bringing our concluding chapter to an end, we return to the work of J.R. Miller and Hopper. The work of these two authors is important to our approach for both general and specific reasons. Generally speaking, it has import for us because they adopt an explicitly psychoanalytic orientation. In addition, each of these clinicians derive their theoretical ideas from the practice of psychoanalytic psychotherapy with addicted patients. And each of these authors present case examples to illustrate their theoretical thinking. As we already stress, the vast majority of the work in the addiction field is *theory heavy* and *case history (or studies) light*. In this regard, Miller and Hopper are exceptions to the rule, and thus are especially deserving of special mention.

For our purposes, however, the import of the work of Miller (1994, 2002) and Hopper (1995) has specific significance. Each of these two authors has something special to offer in support of our approach. For instance, Miller, (1994, 2002) in discussing the case of "Rosalie," concludes that the "positive transference which endured throughout the therapy made it possible [for Rosalie] *to use me as a transitional object*" (p. 762, emphasis added). Miller adopts in this observation of his psychotherapy with Rosalie a Winnicottian and object relational perspective. Nonetheless, we interpret him as adopting an approach that is implicitly consistent with our self-psychological notion of the transitional selfobject transference.

In fact, in the beginning of our book we clarify that our concept of the transitional selfobject transference constitutes a legitimate integration and necessary blending of Winnicottian object relations theory with Kohutian self-psychological theory. (See Adler & Rhine, 1988 and Cooper & Adler, 1990, for first-rate examples of similar attempts at fusing the ideas of British object relations with that of self psychology.) This is an instance that, we believe, counters an idea held by some prominent self psychologists such as A. Goldberg (1988, 1995). According to such theorists, "never shall the twain meet" as far as concerns the blending of self-psychological concepts with those from other psychoanalytic schools of thought. Our opinion is more in line with the thinking of other psychoanalytic theorists, including Bacal (1987, 1990), Smith (1989), Bacal and Newman (1990), and Blass and Blatt (1992). All of these authors accept the legitimacy and appreciate the value of combining Kohut's self psychology with Winnicott's object relations.

Returning to Hopper (1995); he makes the following insightful observation:

> Becoming dependent on, *if not fully addicted to the analyst, psychoanalysis and all its material paraphernalia* is a kind of substitute for the addictive substance, but this process of substitution is slow and tentative and requires a sense of both safety and excitement, which is not easy to provide or to obtain. (p. 1139, emphasis added)

However, in the above passage, Hopper makes an equation that we do not accept as sound. He equates an addicted patient's pathological dependence on a variety of things and activities (that is, "addictive substance") with a healthy reliance on a psychotherapist and the psychotherapy. An addicted patient's transference to the psychotherapist as a transitional selfobject is a form of healthy reliance (versus unhealthy dependence). Such a transitional selfobject transference is necessary and healthy as a replacement or substitute for a psychopathological and unhealthy abuse of the psychoactive functions of ATMs as ersatz selfobject.

Despite our disagreement with Hopper, we believe that he is still on the right track. He recognizes correctly that an addicted patient eventually ought to have, if psychotherapy is to be successful, a special kind of psychoanalytic experience. In sum, an addicted patient ought to gain a healthy reliance on a psychotherapist and psychotherapy as initially equivalent to and later superior to a pathological dependence on ATMs.

References

Abaronovich, E., Liu, X., Nunes, E., & Hasin, D. S. (2002). Suicide attempts in substance abusers: effects of major depression in relation to substance use disorders. *American Journal of Psychiatry, 159 (9)*, 1600–1602.

Abaronovich, E., Nguyen, H. T., Nunes, E. V. (2002). Anger and depressive states among treatment-seeking drug abusers: Testing the psychopharmacological specificity hypothesis. *American Journal on Addiction, 10*, 327–334.

Abraham, K. (1927). *Selected papers of Karl Abraham, M.D.* London: Marsefield Library.

Abraham, K. (1927) [1921]. Contributions to the theory of the anal character. In *Selected papers of Karl Abraham* (pp. 370–392). London: Maresfield Library.

Abraham, K. (1927) [1924]. The influence of oral erotism on character-formation. In *Selected papers of Karl Abraham* (pp. 393–406). London: Maresfield Library.

Abraham, K. (1927) [1925]. Character-formation on the genital level of the libido. In Selected papers of Karl Abraham (pp. 407–417). London: Maresfield Library.

Abraham, K. (1979 [1920]). The narcissistic evaluation of excretory processes in dreams and neurosis. In *Selected papers of Karl Abraham, M.D.* (pp. 318–322). London: Karnac (Books) Ltd.

Abrams, S., & Neubauer, P. B. (1975). Object orientedness: The person or the thing. *Psychoanalytic Quarterly, 45*, 73–99.

Abrams, S., & Neubauer, P. B. (1976). Transitional objects: Animate and inanimate. In S. A. Grolnick, L. Barkin, & W. Muensterberger (Eds.), *Between reality and fantasy: Transitional objects and phenomena* (pp. 133–144). New York: Jason Aronson.

Abse, D. W. (1966). *Hysteria and related mental disorders: An approach to psychological medicine*. Bristol, England: John Wright & Sons, Ltd.

Adams, J. W. (1978). *Psychoanalysis of drug dependence: The understanding and treatment of a particular form of pathological narcissism*. New York: Grune & Stratton.

Adams, V. A. (2001). *The mythological unconscious*. New York: Karnac.

Adams, V. A. (2004). *The fantasy principle. Psychoanalysis of the imagination*. New York: Brunner-Routledge.

Adelman, J. (1992). *Suffocating mothers: Fantasies of maternal origin in Shakespeare's plays, Hamlet to Tempest*. New York: Routledge.

Adelman, S. A. (1993). Pills as transitional objects. In M. Schachter (Ed.), *Psychotherapy and medication: A dynamic integration* (pp. 109–119). Northvale, NJ: Jason Aronson.

Adler, G. (1985). *Borderline psychopathology and its treatment*. Northvale, NJ: Jason Aronson.

Adler, G. (1989a). Transitional phenomena, projective identification, and the essential ambiguity of the psychoanalytic situations. *Psychoanalytic Quarterly, 58*, 81–104.

Adler, G. (1989b). Uses and limitations of Kohut's self psychology in the treatment of borderline patients. *Journal of the American Psychoanalytic Association, 37*, 761–785.

Adler, G., & Buie, Jr., D. H. (1991). The misuses of confrontation in the psychotherapy of borderline cases. In G. Adler & P. G. Myerson (Eds.), *Confrontation in psychotherapy* (pp. 147–162). Northvale, NJ: Jason Aronson.

Adler, N., & Goleman, P. (1969). Gambling and alcoholism; symptom substitution and functional equivalents. *Quarterly Journal of the Study of Alcoholism, 30*, 733–736.

Adler, G., & Rhine, M. W. (1988). The selfobject function of projective identification. *Bulletin of the Menninger Clinic, 52*, 473–491.

Ahearn, C. F., & Carroll, B. J. (2001). Substance abuse in bipolar disorder. *Bipolar Disorders, 3*, 181–188.

Aichhorn, A. (1964). *Delinquency and child guidance: Selected papers.* New York: International Universities Press.

Akiskal, H. S. (1996). The prevalent clinical spectrum of bipolar disorders: beyond DMS-IV. *Journal of Clinical Psychopharmacology, 16 (2)*, 4S–14S.

Alford, C. F. (1988). *Narcissism: Socrates, the Frankfurt school, and psychoanalytic theory.* New Haven, CT: Yale University Press.

Allen, M. H., & Frances R. J. (1986). Varieties of psychopathology found in patients with addictive disorders: A review. In R. E. Meyer (Ed.), *Psychopathology and addictive disorders* (pp. 17–38). New York: Guilford Press.

Alper, G. (1996). *Control games: Avoiding intimacy the singles scene.* Northvale, NJ: Jason Aronson.

American Psychiatric Association. (1980). *Diagnostic and statistical manual of mental disorders* (3rd ed.). Washington, DC: Author.

American Psychiatric Association. (1987). *Diagnostic and statistical manual of mental disorders* (3rd ed., rev.). Washington, DC: Author.

American Psychiatric Association. (1989). *Treatments of psychiatric disorders.* A Task Force Report of the American Psychiatric Association. Washington, DC: Author.

American Psychiatric Association. (1994). *Diagnostic and statistical manual of mental disorders* (4th ed.). Washington, DC: Author.

American Psychiatric Association. (2000). *Diagnostic and statistical manual of mental disorders* (4th ed., rev.). Washington, DC: Author.

Anderson, F. S. (2001). "No matter how hard I try, I can't get through to you!" Dissociated affect in a stalled enactment. In J. Petrucelli & C. Stuart (Eds.), *Hungers and compulsions. The psychodynamic treatment of eating disorders and addictions* (pp. 113–123). Northvale, NJ: Jason Aronson.

Andresen, J. J. (1996). An origin of the inhibition of imagination. *Contemporary Psychoanalysis, 32*, 307–325.

Angst, J., & Cassano, G. (2005). The mood spectrum: Improving the diagnosis of bipolar disorder. *Bipolar Disorders, 7 (Suppl. 4)*, 4–12.

Angst, J., Gamma, A., Benazzi, F., Ajdacic, V., Eich, D., & Rössler, W. (2003). Toward a re-definition of subthreshold bipolarity: epidemiology and proposed criteria for bipolar-II, minor bipolar disorders and hypomania. *Journal of Affective Disorders, 73*, 133–146.

Anthenelli, R. M., & Schuckit, M. A. (1993). Affective and anxiety disorders and alcohol and drug dependence: Diagnosis and treatment. In N. S. Miller (Ed.) *Comorbidity of affective and psychiatric disorders* (pp. 73–87). New York: Haworth Medical Press.

Anthony, D. T., & Hollander, E. (1993). Sexual compulsions. In E. Hollander (Ed.), *Obsessive-compulsive related disorders* (pp. 139–150). Washington, DC: American Psychiatric Press.

Apsler, R. (1978). Untangling the conceptual jungle of drug abuse. *Contemporary Drug Problems, 7*, 55–80.

Arlow, J. A. (1953). Masturbation and symptom formation. *Journal of the American Psychoanalytic Association, 1*, 45–58.

Arlow, J. A. (1969a). Unconscious fantasy and disturbances of conscious experience. *Psychoanalytic Quarterly, 38*, 28–51.

Arlow, J. A. (1969b). Fantasy, memory, and reality testing. *Psychoanalytic Quarterly, 38*, 28–51.

Arlow, J. A. (1991 [1977]). *Psychoanalysis: Clinical theory and practice* (pp. 257–278). Madison, CT: International Universities Press.

Aron, L., & Bushra, A. (1998). Mutual regression: Altered states in the psychoanalytic situation. *Journal of the American Psychoanalytic Association, 46*, 389–412.

Atwood, G. E., & Stolorow, R. D. (1984). *Structures of subjectivity: Explorations in psychoanalytic phenomenology*. Hillsdale, NJ: Analytic Press.

Babor, T. F., Mendelson, J. H., Greenberg, I., & Kuehnle, J. C. (1975). Marijuana consumption and tolerance to physiological and subjective effects. *Archives of General Psychiatry, 32*, 1548–1552.

Bacal, H. A. (1987). British object-relations theorists and self psychology: Some critical reflections. *International Journal of Psycho-Analysis, 68*, 81–98.

Bacal, H. A. (1990). Does an object relations theory exist in self psychology? *Psychoanalytic Inquiry, 10*, 197–220.

Bacal, H. A., & Newman, K. M. (1990). *Theories of object relations: Bridges to self psychology*. New York: Columbia University Press.

Bach, S. (1994). *The language of perversion and the language of love*. Northvale, NJ: Jason Aronson.

Bach, S., & Schwartz, L. (1972). A dream of the Marquis de Sade: Psychoanalytic reflections on narcissistic trauma, decompensation, and the reconstitution of a delusional self. *Journal of the American Psychoanalytic Association, 20*, 451–475.

Back, S., Dansky, B. S., & Coffey, S. F. (2000). Cocaine dependence with and without post-traumatic stress disorder: a comparison of substance use, trauma history and psychiatric comorbidity. *The American Journal on Addictions, 9*, 51–62.

Bader, M. J. (2002). *Arousal: The secret logic of sexual fantasies*. New York: Thomas Dunne Books; St. Martin's Griffin.

Bak, R. C. (1953). Fetishism. *Journal of the American Psychoanalytic Association, 1*, 285–298.

Bak, R. C. (1968). The phallic woman: The ubiquitous fantasy in perversions. *The Psychoanalytic Study of the Child, 23*, 15–36.

Bak, R. C. (1974). Distortions of the concept of fetishism. *The Psychoanalytic Study of the Child, 29*, 191–214.

Baker, H. S., & Baker, M. N. (1996). A self-psychological approach to attention deficit/ hyperactivity disorder in adults: A paradigm to integrate the biopsychosocial model of psychiatric illness. In A. Goldberg (Ed.), *Basic ideas reconsidered. Progress in Self Psychology, 12*, 223–249.

Baladi, P. (2001). *The Shattered self. The end of natural evolution*. Cambridge, MA: MIT Press.

Balter, C., Lothane, Z., & Spencer, J. H. (1980). On the analyzing instrument. *Psychoanalytic Quarterly, 49*, 474–504.

Barnes, G. E. (1979). The alcoholic personality: A reanalysis of the literature. *Journal of Studies on Alcohol, 40*, 571–634.

Barondes, S. H. (1998). *Mood genes. Hunting for origins of mania and depression*. New York: W. H. Freeman.

Barrett, D. (1996). Fantasizers and dissociaters: Two types of high hypnotizables, two different imagery styles. In *Hypnosis and imagination*, R. G. Kunzendorf, N. P. Spanos, B. Wallace (Eds.). (pp. 123–137). Amityville, NY: Baywood.

Bartemeier, L. H. (1954). A psychoanalytic study of pregnancy in an "as if" personality. *International Journal of Psycho-Analysis, 35,* 214–218.

Barth, F. D. (2001). Thinking, talking and feeling in psychotherapy with eating-disordered individuals. In J. Petrucelli & C. Stuart (Eds.), *Hungers and compulsions: The psychodynamic treatment of eating disorders and addictions* (pp. 43–52). Northvale, NJ: Jason Aronson.

Bartholomew, R. E., Basterfield, K., & Howard, G. D. (1991). UFO abductees and contactees: Psychopathology or fantasy proneness? *Professional Psychology: Research and Practice, 22,* 215–222.

Basch, M. F. (1975). Toward a theory that encompasses depression: A revision of existing causal hypothesis in psychoanalysis. In E. J. Anthony & T. Benedek (Eds.), *Depression and human existence* (pp. 485–534). Boston: Little, Brown.

Basch, M. F. (1976). The concept of affect: A re-examination. *Journal of the American Psychoanalytic Association, 24,* 759–771.

Baudry, F. (1983). The evolution of the concept of character in Freud's writings. *Journal of the American Psychoanalytic Association, 31,* 3–33.

Baudry, F. (1989) [1982]. A silent partner to our practice: The analyst's character and attitudes. In R. F. Lax (Ed.) *Essential papers on character neurosis and treatment* (pp. 397–408). New York: New York University Press.

Baudry, F. (1989). Character, character type, and character organization. *Journal of the American Psychoanalytic Association, 37,* 655–686.

Baudry, F. (1990). Character in fiction and fiction in character. *Psychoanalytic Quarterly, 59,* 370–397.

Baudry, F. D. (1999). Introduction-Symposium: On the clinical usefulness of the character concept in evaluating analytic change. October 8th & 22nd, 1996, New York Psychoanalytic Society. *Journal of Clinical Psychoanalysis, 8,* 197–231.

Baumeister, R. F., Heatherton, T. F., & Tice, D. M. (1994). *Losing control: How and why people fail at self-regulation.* New York: Academic Press.

Behar, D., Winokur, G., & Berg, C. J. (1984). Depression in the abstinent alcoholic. *American Journal of Psychiatry, 141, 9,* 1105–1107.

Beitman, B. D. (1991). Medications during psychotherapy: case studies of the reciprocal relationship between psychotherapy process and medication use. In B. Beitman & G. Klerman (Eds.), *Integrating pharmacotherapy and psychotherapy* (pp. 21–43). Washington, DC: American Psychiatric Press.

Bell, D. S., & Trethowan, W. H. (1961). Amphetamine addiction and disturbed sexuality. *Archives of General Psychiatry, 4,* 100/74–104/76.

Belmaker, R. H. (2004). Bipolar disorder. *New England Journal of Medicine, 351,* 476–486.

Bender, L., & Lourie, R. S. (1941). The effect of comic books on the ideology of children. *American Journal of Orthopsychiatry, 11,* 540–550.

Benson, R. M. (1980). Narcissistic guardians: Developmental aspects of transitional objects, imaginary companions, and career fantasies. *American Journal of Psychiatry, 8,* 253–264.

Beres, D., & Arlow, J. A. (1974). Fantasy and identification in empathy. *Psychoanalytic Quarterly, 43,* 26–50.

Berger, L. A. (1991). Substance abuse as symptom: *A psychoanalytic critique of treatment approaches and the cultural beliefs that sustain them.* Hillsdale, NJ: Analytic Press.

Bergler, E. (1942). The psychological interrelation between alcoholism and genital sexuality. *Criminal Psychopathology, 4,* 1–13.

Bergler, E. (1957). *The psychology of gambling.* New York: International Universities Press.

Bergmann, M. S., & Hartman, F. R., (Eds.). (1976). *The Evolution of psychoanalytic technique.* New York: Basic Books.

Berk, M., & Seetal, D. (2005). Bipolar II disorder: A review. *Bipolar Disorders, 7,* 11–21.

Berman, J. (1990). *Narcissism and the novel.* New York: New York University Press.

Bernfeld, S. (1953). Freud's studies on cocaine, 1884–1887. *Journal of the American Psychoanalytic Association, 1,* 581–613.

Bernstein, J. S. (1995). The grandiose character, primary type. *Psychoanalytic Review, 82,* 293–311.

Bettelheim, B. (1955). *Truants from life: The rehabilitation of emotionally disturbed children.* New York: The Free Press.

Bettelheim, B. (1967). *The empty fortress: Infantile autism and the birth of the self.* New York: The Free Press.

Bettelheim, B. (1975). *The uses of enchantment. The meaning and importance of fairy tales.* New York: Vintage.

Bibb, J. L., & Chambless, D. L. (1986). Alcohol use and abuse among diagnosed agoraphobics. *Behaviour Research and Therapy, 24,* 49–58.

Bion, W. R. (1965). *Transformations.* New York: Jason Aronson.

Bion, W. R. (1967). *Second thoughts: Selected papers on psycho-analysis.* Northvale, NJ: Jason Aronson.

Blakeslee, S. (1998, October 13). Placebos prove so powerful even experts are surprised. *New York Times,* p. F1.

Blass, R. B., & Blatt, S. J. (1992). Attachment and separateness. A theoretical integration of object relations theory with self psychology. *The Psychoanalytic Study of the Child, 47,* 189–203.

Bloch, D. (1978). *"So the witch won't eat me": Fantasy and the child's fear of infanticide.* Boston: Houghton Mifflin.

Blos, P. (1963). The concept of acting out in relation to the adolescent process. *Journal of the American Academy of Child Psychiatry, 2,* 118–136.

Blum, H. P. (1986). Psychoanalytic Studies and Macbeth: Shared fantasy and reciprocal identification. *The Psychoanalytic Study of the Child, 41,* 585–599.

Blum, H. P. (1988). Shared fantasy and reciprocal identification, and their role in gender disorders. In H. P. Blum, Y. Kramer, A. K. Richards, & A. D. Richards (Eds.), *Fantasy, myth, and reality: Essays in honor of Jacob A. Arlow, M.D.* (pp. 323–338). Madison, CT: International Universities Press.

Bohn, M. J., & Meyer, R. E. (1994). Typologies of Addiction. In M. Galanter & H. D. Kleber (Eds.), *The American Psychiatric Press textbook of substance abuse treatment* (pp. 11–24). Washington, DC: American Psychiatric Press.

Bollas, C. (1978). The transformational object. *International Journal of Psycho-analysis, 60,* 97–107.

Bollas, C. (1992). *Being a character. Psychoanalysis and self experience.* New York: Hill and Wang.

Bonime, W. (1969). Masturbatory fantasies and personality functioning. In J. H. Masserman (Ed.), *Science and psychoanalysis* (pp. 32–50). New York: Grune & Stratton.

Bonovitz, C. (2004). The co-creation of fantasy and the transformation of psychic structure. *Psychoanalytic Dialogues, 14 (5),* 553–580.

Boon, M. (2002). *The Road of excess: A history of writers on drugs.* Cambridge, MA: Harvard University Press.

Boris, H. (1988). Torment of the object: a contribution to the study of bulimia. In H. J. Schwartz (Ed.), *Bulimia: Psychoanalytic treatment and theory* (pp. 89–110). Madison, CT: International Universities Press.

Bosnak, R. (2003). Embodied imagination. *Contemporary Psychoanalysis, 39,* 683–695.

Bovasso, G. B. (2001). Canabis abuse as a risk factor for depressive symptoms. *American Journal of Psychiatry, 158,* 2033–2037.

Bradlow, P. A. (1973). Depersonalization, ego splitting, non-human fantasy and shame. *International Journal of Psycho-Analysis, 54,* 487–492.

Brady, K. T., & Sinha, R. (2005). Co-occurring mental and substance use disorders: The neurobiological effects of chronic stress. *American Journal of Psychiatry, 162,* 1483–1493.

Brady, K. T., Dansky, B. S., & Sonne, S. C. (1998). Posttraumatic stress disorder and cocaine dependence. Order of onset. *American Journal of Addictions, 7 (2),* 128–135.

Brady, S., Rierdan, J., Penk, W., & Losardo, M. (2003). Posttraumatic stress disorder in adults with serious mental illness and substance abuse. *Journal of Trauma & Dissociation, 4 (4),* 77–90.

Brehm, N. M., & Khantzian, E. J. (1992). A psychodynamic perspective. In J. H. Lowinson, P. Ruiz, R. B. Millman, & J. G. Langrod (Eds.), *Substance abuse: A comprehensive textbook,* (2nd ed, pp. 106–117). Baltimore, MD: Williams & Wilkins.

Breineis, P. (1990). *Tough Jews: Political fantasies and the moral dilemma of American Jewry.* New York: Basic Books.

Brenner, I. (1994). The dissociative character: A reconsideration of "multiple personality". *Journal of the American Psychoanalytic Association, 42,* 819–846.

Brennis, C. B. (1996). Multiple personality: Fantasy proneness, demand characteristics, and indirect communication. *Psychoanalytic Psychology, 13,* 367–387.

Brill, N. Q., Crumpton, E., & Grayson, H. M. (1971). Personality factors in marihuana use: A preliminary report. *Archives of General Psychiatry, 24,* 163–165.

Britton, R. (1998). *Belief and imagination. Explorations in psychoanalysis.* London: Routledge.

Brockman, R. (1998). *A map of the mind. Toward a science of psychotherapy.* Madison, CT: International Universities Press.

Brody, H. (2000). *The Placebo response. How you can release the body's inner pharmacy for better health.* New York: Cliff Street Books.

Brody, J. E. (2003, September 30). Addiction: A brain ailment, not a moral lapse. *New York Times,* p. F8.

Brody, S. (1964). *Passivity: A study of its development and expression in boys.* New York: International Universities Press.

Bromberg, P. M. (1995). Resistance, object-usage, and human relatedness. *Contemporary Psychoanalysis, 31,* 173–191.

Bromberg, P. M. (2001). Out of body, out of mind, out of danger: some reflections on shame, dissociation, and eating disorders. In J. Petrucelli & C. Stuart (Eds.), *Hungers and compulsions: The psychodynamic treatment of eating disorders and addictions* (pp. 67–80). Northvale, NJ: Jason Aronson.

Bromberg, W., & Schilder, P. (1933). Psychologic considerations in alcoholic Hallucinosis-castration and dismembering motives. *International Journal of Psycho-Analysis, 14,* 206–224.

Brondolo, E., & Mas, F. (2001). Cognitive-behavioral strategies for improving medication adherence in patients with bipolar disorder. *Cognitive and Behavioral Practice, 8,* 137–147.

Brook, D. W. (2004). Drug use and the risk of major depressive disorder, alcohol dependence and substance use disorders. *Psychiatric Times,* June 2008, 88.

Brothers, D. (1995). *Falling backwards. An exploration of trust and self-experience.* New York: W. W. Norton.

Brown, E. S. (2005). Bipolar disorder and substance abuse. *Psychiatric Clinics of North America, 28,* 415–425.

Bruch, H. (1977). Depressive factors in adolescent eating disorders. In W. E. Fann et al. (Eds.), *Phenomenology and treatment of depression* (pp. 143–152). New York: Spectrum Publications.

Bruhm, S. (2001). *Reflecting narcissus: A queer aesthetic.* Minneapolis, MN: University of Minnesota Press.

Buie, Jr., D. H., & Adler, G. (1991). The uses of confrontation in the psychotherapy of borderline patients. In G. Adler & P. Myerson (Eds.), *Confrontation in psychotherapy* (pp. 123–146). Northvale, NJ: Jason Aronson.

Burton, N. (2005). Finding the lost girls. Multiplicity and dissociation in the treatment of addictions. *Psychoanalytic Dialogues, 15,* 587–612.

Cabaniss, D. L. (1998). Shifting gears: The challenge to teach students to think *psychodynamically* and psychopharmacologically at the same time. *Psychoanalytic Inquiry, 18,* 639–656.

Cadoret, R., Troughton, E., & Widmer, R. (1984). Clinical differences between antisocial and primary alcoholic. *Comprehensive Psychiatry, 25,* 1–8.

Carlson, J., & Sperry, L. (1998). *The disordered couple.* New York: Brunner/Mazel.

Carmichael, J. S., Linn, M. W., Pratt, T., & Webb, N. (1977). Self-concept and substance abuse treatment. *Comprehensive Psychiatry, 18,* 357–362.

Carnes, P. (1983). *Out of the shadows: Understanding sexual addiction.* Minneapolis, MN: CompCare Publishers.

Carnes, P. (1991). *Don't call it love: Recovery from sexual addiction.* New York: Bantam Books.

Carrere, E. (2000). *The adversary. A true story of monstrous deception.* New York: Metropolitan Books.

Carroll, C. C. (1984 [1865]). *Alice's adventures in wonderland.* Middlesex, England: Puffin Books; Penguin Books, Ltd.

Carroll, K. M. (1996). Integrating psychotherapy and pharmacotherapy in substance abuse treatment. In F. Rotgers, D. S. Keller, & J. Morgenstern (Eds.), *Treating substance abuse. Theory and technique* (pp. 286–318). New York: Guilford Press.

Carroll, K. M. (2001). Combined treatments for substance dependence. In M. T. Sammons & N. B. Schmidt (Eds.), *Combined treatments for mental disorders: A guide to psychological and pharmacological interventions* (pp. 215–237). Washington, DC: American Psychological Association.

Caruth, E. (1968). Hercules and Superman: The modern-day mythology of the comic book. *Journal of the American Academy of Child Psychiatry, 7,* 1–12.

Cassano, G. B., Rucci, P., Frank, E., & Fagiolini, A. (2004). The mood spectrum in unipolar and bipolar disorder: Arguments for a unitary approach. *American Journal of Psychiatry, 161 (7),* 1264–1269.

Cassidy, F., Ahearn, E. P., & Carroll, B. J. (2001). Substance abuse in bipolar disorder. *Bipolar Disorders, 3,* 181–188.

Castle, L. R. (2003). *Bipolar disorder demystified.* New York: Marlowe & Co.

Cath, S. J., & Cath, C. (1978). On the other side of Oz. Psychoanalytic aspects of fairy tales. *Psychoanalytic Study of the Child, 33,* 621–639.

Ceaser, M. A. (1988). Anorexia nervosa and bulimia: An integrated approach to understanding and treatment. In H. Schwartz (Ed.), *Bulimia: Psychoanalytic treatment and theory* (pp. 111–125). Madison, CT: International Universities Press.

Charney, D. A. (2004). Outpatient treatment of comorbid depression and alcohol use disorders. *Psychiatric Times,* February, 32.

Chassell, J. (1938). Family constellation in the etiology of essential alcoholism. *Psychiatry, 1,* 473–503.

Chasseguet-Smirgel, J. (1985). *The ego ideal: A psychoanalytic essay on the malady of the ideal.* New York: W. W. Norton.

Chasseguet-Smirgel, J., & Goyena, A. (1993). Core fantasy and psychoanalytic change. In M. J. Horowitz, O. F. Kernberg, & E. M. Weinshul (Eds.), *Psychic structure and psychic change: Essays in honor of Robert S. Wallerstein,* M. D. (pp. 233–262). Madison, CT: International Universities Press.

Chein, I., Gerard, D. C., Lee, R. S., & Rosenfeld, E. (1964). *The road to H: Narcotics, delinquency, and social policy.* New York: Basic Books.

Chessick, R. D. (1960). The "pharmacogenic orgasm" in the drug addict. *Archives of General Psychiatry, 3,* 545–556.

Chessick, R. D. (1985). *Psychology of the self and the treatment of narcissism.* Northvale, NJ: Jason Aronson.

Chessick, R. D. (1994). What brings about change in psychoanalytic treatment. *Psychoanalytic Review, 81,* 279–300.

Ciolino, C. (1991). Substance abuse and mood disorders. In M. A. Gold & A. E. Slaby (Eds.), *Dual diagnosis in substance abuse* (p. 105). New York: Marcel Dekker.

Clancy, J. (1996). *Anger and addiction: Breaking the relapse cycle.* Madison, CT: Psychosocial Press.

Clark, C. D. (1995). *Flights of fancy, leaps of faith: Children's myths in contemporary America.* Chicago: University of Chicago Press.

Clark, R. E. (2001). Family support and substance use outcomes for persons with mental illness and substance use disorders. *Schizophrenia Bulletin, 27,* 93–101.

Clum, G. A., Nishith, P., & Calhoun, K. (2002). A preliminary investigation of alcohol use during trauma and peritraumatic reactions in female sexual assault victims. *Journal of Traumatic Stress, 15 (4),* 321–328.

Cobb, E. (1993) [1977]. *The ecology of imagination in childhood.* Dallas: Spring Publications.

Cocores, J. (1994). Addictive psychiatric disorders. In N. S. Miller (Ed.), *Treating coexisting psychiatric and addictive disorders: A practical guide* (pp. 127–137). City Center, MN: Hazelden.

Coen, S. J. (1992). *The Misuse of persons: Analyzing pathological dependency.* Hillsdale, NJ: Analytic Press.

Coffey, S. F., Dansky, B. S., Falsetti, S. A., Saladin, M. E., & Brady, K. T. (1998). Screening for PTSD in a substance abuse sample: psychometric properties of a modified version of the PTSD symptom scale self-report. *Journal of Traumatic Stress, 11 (2),* 393–399.

Cohen, J. F. (1991). Myths, questions, and controversies in work with alcoholics. In A. Smaldino (Ed.), *Psychoanalytic approaches to addiction* (pp. 51–64). New York: Brunner/Mazel.

Cohen, M. N. (1995). *Lewis Carroll: A biography.* New York: Alfred A. Knopf.

Compton, III, W. M., Cottler, L. B., Phelps, D. L., Abdallah, M. S., & Spitznagel, E. L. (2000). Psychiatric disorders among drug dependent subjects: are they primary or secondary? *American Journal on Addictions, 9,* 126–134.

Conlan, R. (Ed.). (1999). *States of mind: New discoveries about how our brains make us who we are.* New York: John Wiley & Sons.

Cooper, A. M. (1989). Narcissism and masochism. The narcissistic-masochistic character. *Psychiatric Clinics of North America, 12 (3),* 541–552.

Cooper, A. M. (1993). On empirical research. *Journal of American Psychoanalytic Association, 41,* 381–392.

Cooper, S. H., & Adler, G. (1990). Toward a clarification of the transitional object and selfobject concepts in the treatment of the borderline patient. *Annual of Psychoanalysis, 18,* 133–152.

Coppolillo, H. P. (1967). Maturational aspects of the transitional phenomena. *International Journal of Psycho-Analysis, 43,* 237–245.

Cornoldi, C., Logie, R. H., Brandimonte, M. A., Kaufmann, G., & Reisberg, D. (1996). *Stretching the imagination. Representation and transformation in mental imagery.* New York: Oxford University Press.

Corssen, G., & Domino, E. F. (1966). Dissociative anesthesia: Further pharmacologic studies of the first clinical experience with phencyclkinde derivative C1-581. *Anesthesia & Analgesia, 4,* 29–40.

Council, J. R, Kirsch, I., & Grant, D. L. (1996). Imagination, expectancy, and hypnotic responding. In *Hypnosis and imagination*, R. G. Kunzendorf, N. P. Spanos, B. Wallace (Eds.) (pp. 41–66). Amityville, NY: Baywood.

Cox, B. J., Norton, G. R., Dorward, J., & Fergusson, P. (1989). The relationship between panic attacks and chemical dependencies. *Addictive Behaviors, 14,* 53–60.

Cox, B. J., Norton, G. R., Swinson, R. P., & Endler, N. S. (1990). Substance abuse and panic-related anxiety: a critical review. *Behaviour Research and Therapy, 28,* 385–393.

Cozolino, L. J. (2002). *The neuroscience of psychotherapy. Building and rebuilding the human brain.* New York: W. W. Norton.

Craig, R. J. (1979a). Personality characteristics of heroin addicts: A review of the empirical literature with critique—Part I. *International Journal of the Addictions, 14,* 513–532.

Craig, R. J. (1979b). Personality characteristics of heroin addicts: A review of the empirical literature with critique—Part II. *International Journal of the Addictions, 14,* 607–626.

Currie, G., & Ravenscroft, I. (2002). *Recreative minds. Imagination in philosophy and psychology.* Oxford: Clarendon Press.

Currie, G., & Ravenscroft, I. (2002). *Recreative minds. Imagination in philosophy and psychology.* Oxford: Clarendon Press.

Curry, S. J. (Ed.). (1999). *Psychology of Addictive Behaviors, 13 (2).*

Cohen, D., & MacKeith, S. A. (1991). *The development of imagination. The private worlds of childhood.* London: Routledge.

Daley, D. C., Moss, H., & Campbell, F. (1987). *Dual disorders. Counseling clients with chemical dependency and mental illness* (2nd ed.). City Center, MN: Hazelden.

Davis, W. D. (1990). Reflection on boundaries in the psychotherapeutic relationship. In C. L. Johnson (Ed.), *Psychodynamic treatment of anorexia nervosa and bulimia* (pp. 68–85). New York: Guilford Press.

DeCaria, C. M., & Hollander, E. (1993). Pathological Gambling. In E. Hollander (Ed.), *Obsessive-compulsive related disorders* (pp. 151–171). Washington, DC: American Psychiatric Press.

de Graaf, R., Bijil, R. V., Smit, F., Vollebergh, W. A. M., & Spijjker, J. (2002). Risk factors for 12-month comorbidity of mood, anxiety, and substance use disorders: findings from the Netherlands mental health survey and incidence study. *American Journal of Psychiatry, 159 (4),* 620–629.

Deitz, J. (1995). The self-psychological approach to the bipolar spectrum disorders. *Journal of the American Academy of Psychoanalysis, 23,* 475–492.

Del Bello, M. P., & Strakowski, S. M. (2003). Understanding the problem of co-occurring mood and substance use disorders. In J. T. Westermeyer, R. D. Weiss, D. M. Ziedonis (Eds.), *Integrated treatment for mood and substance use disorders* (pp. 17–41). Baltimore, MD: Johns Hopkins University Press.

Dennis, A. M., & Sansone, R. A. (1990). In C. L. Johnson (Ed.), *Psychodynamic treatment of anorexia nervosa and bulimia* (pp. 68–85). New York: Guilford Press.

Deutsch, H. (1965 [1942]). Some forms of emotional disturbance and their relationship to schizophrenia. In *Neurosis and character types: Clinical psychoanalytic studies* (pp. 262–281). New York: International Universities Press.

Dickes, R. (1963). Fetishistic behavior: A contribution to its complex development and significance. *Journal of the American Psychoanalytic Association, 11,* 303–339.

Dickes, R. (1978). Parents, transitional objects, and childhood fetishes. In S. A. Grolnick, L. Barkin, & W. Muensterberger (Eds.), *Between reality and fantasy: Transitional objects and phenomena* (pp. 307–319). New York: Jason Aronson.

Dickes, R., & Papernik, D. S. (1977). Defensive alterations of consciousness: Hypnoid states, sleep, and the dream. *Journal of the American Psychoanalytic Association, 25,* 635–654.

Dilsaver, S. C., Chen, Y. R., Shoaib, A. M., & Swann, A. C. (1999). Phenomenology of mania: evidence for distinct depress, dysphoric, and euphoric presentations. *American Journal of Psychiatry, 156,* 426–430.

Director, L. (2005). Encounters with omnipotence in the psychoanalysis of substance users. *Psychoanalytic Dialogues, 15,* 567–586.

Distefano, M. K., Pryer, M. W., & Garrison, J. C. (1972). Internal-external control among alcoholics. *Journal of Clinical Psychology, 28,* 36–37.

Dodes, L. M. (1990). Addiction, helplessness, and narcissistic rage. *Psychoanalytic Quarterly, 49,* 398–419.

Dodes, L. M. (1984). Abstinence from alcohol in long-term individual psychotherapy with alcoholism. *American Journal of Psychotherapy, 38,* 248–256.

Dodes, L. M. (1988). The psychology of combining dynamic psychotherapy and alcoholics anonymous. *Bulletin of the Menninger Clinic, 52,* 283–293.

Dodes, L. M. (1995). Psychic helplessness and the psychology of addiction. In S. Dowling (Ed.), *The psychology and treatment of addictive behavior* (pp. 133–145). Madison, CT: International Universities Press.

Dodes, L. M. (1996). Compulsion and addiction. *Journal of the American Psychoanalytic Association, 44,* 815–835.

Dodes, L. M. (2002). *The heart of addiction. A new approach to understanding and managing alcoholism and other addictive behaviors.* New York: Quill.

Dodes, L. M., & Khantzian, E. J. (1991). Individual psychodynamic psychotherapy. In R. J. Frances & S. I. Miller (Eds.), *Clinical textbook of addictive disorders* (pp. 391–405). New York: Guilford Press.

Donald, J. (1989). *Fantasy and the cinema.* London: BFI Publishing.

Donovan, B., Padin-Rivera, E., & Kowaliw, S. (2001). "Transcend": Initial outcomes from a posttraumatic stress disorder/substance abuse treatment program. *Journal of Traumatic Stress, 14 (4),* 757–772.

Doty, W. G. (1993). *Myths of masculinity.* New York: Crossroad Publishing.

Dougherty, D. M., Marsh, D. M., Mathias, C. W., & Swann, A. C. (2005). The conceptualization and role of impulsivity: Bipolar disorder and substance abuse. *Impulse Disorders,* July, 32.

Drover, D. R., Lemmens, H. J., Pierce, E. T., Plourde, G., Loyd, G., Ornstein, E., Prichep, L. S., Chabot, R. J., & Gugino, L. (2001). Titration of delivery and recovery from Propofol, Alfentanil, and nitrous oxide anesthesia. (2002). *Anesthesiology, 97,* 82–89.

Dufresne, R. (1996). Listening to Narcissus (When words alone do not suffice…). *International Journal of Psychoanalysis, 77,* 497–508.

Dunner, D. L., Hensel, B. M., & Fieve, R. R. (1979). Bipolar illness: Factors in drinking behavior. *American Journal of Psychiatry, 136,* 583–585.

Eber, M. (1981). Don Juanism: A disorder of the self. *Bulletin of the Menninger Clinic, 45,* 307–316.

Eccles, J. C. (1994). *How the self controls its brain.* New York: Springer-Verlag.

Edelson, M. (1988). *Psychoanalysis: A theory in crisis.* Chicago: University of Chicago Press.

Edgcumbe, R., & Burgner, M. (1975). The phallic-narcissistic phase: A differentiation between preoedipal and oedipal aspects of phallic development. *The Psychoanalytic Study of the Child, 30,* 161–180.

Eidelberg, L. (1959). The concept of narcissistic mortification. *International Journal of Psycho-Analysis, 40,* 163–169.

Eigen, M. (1979). On the defensive use of mastery. *American Journal of Psychoanalysis, 39,* 279–282.

Eigen, M. (1980). Instinctual fantasy and ideal images. *Contemporary Psychoanalysis, 16,* 119–137.

Eigen, M. (1981). The area of faith in Winnicott, Lacan and Bion. *International Journal of Psycho-Analysis, 62,* 413–433.

Eigen, M. (1982). Creativity, instinctual fantasy and ideal images. *Psychoanalytic Review, 69,* 317–339.

Eigen, M. (1985). Aspects of omnipotence. *Psychoanalytic Review, 72,* 149–159.

Eigen, M. (1986). *The psychotic core.* Northvale, NJ: Jason Aronson.

Eigen, M. (1989). Aspects of omniscience. In M. G. Fromm & B. L. Smith (Eds.), *The facilitating environment: Clinical applications of Winnicott's theory* (pp. 604–628). Madison, CT: International Universities Press.

Eigen, M. (1991). Winnicott's area of freedom: The uncompromisable. In N. Schwartz-Salant & M. Stein (Ed.), *Liminality and transitional phenomena* (pp. 67–88). Wilmette, IL: Chiron Publications.

Eigen, M. (1996). *Psychic deadness.* Northvale, NJ: Jason Aronson.

Eigen, M. (2004 [1980]). Instinctual fantasy and ideal images. In A. Phillips (Ed.), *The electrified tightrope* (pp. 61–75). London: Karnac Books.

Eigen, M. (2004 [1981]). The area of faith in Winnicott, Lacan and Bion. In A. Phillips (Ed.), *The electrified tightrope* (pp. 109–138). London: Karnac Books.

Eigen, M. (2004 [1982]). Creativity, instinctual fantasy and ideal images. In A. Phillips (Ed.), *The electrified tightrope* (pp. 77–94). London: Karnac Books.

Eigen, M. (2004 [1986]). *The psychotic core.* London: Karnac Books.

Eigen, M. (2004 [1991]). The area of freedom: The point of no compromise. In *Psychic deadness* (pp. 69–87). London: Karnac Books.

Eissler, K. R. (1950). Ego-psychological implications of the psychoanalytic treatment of delinquents. *The Psychoanalytic Study of the Child, 5,* 97–121.

Ellman, C., & Reppen, J. (1997). *Omnipotent fantasies and the vulnerable self.* Northvale, NJ: Jason Aronson.

Elson, M. (Ed.). (1987). *The Kohut seminars on self psychology and psychotherapy with adolescents and young adults.* New York: W. W. Norton.

Emde, R., Kubicek, L., & Oppenheim, D. (1997). Imaginative reality observed during early language development. *International Journal of Psycho-Analysis, 78,* 115–118.

Evans, K., & Sullivan, J. M. (1995). *Treating addicted survivors of trauma.* New York: Guilford Press.

Evans, K., & Sullivan, J. M. (2001). *Dual diagnosis. Counseling the mentally ill substance abuser* (2nd ed.). New York: Guilford Press.

Evans, W. N. (1975). The eye of jealousy and envy. *Psychoanalytic Review, 62,* 481–492.

Everill, J. T., Waller, G., & Macdonald, W. (1995). Reported sexual abuse and bulimic symptoms: the mediating role of dissociation. *Dissociation, 8,* 155–159.

Fauconnier, G., & Turner, M. (2002). *The way we think. Conceptual blending and the mind's hidden complexities.* New York: Basic Books.

Feinberg, T. E., & Keenan, J. P. (2004). Not what, but where, is your "self"? *Cerebrum, 6,* 49–62.

Feldman, S. S. (1962). The role of 'as if' in neurosis. *Psychoanalytic Quarterly, 31,* 43–53.

Felix, R. H. (1944). An appraisal of the personality types of the addict. *American Journal of Psychiatry, 100,* 462–267.

Feinberg, T. E. (2001). *Altered egos: How the brain creates the self.* New York: Oxford University Press.

Ferenczi, S. (1926 [1915]). *Further contributions to the theory and technique of psycho-analysis.* New York: Brunner/Mazel.

Ferenczi, S. (1926) [1916/17]. Composite formations of erotic and character traits. In *Further contributions to the theory and technique of psycho-analysis* (pp. 257–258). New York: Brunner/Mazel.

Ferenczi, S. (1952 [1916]). *First contributions to psycho-analysis.* New York: Brunner/Mazel.

Ferenczi, S. (1955 [1930]). Autoplastic and alloplastic adaptation. In *Final contributions to the problems and methods of psycho-analysis* (p. 231). New York: Brunner/Mazel.

Ferenczi, S. (1956 [1913]). Stages in the development of the sense of reality. In *Sex in psychoanalysis (Contributions to psycho-analysis and the development of psycho-analysis)* (pp. 181–203). New York: Dover Publications.

Ferguson, M. (1990). Mirroring processes, hypnotic processes, and multiple personality. *Psychoanalysis and Contemporary Thought, 13,* 417–450.

Fieve, R. R. (1997). *Moodswing.* New York: Bantam Books.

Fine, G. A. (1983). *Shared fantasy. Role-playing games as social worlds.* Chicago: University of Chicago Press.

Fingeroth, D. (2004). *Superman on the couch. What superheroes really tell us about ourselves and our society.* New York: Continuum.

Finstad, S. (2001). *Natasha. The biography of Natalie Wood.* New York: Harmony Books.

Fiorentine, R., & Hillhouse, M. P. (2003). When low self-efficacy is efficacious: Toward an addicted-self model of cessation of alcohol- and drug-dependent behavior. *American Journal on Addictions, 12,* 346–364.

Fischer, H. K. (1973). Some aspects of psychotherapy in patients with addictive personality traits. *Psychosomatics, 14,* 27–32.

Fisher, C. (1954). Dreams and perceptions. *Journal of the American Psychoanalytic Association, 2,* 389–445.

Fisher, C. (1956). Dreams, images, and perceptions. *Journal of the American Psychoanalytic Association, 4,* 5–48.

Fisher, C. (1957). A study of the preliminary steps of the construction of dreams and images. *Journal of the American Psychoanalytic Association, 5,* 5–60.

Fisher, C. (1960). Introduction. In O. Potzl, R. Allers, & J. Teler, *Preconscious stimulation in dreams, associations, and images* (Psychological Issues, Monograph 7, pp. 1–40). New York: International Universities Press.

Fisher, C. (1988). Subliminal (preconscious) perception. The microgenesis of unconscious fantasy. In H. P. Blum, Y. Kramer, A. K. Richards, & A. D. Richards (Eds.), *Fantasy, myth, and reality: Essays in honor of Jacob A. Arlow, M. D.* (pp. 93–108). Madison, CT: International Universities Press.

Fisher, J. V. (1999). *The uninvited guest. Emerging from narcissism towards marriage.* London: Karnac.

Fogarty, J. A. (2000). *The magical thoughts of grieving children. Treating children with complicated mourning and advice for parents.* Amityville, NY: Baywood Publishing.

Forman, M. (1981). Narcissistic personality disorder as a regression to preoedipal phase of phallic narcissism. *Hillside Journal of Clinical Psychiatry, 3,* 45–59.

Forrest, G. G. (1994). *Chemical dependency and antisocial personality disorder: Psychotherapy and assessment strategies.* New York: Haworth Press.

Fox, R. (1967). Alcoholism and reliance upon drugs as depressive equivalents. *American Journal of Psychotherapy, 21,* 585–596.

Frances, R. J., Khantzian, E. J., & Tamerin, J. S. (1988). Psychodynamic psychotherapy. In Treatments of psychiatric disorders (A Task Force Report of the American Psychiatric Association (Vol. 2, pp. 1103–1111). Washington, DC: American Psychiatric Association.

Frances, R. J., Franklin, J., & Borg, L. (1994). Psychodynamics. In M. Galanter & H. D. Kleber (Eds.), *The American Psychiatric Press textbook of substance abuse treatment* (pp. 239–251). Washington, DC: American Psychiatric Press.

Franken, I. H. A., & Hendriks, V. M. (2001). Screening and diagnosis of anxiety and mood disorders in substance abuse patients. *American Journal on Addictions, 10,* 30–39.

Franklin, H. B. (2002). *Vietnam and other American fantasies.* Amherst: University of Massachusetts Press.

Freed, E. X. (1978). Alcohol and mood: An updated review. *International Journal of the Addictions, 13*, 173–200.

Freedman, N. (1985). The concept of transformation in psychoanalysis. *Psychoanalytic Psychology, 2 (4)*, 317–339.

Freeman, L., & Kupfermann, K. (1988). *The Power of fantasy: Where our daydreams come from & how they can help or harm us.* New York: Continuum.

Freeman, E. W., & Rickels, K. (1999). Characteristics of placebo responses in medical treatment of premenstrual syndrome. *American Journal of Psychiatry, 156*, 1403–1408.

Freud, A. (1966 [1936]). The ego and the mechanisms of defense. In *The writings of Anna Freud* (Vol. 2, pp. 3–176). New York: International Universities Press.

Freud, S. (1886). Extracts from the Fleiss papers. In J. Strachey (Ed. & Trans.), *The standard edition of the complete psychological works of Sigmund Freud* [Standard Edition] (Vol. 1, pp. 173–218). New York: W. W. Norton.

Freud, S. (1905). Jokes and their relation to the unconscious. Standard Edition (Vol. 8, pp. 9–236).

Freud, S. (1907). Obsessive actions and religious practices. Standard Edition (Vol. 9, pp. 117–127).

Freud, S. (1908a). Creative writers and day-dreaming. Standard Edition (Vol. 9, pp. 143–153).

Freud, S. (1908b). Character and anal eroticism. Standard Edition (Vol. 9, pp. 169–175).

Freud, S. (1911). Psychoanalytic notes on an autobiographical account of a case of paranoia (dementia paranoids). Standard Edition (Vol. 12, pp. 9–82).

Freud, S. (1913). Totem and taboo. Standard Edition (Vol. 13, pp. 1–161).

Freud, S. (1914). On narcissism: An introduction. Standard Edition (Vol. 14, pp. 67–102).

Freud, S. (1919). "A child is being beaten": A contribution to the study of the origin of sexual perversions. Standard Edition (Vol. 17, pp. 179–204).

Freud, S. (1928 [1927]). Dostoevsky and patricide. Standard Edition (Vol. 21, pp. 177–194).

Freud, S. (1942 [1905 or 1906]). Psychopathic characters on the stage. Standard Edition (Vol. 7, pp. 305–310).

Freud, S. (1953 [1913]) Totem and taboo. In J. Strachey (Ed. & Trans.). *The standard edition of the complete psychological works of Sigmund Freud* [Standard Edition] (Vol. 13, pp. 1–162). London: Hogarth Press.

Freud, S. (1953 [1906]). Psychopathic characters on the stage. Standard Edition (Vol. 7, pp. 305–310).

Freud, S. (1953 [1915–1917]). Introductory lectures on psycho-analysis. Standard Edition (Vol. 16, pp. 243–463).

Freud, S. (1955 [1893–1895]). Studies on hysteria. Standard Edition (Vol. 2, pp. 1–305).

Freud, S. (1955 [1909a]). Analysis of a phobia in a five-year-old boy. Standard Edition (Vol. 10, pp. 5–152).

Freud, S. (1955 [1909b]). Notes upon a case of obsessional neurosis. Standard Edition (Vol. 10, pp. 155–250).

Freud, S. (1955 [1919]). 'A child is being beaten': A contribution to the study of the origin of sexual perversions. Standard Edition (Vol. 17, pp. 179–204).

Freud, S. (1955 [1920]). Beyond the pleasure principle. Standard Edition (Vol. 18, pp. 7–66).

Freud, S. (1958 [1905]). Three essays on the theory of sexuality. Standard Edition (Vol. 7, pp. 135–243).

Freud, S. (1958 [1905]). My views on the part played by sexuality in the aetiology of the neuroses. Standard Edition (Vol. 7, pp. 271–282).

Freud, S. (1958 [1911]). Psycho-analytic notes on an autobiographical account of a case of paranoia (dementia paranoides). Standard Edition (Vol. 12, pp. 9–84).

Freud, S. (1959 [1907]). Creative writers and day-dreaming. Standard Edition (Vol. 9, pp. 143–153).

Freud, S. (1959 [1908a]). Hysterical phantasies and their relation to bisexuality. Standard Edition (Vol. 9, pp. 159–166).

Freud, S. (1959 [1908b]). Character and anal erotism. Standard Edition (Vol. 9, pp. 169–175).

Freud, S. (1961 [1928]). Dostoevsky and parricide. Standard Edition (Vol. 21, pp. 177–194).

Freud, S. (1962 [1894]). Obsessions and phobias: Their psychical mechanism and their aetiology. Standard Edition (Vol. 3, pp. 74–115).

Freud, S. (1962 [1896a]). Heredity and the aetiology of the neuroses. Standard Edition (Vol. 3, pp. 141–158).

Freud, S. (1962 [1896b]). Further remarks on the neuro-psychoses of defence. Standard Edition (Vol. 3, pp. 162–188).

Freud, S. (1962 [1898]). Sexuality in the aetiology of the neuroses. Standard Edition (Vol. 3, pp. 263–286).

Freud, S. (1974). *Cocaine papers*. Introduction, R. Byck (Ed.). New York: Times Mirror.

Freeman, E. W., & Rickels, K. (1999). Characteristics of placebo responses in medical treatment of premenstrual syndrome. *American Journal of Psychiatry, 156,* 1403–1408.

Friedlander, S. (1988). Learned helplessness in children: perception of control and causal attributions. In D. C. Morrison (Ed.), *Organizing early experience imagination and cognition in childhood* (pp. 33–53). Amityville, NY: Baywood Publishing.

Friedman, L. (2005). Flirting with virtual reality. *Psychoanalytic Quarterly, 74,* 639–660.

Friedman, R. A. (2002, June 25). Can the placebo treat depression? That depends. *New York Times,* p. F6.

Frosch, J. (1970). Psychoanalytic considerations of the psychotic character. *Journal of the American Psychoanalytic Association, 18,* 24–50.

Frosch, J. (1990). *Psychodynamic psychiatry: Theory and practice* (Vol. 2). Madison, CT: International Universities Press.

Furman, E. (1992). *Toddlers and their mothers: A study in early personality development.* Madison, CT: International Universities Press.

Furman, E. (1998). *Self-control and mastery in early childhood: Helping young children grow.* Madison, CT: International Universities Press.

Galanter, M. (1976). The "intoxication state of consciousness": A model for alcohol and drug abuse. *American Journal of Psychiatry, 133,* 635–640.

Galatzer-Levy, R. (1988). Manic-depressive-illness: Analytic experience and a hypothesis. In A. Goldberg (Ed.), *Progress in self psychology* (Vol. 3, pp. 87–102). Hillsdale, NJ: Analytic Press.

Gambino, B., & Shaffer, H. (1979). The concept of paradigm and the treatment of addiction. *Professional Psychology, 10,* 207–223.

Garcia, E. E. (1990). A brief note on "Jekyll and Hyde" and MPD. *Dissociation, 3,* 165–166.

Gazzaniga, M. S. (1985). *The social brain discovering the networks of the mind.* New York: Basic Books.

Gediman, H. K. (1995). *Fantasies of love and death in life and art: A psychoanalytic study of the normal and the pathological.* New York: New York University Press.

Gedo, J. E. (1991). *The biology of clinical encounters: Psychoanalysis as a science of mind.* Hillsdale, NJ: Analytic Press.

Gehrie, M. J. (1990). Eating disorders and adaptation in crisis: A hypothesis. In A. Tasman, S. M. Goldfinger, & C. A. Kaufmann (Eds.), *Review of Psychiatry* (Vol. 9, pp. 369–383). Washington, DC: American Psychiatric Press.

Geist, R. A. (1989). Self-psychological reflections on the origins of eating disorders. *Journal of the American Academy of Psychoanalysis, 17,* 5–27.

Gendreau, P., & Gendreau, L. P. (1970). The "addiction-prone" personality: A study of Canadian heroin addicts. *Canadian Journal of Psycho-Analysis, 2,* 18–25.

Geppert, C. M. A., & Minkoff, K. (2004). Issues in dual diagnosis: Diagnosis, treatment & new research. *Psychiatric Times,* April, 103.

Gerzi, S. (2005). Trauma, narcissism and the two attractors in trauma. *International Journal of Psychoanalysis, 86,* 1033–1050.

Glover, E. (1932). On the aetiology of drug-addiction. *International Journal of Psycho-Analysis, 13,* 298–328.

Glover, E. (1933). The relation of perversion-formation to the development of reality-sense. *International Journal of Psycho-analysis, 14,* 486–504.

Glover, E. (1956 [1924]). Notes on oral character formation. In *On the early development of mind* (pp. 25–46). New York: International Universities Press.

Glover, E. (1956 [1925]). The neurotic character. In *On the early development of mind,* 47–66. New York: International Universities Press.

Glover, E. (1956 [1928]). The etiology of alcoholism. In *On the early development of mind* (pp. 81–90). New York: International Universities Press.

Glucksman, M. L. (1998). Altered states of consciousness in the analyst. *Journal of the American Academy of Psychoanalysis, 26,* 197–207.

Gold, M. S., & Slaby, A. E. (Eds.). (1991). *Dual diagnosis in substance abuse.* New York: Marcel Dekker.

Gold, S. N., & Seifer, R. E. (2002). Dissociation and sexual addiction/compulsivity: A contextual approach to conceptualization and treatment. *Journal of Trauma and Dissociation, 3,* 59–82.

Goldberg, A. (1975). A fresh look at perverse behavior. *International Journal of Psycho-Analysis, 56,* 335–42.

Goldberg, A. (1988). *A fresh look at psychoanalysis: The view from self psychology.* Hillsdale, NJ: Analytic Press.

Goldberg, A. (1995). *The problem of perversion: The view from self psychology.* New Haven, CT: Yale University Press.

Goldberg, A. (Ed.). (2000). *Errant selves: A casebook of misbehavior.* Hillsdale, NJ: Analytic Press.

Goldberg, J. F. (2004, October 21). New findings in bipolar disorders. Grand Rounds at Silver Hill Hospital, New Canaan, CT.

Goldberg, J. F., & M. Harrow (Eds.). (1999). *Bipolar disorders: Clinical course and outcome.* Washington, DC: American Psychiatric Press.

Goldhamer, P. M. (1993). The challenge of integration. In M. Schachter (Ed.), *Psychotherapy and medication: A dynamic integration* (pp. 215–224). Northvale, NJ: Jason Aronson.

Goldsmith, R. J. (1993). An integrated psychology for the addictions: Beyond the self-medication hypothesis. In N. S. Miller, & B. Stimmel (Ed.), *Comorbidity of addictive and psychiatric disorders* (pp. 139–154). New York: Haworth Press.

Goleman, D. (1992, March 31). As addiction medicine gains, experts debate what it should cover. *New York Times* (Medical Science), p. C3.

Goleman. D. (1993, August 17). Placebo effect is shown to be twice as powerful as expected. *New York Times.*

Goleman, D. (1995, January 5). An elusive picture of violent men who kill mates. *New York Times,* p. 22.

Gonzalez, R. G. (1988). Bulimia and adolescence: individual psychoanalytic treatment. In H. J. Schwartz (Ed.), *Bulimia: Psychoanalytic treatment and theory.* Madison, CT: International Universities Press.

Good, L. (1995). Addiction as a narcissistic defense: The importance of control over the object. In J. Cooper & N. Maxwell (Eds.), *Narcissistic wounds: Clinical perspectives* (pp. 143–158). Northvale, NJ: Jason Aronson.

Goodman, A. (1993). The addictive process: A psychoanalytic understanding. *Journal of the American Academy of Psychoanalysis, 21,* 89–105.

Goodman, A. (1996a). The addictive process: A neurobiological understanding. (Typescript).

Goodman, A. (1996b). Addictive disorders: An integrated approach. II. An integrated treatment. *Journal of Ministry in Addiction & Recovery, 3,* 49–77.

Goodman, A. (1998). *Sexual addiction: An integrated approach.* Madison, CT: International Universities Press.

Goodsitt, A. (1983). Self-regulating disturbances in eating disorders. *International Journal of Eating Disorders, 2,* 51–60.

Goodsitt, A. (1985). Self psychology and the treatment of anorexia nervosa. In D. M. Garner & P. E. Garfinkel (Eds.), *Handbook of psychotherapy for anorexia nervosa and bulimia* (pp. 55–82). New York: Guilford Press.

Goodwin, D. W. (1988). *Alcohol and the writer.* New York: Penguin Books.

Goodwin, F. K., & Jamison, K. R. (1990). *Manic-depressive illness.* New York: Oxford University Press.

Gordon, K. B. (2002). The treatment of addictive disorders in a private clinical setting. In Shulamith Lafa Ashenberg Straussner (Ed.), *Clinical social work with substance abusing clients* (pp. 88–102). New York: Guilford.

Grapanzano, V. (2004). *Imaginative horizons. An essay in literary-philosophical anthropology.* Chicago: University of Chicago Press.

Grave, R. D., Oliosi, M., Todisco, P., & Bartocci, C. (1996). Trauma and dissociative experiences in eating disorders. *Dissociation, 9 (4),* 274–281.

Green, A. (1986). *On private madness.* Madison, CT: International Universities Press.

Greenacre, P. (1955a). Further consideration regarding fetishism. *The Psychoanalytic Study of the Child, 10,* 187–194.

Greenacre, P. (1955b). *Swift and Carroll: A psychoanalytic study of two lives.* New York: International Universities Press.

Greenacre, P. (1960). Further notes on fetishism. *The Psychoanalytic Study of the Child, 15,* 191–207.

Greenacre, P. (1961). Further notes on fetishism. *The Psychoanalytic Study of the Child, 15,* 191–207.

Greenacre, P. (1969). The fetish and the transitional object. *The Psychoanalytic Study of the Child, 24,* 144–164.

Greenacre, P. (1970). The transitional object and the fetish with special reference to the role of illusion. *International Journal of Psycho-Analysis, 51,* 447–456.

Greenfield, S. F. (2003). The assessment of mood and substance use disorders. In J. J. Westermeyer, R. D. Weiss, & D. M. Ziedonis (Eds.), *Integrated treatment for mood and substance use disorders* (pp. 42–67). Baltimore, MD: Johns Hopkins University Press.

Gregory, R. C. (1987). *The Oxford companion to the mind.* New York: Oxford University Press.

Grilo, C. M. (2001). Pharmacological and psychological treatment of obesity and binge eating disorder. In M. T. Sammons & N. B. Schmidt (Eds.), *Combined treatments for mental disorders. A guide to psychological and pharmacological interventions* (pp. 239–269). Washington, DC: American Psychological Association.

Grimal, P. (1990). *A concise dictionary of classical mythology.* Oxford, England: Basil Blackwell Ltd.

Grosch, W. N. (1994). Narcissism: shame, rage and addiction. *Psychiatric Quarterly, 65,* 49–63.

Grotjahn, M. (1947). About the symbolization of Alice's adventures in Wonderland. *American Imago 47,* 32–41.

Grusky, Z. (1999). Conviction and conversion: The role of shared fantasies about analysis. *Psychoanalytic Quarterly, 68,* 401–430.Washington, DC: American Psychological Association.

Guarner, B. (1994). *Incest addiction: A single case study*. Unpublished paper.

Gustafson, J. (1976). The mirror transference in the psychoanalytic psychotherapy of alcoholism: A case report. *International Journal of Psychoanalytic Psychotherapy, 5,* 65–85.

Guttmann, E. & Maclay, W. S. (1936). Mescalin and depersonalization. Therapeutic experiments. *Journal of Neurology and Psychopathology, 16,* 193–212.

Haertzen, C. A. & Hooks, N. T. (1969). Changes in personality and subjective experience associated with the chronic administration and withdrawal of opiates. *Journal of Nervous & Mental Disease, 148,* 606–614.

Ham, L. S., & Hope, D. A. (2003). Alcohol and anxiety: subtle and obvious attributes of abuse in adults with social anxiety disorder and panic disorder. *Depression and Anxiety, 18,* 128–139.

Hamilton, V. (1982). *Narcissus and Oedipus: The children of psychoanalysis*. London: Karnac (Books) Ltd.

Hanly, C. (1992). On narcissistic defenses. *The Psychoanalytic Study of the Child, 47,* 139–157.

Harrington, A. (Ed.). (1977). *The placebo effect. An interdisciplinary exploration*. Cambridge, MA: Harvard University Press.

Harris, J. E. (1998). *How the brain talks to itself: A clinical primer of psychotherapeutic neuroscience*. New York: Haworth Press.

Hasin, D. S., Tsai, W.-Y., Endicott, J., Mueller, T. I., Coryell, W., & Keller, M. (1996). The effects of major depression on alcoholism. *American Journal of Addictions, 5,* 144–155.

Hausner, R. (1993). Medication and transitional phenomena. In M. Schachter (Ed.), *Psychotherapy and medication: A dynamic integration* (pp. 87–107). Northvale, NJ: Jason Aronson.

Havassy, B. E., Alvidrez, J., & Owen, K. K. (2004). Comparisons of patients with comorbid psychiatric and substance use disorders: Implications for treatment and service delivery. *American Journal of Psychiatry, 161,* 139–.

Heim, M. (1993). *The metaphysics of virtual reality*. New York: Oxford University Press.

Hendin, H. (1975). *The age of sensation: A psychoanalytic exploration*. New York: W. W. Norton.

Hendin, H., Gaylin, W., & Carr., A. (1965). *Psychoanalysis and social research*. Garden City, NY: Doubleday.

Hendin, H., Pollinger, A., Ulman, R., & Carr, A. (1981). *Adolescent marijuana abusers and their families* (National Institute on Drug Abuse, Research Monograph 40). Washington DC: U.S. Government Printing Office.

Hendin, H., Haas, A. P., Singer, P., Ellner, M., & Ulman, R. (1987). *Living high: Daily marijuana use among adults*. New York: Human Sciences Press.

Henrigues, E., Cutter, H., Arsenian, J., & Samaraweera, A. B. (1972). Personality characteristics and drug of choice. *International Journal of Addictions, 7,* 73–76.

Herbert, B. (April 22, 1999). Addicted to violence. *New York Times,* p. A31.

Hien, D. A., Cohen, L. R., Miele, G. M., Litt, L. C., & Capstick, C. (2004). Promising treatments for women with comorbid PTSD and substance use disorders. *American Journal of Psychiatry, 161 (8),* 1426–1432.

Hilgard, J. R. (1965). *Hypnotic susceptibility*. New York: Harcourt, Brace & World.

Hilgard, J. R. (1970). *Personality and hypnosis: A study of imaginative involvement*. Chicago: University of Chicago Press.

Hilgard, J. R. (1974). Toward a neo-dissociation theory: Multiple cognitive controls in human functioning. *Perspectives in Biology and Medicine, 17,* 301–316.

Hill, S. Y., Goodwin, D. W., Schwin, R., & Powell, B. (1974). Marijuana: CNS depressant or excitant? *American Journal of Psychiatry, 131,* 313–315.

Himmelhoch, J. M. (2003). The strengths and weaknesses of the concept 'Bipolar Spectrum.' *Bipolar Disorders, 5,* 443–445.

Hinshaw, S. P. (2002). *The years of silence.* Cambridge, U.K.: Cambridge University Press.

Hollander, E. (1991). Serotonergic drugs and the treatment of disorders related to obsessive-compulsive disorder. In M. T. Pato & J. Zohar (Eds.), *Current treatments of obsessive-compulsive disorder* (pp. 173–191). Washington, DC: American Psychiatric Press.

Hopper, E. (1995). A psychoanalytical theory of drug addiction: Unconscious fantasies of homosexuality, compulsions and masturbation within the context of traumatogenic processes. *International Journal of Psycho-Analysis, 76,* 1121–1142.

Horgan, J. (1999, March 21). Placebo nation. *New York Times,* Op Ed.

Horney, K. (1937). *The neurotic personality of our time.* New York: W. W. Norton.

Howard, J. (2000). *Substance abuse treatment for persons with child abuse and neglect issues: Treatment improvement protocol (TIP) series, #36.* Rockville, MD: U. S. Department of Health & Human Services, Public Health Service. Substance Abuse and Mental Health Services Administration, Center for Substance Abuse Treatment. Washington, DC: U.S. Government Printing Office.

Hudson, J. I., Harrison, Jr., G. P., Jonas, J. M., & Yurgelun-Todd, D. (1993). Phenomenologic relationship of eating disorders to major affective disorder. *Psychiatry Research, 9,* 345–354.

Hughes, J. M. (1994). *From Freud's consulting room: The unconscious in a scientific age.* Cambridge, MA: Harvard University Press.

Hyman, S. E. (2005). Addiction: A disease of learning and memory. *American Journal of Psychiatry, 162,* 1414–1422.

Imhof, J. E. (1991). Countertransference issues in the treatment of drug and alcohol addiction. In W. S. Miller (Ed.), *Comprehensive handbook of drug and alcohol addiction* (pp. 931–946). New York: Marcel Dekker.

Imhof, J. E. (1995). Overcoming countertransference and other attitudinal barriers in the treatment of substance abuse. In A. M. Washton (Ed.), *Psychotherapy and substance abuse: A practitioner's handbook* (pp. 3–22). New York: Guilford Press.

Isakower, O. (1992 [1957] H. H. Wyman & S. M. Rittenberg [Eds.]). The analyzing instrument in the teaching and conduct of the analytic process. *Journal of Clinical Psychoanalysis, 1,* 181–222.

Jacobs, D. F. (1987). A general theory of addictions: Application to treatment and rehabilitation planning for pathologic gamblers. In T. Galsk (Ed.), *Handbook of pathological gambling* (pp. 169–194). Springfield, IL: Charles C. Thomas.

Jacobs, D. F. (1988). Evidence for a common dissociative-like reaction among addicts. *Journal of Gambling Behavior, 4,* 27–37.

Jacobs, D. F. (1989). A general theory of additions: Rationale for evidence supporting a new approach for understanding and treating addictive behaviors. In H. J. Shaffer, S. A. Stern, B. Gambino, & T. N. Cummings (Eds.), *Compulsive gambling: Theory, research, and practice* (pp. 35–64). Lexington, MA: DC Heath and Company.

Jacobs, M. (2000). *Illusion: A psychodynamic interpretation of thinking and belief.* London: Whurr Publishers.

Jacobs, T. J. (1991). *The use of the self: Countertransference and communication in the analytic situation.* Madison, CT: International Universities Press.

Jacoby, M. (1985). *Individuation and narcissism. The psychology of the self in Jung and Kohut.* New York: Routledge.

Jacobsen, L. K., Southwick, S. M., & Kosten, T. R. (2003). Substance use disorders in patients with posttraumatic stress disorder: a review of the literature. *American Journal of Psychiatry, 158 (8),* 1184–1190.

Jamison, K. R. (1991). Manic-depressive illness: The overlooked need for psychotherapy. In B. D. Bettman & G. L. Klerman (Eds.), *Integrating pharmacotherapy and psychotherapy* (pp. 409–420). Washington, D.C.: American Psychiatric Press.

Johanson, C. E. & Ujlenhuth, E. H. (1981). Drug preference and mood in humans: Repeated assessment of d-amphetamine. *Pharmacology Biochemistry & Behavior, 14,* 159–163.

John, E. R. & Prichep, L. S. (2005). The anesthetic cascade. A theory of how anesthesia suppresses consciousness. *Anesthesiology, 102,* 447–471.

John, E. R., Prichep, L. S., Kox, W., Valdes-Sosa, P., Bosch-Bayard, J. Aubert, E., Tom, M. diMichele, F., & Gugino, L. D. (2001). Invariant reversible QEEG effects of anesthetics. *Consciousness & Cognition, 10,* 165–183.

Johnson, B. (1999). Three perspectives on addiction. *Journal of American Psychoanalytic Association, 47,* 791–815.

Johnson, S. L., & Leahy, R. L. (2004). *Psychological treatment of bipolar disorder.* New York. Guilford Press.

Johnson, S. M. (1987). *Humanizing the narcissistic style.* New York: W. W. Norton.

Johnston, P. (1997). *Real fantasies: Edward Steichen's advertising photography.* Berkeley: University of California Press.

Jones, E. (1955). *The life and work of Sigmund Freud: Years of maturity 1901–1919* (Vol. 2). New York: Basic Books.

Jones, E. (1974 [1913]). The God complex: The belief that one is god, and the resulting character traits. In *Psycho-myth, psycho-history: Essays in applied psychoanalysis* (pp. 244–265). New York: Stonehill Publishing.

Jones, S. H., Sellwood, W., & McGovern, J. (2005). Psychological therapies for bipolar disorder: The role of model-driven approaches to therapy integration. *Bipolar Disorders, 7,* 22–32.

Joseph, R. (1992). *The right brain and the unconscious: Discovering the Stranger within.* New York: Plenum Press.

Josephs, L. (1992). *Character structure and the organization of the self.* New York: Columbia University Press.

Kadden, R. M., Kranzler, H. R., & Rounsaville, B. J. (1995). Validity of the distinction between "substance-induced" and "independent" depression and anxiety disorders. *American Journal on Addictions, 4,* 107–117.

Kafka, J. S. (1969). The body as transitional object: A psychoanalytic study of self-mutilating patient. *British Journal of Medical Psychology, 42,* 207–212.

Kahn, D. A. (1993). Medication consultation and split treatment during psychotherapy. In M. Schachter (Ed.), *Psychotherapy and medication: A Dynamic integration* (pp. 225–237). Northvale, NJ: Jason Aronson.

Kalin, R., & McClelland, D. C. (1965). The effects of male social drinking on fantasy. *Journal of Personality and Social Psychology, 1,* 441–452.

Kalin, R., McClelland, D. C., & Kahn, D. A. (1972). The effects of male social drinking on fantasy. In D. C. McClelland, W. N. Davis, R. Kalin, & E. Wanner (Eds.), *The drinking man* (pp. 31–141). New York: The Free Press.

Kaminer, H. (1978). Transitional object components in self and object relations. In S. M. Grolnick, L. Barkin, & W. Muensterberger (Eds.), *Between reality and Fantasy: Transitional objects and phenomena* (pp. 235–243). New York: Jason Aronson.

Kandel, E. R. (2005). *Psychiatry, psychoanalysis, and the new biology of mind.* Washington, DC: American Psychiatric Publishing.

Comorbidity of anxiety disorders with anorexia and bulimia nervosa. *American Journal of Psychiatry, 161,* 2215.

Kantor, S. J. (1993). Depression: When is psychotherapy not enough? In M. Schachter (Ed.), *Psychotherapy and medication: A dynamic integration* (pp. 255–268). Northvale, NJ: Jason Aronson.

Kaplan, E. H., & Wieder, H. (1974). *Drugs don't take people, people take drugs*. Seacaucus, NJ: Lyle Stuart.

Kaplan, H. I., & Sadock, B. J. (1991). *Comprehensive glossary of psychiatry and psychology*. Baltimore, MD: Williams & Wilkins.

Kaplan-Solms, K., & Solms, M. (2002). *Clinical studies in neuro-psychoanalysis* (2nd ed., Introduction to a Depth Neuropsychology). New York: Karnac (Books) Ltd.

Kaptchuk, T., Eisenberg, D., & Komaroff, A. (2002). Pondering the placebo effect. Why do sham treatments work? And what do they tell us about the nature of self-healing? *Newsweek*, December 2, 71.

Karasu, T. B. (1993). Toward an integrative model. In M. Schachter (Ed.), *Psychotherapy and medication: A dynamic integration* (pp. 11–33). Northvale, NJ: Jason Aronson.

Katan, A. (1960). Distortions of the phallic phase. *The Psychoanalytic Study of the Child 15*, 208–215.

Katan, M. (1958). Contribution to the panel on ego-distortion ("as-if" and "pseudo as-if"). *International Journal of Psycho-Analysis 39*, 265–270.

Katzow, J. J., Hsu, D. J., & Ghaemi, S. N. (2003). The bipolar spectrum: A clinical perspective. *Bipolar Disorders, 5*, 436–442.

Kaufman, E. (1994). *Psychotherapy of addicted persons*. New York: Guilford Press.

Kaye, W. H., Bulik, C. M., Thornton, L., Barbarich, N., & Masters, K. (2004).

Kaywin, L. (1968). The evocation of a genie: A study of an "as if" character type. *Psychoanalytic Quarterly, 37*, 22–41.

Kearney, R. J. (1996). *Within the wall of denial: Conquering addictive behaviors*. New York: W. W. Norton.

Kearney-Cooke, A. (1990). The role of the therapist in the treatment of eating disorders: A feminist psychodynamic approach. In C. L. Johnson (Ed.), *Psychodynamic treatment of anorexia nervosa and bulimia* (pp. 295–318). New York: Guilford Press.

Keller, M. (1972). On the loss-of-control phenomenon. *British Journal of Addiction, 67*, 153–166.

Kernberg, O. F. (1975) *Borderline conditions and pathological narcissism*. New York: Jason Aronson.

Kernberg, O. F. (1976). *Object-relations theory and clinical psychoanalysis*. New York: Jason Aronson.

Kernberg, O. F. (1984). *Severe personality disorders: Psychotherapeutic strategies*. New Haven, CT: Yale University Press.

Kershaw, S. (November 7, 2003). 21-Year hunt for killer shapes man and family. *New York Times*, A1, A24.

Khantzian, E. J. (1974). Opiate addiction: A critique of theory and some implications for treatment. *American Journal of Psychotherapy, 28*, 59–70.

Khantzian, E. J. (1975). Self-selection and progression in drug dependence. *Psychiatry Digest*, October, 19–22.

Khantzian, E. J. (1978). The ego, the self and opiate addiction: Theoretical and treatment considerations. *International Review of Psycho-Analysis, 5*, 189–198.

Khantzian, E. J. (1980). The alcoholic patient: An overview and perspective. *American Journal of Psychotherapy, 34*, 4–19.

Khantzian, E. J. (1983). An extreme case of cocaine dependence and marked improvement with methylphenidate treatment. *American Journal of Psychiatry, 140 (6)*, 784–785.

Khantzian, E. J. (1985). The self-medication hypothesis of addictive disorders: Focus on heroin and cocaine dependence. *American Journal of Psychiatry, 142*, 1259–1264.

Khantzian, E. J. (1987). A clinical perspective of the cause-consequence controversy in alcoholic and addictive suffering. *Journal of the American Academy of Psychoanalysis, 15*, 521–537.

Khantzian, E. J. (1995). Self-regulation vulnerabilities in substance abusers: Treatment implications. In S. Dowling (Ed.), *The psychology and treatment of addictive behavior* (pp. 17–41). Madison, CT: International Universities Press.

Khantzian, E. J. (1999). *Treating addiction as a human process*. Northvale, NJ: Jason Aronson.

Khantzian, E. J., & Mack, J. E. (1983). Self-preservation and the care of the self. *The Psychoanalytic Study of the Child, 38,* 289–232.

Khantzian, E. J., & Schneider, R. J. (1986). Treatment implications of a psychoanalytic understanding of opioid addicts. In R. E. Meyer (Ed.), *Psychopathology and addictive disorders* (pp. 323–333). New York: Guilford Press.

Khantzian, E. J., Halliday, K. S., & McAuliffe, W. E. (1990). *Addiction and the vulnerable self: Modified dynamic group therapy for substance abusers*. New York: Guilford Press.

Khantzian, E. J., Mack, J. E., & Schatzberg, A. F. (1974). Heroin use as an attempt to cope. Clinical observations. *American Journal of Psychiatry, 131,* 160–164.

Kipnis, L. (1996). *Bound and gagged: Pornography and the politics of fantasy in America*. New York: Grove Press.

Kircher, T., & David, A. (Eds.). (2003). *The self in neuroscience and psychiatry*. New York: Cambridge University Press.

Klee, G. D. (1963). Lysergic acid diethylamide (LSD-25) and ego functions. *Archives of General Psychiatry, 8,* 461–474.

Klein, M. (1961). *Narrative of a child analysis. The conduct of the psycho-analysis of children as seen in the treatment of a ten-year-old boy*. New York: Delacorte.

Klein, D. F. (1964). Delineation of two drug responsive anxiety syndromes. *Psychopharmacology, 5,* 397–408.

Klein, D. F. (1980). Anxiety reconceptualized. *Comprehensive Psychiatry, 21,* 411–427.

Klein, D. F. (1981). Anxiety reconceptualized. In D. F. Klein & J. Rabkin (Eds.), *Anxiety new research and changing concepts* (pp. 235–265). New York: Raven Press.

Klein, D. F., Rabkin, J. G., & Gorman, J. M. (1985). Etiological and pathophysiological inferences from the pharmacological treatment of anxiety. In A. H. Tuma & J. D. Maser (Eds.), *Anxiety and the anxiety disorders* (pp. 501–532). Hillsdale, NJ: Lawrence Erlbaum.

Klein, M. (1975) [1950]. On the criteria for the termination of a psycho-analysis. In *Envy and gratitude & other works 1946–1963* (pp. 43–47). New York: Delta.

Klein, M. (1975) [1952]. On observing the behaviour of young infants. In *Envy and gratitude & other works 1946–1963* (pp. 94–121). New York: Delta.

Klein, M. (1975) [1955]. On identification. In *Envy and gratitude & other works 1946–1963* (pp. 141–175). New York: Delta.

Klein, M. (1975) [1957]. Envy and gratitude. In *Envy and gratitude & other works 1946–1963* (pp. 176–235). New York: Delta.

Knight, R. P. (1937a). The psychodynamics of chronic alcoholism. *Journal of Nervous & Mental Diseases, 86,* 538–548.

Knight, R. P. (1937b). The dynamics and treatment of chronic alcohol and addiction. *Bulletin of the Menninger Clinic, 1,* 235–250.

Knight, R. P., & Prout, C. T. (1951). A study of results in hospital treatment of drug addictions. *American Journal of Psychiatry, 108,* 303–308.

Knisely, J. S., Barker, S. B., Ingersoll, K. S., & Dawson, K. S. (2000). Psychopathology in substance abusing women reporting childhood sexual abuse. *Journal of Addictive Diseases, 19,* 31–44.

Koenigsberg, H. W., Pollak, C. P., & Ferro, D. (1998). Can panic be induced in deep sleep? Examining the necessity of cognitive processing for panic. *Depression and Anxiety, 8,* 126–130.

Kohut, H. (1966). Forms and transformations of narcissism. In P. H. Ornstein (Ed.), *The search for the self* (Vol. 1, pp. 427–460). New York: International Universities Press.

Kohut, H. (1971). *The analysis of the self: A systematic approach to the psychoanalytic treatment of narcissistic personality disorders*. New York: International Universities Press.

Kohut, H. (1977a). Preface. In J. D. Blaine & D. A. Julius (Eds.), *Psychodynamics of drug dependence* (National Institute on Drug Abuse, Research Monograph Series 12, pp. vii–ix). Washington, DC: U.S. Government Printing Office.

Kohut, H. (1977b). *The restoration of the self*. New York: International Universities Press.

Kohut, H. (1978a [1956]). Discussion of "the role of the counterphobic mechanism in addiction" by Thomas S. Szasz. In P. H. Ornstein (Ed.), *The search for the self* (Vol. 1, pp. 201–203). New York: International Universities Press.

Kohut, H. (1978b [1959]). Introspection, empathy, and psychoanalysis: An examination of the relationship between mode of observation and theory. In P. H. Ornstein (Ed.), *The search for the self* (Vol. 1, pp. 205–232). New York: International Universities Press.

Kohut, H. (1978c [1970]). Narcissism as a resistance and as a driving force in psychoanalysis. In P. H. Ornstein (Ed.), *The search for the self* (Vol. 2, pp. 547–561). New York: International Universities Press.

Kohut, H. (1978d [1972]). Thoughts on narcissism and narcissistic rage. In P. H. Ornstein (Ed.), *The search for the self* (Vol. 2, pp. 615–658). New York: International Universities Press.

Kohut, H. (1978e [1976]). Creativeness, charisma, group psychology: Reflections on the self-analysis of Freud. In P. H. Ornstein (Ed.), *Search for the self* (Vol. 2, pp. 793–843). New York: International Universities Press.

Kohut, H. (1978f [1976]). Preface to *Der falsche Weg zum Selbst, Studien zur Drogen-Karriere* by Jurgen vom Scheidt. In P. H. Ornstein (Ed.), *The search for the self* (Vol. 2, pp. 845–850). New York: International Universities Press.

Kohut, H. (1979). The two analyses of Mr. Z. *International Journal of Psycho-Analysis, 60*, 3–27.

Kohut, H. (1984). *How does analysis cure?* Chicago: University of Chicago Press.

Kohut, H. (1985). *Self psychology and the humanities: Reflections on a new psychoanalytic approach* (C. B. Strozier [Ed.]). New York: W. W. Norton.

Kohut, H., & Wolf, E. S. (1978). The disorders of the self and their treatment: An outline. *International Journal of Psycho-Analysis, 59*, 413–425.

Kolata, G. (2001a, May 24). Placebo effect is more myth than science, study says. *New York Times*, p. XX.

Kolata, G. (2001b, May 27). Putting your faith in science? *New York Times*, p. XX.

Kolb, L. (1925). Types and characteristics of drug addicts. *Mental Hygiene, 9*, 300–313.

Krueger, D. W. (1988). Body self, psychological self, and bulimia: Developmental and clinical considerations. In H. J. Schwartz (Ed.), *Bulimia: Psychoanalytic treatment and theory* (pp. 55–71). Madison, CT: International Universities Press.

Krueger, D. (1997). Food as selfobject in eating disorder patients. *Psychoanalytic Review, 84*, 617–630.

Krueger, D. (2000). The use of money as an action symptom: A psychoanalytic view. In A. Benson (Ed.), *I shop, therefore I am: Compulsive buying and the search for self* (pp. 288–310). Northvale, NJ: Aronson.

Krueger, D. W. (2002). *Integrating body self and psychological self: Creating a new story in psychoanalysis and psychotherapy*. New York: Brunner-Routledge.

Krystal, H. (1966). Withdrawal from drugs. *Psychosomatics, 7*, 299–302.

Krystal, H. (1977). Self and object-representation in alcoholism and other drug dependence: Implications for therapy. In J. D. Blaine & D. A. Julius (Eds.), *Psychodynamics of drug dependence* (National Institute on Drug Abuse, Research Monograph Series 12, pp. 88–100). Washington, DC: U. S. Government Printing Office.

Krystal, H. (1978a). Self representation and the capacity for self care. *Annual of Psychoanalysis, 6,* 209–246.

Krystal, H. (1978b). Trauma and affects. *The Psychoanalytic Study of the Child, 33,* 81–116.

Krystal, H. (1979). Alexithymia and psychotherapy. *American Journal of Psychotherapy, 33,* 17–31.

Krystal, H. (1982a). Adolescence and the tendencies to develop substance dependence. *Psychoanalytic Inquiry, 2,* 581–617.

Krystal, H. (1982b). Alexithymia and the effectiveness of psychoanalytic treatment. *International Journal of Psychoanalytic Psychotherapy, 9,* 353–388.

Krystal, H. (1983). The activating aspects of emotions. *Psychoanalysis and Contemporary Thought, 5,* 605–642.

Krystal, H. (1985). Trauma and the stimulus barrier. *Psychoanalytic Inquiry, 5,* 131–161.

Krystal, H. (1988). *Integration and self-healing: Affect, trauma, alexithymia.* Hillsdale, NJ: Analytic Press.

Krystal, H. (1990). An information processing view of object-relations. *Psychoanalytic Inquiry, 10,* 221–251.

Krystal, H., & Raskin, A. A. (1970). *Drug dependence: Aspects of ego functions.* Detroit, MI: Wayne State University Press.

Kushner, M. G., Sher, K. J., & Erickson, D. J. (1999). Prospective analysis of the relation between *DSM-III* anxiety disorders and alcohol use disorders. *American Journal of Psychiatry, 156,* 723–738.

LaBrussa, A. L. (1994). *Using DSM-IV: A clinician's guide to psychiatric diagnosis.* Northvale, NJ: Jason Aronson.

Lachkar, J. (1992). *The narcissistic/borderline couple. A psychoanalytic perspective on marital treatment.* New York: Brunner/Mazel.

Lachmann, A., & Lachmann, F. M. (1995). The personification of evil: Motivations and fantasies of the serial killer. *International Forum for Psychoanalysis, 4,* 17–23.

Lachmann, F. M., & Beebe, B. (1989). Oneness fantasies revisited. *Psychoanalytic Psychology, 6,* 137–149.

La Farge, L. (2004). The imaginer and the imagined. *Psychoanalytic Quarterly, 73,* 591–625.

Lage, G. A., & Nathan, H. K. (1991). The significance of fantasies. In *Psychotherapy, adolescents, and self psychology.* Madison, CT: International Universities Press.

Landry, M. J. (1994). *Understanding drugs of abuse: The processes of addiction, treatment, and recovery.* Washington, DC: American Psychiatric Press.

Lang, A. R. (1983). Addictive personality: A viable construct? In P. K. Levinson, D. R. Gerstein, & D. R. Malott (Eds.), *Commonalities in substance abuse and habitual behavior* (pp. 157–235). Lexington, MA: DC Heath and Company.

LaPlanche, J., & Pontalis, J.-B. (1988). *The language of psycho-analysis.* London: Karnac Books.

Lasagna, L., von Felsinger, J. M., & Beecher, H. K. (1955). Drug-induced mood changes in man. *Journal of the American Medical Association, 157,* 1006–1020.

Lasch, C. (1979). *The culture of narcissism: American life in an age of diminishing expectations.* New York: W. W. Norton.

Latendresse, J. D. (1968). Masturbation and its relation to addiction. *Review of Existential Psychology and Psychiatry, 8,* 16–27.

Laufer, M. (1976). The central masturbation fantasy, the final sexual organization, and adolescence. *The Psychoanalytic Study of the Child, 31,* 297–316.

Lax, R. F. (1997). Boy's envy of mother and the consequences of this narcissistic mortification. *The Psychoanalytic Study of the Child, 52,* 118–139.

Lear, J. (1990). *Love and its place in nature: A philosophical interpretation of Freudian psychoanalysis.* New York: Farrar, Straus & Giroux.

LeDoux, J. (2002). *Synaptic self. How our brains become who we are.* New York: Penguin.

Leeman, E., & Leeman, S. (2004). Elements of dynamics IV: Neuronal metaphors—probing neurobiology for psychodynamic meaning. *Journal of the American Academy of Psychoanalysis & Dynamic Psychiatry, 42,* 645–659.

Lenoff, L. (1998). Phantasy selfobjects and the conditions of therapeutic change. In A. Goldberg (Ed.), *Progress in Self Psychology* (Vol. 14, pp. 147–167). Hillsdale, NJ: Analytic Press.

Lerner, H. D. (1990). Masochism in subclinical eating disorders. In C. L. Johnson (Ed.), *Psychodynamic treatment of anorexia nervosa and bulimia* (pp. 109–127). New York: Guilford Press.

Lesieur, H. R., & Blume, S. B. (1993). Pathological gambling, eating disorders, and the psychoactive substance use disorders. In N. S. Miller (Ed.), *Comorbidity of addictive and psychiatric disorders* (pp. 89–102). New York: Haworth Medical Press.

Lester, D., Burkman, J. H., Gandica, A., & Narkunski, A. (1976). The addictive personality. *Psychology, 13,* 53–57.

Lettieri, D. J. (1989). Substance abuse etiology. In *Treatments of psychiatric disorders* (Task Force Report of the American Psychiatric Association, Vol. 2, pp. 1192–1202). Washington, DC: American Psychiatric Association.

Levens, M. (1995). *Eating disorders and magical control of the body: Treatment through art therapy.* London & New York: Routledge.

Levin, F. M. (1991). *Mapping the mind: The intersection of psychoanalysis and neuroscience.* Hillsdale, NJ: Analytic Press.

Levin, J. D. (1987). *Treatment of alcoholism and other addictions. A self-psychology approach.* Northvale, NJ: Jason Aronson.

Levin, J. D. (1998). *The Clinton syndrome: The president and the self-destructive nature of sexual addiction forum.*

Levin, J. D. (2001). *Therapeutic strategies for treating addiction: From slavery to freedom.* Northvale, NJ: Jason Aronson.

Levin, K. (1993). *Unconscious fantasy in psychotherapy.* Northvale, NJ: Jason Aronson.

Levy, L. (1925). The psychology of the effect produced by morphia. *International Journal of Psychoanalysis, 6,* 313–316.

Lewin, B. D. (1950). *The psychoanalysis of elation.* New York: W. W. Norton.

Lichtenberg, J. D. (1978). The testing of the reality from the standpoint of the body self. *Journal of the American Psychoanalytic Association, 26,* 357–385.

Lichtenberg, J. D. (1989). *Psychoanalysis and motivation.* Hillsdale, NJ: Analytic Press.

Lichtenberg, J. D., Lachmann, F. M., & Fosshage, J. L. (1992). *Self and motivational systems. Toward a theory of psychoanalytic technique.* Hillsdale, NJ: Analytic Press.

Liebeskind, A. S. (1991). Chemical dependency and the denial of the need for intimacy. In A. Smaldino (Ed.), *Psychoanalytic approaches to addiction* (pp. 65–79). New York: Brunner/Mazel.

Liebowitz, E. B. (1991). Bulimia: A self-psychological study. In A. Smaldino (Ed.), *Psychoanalytic approaches to addiction* (pp. 96–122). New York: Brunner/Mazel.

Lifton, R. J. (1967). *Survivors of Hiroshima.* New York: Basic Books.

Lifton, R. J. (1988). Understanding the traumatized self. Imagery, symbolization, and transformation. In J. P. Wilson, Z. Harel, & B. Kahana (Eds.), *Human adaptation to extreme stress from the Holocaust to Vietnam* (pp. 7–31). New York: Plenum Press.

Lifton, R. J. (1999). Destroying the world to save it. Aum shinrikyo, apocalyptic violence, and the new global terrorism. New York: Metropolitan Books.

Lindner, R. M. (1946). *Stone walls and men.* New York: Odyssey Press.

Lindon, J. A. (1988). Psychoanalysis by telephone. *Bulletin of the Menninger Clinic, 52,* 521–528.

Llinás, R. R. (2001). *I of the vortex: From neurons to self.* Cambridge, MA: MIT Press.

Loewald, H. W. (1960). On the therapeutic action of psychoanalysis. *International Journal of Psycho-Analysis, 41,* 16–33.

Loewald, H. W. (1975). Psychoanalysis as an art and the fantasy character of the psychoanalytic situation. In *Papers on psychoanalysis* (pp. 352–371). New Haven, CT: Yale University Press.

Loewald, H. (1980). *Papers on psychoanalysis.* New Haven: Yale University Press.

Loewald, H. W. (1980 [1955]). Hypnoid state, repression, abreaction, and recollection. In *Papers on psychoanalysis* (pp. 33–42). New Haven: Yale University Press.

Loose, R. (2002). *The subject of addiction psychoanalysis and the administration of enjoyment.* New York: Karnac (Books) Ltd.

Lothane, Z. (1992). *In defense of Schreber: Soul murder and psychiatry.* Hillsdale, NJ: The Analytic Press.

Lydiard, B. R., Brady K., Ballenger, J. C., Howell, E. F., & Malcolm, R. (1992). Anxiety and mood disorders in hospitalized alcoholic individuals. *American Journal on Addictions, 1,* 325–331.

Lynn, S., & Rhue, J. (1988). Fantasy proneness: Hypnosis, developmental antecedents, and psychopathology. *American Psychologist, 43,* 35–44.

Lynn, S., Rhue, J. W., & Green, J. P. (1988). Multiple personality and fantasy proneness: Is there an association or dissociation? *British Journal of Experimental and Clinical Hypnosis, 5,* 138–142.

Lynn, S. J., Neufeld, V., Green, J. P., Sandberg, D., & Rhue, J. (1996). Daydreaming, fantasy, and psychopathology. In R. G. Kuzendorf, N. P. Spanos, & B. Wallace (Eds.), *Hypnosis and imagination,* pp. 67–98. Amityville, NY: Baywood.

Ma, K. (1996). *The modern Madame Butterfly: Fantasy and reality in Japanese cross-cultural relationships.* Rutland, VT: Charles E. Tuttle.

Mackin, P., & Young, A. H. (2004). Rapid cycling bipolar disorder: Historical overview and focus on emerging treatments. *Bipolar Disorders, 6,* 523–529.

MacKinnon, D. F., Zandi, P. P., Cooper, J., Potash, J. B., Simpson, S. G., Gershon, E., Nurnberger, J., Reich, T., & DePaulo, J. R. (2002). Comorbid bipolar disorder and panic disorder in families with a high prevalence of bipolar disorder. *American Journal of Psychiatry, 159,* 30–35.

Mahler, M. S. (1949a). A psychoanalytic evaluation of tics in psychopathology of children: Symptomatic tic and tic syndrome. *Psychoanalytic Study of the Child, 3/4,* 279–310.

Mahler, M. S. (1949b). Remarks on psychoanalysis with psychotic children. *Quarterly Journal of Child Behavior, 1,* 18–21.

Mahler, M. S., Pine, F., & Bergman, A. (1975). *The psychological birth of the human infant. Symbiosis and individuation.* New York: Basic Books.

Maj, M., Pirozzi, R., Formicola, A. M. R., & Tortorella, A. (1999). Reliability and validity of four alternative definitions of rapid-cycling bipolar disorder. *American Journal of Psychiatry, 156,* 1421–1424.

Maj, M., Pirozzi, R., Magliano, L., & Bartoli, L. (2003). Agitated depression in bipolar I disorder: Prevalence, phenomenology, and outcome. *American Journal of Psychiatry, 160,* 2134–2140.

Major, R., & Miller, P. (1984). Empathy, antipathy, and telepathy in the analytic process. In J. Lichtenberg, M. Bornstein, & D. Silver (Eds.), *Empathy II* (pp. 227–248). Hillsdale, NJ: Analytic Press.

Mancia, M. (1993). *In the gaze of Narcissus: Memory, affects and creativity.* London: Karnac Books.

Mantere, O., Suominen, K., Leppämäki, S., Valtonen, H., Arviolmmi, P., & Isometsä, E. (2004). The clinical characteristics of *DSM-IV* bipolar I and II disorders: Baseline findings from the Jorvi Bipolar Study (JoBS). *Bipolar Disorders, 6,* 395–405.

Marcovitz, E. (1964). Bemoaning the lost dream: Coleridge's "Kubla Khan" and Addiction. *International Journal of Psycho-Analysis, 45,* 411–425.

Margulies, A. (1989). *The empathic imagination.* New York: W. W. Norton.

Mark, D., & Faude, J. (1997). *Psychotherapy of cocaine addiction: Entering the interpersonal world of the cocaine addict.* Northvale, NJ: Jason Aronson.

Martin, J. (1988). *Who am i this time? Uncovering the fictive personality.* New York: W. W. Norton.

Martin, J. P. (1992). Psychophysiological experience fulfilling a selfobject experience. *Journal of Psychotherapy Practice and Research, 1,* 160–162.

Martínez-Arán, A., Vieta, E., & Reinares, M. (2004). Cognitive function across manic or hypomanic, depressed, and euthymic states in bipolar disorder. *American Journal of Psychiatry, 161,* 262–270.

Mas, F. (2000). Personal communication.

Mas, F. (2003, October 13). Depression is not simple: Identification and treatment of mixed states in mood disorders. *Moods, No. 3. Newsletter of the Mood Disorders Support Group/New York.*

Mashour, G. A. (2006, January 19). Toward a general theory of unconscious processes in psychoanalysis and anesthesiology. CORST Prize paper presented at The New York Psychoanalytic Institute.

Massing, M. (2000, June 24). Seeing drugs as a choice or as a brain anomaly. *New York Times,* B9 & B11.

Maxman, J. S., & Ward, N. G. (1994). *Essential psychopathology and its treatment* (2nd ed., revised for *DSM-IV*). New York: W. W. Norton.

May, M. (1991). Observations on countertransference addiction, and treatability. In A. Smaldino (Ed.), *Psychoanalytic approaches to addiction* (pp. 1–12). New York: Brunner/Mazel.

Mayes, L. C., & Cohen, D. J. (1992). The development of a capacity for imagination in early childhood. *The Psychoanalytic Study of the Child, 47,* 23–47.

McAuliffe, W. E., & Gordon, R. A. (1974). A test of Lindesmith's theory of addiction: The frequency of euphoria among long-term addicts. *American Journal of Sociology, 79,* 795–841.

McCarthy, J. B. (2000). Psychotic symbol use and nonhuman identities. *Contemporary Psychoanalysis, 36,* 103–119.

McClelland, D. C., Davis, W. N., Kalin, R., & Wanner, E. (Eds.). (1972). *The drinking man.* New York: The Free Press.

McDougall, J. (1985). *Theaters of the mind: Illusion and truth on the psychoanalytic stage.* New York: Basic Books.

McGinn, C. (2004). *Mindsight. Image, dream, meaning.* Cambridge, MA: Harvard University Press.

McGrath, P. J., Nunes, E. V., & Quitkin, F. M. (2000). Current concepts in the treatment of depression in alcohol-dependent patients. *Psychiatric Clinics of North America, 23,* 695–711.

McKowen, J. W., Frye, M. A., Altshuler, L. L., & Gitlin, M. J. (2005). Patterns of alcohol consumption in bipolar patients comorbid for alcohol abuse or dependence. *Bipolar Disorders, 7,* 377–381.

McLellan, A. T., Luborsky, L. Woody, G. E., O'Brien, C., & Kron, R. (1981). Are the "addiction-related" problems of substance abusers really related? *Journal of Nervous and Mental Disease, 169,* 232–239.

McWilliams, N. (1994). *Psychoanalytic diagnosis: Understanding personality structure in the clinical process.* New York: Guilford Press.

Meerlo, J. A. M. (1952). Artificial ecstasy. A study of the psychosomatic aspects of drug addiction. *Journal of Nervous & Mental Disorders, 115,* 246–266.

Meisler, A. W. (1996). Trauma, PTSD, and substance abuse. *PTSD Research Quarterly, 7,* 1–3.

Meissner, W. W. (1980). Addiction and paranoid process: Psychoanalytic perspectives. *International Journal of Psychoanalytic Psychotherapy, 8,* 273–310.

Meissner, W. W. (1985). A case of phallic-narcissistic personality. *Journal of the American Psychoanalytic Association, 33,* 437–469.

Meissner, W. W. (2003). Mind, brain, and self in psychoanalysis. *Psychoanalysis & Contemporary Thought, 26,* 279–386.

Menninger, K. (1938). *Man against himself.* New York: Harcourt Brace Jovanovich.

Menninger, K. (1940). Character disorders. In J. F. Brown (Ed.), *The psychodynamics of abnormal behavior* (pp. 384–401). New York: McGraw-Hill Book Company.

Merritt, R., & Kaufman, J. B. (1993). *Walt in wonderland: The silent films of Walt Disney.* Baltimore, MD: The John Hopkins University Press.

Meyer, R. E. (1986). How to understand the relationship between psychopathology and addictive disorders: Another example of the chicken and the egg. In R. E. Meyer (Ed.), *Psychopathology and addictive disorders* (pp. 3–16). New York: Guilford Press.

Meyer, R. E. (1989). Typologies. In *Treatments of psychiatric disorders* (Task Force Report of the American Psychiatric Association, Vol. 2, pp. 1065–1071). Washington, DC: American Psychiatric Association.

Miliora, M. (1997). A self-psychological study of a shared gambling fantasy in Eugene O'Neill's "Hughie." *Journal of Gambling Studies, 13,* 105–123.

Miliora, M. T. (2000). *Narcissism, the family, and madness: A self-psychological study of Eugene O'Neill and his plays.* New York: Peter Lang Publishing.

Miliora, M. T., & Ulman, R. B. (1996a). Deconstruction and reconstruction: A self-psychological perspective on the construction of meaning in psychoanalysis. In J. R. Brandell (Ed.), *Narration and therapeutic action: The construction of meaning in psychoanalytic social work* (pp. 61–81). New York: Haworth Press.

Miliora, M. T., & Ulman, R. B. (1996b). Panic disorder: A bioself-psychological perspective. *Journal of the American Academy of Psychoanalysis, 24,* 217–256.

Miller, D., & Guidry, L. (2001). *Addictions and trauma recovery. Healing the mind, body, and spirit.* New York: W. W. Norton.

Miller, I. (1969). Unconscious fantasy and masturbatory technique. *Journal of the American Psychoanalytic Association, 17,* 828–842.

Miller, I. (1972). Inhibition of empathy caused by unconscious fantasy. *International Journal of Psychoanalytic Psychotherapy, 1,* 107–116.

Miller, J. (2002). Heroin addiction: The needle as transitional object. *Journal of the American Academy of Psychoanalysis, 30,* 293–304.

Miller, J. R. (1994). Substance abuse: The role of depression and trauma—A case report. *Journal of the American Academy of Psychoanalysis, 22,* 753–764.

Miller, J. R. (2002). Heroin addiction: The needle as transitional object. *Journal of the American Academy of Psychoanalysis, 30 (2),* 293–304.

Miller, L. (1991). *Freud's brain: Neuropsychodynamic foundations of psychoanalysis.* New York: Guilford Press.

Miller, M. C. (Ed.). (2001, April). Bipolar disorder—Part I. *Harvard Mental Health Letter, 17.*

Miller, M. C. (Ed.). (2001, May). Bipolar disorder—Part II. *Harvard Mental Health Letter, 18.*

Miller, M. L. (1991). Understanding the eating-disordered patient: Engaging the concrete. *Bulletin of the Menninger Clinic, 55,* 85–95.

Miller, N. S. (1993). Comorbidity of psychiatric and alcohol/drug disorders: Interactions and independent status. In N. S. Miller & B. Simmel (Eds.), *Comorbidity of addictive and psychiatric disorders* (pp. 5–16). New York: Haworth Medical Press.

Miller, N. S. (1994). *Treating coexisting psychiatric and addictive disorders: A practical guide.* Center City, MN: Hazelden.

Miller, N. S. (1995). *Addiction psychiatry. Current diagnosis and treatment.* New York: Wiley-Liss.

Milligan, B. (1995). *Pleasures and pains: Opium and the orient in nineteenth-century British culture.* Charlottesville, VA: University Press of Virginia.

Milkman, H., & Frosch, W. A. (1973). On the preferential abuse of heroin and amphetamine. *Journal of Nervous and Mental Diseases, 156,* 242–248.

Milkman, H., & Frosch, W. A. (1977). The drug of choice. *Journal of Psychedelic Drugs, 9,* 13–24.

Milkman, H., & Sunderwirth, S. (1982). Addictive processes. *Journal of Psychoactive Drugs, 14,* 177–192.

Milkman, H., & Sunderwirth, S. (1987). *Craving for ecstasy: The consciousness and chemistry of escape.* Lexington, MA: DC Heath and Company.

Milrod, B. L., & Busch, F. N. (1998). Combining psychodynamic psychotherapy with medication in the treatment of panic disorder: Exploring the dynamic meaning of medication. *Psychoanalytic Inquiry, 18,* 702–715.

Miller, M. C. (Ed.). (2001, April). Bipolar disorder—Part I. *Harvard Mental Health Letter,* 1–4.

Miller, M. C. (Ed.). (2001, May). Bipolar disorder—Part II. *Harvard Mental Health Letter,* 1–4.

Mirin, S. M., Meyer, R. E., & McNamee, B. (1976). Psychopathology and mood during heroin use. *Archives of General Psychiatry, 33,* 1503–1508.

Mitchell, P. B., & Malhi, G. S. (2004). Bipolar depression: Phenomenological overview and clinical characteristics. *Bipolar Disorders, 6,* 530–539.

Modell, A. H. (1976). The "holding environment" and the therapeutic action of psychoanalysis. *Journal of the American Psychoanalytic Association, 24,* 285–307.

Modell, A. H. (2003). *Imagination and the meaningful brain.* Cambridge, MA: MIT Press.

Modesto-Lowe, V., & Kranzler, H. (1999). Diagnosis and treatment of alcohol-dependent patients with comorbid psychiatric disorders. *Alcohol Research & Health, 23,* 144–149.

Mondimore, F. M. (1999). *Bipolar disorder: A guide for patients and families.* Baltimore, MD: Johns Hopkins University Press.

Moore, R. A. (1961). Reaction formation as a countertransference phenomenon in the treatment of alcoholism. *Quarterly Journal of Studies on Alcohol, 22,* 481–486.

Moore, S. M., & Ohtsuka, K. (1999). Beliefs about control over gambling among young people, and their relation to problem gambling. *Psychology of Addictive Behaviors, 13 (4),* 339–347.

Moran, C. (1986). Depersonalization and agoraphobia associated with marijuana use. *British Journal of Medical Psychology, 59,* 187–196.

Morrison, D. C. (Ed.). (1988). *Organizing early experience. Imagination and cognition in childhood.* Amityville, NY: Baywood.

Morrison, M. (1989). *White rabbit: A doctor's story of her addiction and recovery.* New York: Crown Publishers.

Muensterberger, W. (1994). *Collecting: An unruly passion: Psychological perspectives.* Princeton, NJ: Princeton University Press.

Mueser, K. T., Noordsy, D. L., Drake, R. E., & Fox, L. (2003). *Integrated treatment for dual disorders: A guide to effective practice.* New York: Guilford Press.

Mullan, M. J., Gurling, H. M. D., Oppenheim, B. E., & Murray, R. M. (1986). The relationship between alcoholism and neurosis: evidence from a twin study. *British Journal of Psychiatry, 148,* 435–441.

Murphy, S. L., & Khantzian, E. J. (1995). Addiction as a "self-medication" disorder: application of ego psychology to the treatment of substance abuse. In A. M. Washton (Ed.), *Psychotherapy and substance abuse: A practitioner's handbook* (pp. 161–175). New York: Guilford Press.

Murray, H. A. (with Morgan, C. D.). (1981 [1935]). A method for investigating fantasies: The thematic apperception test. In E. S. Schneidman (Ed.), *Endeavors in psychology: Selections from the personology of Henry A. Murray* (pp. 390–408). New York: Harper & Row.

Murray, H. A. (with Morgan, C. D.). (1981 [1936]). Techniques for a systematic investigation of fantasy. In E. S. Schneidman (Ed.), *Endeavors in psychology: Selections from the personology of Henry A. Murray* (pp. 366–389). New York: Harper & Row.

Myers, W. A. (1994). Addictive sexual behavior. *Journal of the American Psychoanalytic Association, 42*, 1159–1182.

Myers, W. A. (1995). Sexual addiction. In S. Dowling (Ed.), *The psychology and treatment of addictive behavior* (pp. 115–130). Madison, CT: International Universities Press.

Myrick, H., Cluver, J., Swavely, S., & Peters, H. (2004). Diagnosis and treatment of co-occurring affective disorders and substance use disorders. In N. S. Miller & K. T. Brady (Eds.), *Psychiatric Clinics of North America, Addictive Disorders, 27*, (pp. 649–659).

Nagera, H. (2001). Reflection on psychoanalysis and neuroscience: normality and pathology in development, brain stimulation, programming, and maturation. *Neuro-Psychoanalysis, 3 (2)*, 179–191.

Najavits, L. M. (2002). *Seeking safety: A treatment manual for PTSD and substance abuse.* New York: Guilford Press.

Nakken, C. (1988). The addictive personality. Understanding compulsion in our lives. San Francisco: Harper & Row.

Natterson, J. M. (1976). The self as a transitional object: Its relationship to narcissism and homosexuality. *International Journal of Psychoanalytic Psychotherapy, 5*, 131–143.

Natterson, J. (1991). *Beyond countertransference: The therapist's subjectivity in the therapeutic process.* Northvale, NJ: Jason Aronson.

Nevins, D. B. (1993). Psychoanalytic perspectives on the use of medication for mental illness. In M. Schachter (Ed.), *Psychotherapy and medication: A dynamic integration* (pp. 239–254). Northvale, NJ: Jason Aronson.

Newman, K. (1984). The capacity to use the object. In G. H. Pollock & J. E. Gedo (Eds.), *Psychoanalysis—The vital issues (Clinical psychoanalysis and its implications,* Vol. 2, pp. 149–175). New York: International Universities Press.

Newman, K. (1998). Optimal responsiveness from abstinence to usability. In H. A. Bacal (Ed.), *Optimal responsiveness: How therapists heal their patients* (pp. 97–115). Northvale, NJ: Jason Aronson.

Newman, C. F., Leahy, R. L., Beck, A. T., Reilly-Harrington, N. A., & Gyulai, L. (2002). *Bipolar disorder. A cognitive therapy approach.* Washington, DC: American Psychological Association.

Newman, K. (1999). The usable analyst: the role of the affective engagement of the analyst in reaching usability. *Annual of Psychiatry, 26/27*, 175–200.

Niederland, W. G. (1974). *The Schreber case: Psychoanalytic profile of a paranoid personality.* New York: The New York Times Book Co.

Norris, C. R., & Extein, I. L. (1991). Diagnosing dual diagnosis patients. In M. S. Gold & A. E. Slaby (Eds.), *Dual diagnosis in substance abuse* (pp. 159–184). New York: Marcel Dekker.

Nunberg, H. (1955). *Principles of psychoanalysis: Their application to the neuroses.* New York: International Universities Press.

Nurnberg, G. H., & Shapiro, L. M. (1983). The central organizing fantasy. *Psychoanalytic Review, 70*, 493–503.

Nussbaum, M. C. (1994). *The therapy of desire: Theory and practice in Hellenistic ethics.* Princeton, NJ: Princeton University Press.

Nydes, J. (1950). The magical experience of the masturbation experience. *American Journal of Psychotherapy, 4,* 303–310.

Obitz, F. W., & Swanson, M. K. (1976). Control orientation in women alcoholics. *Journal of Studies on Alcohol, 37,* 694–697.

Odier, C. (1956). *Anxiety and magic thinking.* New York: International Universities Press.

O'Donnell, M. (2004, March 20). Increase seen in treatment for firefighters. A possible 9/11 link to substance abuse. *New York Times,* pp. B1, B4.

Ogden, T. H. (1982). *Projective identification and psychotherapeutic technique.* Northvale, NJ: Jason Aronson.

Ogden, T. H. (1986). *The matrix of the mind. Object relations and the psychoanalytic dialogue.* Northvale, NJ: Jason Aronson.

Ogden, T. H. (1997). Reverie and interpretation. *Psychoanalytic Quarterly, 66,* 567–595.

O'Neil, J. (2003, June 24). Drug addiction as a developmental disorder. *New York Times,* F8.

O'Neill, E. (1967 [1946]). *The iceman cometh.* New York: Vintage Books.

Orange, D. M., Atwood, G. E., & Stolorow, R. D. (1997). *Working intersubjectively. Contextualism in psychoanalytic practice.* Hillsdale, NJ: Analytic Press.

Orlandini, A. (2004). Repetition compulsion in a trauma victim: Is the "Analgesia Principle" beyond the Pleasure Principle? Clinical implications. *Journal of the American Academy of Psychoanalysis and Dynamic Psychiatry, 32 (3),* 525–540.

Ornstein, A. (1974). The dread to repeat and the new beginning: A contribution to the psychoanalysis of the narcissistic personality disorders. *Annual of Psychiatry, 2,* 231–248.

Ornstein, A. (1983). Fantasy or reality? The unsettled question in pathogenesis and reconstruction in psychoanalysis. In A. Goldberg (Ed.), *The future of psychoanalysis: Essays in honor of Heinz Kohut* (pp. 381–396). New York: International Universities Press.

Ornstein, A. (1991). The dread to repeat: comments on the working-through process in psychoanalysis. *Journal of the American Psychoanalytic Association, 39,* 377–398.

Ornstein, A. (1992). The curative fantasy and psychic recovery: Contributions to the theory of psychoanalytic psychotherapy. *Journal of Psychotherapy Practice and Research, 1,* 16–28.

Ornstein, A. (1995a). The fate of the curative fantasy in the psychoanalytic treatment process. *Contemporary Psychoanalysis, 31,* 113–123.

Ornstein, A. (1995b). Erotic passion: A form of addiction. In S. Dowling (Ed.), *The psychology and treatment of addictive behavior* (pp. 101–114). Madison, CT: International Universities Press.

Ornstein, P. A. (1981). The bipolar self in the psychoanalytic treatment process: Clinical–theoretical considerations. *Journal of the American Psychoanalytic Association, 29,* 353–375.

Ortman, D. C. (1997). *The dually diagnosed: A therapist's guide to helping the substance abusing, psychologically disturbed patient.* Northvale, NJ: Jason Aronson.

Ostow, M. (1954). A psychoanalytic contribution to the study of brain function. I. The frontal lobes. *Psychoanalytic Quarterly, 23,* 317–338.

Ostow, M. (1955). A psychoanalytic contribution to the study of brain function. II. The temporal lobes. *Psychoanalytic Quarterly, 24,* 383–423.

Ostow, M. (1962). *Drugs in psychoanalysis and psychotherapy.* New York: Basic Books.

Ostow, M. (Ed.). (1979). *The psychodynamic approach to drug therapy.* New York: Psychoanalytic Research and Development Fund.

Ostow, M. (1992). Comments on the Panel: Use of medication with patients in analysis. *Journal of Clinical Psychoanalysis, 1,* 57–68.

Ouimette, P., & Brown, P. J. (Eds.). (2003). *Trauma and substance abuse causes, consequences, and treatment of comorbid disorders*. Washington, DC: American Psychological Association.

Oziel, L. J., & Obitz, F. W. (1975). Control orientation in alcoholics related to extent of treatment. *Journal of Studies on Alcohol, 36,* 158–161.

Paley, V. G. (1984). *Boys and girls: Superheroes in the doll corner*. Chicago: University of Chicago Press.

Paley, V. G. (1988). *Boys and girls: Superheroes in the doll corner*. Chicago, IL: The University of Chicago Press.

Paley, V. G. (1990). *The boy who would be a helicopter: The uses of storytelling in the classroom*. Cambridge, MA: Harvard University Press.

Palombo, J. (2001). *Learning disorders & disorders of the self in children & adolescents*. New York: W. W. Norton.

Pandina, R. J., Johnson, V., & Labaouvie, E. W. (1992). Affectivity: A central mechanism in the development of drug dependence. In M. Glanta & R. Pickens (Ed.), *Vulnerability to drug abuse* (pp. 179–209). Washington, DC: American Psychological Association.

Panksepp, J. (1999). Emotions as viewed by psychoanalysis and neuroscience: An exercise in consilience. *Neuro-Psychoanalysis, 1 (1),* 15–38.

Paredes, A., Hood, W. R., Seymour, H., & Gollob, M. (1973). Loss of control in alcoholism: An investigation of the hypothesis, with experimental findings. *Quarterly Journal of the Study of Alcoholism, 34,* 1146–1161.

Paul, M. I., & Carson, I. M. (1997). Transformational aspects of phantasy in relation to dyadic communication under the influence of marijuana. *Journal of Melanie Klein and Object Relations, 15,* 195–212.

Pearson, M. N., & Little, R. B. (1969). The addictive process in unusual addictions: A further elaboration of etiology. *American Journal of Psychiatry, 125,* 60–65.

Peele, S. (1982). Love, sex, drugs and other magical solutions to life. *Journal of Psychoactive Drugs, 14,* 125–131.

Peele, S. (1985). *The meaning of addiction: Compulsive experience and its interpretation*. Lexington, MA: DC Heath and Company.

Pekala, R., Kumar, V. K., & Anislie, G. (2000). Dissociation as a function of a child abuse and fantasy proneness in a substance abuse population. *Imagination, Cognition and Personality, 19,* 105–129.

Peller, L. (1954). Libidinal phases, ego development, and play. *Psychoanalytic Study of the Child, 9,* 178–198.

Penk, W. E., Flannery, R. B., & Irvin, E. (2000). Characteristics of substance-abusing persons with schizophrenia: the paradox of the dually diagnosed. *Journal of Addictive Diseases, 19,* 2–30.

Person, E. S. (1995). *By force of fantasy: How we make our lives*. New York: Basic Books.

Perugi, G., & Akiskal, H. S. (2002). The soft bipolar spectrum redefined: Focus on the cyclothymic, anxious-sensitive, impulse-dyscontrol, and binge-eating connection in bipolar II and related conditions. *Psychiatric Clinics of North America, 25,* 713–737.

Pesce, M. (2000). *The playful world: How technology is transforming our imagination*. New York: Ballantine Books.

Petrakis, I., Gonzalez, G., Rosehneck, R., & Krystal, J. (2002). Comorbidity of alcoholism and psychiatric disorders. An overview. *Alcohol Research & Health, 26,* 81–89.

Petry, N. M. (2005). *Pathological gambling. Etiology, comorbidity, and treatment*. Washington, D.C.: American Psychological Association.

Phillips, A. (2001). On preferring not to: The aesthetics of defiance. In J. Petrucelli & C. Stuart (Ed.), *Hungers and compulsions: The psychodynamic treatment of eating disorders and addictions* (pp. 83–94). Northvale, NJ: Jason Aronson.

Phillips, J., & Morley, J. (Eds.). (2003). *Imagination and its pathologies*. Cambridge, MA: MIT Press.

Piaget, J. (1959). *The language and thought of the child*. New York: Humanities Press.

Piaget, J. (1962). *Play, dreams and imitation in childhood*. New York: W. W. Norton.

Piaget, J. (1973). *The child and reality*. New York: Penguin.

Pines, D. (1993). *A woman's unconscious use of her body*. New Haven, CT: Yale University Press.

Piran, N., Kennedy, S., Garfinkel, P. E., & Owens, M. (1985). Affective disturbance in eating disorders. *Journal of Nervous and Mental Disease, 173,* 395–400.

Plant, S. (1999). *Writing on drugs*. New York: Farrar, Straus & Giroux.

Platt, J. J. (1975). "Addiction proneness" and personality in heroin addicts. *Journal of Abnormal Psychology, 84,* 303–306.

Pleij, H. (1997). *Dreaming of cockaigne medieval fantasies of the perfect life*. New York: Columbia University Press.

Plumb, M. M., D'Amanda, C., & Taintor, Z. (1975). Chemical substance abuse and perceived locus of control. In D. J. Lettieri (Ed.), *Predicting adolescent drug abuse: A review of issues, methods and correlates* (pp. 225–261). Washington, DC: U.S. Government Printing Office.

Polivy, J., & Otterman, C. P. (1993). Etiology of binge eating: Psychological mechanisms. In C. G. Fairburn & G. R. Wilson (Ed.), *Binge eating: Nature, assessment, and treatment* (pp. 173–205). New York: Guilford Press.

Powell, A. D. (2001). The medication life. *Journal of Psychotherapy Practice & Research, 10,* 217–222.

Powers, S. M. (1991). Fantasy proneness, amnesia, and the UFO abduction phenomenon. *Dissociation, 4,* 46–54.

Quitkin, F. M., Rifkin, A., Kaplan, J., & Klein, D. F. (1972). Phobic anxiety syndrome complicated by drug dependence and addiction. *Archives of General Psychiatry, 27,* 159–162.

Racker, H. (1968). *Transference and countertransference*. New York: International Universities Press.

Rader, C. M., Kunzendorf, R. G., & Carracino, C. (1996). The relation of imagery vividness, absorption, reality boundaries and synthesia to hypnotic states and traits. In *Hypnosis and imagination*, R. G. Kunzendorf, N. P. Spanos, B. Wallace (Eds.) (pp. 99–122). Amityville, NY: Baywood.

Rado, S. (1926). The psychic effects of intoxicants: An attempt to evolve a psycho-analytical theory of morbid cravings. *International Journal of Psychoanalysis 7,* 396–413.

Rado, S. (1933). The psychoanalysis of psychothymia (drug addiction). The clinical picture. *The Psychoanalytic Quarterly, II,* 1–23.

Rado, S. (1957). Narcotic bondage: A general theory of the dependence on narcotic drugs. *American Journal of Psychiatry, 114,* 165–172.

Rado, S. (1963). Fighting narcotic bondage and other forms of narcotic disorder. *Comprehensive Psychiatry, 4,* 160–167.

Rado, S. (1969). *Adaptational psychodynamics: Motivation and control*. New York: Science House.

Randall, C. K., Johnson, M. R., & Thevos, A. K. (2001). Paroxetine for social anxiety and alcohol use in dual-diagnosed patients. *Depression and Anxiety, 14,* 255–262.

Rauschenberger, S., & Lynn, S. J. (2003). Fantasy-proneness, negative affect, and psychopathology. *Imagination, Cognition and Personality, 22 (3),* 239–255.

Reich, W. (1945). *Character analysis*. New York: Farrar, Straus & Giroux.

Reich, A. (1960). Pathologic forms of self-esteem regulation. *The Psychoanalytic Study of the Child, 15,* 215–232.

Renik, O. (1992). Use of the analyst as a fetish. *Psychoanalytic Quarterly, 61,* 542–563.

Rescher, N. (2003). *Imagining irreality. A study of unreal possibilities*. Chicago: Open Court.

Restak, R. (1991). *The brain has a mind of its own: Insights from a practicing neurologist*. New York: Harmony Books.

Reto, C. S., Dalenberg, C. J., & Coe, M. T. (1996). Dissociation and physical abuse as predictors of bulimic symptomatology and impulse dysregulation. In M. F. Schwartz & L. Cohn (Eds.), *Sexual abuse and eating disorders* (pp. 52–67). New York: Brunner/Mazel.

Rice, E. (1985/6). The role of the oedipal fantasy in masturbatory and suicidal phenomena. *International Journal of Psychoanalytic Psychotherapy, 11,* 243–267.

Richards, H. J. (1993). *Therapy of the substance abuse syndromes*. Northvale, NJ: Jason Aronson.

Riker, J. H. (1996). The philosophical importance of Kohut's bipolar theory of the self. In A. Goldberg (Ed.), *Progress in Self Psychology, 12,* 67–83. Hillsdale, NJ: Analytic Press.

Ring, K. (1990). Fantasy proneness and the kitchen sink: Response to Bartholomew and Basterfield. *Journal of UFO Studies, 2,* 186–187.

Robbins, P. R. (1974). Depression and drug addiction. *Psychiatry Quarterly, 48,* 374–386.

Rochlin, G. (1973). *Man's aggression: The defense of the self*. New York: Dell.

Rodman, F. R. (2002). The psychoanalytic imagination. *Journal of Clinical Psychoanalysis, 11,* 419–440.

Róheim, G. (1930). *Animism, magic, and the divine king*. New York: International Universities Press.

Róheim, G. (1955). *Magic and schizophrenia*. Bloomington, IN: Indiana University Press.

Rosenfeld, H. A. (1959). On drug addiction. *International Journal of Psycho-Analysis, 41,* 467–475.

Roose, S. P., & Johannet, C. M. (1998). Medication and psychoanalysis: Treatments in conflict. *Psychoanalytic Inquiry, 18,* 606–620.

Rosenfeld, H. A. (1964). The psychopathology of drug addiction and alcoholism. In *Psychotic states: A psychoanalytical approach* (pp. 217–242). New York: International Universities Press.

Rosenfeld, I. (2000). *Freud's megalomania: A novel*. New York: W. W. Norton.

Rosenman, S. (1981). Narcissus of the myth: An essay on narcissism and victimization. In S. Tuttman, C. Kaye, & M. Zimmerman (Eds.), *Object and self: A developmental approach—essays in honor of Edith Jacobson* (pp. 527–548). New York: International Universities Press.

Rosenthal, R. J., & Rugle, L. J. (1994). A psychodynamic approach to the treatment of pathological gambling: Part I. Achieving abstinence. *Journal of Gambling Studies, 10,* 21–42.

Ross, N. (1967). The "as if" concept. *Journal of the American Psychoanalytic Association, 15,* 59–82.

Rothstein, A. (1984a). *The narcissistic pursuit of perfection* (2nd rev. ed.) New York: International Universities Press.

Rothstein, A. (1984b). The fear of humiliation. *Journal of the American Psychoanalytic Association, 32,* 99–116.

Rozen, D. L. (1993). Projective identification and bulimia. *Psychoanalytic Psychology, 10,* 261–273.

Rubin, J. (2001). Countertransference factors in the psychology of psychopharmacology. *Journal of the American Academy of Psychoanalysis, 29,* 565–573.

Rugle, L. J., & Rosenthal, R. J. (1994). Transference and countertransference reactions in the psychotherapy of pathological gamblers. *Journal of Gambling Studies, 10,* 43–65.

Ruiz, P., Lile, B., & Matorin, A. A. (2002). Treatment of a dually diagnosed gay male patient: a psychotherapy perspective. *American Journal of Psychiatry, 159,* 209–215.

Rundshagen, I., Schroder, T., Prichep, L. S., John, E. R., & Kox, W. J. (2004). Changes in cortical electrical activity during induction of anaesthesia with thiopental/fentanyl and tracheal intubation: A quantitative electroencephalographic analysis. *British Journal of Anaesthesia, 92*, 33–38.

Sacks, S., & Reis, R. K. (2005). *Substance abuse treatment for persons with co-occurring disorders*. Rockville, MD: Substance Abuse and Mental Health Services Administration, Washington, DC, U. S. Government Printing Office.

Sammons, M. T. (2001). Combined treatments for mental disorders: clinical dilemmas. In M. T. Sammons & N. B. Schmidt (Eds.), *Combined treatments for mental disorders: A guide to psychological and pharmacological interventions* (pp. 11–32). Washington, DC: American Psychological Association.

Sandberg, L. S. (1998). Analytic listening and the act of prescribing medication. *Psychoanalytic Inquiry, 18*, 621–638.

Sands, S. (1989). Female development and eating disorders: A self-psychological perspective. In A. Goldberg (Ed.), *Progress in self psychology* (Vol. 5, pp. 75–103). Hillsdale, NJ: Analytic Press.

Sands, S. (1991). Bulimia, dissociation, and empathy: A self-psychological view. In C. Johnson (Ed.), *Psychodynamic treatment of anorexia nervosa and bulimia* (pp. 34–50). New York: Guilford Press.

Sands, S. (1994). What is dissociated? *Dissociation, 7*, 145–152.

Sansone, R. A., & Johnson, C. L. (1995). Treating the eating disorder patient with borderline personality disorder: Theory and technique. In J. P. Barber & P. Crits-Christoph (Eds.), *Dynamic therapies and psychiatric disorders: (Axis I)* (pp. 230–266). New York: Basic Books.

Sartre, J.-P. (2004 [1940]). *The imaginary. A phenomenological psychology of the imagination*. London: Routledge.

Satel, S. L. (1999, May). Drug addiction is not a brain disease. *Psychiatric Times, 6 & 10*.

Satel, S. L. (2000, July 14). Learning to say "I've had enough." *New York Times*, A25.

Satel, S. L., & Goodwin, F. K. (1998). Is drug addiction a brain disease? *Program on Medical Science and Society*, Washington, DC: Ethics and Public Policy Center.

Satel, S. L., & Goodwin, F. K. (1998). *Is drug addiction a brain disease?* Program on Medical Science and Society. Washington, DC: Ethics and Public Policy Center.

Savage, C. (1955). Variations in ego feeling induced by D-lysergic acid diethylamide (LSD-25). *Psychoanalytic Review, 42*, 1–17.

Sawyer, R. K. (1997). *Pretend play as improvisation: Conversations in the preschool classroom*. Mahwah, NJ: Lawrence Erlbaum Associates.

Schell, O. (2000). *Virtual Tibet: Searching for Shangri-La from the Himalayas to Hollywood*. New York: Metropolitan Books.

Scheller-Gilkey, G., Thomas, S. M., Woolwine, B. J., & Miller, A. H. (2002). Increased early life stress and depressive symptoms in patients with comorbid substance abuse and schizophrenia. *Schizophrenia Bulletin, 28*, 223–231.

Schildner, P. (1938). Psychoanalytic remarks on "Alice in Wonderland" and Lewis Carroll. *Journal of Nervous and Mental Diseases, 87*, 159–168.

Schiraldi, G. R. (2000). *The post-traumatic stress disorder sourcebook: A guide to healing, recovery, and growth*. Los Angeles: Lowell House.

Schore, A. N. (1994). *Affect regulation and the origin of the self: The neurobiology of emotional development*. Hillsdale, NJ: Lawrence Erlbaum Associates.

Schore, A. N. (2003a). *Affect dysregulation & disorders of the self*. New York: W. W. Norton.

Schore, A. N. (2003b). *Affect regulation & the repair of the self*. New York: W. W. Norton.

Schreiber, S. (1974). A filmed fairy tale as a screen memory. *Psychoanalytic Study of the Child, 29*, 389–412.

Schuckit, M. A. (1973). Alcoholism and sociopathy—diagnostic confusion. *Quarterly Journal of Studies on Alcoholism, 34,* 164–197.

Schuckit, M. (1983). Alcoholic patients with secondary depression. *American Journal of Psychiatry, 140, 6,* 711–714.

Schultz, M. G. (1971). The "strange case" of Robert Louis Stevenson. *Journal of the American Medical Association, 216,* 90–94.

Schwartz, M. F., & Cohn, L. (Eds.). (1996). *Sexual abuse and eating disorders.* New York: Brunner/Mazel.

Schwartz-Salant, N. (1982). *Narcissism and character transformation: The psychology of narcissistic character disorders.* Toronto: Inner City Books.

Scull, A. (2005). *Madhouse. A tragic tale of megalomania and modern medicine.* New Haven: Yale University Press.

Searles, H. F. (1960). *The nonhuman environment in normal development and in schizophrenia.* New York: International Universities Press.

Searles, H. F. (1979 [1976]). Transitional phenomena and therapeutic symbiosis. In *Countertransference and related subjects* (pp. 503–576). New York: International Universities Press.

Segal, B. (1974). Drug use and fantasy processes: Criterion for prediction of potential users. *The International Journal of the Addictions, 9,* 475–480.

Segal, B., & Feger, G. (1973). Drug use and fantasy processes in college students. *Journal of Altered States of Consciousness, 1,* 5–14.

Segal, B., Huba, G. J. & Singer, J. C. (1980). *Drugs, daydreaming, and personality: A study of college youth.* Hillsdale, NJ: Lawrence Erlbaum Associates.

Segal, J. (1985). *Phantasy in everyday life: A psychoanalytical approach to understanding ourselves.* Harmondsworth, Middlesex, England: Penguin Books.

Segal, M. M. (1963). Impulsive sexuality: Some clinical and theoretical observations. *International Journal of Psycho-Analysis, 44,* 407–418.

Seligman, M. (1975). *Learned helplessness: On depression, development, and death.* San Francisco: W. H. Freeman.

Serban, G. (1982). *The tyranny of magical thinking: The child's world of belief and adult neurosis.* New York: E. P. Dutton.

Seymour, P. M. (2003). Long-term treatment of an addictive personality. *Bulletin of the Menninger Clinic, 67,* 328–346.

Shane, M., & Shane, E. (1990). Unconscious fantasy: Developmental and self-psychological considerations. *Journal of the American Psychoanalytic Association, 38,* 75–92.

Sharoff, R. L. (1969). Character problems and their relationship to drug abuse. *American Journal of Psychoanalysis, 29,* 186–193.

Shay, J. (1994). *Achilles in Vietnam: Combat trauma and the undoing of character.* New York: Atheneum.

Shedler, J., & Block, J. (1990). Adolescent drug use and psychological health. *American Psychologist, 45,* 612–630.

Sherwood, V. R., & Cohen, C. P. (1994). *Psychotherapy of the quiet borderline patient: The as–if personality revisited.* Northvale, NJ: Jason Aronson.

Shevrin, H. (Ed.). (2003). *Subliminal explorations of perception, dreams, and fantasies: The pioneering contributions of Charles Fisher.* Madison, CT: International Universities Press.

Shevrin, H., Bond, J. A., Brakel, L. A. W., Hertel, R. K., & Williams, W. J. (1996). *Conscious and unconscious processes. Psychodynamic, cognitive, and neurophysiological convergences.* New York: Guilford Press.

Shivani, R., Goldsmith, R. J., & Anthenelli, R. M. (2002). Alcoholism and psychiatric disorders. Diagnostic challenges. *Alcohol Research & Health, 26,* 90–98.

Siegel, D. J. (1999). *The developing mind. Toward a neurobiology of interpersonal experience*. New York: Guilford Press.

Siegel, E. V. (1991). But I must have you in my life: Thoughts about the addictive quality of some object relationships. In A. Smaldino (Ed.), *Psychoanalytic approaches to addiction* (pp. 13–27). New York: Brunner/Mazel.

Siegel, R. K. (1989). *Intoxication: Life in pursuit of artificial paradise*. New York: E. P. Dutton.

Siever, L. J., with Frucht, W. (1997). *The new view of self. How genes and neurotransmitters shape your mind, your personality, and your mental health*. New York: Macmillan.

Silber, A. (1970). An addendum to the technique of psychotherapy with alcoholics. *Journal of Nervous and Mental Disease, 150,* 423–437.

Silber, A. (1974). Rationale for the technique of psychotherapy with alcoholics. *International Journal of Psychoanalytic Psychotherapy, 3,* 28–46.

Silverman, D. K., & Gruenthal, R. (1993). Fantasy: A consolidation. Psychoanalytic Psychology, *10,* 39–60.

Silverman, J. (1968). A paradigm for the study of altered states of consciousness. *British Journal of Psychiatry, 114,* 1201–1218.

Silverman, L. H. (1978/9). Unconscious symbiotic fantasy: A ubiquitous therapeutic agent. *International Journal of Psychoanalytic Psychotherapy, 7,* 562–585.

Silverman, L. H. (1979). Unconscious fantasy as therapeutic agent in psychoanalytic treatment. *Journal of the American Academy of Psychoanalysis, 7,* 189–218.

Silverman, L. H. (1982). A comment on two subliminal psychodynamic activator experiments. *Journal of Abnormal Psychology, 91,* 126–130.

Silverman, L. H. (1983). The subliminal psychodynamic activation method: Overview and comprehensive listing of studies. In J. Masling (Ed.), *Empirical studies of psychoanalytic theories* (Vol. 1, pp. 69–100). Hillsdale, NJ: Analytic Press.

Silverman, L. H., & Weinberger, J. (1985). Mommy and I are one: Implications for psychotherapy. *American Psychologist, 40,* 1296–1308.

Silverman, L. H., Lachmann, F. M., & Milich, R. H. (1982). *The search for oneness*. New York: International Universities Press.

Silverman, L. H., Lachmann, F. M., & Milich, R. H. (1984). Unconscious oneness fantasies: Experimental findings and implications for treatment. *International Forum for Psychoanalysis, 1,* 107–152.

Simmel, E. (1920). Psychoanalysis of the gambler. *International Journal of Psycho-Analysis, 1,* 352–353.

Simmel, E. (1948). Alcoholism and addiction. *Psychoanalytic Quarterly, 17,* 6–31.

Skinner, J. (1947). Lewis Carroll's adventures in Wonderland. *American Imago, 4,* 3–31.

Skodol, A. E., Oldham, J. M., & Gallaher, P. E. (1999). Axis II comorbidity of substance use disorders among patients referred for treatment of personality disorders. *American Journal of Psychiatry, 156,* 733–739.

Sloan, J. P. (1996). *Jerzy Kosinski: A biography*. New York: Dutton.

Slochower, J. A. (1994). The evolution of object usage and the holding environment. *Contemporary Psychoanalysis, 30,* 135–151.

Smail, P., Stockwell, T., Canter, S., & Hodgson, R. (1984). Alcohol dependence and phobic anxiety states. *British Journal of Psychiatry, 144,* 53–57.

Smaldino, A. (1991). Substance abuse nightmares and the combat veteran with PTSD: a focus on the mourning process. In A. Smaldino (Ed.), *Psychoanalytic approaches to addiction* (pp. 28–50). New York: Brunner/Mazel.

Smaldino, C. (1991). Desperate worship: a view of love addiction. In A. Smaldino (Ed.), *Psychoanalytic approaches to addiction* (pp. 80–95). New York: Brunner/Mazel.

Smith, B. L. (1989). Winnicott and self psychology. In M. G. Fromm & B. L. Smith (Eds.), *The facilitating environment: Clinical applications of Winnicott's theory* (pp. 52–87). Madison, CT: International Universities Press.

Smith, G. M., & Beecher, H. K. (1962). Subjective effects of heroin and morphine in normal subjects. *Journal of Psychopharmacology & Experimental Therapeutics, 136*, 47–52.

Smith, H. F. (2004). The analyst's fantasy of the ideal patient. *Psychoanalytic Quarterly, 73*, 627–658.

Socarides, D. D., & Stolorow, R. D. (1984/5). Affects and selfobjects. *Annual of Psychoanalysis, 12/13*, 105–119.

Solms, M., & Turnbull, O. (2002). *The brain and the inner world: An Introduction to the neuroscience of subjective experience*. New York: Other Press.

Solomon, I. (1992). *The encyclopedia of evolving techniques in dynamic psychotherapy: The movement to multiple models*. Northvale, NJ: Jason Aronson.

Solomon, M. F. (1989). Narcissism and intimacy. Love and marriage in an age of confusion. New York: W. W. Norton.

Sonne, S. C., & Brady, K. T. (1999). Substance abuse and bipolar comorbidity. *Psychiatric Clinics of North America, 22*, 609–627.

Sonne, S. C., & Brady, K. T. (2002). Bipolar disorder and alcoholism. *Alcohol Research and Health, 26*, 103–108.

Sonne, S. C., Back, S. E., & Zuniga, C. D. (2003). Gender differences in individuals with comorbid alcohol dependence and post-traumatic stress disorder. *American Journal on Addictions, 12*, 412–423.

Spence, M. J. (1988). Experiencing and recovering transitional space in the analytic treatment of anorexia nervosa and bulimia. In H. J. Schwartz (Ed.), *Bulimia: Psychoanalytic treatment and theory* (pp. 73–88). Madison, CT: International Universities Press.

Spencer, C., Castle, D., & Michie, P. T. (2002). Motivations that maintain substance use among individuals with psychotic disorders. *Schizophrenia Bulletin, 28 (2)*, 233–247.

Sperling, M. (1963). Fetishism in children. *Psychoanalytic Quarterly, 32*, 374–392.

Spiegel, A. (2005, January 3). The dictionary of disorder. How one man revolutionized psychiatry. *New Yorker*, pp. 56–63.

Spotts, J. V., & Shontz, F. C. (1976). *The life styles of nine American cocaine users: Trips to the land of cockaigne* (Research Issues 16). U. S. Department of Health, Education and Welfare. Washington, DC: U. S. Government Printing Office.

Spotts, J. V., & Shontz, F. C. (1982). Ego development, dragon fights, and chronic drug abusers. *International Journal of the Addictions, 17 (6)*, 945–976.

Spotts, J. V., & Shontz, F. C. (1983). Psychopathology and chronic drug use: A methodological paradigm. *International Journal of the Addictions, 18 (5)*, 633–680.

Stamm, J. S. (1962). Altered ego state allied to depersonalization. *Journal of the American Psychoanalytic Association, 10*, 762–783.

Stein, A. (2003). Dreaming while awake. The use of trance to bypass threat. *Contemporary Psychoanalysis, 39*, 179–197.

Steiner, R. (1999). Some notes on the 'heroic self' and the meaning and importance of its reparation for the creative process and the creative personality. *International Journal of Psycho-Analysis, 80*, 685–718.

Steiner, R. (Ed.). (2003). *Unconscious phantasy*. New York: Karnac (Books) Ltd.

Steiner-Adair, C. (1990). New maps of development, new models of therapy: the psychology of women and the treatment of eating disorders. In C. L. Johnson (Ed.), *Psychodynamic treatment of anorexia nervosa and bulimia* (pp. 225–244). New York: Guilford Press.

Sterba, R. F. (1934). The fate of the ego in analytic therapy. *International Journal of Psycho-Analysis, 15*, 117–126.

Sterba, E. (1949). Analysis of psychogenic constipation in a two-year-old. *Psychoanalytic Study of the Child, 3,* 227–252.

Stern, J. (2003). Cyclones, bi-cycle, and psychoanalysis: The witch-of-us? Complex and "The Wizard of Oz." *Journal of the American Psychoanalytic Association, 51,* 1241–1261.

Stern, S. (1990). Managing opposing currents: an interpersonal psychoanalytic technique for the treatment of eating disorders. In C. L. Johnson (Ed.), *Psychodynamic treatment of anorexia nervosa and bulimia* (pp. 86–105). New York: Guilford Press.

Stevenson, O. (1954). The first treasured possession. A study of the part played by specially loved objects and toys in the lives of certain children. *Psychoanalytic Study of the Child, 9,* 199–217.

Stevenson, R. L. (1987 [1886]). *The strange case of Dr. Jekyll and Mr. Hyde.* Philadelphia, PA: Running Press.

Stewart, C. T. (2001). *The symbolic impetus: How creative fantasy motivates development.* London: Free Association Books.

Stolorow, R. D., & Atwood, G. E. (1989). The unconscious and unconscious fantasy: An intersubjective developmental perspective. *Psychoanalytic Inquiry, 9,* 364–374.

Stolorow, R. D., & Atwood, G. E. (1992). *Contexts of being. The intersubjective foundations of psychological life.* Hillsdale, NJ: Analytic Press.

Stolorow, R. D., & Grand, H. (1973). A partial analysis of a perversion involving bugs. *International Journal of Psycho-Analysis, 54,* 349–350.

Stolorow, R. D., & Lachmann, F. M. (1980). *Psychoanalysis of developmental arrests. Theory and treatment.* New York: International Universities Press.

Stolorow, R. D., Brandschaft, B., & Atwood, G. E. (1987). *Psychoanalytic treatment: An intersubjective approach.* Hillsdale, NJ: Analytic Press.

Strachey, J. (1934). The nature of the therapeutic action of psycho-analysis. *International Journal of Psycho-Analysis, 15,* 127–159.

Striegel-Moore, R. H. (1993). Etiology of binge eating. A developmental perspective. In C. G. Fairburn & G. T. Wilson (Eds.), *Binge Eating: Nature, assessment, and treatment* (pp. 144–172). New York: Guilford Press.

Strober, M. (1990). Disorders of the self in anorexia nervosa: an organismic-developmental paradigm. In C. L. Johnson (Ed.), *Psychodynamic treatment of anorexia nervosa and bulimia* (pp. 354–373). New York: Guilford Press.

Stunkard, A., Faith, M. S., & Allison, K. C. (2004). Depression and obesity: A complex relationship. *Psychiatric Times,* October, 81.

Sugarman, A. (1990). Bulimia: A displacement from psychological self to body self. In C. L. Johnson (Ed.), *Psychodynamic treatment of anorexia nervosa and bulimia* (pp. 3–33). New York: Guilford Press.

Sugarman, A., & Kurash, C. (1981). The body as a transitional object in bulimia. *International Journal of Eating Disorders, 1,* 57–67.

Sugerman, D. (1989). *Wonderland Avenue: Tales of glamour and excess.* New York: William Morrow and Co.

Sutherland, E. H., Schroeder, H. G., & Tordella, C. K. (1950). Personality traits and the alcoholic: A critique of existing studies. *Quarterly Journal of Studies of Alcoholism, 11,* 547–561.

Swann, A. C. (2005). Bipolar disorder and substance abuse: Two disorders or one? *Journal of Dual Diagnosis, 1,* 9–23.

Swann, A. C., Dougherty, D. M., Pazzaglia, P. J., Pham, M., & Moeller, F. G. (2004). Impulsivity: a link between bipolar disorder and substance abuse. *Bipolar Disorders, 6,* 204–212.

Swift, W. J. (1990). Bruch Revisited: the role of interpretation of transference and resistance in the psychotherapy of eating disorders. In C. L. Johnson (Ed.), *Psychodynamic treatment of anorexia nervosa and bulimia* (pp. 51–67). New York: Guilford Press.

Syme, L. (1957). Personality characteristics and the alcoholic: A critique of current studies. *Quarterly Journal of Studies of Alcoholism, 18,* 288–302.

Talbot, M. (2000). Astonishing medical fact: Placebos work! So why not use them as medicine? *New York Times Magazine,* January 9.

Tamerin, J. S., Tolor, A., Holson, P., & Neumann, C. P. (1974). The alcoholic's perception of self: A retrospective comparison of mood and behavior during states of sobriety and intoxication. *Annals of the New York Academy of Sciences, 233,* 43–60.

Tamminga, C. A. (2004a). Drug dependence and addiction. Neural substrates. *American Journal of Psychiatry, 161,* 223.

Tamminga, C. A. (2004b). Drug dependence and addiction, II. Adult neurogenesis and drug abuse. *American Journal of Psychiatry, 161,* 426.

Taylor, G. J. (1987). *Psychosomatic medicine and contemporary psychoanalysis.* Madison, CT: International Universities Press.

Tansey, M. J., & Burke, W. F. (1989). *Understanding countertransference: From projective identification to empathy.* Hillsdale, NJ: Analytic Press.

Tartakoff, H. H. (1966). The normal personality in our culture and the nobel prize complex. In R. M. Lowenstein, L. M. Newman, M. Schur, & A. J. Solnit (Ed.), *Psychoanalysis—A general psychology: Essays in honor of Heinz Hartmann* (pp. 222–252). New York: International Universities Press.

Tausk, V. (1948 [1919]). On the origin of the "influencing machine" in schizophrenia. In R. Fliess (Ed.), *The psychoanalytic reader* (pp. 31–63). New York: International Universities Press.

Tellegen, A., & Atkinson, G. (1974). Openness to absorbing and self-altering experience ("absorption"), a trait related to hypnotic susceptibility. *Journal of Abnormal Psychology, 83,* 268–277.

Theweleit, K. (1987). *Male fantasies* (Volumes 1 & 2). Minneapolis, MN: University of Minnesota Press.

Tismaneanu, V. (1998). *Fantasies of salvation democracy, nationalism, and myth in post-communist Europe.* Princeton, NJ: Princeton University Press.

Tobin, D. L. (1993). Psychodynamic psychotherapy and binge eating. In C. G. Fairburn & G. T. Wilson (Eds.), *Binge eating: Nature, assessment, and treatment* (pp. 287–313). New York: Guilford Press.

Tohen, M., & Zarate, Jr., C. A. (1999). Bipolar disorder and comorbid substance use disorder. In J. F. Goldberg & M. Harrow (Eds.), *Bipolar disorders clinical course and outcome.* Washington, DC: American Psychiatric Press.

Tokar, J. T., Brunse, A. J., Stefflre, V. J., Napior, D. A., & Sodergren, J. A. (1973). Emotional states and behavioral patterns in alcoholics and nonalcoholics. *Quarterly Journal of the Study of Alcohol, 34,* 133–143.

Tolpin, M. (1971). On the beginnings of a cohesive self. An application of the concept of transmuting internalization to the study of the transitional object and signal anxiety. *The Psychoanalytic Study of the Child, 26,* 316–352.

Tolpin, M. (1974). The Daedalus experience: A developmental vicissitude of the grandiose fantasy. *Annual of Psychoanalysis, 2,* 213–228.

Tolpin, M., & Kohut, H. (1980). The disorders of the self: The psychopathology of the first years of life. In S. I. Greenspan & G. H. Pollock (Eds.), *The course of life: Psychoanalytic contributions toward understanding personality development (Infancy and early childhood)* (Vol. 1, pp. 425–442). Washington DC: National Institute of Mental Health.

Tolpin, P., & Tolpin, M. (Eds.). (1996). *Heinz Kohut: The Chicago Institute lectures.* Hillsdale, NJ: Analytic Press.

Tolpin, P. (1974). On the regulation of anxiety: Its relation to "the timelessness of the unconscious and its capacity for hallucination." *Annual of Psychoanalysis, 2,* 150–177.

Tonneatto, T., Negrete, J. C., & Calderwood, K. (2000). Diagnostic subgroups within a sample of comorbid substance abusers: correlates and characteristics. *American Journal on Addictions, 9,* 253–264.

Torda, C. (1968). Comments on the character structure and psychodynamic processes of heroin addicts. *Perceptual and Motor Skills, 27,* 143–146.

Tucker, P., & Westermeyer, J. (1990). Substance abuse in patients with comorbid anxiety disorder. A comparative study. *American Journal on Addictions, 4,* 226–233.

Tuma, R. S. (2002). Placebo and depression. A dose of caution. *BrainWork,* July/August, 5–6.

Ulman, R. B. (1988). The transference-countertransference in psychoanalysis: The intersubjective context of dream formation. In N. Slavinoka-Holy (Ed.), *Borderline and narcissistic patients in therapy* (pp. 203–219). Madison, CT: International Universities Press.

Ulman, R. B., & Brothers, D. (1987). A self-psychological reevaluation of posttraumatic stress disorder (PTSD) and its treatment: Shattered fantasies. *Journal of the American Academy of Psychoanalysis, 15,* 175–203.

Ulman, R. B., & Brothers, D. (1988). *The shattered self: A psychoanalytic study of trauma.* Hillsdale, NJ: Analytic Press.

Ulman, R. B., & Miliora, M. T. (2000). Obsessive compulsive disorder (OCD) and obsessive compulsive personality disorder (OCPD): A bioself-psychological perspective. Unpublished paper.

Ulman, R. B., & Paul, H. (1989). A self-psychological theory and approach to treating substance abuse disorders: The "intersubjective absorption" hypothesis. In A. Goldberg (Ed.), *Progress in self psychology* (Vol. 5, pp. 121–141). Hillsdale, NJ: Analytic Press.

Ulman, R. B., & Paul, H. (1990). The addictive personality and "addictive trigger mechanisms" (ATMs): The self psychology of addiction and its treatment. In A. Goldberg (Ed.), *Progress in self psychology* (Vol. 6, pp. 129–156). Hillsdale, NJ: Analytic Press.

Ulman, R. B., & Paul, H. (1992). Dissociative anesthesia and the transitional selfobject transference in the intersubjective treatment of the addictive personality. In A. Goldberg (Ed.), *Progress in self psychology* (Vol. 8, pp. 109–139). Hillsdale, NJ: Analytic Press.

Ulman, R. B., & Stolorow, R. D. (1985). The "transference-countertransference neurosis" in psychoanalysis: An Intersubjective viewpoint. *Bulletin of the Menninger Clinic, 49,* 37–51.

Valliant, G. E. (1970). The natural history of narcotic drug addiction. *Seminars in Psychiatry, 2,* 486–498.

Valliant, G. E. (1975). Sociopathy as a human process: A viewpoint. *Archives of General Psychiatry, 32,* 178–183.

Valliant, G. E. (1978). Alcoholism and drug dependence. In A. M. Nicholi, Jr. (Ed.), *The Harvard guide to modern psychiatry* (pp. 567–577). Cambridge, MA: Belknap Press of Harvard University Press.

Valliant, G. E. (1983). *The natural history of alcoholism.* Cambridge, MA: Harvard University Press.

Valliant, G. E. (1995). *The natural history of alcoholism—Revisited.* Cambridge, MA: Harvard University Press.

Valliant, G. E., & Milofsky, E. S. (1982a). The etiology of alcoholism: A prospective viewpoint. *American Psychologist, 37,* 494–503.

Valliant, G. E., & Milofsky, E. S. (1982b). Natural history of male alcoholism. *Archives of General Psychiatry, 39,* 127–133.

van der Kolk, B. A. (1987). *Psychological trauma.* Washington, DC: American Psychiatric Press.

van der Kolk, B. A., & van der Hart, O. (1995). The intrusive past: the flexibility of memory and the engraving of trauma. In C. Caruth (Ed.), *Trauma explorations in memory* (pp. 158–182). Baltimore, MD: The Johns Hopkins University Press.

Vanderlinden, J., & Vandereycken, W. (1997). *Trauma, dissociation, and impulse dyscontrol in eating disorders.* New York: Brunner/Mazel.

Vannicelli, M.-L. (1972). Mood and self-perception of alcoholics when sober and intoxicated. *Quarterly Journal of the Study of Alcohol, 33,* 341–357.

Vaughan, S. C. (1997). *The talking cure. The science behind psychotherapy.* New York: Putnam.

Viorst, J. (1998). *Imperfect control: Our lifelong struggles with power and surrender.* New York: Simon & Schuster.

Volkan, K. (1994). *Dancing among the maenads: The psychology of compulsive drug use.* New York: Peter Lang.

Volkan, V. D. (1973). Transitional fantasies in the analysis of a narcissistic personality. *Journal of the American Psychoanalytic Association, 21,* 351–376.

Volkan, V. D. (1976). *Primitive internalized object relations: A clinical study of schizophrenic, borderline, and narcissistic patients.* New York: International Universities Press.

Volkan, V. D., & Kavanaugh, J. G. (1978). The cat people. In S. A. Grolnick, L. Barkin, & W. Muensterberger (Ed.), *Between reality and fantasy: Transitional objects and phenomena* (pp. 289–303). Northvale, NJ: Jason Aronson.

Volkow, N. D. (2001). Drug abuse and mental illness: progress in understanding comorbidity. *American Journal of Psychiatry, 158 (8),* 1181–1183.

Volkow, N. (2004c). Drug dependence and addiction, III. Expectation and brain function in drug abuse. *American Journal of Psychiatry, 161,* 621.

Volpicelli, J., Balaraman, G., Hahn, J., Wallace, H., & Bux, D. (1999). The role of uncontrollable trauma in the development of PTSD and alcohol addiction. *Alcohol Research & Health, 23,* 256–262.

Vyse, S. A. (1997). *Believing in magic: The psychology of superstition.* New York: Oxford University Press.

Walant, K. B. (1995). *Creating the capacity for attachment: Treating addictions and the alienated self.* Northvale, NJ: Jason Aronson.

Wallerstein, R. S. (1981). The bipolar self: discussion of alternative perspectives. *Journal of the American Psychoanalytic Association, 29,* 377–394.

Walter, P. (1995). *Batman and Catwoman. Megalomania and cross-dressing.* Unpublished paper.

Wang, J., & Patten, S. B. (2002). Prospective study of frequent heavy alcohol use and the risk of major depression in the Canadian general population. *Depression and Anxiety, 15,* 42–45.

Warner, M. (2002). *Fantastic metamorphoses, other worlds: Ways of telling the self.* Oxford: Oxford University Press.

Warren, G. H., & Raynes, A. E. (1972). Mood changes during three conditions of alcohol intake. *Quarterly Journal of the Study of Alcohol, 33,* 979–989.

Wegner, D. M. (2002). *The illusion of conscious will.* Cambridge, MA: MIT Press.

Weil, J. L. (1992). *Early deprivation of empathic care.* Madison, CT: International Universities Press.

Weininger, O. (1989). *Children's phantasies: The shaping of relationships.* London: Karnac (Books) Ltd.

Weiss, J. (1966). Clinical and theoretical aspects of "as if" characters. *Journal of the American Psychoanalytic Association, 14,* 569–590.

Weiss, R. D. (2003). Pharmacotherapy for co-occurring mood and substance use disorders. In J. T. Westermeyer, R. D. Weiss, & D. M. Ziedonis (Eds.), *Integrated treatment for mood and substance use disorders* (pp. 122–139). Baltimore, MD: Johns Hopkins University Press.

Weissman, G. (2004). *Fantasies of witnessing: Postwar efforts to experience the holocaust.* Ithaca, NY: Cornell University Press.

Weissman, M. M., Pottenger, M., Kleber, H., Ruben, H. L., Williams, D., & Thompson, W. D. (1977). Symptom patterns in primary and secondary depression. A comparison of primary depressives with depressed opiate addicts, alcoholics, and schizophrenics. *Archives of General Psychiatry, 34,* 854–862.

Weissman, S. M. (1989). *His brother's keeper: A psychobiography of Samuel Taylor Coleridge.* Madison, CT: International Universities Press.

Werner, H., & Levin, S. (1967). Masturbation fantasies: Their changes with growth and development. *The Psychoanalytic Study of the Child, 22,* 315–328.

Westermeyer, J. T. (2003). Addressing co-occurring mood and substance use disorders. In J. T. Westermeyer, R. D. Weiss, & D. M. Ziedonis (Eds.), *Integrated treatment for mood and substance use disorders* (pp. 1–16). Baltimore, MD: Johns Hopkins University Press.

Westermeyer, J., Tucker, P., & Nugent, S. (1995). Comorbid anxiety disorder among patients with substance abuse disorders. Risk factors on initial evaluation. *American Journal on Addictions, 4,* 97–106.

Whiteside, R. G. (1998). *The art of losing and using control: Adjusting the therapeutic stance.* New York: Brunner/Mazel.

Whybrow, P. C. (1997). *A mood apart: Depression, mania, and other afflictions of the self.* New York: Basic Books.

Widzer, M. (1977). The comic-book superhero. A study of the family romance fantasy. *The Psychoanalytic Study of the Child, 32,* 565–603.

Wieder, H., & Kaplan, E. H. (1969). Drug use in adolescents: Psyochodynamic meaning and pharmacogenic effect. *The Psychoanalytic Study of the Child, 24,* 399–431.

Wilens, T. E. (2004). Attention-deficit/hyperactivity disorder and the substance use disorders: The nature of the relationship, subtypes at risk, and treatment issues. In N. S. Miller & K. T. Brady (Eds.), *Psychiatric Clinics of North America, Addictive Disorders, 27,* 283–301.

Wilsnack, S. C. (1974). The effects of social drinking on women's fantasy. *Journal of Personality, 42,* 43–61.

Wilson, S. C., & Barber, T. X. (1981). Vivid fantasy and hallucinatory abilities in the life histories of excellent hypnotic subjects ("somnabules"): Preliminary report with female subjects. In E. Klinger (Ed.), *Imagery* (Vol. 2, pp. 133–149). New York: Plenum.

Wilson, S. C., & Barber, T. X. (1983). The fantasy-prone personality: Implications for understanding imagery, hypnosis, and parapsychological phenomena. In A. Sheikh (Ed.), *Imagery: Current theory, research, and applications* (pp. 340–387). New York: Wiley.

Winnicott, D. W. (1969). The use of an object. *International Journal of Psycho-Analysis, 50,* 711–716.

Winnicott, D. W. (1971 [1969]). *Playing and reality.* London: Routledge.

Winnicott, D. W. (1975 [1951]). Transitional objects and transitional phenomena. In *Through pediatrics to psycho-analysis* (pp. 229–242). New York: Basic Books.

Winnicott, D. W. (1989 [1959]). The fate of the transitional object. In C. Winnicott, R. Shepherd, & M. Davis (Eds.), *D. W. Winnicott: Psycho-analytic explorations* (pp. 53–58). Cambridge, MA: Harvard University Press.

Winokur, G. (1991). *Mania and depression: A classification of syndrome and disease.* Baltimore, MD: The John Hopkins University Press.

Winokur, G. (1999). Alcoholism in bipolar disorder. In J.F. Goldberg & M. Harrow (Eds.), *Bipolar disorders. Clinical course and outcome* (pp. 185–197). Washington, DC: American Psychiatric Press.

Winter, A. (1998). *Mesmerized powers of mind in Victorian Britain.* Chicago: University of Chicago Press.

Wolf, E. (1980). On the developmental line of selfobject relations. In A. Goldberg (Ed.), *Advances in self psychology* (pp. 117–130). New York: International Universities Press.

Wolf, N. S., Gales, M., Shane, E., & Shane, M. (2000). Mirror neurons, procedural learning, and the positive new experience: a developmental systems self psychology approach. *Journal of the American Academy of Psychoanalysis, 28,* 409–430.

Wolf, N. S., Gales, M., Shane, E., & Shane, M. (2001). The developmental trajectory from amodal perception to empathy and communication: The role of mirror neurons in this process. *Psychoanalytic Inquiry, 21,* 94–112.

Wolin, S. J., & Mello, N. K. (1973). The effects of alcohol on dreams and hallucinations in alcohol addicts. *Annals of the New York Academy of Sciences, 215,* 266–302.

Woodham, R. L. (1987). A self-psychological consideration in cocaine addiction. *Alcoholism Treatment Quarterly, 4,* 41–46.

Woodruff, R. A., Guze, S. B., Clayton, P. J., & Carr, D. (1973). Alcoholism and depression. *Archives of General Psychiatry, 28,* 97–100.

Woody, G. E., Luborsky, L., McLellan, A. T., & O'Brien, C. P. (1989). Individual psychotherapy of substance abuse. In *Treatments of psychiatric disorders* (Task Report of the American Population Association (Vol. 2, pp. 1413–1417). Washington, DC: American Psychiatric Association.

Woody, G. E., Mercer, D., & Luborsky, L. (1994). Individual psychotherapy: Other drugs. In M. Galanter & H. D. Kleber (Eds.), *The American Psychiatric Press textbook of substance abuse treatment* (pp. 275–284). Washington, DC: American Psychiatric Press.

Woody, G. E., O'Brien, C. P., & McLellan, A. T. (1979). Depression in narcotic addicts: Possible causes and treatment. In R. W. Pickens & L. L. Heston (Eds.), *Psychiatric Factors in Drug Abuse* (pp. 105–152). New York: Grune & Stratton.

Wooley, S. C. (1990). Uses of countertransference in the treatment of eating disorders: A gender perspective. In C. L. Johnson (Ed.), *Psychodynamic treatment of anorexia nervosa and bulimia* (pp. 245–294). New York: Guilford Press.

Wullschläger, J. (1995). *Inventing wonderland: The lives and fantasies of Lewis Carroll, Edward Lear, J. M. Barrie, Kenneth Grahame, and A. A. Milne.* New York: Free Press.

Wurmser, L. (1968). Drug addiction and drug abuse. *Maryland State Medical Journal 17,* 68–80.

Wurmser, L. (1970). Why people take drugs: Escape and search. *Maryland State Medical Journal, 19,* 62–64.

Wurmser, L. (1974a). Personality disorders and drug dependency. In J. R. Lion (Ed.), *Personality disorders: Diagnosis and management* (pp. 113–142). Baltimore, MD: Williams & Wilkins.

Wurmser, L. (1974b). Psychoanalytic considerations of the etiology of compulsive drug use. *Journal of the American Psychoanalytic Association, 22,* 820–843.

Wurmser, L. (1977). Mr. Pecksniff's horse? (Psychodynamics in compulsive drug use). In *Psychodynamics of drug dependence.* NIDA Research Monograph 12 (pp. 36–72). Washington, DC: U. S. Government Printing Office.

Wurmser, L. (1978). *The hidden dimension: Psychodynamics in compulsive drug use.* New York: Jason Aronson.

Wurmser, L. (1980). Phobic core in the addictions and the paranoid process. *International Journal of Psychoanalytic Psychotherapy, 8,* 311–335.

Wurmser, L. (1995). Compulsiveness and conflict: The distinction between description and explanation in the treatment of addictive behavior. In S. Dowling (Ed.), *The psychology and treatment of addictive behavior* (pp. 43–64). Madison, CT: International Universities Press.

Wurmser, L., & Spiro, H. R. (1969). Factors in recognition and management of sociopathy and the addictions. *Modern Treatment, 6,* 704–719.

Wylie, H. W., & Wylie, M. L. (1993). An effect of pharmacotherapy on the psychoanalytic process. In M. Schachter (Ed.), *Psychotherapy and medication: A dynamic integration* (pp. 271–278). Northvale, NJ: Jason Aronson.

Wyman, H. M., & Rittenberg, S. M. (1992). Introduction. *Journal of Clinical Psychoanalysis, 1,* 3–10.

Yager, J. (1991). Bulimia nervosa. In B. D. Beitmen & G. K. Klerman (Eds.), *Integrating pharmacotherapy and psychotherapy* (pp. 253–270). Washington, DC: American Psychiatric Press.

Yeazell, R. B. (2000). *Harems of the mind: Passages of western art and literature.* New Haven, CT: Yale University Press.

Yochelson, J., & Samenow, S. (1986). *The criminal personality (The Drug User,* Vol. 3). Northvale, NJ: Jason Aronson.

Zerbe, K. J. (1983). *The body betrayed: Women, eating disorders, and treatment.* Washington, DC: American Psychiatric Press.

Ziedonis, D. M., & Krejci, J. A. (2003). Dual recovery therapy: Blending psychotherapies for depression and addiction. In J. T. Westermeyer, R. D. Weiss, & D. M. Ziedonis (Eds.), *Integrated treatment for mood and substance use disorder* (pp. 90–121). Baltimore, MD: Johns Hopkins University Press.

Zonis, M. (1991). *Majestic failure: The fall of the shah.* Chicago: University of Chicago Press.

Index

A

Abuse of children, 452–453; *see also*
  Rageaholism; Teddy
*Achilles in Vietnam: Combat Trauma and
  the Undoing of Character* (Shay), 7
Acting-in, 343–344, 349
Acting out, 348
Adaptation and assimilation in fantasy,
  364–365
Addict family
    case study, 373–385, 437–438; *see also*
      Megworth (Meggy)
    etiology of addiction and, 126, 247, 252
Addiction; *see also* Addicts; *specific
    addictions (e.g., alcoholism); specific
    topics beginning with addictive; specific
    topics listed for additional detail (e.g.,
    fantasy, megalomania)*
    acting out and, 348
    affect and, 297–299, 361
    alexithymia and, 297–299
    allegory for dangers of, 7–11
    case illustration, *see* Addiction paper
      trilogy; Cases
    comorbidity in, 86, 397, 400–410, 454
    cross-over, 233
    denial and, 456
    depression and, 278
    dissociative identity disorder vs., 420
    DSM-IV-TR on, 454–455
    eating disorders as, 413–414
    empathy and, 28, 201

etiology and pathogenesis of, *see* Etiology
  and pathogenesis of addiction
fantasy and, 12–13, 288–294
fetish and, 51, 102
forced action of, 97
libido and, 351
literature on, *see* Theoretical origins
  under specific topics
masturbation and, 80–81, 215,
  276–277, 350–351
megalomania and, 28
methodology on, 68–73, 238–239,
  331–332, 335–337, 456
model of, *see* Model of addiction
mothers and, 288–294, 297–300
as narcissistic behavior disorder,
  4, 29, 51–52, 109, 301–304
perversion and, 102, 228, 355–356
phenomenology of, *see* Phenomenology
  of addiction
polyaddiction, 397
psychoanalytic psychotherapy for, *see*
  Psychoanalytic psychotherapy
psychosis vs., 142, 275–276
self-caring functions and, 291–292,
  296–297
as self-indulgence, 47
as self-medication, 31–32
as suicide, 156, 168
trauma and, *see* Addiction and trauma
typology of, *see* Typology of addiction
unconscious meaning of, 29, 449
urgency quality of, 95–96

U